Klara Glowczewski   2.95

W9-AZY-560

Introduction to
Modern Behaviorism

Introduction to

Modern Behaviorism

Howard Rachlin

*State University of New York
at Stony Brook*

W. H. FREEMAN AND COMPANY

San Francisco

Copyright © 1970 by W. H. Freeman and Company

No part of this book may be reproduced
by any mechanical, photographic, or electronic process,
or in the form of a phonographic recording,
nor may it be stored in a retrieval system, transmitted,
or otherwise copied for public or private use
without written permission of the publisher.

Printed in the United States of America
Library of Congress Catalog Card Number: 70–117974

International Standard Book Number: 0–7167–0928–7 (cloth)
0–7167–0927–9 (paper)

9 8 7 6 5 4

Preface

This introduction to modern behaviorism is designed to supplement standard textbooks in introductory psychology and animal learning. Such texts are notoriously weak in their discussions of the topics covered in this volume. Indeed, because of the deficiencies of standard texts and because of the importance of the historical and philosophical background of behaviorism to the study of animal behavior and learning, this book may also prove useful at the beginning of some intermediate courses.

At the outset, it should be pointed out that many of the historical statements made here as though they were incontrovertable facts and many of the experiments cited here as though they were the last word on the subject are actually matters of some dispute. From time to time in the text it is indicated that there has been little agreement on certain important issues among psychologists and philosophers; in a few cases both sides of an argument are presented. However, an introductory book is no place for tracing out the details of esoteric debates. The main purpose of this volume is simply to give the reader an idea of what sort of things psychologists who call themselves behaviorists do and why they do them.

If there are any ideas in this book that are new and worthwhile, they arose from conversations with Richard Herrnstein and with graduate students in the animal behavior laboratory at Harvard University. I would also like to thank the following people who read and criticized parts of the manuscript: William Baum, Robert Boakes, David Cross, Marvin Frankel, Charles Gross, Peter Killeen, John Schneider, and Richard Solomon.

Stony Brook, New York   HOWARD RACHLIN
October, 1970

Contents

Chapter 1

Background

Organisms try to influence the behavior of other organisms by a variety of means and for a variety of purposes. Indeed, much of the interaction among humans and other living creatures consists in efforts to influence behavior. Consider a cow nudging its newborn calf, or for contrast, a victorious alley cat driving an intruder from its territory.

Of course, not all interactions are so one-sided. Organisms often simultaneously modify each other's behavior. Even when one organism is clearly dominant over another, as in the relations between ant and aphid or doctor and patient, there may still be an element of mutual influence. If we examine the teacher-student relationship, which, in formal terms at least, seems rather one-sided, we may find that a given student is trying to get a good grade as actively as his teacher is trying to impart information and stimulate thinking. Thus what the teacher sees as learning on the part of the student may be, from the student's point of view, simply a means of influencing the teacher and obtaining a good grade.

Given a situation in which one organism is trying to influence the behavior of another organism, the purpose of the effort may not be readily apparent. A parent may spank a child to keep him from playing in the street. This punishment is intended "for the child's own good." On the other hand, if a parent spanks a child for not making his bed or cleaning his room, it may be the parent himself who hopes to benefit from the change in the child's behavior. Thus the motives behind the modification of behavior and the benefit to be derived from the modified behavior may critically determine the nature of a given interaction.

Let us consider one final example along these lines. A radio announcer may urge us to "Eat apples for health!" because he is paid to advertise apples. If the speaker were an apple grower, instead of a radio announcer, the same statement might be a form of benign propaganda. But if a nutritionist or doctor gives us this advice, the statement may express more concern for our health than for the selling of apples. The very same statement could be used in all three attempts to modify our behavior.

The type of relationship between organisms that will be discussed in this book is that of experimenter and subject. On the surface this relationship is one-sided, with the experimenter apparently observing, modifying, and manipulating the behavior of the subject. But in a deeper sense a truly reciprocal interaction occurs, for the subject helps determine the experimenter's behavior and causes him to modify old theories, to formulate new theories, and to design new experiments.

If we look over the titles of articles in the journals that publish studies by behaviorists (those who are engaged in the experimental study of behavior), we will find clues to their objectives. Here, for example, is a hypothetical set of titles corresponding to the experimental observations shown in Figure 1.1:

  a. Variables influencing the rate of motor learning
  b. The sense of time
  c. A study of appetite
  d. Anxiety as a determiner of performance

Although authors almost always qualify such broad titles in subtitles or introductions, the titles do reveal the questions that the experimental reports are meant to elucidate.

Behaviorists seem to have rather grand expectations for the data they gather in laboratories. Looking at Figure 1.1, it seems that they study narrowly defined bits of behavior. How, then, do they justify their expectations?

This chapter will be devoted to the theoretical and historical influences

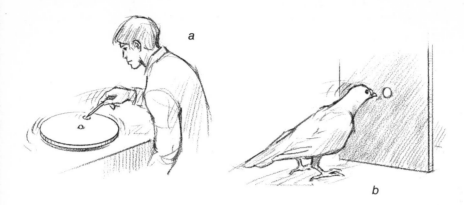

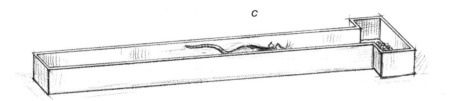

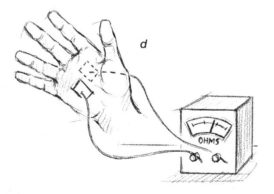

Figure 1.1 *Four forms of behavior observed in the laboratory: (a) a man following a moving spot with a stylus; (b) a pigeon pecking at an illuminated disk on the wall; (c) a rat running down a straight alley with food at the end; (d) a change in electrical resistance due to sweat secreted on the palm of a hand.*

that guide behaviorists' research. Because the history of psychology is lengthy and complex, we shall concentrate primarily on one central problem: What kinds of events should a psychologist study? Through an understanding of some of the intellectual roots of modern psychology, we may come to understand the behaviorist's purpose when he observes a human following a moving spot with a stylus, when he observes a pigeon pecking at an illuminated disk on the wall, when he observes a rat running down a straight alley to reach some food, or when he observes a man's sweating palm.

CARTESIAN DUALISM

In the Middle Ages, the theology of Western Christendom viewed reason as a handmaiden to faith. Faith had resolved the essential nature of man; reason's job was to support faith. Clearly, the intellectual climate was not hospitable to the scientific study of human behavior.

At the dawning of the modern age, science began to question many traditional beliefs. For example, in 1616, Galileo Galilei (1564–1642) earned harsh censure from established authority for denying the theological truth that the earth was fixed at the center of the universe. René Descartes (1596–1650) was about twenty years old when the Church first censured Galileo. When Descartes later undertook to study the nature of man, he found a way to compromise with tradition rather than clashing with it head on.

Descartes was already a great mathematician and philosopher when he published his first essays concerning human and animal behavior. In these essays, he felt obliged to reconcile his findings with the fundamental precepts of theology. Descartes thus took the position—a position adopted by most subsequent philosophers*—that there are two broad classes of human behavior: voluntary and involuntary. Descartes said that voluntary behavior is governed by the mind (a nonphysical entity) and that involuntary behavior has nothing to do with the mind, but instead is purely mechanical—as mechanical as the behavior of animals. According to theology, animals had no souls; Descartes therefore considered them to be essentially like clockwork mechanisms. For this reason, their behavior could be studied directly.

Descartes may have gotten the idea that many human behaviors could

---

* The term "scientist" was not coined until 1840.

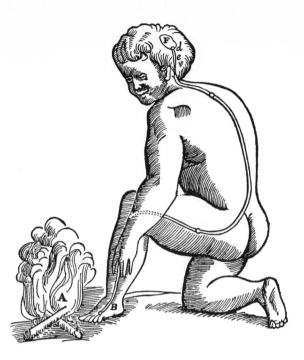

Figure 1.2 *This illustration from Descartes'* De Homine *was designed to show the response of an organism to a stimulus.* [*From F. Fearing, 1930.*]

also be mechanical from the movements of mechanical statues. Ingenious seventeenth-century architects and hydraulic engineers constructed such statues. Many of these grotesque figures were activated, like the chimes of clocks, by internal forces, but some had a unique feature—they were triggered unknowingly by the observer of the mechanism. For instance, as the observer walked down a path he stepped on a hidden treadle that activated a hydraulic mechanism that, in turn, caused a grinning Saracen automaton to emerge from the bushes brandishing a sword. (Similar mechanisms are still to be found at amusement parks like Disneyland). To Descartes, this feature of the mechanisms, their response to a signal from the environment, was critically important. He reasoned that if human behavior could be simulated so well by these mechanical figures, then perhaps some of the principles by which the mechanisms were built also applied to the humans they were designed to imitate.

Figure 1.2 is a diagram by which Descartes showed an example of the operation of an involuntary, purely mechanical, act. The overall effect is that the fire (A), touching the foot (B) of the boy, causes him to

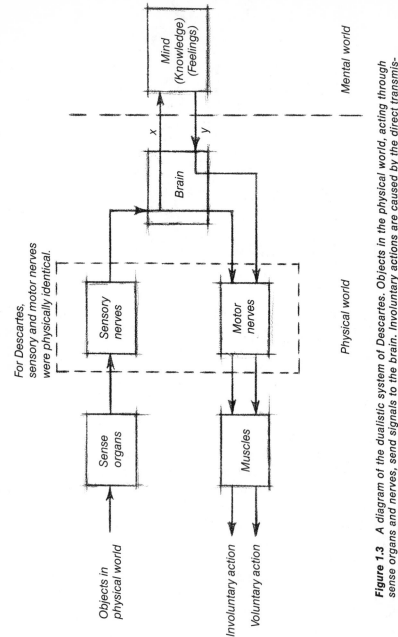

Figure 1.3 *A diagram of the dualistic system of Descartes. Objects in the physical world, acting through sense organs and nerves, send signals to the brain. Involuntary actions are caused by the direct transmission through the brain of signals to the motor nerves and muscles. The mind can sense input through arrow X. Voluntary actions are caused by the mind, which sends out signals at Y.*

withdraw his foot. The mechanism acts through the nerve. The lower end of the nerve is set in motion by the fire, and this motion is transmitted upwards to the brain (de) ". . . just as, by pulling one of the ends of a cord, you cause a bell attached to the other end to ring at the same time." At the brain, a substance (which Descartes called "animal spirits") is released from the cavity (F). The animal spirits travel back down the nerve, swell the muscle in the calf, and cause the foot to be pulled back. At the same time, animal spirits go to the eyes, head, and hand to direct them toward the fire. While this primitive explanation is crude by today's standards, it was a great departure from earlier conceptions of the workings of the body in that it tried to explain the boy's action in physical terms—without recourse to his will, his mind, or his emotions.

The dualism of Descartes' psychology is the feature that is essential to our understanding of the history of psychology. As we have noted, both mind and body were considered necessary to explain the totality of human behavior. Figure 1.3 is a schematic diagram of human behavior as it was conceived by Descartes. In his view, objects in the physical world affect the sense organs, which send messages through the nerves to the brain. At the brain, two things happen. First, in a purely mechanical way, the brain causes action by sending animal spirits through the nerves to the muscles. (This mechanical chain of effects from the sense organs to the brain and back to the muscles, by means of the nerves, eventually became known as a *reflex arc*.) At the same time, the body interacts with the mind at the pineal gland, near the center of the brain. This interaction allows the mind to be aware of both kinds of the body's actions—reflex, involuntary actions, over which it has no control, as well as voluntary actions, over which it exercises complete control. All actions involve the same nerves and muscles, but voluntary actions originate in the mind, a nonphysical realm, and involuntary actions originate in objects in the physical world. Only humans possess the extra pathway that leads to voluntary action (Figure 1.3). According to Descartes, since much behavior (including all animal behavior) is as mindless as the behavior of a stone, it can be considered subject to the same physical laws that govern a stone's behavior. On the other hand, the actions of the mind are not subject to physical laws but are determined by other laws, unknown, and perhaps unknowable.

The effect of Descartes' dualism was to divide up the study of behavior: involuntary behavior came to be studied by physiologists specializing in the study of the body; voluntary behavior remained in the realm of philosophers. These two branches of study had, at first, virtually nothing in common. They are of interest here because they gave rise to two distinct methods of collecting psychological data. We will discuss first the mental branch of study and then the physical branch of study that grew out of Descartes' dualism.

THE MIND

Psyche is a Greek word meaning breath, spirit, or soul. Originally, psychology was that branch of knowledge that dealt with the human soul or mind. (Although "soul" and "mind" are not synonyms, the concepts are inextricably linked and the terms are often used interchangeably.) According to the dualism of Descartes, the mental world (which was identified with the soul) was the true realm of psychology, and the physical world—including the human body—was outside that realm.*

Introspection

In the age of Descartes, the concept of mind provided the very basis of philosophical speculation concerning human nature. How could the mind be studied? As we have noted, the study of mind through behavior was held to be impossible because (1) involuntary behavior was not determined by the mind; (2) voluntary behavior, which was governed by the mind, was considered to be unpredictable, determined by man's free will. Since the only observation a philosopher could make of others was their behavior (speech being included as a form of behavior), the minds of others were closed to him.

The most that one can do, these philosophers contended, is to study one's own mind by looking inward. Such a study was thought to be reliable because the information carried from the body to the mind (arrow X, Figure 1.3) was considered to be orderly and to affect the mind in orderly ways.

To this day introspection remains a common technique for studying mental activity.

---

* The modern behaviorist turns these priorities around: for him, the object of psychology is to study behavior. He feels required to look for the explanation of all human and animal behavior wherever his quest takes him. His ultimate objective is to explain behavior. If the concept of mind is useful in that respect, it must be part of his explanation. If it proves not to be useful, he is free to ignore it.

Innate Ideas

If we accept, for the time being, the notion that the mind can be examined by introspection, and that the object of the examination is to determine the nature and origin of its contents, we can focus on one of the key questions that troubled Descartes and the philosophers who came after him. That is, to what extent does the information entering the mind from the senses (arrow X in Figure 1.3) determine the contents of the mind? In other words, what is the effect of experience on ideas and emotions?

All philosophers agree that experience plays an important part in forming ideas. As we learn more about the world around us, our ideas change radically. A baby, for instance, sees a coin as a toy or as something to put in his mouth; an adult sees it quite differently. The question under debate was not whether experience modifies our ideas, but *to what extent* it modifies our ideas. Descartes himself, while believing that experience played a role in forming some of our concepts of the world, held that our most basic ideas are innate. That is, they are common to all human beings simply because they are qualities of the soul and because all human beings possess a soul. The idea of God, the idea of the self, the geometrical axioms (e.g., that a straight line is the shortest distance between two points), the ideas of space, time, and motion are thus all said to be innate; experience is thus believed to fill in the details. (For example, experience can tell you what sort of objects move fast and what sort of objects move slowly or stay still, but the basic idea of motion in the world is present before experience.)

Those who hold that there are innate ideas, or that innate ideas are more basic and important than what is learned from experience are called "nativists." Those who deny the existence of innate ideas or hold that the idea of innate ideas is relatively unimportant are called "empiricists." The controversy between nativists and empiricists is a theme that runs through philosophy and psychology to the present day. However, contemporary psychologists (who de-emphasize *mind* as an explanatory concept) argue not about innate ideas but about innate *patterns of behavior*. Note that the nativism-versus-empiricism dispute can apply to both halves of Descartes' bifurcated model of man. Although we have been discussing innate ideas, i.e., inborn mental qualities, there are also innate physical qualities. Just as one can argue about the extent to which the idea of space is modified by experience, one can also argue about the extent to which the structure of the nervous system is modified by the environment. By and large, the beliefs of most contemporary psychologists fall somewhere between extreme nativism and extreme empiricism. Descartes, who is usually considered a nativist, played a role in the development of empiricism. For example, although he held that the idea of space was innate, he showed how experience might give rise to the ideas of size and distance.

The more extreme view, that all or almost all ideas are due to experience, was not formulated until after Descartes' death. The development of this more extreme form of empiricism took place in England, and its adherents came to be known as the "British Associationists." This school of philosophy was a direct predecessor of experimental psychology, and we will turn to it next (after a cautionary note).

Warning. Because this chapter is about the historical background of behaviorism, we shall discuss a number of doctrines. So far we have mentioned mentalism, nativism, empiricism, and British Associationism. Once we grasp the principles that underlie such doctrines, we are tempted to use "isms" as handy categories in which to group various philosophers and psychologists. This tendency should be resisted. Nativism and empiricism, for instance, should not be regarded as two boxes into which philosophers may be sorted. These two terms are better regarded as marking ends of a continuum that has an infinite number of gradations. Although, in our frame of reference, we see that philosophers X and Y are both relatively nativistic, X may have seen Y as an empiricist and may have spent most of his life arguing against Y's empiricism. The relativity of such perspectives is especially important when we discuss the British Associationists. From our point of view, two centuries later, it seems that they had so much in common that their thinking can be labeled with one "ism." We therefore ignore many of their differences. Nevertheless, we must be aware that there *were* differences; that the differences were sometimes important; that when we class a given philosopher as a British Associationist, we are not saying all there is to say about the characteristics of his individual philosophy.

Principles of Association

The British empiricists accepted Descartes' idea of human nature (Figure 1.3). They found his division of man into a mind and a body to be reasonable. They also accepted Descartes' belief that the seat of knowledge is in the mind; they generally agreed with him that the proper subject for psychological study is the mind of man; they accepted his idea that the mind could be known by "reflection upon itself," in other words, by introspection. However, they did not accept Descartes' notion that man is born with a set of ideas. Their basic axiom was that all knowledge must come from the senses. Man may be born with the capacity to acquire knowledge, but everything we know, they held, comes from our experience. If we lived different lives, if our experiences were different, if we had been transported to a foreign land in infancy, then our knowledge would be different, and we would be, essentially, different people. This assumption is stated clearly by John Locke, one of the earlier associationists, in 1690 in *An Essay Concerning Human Understanding:*

> Let us then suppose the Mind to be, as we say, white Paper, void of all Characters, without any *Ideas;* How comes it to be furnished? Whence comes it by that vast store, which the busie and boundless Fancy of Man has painted on it, with an almost endless variety? Whence has it all the materials of Reason and Knowledge? To this I answer, in one word, From *Experience:* In that, all our Knowledge is founded; and from that it ultimately derives it self. Our observation employ'd either about *external, sensible Objects; or about the internal Operations of our Minds, perceived and reflected on by our selves, is that, which supplies our Understandings with all the materials of thinking.* These two are the Fountains of Knowledge, from whence all the *Ideas* we have, or can naturally have, do spring.

The empiricists held that all knowledge comes from the senses. But the senses, by themselves (unaided by innate ideas), could provide only sensations: eyes alone could detect a spot of color but could hardly provide the knowledge that the spot of color is a round red ball.

The empiricists faced a dilemma. If we have no innate idea of a book, how do we know that a patch of light that is before us is an object that can be opened and read? that when we open it we can expect to find print on the pages? that the pages will be numbered consecutively? How do we know, in fact, that this object will not disappear after we have touched it? that it is capable of being lifted up without falling apart? or, for that matter, that it won't bite us or explode and destroy us? In other words, how is the mere sight of the object associated with sensations we do not feel but can *expect* to feel once we have lifted the object, opened it, and started to read it?

What the empiricists needed to find was some sort of "mental glue" to hold together all of the sensations capable of being experienced from a given object. "Association"—hardly a new idea—served this purpose. Aristotle (384–322 B.C.) formulated one of the first sets of associationist principles. He said that we remember things together (1) when they are similar, (2) when they contrast, and (3) when they are contiguous. This last principle, that of "contiguity" is by far the most important, since all

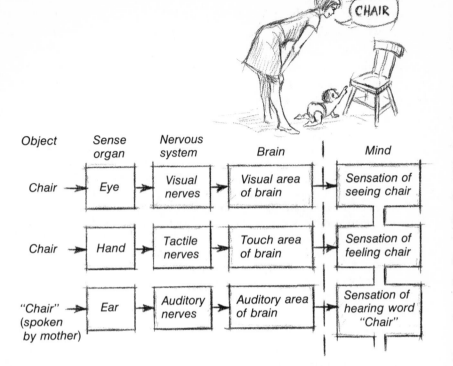

Figure 1.4a *A common view of the way meaning becomes established through association. The sketch shows a child touching a chair and hearing his mother say the word "chair." The diagram shows the inputs to the various sensory systems of the child. The three sensations occur together and are associated with one another by the child.*

subsequent formulations of the principles of association contain it. It is perhaps worth stating formally:

> If two (or more) sensations are felt at the same time often enough, then one alone felt later can invoke the memory of the other (or others).

To summarize, then, the empiricists took as their basic axiom: All knowledge comes from the senses. Realizing that isolated sensations cannot convey the meanings or the connotations of objects, these philosophers adopted a further principle to explain how sensations are connected. This principle was the principle of association by contiguity: If sensations occur together often enough, one alone can cause the memory of the rest.

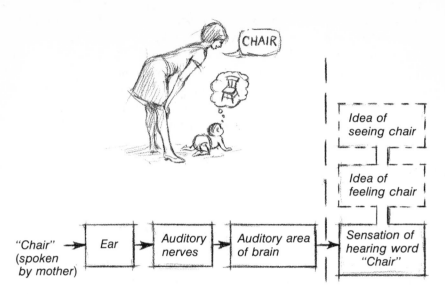

Figure 1.4b *This sketch shows the child at a later time, hearing the word "chair" when there is no chair present. The diagram shows that the word "chair" is now associated with past visual and tactile sensations.*

The task of the empiricists then became to explain how the principle of contiguity acts in particular instances to produce complex experiences from simple sensations.

Visual Distance

One kind of complex experience that concerned the associationists was the experience of distance. The world appears to us in three dimensions, yet the retina of the eye is a thin, fairly flat surface. How does the three-dimensionality of experience come from impressions on the retina? According to the associationist George Berkeley (1685–1753), one possibility was that our idea of visual distance comes from the sensation of moving the pupils of the eyes together. Here is Berkeley's argument. For closer objects we have to move our eyes closer together to focus the objects; for farther objects we must move them apart. The sensations in the muscles of the eyes correspond to the distance of the objects. Other, nonvisual sensations corresponding to distance are those involved in reaching for or walking to the object. These sensations of walking, reaching, and so forth, become attached to the sensations in the muscles of the eyes by association by contiguity. In other words, whenever we have to reach only a short distance to touch an object, our pupils have to move close together to focus on the object. Whenever we have to reach far to touch an object, our pupils must move farther apart. Thus, the movement of our pupils and the movement of our hands become associated, and when we look at an object without touching it and only our pupils move, we remember the other sensation—that of our hands moving. This memory of our hands' greater or lesser movement is, according to Berkeley, what we mean when we say an object is far away from us or near.*

Meaning

Another problem faced by the associationists was that of meaning. How do we learn, for instance, the meaning of the word "chair?" The solution of this problem by the associationist James Mill (1773–1836) was essentially an extension of Berkeley's solution of the problem of perceived distance. Here, in brief, is James Mill's reasoning. As we experience chairs in our lifetime, we see them, touch them, sit on them, and so forth. All these activities in relation to chairs produce their own sensations as well as containing many sensations in common. The "sittableness" of a chair is an association of the visual experience of chairs with the kinesthetic sensation of sitting. Also, simultaneously seeing and hearing the word "chair" produce sensations that become associated with each other and with the sensations resulting from the sight and touch of chairs. These all mix together in a huge bundle so that when we hear the word "chair" the memories or ideas of all the other sensations come to our minds. These memories and ideas were conceived by Mill to be less vivid than the actual sensations, but otherwise identical to them. The meaning of a word would thus be nothing but the bundle or total sum of associated ideas called to mind when the word is spoken or read. (Figure 1.4 illustrates the process by which meaning is established.)

Mental Chemistry

A more sophisticated concept of meaning was advanced by James Mill's son, John Stuart Mill (1806–1873), whose thinking was clearly influenced by the advancing science of chemistry. The younger Mill suggested that simple ideas might interact in a way more analogous to a chemical process rather than by simply mixing together like salt and pepper. John Stuart Mill argued that just as the properties of water differ from those of its

---

*Berkeley seems to have favored different explanations at different times. This account of his argument is based on proposition 45 in "An essay towards a new theory of vision," Dublin: 1709. Reprinted in Berkeley, *Works on Vision* (Indianapolis: Bobbs-Merrill, 1963, p. 39).

elements, hydrogen and oxygen, the properties of the meaning or conno-
tation of a word could differ from the properties of the sensations that
went into forming it. As he wrote,

> When many impressions or ideas are operating in the mind together,
> there sometimes takes place a process, of a similar kind to chemical com-
> bination. When impressions have been so often experienced in conjunc-
> tion, that each of them calls up readily and instantaneously the ideas of
> the whole group, those ideas sometimes melt and coalesce into one an-
> other, and appear not several ideas but one . . . [Mill, 1843]

The idea that the operations of the mind could be studied in an
experiment was a direct outgrowth of such speculations by the British
Associationists. The groundwork for experimental psychology was laid
when the apparent chaos of our thoughts, the infinitude of images and
ideas that seem to float so haphazardly in our minds, was seen to be a
function of a restricted set of elements ("sensations") and of principles of
association. The early experiments in mental experimental psychology
took two forms: studies of sensations themselves and studies of their
combination.

Studies of Sensation

The idea that a sensation, as it occurs in the mind, is not identical to a
sensory process in the body had been present since ancient times, but the
idea that sensation as a mental phenomenon could be studied and measured seems to have come into being in German universities in the nineteenth century. It is to that time and place that most experimental
psychologists today trace the origins of their science.

The first psychological experiments sought to explain the way in which
sensory impulses pass from the physical world to the mental world
(arrow X in Figure 1.3). Two lines of investigation started separately and
eventually fused. One line studied the intensity of sensations and the other
studied the quality of sensations. Let us discuss each of them in turn.

Intensity of Sensations

To some early investigators, the mental world, in contrast to the physical
world, seemed discontinuous. Consider the following hypothetical experiment. Imagine a light controlled by a dial capable of producing a continuous range of intensity from complete blackness to blindingly intense light
(Figure 1.5). An experimenter, starting at zero, turns the dial up very
slowly until a subject reports that he can see some light. The amount that
the intensity must increase from zero before light is reported is called the

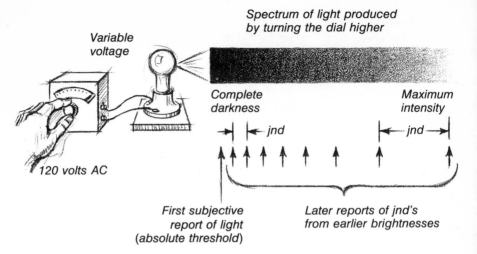

Figure 1.5 *A light used to measure* just noticeable differences *(jnd's) of brightness. The arrows across the bottom of the brightness spectrum indicate points at which a subject reported a difference in brightness as the brightness was gradually increased. Note that the jnd's at the dark end of the spectrum are smaller than those at the bright end.*

absolute threshold (or "absolute limen"). Then the dial is turned farther, until the subject reports that it is noticeably brighter than it was before. Then it is turned farther still, until the subject again reports an increase in brightness. Each interval of brightness between reports is called a *just noticeable difference* (jnd). As the light is continuously increased in physical intensity, the intensity of the sensation (brightness) seems to go up in discrete jumps each jump corresponding to a jnd. It was noticed by Ernst Heinrich Weber (1795–1878) that for many different stimuli there was an orderly relation of jnd's to the magnitude of the stimulus. The bigger the stimulus, the bigger the increase required to notice that the stimulus increased. This relationship, in rough form, is quite obvious in everyday life. If a goldfish grows two inches longer overnight, its owner is likely to notice it the next morning; however, if an elephant grows two inches longer, no one is likely to notice it—even if it takes place in front of his eyes. Weber's significant contribution was that he quantified this observation. He stated that the increase in the stimulus for one jnd was exactly proportional to the intensity (or size) of the stimulus. The importance of this correlation was seen by Gustav Theodor Fechner (1801–1887). He reasoned that since all jnd's had in common the fact that they were the smallest increment it was possible to see, then, as far as the subject who is watching for a change is concerned, any jnd is equivalent

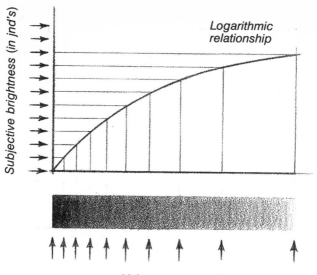

Figure 1.6 *This graph shows the relationship between jnd's in brightness and the magnitude of the stimulus (measured by the voltage regulator). All jnd's are considered to be subjectively equal.*

to any other (in other words, Fechner reasoned that all jnd's are subjectively equal). But, whereas the jnd's may be *subjectively* equal, they were not *physically* equal. If the jnd's vary in the physical dimension as Weber's theory states, and if all jnd's are subjectively equal, then the relation of subjective to physical size can be plotted (as in Figure 1.6). According to Fechner, in this relationship ". . . one has a general dependent relation between the size of the fundamental stimulus and the size of the corresponding sensation. . . . This permits the amount of sensation to be calculated from the relative amounts of the fundamental stimulus and thus we have a measurement of sensation [Fechner, 1860]." Fechner believed that their relation bridged the gap between the mental (psychic) and physical worlds (arrow X in Figure 1.3). Accordingly he chose the name *psychophysics* for this new science of the measurement of sensations, a name that persists today for the study of sensory magnitude.

Quality of Sensations

The theory of the associationists was that complex mental phenomena could be constructed from a limited group of elements. What, then, are the elements? How can they be distinguished from complex mental phenomena?

Johannes Müller (1801–1858), another German scientist, made the argument that the thing that distinguishes one sensation from another is not the stimulus itself, but the particular nerve stimulated. In other words, a sound seems different to us from a light, not because sound energy is essentially different from light energy, but because sound and light activate different nerves. Here are Müller's views. The mind decides whether a given stimulus was a light or a sound; if a light, what color; if a sound, what pitch. But the mind has no contact with the light or sound themselves. The mind can only be sensitive to the nervous impulses leading from the receptors to the brain. The nerves alone tell the mind what sort of stimulation is impinging on the body. Any one of a certain group of nerves can signal that a sound has occurred (the particular activated nerve corresponds to the pitch of the sound). The ear is constructed so that it allows sounds of only that particular pitch to stimulate that particular nerve. But, Müller argued, under certain circumstances the mind can be fooled. If the energy that usually goes to our ears and causes us to hear a sound could be made instead to stimulate the nerve that goes from our eye to our brain, we would experience the sound as a light. In fact any form of energy that succeeds in striking the nerve that corresponds to a given sensation would be capable of causing that sensation. He pointed out that electricity as well as sound energy could cause us to hear sounds when it was applied to the nerves of the ears. Müller's contention that the nerve rather than the stimulus determines the quality of sensation became the doctrine of specific nerve energies. This principle led to more questions. How many specific nerve energies are there? In vision, for instance, is there one for each color? In hearing, is there one for each tone?

A great deal of subsequent experimentation was directed towards answering such questions. In vision, for instance, all the colors were shown capable of being constructed by various combinations of three elementary colors, the primaries, red, green, and blue. These, then, could be the elementary sensations that reach the mind, and the vast array of colors that we see could be products of mental chemistry. Similar research was carried out for the other senses. Usually the method used was introspection and verbal report. Early experimental psychologists believed that a person could be trained to analyze his complex experience into its elements. For instance, an untrained observer experiences *wetness* as a unitary sensation, but observers experienced in introspection could analyze the experience of wetness into *pressure* and *cold*. As a check on this analysis it was shown that a dry, cold, uniform pressure on the finger, for instance, cannot be distinguished by a blindfolded observer from actual wetness.

Experiments in the analysis of sensations are still being carried on today, albeit in a more sophisticated way than those described here.

Secondary Laws of Association

Once it is accepted that simultaneously experienced sensations become associated in the mind, there is nothing more that the simple, unvarnished law of association has to say about them. How many times must they be experienced together before becoming associated? Which of several simultaneous sensations are more likely to become associated, or will they all become equally associated? Do sensations, once they become associated, remain so forever, or do they eventually separate again? These questions were not of great importance to the British Associationists. However, the early experimental psychologists deemed them to be important because only by answering such questions would they be able to measure associations, and only by measurement would they be able to predict the occurrence of an association. It was the Scottish philosopher Thomas Brown (1778–1820) who first tried to answer these questions by formulating nine laws he called secondary laws of association (the three primary laws being those of Aristotle: contiguity, similarity, contrast). The secondary laws were held to modify the primary laws and to enable one to predict which sensations out of a group of sensations were more likely to become associated. Because of their importance for psychology it is worth listing Brown's secondary laws. They stated that association between sensations is modified by

1. the length of time during which the original sensations endured.
2. the intensity of the original sensations.
3. the frequency of their pairing.
4. the recency of their pairing.
5. the number of other associations in which the sensations to be paired are involved.
6. the abilities, capacities, and dispositions of the person experiencing the sensations.
7. the emotional state of the person experiencing the sensations.
8. the bodily state of the person experiencing the sensations.
9. the similarity of the association itself to other, previously acquired, associations.

The nine secondary laws of association set forth by Brown, as he himself recognized, contained no new facts but were merely a new way to organize facts that separately were well known. However, new facts about association did come from Hermann Ebbinghaus (1850–1909), who was the first to perform formal experiments in learning. His object was to study the quantitative relations implied by the nine secondary laws of association, particularly the third and fourth, which state that the mental association of two elements is modified by the frequency and recency of their pairing. Ebbinghaus chose nonsense syllables to be the elements he would use in his research and prepared lists of them to be memorized.

Ebbinghaus's nonsense syllables were three-letter combinations like BIV, RUX, JIC, and KEL, with the first letter a consonant, the second a vowel, and the third another consonant. It is worth knowing the claims Ebbinghaus made for nonsense syllables, because similar claims have frequently been made by psychologists about the kinds of material they use in their experiments and about the kinds of behavior they choose to study. In fact, the various, apparently trivial, observations depicted in Figure 1.1 are used in psychological experiments today for some of the same reasons that nonsense syllables were used in Ebbinghaus's classic studies. (Indeed, nonsense syllables themselves are still used in many studies of learning.) The advantages claimed for such materials are:

1. *They are relatively simple.* (It is important to understand the reason behind the search for simplicity in psychology. Many of the experiments that psychologists do will otherwise seem incomprehensible. Essentially, the reason that simplicity is sought is that psychologists hope that the underlying laws of behavior will prove to be simple and that the complexity we observe in everyday life will prove to be the result of the concatenation of simple basic processes. The reason for this hope is that in other sciences a similar hope has occasionally been fulfilled. For example, it is virtually impossible for a physicist to predict the everyday behavior of physical objects except in a most general way. When a piece of paper is dropped in a room, it is impossible to predict the path it will take as it flutters to the floor. But it is relatively easy to predict the path the paper would follow if it were dropped in a vacuum, a simplified environment where several second-order phenomena—like friction and air resistance—are not present. The vacuum is artificial, so is the nonsense syllable. The hope of scientists, however, is the same in both cases: to find an area in which laws operate simply and directly and in which behavior can be easily predicted. Psychologists are continu-

ally seeking to devise a test condition that is the psychological equivalent of a physical vacuum, and many of their methods reflect this
effort. Just as the vacuum eliminates friction and air resistance, the
nonsense syllable, according to Ebbinghaus, eliminates meaning. For
Ebbinghaus, as for the earlier associationists, meaning was equivalent
to the accumulation of sensations attached to a given word. Because
the syllables he devised were not words, not associated with any
objects, and therefore not associated with any particular sensations,
they had no meaning.)

2. *They are relatively homogeneous.* (This means simply that no one
nonsense syllable stands out from the rest.)
3. *They form an inexhaustible amount of new combinations, each of
which can be compared to the other.* (In other words, a given list of
ten nonsense syllables has no more meaning than any other list of
ten nonsense syllables. Also, they may be compared in reverse. That
is CEV MEB has no more meaning than MEB CEV.)
4. *They are capable of quantitative variations, and may be divided at
any point.* (The only difference between a list of 5 nonsense syllables
and a list of 10 nonsense syllables no matter how they are arranged
is that the latter is twice as long. On the other hand, consider the differences between these two lists:

I	II
TOM	BUT
MEN	SIX
SIX	MEN
BUT	SAW
HIS	TOM
	GET
	HIS
	BIG
	RED
	CAR

The difference between them is not only that the second is twice as
long, but that it is a meaningful sentence whereas the first is not. The
second list, although twice as long as the first, is easier for most people to memorize because of its meaning.)

The object of Ebbinghaus's experiments was to use nonsense syllables in
a quantitative analysis of the development of associations. He was not
satisfied to know merely that greater frequency of pairing leads to greater

Order of remoteness from original list

Original list	0-Order	1st-Order	2nd-Order	3rd-Order	7th-Order
1 ZEP	ZEP	ZEP	ZEP	ZEP	ZEP
2 LAN	LAN	NUR	VEL	REG	ROL
3 NUR	NUR	REG	DEM	ROL	LAN
4 VEL	VEL	LEM	BUF	SID	BUF
5 REG	REG	ROL	SID	LAN	NUR
6 TAV	TAV	CES	FAX	TAV	CES
7 DEM	DEM	SID	LAN	BUF	VEL
8 MOC	MOC	GIZ	REG	PEB	VAM
9 ROL	ROL	LAN	MOC	NUR	REG
10 BUF	BUF	VEL	CES	DEM	SID
11 CES	CES	TAV	QEB	CES	TAV
12 VAM	VAM	MOC	NUR	GIZ	QEB
13 SID	SID	BUF	TAV	VEL	DEM
14 QEB	QEB	VAM	ROL	MOC	GIZ
15 GIZ	GIZ	QEB	VAM	VAM	MOC
16 FAX	FAX	FAX	GIZ	FAX	FAX

Weak association   Strong association

Strong associations present   Mostly weak associations

Figure 1.7 *Lists of nonsense syllables prepared by Ebbinghaus.*

association. He wanted to know exactly how much pairing was necessary before an association would be formed.

In the course of his investigations, Ebbinghaus studied many different aspects of association. To better understand his method, let us consider one of his experiments. The purpose of this particular experiment was to test the conception that an association is formed in the mind of a subject between all members of a list of nonsense syllables when he reads that list, and that the association is stronger for items on the list that are closer together and weaker for items on the list that are further apart. Consider the "original list" in Figure 1.7. According to Ebbinghaus, once the list is memorized, associations are formed between each item and all the other items. The association between neighboring items is strongest; the association between distant items is weak. This would imply, for instance, that ZEP LAN becomes strongly associated, ZEP NUR moderately associated, and ZEP ROL only weakly associated. In order to test this notion, Ebbinghaus invented what is called the *savings method*. He memorized several lists like those in the left-hand column of Figure 1.7; 24 hours later, he tried to relearn the same lists. The relearning of the lists, he found, took an average of 420 seconds less than the learning of the original list. The 420 seconds he saved he considered to be a measure of the strength of the associations 24 hours after they were formed. He reasoned that if he had forgotten the list completely he would have shown no saving (learning and relearning times would be equal), and if he had remembered the list completely he would have maximum saving (relearning time would equal zero). Thus, the amount of time saved would be an index of how well he had remembered the list.

Then he constructed, from the original list, a series of derived lists. "A derived list of zero order" is simply the original list. A derived list of the first order contains the items of the original list so arranged that all but one of the adjacent items in the derived list were separated by one item in the original list. A derived list of the second order is arranged so that most of the adjacent items in the new list were originally separated by two items. Higher order derived lists were constructed by the same principle. If, as Ebbinghaus theorized, the association on the original list was greatest for adjacent items, then a zero-order derived list, which retains the same adjacent items, should produce the most saving. A first-order derived list, which contains items from the original list spaced one item apart, should produce less saving. A second-order derived list with items spaced two apart should show still less, and so on. When the experiment was performed, this was exactly what Ebbinghaus found. A graph showing the decreasing amount of saving as the associations on the list became more remote is shown in Figure 1.8.

The experiments of Ebbinghaus were the first formal experiments in association, just as the experiments of Weber and Fechner were the first formal experiments in sensation. The goal of these experiments was to describe and measure scientifically the properties of the mind. The subjects were invariably human. The data collected was in the form of verbal reports. The preferred method of obtaining this data was by introspection on the part of the subject, although whether Ebbinghaus's experiments really relied on introspection is open to question. The introspective method in which the experimenter and subject are the same person was so influential, however, that even in his rather objective experiments, Ebbinghaus always served as his own subject.

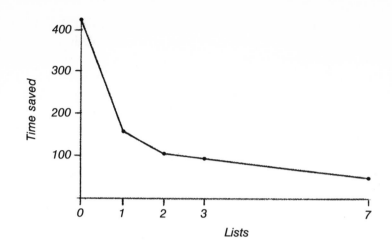

Figure 1.8 *Results of Ebbinghaus's experiment. This graph shows that the amount of time saved in relearning lists decreases as a function of their remoteness from the original list (0). The time saved is the number of seconds required to learn the original list minus the number of seconds required to learn one of the derived lists 24 hours later.*

For many years all scientists who called themselves psychologists were engaged in studying mental phenomena by methods like these. In the early part of the present century, however, such methods were seriously challenged by physiologists who claimed that pheomena such as memory, emotion, and knowledge, hitherto seen as mental, were actually capable of being explained as bodily functions. Thus, they contended, the proper people to study such phenomena were not psychologists trained in introspection, but physiologists trained in analyzing the discrete and delicate functions of the body and, in particular, the system of nerves that regulate bodily functions.

THE BODY

For a hundred years after Descartes, the methods of investigating the mind and the body could not have been more widely separated. On the one hand, the British associationists and the German experimental psychologists studied the mind of man by means of introspection. On the other hand, physiologists studied the body by methods akin to those of physics. In general, the physiologists accepted Descartes' division: psychology, the study of the mind; physiology, the study of the body.

However, as their science gained precision, physiologists could account for much of the behavior previously thought to be controlled by the mind. For instance, in the seventeenth century, physiologists showed that after death (when, presumably, the soul had left the body) hearts could be kept beating. In fact, instances of hearts beating when removed entirely from the body were reported. Today we know that the heart operates like a muscle and that muscles can be activated by stimulating them appropriately even when they are detached from the body, but in the seventeenth century most people believed that the soul gave life to the heart. There are two possible resolutions to the problem that was posed by the observation that the heart, the muscles, and other organs were capable of functioning separately from the body. First of all, one could say that each of these organs had a soul—an animating force—of its own. This resolution was counter to the traditional belief that a human soul was in essence an *immortal entity:* such an entity obviously could not be divided up into several bits and pieces, some of which remained in human organs after death. The other solution to the problem was to deny that the soul had anything to do with the operation of the organs and to say that human organs worked "mechanically," like those of animals. This was the position that most physiologists took and the notion that is generally accepted today. (Not many people object to heart transplant operations on the grounds that they interfere with a patient's soul.)

With each new advance, the physiologists found mechanistic explanations for processes that were traditionally held to be controlled by the mind. Some people reasoned that physiology might continue to advance until it eventually captured the entire province of the mind. Might not all human behavior eventually be explained in mechanistic terms? By this reasoning, to say that a function was "controlled by the mind" was the same as saying that its causes were unknown, and that physiology had not yet advanced far enough to explain it. Perhaps Descartes' dualism was wrong, ran this mechanistic reasoning, and perhaps human behavior as well as animal behavior could eventually be explained without any reference to an animating force like the mind or the soul. In the words of Julian Offray De La Mettrie (1709–1751), one of the first thinkers to espouse a completely mechanical explanation of behavior—

> To be a machine, to feel, to think, to know how to distinguish good from bad, as well as blue from yellow, in a word, to be born with an intelligence and a sure moral instinct, and to be but an animal, are therefore characters which are no more contradictory, than to be an ape or a parrot and to be able to give one's self pleasure . . . I believe that

thought is so little incompatible with organized matter, that it seems to be one of its properties on a par with electricity, the faculty of motion, impenetrability, extension, etc. [La Mettrie, 1748]

Most physiologists did not go so far as La Mettrie, preferring mechanical explanations for those functions of the body that they could bring under their scrutiny, and mental explanations for those functions that they had not yet investigated.

The subsequent physiological investigations that had the greatest effect on psychology were those that dealt with the reflex, that is, with the direct response of an organism to a stimulus in the environment. (We recall Descartes' example of the boy recoiling from the fire.)

As recently as the beginning of the twentieth century, there were still two principal areas of behavior that remained virtually unaffected by physiological research and almost wholly within the province of the mind:

1. Behavior seeming to arise from within the person himself, such as (*a*) an apparently voluntary raising of the arm for which no cause or stimulus can be found in the environment or (*b*) complex behavior (singing an operatic aria in the shower, for instance) for which no correspondingly complex environmental stimulus can be found.
2. Learning. Most reflexes seem to be permanently fixed in the body. How can they explain learning to sing a song, for instance, or learning a whole repertoire of songs?

However, it was in the late nineteenth century and early twentieth century that the Russian physiologists Ivan Michailovich Sechenov (1829–1905) and Ivan Petrovich Pavlov (1849–1936) asserted that even these two areas of behavior could be understood in terms of reflexes.

In the next several sections, we will trace the history of the physiological investigation of the reflex. We shall see how the concept of the reflex has become vital in psychology, especially in the study of learning. Let us begin by returning to the world of Descartes to look for the origins of the concept of reflex action in early discussions of nervous conduction.

Nervous Conduction

In general, early theories of nervous conduction held that the mind governs behavior through the transmission of some kind of vapor or substance to the muscles. Such theories reflected both traditional doctrine

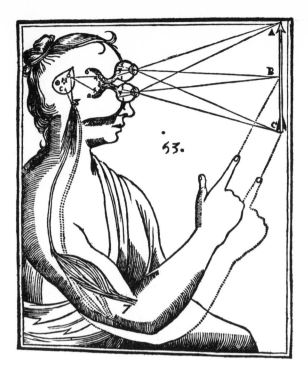

Figure 1.9 *The central role of the pineal gland in Descartes' physiology is shown in this diagram from l'Homme. Images fall on retinas (5, 3, 1) and are conveyed to the cerebral ventricles (6, 4, 2); these then form a single binocular image on the pineal gland (H), the site from which the soul controls the body. Stimulated by the image, the soul inclines the pineal gland, activating the "hydraulic system" of the nerves (8), causing a muscle to move (at 7).[Courtesy of the Curators of Bodlein Library, Oxford University.]*

and the state of knowledge in the physical sciences. For Descartes, nervous conduction was based on a hydraulic model. As we recall, his opinion was that the soul interacts with the body in the pineal gland, near the middle of the brain. This gland, he thought, directs "animal spirits" through the nerves to activate the muscles mechanically. In 1662, he wrote that even though animal spirits must be "very mobile and subtle, they nevertheless have the force to swell and tighten the muscles within which they are enclosed, just as the air in a balloon hardens it and causes the skin containing it to stretch." (See Figure 1.9.)

Descartes' views were highly influential. For a hundred years, controversy raged, not about whether animal spirits existed, but rather about what they consisted of. Some physiologists rejected Descartes' hydraulic model and adopted a pneumatic model; that is, they claimed that a gas,

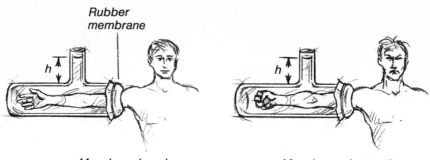

Rubber membrane

Muscles relaxed   *Muscles under tension*

Figure 1.10 *Glisson's attempt to show that muscles do not gain in substance when they are contracted. The height of the water, h, is identical whether the subject's arm is tensed or relaxed.*

rather than a liquid, runs from the nerves to the muscles. Some (called iatro-physicists) claimed that there is a mechanical transmission of force, and others (called iatro-chemists) claimed that the phenomenon is basically a chemical process. This speculation was generally nonexperimental. A clear experimental advance, however, was made by Francis Glisson (1597–1677), who showed in 1677 that whatever nervous conduction occurs when muscles contract, it does not consist of the transfer of a substance, either liquid or gas, from the nerves to the muscles. Glisson's experiment was simple. He had a subject put his hand in a tube full of water, as shown in Figure 1.10, and then contract and relax his muscles. When the muscles were contracted Glisson found that the height of the water did not increase above the height for relaxed muscles, showing that no substance could be flowing into the muscles when they were contracted. From this evidence, it followed that muscles work by themselves once they receive proper stimulation. The question that remained was: what sort of stimulation do the nerves supply to the muscles?

Actually, a more sophisticated experiment had been done by John Swammerdam (1637–1680), prior to Glisson's work, but had not become widely known. In 1660 Swammerdam had surgically isolated a nerve and muscle of a frog and had shown that mechanical stimulation of the nerve was sufficient to contract the muscle. In other words, no infusion of animal spirits or any other substance was necessary for the contraction of the muscle; simple irritation of the nerve was sufficient. Whether such a mechanical irritation is the actual process that takes place in the body when a muscle is contracted was another question. Figure 1.11 shows

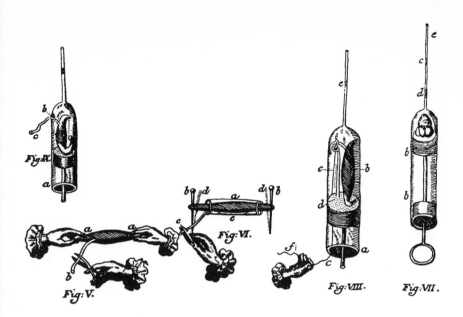

Figure 1.11 *Early illustrations of Swammerdam's experiments. [From Fearing, 1930.]*

some of the illustrations of Swammerdam's experiments with nerves and muscles of frogs—experiments that have been repeated by countless students of elementary physiology.

In general, until late in the eighteenth century, some kind of mechanical conduction of energy was held to activate muscles, but the question of the exact nature of the energy was not resolved. For instance, according to David Hartley (1705–1766)—whose ideas we shall discuss again later—the nervous impulse consisted of minute mechanical vibrations transmitted through the nerve like a wave. By the beginning of the nineteenth century, physiologists came to agree that however nerves might work, they were not adequately explained by references to animal spirits, mind, or soul.

Around 1800 there was great interest in electricity and much fruitful study of the subject. Some scientists speculated that nervous conduction might be electrical. As research progressed in the middle of the nineteenth century, it became increasingly clear that some form of electrical impulse was present in the nerve. Today, the nerve impulse is thought to be a combination of electrical and chemical events.

So we have, in the history of speculation about nervous conduction and research into its nature, a progression of theories—hydraulic to pneumatic to vibratory to electrical and chemical. These theories became more sophisticated and complex as the physical sciences offered successively better ways to understand the way the human body functions.

The Reflex Arc

To those who have considered animal behavior (and much of human behavior) to be machinelike, the basic element of that machinelike behavior has been the *reflex arc*, the pathway leading from the sense organs through the nerves to the muscles. Descartes thought that sensory and motor signals travel through the same nerve. According to him, the sensory signal from the sense organ to the brain operated like a pull chain; the motor signal was hydraulic, consisting of the flow of animal spirits down through the nerve and into the muscle.

After Descartes' time, experimenters began to dissect animals to look for the organs necessary for various reflex functions. They found that certain parts of the nervous system (for instance, the cerebrum of the brain) could be entirely removed without destroying most reflexes; but they also found that severing some parts (notably, the spinal cord) immediately destroyed reflexes. This kind of investigation of the body may be compared to a mechanical investigation of an unknown machine. In order to discover whether a certain part of the machine is necessary for a certain function, you could remove or disconnect that part and see what functions are impaired. Does the carburetor of an automobile belong to its steering mechanism? One way to find out is to remove the carburetor and see if you can still steer the automobile. Because of experiments of this nature with animals, physiologists began to look upon the spinal cord and the base of the brain—but not the cerebrum—as necessary centers of reflex action. But what happens in the spinal cord or base of the brain between the input and output was still a matter for speculation. According to George Prochaska (1749–1820), an early reflexologist, "This part, in which, as in a centre, the sensoral nerves, as well as the motor nerves, meet and communicate, and in which the impressions made on the sensorial nerves are reflected on the motor nerves, is designated by a term, now adopted by most physiologists, the *sensorium commune* [Prochaska, 1784]." But it was not clear in Prochaska's time, nor is it fully clear today, exactly what occurs in the *sensorium commune*, now called the central nervous system.

Although information on the central nervous system was scanty in the eighteenth century, physiologists were able to make lists of types of behavior that they thought were governed by reflexes. Here is one made in 1749 by Hartley, classified according to the sense organ stimulated:

Special sense	Automatic motion
1. "Feeling"—touch, pain	Crying, distortion of face, laughter following tickling, grasping, putting muscles into contraction following painful stimulation.
2. Taste	Sucking, mastication, deglutition, distortion of mouth, peristaltic motion of stomach and bowels, vomiting, hiccough, expulsion of faeces, spasms.
3. Smell	Inspiration of air to "increase" odor, contraction of the fauces and gullet, sneezing.
4. Sight	Motions of globe of eye, motions of the eyelid, contractions of the lacrymal glands, contractions of the muscular rings of the iris, and the ciliar ligaments.
5. Hearing	Contraction of small muscles of the auricle in adjusting to sound, contraction of muscles belonging to small bones of the ear.

In the early nineteenth century, physiologists began to develop a better picture of reflex mechanisms. In independent experiments with animals, François Magendie (1783–1855) and Charles Bell (1774–1842) discovered that when they cut the posterior branch of spinal nerves in an experimental animal, the animal could still move the innervated limb but did not react to a pinprick on the limb, whereas, when they cut the anterior branch of nerves, the animal responded to a pinprick but was not able to move the limb. This discovery established a clear distinction between nerves with a sensory function and nerves with a motor function. Meanwhile, lists of reflexes such as Hartley's were being expanded. Postural reflexes, such as those that allow a man to walk on a tilting ship or allow a cat to land on its feet when dropped upside down, and tendon reflexes, such as the knee jerk, were studied in detail. However, no matter how the list of automatic actions was extended, there still remained a host of actions, including most of the complex actions of everyday life, such as speaking, reading, and writing, that were unexplained by the physiologists and therefore classified as volutary acts. We now turn to the attempt by the Russian physiologists Sechenov and Pavlov to explain such complex acts mechanistically.

Complex Behavior

Although the notion that all behaviors could be classified as either voluntary or involuntary (automatic) was a basic legacy of the dualism of Descartes, many observable behaviors simply could not be fit into either classification. Sneezing and laughing seem involuntary enough, yet they can be suppressed; with much practice, some people have even learned to exert some control over the size of the pupils of their eyes. And what about breathing? We normally consider it to be quite automatic. But when a doctor puts a stethoscope to our chest we breathe in and out at his command; we can also hold our breath at will for short periods of time.

A different type of hard-to-classify behavior is represented by fast and accurate typing. Most skilled typists say that fast typing is automatic, and that they do not concentrate on the pressing of each individual key. In fact, if they try to think of each key, they slow down considerably. Yet, clearly, when someone starts learning to type, he or she must concentrate on each key that is struck. This voluntary effort seems to become involuntary with practice. A similar shift from voluntary to automatic behavior can be seen in the acquisition of almost any skill. As an advertisement for a standard-shift Volkswagen puts it, "After a while, it becomes automatic."

Recognizing (1) the tendency of many voluntary acts to develop into involuntary acts and (2) the modifiability of many involuntary acts, nineteenth-century physiologists had to admit that they knew little or nothing about many forms of behavior. Nevertheless, they persisted in their hope that the idea of reflexes would eventually explain all behavior of organisms.

It was Sechenov who attempted to show how complex, apparently voluntary acts, can, in a broad frame of reference, be understood to be essentially involuntary. To demonstrate this, Sechenov had addressed himself to the problem of energy. One of the most basic laws of physics is that of the conservation of energy: any energy that crosses the boundaries into a system must either remain in the system or come out in some other form. For instance, in an automobile engine, the energy contained in the gasoline that enters the engine eventually may leave it in the form of kinetic energy—the energy involved in the motion of the automobile—or in the form of heat lost to the environment, in the form of sound energy,

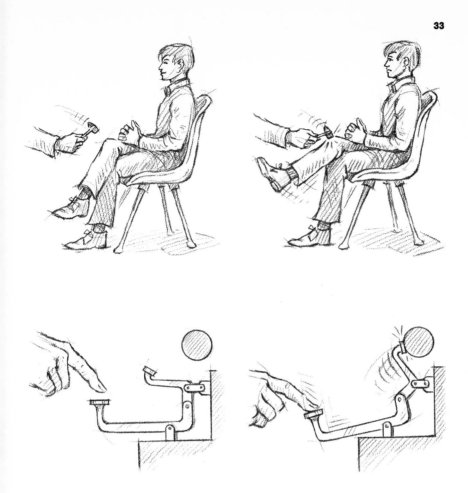

Figure 1.12 *The reflex conceived of as a simple mechanism. Above, a high-energy stimulus from the environment causes a high-energy response in the form of a knee jerk. Below, a high-energy blow on a typewriter key causes a typebar to strike the roller.*

and in the form of the chemical energy remaining in the exhaust gases. If you could keep a record of all the energy going into and coming out of the engine—or any system—you would find that the two amounts are equal.

Many movements of organisms are caused by direct stimuli in the environment. A tap on a human knee, for instance, causes a reflex jerk in the leg. The energy input here is great enough so that it does not stretch the imagination to attribute the energy output of the knee jerk to the energy input of the blow on the knee. This view of the operation of this reflex is illustrated in Figure 1.12. Even though we now know it to be

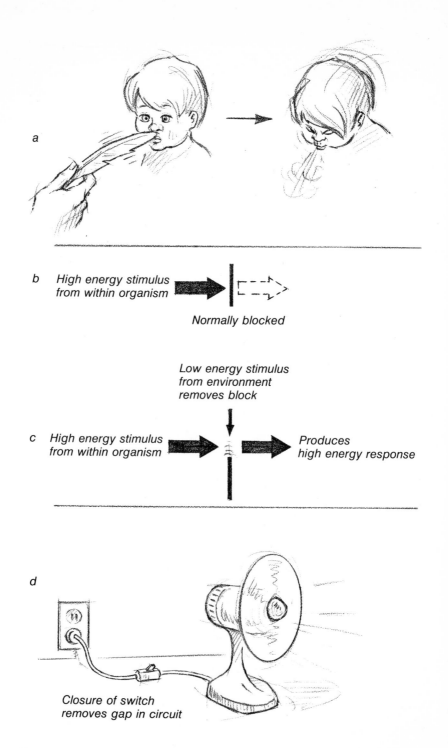

a

b   *High energy stimulus*
    from within organism

    Normally blocked

    Low energy stimulus
    from environment
    removes block

c   *High energy stimulus*   *Produces*
    from within organism   *high energy response*

d

    Closure of switch
    removes gap in circuit

a gross oversimplification, it was nevertheless possible for early physiologists to think of the knee jerk as a mechanism that connected the stimulus to the response by various linkages within the body, and provided the energy for the response, just as a blow on a key of a standard typewriter provides the energy for a typebar to strike the paper. But consider another reflex: a baby's sneeze. Where is the stimulus that provides the tremendous energy exhibited in a good satisfying sneeze? Could all that energy come from a mote of dust tickling the inside of the baby's nostril? It did not seem to Sechenov that it could. Instead, he proposed another kind of mechanism, one that we can compare to the electric switch that starts a fan. The energy that operates the fan is not supplied by the movement of the switch. The switch merely releases electrical energy to the fan, energy that is far greater than that required to turn the switch. While the switch is turned off, the pathway of electric current is blocked; turning on the switch removes the block. (In the nervous systems of organisms such blocking is called *inhibition,* and the stimulus that removes the inhibition is called a *releasing stimulus.*) Returning to the example of the baby's sneeze, we can think of the energy for the sneeze as stored up in the body of the baby, perhaps from milk drunk the previous day, ready to activate a sneeze at any moment—but normally inhibited from doing so. When the baby's nose is tickled, the energy is released and the baby sneezes. Figure 1.13 illustrates the mechanism. For a long time, explanations of complex behaviors had relied on the idea of inhibitory and releasing mechanisms, but Sechenov was among the first actually to locate them in the body.

In one series of experiments Sechenov measured the time taken by a frog to remove its foot reflexively when an acid stimulus was applied to its extended leg. Then he showed that this reflex could be modified by removing various portions of the frog's brain. Sechenov found, essentially, that the stimulus-response reaction time decreased when he removed certain areas of the brain—indicating that he had removed an inhibitory mechanism. When he put salt on parts of the frog's brain, the stimulus-re-

Figure 1.13 *A low-energy stimulus can produce a high-energy response. (a) Gentle tickling produces a violent sneeze. (b) This diagram suggests that the main source of energy is within the organism but that it is normally blocked. (c) This diagram suggests that a low-energy stimulus like a gentle tickle may temporarily remove the block and thus permit a high-energy response like a sneeze. (d) This sketch shows how a low-energy stimulus might be analogous to the simple act of pressing a switch. By closing a little gap in the circuit, the switch releases electrical energy and produces the high-energy movement of an electric fan.*

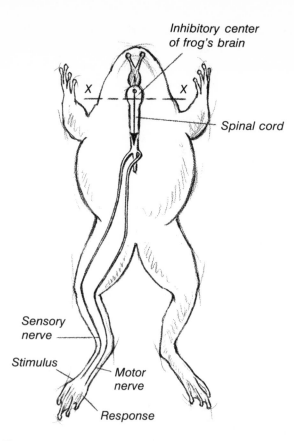

Figure 1.14 *Sechenov's experiments on inhibition. Sechenov observed that (1) salt applied to "an inhibitory center" in the frog's brain slowed down the withdrawal of its leg from an acid, and (2) severing the frog's nerves at X—X speeded up the withdrawal.*

sponse reaction time was increased—showing that he had excited an inhibitory mechanism. Figure 1.14 shows how Sechenov supposed this mechanism to work. In a series of experiments with humans, Sechenov showed that people's reflexes work slower when they are tickled than when they are not tickled; furthermore, the more tickling the slower the reflexes. In other words, tickling serves to increase the inhibition of reflexes.

Sechenov reasoned that if stimuli with little energy could trigger off and control such relatively violent reactions, then perhaps all of those complex actions that appear to be voluntary (controlled from within the organism by the mind) are actually controlled from outside the organism by stimuli that have so little energy that the organism is not aware of its responses to them. Although the reactions to low-energy stimuli may be slight, they are present, and are, according to Sechenov, purely mechanical. In other words, the small, unnoticed external stimuli have two functions. First, they cause reactions within the brain, reactions we have come to call thoughts. Secondly, they activate or release inhibitions on gross motor reactions. Sechenov says of this sequence:

> It is generally accepted that if one act follows another, the two acts stand in causal relationship (post hoc—ergo propter hoc); *this is why thought is generally believed to be the cause of behaviour;* and when the external sensory stimulus remains unnoticed—which happens quite frequently— *thought is even accepted as the initial cause of behaviour.* Add to this the extremely subjective character of thought, and you will understand how firmly man must believe in the voice of self-consciousness, when it tells him such things. In reality, however, this voice tells him the greatest of falsehoods: *the initial cause of all behaviour always lies, not in thought, but in external sensory stimulation, without which no thought is possible.* [Sechenov, 1863]

By this reasoning, Sechenov attempted to draw all the complexity of behavior within the realm of reflexology. No longer was a reflex seen to be a simple chain from stimulus to response; instead, it was seen as a complex machinelike process modified by unnoticed signals from the environment—much like the process by which a radio receives low-energy electromagnetic waves and uses them to modify the high energy from its battery or from an electric outlet so as to generate signals loud enough to be audible. But no matter how complex a radio may be, it is nevertheless fixed in its construction. If the signal to a radio is repeated, its response will be the same. In this respect, the behavior of an animal cannot be explained by Sechenov's theory. An animal does not always respond in the same way to a repeated stimulus. Its responses are modified, as we have seen, by experience; furthermore, the way in which responses are modified depends on the nature of the experience. It was another Russian physiologist, Pavlov, who was to show how reflexes could be modified by experience.

Pavlov realized that inborn reflex mechanisms, no matter how precise and complex, were not enough to explain the various adjustments that organisms make to their environments. In particular, such mechanisms could not explain the process that the psychologists who studied mental phenomena called *association.* For example, how could an inborn reflex explain the fact that people react strongly not only to heat on their skin, but to the sight of a fire, the smell of smoke, the word "fire" shouted in a loud voice, and the sound of fire engines in the street? Certainly it was too much to imagine that each of these stimuli is connected to an inborn reflex of its own; more likely, such groups of stimuli become associated through experience. But how? Pavlov's investigations were directed mainly towards this question.

The particular reflex that Pavlov and his students studied most closely was the salivary reflex in dogs. (We shall describe these experiments in more detail in Chapter 2.) In general, Pavlov found that dogs salivate when any stimulus is presented, such as a bell, a light, the experimenter, or a geometrical pattern, provided that the stimulus has been presented together with food a sufficient number of times. There are parallels between Pavlov's work and Ebbinghaus's. Ebbinghaus presented two nonsense syllables together and observed association. Pavlov presented a neutral arbitrary stimulus (such as a bell) together with a stimulus (food) that was closely linked to a response. Like Ebbinghaus, Pavlov found that the more the paired stimuli are presented together, the greater is the strength of the association. The strength of the association was determined by Pavlov by measuring the amount of saliva secreted when the bell was sounded. As the amount secreted at the sound of the bell approached the amount secreted when food itself was present, the strength of the association was said to be increasing.

Pavlov decided that all organisms must possess two sets of reflexes:

1. *A fixed, innate set of relatively simple reflexes.* (According to Pavlov, the path of these reflexes runs from the sensory nerves through the spinal cord to the motor nerves; these simple reflexes can be modified by innate inhibitory mechanisms, as Sechenov had shown, but essentially they are fixed.)
2. *A set of acquired reflexes.* (These reflexes, called *conditioned* reflexes by Pavlov, are formed by pairing previously neutral stimuli with a stimulus that triggers off an innate reflex; the path of these acquired reflexes goes through the upper parts of the brain, the cerebral hemispheres; when these parts of the brain are removed, the acquired reflexes disappear, leaving only the simple innate reflexes.)

It was Pavlov's view that

> the basic physiological function of the cerebral hemispheres throughout the . . . individual's life consists in a constant addition of numberless signalling conditioned stimuli to the limited number of the initial inborn

unconditioned stimuli, in other words, in constantly supplementing the unconditioned reflexes by conditioned ones. Thus, the objects of the instincts [our desires for food, etc.] exert an influence on the organism in ever-widening regions of nature and by means of more and more diverse signs or signals, both simple and complex; consequently, the instincts are more and more fully and perfectly satisfied, i.e., the organism is more reliably preserved in the surrounding nature. [Pavlov, 1955, p. 273]

Pavlov held that we (organisms) steer ourselves through our environments by means of signals conditioned through experience to remove us from trouble and to lead us to the things we need. He contended that all complex learned behavior is brought about through the combination of several simple conditioned reflexes, which are physiological—not mental—processes. He believed that through objective investigations, physiologists would eventually be able to predict all of the behaviors of animals and humans.

THE RELATION OF PHYSIOLOGICAL PSYCHOLOGY TO MENTAL PSYCHOLOGY

In regard to the associationists we pointed out that the parties to theoretical disputes are often seen from the perspective of time as essentially similar in basic outlook. To some extent, this applies to the reflexologists versus the associationists. The reflexologists, like Sechenov and Pavlov, thought that all complex behavior is mechanical; the associationists, like Ebbinghaus, thought that all complex behavior is influenced by the mind. While these theorists differed in many obvious respects, they nevertheless retained several basic similarities.

Both the associationists and reflexologists believed that complex behavior is the result of the combination of simple elements. The associationists believed that the elements are simple sensations or ideas, that a complex idea is the combination of a group of simple ideas, that the blending of simple ideas into complex ones takes place in the mind. The reflexologists believed that the elements are simple reflexes, that a complex action or behavior is the combination of a group of simple reflexes, that the blending of simple reflexes into complex ones takes place in the brain.

The parallels between the basic concepts of these two outgrowths of Descartes' dualism, although often obscured, were not unnoticed at the time. Both the mentalists and Pavlov claimed that conditioned reflexes might shed light on the concept of association. Even as early as the eighteenth century, the associationist philosopher Hartley, who was also a physician and a physiologist, attempted to explain all of human behavior in terms of both association and physiology. He believed that mental and physical processes could exist side by side, that together they could account for all complex phenomena, each on its own terms, without interaction between them: in Hartley's book *Observations on Man . . .* (1750) the chapters alternate, one on the physical explanation of a phenomenon and the next on the mental explanation of that phenomenon. There is one chapter on the mental association of ideas and a tandem chapter—which anticipates Pavlov—on associative interactions within the brain.

An important point about both mental association and physiology as explanations of complex behavior is their common *structural* nature. Both systems have elements; the research pertinent to both systems has to do with the rules for the combination of these elements and the nature of the compound formed from the elements. In both systems the repeated pairing or grouping of stimuli attaches elements together in some way to build compounds. The general term for such systems is *structuralism*.

The next section is concerned with an alternative to and an attack on the structural method of analyzing behavior.

Molarism

So far, what we have said about psychology can be understood in terms of Figure 1.3, Descartes' system for understanding man. We have examined Ebbinghaus's and Pavlov's work. Since both of these experimentalists relied on the idea that elements become combined into complex entities, both are described as structuralists.

Structuralism is surely not the only doctrine by which man may be understood. For example, consider again how we might come to understand such a complex entity as an automobile.

The engineer who built the automobile knows the relation between the temperature in the combustion chamber and the power output, and he knows the diameter of each opening in the carburetor. The mechanic who regularly repairs the automobile knows that it needs a little extra oil in certain areas where leaks occur, that wheels are currently out of line, and that the exhaust system has another thousand miles to go. The driver knows that the car is hard to start unless the choke is pulled out just so far, that the steering is rather loose, that the back seat is cramped, and that the windshield washers and the clock do not work. If we offered $1000 to the person who knows the car best, who would be entitled to the prize?—the engineer, the mechanic, or the driver? They all "know" the car quite well, and no one area of knowledge is really more "basic" than the others. The engineer may argue that his knowledge is the most basic because without him the car wouldn't exist. But the driver might claim that since the ultimate purpose of a car is to be driven, to know how to drive an automobile well is to know an automobile in its most basic sense. There is much room for heated—and unproductive—argument here. One must finally accept the fact that the ways in which the engineer, the mechanic, and the driver know the automobile are all valid ways of knowing automobiles, and that, in fact, there are other valid ways to know automobiles. Consider the traffic policeman, the road-builder, the city planner, the traffic engineer, the automobile salesman, to name a few.

Similarly, there are many ways in which the behavior of animals and man may be studied and known. The structural approach, whether mental or physiological, corresponds to an engineer's understanding of a car—the structuralist wishes to know the components and how they are put together. *Molarism* is another approach in psychology, one that attempts to know man as a whole. To return to our analogy, we might say that a driver has a molar view of a car's steering, acceleration, and braking characteristics. When a psychologist says he is a molarist, we can understand him to mean that he studies large units of behavior rather than looking for discrete "building blocks." The molarist also differs from the structuralist in the way in which he goes about his study and especially in the kind of data he collects and the kind of observations he makes.

The molarist observes a large psychological unit (like "personality") directly, without trying to break it into its elements, and, just as there are structuralists on both the mental and physical sides of Descartes' dualism (e.g., Ebbinghaus versus Pavlov), there are also molarists on both sides. A group of molarists who addressed themselves to mental phenomena were the Gestalt psychologists.

Gestalt Psychology

In Germany in the early twentieth century the predominant approach in psychology was both mental and structural. The research was similar to that which had been done previously by Ebbinghaus, Weber, and Fechner, and mainly consisted in trying to discover laws pertaining to the association of mental elements such as sensations and ideas.

Gestalt psychology arose in reaction to the structural aspect of German psychology. The emphasis of the Gestalt psychologists was on the study of whole entities rather than parts. However, the Gestaltists did not object to the mentalism of earlier German psychology; in fact, they emphatically stated their desire to study the mind and consciousness. As mentalists, their chosen method of observation was introspection. As molarists, they did not try to analyze mental phenomena into elements but rather attempted to study properties of the entire mind as it interreacted with the environment.

Let us consider a specific example of a phenomenon to which the Gestalt psychologists felt their argument was relevant: melody. The elements of a melody are tones. But, according to the Gestaltists, the essence of a melody is its organization. After all, a melody may be played in a low key or a high key (with completely different sets of tones). It may be sung by various singers, played on various instruments, and rendered in various styles. Yet it remains the same melody.

If we try to break a melody down into discrete tones, we lose the very quality by which we can identify it—the way in which it organizes tones. It is fruitless, according to Gestalt psychologists, to study a complex process like a melody by trying to list its elements. We must instead listen to the melody as a whole and concentrate on its organization.

Let us consider another example offered by the Gestaltists. When we recognize a friend, we recognize him all at once. We don't stop to compare his eyes with our memory of his eyes, his nose with our memory of his nose, his mouth with our memory of his mouth, and so forth. According to the Gestalt point of view, we recognize our friend by comparing the whole organization of elements before us with an equivalent organization in our memory; this recognition of our friend's identity is primary and basic and does not depend on the analysis of what we see into particular elements. If we do analyze our recognition into elements, said the Gestaltists, we do it after it occurs, not before.

As we have indicated, the Gestaltists felt that data could be collected through introspection. After all, they studied the mind, and what better way was there to learn about the operations of the mind than for the mind to reflect upon its own operations? Instead of breaking down a stimulus, a geometrical figure for instance, into its elements of color, form, intensity, and so forth, the observer was asked to judge the stimulus simply and naively as it appeared to him along with other stimuli. The Gestalt psychologists realized that subjective judgments of qualities depend on relationships and patterns of organization. (For instance, the headlights of an oncoming car seem very bright at night when the surroundings are dim, but they seem less bright in the daytime when the surroundings are bright. The important determinant of the brightness of

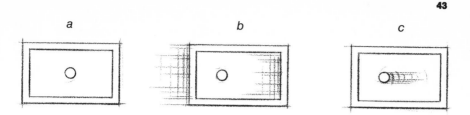

a *b* *c*

Figure 1.15 *Duncker's experiment with "induced movement." (a) Spot of light within a frame in a dark room. (b) Experimenter moves frame slowly to the right, but (c) subject reports seeing spot move slowly to the left.*

the headlights as we experience it is not the constant intensity of the headlights themselves, as structuralism might lead us to believe, but rather the relationship of that intensity to the intensity of the surrounding light. In other words, the total organization is what we experience.) Consider this experiment by the Gestalt psychologist Karl Duncker (1903–1940). In a dark room, the subject was shown only a spot of light located within a square frame. The frame was then moved while the spot was kept still. But the subject always thought that the spot moved within an immobile frame (Figure 1.15). Duncker called the apparent movement of the spot "induced movement." The Gestalt psychologists saw this experiment as proof that movement is seen subjectively in the relationships of an object (the spot) with its environment (the frame) and not in terms of isolated sensations. As regards their method of collecting psychological data, the Gestalt psychologists called themselves *phenomenologists;* the kind of introspection that tries to look at the contents of the mind as a whole, naively, without analysis is called *phenomenology.*

The Gestalt psychologists were mentalists, to be sure, but they broke with tradition on an important point. Although they were studying the mind and although they maintained that the mind could influence behavior (as indicated by arrow Y, Figure 1.3), they also maintained that there were no "mental processes." Recall the structuralist view: The mind receives isolated sensations, then (on the right side of the dotted line in Figure 1.3), these sensations are combined by the process of association—a mental phenomenon—that takes place in the mind but not necessarily in the brain. The Gestaltists denied the existence of such processes. According to them, consciousness is isomorphic to (has the same form as) processes in the brain. But if we have no conscious processes, if everything we think of or are aware of has a physical counterpart in our brains, how can we explain those instances where our consciousness does not reflect the real world? For instance, how can we explain the misperception of movement in Duncker's experiment (as illustrated in Figure 1.15)? Previous mental psychologists would have said that the misperception occurs in the mind, but the Gestalt psychologists explicitly denied that anything could occur in the mind. If we see the spot of Duncker's experiment as moving, its representation in our brains must be a moving representation, and the representation of the frame must be standing still. When the perception of things differs from reality, the distortion occurs, not in our minds, but in internal physical processes. The Gestalt psychologists went on to postulate certain physical processes in the brain that they believed might explain some of the phenomena they had discovered.

In the early twentieth century physicists had begun to study electromagnetic fields. The Gestalt psychologist Wolfgang Köhler (1887–1967) thought that many of the processes of electromagnetic fields had parallels in human perception of form and motion. For instance, he contended, distortions in electromagnetic fields tend to become spherical and symmetrical just as our memory of figures tends towards symmetry. Köhler knew that people often remember ellipses as circles or open circles as closed circles, and in general tend to remember complex assymetrical figures as simpler symmetrical figures. He surmised that the brain contains electromagnetic fields in which our memories are stored and onto which the nerves cause our sensory impressions to impinge.

Physical Molarism

The influence of the Gestalt psychologists was not limited to their attack on the structural doctrine of the mental psychologists. The Gestaltists' idea that the best way to study any process is to look at the organization of that process as a whole was extended to the behavior of the body as well as that of the mind, as other psychologists, studying behavior in terms of discrete movements, began to question whether they could ever explain very complex behavior.

Let us consider how reflexologists might try to explain the path taken by Mr. X, who walks to work every morning. From the time he kisses his wife goodbye to the time he greets his co-workers, X's behavior can be described as a series of movements—of steps, left turns, right turns, stops, and starts—that might well be interpreted as a series of reflexes learned by constant repetition.

Yet suppose one morning there is construction on the street X usually takes, and that he must detour through a completely strange back alley. If he is a reasonably clever man, his detour will be successful and he will end up once more on the familiar street with the construction behind him.

How could X have possibly made this detour if his behavior was running off mechanically as a series of reflexes, each triggered by a familiar stimulus? Some psychologists reasoned that such behavior could not be satisfactorily explained in terms of the kind of simple reflexes that the physiologists Sechenov and Pavlov studied. They claimed that X has, in fact, never acquired such reflexes, but rather that he has learned a *strategy*, an overall plan for getting to work, a sort of complex set of instructions to himself that takes into account, before they happen, the various possible environmental obstacles. What exactly the learning of such complex contingencies consists of remains a matter of dispute.

Some psychologists would say the unifying theme of X's behavior is his purpose—getting to work, and that we must therefore study behavior in terms of purposes. They would contend that meaningful rules and laws of behavior will never be expressed in terms of discrete reflexive actions—but always in terms of aims and goals. X's ordinary path and his detoured path have one thing in common—their destination. Change his destination and you will change his behavior in a fundamental sense; keep his destination the same and all paths to the destination can be studied as a single kind of behavior.

Still other psychologists see X's detour as evidence that explanations of behavior in purely physical terms will never succeed—that we must stick to a study of man in terms of his mental life. What X acquires when walking to work is a cognitive or mental map of the path to work and his detour is made with reference to the map that he has learned and carries around in his mind. One need not talk about his purpose in walking to work, these psychologists argue, for he would have acquired this mental map even while strolling aimlessly around the neighborhood.

The Gestalt psychologists themselves would have claimed that X's successful detour was a product of *insight*. One characteristic of conditioned reflex behavior is that it is gradually acquired by repeated pairings. Yet, according to the Gestaltists, the man's solution to the problem of the detour on his way to work was sudden and immediate. Insight is not something that is gradually learned by repeated pairings, but comes about by looking at a situation in a novel way, so as to grasp the structural and functional relationships of the problem.

Köhler, the Gestalt psychologist whose field theory of the brain we previously mentioned, was detained during World War I on Tenerife, an island that possessed a colony of apes for scientific study. Köhler performed a series of experiments with these apes that mainly consisted of setting problems for them and observing their solutions. Köhler almost

Drawing by W. Steig. © 1968. The New Yorker Magazine, Inc.

Figure 1.16

invariably found that when they were given complicated problems the apes would persist in an incorrect solution or merely do nothing until they suddenly would perform the correct act without hesitation. Köhler ascribed this sudden change in the apes' behavior to insight—the seeing of a relationship between the elements of the problem. For instance, when a banana was hung out of reach of the chimpanzees in a room containing only an open box placed on the floor,

> All six apes vainly endeavoured to reach their objective by leaping up from the ground. Sultan [one of the apes] soon relinquished this attempt, paced restlessly up and down, suddenly stood still in front of the box, seized it, tipped it hastily straight toward the objective, but began to climb upon it at a horizontal distance of half a meter, and springing upwards with all his force, tore down the banana. About five minutes had elapsed since the fastening of the fruit; from the momentary pause before the box to the first bite into the banana, only a few seconds elapsed, a perfectly continuous action after the first hesitation. Up to that instant, none of the animals had taken any notice of the box; they were all

far too intent on the objective; none of the other five took any part in carrying the box; Sultan performed the feat single-handed in a few seconds. [Köhler, 1925, p. 40]

In Figure 1.16, we observe an ape faced with a somewhat more difficult problem.

The Gestaltists' objections to the analysis of behavior into discrete elements convinced most contemporary psychologists that although it was useful and important to study reflexes in the way that Sechenov and Pavlov had studied them, reflexes could not be regarded as the simple building blocks of all behavior (the behavior of Köhler's apes for example). Something more than the conditioned reflex was needed to account for truly complex behavior. It thus seemed necessary to modify radically the concept of the reflex or even to abandon it altogether as a basic mechanism of complex behavior. Most of the theoretical and experimental work on this problem was and is now being done by American psychologists, as we shall see in subsequent chapters.

The "Gestalt revolution" in psychology was only partially successful. Its negative purpose succeeded, for it demonstrated the inadequacy of a structural account of all behavior. However, its positive purpose failed, for it did not produce a completely molar account of behavior. Most psychologists see the value of both structural and molar analysis and are convinced that behavior can be understood on many different levels.

Functionalism

We have seen how Gestaltism, with its emphasis on the study of molar behavior, brought into question the premises of both physiological and mental structuralism. We now come to an even more influential doctrine, that of *functionalism*, which has flourished in the United States. The functional and molar revolutions in psychology overlapped considerably. Which came first is difficult to determine. Both made headway slowly, by fits and starts; the ultimate origins of both may be traced to historical arguments within philosophy and the physical sciences.

Functionalism stems from the theory of evolution put forward by the biologist Charles Darwin (1809–1882) a little over one hundred years ago. Darwin's theory, in capsule form, is that those organisms that are best able to survive in their environment tend to increase in number, and those that are least able to survive in the environment tend to decrease in number. Because organisms within a species naturally vary in physical

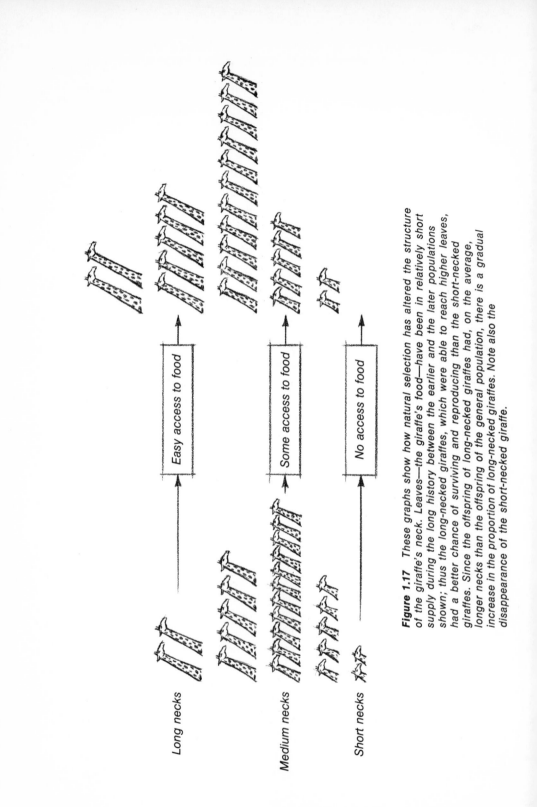

Figure 1.17 These graphs show how natural selection has altered the structure of the giraffe's neck. Leaves—the giraffe's food—have been in relatively short supply during the long history between the earlier and the later populations shown; thus the long-necked giraffes, which were able to reach higher leaves, had a better chance of surviving and reproducing than the short-necked giraffes. Since the offspring of long-necked giraffes had, on the average, longer necks than the offspring of the general population, there is a gradual increase in the proportion of long-necked giraffes. Note also the disappearance of the short-necked giraffe.

qualities and behavior patterns, those organisms that are better able to survive than others will survive and reproduce—and their distinct adaptive qualities will tend to become preponderant; by this process the whole species will gradually change so as to become better fitted to cope with its environment.

Let us consider one common illustration of the action of evolution: the origin of the extreme length of the giraffe's neck. To begin with, (1) all giraffes, no matter how long their necks, depend on foliage for food, and (2) foliage is sometimes in short supply. In the course of natural variation, some early giraffes were born with longer-than-average necks—just as some humans are born very tall, even, occasionally, when they have parents of average height. Those giraffes with long necks were better able to eat leaves on the high trees in their environment and lived longer and produced more offspring. Those with short necks were unable to reach the leaves on the upper parts of the trees and tended to die earlier and to produce less offspring. Thus, as the generations went on, there were more and more offspring of long-necked giraffes, who tended on the average to be long-necked—just as the children of tall human parents tend on the average to be tall.

Darwin saw natural selection as a process similar to the artificial selection used by animal breeders; for instance, a race of plump chickens or turkeys can be created by breeding plump fowl and not breeding lean or stringy birds. Figure 1.17 shows how the process of natural selection works in the case of giraffes. Note that this process is contrary to the notion that (1) giraffes were constantly stretching their necks to reach the high leaves on trees, (2) this stretching made their necks longer, (3) they passed this trait on to their young.

A profound implication of the theory of evolution is that all living creatures share a common biological inheritance. After Darwin, species were no longer regarded as immutable, and there was no longer a sharp boundary separating "higher animals" from "lower animals"—or even men from animals. In regard to human life, evolution meant that the traits humans possess must have evolved from traits their ancestors once possessed.

One of the first effects of this principle of *biological continuity* on psychology was the acceptance of the notion that because humans have minds and consciousness, then other animals also have minds and consciousness, although of a more rudimentary kind. This led psychologists who were studying the mentality of humans to become interested also in the mentality of animals. The evidence for mentality in animals had long

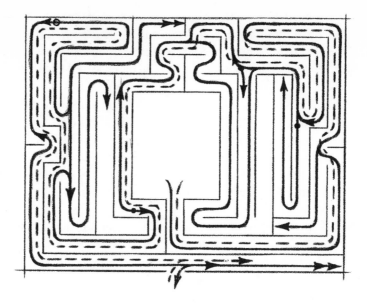

Figure 1.18 *Floorplan of Small's maze. Small studied the "mental processes" of rats with this maze, which he based on the maze in the gardens at Hampton Court Palace in England.*

rested on anecdotes about the clever actions of pets and farm animals. However, a group of American psychologists (the functionalists) began to investigate animal behavior in laboratories, especially at the University of Chicago. One of the tools they devised to study the mental processes of animals was the maze, and some of the first animals to be studied in mazes were rats.

In 1901, in a paper entitled "Experimental Study of the Mental Processes of the Rat," Willard Stanton Small (1870–1943) introduced the rat in the maze to psychology. Small's maze was modeled on the Hampton Court Maze, a garden maze created for the amusement of the English nobility. (These mazes are shown in Figures 1.18 and 1.19.) The object of Small's maze was to determine the conscious state of an animal by observing its behavior. In the following description of a rat's behavior, Small's observations of behavior and his conclusions about the rat's conscious states are italicized. It might be instructive for the reader to try to list those italicized words that seem to him to be direct observations of behavior—as opposed to those that seem to express conclusions drawn by Small about the conscious state of the rat.

View from above

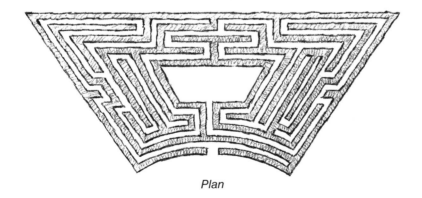

Plan

Figure 1.19 *The Hampton Court maze.* [*Crown copyright.*]

Analyses of Results

In appreciating the results of this series of experiments, . . . the [following] . . . facts come into view. . . . *the initial indefiniteness of movement* and the *fortuitousness of success;* the just *observable profit from the first experiences;* the gradually increasing *certainty of knowledge* indicated by *increase of speed and definiteness,* and the *recognition of critical points* indicated by *hesitation* and *indecision;* the lack of *imitation* and the improbability of *following by scent;* the outbreak of the instincts of *play* and *curiosity* after the edge of *appetite* is dulled. In addition are to be noted the further observations upon the contrast between the *slow and cautious entrance* into, and the *rapid exit* from the blind alleys, after the first few trials; the appearance of *disgust* on reaching the end of a blind alley; the clear indication of centrally excited *sensation* (images) of some kind; *memory* (as I have used the term); *the persistence of certain errors;* and the almost *automatic character of the movements* in the later experiments.

The historical importance for psychology of the notion of biological continuity is that it stimulated much research in comparative psychology —the study of the behavior of one species as compared to another species. At first the purpose of this research was to affirm or deny Darwin's theories by comparing the mental qualities of one species with another— to answer the question, for instance: Which animal has the higher developed mentality, the dog or the horse?—and to thereby rank the various species in terms of the properties of their minds. Contemporary comparative research ignores the relative "mental development" of species and concentrates more on the comparison of various complex behavior patterns.

The general principle that the process of natural selection embodies is critically important in modern psychology, as well as in other sciences; it is the principle of *feedback.* In a feedback system, a process is regulated through testing the actual state of the process against a selected potential state.

In Figure 1.20 the dotted lines represent a feedback loop whereby information about the actual state of an ongoing process is compared with information about a potential state of the process. In the case of the natural selection of long-necked giraffes, a potential state was signaled by the height of the leaves on the trees. Time after time, this potential state was compared with the actual state of the length of the giraffe's necks. The long-term result of this process was attainment of a new actual state: a population of long-necked giraffes.

Feedback is a very common process in everyday experience. Consider a household thermostat. In this case, a desired state is represented by the setting on the thermostat, say 72°. The actual state is the current temperature of the house, say 65°. The ongoing comparison of these two states controls a process—the burning of coal, gas, or oil to warm the house. As soon as the difference disappears—that is, as soon as the house becomes as warm as the setting on the thermostat indicates it should be—the heater or furnace is turned off. Figure 1.21 shows such a thermostat mechanism.

Such self-adjusting systems embody simple *negative* feedback (a term

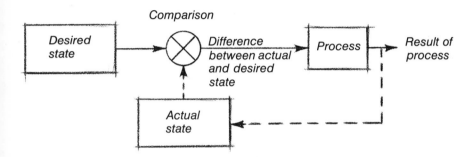

Figure 1.20 *A diagram of a simple feedback system.*

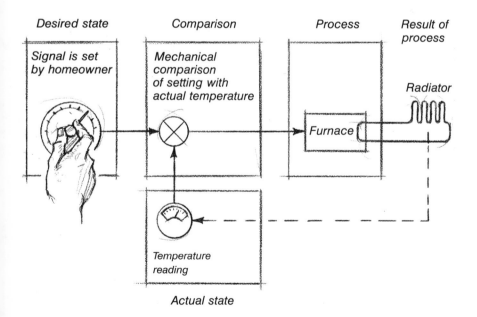

Figure 1.21 *A diagram showing the operation of a household thermostat.*

borrowed from engineering usage). The feedback is called negative simply because the ongoing comparison tends to decrease the difference between the actual state of the system and the selected potential state of the system. Both the system of natural selection and the thermostat can eventually reach *equilibrium* when the actual and signaled states are identical, and the process terminates. However, it is possible to have other kinds of feedback. *Positive* feedback tends to amplify the difference between the actual state and the selected potential state, producing a runaway process. Suppose, for instance, that the thermostat we have been considering got connected by mistake to the air conditioner instead of the furnace. Then, the difference in temperature between the desired 72° and the actual 65° would activate the air conditioner, causing the actual temperature to drop further, increasing the difference. The thermostat feeds more power to the air conditioner, which in turn decreases the temperature still further, and so forth. Positive feedback in everyday situations often causes havoc. A young man, for instance, thinks that a young woman is cool to him because he is not forward enough, whereas the reverse is actually true. He increases his forwardness and finds her cooler. He interprets this continued coolness as a sign that he is still not forward enough, increasing his advances in proportion to the degree of coolness his very advances are generating. Such miscalculations between persons can result in something unpleasant, like a slap on the face. In the case of an international arms race, they could lead to disaster.

The feedback principle, showing how a process could be controlled by a desired end or function, formed the basis for functional psychology. The functionalists, inspired by Darwin's theory, believed that mental processes had evolved to serve various useful functions for organisms struggling to cope with their complex environments. According to the philosopher and psychologist William James:

> Mental facts cannot be properly studied apart from the physical environment of which they take cognizance. The great fault of the older rational psychology was to set up the soul as an absolute spiritual being with certain faculties of its own by which the several activities of remembering, imagining, reasoning, willing, etc., were explained, almost without reference to the peculiarities of the world with which these activities deal. But the richer insight of modern days perceives that our inner faculties are adapted in advance to the features of the world in which we dwell, adapted, I mean, so as to secure our safety and prosperity in its midst. Not only are our capacities for forming new habits, for remembering sequences, and for abstracting general properties from things and associating their usual consequences with them, exactly the

faculties needed for steering us in this world of mixed variety and uniformity, but our emotions and instincts are adapted to very special features of that world. In the main, if a phenomenon is important for our
welfare, it interests and excites us the first time we come into its presence. Dangerous things fill us with involuntary fear; poisonous things
with distaste; indispensable things with appetite. Mind and world in short
have been evolved together, and in consequence are something of a mutual fit. [James, 1893, p. 4]

Notice that the adaptation between our minds and environments is said
to take place *in advance*. That is, our emotions and desires, which help us
survive, are inborn, so that we are interested in an object that is important
for our welfare "the first time we come into its presence." Furthermore,
note that the locus of our sense that the object is important is said to be in
the mind—considered a separate "organ" whose propeties are as subject
to the action of evolution as the length of the giraffe's neck, but which,
like Descartes' concept, is still not to be found in the physical world (see
Figure 1.3).

From the notion that the mind (1) is subject to evolutionary changes
and (2) develops in response to the environment, it follows that complex
behavior, which the mind controls, also must change with the generations
of species, so that individuals cope better with their environments. This
notion gave rise to research such as Small's, whereby the complex behavior patterns of various organisms were studied with a view towards
determining their mental qualities. To return briefly to the principle of
biological continuity, recall that this principle implies that consciousness
is not a purely human trait, and, if possessed by humans, it must be
possessed by other animals, at least to some degree. By 1912, some
American psychologists had discovered the other side of the same coin.
They observed that since both biologists and psychologists were studying
animal behavior fruitfully without recourse to the notion of consciousness, then perhaps much of human behavior could also be explained
without having to analyze or even refer to consciousness. The Russian
reflexiologists had previously abandoned the idea altogether as an explanatory concept. The important point for our discussion is not whether there
really is such a thing as consciousness but that, when attention was no
longer focused on consciousness, introspection lost its position as the
prime method of psychological investigation.

John Broadhus Watson (1878–1958) studied at the University of Chicago when the functionalist school of psychology flourished there. He
was trained to perform animal experiments similar to Small's experiments

with rats in a maze. Watson soon became convinced that he could separate his observations into (1) those that could be verified by other psychologists and (2) those that could not be so verified. In the former category, he placed observations of the overt behavior of animals—where and how they moved. Watson knew that such observations yielded general agreement. In the second category, he placed observations of the conscious states of animals. He knew that these observations consistently failed to yield much agreement. (In other words, Watson found it far more likely that three observers would agree on whether a rat turned left or right in a maze than on whether the rat was happy or sad while it was turning.)

Whereas some functionalists faulted each other's introspective training, Watson held that introspection itself was the source of the prevalent disagreement about animals' mental states. Watson declared that introspection should be banished from psychology and that psychological observations should be restricted, like other scientific observations, to overt behavior.

Because Watson focused on observable behavior, he called himself a "behaviorist" and broke away from the other functionalists at Chicago. As Watson's position gained adherents, behaviorism emerged as a successor to functionalism. Both approaches share a common attitude toward biological continuity, and both stress the adaptive function of behavior, but whereas functionalism was devoted to examining the *mental life* of men and animals, behaviorism is devoted to examining their *overt activities*. As time has gone by, behaviorism has become predominant in American psychology.

Bibliography

The best way to get an idea of the history of psychology is to read the original sources. A good place to start is R. J. Herrnstein and E. C. Boring's *A Source Book in the History of Psychology* (Cambridge, Massachusetts: Harvard University Press, 1965). The material that introduces each section is particularly illuminating. Most of the quotations in the present volume come from selections in Herrnstein and Boring. From the source book one can go to more comprehensive original sources.

There are two classic history books of experimental psychology by E. G. Boring: *A History of Experimental Psychology* (New York: Appleton-Century-Crofts, 1950) and *Sensation and Perception in the History of Experi-*

mental Psychology (New York: Appleton-Century-Crofts, 1942). The attitude toward the history of psychology in the present volume comes basically from that of Boring's two history books; the approach in these books is to follow the history of psychology from Descartes through the British associationists to modern psychology. For an approach centered around studies of behavior *per se*, see J. R. Kantor, *The Scientific Evolution of Psychology* (2 vols., Chicago: The Principia Press, 1963–1969). For a history of studies on the reflex, see F. Fearing, *Reflex Action* (New York: Hafner Publishing Company, 1930).

The material quoted in this chapter is from the following sources:

Descartes, René, *De Homine*. Leiden: 1662. Reprinted in Herrnstein and Boring, p. 269.

Fechner, G. T., *Elemente de psychophysik*. Leipzig, 1860. Reprinted in Herrnstein and Boring, p. 75.

Hartley, David, *Observations on man, his frame, his duty, and his expectations*. London and Bath: 1749. Reprinted in Fearing, p. 86.

James, W. *Psychology*. New York: Henry Holt, 1893.

Köhler, W. *The mentality of apes*. Translated by E. Winter. New York: Harcourt, Brace and Company, 1925.

La Mettrie, J. O. de, *L'homme machine*. Leiden: 1748. Reprinted in Herrnstein and Boring, p. 278.

Locke, John, *An essay concerning human understanding: in four books*. London, 1690. Reprinted in Herrnstein and Boring, p. 584.

Mill, J. S., *A system of logic, ratiocinative and inductive, being a connected view of the principles of evidence, and the methods of scientific investigation*. London, 1843. Reprinted in Herrnstein and Boring, p. 379.

Pavlov, I. P., *Pavlov: selected works*. Translated by S. Belsky. Moscow: Foreign Languages Publishing House, 1955.

Prochaska, George, *De functionibus systematis nervosi*. Prague, 1784. Reprinted in Herrnstein and Boring, p. 294.

Sechenov, I. M., *Refleksy golovnogo mozga*. St. Petersberg, 1863. Reprinted in Herrnstein and Boring, p. 321.

Small, W. S., Experimental study of the mental processes of the rat. *American Journal of Psychology*, 1901, **12**, 218–220. Reprinted in Herrnstein and Boring, pp. 552–553.

Chapter 2

Basic Procedures
and Techniques

The emergence of behaviorism in the early twentieth century brought fresh approaches to the question: How do organisms learn? There began a series of attempts to provide a systematic and thorough answer based on behaviorist principles. American behaviorists Edwin R. Guthrie (1886–1959), Clark L. Hull (1884–1952), Edward C. Tolman (1886–1959), and B. F. Skinner (b. 1904), among others, published influential works in which they tried to identify and fit together the pieces of this subtle and complex puzzle. We shall note in passing some of the experimental methods their systems have contributed to the study of behavior.

In general, contemporary behaviorists tend to set aside vast theoretical questions and to ask instead how a particular organism acquires a particular behavior. In their work, they make free use of one or another of the many methods developed by various theorists and innovators. In other words, psychologists seem to have abandoned—at least temporarily—the effort to systematize and unify their field of study; they favor piecemeal attacks on specific areas of behavior, for which they use whatever tools are convenient and effective.

The aim of this chapter is to give the reader an appreciation of the basic procedures and techniques that are the essential features of modern behaviorism. We shall first discuss *classical conditioning*, then we shall take up *instrumental conditioning.** We shall compare these two commonly followed procedures. Finally, we shall discuss techniques for measuring behavior in the laboratory.

CLASSICAL CONDITIONING

Pavlov's Experiments

Seven decades ago the Russian physiologist Pavlov was studying the salivation reflex in dogs when he discovered that systematic changes in the dogs' reflexes were clearly linked to his own pattern of behavior in the laboratory. Pavlov began to study this intriguing phenomenon and subsequently produced the first empirical reports on the conditioned reflex.

Pavlov had initially set out to investigate the physiology of the secretion of various fluids within the mouth and stomach. By ingenious surgical techniques he was able to implant tubes leading from various points along the digestive tracts of dogs out through the skin. Part of the secretion of fluids in the digestive tracts passed into the tubes and was collected and its amount was measured. In effect, the questions that Pavlov asked were: "If I give the dog some food to eat, how soon will the food, acting as a stimulus, cause the mouth and the stomach to secrete their various digestive fluids?" "What is the mechanism that links the insertion of food in the mouth and the secretion of saliva?" "What is the function relating the amount of food and the amount of saliva secreted?" "As the food reaches the stomach, how long does the stomach take to secrete the acids necessary to digest the food?" Such physiological questions seemed unrelated to psychology.

However, Pavlov began to be plagued by a bothersome annoyance in the course of his research: As dogs became familiar with the experimental situation, they would often begin to salivate and secrete stomach acids as soon as Pavlov walked into the room. Pavlov called these premature

---

* Other names for classical conditioning include *Pavlovian conditioning*, and *respondent conditioning*. Instrumental conditioning is also known as *instrumental learning* and *operant conditioning*. Some psychologists distinguish between instrumental conditioning, instrumental learning, and operant conditioning on the basis of the kind of response (locomotor versus nonlocomotor) or the procedure (trial-by-trial versus continous observation of behavior). There is more similarity than difference among these techniques, however, and we will treat them alike here under the rubric of *instrumental conditioning*.

secretions "psychic" secretions because he believed at first that they resulted from the dogs' psychic (mental) activity. Later, he realized that these "annoyances" bore certain similarities to the physiological reflexes he had been measuring, and he decided to study them.

One of the first of Pavlov's experiments on psychic secretions is particularly instructive. A dog's secretion of stomach acids, following the introduction of food in its mouth, increases and then decreases over the course of four hours, as shown in curve (a) in Figure 2.1. This curve represents (1) whatever was secreted as a direct result of the stimulation of food in the stomach *plus* (2) whatever was secreted before food reached the stomach (the "psychic secretions"). Pavlov wished to measure these two components of the curve separately. In order to plot the curve of direct secretions only, Pavlov introduced food not through the dog's mouth, but directly into its stomach through a tube (called a fistula), which bypassed the normal routes from the mouth and led directly to the dog's stomach. When food was introduced through the fistula into the stomach, the gastric secretion was much less than when food was eaten in a normal way. Curve (b) in Figure 2.1 shows the amount of secretion under this special condition. This, then, represented one component of the total secretion—the secretion that followed direct stimulation of the stomach by food. The second component of curve (a) was determined by a method called *sham-feeding*. The dog ate food in the normal way, chewing and swallowing it, but the food was not allowed to pass into its stomach. Instead, the food was removed through another fistula before reaching the stomach. Despite the fact that no food reached the stomach, there was a secretion of stomach acids as shown by curve (c). Curve (d), which is the sum of curves (b) and (c), is similiar to curve (a). Thus, the experiment confirmed Pavlov's suspicion that total stomach secretion derived about equally from direct stimulation and "psychic" stimulation.

Now let us turn to another of Pavlov's experiments. Pavlov knew that his dogs began to salivate when they merely saw food, just as a hungry man begins to salivate when he enters a restaurant or passes a bakery. Pavlov wondered whether such premature salivation was caused only by the sight of food in particular or whether *any* stimulus, such as the sounding of a tone, would cause this premature salivation if followed often enough by actual eating. To answer this question, Pavlov constructed the apparatus shown in Figure 2.2. A hungry dog was isolated from as many extraneous stimuli as possible. Then Pavlov struck a tuning fork, which produced a tone, and after half of a second, fed the dog. He

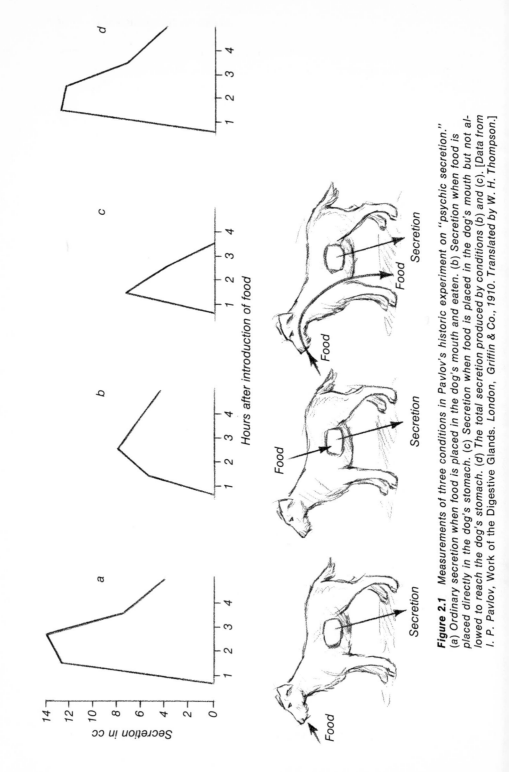

Figure 2.1 Measurements of three conditions in Pavlov's historic experiment on "psychic secretion." (a) Ordinary secretion when food is placed in the dog's mouth and eaten. (b) Secretion when food is placed directly in the dog's stomach. (c) Secretion when food is placed in the dog's mouth but not allowed to reach the dog's stomach. (d) The total secretion produced by conditions (b) and (c). [Data from I. P. Pavlov, Work of the Digestive Glands. London, Griffin & Co., 1910. Translated by W. H. Thompson.]

repeated these pairings of tone and food several times, measuring salivation all the while through a tube leading from the dog's cheek to a small container. At first, the dog salivated only after the food was inserted into its mouth. But it gradually salivated earlier and earlier in the procedure, until salivation finally appeared somewhat *before* the dog was fed, but after the tone. Pavlov found that such "psychic" secretions could be established in this manner for many kinds of stimuli.

It is important to recognize the difference between Pavlov's earlier experiment with sham feeding and his later one with the dog and the tone. In the first experiment, Pavlov observed a "psychic" secretion linked to food, a stimulus that had already been established and (for all Pavlov knew) had been established even before the dog was born. In the second experiment, however, Pavlov observed a "psychic" secretion that followed a wholly new and arbitrarily chosen stimulus. This process—the forging of a connection between a new stimulus (like a tone) and an existing reflex process (like salivation to food in the mouth)—Pavlov called *conditioning*.

Elements of Classical Conditioning

It is worth examining Pavlov's classical procedure more closely, in order to learn the traditional nomenclature for its various elements.

The first necessary element is an established reflex. A reflex consists of a stimulus and a response, when the response is reliably elicited by the stimulus. In Pavlov's experiment the response was salivation and the stimulus was the presence of food in the mouth. The stimulus part of this reflex—the presence of food in the mouth—is traditionally called the *unconditioned stimulus* or, more briefly, the US. The next requirement for classical conditioning is a neutral stimulus, anything that will not by itself cause the response before the experiment begins. This neutral stimulus is called the conditioned stimulus (CS). Besides tones, Pavlov used lights, pictures and other objects as CS's. Indeed, Pavlov himself became a CS for his dogs. (This was the bothersome effect that launched Pavlov's research into conditioning.)

The US-response connection and the CS are the two basic components of any classical conditioning experiment. The schematic sketches in Figure 2.2 show their relationship in time.

The end result of the conditioning procedure is the conditioned reflex. The conditioned reflex in Pavlov's experiments was salivation in response to a previously neutral stimulus. Parts (b) and (c) of Figure 2.2 show two measurable effects of classical conditioning, both of which were studied

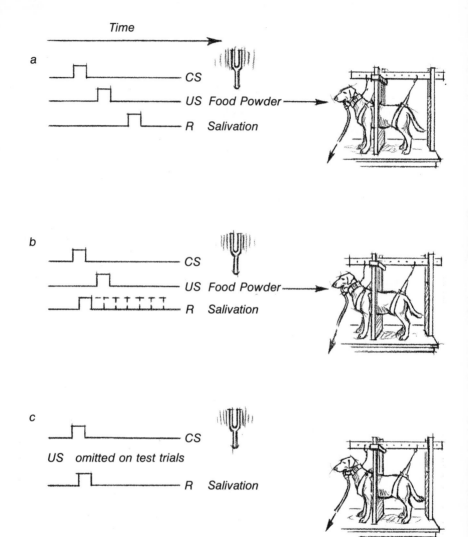

Figure 2.2 Classical conditioning. (a) Procedure for the establishment of conditioning. (b) One test for conditioning: Does the response come to precede the US? (c) Another test for conditioning: Does the response occur in the absence of the US?

by Pavlov. Part (b) shows the salivation response occurring progressively earlier until it occurs before the US; Part (c) shows the occurrence of the response with the US omitted. In order for the response to occur with the US omitted, the sequence in (a) is presented repeatedly—except that, according to a prearranged schedule, the US is occasionally omitted. As the experiment progresses, the usual observation is that the response without the US becomes almost but not quite as large in magnitude as the response with the US. Measurement of the effect shown in (b) emphasizes the latency of the response; measurement of the effect shown in (c) emphasizes the *magnitude* of the response. (As classical conditioning proceeds, one finds that the latency of the response to the CS becomes shorter and its magnitude becomes larger.)

Pavlov saw conditioning as the establishment of a new reflex by the addition of a new stimulus to the group of stimuli that are capable of triggering a response.

Classical conditioning, Pavlov believed, shed new light on the process of association. In associ̇on, as studied by Ebbinghaus with nonsense syllables for instance, there are all the elements of classical conditioning. One syllable is presented to the subject first (the CS). Then another is presented to the subject (the US). These pairings are repeated, and, finally, the subject can say the name of the second syllable (the response) when he is presented with the first. Pavlov maintained that psychologists like Ebbinghaus who were studying association were really doing experiments in classical conditioning, but with the stimuli and responses not as well controlled as they were in Pavlov's laboratory.

Although Pavlov's original experiments used the secretion of saliva to food in a dog's mouth as the basic reflex, to which a neutral CS was attached, the classical conditioning procedure has since been carried out with many other kinds of reflexes. Mild electric shock has often been used as a US because it produces a host of measurable responses. For example, after electric shock, the rate of breathing increases, the heart rate increases, and the part of the body being shocked is withdrawn. In one experiment performed at Cornell University, sheep were shocked briefly on their foreleg, causing them to breathe faster and deeper and also to raise the leg (even though the wires delivering the shock were attached to it.) The experimenters decided to set a metronome ticking a few seconds before the shock was given. After this was done four or five times, a sheep would lift its leg and begin breathing faster as soon as the metronome started ticking. The shock was the US; the metronome ticking was the CS; the leg-raising and faster breathing were responses.

Extinction

So far we have been talking about conditioning as if it were a one-way process. By a procedure such as that shown in Figure 2.2 we have conditioned the behavior of a dog. The dog salivates when it hears a tone. Is that dog fated, then, for the rest of its life, to salivate when it hears the tone? No, it is not. Any response can be eliminated if the CS occurs a sufficient number of times without the US following. We recall that the CS was occasionally presented alone in the test trials of part (c) of Figure 2.2. However, it was isolated like an island amid a sea of conditioning trials, like those in part (a) of Figure 2.2. Suppose we arranged large blocks of trials in which the CS is always presented alone. What would happen to the response? We would find that the response would begin to decrease in magnitude so that eventually it would cease to appear. This process is called *extinction* of the response. A typical extinction curve is shown in Figure 2.3.*

Clearly the procedure for extinguishing a response is quite straightforward. The US is simply omitted from the normal conditioning procedure.

In order to clarify the nature of the process of extinction, let us pay an imaginary visit to Pavlov's laboratory. Suppose we bring a dog with us, one that has never been exposed to any laboratory conditioning procedure; if we prevail upon Pavlov to sound his tuning fork, our dog will not salivate. Suppose another dog, one of Pavlov's, was previously conditioned so that it salivated to a tuning-fork tone but that its response was subsequently extinguished. When Pavlov sounds his tuning fork, his dog salivates as little as ours. It seems as though the conditioning of Pavlov's dog has been "wiped away" by the process of extinction and that no one could ever tell the two dogs apart on the basis of their behavior.

In fact, Pavlov found that he *could* distinguish between two such dogs if he presented the tone and then sounded a loud noise suddenly and unexpectedly. The dog with the extinguished response (Pavlov's, in our example) would salivate, and the other dog (ours) would not salivate. Pavlov reasoned that extinction did not simply "wipe away" conditioning

---

* The galvanic skin response (GSR) of Figures 2.3 and 2.5 is a change in electrical resistance between one area of the skin and another. It is often measured between the front and the back of the hand (as shown in Figure 1.1). This change in resistance may be caused by sweating of the palm, but there is dispute as to whether sweatiness is the only factor involved. In any case the GSR reliably follows electric shock and other painful stimuli and is frequently the measured response in classical conditioning experiments with humans.

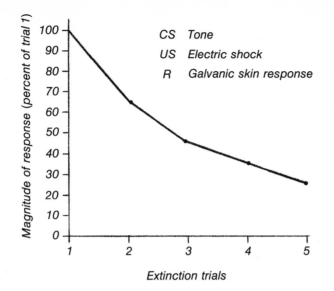

Figure 2.3 *Typical extinction curve. Each extinction trial is a presentation of the CS alone. In this case the curve shows the extinction of the galvanic skin response following 24 conditioning trials. Each point represents the average response of 20 human subjects.* [*Data replotted from C. I. Hovland, "Inhibition of reinforcement and phenomena of experimental extinction." Proc. Nat. Acad. Sci. 22, 430–433, 1936.*]

but that it added another force equal and opposite to the force of conditioning. He called the force added by extinction an *inhibitory force*. He thought that the sudden loud noise somehow temporarily removed the inhibitory effect of extinction and allowed salivation to begin.

Pavlov had discovered that if the noise was sounded during conditioning it stopped salivation. In other words, the noise acted in the opposite direction to whichever process was going on. It could not do this if a response that had been both conditioned and extinguished was identical to an unconditioned response. Pavlov called the extinction process a form of *internal inhibition*. The sounding of the loud noise during extinction which produced salivation, he called *disinhibition*, the release of inhibition. When the loud noise was sounded during conditioning and served to inhibit salivation, the process was called *external inhibition*.

The process of internal inhibition may be compared to a system of weights and counterweights. Imagine a weight attached to a block of wood (as in Figure 2.4) and tending to pull it towards the left. There are

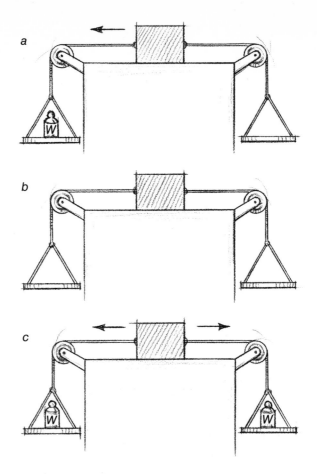

Figure 2.4 *This system of weights shows how extinction might operate as either a negative or a positive process. (a) If conditioning is seen as the pull of a weight, extinction can be either (b) a negative process that simply removes the weight, or (c) a positive process that adds a new weight to the system to counterbalance the effect of conditioning.*

two ways to stop the block from moving towards the left. One is to cut the string or otherwise remove the weight (an analogy to "wiping away" conditioning). Another way is to add another weight on the other side (an analogy to a force of inhibition). Both procedures produce a stationary block (extinction). If the weights and strings are hidden from view, how can you tell which system applies? You can distinguish between conditions (b) and (c) in Figure 2.4 by cutting one of the strings or removing one of the weights (an analogy to the disinhibitory effect of the loud noise). If this is done to the apparatus shown in (b), nothing will happen to the block. But if it is done to the apparatus in (c), the block *will move suddenly* in one direction (this is analogous to the reappearance of the response).

Generalization and Discrimination

There is bound to be some *generalization* in a process through which a new pattern of behavior is acquired. For instance, if a dog's behavior is modified in a laboratory so that it salivates when it hears a tone sounded by a tuning fork, another tone slightly higher or lower in pitch will also make it salivate. Generalization also occurs when a child, sometimes to the embarrassment of his parents, calls every man he meets "Daddy." Of course, the child will eventually learn to reserve the name "Daddy" for his male parent. When this occurs, we say he has learned to make a *discrimination*.

Let us consider an experiment performed in the United States in 1934 on the generalization of a classically conditioned response. The behavior of a group of college students was conditioned, with mild electric shock as the US and sweating of the palms as the response. The CS was a vibrating instrument applied to the skin. For some subjects the instrument was applied to the shoulder and for others it was applied to the calf. As training progressed the amount of sweating measured on test trials (when the CS occurred without the shock) was seen to increase. Then, on later test trials, the instrument was occasionally applied at places on the skin *other* than where conditioning was originally established. The further away the instrument was applied on these later test trials, the less was the response. Figure 2.5 shows the magnitude of the response as a function of the distance from the original point of application. The kind of curve shown in Figure 2.5 is called a *generalization gradient.**

Generalization gradients like the one in Figure 2.5 are by no means unalterable. Suppose we have a set of several similar stimuli, only one of which we want to be a CS. Suppose that, even though we use only the desired stimulus as the CS in a classical conditioning experiment, we find that the subject generalizes and responds to the other stimuli too. How can we eliminate responses to these other stimuli but retain responses to the one we want to be a CS? We may try alternating conditioning trials that contain both the desired CS and the US with extinction trials that contain no US—only the unwanted stimuli. Our hope is that the organism

---

* The specific spot at which the vibrating stimulus was applied is not important in determining the gradient; what was important was the distance from the original CS, wherever that CS may have been applied.

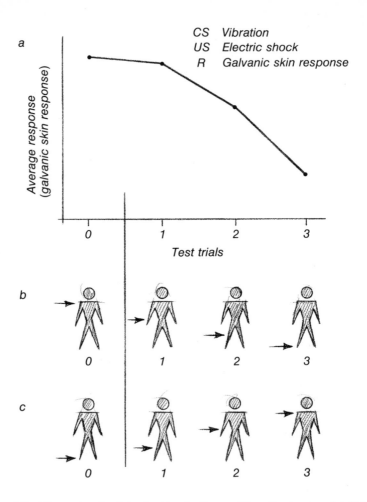

Figure 2.5 *The generalization of a classically conditioned response. (a) This graph shows the decline of a galvanic skin response to vibration as the vibration is moved progressively farther from the original site of conditioning. (b) Some subjects were initially conditioned on the shoulder. (c) Some subjects were initially conditioned on the ankle. [Data from M. J. Bass and C. L. Hull, "The irradiation of a tactile conditioned reflex in man." J. of Comparative Psychology, 1934, 17, 47–65.]*

will learn to discriminate the particular stimulus to which we want it to respond from the unwanted stimuli. This procedure works—but, significantly, it works only up to a point.

We know Pavlov's view that extinction is an active process of inhibition, not just a matter of "wiping away" old conditions but more like adding counterweights to a hypothetical system of weights (Figure 2.4). Keeping this in mind, consider the following experiment, performed by one of Pavlov's students, Dr. Shenger-Krestovnikova. She trained dogs to salivate by a method similar to Pavlov's except that instead of a tone she used a circle drawn on a card as the CS. She found that after being conditioned to salivate when they saw a circle, the dogs generalized to the extent that they would also salivate when they saw an ellipse, like those in Figure 2.6. In order to condition discrimination between (a) and (b), (a) was presented with the US while (b) was presented without the US. Following this procedure the dog would salivate in response to (a) but not in response to (b). Then the same procedure was repeated with (a) and (c), then (a) and (d)—(d) being an ellipse very much like the circle. According to Pavlov, this is what happened when (a) and (d) were discriminated:

> In this case, although a considerable degree of discrimination did develop, it was far from being complete. After three weeks of work upon this differentiation not only did the discrimination fail to improve, but it became considerably worse, and finally disappeared altogether. At the same time the whole behaviour of the animal underwent an abrupt change. The hitherto quiet dog began to squeal in its stand, kept wriggling about, tore off with its teeth the apparatus for mechanical stimulation of the skin, and bit through the tubes connecting the animal's room with the observer, a behaviour which never happened before. On being taken into the experimental room the dog now barked violently, which was also contrary to its usual custom; in short it presented all the symptoms of acute neurosis. On testing the cruder differentiations they were also found to be destroyed. . . . [Pavlov, 1927, p. 291]

One cannot help but draw a parallel to the behavior of humans when they are required to perform for long periods of time at the limit of their discriminative capacities. We humans can make just so many discriminations, until, like Pavlov's dogs, or rather like those of Shenger-Krestovnikova, we start making mistakes and are unable to perform tasks that were previously easy for us. In extreme cases we may develop the "symptoms of acute neurosis" to which Pavlov refers.

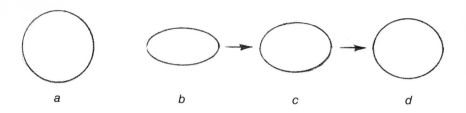

Figure 2.6 *Shenger-Krestovnikova's stimuli. Dogs were conditioned to respond to a circle (a). Their responses to an ellipse (b) were extinguished. As the ellipse was gradually changed to look more like a circle, as in (c) and (d), the dogs' ability to discriminate broke down, and, in Pavlov's words, their behavior "presented all the symptoms of acute neurosis."*

Noninstantaneous Stimuli and Responses

In most of Pavlov's conditioning experiments each stimulus and response was considered to be a fairly discrete event. A buzzer was sounded for an instant, or a light was flashed and an increase in salivation occurred for only 1 or 2 seconds. However, there is no need for the US, CS, or response to be instantaneous discrete events for the conditioning procedure to be effective. Indeed, the CS and the US may be ongoing processes. For instance, let us consider the relation between temperature and a dog's rate of breathing. These two processes are clearly correlated. (That is, temperature and rate of breathing tend to rise and fall together. When the temperature is high, dogs breathe fast; when the temperature is low, dogs breathe slowly.) In this case there is no reason to look for a specific stimulus for each breath—we merely consider the dog's rate of breathing as the response and the temperature to be a US. Let us add a CS to the situation: a light that signals high temperatures. In this case the response can be considered to be the *rate* of a series of fairly discrete events—after a while, to test the CS, we turn on the light without raising the temperature and observe the rate of breathing.

Here is another, similar conditioning experiment with dogs: the *rate* of buzzer sounds is correlated with *rate* of presentation of food, and the response is measured as the *rate* of salivation. All three events—buzzers, food presentations, and salivation—occur over the same time span. A high rate of buzzer presentation is used to signal a high rate of food presentations and a low rate of buzzer sounds is used to signal the reverse. Learning then consists of a dog's changing its rate of salivation in accordance with the rate of buzzer presentations. We can see how the concept of classical conditioning can be extended to familiar, everyday situations, in which behavior often adjusts to overall rates of environmental events instead of to each separate event as it occurs.

INSTRUMENTAL CONDITIONING

The Law of Effect

In 1898, the American psychologist E. L. Thorndike laid the groundwork for a simple but important principle, which he named the "law of effect." Here is a contemporary paraphrase of his principle: One effect of a successful behavior is to increase the probability that it will occur again in similar circumstances. Thorndike based this conclusion on experiments with cats, dogs, and chicks, which he placed in puzzle boxes like the one shown in Figure 2.7. In these experiments, a hungry animal was confined in a box with food placed outside of the box and within view of the animal. In order to escape from this confinement and get the food, the animal had to step on a lever or pull out a bolt, or perform some other mechanical task. Thorndike found that the animal, in the course of its behavior in the box, would sooner or later make the correct movement and get out of the box. He measured the *latency* of the correct movement —how long it took the animal to escape. He repeatedly put the animal back in the box and measured how long it took to escape. Thorndike found that, in general, there was a negative correlation between the number of times an animal had escaped from the box and the length of time it took to escape—the more trials, the less time to escape. After many repeated trials, the animal would solve the puzzle and get out of the box almost immediately. (The graphs in Figure 2.8 show how latency decreased with repeated trials.)

Now let us consider the following hypothetical experiment, which is rather similar to Thorndike's and perhaps further clarifies the "law of effect." Suppose we construct a puzzle box like Thorndike's, except that we make the ceiling somewhat higher. And, suppose that, like Thorndike, we put a cat into the box. But now, instead of letting it out after solving a puzzle, we merely observe its behavior while inside, and we especially concentrate on observing its jumping. (Thorndike reported that one common behavior of a hungry cat in a box is jumping.) In fact, if we measure the height of each jump and plot them as a distribution (see the lower left portion of Figure 2.9), we will probably find some very low

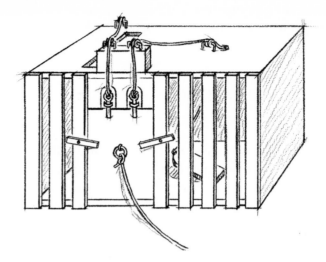

Figure 2.7 *Thorndike's puzzle box. Cats that were placed inside this box learned to unbolt the door and then to press the door outward to escape. [From E. L. Thorndike,* Animal Intelligence. *New York, Macmillan Publishing Co., 1911.]*

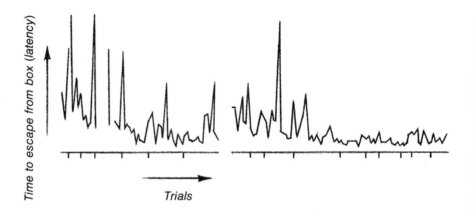

Figure 2.8 *These two curves show the performances of two cats in Thorndike's box. [From E. L. Thorndike,* Animal Intelligence. *New York, Macmillan Publishing Co., 1911.]*

jumps and some very high ones but a generally bell-shaped distribution with a relatively large proportion of medium jumps. Suppose that we open the door to the box after each jump greater than some arbitrary height, a little above average, say 13 inches, and feed the cat before putting it back in the box. At first, we find the usual number of 13-inch jumps. But as the experiment progresses, we find more and more jumps of 13 inches and above. In fact, the distribution will probably change to one resembling that on the lower right of Figure 2.9.

Thorndike's puzzle box experiments were comprised of the following steps: (1) The experimenter provided a stimulus to the organism and observed the organism's behavior in its presence. (2) If the behavior was "appropriate," in the sense that it conformed to criteria set by the experimenter, he rewarded the organism. (3) This, in turn, increased the likelihood of the behavior recurring and producing more rewards. (In this sense, a reward to the organism is said to *reinforce* its behavior.) Today, Thorndike's experimental procedure is considered a major variant of *instrumental conditioning*, so called to distinguish it from Pavlov's classical conditioning procedure, which we discussed previously.

It is important to realize the purpose of the highly artificial situation in which Thorndike put his animals. He believed that the "law of effect" was not limited to such artificial situations but was a general law of nature. In his view the environment usually sets the conditions of the "puzzle" for individual organisms. Thorndike reasoned that a fox learns how to enter a barnyard in the same way that he learns to get out of a puzzle box. The reason Thorndike built his puzzle box was to isolate the phenomenon of learning and measure its progress. The conditions he set in the laboratory were meant to parallel the conditions of the environment, but to be less complicated. If the puzzle box seems to be an artificial way to study behavior, we should remember that all experiments are inherently artificial because they isolate from the complexity of the environment those particular variables that are of interest to the experimenter.

Much as the physicist, when he studies the behavior of falling bodies, prefers to work with a hypothetical vacuum, where air resistance is eliminated, Thorndike tried to isolate the mechanism of the influence of reward by removing environmental distractions.

The early experiments of Thorndike are important for many of the same reasons as are the early experiments of Ebbinghaus, which we discussed in the first chapter. Unlike the casual observations of their predecessors, the experiments of Ebbinghaus and Thorndike were systematic enough to be

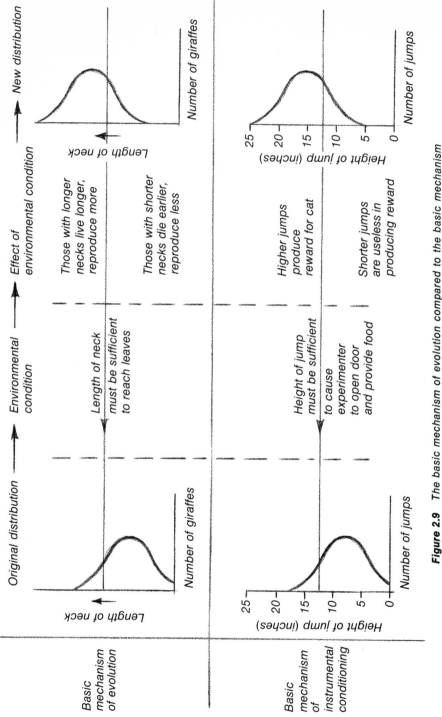

Figure 2.9 The basic mechanism of evolution compared to the basic mechanism of instrumental conditioning. The two examples used are (top) the natural selection of long-necked giraffes and (bottom) the jumping-cat experiment.

replicable. Their experiments have been repeated; as long as the same procedures have been followed, similar results have always been obtained.

We turn now to the topic "learning and evolution." Thorndike, who helped lay the foundation of instrumental conditioning, saw a direct connection between individual adaptation—the selection of successful behaviors from an organism's repertoire—and species adaptation. Indeed, the "law of effect" is simply natural selection at work within the life history of a single organism.

Learning and Evolution

Both species structures and species behaviors evolve. If the environment changes slowly, and is the same for all members of the species, evolution from generation to generation works well. The spider's web-spinning and the social interaction of bees, ants and other insects are behaviors that have been brought about by natural selection.

But this evolutionary process, which takes generations to do its work, is too slow to solve some of the problems faced by some species. Take foxes for example. If a farmer devises a new fence for his barnyard, a particular fox must change its behavior to get past that particular fence. If the fence is too high to jump over, the fox must learn to climb over it or to tunnel under it or to gnaw through it. Since there are many foxes, many farmers, and many kinds of fences, there is little chance for the evolution of a whole breed of foxes whose specific "fence-climbing behavior" would be just suited to the peculiarities of any single fence. If such a breed of foxes did come into being, the farmer would replace the fence with another fence that the new breed could not climb over, and the process would have to begin again. In other words, given their relatively change-able environment, the only hope for foxes lies in individual adaptation rather than in species adaptation. Each fox must respond to its own specific environmental conditions. Individual adaptation, the ability of an organism to change its behavior in relation to changes in the environment, is nothing more or less than learning. This relatively rapid adaptabil-ity of individual behavior complements the more gradual adaptability of species structure and species behavior we find in the long-term evolution-ary process and is, itself, a product and a part of that process.

Complex Behavior

Because an action cannot be rewarded or punished unless it occurs, we infer that the mechanism of the "law of effect" can only strengthen acts that *do already* occur. This being the case, how could a man teach a dog to run to the closet and fetch his slippers? The man would probably have to wait a long time before this rather complex behavior occured fortuitously so he could reward it. Instead, he must begin by rewarding the dog for simple acts already within its repertoire. As these simple acts are strengthened, other acts will appear in the repertoire more like the desired final behavior. The "law of effect" works rather subtly and rather slowly in regard to complex patterns of behavior; these complex patterns evolve from simpler patterns, just as complex species structures evolve from simpler structures. In our hypothetical experiment with the jumping cat, we would have to wait a very long time for a jump over 20 inches to occur when the cat is first put in the box. Thus, if we tried to strengthen 20-inch jumps by rewarding them initially, we might not succeed. If, however, we first trained 12-inch jumps, we see from the revised distribution of the lower right of Figure 2.9 that 20-inch jumps would become fairly frequent. *Then*, if we rewarded 20-inch jumps we would be likely to succeed in strengthening them. By this method of *successive approximations* to our goal, we could finally train the cat to consistently jump at the very limits of its capacity.

So, it is clear that complex patterns of behavior can evolve within the life history of a single organism through the mechanism described by the "law of effect." Thorndike called such evolved patterns of behavior *habits*. He felt that the particular habits of an individual organism depend on the history of that organism. Thorndike believed that the complex patterns of behavior that enable one person, say, to operate a lathe and another person to quarterback a football team cannot arise wholly from inheritance but must be largely due to the unique patterns of experience of the two people.*

Kinds of Instrumental Conditioning

There are four basic principles used in instrumental conditioning, all of which are related to the evolution of individual behaviors. In capsule form, we can describe the four principles as *reward, punishment, escape,* and *omission.*

---

* We must not neglect another source of complex patterns of behavior. Complex behaviors can also evolve gradually from generation to generation. Such behaviors, said to be *instincts*, are much the same from generation to generation and from organism to organism within an entire species. As organisms within the species mature, they acquire the complex behaviors that are specific to their species. Much of the complex behavior of species of insects, for example, consists of unvarying sequences of acts that are adaptive as long as relatively constant environmental conditions are not disrupted. Unlike foxes, however, a species of insect might essentially have only *one way* to solve a problem (to build nests, for example).

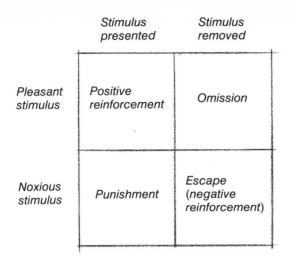

	Stimulus presented	Stimulus removed
Pleasant stimulus	Positive reinforcement	Omission
Noxious stimulus	Punishment	Escape (negative reinforcement)

Figure 2.10 *Four basic kinds of instrumental conditioning are classified by the consequences of a specific act. For example, if a specific act is followed by the presentation of a pleasant stimulus (a reward), the instrumental conditioning is classified as positive-reinforcement conditioning.*

1. The principle of reward was stated in Thorndike's "law of effect"— a reward tends to increase the probability that the response it follows will recur. In conditioning experiments, a reward is called *positive reinforcement*.
2. The principle of punishment is the inverse of Thorndike's law—an aversive, (or painful), stimulus tends to decrease the probability that the response it follows will recur.
3. In what is called escape conditioning, a particular response is followed by escape from an aversive stimulus. Escape from an aversive stimulus increases the probability that the response will recur. For example, Thorndike found that his cats would often learn to solve the puzzle in the box even when they were not fed afterwards. In other words, they learned to respond solely in order to escape confinement. This type of conditioning is called *negative reinforcement*.
4. Omission of reward occurs when a reward, usually present in the environment, is absent after the response. The omission of a reward tends to decrease the probability that the response will recur.

Figure 2.10 is a diagram showing basic relationships among the four kinds of instrumental conditioning.

(Later in this chapter, when we discuss the aversive control of behavior, we shall have something to say about which of these methods can best be used in a given situation to increase or decrease the occurrence of various kinds of behavior.)

CLASSICAL AND INSTRUMENTAL CONDITIONING COMPARED

How are classical conditioning and instrumental conditioning related? No definitive answer to this question is generally accepted by modern behaviorists. Without going into the details of the theoretical disputes in this area, we can observe that classical conditioning and instrumental conditioning are two closely related but distinguishable phenomena.

Differences between classical and instrumental conditioning experiments can be found (1) in the organism's influence on reinforcement and (2) in the way behavior is classified by the experimenter.

The Organism's Influence on Reinforcement

Let us take food as an example of a reinforcer. In a classical conditioning experiment, the organism's influence on the appearance of food is negligible. The experimenter decides the time for the delivery of food. By contrast, instrumental conditioning experiments are arranged so that the organism can produce food by a particular response. In Pavlov's experiments food was presented on each trial, whatever the organism did. If one of Pavlov's dogs had been trained with food withheld until salivation occurred, the classical conditioning experiment would have been transformed into an instrumental conditioning experiment.

If we consider the organism to be a single unitary system, we find that there are three elements in both the classical and instrumental conditioning procedures that cross the boundary of this system. (See Figure 2.11.) Because the US in classical conditioning and the reward in instrumental conditioning are parallel elements, they share a common name—reinforcement. In both procedures the presence of reinforcement serves to determine conditioning and its absence serves to define extinction. (In both classical and instrumental conditioning, we speak of the response as being reinforced. We say "The dog was rewarded for opening the latch" or "The latch-opening response of the dog was reinforced" not "The dog was reinforced." or "The response was rewarded."). When reinforcement is mentioned in connection with classical conditioning, the speaker is referring to the US. Thus, in classical conditioning, an unreinforced trial

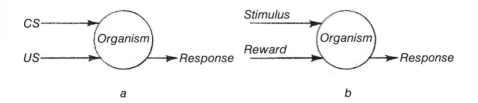

Figure 2.11 *Classical conditioning and instrumental conditioning compared with respect to inputs to the organism and outputs from the organism. (a) Classical conditioning. (b) Instrumental conditioning.*

is either a test trial, as in Figure 2.2b, or part of a block of extinction trials.

Whether reinforcement in classical conditioning acts functionally in a manner similar to reinforcement in instrumental conditioning is a question about which there is some dispute. Although Figure 2.11, which shows the organism as a system, reveals a similarity with respect to the inputs and outputs of the system, the difference between the two methods lies in the interaction between the organism and conditions in its environment. Figure 2.12 shows the system in Figure 2.11 with the experimenter also diagrammed. The difference between the two parts of Figure 2.12 is the dotted feedback loop in the instrumental conditioning diagram. In classical conditioning the temporal relation between the CS and US is determined by the experimenter in advance, and nothing the subject does will change it. In any classical conditioning trial the CS and US are both always present. Reinforcement is always present. The critical prerequisite for conditioning is the invariable occurrence of the response whenever the US is presented. In instrumental conditioning, on the other hand, reinforcement is *not* given every time the stimulus is presented. It is only given when the response is made. Thus, *the critical prerequisite for instrumental conditioning is the experimenter-determined relation between response and reinforcement.* In some early experiments on conditioning this critical difference was not realized. Consider the following two experiments diagrammed in Figure 2.13. In both experiments, a tuning fork is sounded and electric shock is delivered to the dog's paw. In one case, the circuit is arranged so that lifting the paw serves to break the circuit. In the other, lifting the paw does not break the circuit. The procedure shown at the bottom of the figure is instrumental conditioning:

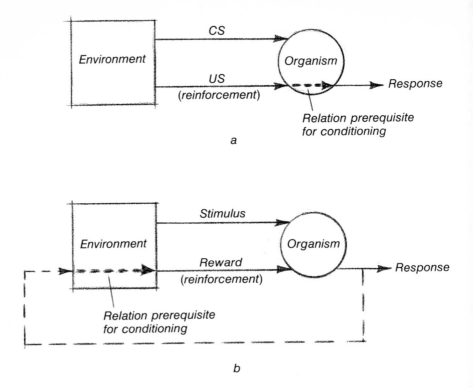

Figure 2.12 *Classical and instrumental conditioning compared with respect to interaction between the organism and its environment. (a) Classical conditioning. (b) Instrumental conditioning.*

the subject's behavior here serves to determine the presence or absence of the shock. The procedure sketched at the top is classical conditioning: the subject's behavior has no effect on the shock, but the pairing between the tuning fork stimulus, the shock, and the withdrawal of the leg is always maintained.

We discussed extinction previously in relation to classical conditioning. Extinction consisted in eliminating the US (the reinforcement). Extinction in instrumental conditioning also consists in eliminating the reinforcement. In order to extinguish an instrumentally conditioned response, we stop rewarding the animal for making the response. The results are the same for classical and instrumental conditioning—the probability that the response will recur decreases.

We have spoken of the *probabilities* that responses will recur. One

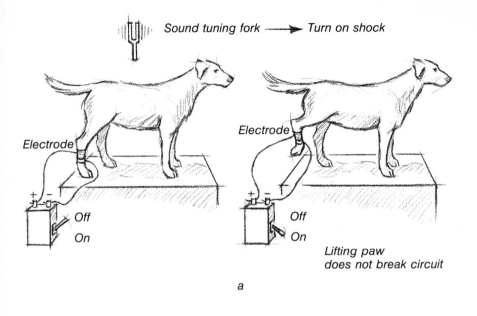

a

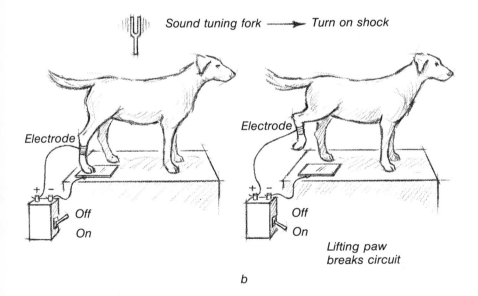

b

Figure 2.13 *The difference between classical conditioning and instrumental conditioning illustrated by a minor change in an electric-shock circuit. (a) Classical conditioning. (b) Instrumental conditioning.*

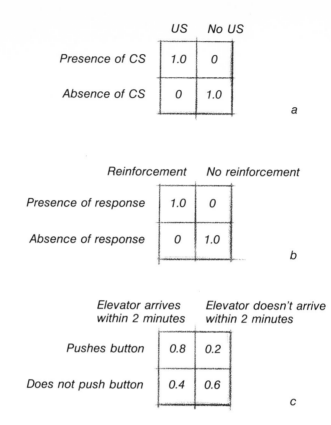

Figure 2.14 Contingency tables (a) for a standard classical conditioning
experiment, (b) for a standard instrumental conditioning experiment, and
(c) for elevator arrivals versus button pushing. The values in the tables are
conditional probabilities. In (c), for instance, 0.8 is the probability that a certain
elevator will arrive within 2 minutes of pressing the button.

difference between classical and instrumental conditioning can be seen in
the different contingencies involved. A contingency is a set of conditional
probabilities, the probability that, given one event, another event will
occur. A contingency table that could apply for a classical conditioning
experiment is shown in part (a) of Figure 2.14. It shows that when the CS
is presented, the probability of the US is 1.0 and that when the CS is
absent the probability of the US is zero; that is, the US (the reinforcement) is completely dependent on the CS. With instrumental conditioning the contingency set by the experimenter is between the response and
the reinforcement. The table in part (b) of Figure 2.14 says that when a
response is made, the probability of reinforcement is 1.0 and that when no
response is made the probability of reinforcement is zero; that is, the

reinforcement is completely dependent on the response. The reinforcer is omitted during extinction of both kinds of conditioning, and all the terms in the first column of the table would be zero.

One advantage of this way of formulating the two types of conditioning is that other, nonzero and nonunity values may be put in the table and their effect on conditioning studied. In everyday life we rarely find the complete dependencies shown in parts (a) and (b) of Figure 2.14. Responding that usually produces reinforcement sometimes fails to work and nonresponding that usually fails to produce reinforcement sometimes produces reinforcement. Occasionally, pushing the button and waiting fails to bring an elevator and occasionally elevators arrive without any button-pushing at all. The contingency of elevator arrivals on button pushing might be as shown in Figure 2.14c. Clearly, pushing a button makes elevator arrivals more probable, but it by no means makes them certain.

Classifying Behavior

The ever-changing pattern of events that comprise an organism's behavior are sometimes analyzed into relatively large chunks (like "sleeping," "resting," and "eating") and sometimes into relatively small bits (like "heartbeats," "breaths," "blinks," and "nerve impulses"). Obviously there is no single correct way to classify behavior. How one classifies the behavior of a particular organism depends largely on one's point of view and on the degree of one's interest in the organism.

For most of us, a man's eye movements in his sleep is a detail scarcely worthy of note; we are content with the observation that the man seems to be asleep. On the other hand, if we were studying the nature of sleep, we might attempt to keep a careful record of such bits of behavior, and eye movements and other muscular spasms might turn out to be significant classifications of behavior within the context of our study.

If we observe someone, say a businessman, for a considerable period, how should we group the events we observe? Our businessman is always doing something, always breathing for instance. Will that form an important part of our description? Should we describe in detail the nervous mechanism involved in each breath? or should we ignore his breathing entirely and concentrate on molar actions, like his work or his eating? We also face the probem that at any given time our subject may be doing *many* things—breathing, writing, working, earning money, digesting his food, advancing his career, biting his upper lip, blinking, hoping, thinking, and sitting.

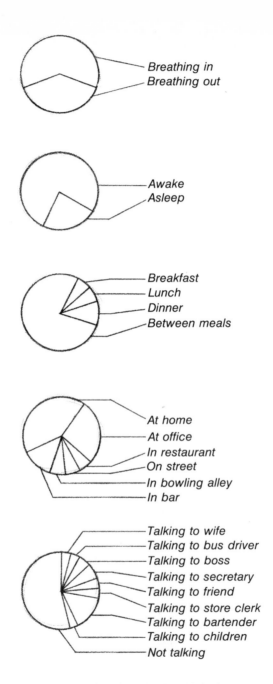

Figure 2.15 *Several ways in which observers could classify a man's behavior.*

Figure 2.15 shows how different observers might describe what the businessman did in a single day. Some of these descriptions are relatively molecular in the sense that they go into some detail about bits of his behavior. Some are more molar in the sense that they divide his behavior into relatively large chunks, but all are fairly consistent and reasonable ways to look at what he is doing. The businessman's associates may describe his behavior in terms of his business activities. His wife may describe his behavior in terms of his domestic activities. His doctor, his insurance agent, his banker, will each have a particular outlook. Each will describe the behavior of the man in terms of his interest in the man. As psychologists, though, where do *we* draw the line? How can we bring some organization to this complex ongoing process, (Indeed, how shall we classify *all* the possible behaviors of *all* possible organisms?) If we are interested in the *modification of behavior,* then we must find a way to classify behavior in terms of its modifiability.

We have described two methods of modifying behavior—classical conditioning and instrumental conditioning. What do they tell us about how to classify the businessman's behavior (and behavior in general)? Figure 2.16 shows how the contingencies of reinforcement in the two methods aid in the classification of behavior.

In classical conditioning, reinforcement is the presentation of an unconditioned stimulus that invariably elicits a response. Thus, responses in classical conditioning must be grouped into a class, or category, on the basis of their common elicitation by a certain type of stimulus. (The stimulus thus defines the category.) As our hypothetical businessman goes through his day some of the things he does fall into such stimulus-defined categories.

For instance, when a light is turned on, the man's pupils contract, and there is some electrical activity in the cortex of his brain. When he hears a sudden loud noise, he withdraws from it, shows increased heart rate, and a group of other measurable phenomena. Each stimulus has a set of behavioral and physiological responses that follow it. With respect to classical conditioning, *the group of measurable phenomena elicited by a particular stimulus are classified together as the response to that stimulus.* Only a limited set of responses, however, can be so classified. Most of the man's behavior, especially that part that appears to be "voluntary" cannot be elicited by any particular stimulus. The techniques of classical conditioning are difficult to apply to such behavior. For instance, if our businessman were head of a construction company engaged in building a dam, we would be hard put to find any unconditioned stimulus that elicited the

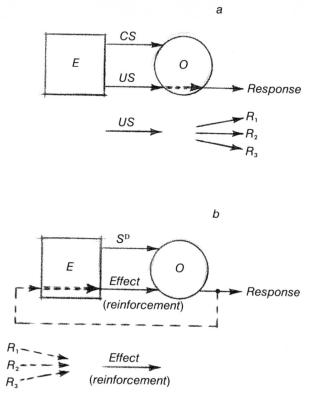

Figure 2.16 *Classification of behavior in terms of classical conditioning and instrumental conditioning. (a) Classical conditioning. Any acts that are invariably elicited by a single stimulus can be grouped together. Thus we can identify "leg-withdrawal following electric shock," and distinguish it, as a category, from other muscular movements. (b) Instrumental conditioning. Any acts that produce the same effect can be grouped together. Such a category is called an operant. An operant could include such diverse actions as pressing an elevator button with one's thumb, one's forefinger, or one's elbow or even asking another person to press the button—in short, any action that moves the button.*

behavior of dam-building in the businessman.* The psychologist who is interested in classical conditioning does not talk about the response of dam-building. If he wants to describe dam-building at all in terms of classically conditioned behavior, he must break the entire process down into smaller responses such as the movements of certain muscles, each of which itself *can* be elicited by known stimuli.

In instrumental conditioning, on the other hand, we need not limit

---

* However, in the case of certain organisms like the beaver, dam-building might be an innate pattern of behavior capable of being elicited by certain stimuli.

ourselves only to behavior known to be elicited by certain stimuli. We are free to work with any behavior that the organism will emit. The only requirement is that we be able to measure the behavior so as to reward or punish the organism when the behavior is emitted. The dam-building of our businessman can be measured, and reinforcement may be programmed for it. Dam-building is, thus, a legitimate category of behavior for instrumental conditioning.

In order to measure a given class of behavior, all the members of that class must have some common environmental effect. For instance, all dam-building behavior must potentially result in a completed dam. The businessman's contract, which determines the conditions of his reward, sets forth only specifications of the completed dam. How the dam is built is up to the businessman. There may be an infinite number of ways in which this contract could be fulfilled. Similarly, an experimenter might be training a rat to press a bar. He programs reinforcement for bar-pressing, but he does not specify how the bar must be pressed. The rat may press the bar with its left paw, its right paw, its head, its tail, or in an infinite number of different ways. What these infinite different actions of the rat have in common is that they all change a certain portion of the environment in the same way—they all succeed in moving the bar through a certain angle, and they all may produce reward. Any class of behavior that produces such a common effect on the environment is called an *operant*. The term was coined by the American psychologist B. F. Skinner, who first proposed that instrumental behavior consists of *emitted* acts, which are classified according to their effect on the environment (as opposed to classically conditioned behavior, which consists of elicited acts, which are classified according to the stimulus that elicits them). In this chapter, we shall deal with several operants, including bar pressing, key pecking, door opening, the breaking of photocell beams, and even running from one place to another. All are operants in the sense that they are categories that describe an infinite set of individual acts having a common effect on the environment.

Classical and Instrumental Conditioning in the Same Experiment

In a given situation, both classical and instrumental responses may be reinforced simultaneously. In other words, Response A may be required to produce the reinforcement, and Response B may be elicited by the very same reinforcement.

An experiment by Gaylord D. Ellison and Jerzy Konorski produced classical and instrumental conditioning with the same reinforcer, and studied the two kinds of responses separately. Their method was to train a dog to press a lever during a light in order to produce, not food directly, but a buzzer (CS) followed by food. They could measure both lever presses and salivation during the light and during the CS. When the light was introduced, the dog had to press the lever nine times. This turned off the light and produced the buzzer. Eight seconds later the food was automatically presented.

This somewhat complicated procedure enabled Ellison and Konorski to measure rates of salivation (classically conditioned) and bar pressing (instrumentally conditioned) separately. First, they measured salivation and bar pressing before all of the nine presses were made. (At this point, bar pressing was the appropriate response since it was required to produce the reinforcement. Second, they measured salivation and bar pressing after the nine presses were made (and after the CS was presented) but *before* the US (food) was presented. By then bar presses had no effect, but the CS produced salivation. Figure 2.17 shows their results. Bar-presses, the instrumental response, were high during the light and low during the buzzer; salivation was high during the buzzer and low during the light. Thus, within a single experimental situation, both classical and instrumental responses can be measured separately and made to occur with maximum force at different times depending on the conditioning procedure that generated them.

Anatomical Correlates of Classical and Instrumental Conditioning

Some psychologists believe that classical and instrumental conditioning may be distinguished by the part of the nervous system in which they can act. Classical conditioning is said to work better with autonomic functions such as glandular secretions, and instrumental conditioning is said to work better with nonautonomic responses such as muscular movements. Ellison and Konorski's experiment provides an example of this distinction. The classical component was autonomic (salivation) while the instrumental component was muscular (lever pressing).

These anatomical boundaries, however, have been crossed many times. Classical conditioning experiments have been performed with muscular responses such as eyeblink, and Neil Miller and his students at Rockefeller University have recently instrumentally conditioned autonomic responses. For instance, when an animal's heart rate is measured and it is given reward (feedback) only when its heart rate varies within a certain range,

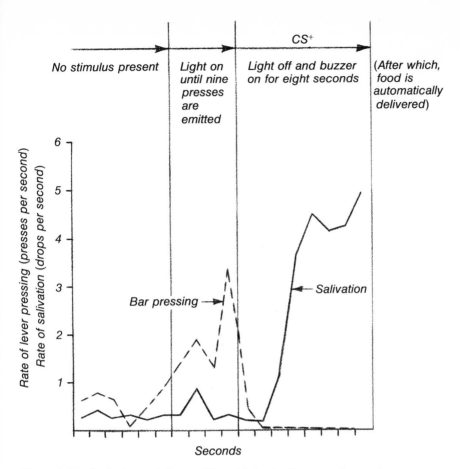

Figure 2.17 *An instrumentally conditioned behavior (bar pressing) and a classically conditioned behavior (salivation) occurring simultaneously in the same experiment. [Data from G. D. Ellison and J. Konorski, "Separation of the salivary and motor responses in instrumental conditioning." Science, 1964, 146, 1071–1072. Copyright 1964 by American Association for the Advancement of Science.]*

the heart rate tends to stay within that range more than it does if rewards are delivered randomly. Apparently, the characteristic of autonomic behavior that normally makes instrumental conditioning difficult is lack of feedback to the behaving organism.

This area of research holds practical promise since it implies that people can learn to keep blood pressure, stomach acidity, and so forth, at nonharmful levels provided they have feedback informing them of the state of these autonomic functions. Indeed, such feedback could be provided electronically.

PSEUDOCONDITIONING

Pseudoconditioning in Classical Experiments

What does it mean to say that classical conditioning has taken place? In one sense it means merely that a dog, perhaps, has been exposed to a certain procedure, as in Figure 2.2a. In another sense it means that not only has the dog been exposed to the procedure but also that the procedure has worked—after all, attempts at classical conditioning do not always work. For example, consider a reflex such as the knee jerk caused by striking the knee with a hard rubber hammer. If we shine a red light into a volunteer's eyes before striking his knee, and then present a test trial in which we shine the light only, what happens? Very likely, nothing. The knee-jerk reflex is a particularly difficult one to condition. Successful conditioning depends on a great many factors: the kind of stimulus, the kind of response, the techniques of measurement, and the skill of the experimenter.

Well, then, suppose we do select a CS, a US and a response, present them, test them, and find that we actually get a response to the CS (as in Figure 2.2). Can we then safely assume that conditioning has transpired? Unfortunately, no. If conditioning is to be successful, we must be assured that somehow we have created a connection that has not existed before. In some cases the US-response presentation can change the state of the organism so that the CS produces the response by itself without any necessary connection to the US-response. Remember that a critical part of classical conditioning is the *pairing of the CS and the US*. If this pairing is shown to have been unnecessary, we cannot call the process classical conditioning.

One must be especially careful regarding pseudoconditioning when electric shock is the US and a vibratory tactile stimulus is the CS. Consider the following experiment. First, vibrations are applied to one

Figure 2.18 *An example of a test for pseudo classical conditioning. If the results of these two procedures* (left and right) *are withdrawals similar in latency and extent, then it is possible that none of the withdrawals is a classically conditioned response. However, if there is no withdrawal after the test procedure* (bottom right) *even though there is a withdrawal after the classical conditioning procedure* (bottom left), *then the response at bottom left is a genuine classically conditioned response. In this case, "V" stands for a vibration and "S" stands for a shock.*

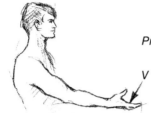

Present vibrating stimulus alone
Observe no withdrawal

Classical conditioning? | Pseudoconditioning test

Pair V with S

Present S alone

Observe withdrawal

Observe withdrawal

Present V alone

Present V alone

Observe withdrawal

Observe withdrawal

hand of a human subject. No effect is found. Then vibrations are paired with shock to the hand, and we observe a withdrawal of the hand. Then vibrations are applied alone, and again the hand is withdrawn. Is this effect the result of classical conditioning? The test is to get another subject, apply electric shock alone (unpaired with vibrations), then apply vibrations alone and see if the hand is now withdrawn. If it is, we can be fairly sure that the shock merely made the hand more sensitive to the vibrations, and that we did not observe classical conditioning in the first subject.

A critical test of classically conditioned behavior is to determine whether *pairings of the CS and US* are necessary to produce it. When we perform a classical conditioning experiment, observe a response, and then test and find that pairings were not necessary to produce that response, we have merely observed *pseudoconditioning*. (It is always important to test classical conditioning experiments to see if they can be explained on the basis of pseudoconditioning. Figure 2.18 shows the sequence of the pseudoconditioning test.)

Pseudoconditioning in Instrumental Experiments

In instrumental conditioning, any response that would occur without *pairings of response and reinforcement* is a pseudoconditioned response. Consider the following hypothetical experiment. The experimenter puts a rat in a chamber. The chamber has a bar protruding into it. Eventually the rat, in the course of its normal movements about the chamber, will press the bar. When this happens the experimenter sprays the rat with a powder that makes it itch. As a result, the rat jumps vigorously about the chamber. Because of these vigorous jumps, the rat hits against the bar sooner than before and the experimenter records a reduced latency of bar pressing. After the second press, the experimenter again sprays in the itching powder, causing still more jumping about and, hence, an even faster rate of bar presses. This continues until the rat is exhausted. Can we say that itching powder is rewarding to the rat and that we have here a genuine case of instrumental conditioning of the bar-press response? We cannot, until we have tested for pseudoconditioning.

How can we perform such a test? In order to test for pseudoconditioning we have to find out whether the same response would occur without the critical element, the pairings, of response with reinforcement. In the case of the rat and the itching powder, it would be easy to prove that itching powder was not instrumentally conditioning bar presses. We would merely take another rat and place it in an identical chamber. This

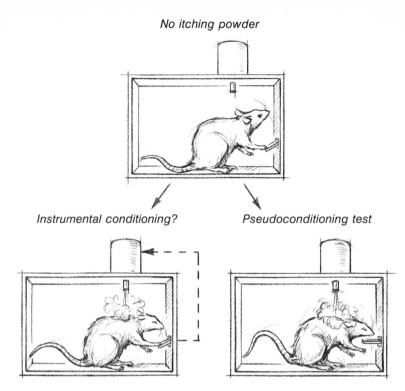

No itching powder

Instrumental conditioning?   *Pseudoconditioning test*

Itching powder follows bar presses   *Itching powder emitted randomly*

Figure 2.19 *A hypothetical example of a test for pseudo instrumental conditioning. At top, a rat's bar-presses are observed in the absence of reward or punishment. At bottom left, itching powder is sprayed on the rat whenever it presses the bar. At bottom right, itching powder is sprayed on the rat at random regardless of its bar-presses. The situation shown at bottom left may look like true instrumental conditioning—the rat seems to press the bar repeatedly to get sprayed by itching powder. However, the situation shown on the bottom right results in an equal increase in bar pressing, simply because the rat is agitated by the itching powder, thus revealing that the behavior at bottom left is not truly conditioned.*

time we would ignore the bar. We would spray the second rat periodically with itching powder, just as we sprayed the first rat with itching powder. (Of course, the systematic relation of the spraying of itching powder and pressing the bar would be absent.) If this rat's rate of pressing increased as much as the first rat's (as it is likely to do), we could assume that the increase in pressing we observed for the first rat was not a result of the pairing of responses with reinforcement but merely an artifact of the reinforcement (in this case, the itching powder) itself.

This, then, would be a case of pseudoconditioning. Figure 2.19 shows the procedure for testing for pseudoconditioning in instrumental conditioning experiments.

METHODS OF MEASUREMENT

Techniques for measuring behavior are the tools of the behaviorist's trade; they are as important to him as a hammer and saw are to a carpenter. Indeed, at times they seem so important that psychologists become more interested in the operation of the tools themselves than in the functions they have been designed to perform. But it is important to have a general understanding of these tools and what they measure.

Techniques for measuring responses that have been classically conditioned are identical to techniques for measuring unconditioned reflexes. One obvious example is the fistula and receptacle Pavlov devised for measuring salivation. Other reflexes, such as the eyeblink, knee jerk, and GSR can be measured by specialized electronic devices.

Instrumental conditioning responses are grouped according to their common effect on the environment. In the laboratory, this common effect is determined by the experimenter. Hence the problem of measurement in instrumental conditioning is not to *discover* the response already being made to a stimulus, as it is in the case of classical conditioning, but to *invent* an environmental event that will be sensitive to the organism's behavior. The latitude for such inventions is great, and there have been many widely different kinds of apparatus used. We shall describe a few of the most common kinds of measurements here.

Latency

The latency of any sort of behavior is the time between some signal and the occurrence of the behavior. The latency of an instrumental response will depend on the condition of the subject and the reinforcement being presented. For instance, when a mother calls her little boy to dinner, he is liable to come faster when he is hungry than when he is not, faster for hamburgers than for liver, and faster on rainy days than on sunny days. Latency has been a popular dependent variable for instrumental conditioning experiments and was, in fact, the measure of learning used by Thorndike in his original instrumental conditioning experiments.

Thorndike measured the interval from the time the animal was put into the puzzle box until it solved the puzzle and got out. (One difficulty with the puzzle box is that it is impossible to specify exactly *when* the response occurs. At what instant is the puzzle solved?—when the animal starts to pull the bolt out of the latch? or when it finishes?)

Since Thorndike's time, puzzle boxes have been simplified. One modification of the puzzle box has been the shuttle box invented by Neal Miller and O. Hobart Mowrer. A form of this device is a box with a barrier in the center. Instead of solving a puzzle and escaping to freedom and food, the animal jumps over the barrier from one side of the box to the other. The experimenter may put food in the other side of the box or he may put some aversive stimulus in the side with the animal. One common aversive stimulus is electric shock. When electric shock is used, the animal jumps over the barrier into, say the right side of the box to escape the shock on the left side, and the experimenter is able to measure the time between the onset of the shock and the jump. Then the animal is shocked on the left and the time between shock and jump measured again. One would expect an animal to become experienced with this procedure and jump faster and faster to escape shock. This is exactly what happens. In fact, if a signal precedes the shock, the animal does not wait for the shock to come on, but eventually learns to jump at the signal so that it avoids the shock altogether.

The shuttle box has two big advantages over the puzzle box. First of all, the behavior of the animal can be measured without the experimenter handling it between trials. (When the experimenter handles the animals he is likely to affect their behavior.) Secondly, the response of jumping is fairly discrete, in the sense that the response takes only a split second, so the latency from a signal to the beginning of the jump is about the same as the latency to the end of a jump.

Another isolation chamber in which latency may be measured is the lever box, or Skinner box, invented by B. F. Skinner (see Figure 2.20). Here, instead of shuttling over a divider, the animal has a lever to press. In a Skinner box, the response takes even less time than in the shuttle box. A further convenience of the Skinner box is the fact that the lever may be connected to a switch automatically delivering food or stopping electric shock.

Rate of Response

Sometimes every response is preceded by a signal. The running of a race, for instance, is formally started by the sound of a gun. In that case, the proper measure of responding is the time between the signal and the completion of the response. At other times, however, a certain form of

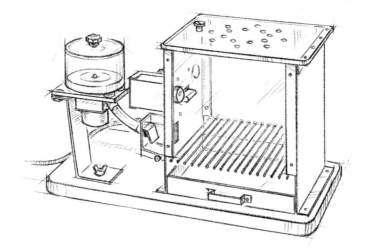

Figure 2.20 *A lever box, or Skinner box.*
[*Courtesy of Ralph Gerbrands Co., Arlington, Mass.*]

behavior is repeated many times in the presence of a single signal. For instance, suppose that the little boy in our previous example has finally come home to dinner. He begins to eat, lifting a forkful of food. The signal for this first forkful is a plate of food, which remains present during repeated instances of the same response. Although we can measure the latency of his first forkful of food, we must turn to *rate of response* if we want to quantify the rest of his eating. His rate of eating (like his latency in coming home) may be expected to vary with his hunger and his food preferences. When he is hungry he needs no coaxing to eat heartily, but when he is not hungry he is liable to eat listlessly or not at all.

Perhaps the simplest way to measure rate of response is to measure the speed with which an organism gets from one point to another. A device used for this purpose is called a *straight alley* and is, indeed, nothing but an alley with a box at either end. The animal runs from one box to the other, and its rate of running (its speed) can be measured automatically as it interrupts the light beams of a series of photocells. The straight alley is good for measuring the speed with which an animal runs toward a goal or away from a painful stimulus. However, if we were interested in continuously measuring an animal's running speed 1, 2, and 3 hours after an injection of a drug such as caffeine, we would need an impossibly long straight alley to allow a rat to run as far as it could. In order to measure rate of running over such long periods we use a device called a *running*

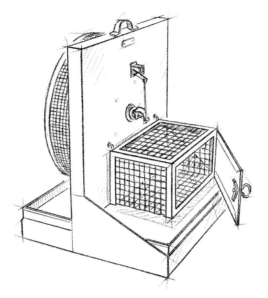

Figure 2.21 A running wheel. [Courtesy of Wahmann Manufacturing Co., Baltimore, Md.]

wheel (Figure 2.21). As far as the animal (usually, a rat) is concerned, the running wheel is an infinitely long straight alley, with the convenience to the experimenter that no matter how fast or far the rat runs, it remains in the same place. The rat's speed of running is easy to obtain by timing the wheel's revolutions.

The Skinner box is frequently employed to study rate of responding as well as to measure latency. To use this device to measure rate of responding, we leave the signal on continuously and stipulate that, while the signal is on, pressing the lever will be reinforced. Figure 2.22a shows a record of lever-presses by a rat when each lever-press was followed by a pellet of food. We can get a better picture of the changes in rate of response if we plot the responses cumulatively as in the Figure 2.22b. In such a cumulative record, a steep slope represents a rapid rate of responding and a shallow slope represents a slow rate of responding. A machine for plotting cumulative records directly is shown in the Figure 2.24b.

Choice

Choice is a relative measure, a measure of *ratios* rather than *absolute values*. The devices by which choice is measured in the psychological laboratory will illustrate the point.

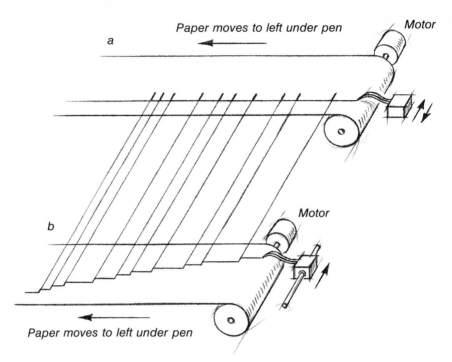

Figure 2.22 (a) An event recorder. A pen makes a regular tick for each response. (b) A cumulative recorder. A pen moves in one direction along a slide for each response and automatically drops back to the starting position when it reaches the edge of the roll of paper.

Small's maze embodied the principle of choice (Figure 1.18 in Chapter 1). Since Small's time, mazes for psychological experiments have become much simpler. One much-used maze is the T-maze shown at the top of Figure 2.25. The T-maze consists of a single central alley down which an animal (again usually a rat) runs until he reaches the cross of the T, where he must choose which of the two arms to run down next. This point is called the *choice point*. The two arms of the T are essentially two separate straight alleys that the rat can choose between. (Most of the devices that measure choice, in fact, are combinations of two or more rate-of-response devices.) At the choice point, the experimenter may provide the rat with a cue, for instance, a card, one side of which is painted red, and the other side green. At the ends of the arms lie two goal boxes, in which the rat may be rewarded or punished. Almost always, the events in the two goal boxes will be different. For instance, every time the rat runs down the arm corresponding to the green part of the card it might be rewarded in the goal box with a pellet of food. But if it runs

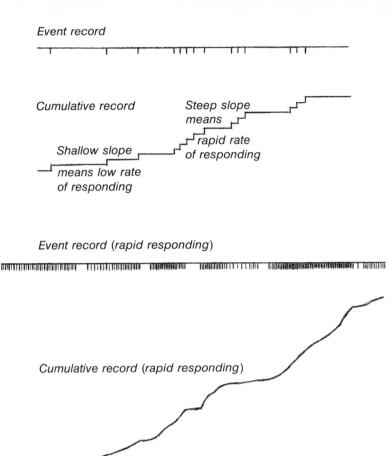

Figure 2.23 *Event records and cumulative records of responding. When responding is rapid compared to the speed of the paper and the size of the steps, the cumulative recorder draws a relatively smooth line whose slope is proportional to the rate of responding at any instant.*

down the arm corresponding to the red part of the card, it might be punished in the goal box with electric shock. In this case, the experimenter would measure the number of trials required for the rat to learn always to run down the arm indicated by the color green. The green card could always be on the left, but it could also be shifted from left to right on various trials.

With a device such as the T-maze, the experimenter can measure the ability of an animal to respond differentially to various stimuli at the choice point, that is, to discriminate between two stimuli by always

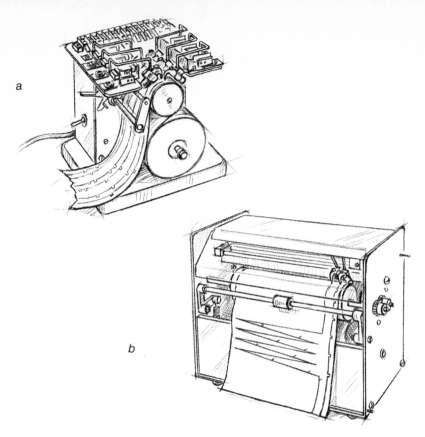

Figure 2.24 (a) An event recorder. (b) A cumulative recorder. [*Courtesy of Ralph Gerbrands Co., Arlington, Mass.*]

running down the arm corresponding to one of them. For instance, if the rat in the above example were color blind, it might never learn to run down the arm corresponding to green. The greater the rat's ability to discriminate between the stimuli at the choice point, the more quickly it could be expected to learn always to choose the arm corresponding to the preferred reward.

The experimenter could also determine the priorities of various rewards or punishments for the rat. For instance, suppose the rat was given twice as much food in Goal Box A as in Goal Box B, but was also shocked in Goal Box A, whereas no shock was given in Goal Box B. Which would it choose? Would its choice depend on how long it had been since the rat last ate? These kinds of questions can be answered with the help of a T-maze.

Because the T-maze measures Behavior A *relative* to Behavior B, the kind of psychological data that the T-maze produces is called a *behavior ratio*. The behavior ratio is simply the percentage of trials that the animal

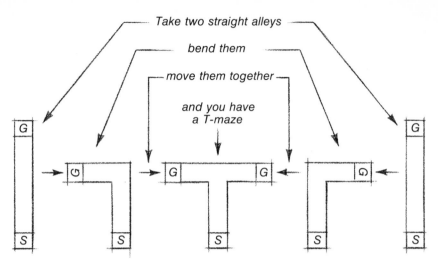

Take two straight alleys

bend them

move them together

and you have
a T-maze

where choice can be measured

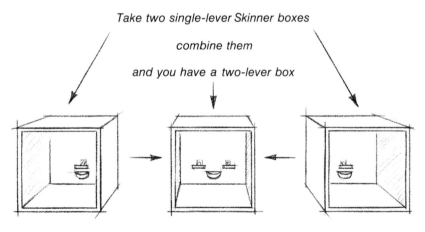

Take two single-lever Skinner boxes

combine them

and you have a two-lever box

where choice can be measured

Figure 2.25 In principle, each of these two-choice devices combines two simpler rate-of-response devices.

goes to one side or the other. (For instance, if food is in the left goal box of the T-maze while the right goal box is empty, the animal will learn to choose the left alley on 100 percent of the trials. Thus, the behavior ratio is 100 percent. If the animal were indifferent between left and right, the behavior ratio would be 50 percent; if he always chose the right, the behavior ratio would be 0 percent with reference to the left goal box.)

A fairly obvious example of a combination of two rate-of-response devices into a single device that will measure choice is the Skinner box containing two response levers instead of one. Pressing one lever might cause food to be delivered, and pressing the other might cause water to be delivered. With one lever, the relevant measure of behavior is the rate at which the lever is pressed. With two levers, the relevant measure is again a behavior ratio. Whatever percentage of the total number of presses are made on one lever determines the behavior ratio with respect to that lever. As with the T-maze, behavior ratio varies anywhere from zero to 100 percent.

We do not know at present which is more important, absolute measures (such as latency or rate of responding), or relative measures (such as choice measured by the behavior ratio). In common experience, sometimes one and sometimes the other is the most useful. (A candidate for public office may need a certain absolute number of signatures on a nominating petition. But, in order to be elected, he needs more votes than his opponent regardless of the absolute number of votes. The techniques for obtaining nomination may, in fact, be different from those for getting elected simply because of the absolute versus relative requirements of the two endeavors.)

Another device often used to measure choice is called the Lashley jumping stand (Figure 2.26), invented by Karl Lashley around 1938. A rat is placed on the jumping stand, in front of which is a vertical wall in which two cards are inset. If the rat jumps at the correct card, the card gives way and the rat lands on another platform, where he may be fed. If the rat jumps at the wrong card, the card does not give way and the rat falls into a net. When this device is used discriminations between two given stimuli (for instance, vertical versus horizontal stripes) are learned more rapidly than with the T-maze. It is worth examining the differences between the two devices for clues as to why this should be so. There are three essential differences between the devices: (1) In the Lashley jumping stand the animal must look at the patterns to be discriminated because he must look where he is jumping. (2) With the jumping stand, reward

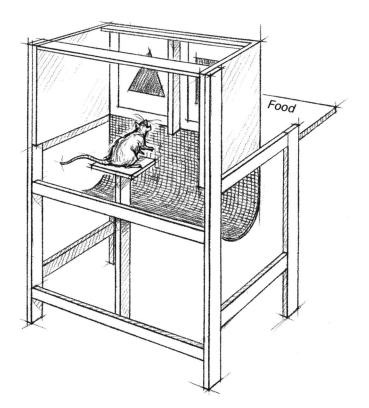

Figure 2.26 *The Lashley jumping stand. [After K. S. Lashley, "The mechanism of vision, XV. Preliminary studies of the rat's capacity for detailed vision." J. of Gen. Psych., 1938, 18, 126.]*

or punishment immediately follows choice. In the T-maze, the animal must take the time to run down an arm of the maze before it reaches the consequences of its choice; on the jumping stand, it has but to jump. The principle at work here is *delay of reward:* the longer that rewards are delayed following responses, the less effective they tend to be. (3) In the jumping stand procedure, there is an immediate aversive consequence of jumping at the wrong door. There is usually no such built-in punishment for the wrong response in the T-maze. In the usual T-maze discrimination, one box contains food, the other, nothing. It is interesting to note that when rats are punished for entering the wrong goal box in a T-maze (as well as rewarded in the right goal box), they learn to discriminate more rapidly.

Bibliography

Pavlov's works have received excellent translations, are easy to read, and ought to be fully comprehensible to beginning students. I. P. Pavlov, *Conditioned Reflexes*, originally published in English in 1927 by Oxford University Press, is available as a paperback (New York: Dover, 1960). An introductory learning text with an approach similar to the one taken here is J. R. Millenson, *Principles of Behavioral Analysis* (New York: Macmillan Co., 1967). Another introduction to operant conditioning techniques, excellent within its limited area, is G. S. Reynolds, *A Primer of Operant Conditioning* (Glenview, Illinois: Scott, Foresman & Co., 1968).

A comparison of instrumental and classical conditioning can be found in G. A. Kimble, *Hilgard and Marquis' Conditioning and Learning* (New York: Appleton-Century-Crofts, 1961). Kimble's book is detailed and not well organized, but it is the *most* comprehensive book on conditioning and learning. It describes a large proportion of the significant work in the area. Any student wishing to progress beyond the elementary level of the present volume must master the material in Kimble's book. A brief overview of learning theories can be found in E. R. Hilgard and G. H. Bower, *Theories of Learning* (New York: Appleton-Century-Crofts, 1966). One can start from Hilgard and Bower, but the best way to find out about a theoretical outlook is to read the original source. Here are some works by behavioral theorists:

Guthrie, E. R. *The Psychology of Learning.* Revised. New York: Harper & Row, 1952.

Hull, C. L. *A Behavior System: An Introduction to Behavior Theory Concerning the Individual Organism.* New Haven: Yale University Press, 1952.

Skinner, B. F. *The Behavior of Organisms: An Experimental Analysis.* New York: Appleton-Century-Crofts, 1938.

Tolman, E. C. *Purposive Behavior in Animals and Man.* New York: Appleton-Century-Crofts, 1932.

The experiment of Ellison and Konorski that used classical and instrumental conditioning together may be found in G. D. Ellison and J. Konorski, "Separation of the salivary and motor responses in instrumental conditioning" [*Science, 146* (No. 3647), 1071–1072, 1964]. Konorski has also recently written a book about conditioning from a physiological viewpoint called *Integrative Activity of the Brain* (Chicago: University of Chicago Press, 1967).

The various items of apparatus described in the section "Methods of Measurement" are more fully described in J. B. Sidowski, *Experimental Methods and Instrumentation in Psychology* (New York: McGraw-Hill, 1966).

Chapter 3

Reinforcement and Punishment

One of the principal functions of science is to make valid predictions. Astronomers predict positions of heavenly bodies; physicists predict the behavior of physical objects; chemists predict the products of various combinations of elements. Science, to be meaningful, must go beyond the explanation of events after they have happened and make predictions about future events.

Since the very heart of the conditioning process is reinforcement, psychologists have concerned themselves with predicting whether a given stimulus will reinforce a given behavior. We have been talking loosely about positive reinforcers such as food for hungry organisms or water for thirsty organisms, but we have not specified any characteristic that food and water have in common to make them reinforcing. If we knew what this characteristic was we could make true behavioral predictions; we would predict that a new stimulus with the characteristic would be reinforcing (that it would increase the probability of behavior it followed), while a new stimulus without the characteristic would not be reinforcing.

Theories of reinforcement are attempts to specify this characteristic. Let us consider a few of them.

THEORIES OF REINFORCEMENT

Four of the more influential theories of reinforcement that have emerged from the prolific speculation about the relation of reinforcement to organism are these: (1) *Need reduction.* This theory says that every reinforcer ultimately satisfies some vital need of the organism and "reduces the need" (that is, reduces the amount of the substance or thing needed) through a process of negative feedback. (2) *Tension reduction.* The tension-reduction theory says that every reinforcer ultimately lessens some tension in the organism through a process of negative feedback. (3) *Brain stimulation.* According to this theory, every reinforcer ultimately stimulates certain parts of the brain. (4) *Response as reinforcement.* This theory holds that responses are reinforced by the ability to make other responses, for example, that bar pressing is reinforced by the act of eating.

Before we discuss these four theories, we should note that each seems to contain at least a grain of truth but that none has succeeded, by itself, in accounting for all of the ways in which a response can be reinforced.

Need Reduction

Organisms need certain things to survive—food and water, for instance, oxygen to breathe, and specific temperature ranges outside of which they will perish. It is argued that all reinforcers must ultimately reduce one or the other of these physiological needs. (In other words, if the psychologist wants to know whether a certain substance is rewarding to a certain organism, it would seem that all he has to do is call up the biology department of his university and ask whether the substance satisfies a physiological need. If so, then it must be rewarding. If the biologist tells the psychologist that a platypus needs the chemicals found in bananas in order to survive, then bananas must be rewarding to the platypus.) Unfortunately, this theory is inconsistent with several well-known facts. Take the case of saccharine. There is no question that artificial sweeteners such as saccharine can be reinforcing. Rats will learn to run down the alley of a T-maze leading to a goal box with a saccharine solution in it although they have plenty of water available. Rats will learn to press a bar to receive a saccharine solution and humans will gladly put a dime in a slot to receive a cupful of carbonated water mixed with artificial flavoring and saccharine even when a water fountain is nearby. Yet, such artificial sweeteners are passed through the body virtually unchanged. This is but one of many reinforcers that do not appear to satisfy any vital need.

Tension Reduction

Another theory, one closely related to "need reduction," is that anything that immediately lessens tension of some kind in the organism is a reinforcer. Hunger, for instance, can be seen as a kind of tension that is lessened by eating. The trouble with this theory is that many things that seem to immediately increase tension are reinforcing. For instance, it may seem like cruel and unusual punishment to allow a male rat to copulate with a female and then to remove him before he has a chance to ejaculate. Nevertheless, male rats will repeatedly run down the alley of a T-maze leading to such treatment as opposed to lacking female rats altogether. Animals of all kinds will work hard at tasks which lead to no more startling reward than the sight of another animal or the opportunity to do a more complex task. For instance, monkeys will press a bar repeatedly to open a window that allows them to see activity in the laboratory. Monkeys will also solve puzzles with no reward involved other than the solution of the puzzle. It is difficult to classify all of these rewards in terms of tension reduction. If anything, presentation of some rewards seems to increase tension.

Of course, a tension-reduction theorist could argue that *immediate* tension reduction is not necessary for reinforcement. All that is necessary is *eventual* tension reduction. Then he could trace each reinforcement to its eventual tension-reducing act. But the problem with such theoretical maneuvering is that when a theory is stretched and stretched—even to cover cases like these—it becomes nebulous, does not allow us to make predictions, and does not advance our understanding a great deal.

Brain Stimulation

In 1954, two physiologists, James Olds and Peter Milner, found that rats would press a lever in order to deliver a mild electric shock to a certain area of their brain, the midbrain generally. The experiment is shown in Figure 3.1. The rat was enclosed in a cage with a lever attached to an electrical switch that sent current through a wire to certain areas of its brain. Each time the rat pressed the lever, a very mild current (of about 1/10,000 ampere) was turned on for less than half a second. Olds found

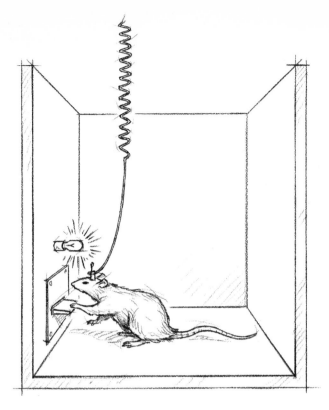

Figure 3.1 *Olds' self-stimulation experiment. [After "Pleasure Centers in the Brain," by James Olds. Copyright © 1956 by Scientific American, Inc. All rights reserved.]*

that rats would press the bar thousands of times an hour for periods of 12 hours or more to receive this stimulation. Evidently the current in the rat's brain was reinforcing. This experiment led to the speculation that perhaps a common element in all rewards is an ability to stimulate certain locations in the brain. Olds called these areas "pleasure centers," reasoning that anything that stimulated them resulted in the feeling of pleasure.

The brain is so complicated and knowledge of its functioning so vague, that we cannot tell whether any given stimulus branches to the pleasure center or not. In other words, we still have no operation that will predict what will or will not be reinforcing. While Olds' experiment seems to promise an eventual answer, it may be a long time before the promise is fulfilled.

Response as Reinforcement

Although it is convenient to call a stimulus *a reinforcer,* some psychologists argue that it would be more accurate to designate responses with this term. (Thus they might prefer to say "eating the pudding is a reinforcer" to "the pudding is a reinforcer.") This theory, that reinforcement lies in the *act* of consuming a needed substance, rather than in the substance itself is called a *consummatory-response* theory. According to this theory, certain acts and the sensations involved in performing these acts are said to be innately reinforcing to organisms. The reason that bar-presses of a hungry rat will increase when they are followed by food is not because the bar-presses produce food but because they give the rat the opportunity to eat. Thus, *eating* and *drinking* are sources of reinforcement, as opposed to food and water themselves.

This theory, unlike the need-reduction theory, is consistent with the reinforcing powers of substances like saccharine, since the act of consuming saccharine and the sensations involved therein are the same as the act of consuming other substances that do reduce needs. While sugar and saccharine are different with respect to their *need-reducing* powers, they are similar with respect to their *consummatory response.*

Another response theory of reinforcement, proposed by the psychologist David Premack, is called the *prepotent-response* theory. This theory is similar to the consummatory-response theory in the sense that responses are said to be reinforced only by the opportunity to make other responses. It differs from the consummatory-response theory, however, because it postulates no innately reinforcing responses (like eating and drinking). Instead, any response may be reinforcing. The power of one response to reinforce another is determined only by the relative strength of the two responses, the stronger response being capable of reinforcing the weaker. Relative strength, in turn, is measured by the relative time that the organism spends performing the acts if both acts are continuously available. One of Premack's experiments illustrates the point. He allowed several children free access to candy and to pinball machines. He found that many of the children spent a greater proportion of time playing the pinball machines than eating the candy. He reasoned that, for these children, playing with the machines was a stronger response than eating the candy. According to his theory a stronger response should reinforce a weaker one. When he tested this by allowing the children to play with the machines only after they had eaten a certain amount of the candy, he found that eating candy increased. In other words, playing with pinball machines reinforced eating. Note that this is a reversal of the usual situation where eating is the reinforcer and some other act is reinforced.

Two advantages of Premack's theory are (1) that it takes the relative nature of reinforcers into account. It treats reinforcement as a *relation* between behavior and its consequences rather than an absolute fact, and (2) it provides an independent measure of reinforcing power by observation of the relative time an organism is engaged in the reinforcing and to-be-reinforced acts.

The argument against both the consummatory-response theory and the prepotent-response theory is that reinforcement often can be achieved by by-passing any response. Normally, when food is used as reinforcement, the presentation of food and eating of the food go together. It is possible, however, to separate them. When food is delivered without eating, by injecting it directly into the stomach, the food is still reinforcing. Rats will learn to press a lever that results in the injection of food into their stomachs. Also, animals will learn to press a lever to get a higher proportion of oxygen to carbon dioxide in the air of a stuffy room despite the fact that more oxygen in the air causes less breathing—in other words, less responding (whether consummatory or prepotent). We must conclude, then, that animals can be rewarded in other ways than by making a response.

Which Theory is Correct?

The above are only a sample of the many theories about how positive reinforcers function. Even within the area of positive reinforcement, however, we have not been able to arrive at a simple classification. Theories help to give us insight about how to choose reinforcers in specific instances, since they are all correct up to a point, and, between them, they cover most of the reinforcers we have so far found. The point to be remembered here, though, is that none, by itself, is sufficient to account for all known reinforcers. This means that the best way to tell if a stimulus is reinforcing is to try it out in an instrumental conditioning experiment.

One consolation for the lack of a unifying principle that would enable us to predict the things that are reinforcing is the general consistency in the way reinforcers act once they are known to be reinforcing. A reinforcer for one response will generally be a reinforcer for other responses of the same organism. If you can teach your dog to give you his paw by rewarding him with a dog biscuit, you probably can also teach him to roll over with the same type of reward. But whether dog biscuits are rewarding in the first place can only be determined by trying them out.

REINFORCEMENT SCHEDULES

One of the earliest experiments relating to schedules of reinforcement was done more-or-less by accident by B. F. Skinner around 1932. In order to study the eating behavior of rats, he trained them to press a lever to receive a pellet of food and measured their rate of pressing, hence, their rate of eating, after various periods of food deprivation. One day, Skinner found that his supply of pellets was low. This inspired him to set up the apparatus so that instead of every press producing reinforcement, only one press a minute would be reinforced, no matter how many times a rat pressed the lever.

Not only did the rats keep pressing the lever but their rate of pressing was considerably higher than when every press was reinforced. This increase in rate of responding is evidence against the notion that less reinforcement would simply produce less responding. Skinner inferred that the schedule (or rule) according to which reinforcement is presented could be a powerful way to control behavior and is a worthwhile subject of study in and of itself. The name for the particular reinforcement schedule used by Skinner is a "fixed interval" schedule. Let us now consider a method for expressing the requirements of Skinner's schedule and the animal's performance with this schedule in graphic form.

Fixed-Interval Schedules

In order to diagram fixed-interval (FI) schedules of reinforcement, we construct a graph with number of presses on the vertical axis and time on the horizontal axis, as in part (a), Figure 3.2. Furthermore, we represent the conditions of reinforcement by a line on the graph. In Skinner's experiment, the requirement is that one minute elapse since the last reinforcement. Assuming that the rat presses the lever often enough, one response would be reinforced every minute. This could be represented by a vertical line at each minute on the horizontal axis. Starting at the origin, then, we can draw a cumulative record, as in part (b), Figure 3.2, of the responses until they reach the required interval. Each response raises the cumulative record another step. The width of the step is the time between responses. When the first minute is reached, reinforcement is given (rep-

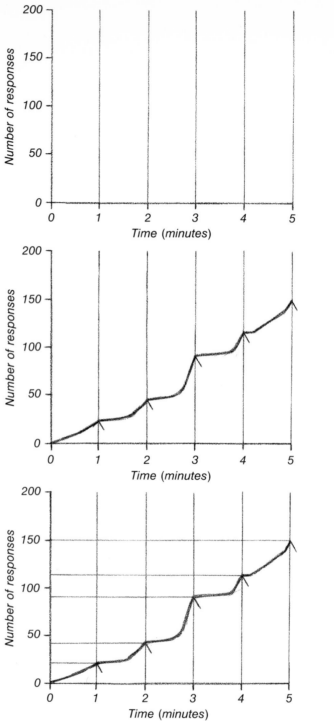

Figure 3.2 *Cumulative record of lever presses by a rat reinforced on a one-minute fixed-interval schedule. (Ticks mark reinforcements.) (a) The vertical lines mark the locus of each reinforcement; reinforcement is available once at the end of each minute no matter how many times the rat presses the lever. (b) Cumulative record of responding, showing reinforcements received by the rat. (c) Projection of the results to the vertical axis. The distances between the horizontal lines show how many responses occurred for each reinforcement.*

resented by a downward slash on the graph) after the next response and so on for the other intervals. If we project the slashes across to the vertical axis, as in Figure 3.2c, we get a picture of the number of responses between reinforcements. In a one-minute fixed-interval schedule (an FI-1′ schedule) the organism has only to respond once every minute to receive the maximum reward. Any additional responses during the minute have no effect. The kind of behavior often observed with fixed-interval schedules, and shown by the cumulative records of Figure 3.2, is a pause after reinforcement and then an increase in rate of responding until a high rate is reached just as the interval is about to end. This pattern (called scalloping) is found with many organisms and many responses. (An example of human behavior which conforms to the same pattern might be the frequency with which one looks at a pot of water when one is impatient for it to boil, or the frequency with which the oven door is opened to test the turkey while a hungry family is waiting.)*

Fixed-Ratio Schedules

Another kind of schedule much studied in the laboratory is the fixed-ratio (FR) schedule. Here, the organism is rewarded only after making a certain fixed number of responses. For instance, a rat may be rewarded for every fourth press instead of for every press. Figure 3.3a shows a cumulative record of a pigeon rewarded with three seconds of access to food for every 50 pecks on an illuminated disk. (This is called an FR-50 schedule.) The lines showing the locus of reinforcement are horizontal instead of vertical, reflecting the fact that fixed numbers of responses rather than intervals of time determine the availability of reinforcement. Each response raises the cumulative record a small step. When the step is reached corresponding to the ratio, reinforcement is given; reinforcement is represented by a slash on the graph. If we project the slashes downward to the horizontal axis, as in Figure 3.3b, we get a

---

* Recent experiments have shown that in many fixed-intervals schedules the change from pausing to rapid responding is quite sudden.

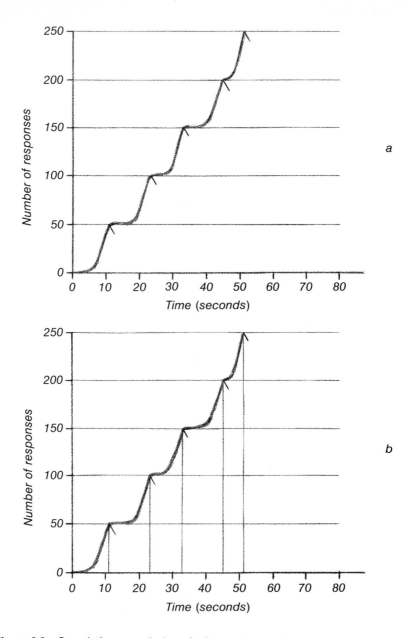

Figure 3.3 Cumulative record of pecks by a pigeon reinforced on a fixed-ratio schedule of one reinforcement for each 50 pecks. (a) Cumulative record with horizontal lines marking the locus of each reinforcement and ticks representing actual reinforcements. (b) Projection to the vertical axis, showing time between reinforcements.

picture of the rate of reinforcements in time. If the reinforcements are close together, they are coming rapidly; if they are far apart, they are coming slowly. Note that after each reinforcement the pigeons pause before beginning to respond again. This pattern of a rapid burst of responding which fulfills the ratio and then a pause after reinforcement is found for pigeons pecking a disk, rats pressing a lever, monkeys pressing a disk, humans tapping a telegraph key and innumerable other responses.

Compound Schedules

The basic fixed-interval and fixed-ratio schedules may be combined in various ways. In the fixed-ratio, a certain *number* of responses must appear before reinforcement occurs. In the fixed-interval, a fixed time must elapse. Suppose we specify that a fixed number of responses must occur *or* a fixed time must elapse before reinforcement. This type of schedule is diagrammed in Figure 3.4a. The patterns of behavior shown by the two cumulative records would be rewarded at points (p) and (q). Pattern (p) would be rewarded sooner, but at the cost of more responses; pattern (q) would be rewarded later, but with less responses.

If we were to stipulate that both the interval *and* ratio requirements must be met for reinforcement to occur we would have the situation diagrammed in Figure 3.4b. The same patterns of responding would not be reinforced at (p) or (q), where only the ratio or interval requirements are met, but at (r) or (s) where both requirements are met.

A third, and more complex kind of compound schedule is the interlocking schedule diagrammed in Figure 3.4c. For this schedule, the requirement is that a certain *sum* of responses and seconds must occur before a response can be reinforced. This schedule works on the same principle as a taximeter, which adds the time of the ride to the distance travelled to determine the fare. In the schedule, the time is added to the number of responses. When they reach a certain sum, reinforcement will be available at the next peck.

Variable Schedules

The fixed patterning of responses that occurs when fixed-interval or fixed-ratio schedules are imposed does not appear with variable-interval and variable-ratio schedules. A variable-interval (VI) schedule makes reinforcement available sometimes after short intervals and sometimes after long intervals. Figure 3.5 shows cumulative records of pigeons pecking a key for variable-interval and variable-ratio schedules of reinforcement. When we refer to a fixed-interval schedule of one minute

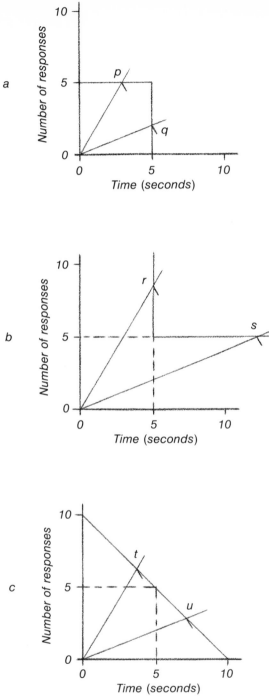

Figure 3.4   *Compound schedules of reinforcement. (a) Locus of reinforcement*
for 5 responses or a 5-second interval. At p, behavior is reinforced after
5 responses in less than 5 seconds. At q, behavior is reinforced after 5 seconds
and fewer than 5 responses. (b) Locus of reinforcement for 5 responses plus
a 5-second interval. At r, behavior is reinforced after more than 5 responses
in 5 seconds. At s, behavior is reinforced after 5 responses in more than 5
seconds. (c) Locus of reinforcement for 10 responses or 10 seconds or any
number of responses and seconds totalling 10. At t, behavior is rewarded for
6 responses in 4 seconds. At u, behavior is rewarded for 3 responses in 7 seconds.

(FI-1'), we mean that each reinforcement is made available after a
one-minute interval. When we speak of a variable-interval schedule of
one minute (VI-1'), we mean only that the *average* of the intervals used
in that schedule is one minute.

When variable-interval and variable-ratio schedules are used, responses
usually occur at a fairly constant rate. Note that the rate of responding
with the variable-ratio schedule in Figure 3.5 is quite a bit faster than the
rate for the variable-interval schedule. Because of the slow steady rate of
responding on variable-interval schedules, these schedules are often used
as baselines to gauge the effects of other variables on behavior. A rat on a
variable-interval schedule, for instance, responds more rapidly after being
given an injection of dexedrine, a stimulant, than after being given an
injection of pentobarbital, a depressant.

Extinction after Partial Reinforcement

We know that the withdrawal of reinforcement from an instrumental
response extinguishes the response. In other words, it gradually comes to
be no longer emitted. We might ask how extinction of responses that have
been conditioned under various schedules of reinforcement we have
discussed compares with extinction of responses conditioned under a
schedule of constant reinforcement (where each response is reinforced).
Our line of thinking might run as follows: The more reinforcement for a
response, the stronger that response should be. The stronger a response is,
the better it should resist extinction. The better a response resists extinction, the more responses one should observe after reinforcement has been
withdrawn. This line of reasoning seems logical, but, as a matter of fact,
exactly the opposite holds true. When a response has been constantly
rewarded, extinction is usually much faster than when the same response
has been rewarded only part of the time. This result so surprised psychologists that they called it "Humphreys' paradox" (after Lloyd G. Humphreys, the man who first demonstrated it experimentally). Yet, this
seeming paradox is a most reliable, reproducible, and significant effect.

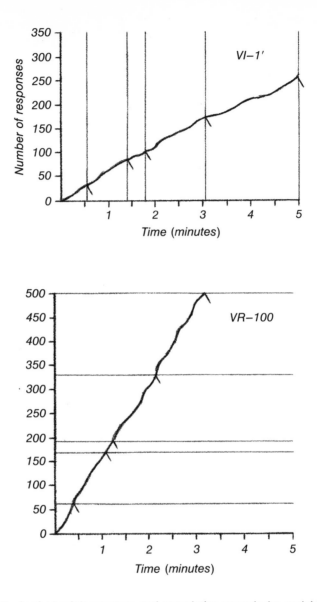

Figure 3.5 Loci of reinforcements and cumulative records for variable-interval and variable-ratio schedules of reinforcement of a pigeon's pecking. (*Ticks mark reinforcements.*) *VI-1': This graph shows a variable-interval schedule in which a reinforcement is available at the average rate of once per minute. VR-100: This graph shows a variable-ratio schedule in which a reinforcement is available at the average ratio of one per 100 responses.*

Perhaps we can gain an insight into Humphreys' paradox from this example:

There are two hypothetical Coke machines. One, in Building A, produces a drink for every dime inserted. The other, in Building B, is partially broken. Occasionally, when a dime is inserted, nothing happens. The people in Building B complain repeatedly but ineffectually about the situation, but they seem to be willing to lose their dimes once in a while as long as they eventually get a Coke. Now, suppose both machines break down completely. Which one will receive more dimes before the dimes stop altogether? Probably the machine in Building B, which has been only partially reinforcing the "dime-inserting behavior." It will take a while before the people in Building B realize that the machine is completely inoperative. The people in Building A, on the other hand, will immediately realize that there is something wrong and stop inserting dimes.

To be more general, the Coke-machine example shows that organisms must learn to discriminate between conditions of reinforcement and conditions of extinction, and that anything that helps them to do this will speed up extinction. Partial reinforcement on some schedule is more like extinction than is constant reinforcement and, hence, harder to tell from extinction. To the extent that conditions of reinforcement resemble conditions of extinction, there will be more responses during extinction.

But when we say that an organism responds to conditions, that the conditions of extinction must be discriminated from the conditions of reinforcement, what do we mean? Simply that organisms can discriminate between general situations as well as between particular stimuli. Once more, this is the problem of molecularity versus molarity. At the beginning of this chapter we discussed the problem of categorizing an organism's behavior. Let us return to this problem and consider the following example: Two people might describe the behavior of the same man as "building a house" or as "laying bricks" depending on their point of view. One continuum upon which these descriptions could be located is that of molarity–molecularity. The molar view is broad and encompassing; the molecular view is narrow and detailed. In the same way that the experimenter (or the environment) may react to the molar or molecular behavior of the subject, so the subject may react to molar or molecular aspects of the environment. If a person moves from Alaska to Florida, he probably does not do so because it happened to snow in Alaska one day, but he might do so because it is generally snowy in Alaska. He is more likely to react to the *rate* of snowing than to an individual snowstorm.

Similarly, any animal may react to the *rate* of reinforcements, or some other collective property of reinforcements rather than to each reinforcement as it occurs.

More direct evidence that the problem of extinction is actually one of discriminating between conditions of reinforcement and conditions of extinction is that, when cues are provided during extinction, the extinction process is speeded up. For instance, in a Skinner box, if the color of the illumination of the test chamber is changed when reinforcement is withdrawn, extinction is faster. Any signal that is present during extinction and not present during conditioning will speed up extinction. Another piece of evidence is the fact that extinction is faster for fixed-interval and fixed-ratio schedules than for variable-interval and variable-ratio schedules. In the fixed schedules, disruption of the pattern of regular reinforcements signals extinction; in the variable schedules, there is no pattern to disrupt.

The assumption in the original reasoning that led to Humphreys' paradox is that strong conditioning of a response would produce more responses in extinction. This assumption is based on the notion that latency of response, magnitude of response, and resistance to extinction are all measures of the same thing, namely, the "strength" of the response. Apparently responses in extinction are not exclusively determined by the "strength" of a response—but also reflect a failure to discriminate between conditions of extinction and conditions of reinforcement. Where enough cues to this discrimination are provided, there are relatively few responses after reinforcement is withdrawn.

SECONDARY REINFORCEMENT
AND CHAINS OF BEHAVIOR

It may have occurred to the reader by now that there are few human actions that are directly reinforced by primary reinforcers such as food. "Man does not live by bread alone," the saying goes. But then, what *does* he live by? At the risk of impiety, behaviorists must answer: Man lives largely by *secondary reinforcers*.

The idea of a secondary reinforcer is really quite simple and is based on common sense. In classical conditioning, a neutral stimulus (which becomes the CS) is always followed by primary reinforcement. In instrumental conditioning a neutral stimulus will always be followed by primary reinforcement, provided the correct response is made in its presence. Thus from the subject's point of view it is sufficient to obtain the neutral stimulus in order to be sure of eventual primary reinforcement. If a child is fed (primary reinforcement) whenever he is seated in a certain chair (the neutral stimulus) he will soon learn to climb into the chair when he is hungry and will direct his efforts to sitting in the chair. To a visitor who did not know that the child was fed in that chair it would seem as if the chair itself was reinforcing. The visitor would see the child strain to climb into it and cry until he was placed in it. In this sense, the chair is a secondary reinforcer. (If the child's mother eventually stopped feeding him there, the chair would lose its secondary reinforcing properties.)

Secondary reinforcement bridges the gap between laboratory procedures and complex human and animal behavior. It is a process by which things and events that formerly did not reinforce behavior can become apparently reinforcing. A newborn baby's rewards are easy to enumerate: milk, a change of diapers, and a certain amount of fondling by its parents. As the baby grows up, the list of things that he will work to produce may be enlarged to include praise, money, fame, achievement, and so forth. A dollar bill may not be as rewarding to a baby as a shiny dime. As he grows older, though, the dirty green piece of paper may become relatively more sought after. It is reasonable to explain this change as a case of secondary reinforcement—the dollar has become linked to other reinforcements.

Wolfe's Experiment

An illuminating study of how secondary reinforcement becomes effective was done by John B. Wolfe in 1936. Chimpanzees, like babies, are initially quite indifferent to money, but Wolfe showed how money could come to reinforce behavior. The "money" used by Wolfe in his experiment consisted of poker chips. In a corner of the chimpanzees' cage, there was a vending machine that provided a grape every time the chimpanzees inserted a poker chip. After the chimpanzees learned to put a chip in the slot for the grape, Wolfe found that he could teach them to do other tasks, such as pressing a lever, or pulling on a string in order to receive poker chips. Thus, the poker chips, to which the chimpanzees were initially indifferent, took on the properties of reinforcement. In fact, even when the vending machine was not present, the chimpanzees would continue to work to accumulate chips that they could use to operate the machine later.

One can think of various ways of extending Wolfe's experiment. Suppose the vending machine only produced a grape if a blue chip was

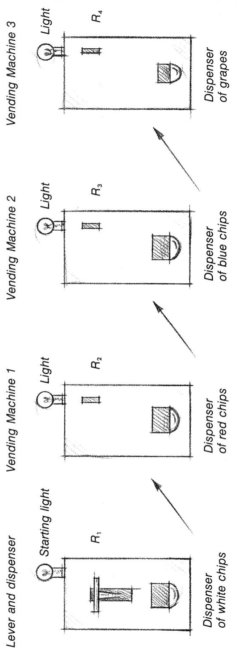

Figure 3.6 Hypothetical extension of Wolfe's experiment to produce an extended chain of behavior. The light on the dispenser at left signals a chimpanzee that a white chip is available. The chimp responds (first response, R_1) by pulling a lever. The light on Vending Machine 1 signals the availability of a red chip. The chimp now responds (R_2) by inserting the white chip in Machine 1. When the light on Vending Machine 2 comes on, he responds (R_3) by inserting the red chip in the machine. He receives a blue chip that may then be inserted (R_4) in Vending Machine 3 when its light signals that a grape is available.

inserted. We could install another vending machine that would produce blue chips—but only if a red chip were inserted. We could install still another machine that would produce red chips if white chips were inserted. It is likely that the chimpanzees could then learn still another task to get the white chips. By such means highly complex instrumental behaviors are established.

The entire sequence, starting with the response that earns the white chip and ending with the response that earns the grape, is called a *chain of behavior*. We could reinforce each response in the chain only under certain specified conditions. For instance, the vending machines could be made inoperative except when a light is on above the slot. Then the chimpanzees would have to insert chips in slots only when the light is on above them. Figure 3.6 is a diagram of such conditions. While this particular chain is discontinuous, with each step clearly signaled by a specific stimulus and clearly delineated from the step before, chains of behavior may become quite continuous. (For instance, the sequence of movements involved in playing the piano eventually take on a continuous quality.)

The important rule in establishing chains is to start with the last response—the one that is rewarded with primary reinforcement. Wolfe *first* taught his chimps to put a token in the slot for the grape and *then* taught them to work for the tokens. If you want to teach a dog to fetch your slippers and drop them in front of you, *first* teach him to drop the slippers and *then* teach him to fetch them.

Extinction of Chains of Behavior

If the final primary reinforcement is eliminated from the chain, the entire chain of behavior will often disintegrate and eventually cease to occur. But what happens if the chain is interrupted in the middle? In other words, what happens if one of the secondary reinforcements is eliminated? In Figure 3.6 suppose that the lever and Vending Machine 1 remained operative but that Vending Machine 2 got clogged so that even when its light went on, depositing a red chip produced nothing but the loss of the chip. Our own experience in such situations tells us that the chimpanzee, after hitting the machine or shaking it or sticking his finger as far into the slot as it will go, will eventually stop depositing red chips. Soon after, he will stop operating the lever to produce the white chips. In other words, all behavior leading to the point at which the chain is broken will be extinguished. But what about the behavior after the point at which the chain is broken? This, generally, will remain intact. If, after the above extinction process were carried out, we gave the chimpanzee a red chip he would probably reject it. But, if we gave him a blue chip, he would be likely to operate Vending Machine 3 with it, showing that his behavior after the point of the interruption of the chain was not extinguished.

Do Secondary Reinforcers Acquire the Properties of Primary Reinforcers?

We implied that in the case of the child who cries to be put in his chair, the chair serves as a substitute for food and that it thereby takes on reinforcing properties. It is time now to examine this implication more closely.

We have to be careful before we attribute the properties of primary reinforcers to secondary reinforcers. In general, secondary reinforcers (reinforcers that have attained their power to strengthen the behavior that produces them because they, in turn, lead to primary reinforcement) will lose this power gradually if the primary reinforcer is withdrawn. The child's chair in our example is like a promissory note for food. As long as the promise is eventually fulfilled, or as long as it is fulfilled in a reasonable precentage of the cases, the chair will be sought after as if it was primary. However, if the child is no longer fed in the chair, his pleas to be put in the chair will eventually be extinguished. Similarly, we will drop only so many dimes into a broken Coke machine before we give up.

As a further illustration, let us suppose that there are two hotels identical in all respects except for one thing. In Hotel A each meal is invariably preceded by a dinner bell. In Hotel B the same meals are served, each preceded by a dinner bell, but the man who rings the dinner bell overdoes his job and frequently rings the bell between meals as well as before each meal. In both hotels the same meals are served, but in Hotel B there are many more dinner bells. Given experience with both hotels, which hotel do people prefer? Surely Hotel A. Meals are primary reinforcers for people, and since each meal in both hotels is always preceded by a dinner bell, dinner bells must be secondary reinforcers. In Hotel A there are fewer of these secondary reinforcers than in Hotel B. While it is reasonable to assume that in Hotel B people spend more time walking toward the dining room, one might expect people to prefer Hotel A where dinner bells reliably precede meals. In other words, one might expect that secondary reinforcement (dinner bells) is reinforcing in this case only insofar as it is followed by primary reinforcement (meals).

A recent experiment by Richard Schuster with pigeons parallels the situation of the two hotels.

Schuster allowed his pigeons to chose between a few minutes of exposure to either of the following two conditions:

A. A condition where pecking a key occasionally (on a variable-interval schedule) produced a blue light and buzzer followed by food (corresponding to Hotel A).
B. A condition identical to the first (where pecking produced the blue light and buzzer followed by food) except that, in addition, pecking sometimes produced extra pairs of blue lights and buzzers that were not followed by food (corresponding to Hotel B).

Figure 3.7 illustrates the choice the pigeons were required to make. Suppose, on a given exposure to Condition A for one minute the pigeon pecked the key 60 times, and three of those pecks were followed by a blue light and a buzzer, followed in turn by reinforcement. Thus, there were three primary reinforcements each preceded by a secondary reinforcement. Suppose on a given exposure to Condition B for one minute,

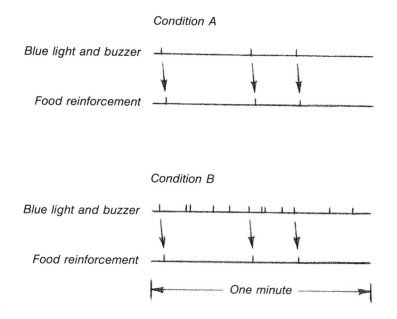

Figure 3.7 *Examples of the two conditions between which pigeons chose in Schuster's experiment. (All reinforcements are shown by ticks.) Condition A = each reinforcement preceded by a secondary reinforcement. Condition B = each reinforcement preceded by a secondary reinforcement plus extra secondary reinforcements.*

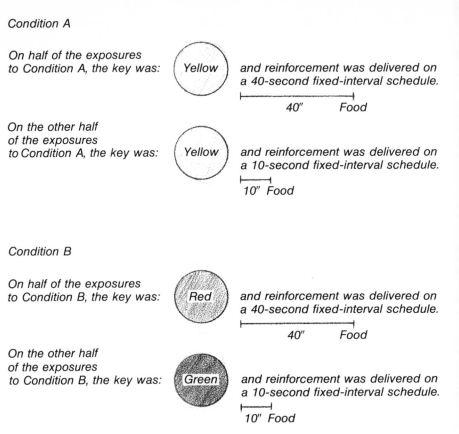

Figure 3.8 *Bower, McLean, and Meacham's experiment on the value of knowing when reinforcement is due. Pigeons chose between Conditions A and B.*

the pigeon also pecked the key 60 times. In Condition B suppose fifteen of the pecks produced a blue light and buzzer, but only on three occasions was the blue light and buzzer followed by food. Thus, there were again three primary reinforcements, each preceded by a secondary reinforcement, but there were twelve extra secondary reinforcements.

Schuster reasoned that if the buzzer and blue light had the properties of primary reinforcers, the pigeons should prefer Condition B, in which there were more of them, but if they were only reinforcing to the extent that they signaled, or promised, food, the pigeons should be indifferent or actually prefer Condition A, where the promise was more reliably fulfilled. Schuster found that although the pigeons pecked more during

Condition B, they preferred Condition A (when they were given the opportunity to choose between the two conditions), indicating that the buzzer and light were only reinforcing to the extent that they reliably indicated that food was to come.

One useful way to characterize secondary reinforcers is not in terms of some reinforcement value that they acquire by association with primary reinforcers, but in terms of their power to give the subject information about the coming of a primary reinforcer. We may talk figuratively here about "promissory notes," "cues" and "signals," but there is a more exact way of specifying how much information a certain event in the environment conveys to a subject—that is, in terms of the degree to which that event reduces uncertainty.

There is some evidence that organisms prefer situations where uncertainty about reinforcement is low to situations where uncertainty is high even though the two situations involve the same reinforcement. (Schuster's experiment is one instance.) A study by Gordon H. Bower, Jim McLean, and Jack Meacham was called. "The value of knowing when reinforcement is due." They had pigeons choose between two identical reinforcing conditions. Their experiment is illustrated in Figure 3.8. In Condition A reinforcement was delivered on one of two fixed-interval schedules, a fixed-interval 10-second (FI-10″) schedule or a fixed-interval 40-second (FI-40″) schedule. Which of these schedules was in effect was determined randomly. The key was yellow during both schedules and there was no signal to indicate which of the two FI schedules was in effect. In Condition B reinforcement was also delivered on one of two fixed-interval schedules, and which of these two schedules was in effect was also determined randomly. However, if the pigeons chose Condition B, the key turned red when the FI-40″ schedule was in effect and green when the FI-10″ schedule was in effect.* The experimenters argued that the pigeons were choosing between an informative and a noninformative situation. Condition A provides no information about the schedule in effect while Condition B provides information. In other respects the two conditions are identical. The pigeons showed a strong preference for Condition B, the one with more information about reinforcement.

It is to the extent that secondary reinforcers convey information about reward that they, themselves, can be reinforcing.

---

* Choice in the Bower, McLean, and Meacham experiment (and in Schuster's experiment) was measured by pecking during still another condition when two responses were available, one leading to Condition A and the other to Condition B.

DELAY OF REINFORCEMENT

What happens when the temporal relation between response and reinforcement is varied so that reinforcement is delayed? The answer is that in almost all cases a delayed reinforcement is worth less than immediate reinforcement during acquisition of a habit. Let us first consider the power of delayed reinforcement to strengthen an individual response. Then we will consider choice between long and short delays of reinforcement.

Learning with Delayed Reinforcement

The main problem for an experimenter is to define experimentally the delay interval and its attributes. He must decide what sort of thing he wants to happen during the delay period. One point of view says that nothing at all should happen during the delay. But, if nothing happened, if in a strict sense all motion of any kind were suspended and all processes halted, then by definition delay could have no effect. Any effect it would have must be the result of some process (be it "forgetting" or "interference by other responses") during the delay period. In other words, to say that nothing must happen during the delay period is to say that the delay period can have no effect. It is as if you were instantly to freeze the universe in its motion for the delay period and then allow it to move again when the delay was over.

Another alternative would be to allow many events of all kinds during the delay period. For instance let us go back to the chain of responses illustrated in Figure 3.6. Suppose we consider the first response in the chain, pressing the lever to receive a white chip, as a response which is ultimately reinforced by the grape delivered at the end of the chain. The other responses, the placing of the various chips in the slots, would be merely ways of filling up the delay period between the lever press and the reinforcement. One criticism that has been made of this kind of experiment is that there really would be no delay of reinforcement even for responses at the beginning of the chain. The various poker chips would serve as secondary reinforcers which could effectively signal the coming of the food. Since poker chips had been repeatedly associated with food, the chimpanzee's behavior would be reinforced as much by the sight of the poker chips as it would have been by the sight of the food. The chimpanzee in this situation is much like the television quiz show winner who is presented with a check instead of prizes. Although the check is only a piece of paper, the recipient is as rewarded as the person who receives a refrigerator or television set because he will be able to cash the check and get the prizes in the future. In terms of information theory, we may say that the poker chip reduces uncertainty about whether food will be presented. Even should we cause a delay between acquisition of the poker chip and its insertion in the machine, the chimpanzee still has the poker chip (the promissory note) in his hand during the delay period. When Wolfe did cause such a delay (Figure 3.9b) the chimpanzees responded just as fast to get poker chips as when there was no delay. However, when Wolfe caused a delay between insertion of the poker chip and delivery of the food (Figure 3.9c), when the chimpanzee has to wait during the delay period with no poker chip in his hand, responding for poker chips fell off sharply.

Experimenters have tried to eliminate secondary reinforcement from delay-of-reinforcement experiments. G. Robert Grice (1948) provided food to rats in a device similar to a T-maze. The floor of one arm was white and the floor of the other arm was black. The arms were reversed occasionally so that the white and black arms were not consistently associated with the left and right sides. After running down either arm, the rats were kept in one of a pair of identical grey delay boxes for periods which varied for different groups of rats. Then they were allowed into a goal box. If they had originally run down the white arm, they were then fed in the goal box. If they had originally run down the black arm, they were not fed. Figure 3.10 is a diagram of Grice's experiment. When there was no delay, the rats learned fairly easily to go in the direction corresponding to the white arm. However, when the delay was longer than five seconds, none of the rats in the delay group could learn to run consistently down the white arm to food.

Like the chimps in Wolfe's experiment (Figure 3.9c), the rats in Grice's experiment (Figure 3.10b) had nothing during the delay period that signaled reinforcement to come. When Grice provided one delay box following a choice of white and another, distinctly different box following a choice of black (Figure 3.10c), the performance of the rats improved considerably, even with longer delays than the original five seconds.

The reason the rats in the conditions of Figure 3.10b did not learn the maze is that no stimulus in the grey delay box was reliably correlated with either alley. An organism could, however, provide such correlated stimuli by its own actions.

A human child in similar circumstances to those shown in Figure 3.10b

Normal sequence

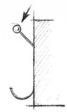 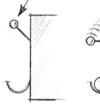 

Handle down   Chip out   Chip in slot   Grape out

a

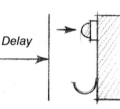

b

c

Figure 3.9 *How the point of delay affected lever pressing in Wolfe's experiment. (a) Normal sequence without a period of delay. (b) Delay between collecting chip and inserting it in slot. In this sequence, the chimp has the chip during the delay, and the delay does not slow down the chimp's lever pressing. (c) Delay between placing poker chip in slot and collecting grape. In this sequence, the chimp has no chip during the delay, and the delay does slow down lever pressing.*

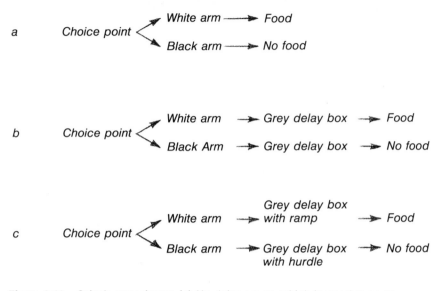

Figure 3.10 *Grice's experiment. (a) No-delay group, which learned to go to the white arm. (b) Delay group, which could not learn to go to the white arm when delayed longer than 5 seconds. (c) Secondary-reinforcement group, which learned to go to the white arm.*

might learn to put his hands in his pockets whenever he turned in the direction of a white passageway and keep them there until he was finally permitted to enter the goal room. Correspondingly, he could put his hands on his head whenever he turned down the black passageway and keep them there until he entered the goal room. He would soon learn that he was rewarded whenever he had his hands in his pockets and unrewarded whenever he had his hands on his head. This mediating response would serve to connect the situation at the choice point with that in the goal room and enable him to make the correct response easily. In other words, he could provide differential cues for himself like those Grice provided for some of his rats (Figure 3.10c).

Most of the mediating responses that humans use to bridge gaps between response and reinforcement are verbal. Instead of putting our hands in our pockets or on our heads we would probably solve the problem by saying to ourselves "I'll go to the white side now" or "I'll go to the side opposite to the white now." If, when reinforcement came, we had been saying some such phrase, we would be likely to remember what we were saying the next time we reach the choice point and use the phrase to guide our choice behavior. The use of repeated verbal responses is a common

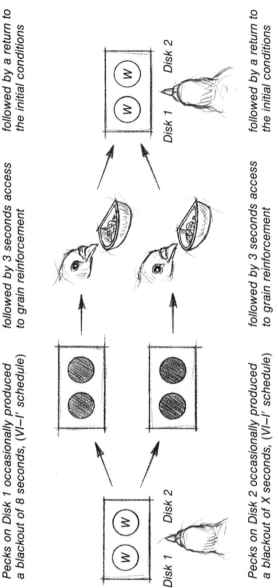

Pecks on Disk 1 occasionally produced a blackout of 8 seconds, (VI–I' schedule)

followed by 3 seconds access to grain reinforcement

followed by a return to the initial conditions

Disk 1   Disk 2

Pecks on Disk 2 occasionally produced a blackout of X seconds, (VI–I' schedule)

followed by 3 seconds access to grain reinforcement

followed by a return to the initial conditions

Figure 3.11 Diagram showing the procedure used by Chung and Herrnstein to study delay. Pigeons could peck at either or both illuminated disks.

technique for bridging gaps in time. The shopping list repeated over and over again by a child as he walks to the store or the phone number repeated over and over again between the telephone book where we have looked it up and the telephone where we dial it are examples.

Choice Between Short and Long Delays

The choice in the Grice experiment was between a delayed reinforcement and no reinforcement at all. Grice was interested in whether an animal could learn to make a response when reinforcement was delayed. Another question we might ask is: After a response is learned, to what extent is a short delay of reinforcement preferred over a long delay of reinforcement? In this case, we are interested not in the acquisition of a response, but in the choice between two conditions of reinforcement. The difference between the two questions is like the difference between the questions: (1) To what extent is it easier to learn to drive a car with automatic than manual shift? and (2) After learning both automatic and manual driving, which is preferred, and how much is it preferred? We have just discussed the first kind of question, and we found that it is easier to learn a task when the reinforcement is immediate than when it is delayed.

The second kind of question was asked by Shin Ho Chung and Richard Herrnstein (1967). These experimenters studied the pecking of pigeons in a box containing two disks, both illuminated with white light. Figure 3.11 illustrates the procedure. When the pigeons pecked on either of these disks (Disk 1 or Disk 2) they were rewarded on a one-minute variable-interval (VI-1′) schedule. That is, on the average of once a minute a peck on either disk would produce three seconds of access to grain. If the pigeons pecked at both disks, they would receive an overall average of reinforcement every 30 seconds (once a minute from each of two disks). A pigeon pecking at two disks is somewhat like a farmer who has two chickens who each lay an egg every 24 hours on the average. The farmer will collect from his two chickens an average of two eggs a day.

The significant aspect of Chung and Herrnstein's experiment is that the peck that produced reinforcement was not followed immediately by reinforcement. Instead, all illumination in the box was turned off. Illumination was restored and reinforcement was presented to the pigeons after a period of delay. For Disk 1, this delay period was always eight seconds. For Disk 2, this delay period varied between 1 second and 30 seconds. Sometimes then the delay was longer for Disk 1 than for Disk 2 (when the Disk 2 delay was 1 second) and sometimes the delay was longer for Disk 2 than for Disk 1 (when the Disk 2 delay was 30 seconds). Under these

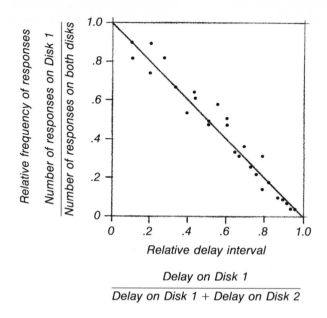

Figure 3.12   *Proportion of pecks on Disk 1 as a function of the relative delay on that disk. [From S. H. Chung and R. J. Herrnstein, "Choice and delay of reinforcement." J. Exp. Analysis Behavior, 1967, 10, 69.]*

conditions, all of the pigeons pecked at both disks. The question asked by Chung and Herrnstein was: What percentage of the total pecks were made on each disk as the delay of reinforcement for pecking on Disk 2 varied? (i.e., What was the behavior ratio?) The answer is that the pigeons always pecked more frequently on whichever disk represented shorter delays of reward. The curve of Figure 3.12 is a quantitative expression of the degree of preference for shorter delays. The 45° straight line drawn through the points shows that the relative frequency of responding on Disk 1 is inversely proportional to the relative delay on that disk. In other words, pigeons will always choose to get their food sooner than later, and the degree of their choice is proportional to how much sooner. If Disk 1 delivers food twice as soon as Disk 2, then Disk 1 will be pecked twice as often as Disk 2.

The purpose of this discussion of delay of reinforcement has been to provide an example of the kinds of questions that one can ask regarding the major variables that in combination determine the character of reinforcement. It represents only one part of the study of one such parameter, delay of reinforcement. Similar kinds of investigations have been made into such parameters as rate of reinforcement, and amount of reinforce-. ment, and the degee to which presentation of reinforcement depends on occurrence of a response.

We have not nearly exhausted the kinds of questions that can be asked about delay of reinforcement alone. We have simply asked whether a response could be learned as well when reinforcement is delayed as when reinforcement is immediate. The answer is: No. We have also asked to what extent short delays are preferred to long delays. The answer is that preference varies directly in proportion to the relative shortness of delay. We could have asked: What effect does delay have on rate of responding, or on extinction of a response? How does delay interact with rate or amount of reinforcement?

Note that we have not asked how delay of reinforcement affects the strength of a response. As Humphrey's paradox revealed, "response strength" is an ambiguous notion. (See the second paragraph on page 122.) After all, we could argue that immediately reinforced responses are "stronger" than others because organisms guickly learn to recognize immediate rewards and prefer them to delayed rewards. However, we could also argue that responses that are acquired when rewards are delayed and only loosely correlated with responses (as is true of pushing buttons for elevators) are, in another sense, "stronger" because they are far more difficult to eradicate.

PUNISHMENT AND NEGATIVE REINFORCEMENT

So far, in our discussion of reinforcement, we have been dealing mostly with positive reinforcers, stimuli or objects that most organisms will approach, such as food, water, and sexual partners. These are shown in the top two boxes of Figure 2.10 where the types of instrumental conditioning are diagrammed. The bottom boxes of the figure show processes using aversive stimuli, stimuli which most organisms will escape from or avoid. Control of behavior with such aversive stimuli can be just as effective as control with positive stimuli. If we spend less time on aversive control it is because we have already covered basic principles applicable to both aversive and positive control, not because aversive control is unimportant.

Before we begin a discussion of experimental findings, let us repeat a few definitions made earlier. Figure 3.13 shows in a highly diagrammatic

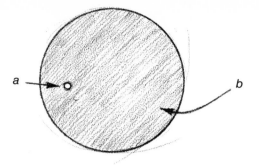

Figure 3.13 *Specific and nonspecific definitions of behavior. (a) A specific behavior, like pressing a lever. (b) All other potential behavior.*

form a particular way of looking at the behavior of an animal in a laboratory situation. Suppose the animal is a rat in a Skinner box with a lever. The entire large circle represents all the behavior of which the rat is capable: scratching, biting, jumping, and so forth. The small white circle within the large one represents a particular portion of the total—presses of the lever. This portion is what we have previously defined as an operant—it represents, small as its area in the diagram is, a class of still smaller kinds of behavior, all of which somehow depress the lever. If pressing the lever is followed by aversive stimulation the process is called punishment. If anything the animal does *except* pressing the lever is followed by aversive stimulation, the process is called negative reinforcement. For example, referring to Figure 3.13, if we shocked the rat for behavior included in the small white circle (after each lever press), we would be punishing the lever-pressing behavior. If we shocked the rat for all behavior included in the large grey part of the circle (that is, *except* after a lever press), we would be negatively reinforcing the lever press. Punishment will tend to decrease the rate of lever pressing and negative reinforcement to increase it. According to common usage, when we refer to positive reinforcement, we frequently just say "reinforcement" while when we refer to negative reinforcement we always say "negative reinforcement." (A similar convention exists with respect to positive and negative numbers. We often say "three" for "plus three" but we always say "minus three.") If we shocked the rat for all behavior in the big circle including that in the small circle, we would be delivering shock independently of the behavior of the rat.

What is an Aversive Stimulus?

The problem of defining an aversive stimulus is symmetrical to the problem of defining the nature of positive reinforcement, and the attempted solutions have also been symmetrical. Just as there is a need-reduction theory of positive reinforcement, there is a need-increase theory of aversive stimulation. Just as there are response theories of positive reinforcement, there are response theories of aversive stimulation. Defining aversive stimuli as "painful" and positive reinforcers as "pleasurable" does not help. Such definitions suffer from the same drawbacks as other mentalistic concepts, they give us no guidelines to tell what is painful or pleasurable to another organism.

It would be pointless to trace through a series of "aversive-stimulation theories" because our conclusion would be symmetrical to the one we reached about positive reinforcement: There is no unifying principle that would enable us to predict the things that are aversive. Our consolation, however, is also the same; a stimulus that proves to be aversive in one situation will generally be aversive in others. If beating a dog with a rolled-up newspaper is an effective punishment for defecating in the house, chances are it will also be effective punishment for jumping on the laps of guests. If electric-shock punishment reduces the rate of bar pressing in rats, it will also reduce the rate of wheel-running.

Punishment

Just as positive reinforcement tends to increase the rate at which a behavior is emitted, punishment tends to decrease the rate. Figure 3.14a shows a cumulative record of the lever-presses of a rat in a Skinner box where lever-presses have no effect. The low slope of the line means that the rat occasionally presses the lever, even with no positive reinforcement, but the rate of pressing is very low. Figure 3.14b shows a cumulative record of presses that are *positively* reinforced according to a variable-interval schedule. The steep slope of the line shows that the rate of pressing is much more rapid for positive reinforcement than for no reinforcement at all. Figure 3.14c shows cumulative records when lever-presses are rewarded *and* punished. In this case, the punishment was a brief electric shock following each press. The particular intensity of punishment used caused a slow-down, or suppression, of the rate of pressing shown by a slope intermediate between the rate of pressing for reward only, and the rate of pressing for neither reward nor punishment. The amount of

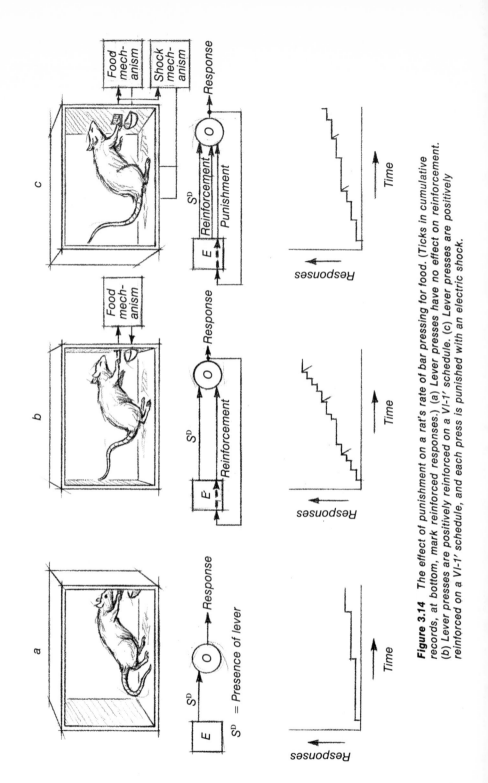

Figure 3.14 The effect of punishment on a rat's rate of bar pressing for food. (Ticks in cumulative records, at bottom, mark reinforced responses.) (a) Lever presses have no effect on reinforcement. (b) Lever presses are positively reinforced on a VI-1' schedule. (c) Lever presses are positively reinforced on a VI-1' schedule, and each press is punished with an electric shock.

suppression depends on the intensity of punishment. Figure 3.15 shows how the intensity of punishment determines the suppression in the rate at which pigeons peck a key. At higher intensities of shock, the rate of responding can be suppressed to zero.

Is Punishment a Form of Instrumental Conditioning?

In the last chapter, we discussed pseudoconditioning. We introduced pseudoconditioning in instrumental conditioning experiments with the hypothetical example of itching powder as a reinforcer for bar pressing in a rat. The test of itching powder as a pseudoreinforcer is whether the same increases in bar pressing occur when the injection of itching powder is dependent on, and independent of, a bar-press. If the powder causes just as many bar-presses when it is delivered randomly as when it follows each bar-press, then we do not have a case of instrumental conditioning.

It is also possible that the process of punishment may not be a form of instrumental conditioning. With positive reinforcement we are trying to train the animal to *do* something. With punishment we are trying to train the animal *not* to do something. When a hungry animal is presented with food, the behavior that one observes is eating. In order to get the animal to perform some act other than eating (like pressing a bar), the food must be made dependent on the bar-press. When an animal is shocked, the behavior that one observes is jumping or running, or freezing in position, but *not* bar pressing. In other words, shock can itself produce "nonperformance" of bar pressing, the very effect we are trying to condition. In order to get the animal to *stop* pressing a bar, all one needs to do is shock the animal. But we said previously that true instrumental conditioning must involve a *relation* between responding and its consequences, not simple presentation of those consequences. It is at least conceivable that to reduce responding there may be no need to shock the animal in any relation to its responses.

The question then becomes: Will aversive stimulation delivered independently of responding suppress behavior as much as aversive stimulation delivered only when a response is made? If it does, then punishment does not have the properties of instrumental conditioning. If it does not—if aversive stimulation must follow responding to have its maximum effect—then punishment does have the properties of instrumental conditioning. Many experiments have been performed to answer this question, and their answer has been almost unanimous—aversive stimulation delivered independently of responding has some suppressive effect to be sure, but nowhere near as much as when it follows immediately after each

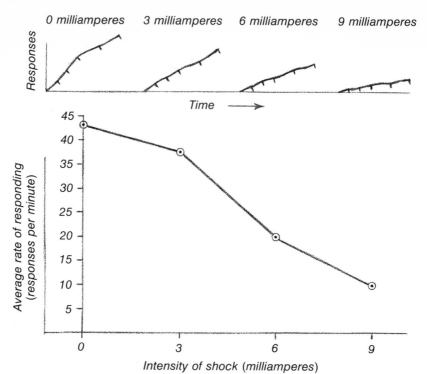

Figure 3.15 *The effect of punishment on the rate of key pecking in pigeons.* Top, *cumulative records of pigeons pecking a key for reinforcement on a VI-1′ schedule. (Ticks mark reinforcements.) The graph at left shows a no-shock condition; the second graph shows the effect of a 3-milliampere shock; the third graph shows the effect of a 6-milliampere shock; the fourth graph shows the effect of a 9-milliampere shock.* At bottom, *a function showing that the rate of responding decreased as the intensity of the electric shock increased.*

response. To the extent that there is a difference, then, between the effects of response-produced aversive stimulation and response-independent aversive stimulation, punishment is a form of instrumental conditioning.

Curve B in Figure 3.16 shows rate at which a pigeon pecked a key where pecks were reinforced with food on a one-minute variable-interval schedule, and inescapable shocks were delivered twice per second. As the intensity of shock increased, the rate of pecking decreased slightly. Curve A in Figure 3.16 is a repetition of Figure 3.15, showing the rate at which another pigeon pecked a key when pecks were reinforced with food on the same schedule but shock was delivered only when the pigeon pecked the key. As the intensity of shock increased, the rate of pecking decreased drastically. The difference in the slopes of these two curves shows the instrumental effect of shock.

Punishment of Human Behavior

What implications can we draw from these empirical findings with regard to human behavior? Does it mean that our grandfathers were right when they said "Spare the rod and spoil the child?" Is modern child-rearing, with its deemphasis on punishment, all wrong? Not necessarily. There is no question that punishment works—the trouble with punishment may be not that it doesn't work but that it works only too well. A single intense shock to a pigeon following a peck on a key can suppress key pecking permanently without disturbing other behavior. If we severely punish a child for "being fresh" we must ask ourselves whether we want to suppress his outspokenness completely and permanently. Another implication to be drawn from this research is that random presentation of aversive stimulation has little positive effect. Consider the mother who is constantly spanking, shaking or slapping her child for reasons that are only tenuously related to his specific acts. She will never understand why he is so naughty despite her constant attempts at discipline. If a child is to be spanked, he should be spanked immediately after the offense. Otherwise, any acts performed between the offense and the spanking are liable to be suppressed along with or instead of the act the mother intends to suppress. If a child is innocently reaching for a lollypop at the moment it occurs to his mother that he ought to be punished for something he did an hour before, and she suddenly slaps his hand, it may be a long time before he again reaches for a lollypop.

Furthermore, one must be certain that "the punishment fits the crime." The classic example of an inappropriate punishment is spanking a child for crying. The spanking generates still more crying, which, in turn, is punished by still more spanking, and so on, until the child or the parent becomes exhausted. (Such "vicious circles" indeed may be responsible for some otherwise inexplicable cases of child abuse by parents.)

In general, with regard to both reward and punishment, the more specific and discrete the response, the more likely it is that reward and punishment will work. Punishment of a child for "being a bad boy that day" or reward for "being a good boy that day" will be much less effective than an immediate punishment for carelessly breaking a vase or an immediate reward for saying "please." When you want a specific response from a fellow organism, it is far more effective to reward the occurrence of the behavior than to punish its absence. When you want an organism *not* to do something specific, it is more effective to punish the occurrence of the behavior than to reward its absence. Referring to Figure 3.13, it is more effective, usually, to apply either reward or

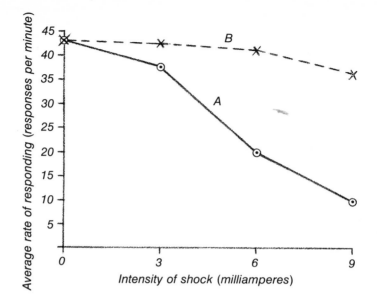

Figure 3.16 *Curve A is repeated from the bottom portion of Figure 3.15, showing the rate of response as punishment increases. Curve B shows the rate of response under the same conditions of reinforcement but with the shocks delivered independently of the responses. The rate of delivery of the independent shocks was 120 per minute.*

punishment to the operant represented by the small white area of the circle rather than to the large grey area. When reward and punishment are applied to the grey part, it is hard for the organism to distinguish the situation from one in which reward and punishment are applied to white and grey together—in other words, a situation in which reward and aversive stimulation are independent of any response. In the next sections, on escape and avoidance, we will look at what happens when punishment is applied to large, general classes of behavior such as those represented by the large grey part of Figure 3.13.

Escape (Negative Reinforcement)

In the typical escape-conditioning experiment, an aversive stimulus is presented and the experimenter waits until the subject performs some act that the experimenter has specified in advance. When the act is performed, the aversive stimulus is removed. For example, a dog may be placed in a shuttle box (one with a hurdle in the middle that the dog can leap over). When the dog is on one side of the box, he may be shocked until he leaps over the hurdle. Dogs in such situations quickly learn to jump over the hurdle.

Negative reinforcement is a synonym for escape. Although the word "escape" vividly describes what is happening in a typical negative reinforcement experiment, we shall use the phrase "negative reinforcement" to remind us of the relation between this process and that of positive reinforcement. Both kinds of reinforcement will strengthen whatever acts they follow. Positive reinforcement reinforces by adding a positive stimulus; negative reinforcement reinforces by taking away a negative stimulus. The line between these two processes is not always easy to draw. (Is turning on the heater on a cold day reinforcing because it gives us warmth or because it removes our feeling of cold?)

One theory of reinforcement (the need-reduction theory that we mentioned previously) holds that all reinforcement is negative reinforcement. The eating of food, for instance, is thus "escape from hunger," and the drinking of water is "escape from thirst."

Nevertheless, the behavior of animals when exposed to aversive stimuli is different from that of animals who are deprived of food or water. A pigeon who is being shocked will jump around the area in which it is confined and flap its wings violently; a pigeon deprived of food will engage in more deliberate searching and pecking motions. It may be that one difference between aversive stimuli (such as electric shocks or loud noises) and such feelings as hunger or thirst is that the former originate suddenly outside the organism while the latter originate gradually within it. Because of the violent behavior generated by aversive stimuli, it is difficult to train an animal to perform delicate, subtle or complicated acts to escape them. It is difficult, for instance, for organisms to react nonviolently to aversive stimuli even though, in many cases, nonviolence may be the best means of escaping it. Only a great deal of self-control and previous training enables people in a crowded auditorium to keep from running to the exits to escape a fire. Similarly, although it is easy to train a pigeon to peck a key to obtain food, it is difficult to train a pigeon to perform the same act to escape from electric shock. (On the other hand, it is easy to train a pigeon to flap its wings, to run around a cage or to raise its head to escape electric shock.)

A great deal of patience is required to train an organism to react to aversive stimuli in nonviolent ways. One must find the precise value of intensity that will be aversive enough to facilitate escape, yet not so intense as to trigger violent reactions. In everyday life, we are often faced with similar problems. Perhaps prisons should be aversive enough relative

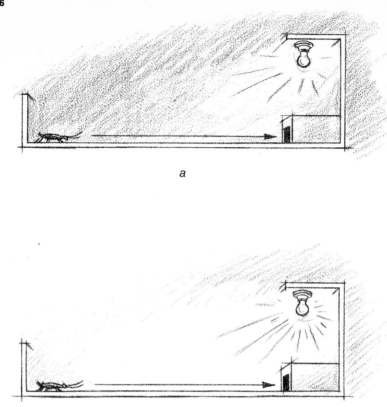

Figure 3.17 *Teaching a cockroach to approach a bright light. (a) The roach learns to go to the dark box. The intensity of the light is gradually increased over many trials until (b) the roach goes to the dark box in spite of a bright light.*

to the outside world so that people do not want to stay in them, yet not so aversive that prisoners become more bitter or violent than they were before their incarceration.

It is possie to train an animal to perform an act it would not ordinarily perform under aversive stimulation. For example, the cockroach will ordinarily run away from light, yet this photonegative insect can, in the course of repeated trials, learn to go to a dark box situated under a light. Figure 3.17 diagrams the experiment. The roach is placed in one end of an alley with a very weak light above a covered box at the other end. In order to get to the box, which is in complete shade, the roach must move toward the light. If the light is made very bright initially, the roach will stay at the end of the alley where it is put, and not move. However, if the light is very dim, the roach will adapt to the light and move down the alley and find the dark box. Once the roach learns to run to the dark box when the light is dim, the intensity of the light can be increased slowly. The roach will eventually learn to approach a bright light to get to the dark box.

Avoidance

An experiment by Richard Solomon and L. C. Wynn illustrates the relation of avoidance to escape. They trained dogs in the shuttle box diagrammed in Figure 3.18. When the dogs were in Side A, they were severely shocked. The electricity remained on until the dogs jumped to Side B. However, 10 seconds before each shock, a light in the box went out. Gradually, the dogs were conditioned to jump when the light went out, *before* the shock came on, thus avoiding the shock altogether.

The relation between avoidance and escape bears a certain similarity to the relation between secondary reinforcement and primary reinforcement.

In secondary reinforcement experiments we concluded that one of the values of secondary reinforcers is that they signal to the organism "when reinforcement is due." Avoidance procedures perform a similar function; they tell the organism when aversive stimulation is due. In both secondary reinforcement and avoidance situations the signal makes a certain kind of behavior appropriate. Secondary reinforcing signals are part of a chain culminating in positive reinforcement. Avoidance signals are part of a chain culminating in nonpresentation of an aversive stimulus.

If we look upon organisms as reacting to overall molar features of the environment, we can see how avoidance behavior may easily come about. One man may react to the fact that the sun is shining and dress accordingly, while, on the same morning, another may react to the fact that it is the month of April and hence carry an umbrella even if the sun is shining at that particular moment. If a man reacts to the fact that the month is April and carries an umbrella despite the sunny weather at the moment, he is, in essence, avoiding getting wet, just as Solomon and Wynne's dogs avoided shock by responding even when shock was not present at the moment. For some of Solomon and Wynne's dogs, the transition from escape of shock (reaction to the shock itself) to avoidance of shock (reaction to the stimulus that indicated shock was to come) was rapid (Dog A); for other dogs this transition was more gradual (Dog B).

The invariable correlation between the light-out signal and the shock in

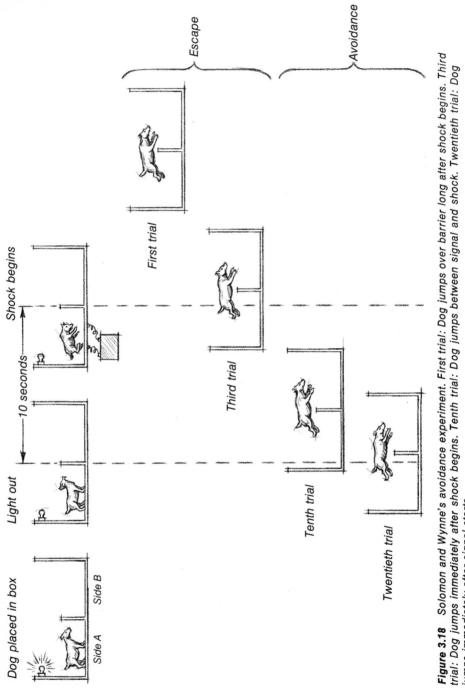

Figure 3.18 Solomon and Wynne's avoidance experiment. First trial: Dog jumps over barrier long after shock begins. Third trial: Dog jumps immediately after shock begins. Tenth trial: Dog jumps between signal and shock. Twentieth trial: Dog jumps immediately after signal starts.

Solomon and Wynne's experiment is not always paralleled in everyday life "avoidance situations." Just because it is April, it will not necessarily rain. Sometimes the man who responds to the more molecular aspects of his environment, who leaves his umbrella home on sunny days, even in April, is better off than his more foresighted brother. People obviously have to strike a general balance between a molecular and molar view of life, and sometimes this can be difficult.

It is generally true that children find it difficult to respond to the molar conditions of their environment. As we grow older we sometimes have difficulties in the other direction. The man who can never take a vacation, for instance, or the woman who worries and cannot enjoy herself while her children are away at camp are examples of people who are responding to aversive molar aspects of their environment at the expense of the molecular. To put it another way, there are those who cannot see the forest for the trees and those who cannot see the trees for the forest.

An experiment that illustrates how rats can avoid electric shock by responding to molar rather than molecular aspects of their environment was done recently by Herrnstein and Philip Hineline, who used rats in a Skinner box containing a lever and a grid floor (see Figure 3.20). There were two machines that could deliver shock to the rat through the grid floor, but only one was connected at a time. The shocks delivered by each machine were fairly intense, very brief, and came at irregular intervals. The only difference between the two was that Machine A produced shocks at a fairly rapid rate and Machine B produced shocks at a fairly slow rate. In other words, the probability of shock at any time was greater for A than for B. If we stretch our imaginations to conceive of snowstorms as analogous to shocks, it is as if one machine produced the snowstorms of January (a high rate of snowstorms) while the other produced the snowstorms of November (a low rate). Ordinarily, Machine A, which produces shocks at a high rate is connected, and Machine B is not connected. A press of the lever, however, disconnects Machine A and connects Machine B, which stays connected until a shock is received and then it is disconnected, and Machine A is connected. It is as if someone who disliked snowstorms could press a lever during January to restore the conditions of November which lasted until a November snowstorm occurred and then reverted to January. It is possible under these conditions that immediately after pressing the lever, Machine B would produce a shock (this would happen if the rat had pressed the lever at X—X in Figure 3.20). Just as, if one could switch from January to November, there would be no guarantee it would not snow the next day

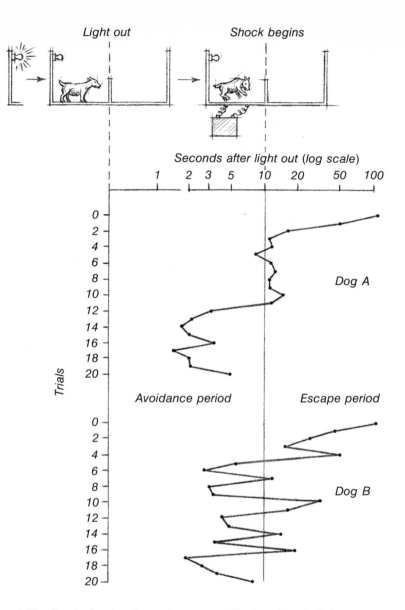

Figure 3.19 Graph showing the performance of the two dogs in Solomon and Wynne's experiment. (Each point represents a jump over the barrier.) Dog A shifted rapidly from escape to avoidance. Dog B shifted gradually from escape to avoidance. [Data from R. L. Solomon and L. C. Wynne, "Traumatic avoidance learning: Acquisition in normal dogs." Psychol. Monogr., 1953, 67 (No. 354)]

—even in November. Thus, pressing the lever did not avoid shocks completely. All it did was to change conditions so that the overall rate of shocks was less. In the Herrnstein and Hineline experiment, all the rats learned to press the lever for such molar negative reinforcement.

Extinction of Escape and Avoidance

When extinction of escape and avoidance is carried out in a way parallel to extinction of positively reinforced behavior, the reinforced response disappears quite rapidly. For instance, suppose one of Solomon and Wynne's dogs learned to jump over a barrier to escape—and then to avoid—shocks. Suppose we want to extinguish this behavior. During extinction the jumps would no longer be reinforced by escape or avoidance—we would shock the animal no matter what it did. When this procedure is followed, the jumps eventually stop. In fact, responses extinguished in this manner are often extinguished so thoroughly that it is difficult to get the animal to respond again, even when extinction is discontinued and conditioning is reinstated.

There is another procedure that one may follow in an attempt to reduce the rate of avoidance behavior that produces exactly the opposite results. Suppose again that an animal has learned to jump over a barrier to avoid shocks, as in the Solomon and Wynne study. Then, suppose the experimenter maintains the same conditions—the same box, the same signal, and the same jump before the shock comes on—except that the shock apparatus is unplugged. When Solomon and Wynne tried unplugging their electrical apparatus, they found that the dogs kept jumping; the dogs would jump literally hundreds of times after shock had been discontinued. Eventually, the avoidance behavior will slow down and stop under these conditions, but the process was a lengthy one, especially as compared to the normal extinction procedure. It is easy to understand why the second extinction process was so inefficient if we remember what was said about extinction of positively reinforced responses: *The easier it is to discriminate the reinforcement situation from the extinction situation, the faster extinction will be.* In the case of the two extinction processes for avoidance, the first is easily distinguished from reinforcement. As soon as the dog makes the previously reinforced jumping response, and the shock is maintained nevertheless, the conditions of reinforcement are obviously at an end. However, in the second procedure, when the dog jumps and is not shocked, the conditions are identical to those of reinforcement. With the second method of extinction, as long as the reinforced response is maintained, the conditions of reinforcement and extinction are identical.

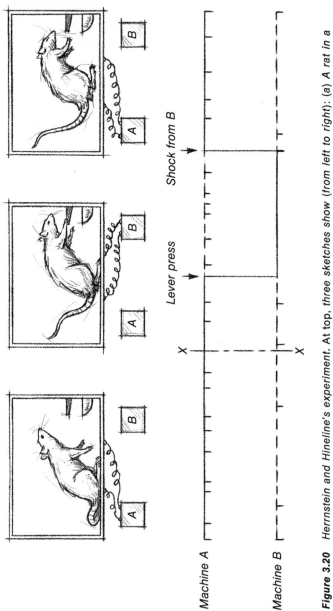

Figure 3.20 Herrnstein and Hineline's experiment. At top, three sketches show (from left to right): (a) A rat in a Skinner box to which Machine A is attached; (b) the rat presses a lever that disconnects Machine A and connects Machine B; (c) the rat receives a shock from B, which now disconnects B and connects A. At bottom, two horizontal lines with vertical ticks show the electric shocks programmed by Machine A and Machine B. Solid line shows which machine was connected to the box at a given time and thus which shocks were actually received. (This means, for instance, that if the rat had pressed the lever at point X—X, it would have been shocked immediately.)

Even when the previously reinforced response is prevented by physical restraint, it is not extinguished by this method. (With respect to chains of behavior, we noted that a conditioned response in the chain will be preserved even though other responses preceding it are extinguished. This is true for responses that are restrained as well as for responses that are not made because the signal for their occurrence is never given.)

To illustrate the two methods of extinction, consider the behavior of two children who learn to hit or otherwise interfere with the pleasure of other children in order to prevent the other children from taking their toys. One child is then put among older children who will take his toys regardless of how aggressively he behaves. The other child is put among younger children who will not take his toys, no matter how meekly he behaves. It is reasonable to suppose that the aggressive behavior of the first child will stop while that of the second child will continue; a model example, perhaps, of how a neighborhood bully is created. In fact, the slow, inefficient extinction of avoidance is seen by some behavioral therapists as a major parameter in much adult human neurotic behaviors. As children, people learn many avoidance behaviors. Sometimes, as adults, they continue to perform these behaviors even though the sources of aversive stimulation have long been absent. For instance, if a boy is punished in his youth for open displays of emotion, as an adult he is likely to inhibit such display, perhaps inappropriately, to the detriment of his relations with his wife and children. In this case, a therapist might encourage his patient to express his emotions openly in a permissive atmosphere in the hope of extinguishing the heavy-handed childhood conditioning.

Bibliography

Books on the nature of reinforcement usually have the word "motivation" in the title. The sections on motivation and reinforcement in Kimble's book on conditioning and learning (previously cited) are excellent. A book by D. Bindra, *Motivation*, (New York: Ronald Press, 1959), gives an overview of the various topics usually collected under this rubric. A collection of the classic articles on reinforcement is available in paperback in R. C. Birney and R. C. Teevan (Eds.), *Reinforcement* (Princeton: Van Nostrand, 1961).

The parameters of reinforcement, schedule, delay, secondary reinforcement, and so forth, are discussed in detail in Kimble's book on conditioning and learning, and in a collection of original essays by students of B. F. Skinner: W. K. Honig (Ed.), *Operant Behavior: Areas of Research and Application*

(New York: Appleton-Century-Crofts, 1966). Punishment and aversive control are treated skimpily in the Kimble book, but not in the Honig collection. I particularly recommend the article "Punishment" by N. H. Azrin and W. C. Holz (in Honig's book). A systematic account of the investigation of parameters of reinforcement and punishment can be found in paperback in F. A. Logan and A. R. Wagner, *Reward and Punishment* (Boston: Allyn and Bacon, 1965).

Schuster's experiment with secondary reinforcement is available in D. P. Hendry (Ed.), *Conditioned Reinforcement* (Homewood, Ill.: Dorsey, 1969). The Bower, McLean, and Meacham experiment called "The value of knowing when reinforcement is due" appears in the *Journal of Comparative and Physiological Psychology* (*62*, 1967, 184–192). The Wolfe and Grice experiments are described in Kimble's book, but it is instructive to read Wolfe's own descriptions of his experiments to be found, unfortunately, only in J. B. Wolfe, "Effectiveness of token-rewards for chimpanzees," *Comparative Psychology Monographs*, *12*, No. 60, 1936. The Chung and Herrnstein experiment is from the *Journal of the Experimental Analysis of Behavior* (*10*, 1967, pp. 67–74). The Solomon and Wynne experiment has been reprinted extensively and is described in most texts on learning. The original source is *Psychological Monographs* (*67*, No. 354, 1953). The Herrnstein and Hineline experiment, "Negative reinforcement as shock-frequency reduction," appears in the *Journal of the Experimental Analysis of Behavior* (*9*, 1966, 421–430).

Chapter 4

Relations Between Stimuli, Responses, and Reinforcement

CONNECTIONS AND CORRELATIONS

Association by Contiguity

In this chapter we will focus on the relations between major variables (stimuli, responses, and reinforcement) in classical and instrumental conditioning. In classical conditioning the experimenter controls the relation between the CS and the US. In instrumental conditioning the experimenter controls the relation between response and reinforcement. What property of these relationships is most critical in determining behavior?

The first, most obvious, and most popular answer to this question is "temporal contiguity." In classical conditioning the CS and the US are presented together. When a dog is exposed to a bell and then food powder, it is the conjunction in time, the 1:1 correspondence between the bell and the food powder, that is said to increase the probability of salivation the next time, when the bell is presented alone. In instrumental conditioning, when a rat is given a pellet of food immediately after pressing a lever, it is the conjunction in time, the 1:1 correspondence between the bar-press and the pellet, that is said to increase the rate of bar pressing. This is nothing more or less than the principle of *association by contiguity*, which we discussed in the first chapter, a principle that has served psychologists long and well.

By and large, "association by contiguity" is still the way most psychologists describe what subjects learn when they are instrumentally or classically conditioned. The dog learns the connection between the bell and the food powder. The rat learns the connection between the bar-press and the food pellet. It is hard to talk about learning at all without implying some form of association by contiguity. Recently, however, behaviorists have become somewhat suspicious of temporal contiguity as an universal description of all relations between stimuli, responses, and reinforcement. What is wrong with assuming a 1:1 relationship between stimulus and response or between response and reinforcement? What is wrong with describing these relations solely as connections?

The Relation Between Stimuli and Responses

To say there is a 1:1 correspondence between stimuli and responses, for example, is to say that each occurrence of a conditioned response must be caused by a specific stimulus. But consider the instrumental act of a fireman shoveling coal into the boiler of a locomotive. We may reasonably ask: Where is the 1:1 stimulus for this behavior? This stimulus can be considered to consist of those elements of the environment, the gauges and dials on the boiler, that tell the man the pressure is low. These dial or gauge readings are measurable. An observer may notice a correlation between the dial reading and the rate of shoveling. At this level we usually find the most consistent relationships between stimuli and responses.

At a more molecular level, are we able to account for each shovelful of coal in terms of its own special stimulus? In order to do this, we would be forced to hypothesize about the *proprioceptive* feedback from muscular movements and attempt to relate that feedback to internal stimuli provided by the fireman's central nervous system or his thoughts, wishes, ideas, and intentions. However, none of these hypothetical internal stimuli are at present easily measurable, and if the behaviorist relies on anything, it is the desirability of measuring the effects he studies. Therefore, until more precise techniques are developed to provide meaningful 1:1 relationships between each response and its stimulus, we should be satisfied to describe the stimulus-response relation in these complex cases in terms of a correlation between events such as (1) the reading on the fireman's pressure gauge and (2) his rate of shoveling.

It is often the case that order is found on a molar level but not on a more molecular level. The physicist finds order in the relations between the pressure, volume, and temperature of a gas although the individual molecules of gas move in random and unpredictable ways; the economist can estimate reasonably well the total amount of money in savings banks in the United States next year without being able to tell whether or not a given individual will deposit or withdraw money. Similarly, the behaviorist does not need to refer to unmeasured stimuli within the organism or to refer to unmeasured thoughts, hopes or dreams within the organism in order to justify his molar descriptions of behavior.

Some classically conditioned responses may have a specific stimulus by which they are elicited, much like the unconditioned knee jerk, which is elicited by striking the knee with a rubber hammer. However, some responses are elicited by more molar environmental events. As we noted, the rate at which a dog breathes is correlated with temperature; a high temperature existing over a relatively long span of time can be a US, with rate of breathing (only measurable over a relatively long time span) as the response with which it is correlated.

In instrumental conditioning (and in the case of the fireman stoking coal), the stimulus signals the existence of a certain relationship between behavior and reinforcement; the gauges tell the fireman whether shoveling will be reinforced.

The Relation Between Responses and Reinforcement

Virtually the same argument applies to the relation between response and reinforcement as to that between stimulus and response. According to the principle of association by contiguity, we ought to find a 1:1 correspondence between response and reinforcement; if it appears that a response is acquired, then it must be reinforced somehow; each instrumental act must have its own reinforcement. The trouble with this notion is the same as the trouble with the supposed 1:1 correspondence between stimulus and response: in everyday life it is hard to find such correspondence.

Consider again the man stoking coal. What is the reinforcement for this response? Possibly the increase in speed of the locomotive. Taking a broader view, the reinforcement could be the fireman's salary or the things he buys with his salary. In any case, we would be hard put to find a specific reinforcer for each shovelful of coal. What we do find is a general correlation between coal shoveling and speed of the locomotive. The faster the coal is shoveled the faster the locomotive goes. As long as the locomotive goes fast enough, the fireman will be paid every week and he will be able to feed himself and his family. As soon as we try to go beyond these correlations—as soon as we try to discover reinforcers for each response—we find ourselves making unverifiable hypotheses about unmeasurable events within the organism. It is indeed a stimulating exercise to speculate about what sort of events could be reinforcing each response. One theory has it that the fireman's sense of his own muscular effort in lifting the shovel becomes associated with the increased speed of the locomotive (the reinforcing event), and, hence, is reinforcing in itself. Thus the reinforcer for each response becomes the feeling of having made that response. Another theory about the reinforcer for each response is that the fireman is rewarded by the satisfaction of accomplishment after each shovelful of coal. These theories, however, contain dangerous pitfalls for the behaviorist, since they involve unmeasured entities within the organism.

Do Organisms Learn Correlations?

If we reject the notion of 1:1 correspondence, we can offer in its place the possibility that the organism learns a set of correlations. (Again, we use the term "learning" with the proviso that it corresponds to overt behavioral effects. We need not posit anything within the organism's mind or even within its nervous system.)

Figure 4.1 shows the correlation between stimulus and reinforcement in simple classical conditioning. A bell is paired with food powder as it is presented to a dog. One unalterable feature of this pairing is that whatever the frequency of the bell, the frequency of the food powder goes along with it. Short intervals between successive bells are accompanied by short intervals between successive presentations of food powder, and *vice versa*.

Figure 4.1 also shows the correlation between response and reinforcement in simple instrumental conditioning in which a rat is reinforced for each bar-press by a pellet of food. With the 1:1 correspondence specifically provided in the experiment (and shown on the left side of Figure 4.1) goes the correlation of frequencies shown on the right. Let us consider the rat that is in a chamber with the bar. Sometimes the rat presses the bar at a slow rate and sometimes at a rapid rate. When the bar is pressed at a slow rate, food comes at a slow rate. When the bar is pressed at a rapid rate, food comes at a rapid rate. We notice that in situations of this kind, rats tend to press the bar rapidly. It is possible that the critical feature of the relationship between response and reinforcement is their correlation in rate.

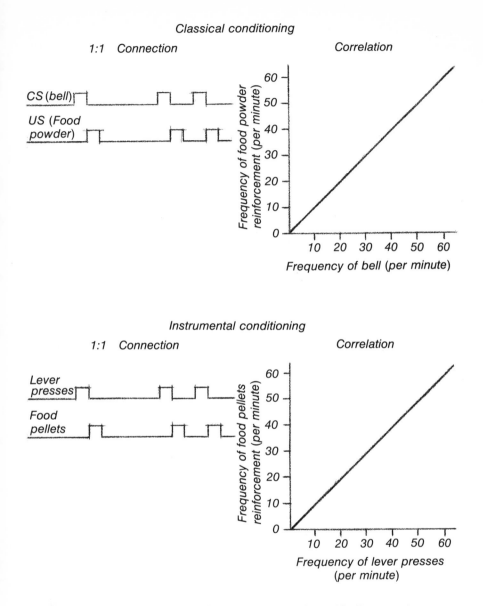

Figure 4.1 *Repeated 1:1 connections are expressed graphically as perfect correlations. The top half of the figure illustrates a perfect correlation in classical conditioning; the bottom half illustrates a perfect correlation in instrumental conditioning.*

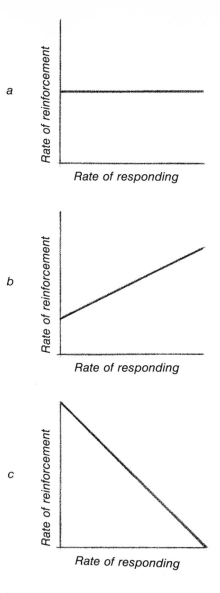

Figure 4.2 *An organism may learn to respond to these kinds of correlations between rate of responding and rate of reinforcement. (a) Zero correlation between response and reinforcement. (b) Slight positive correlation between response and reinforcement. Some reinforcement occurs without responding; reinforcement is increased slightly by responding. (c) Negative correlation between response and reinforcement. The more responding, the less reinforcement.*

The particular kind of correlation in Figure 4.1b (where a response is followed immediately by a reinforcement) represents the most common experimental learning situation, but other correlations can also be learned. For instance, when the correlation between responding and reinforcement is zero, when the reinforcements are programmed at a given rate no matter what the rate of responding, this fact too is learned. Figure 4.2a shows such a zero correlation. This would apply, for instance, to any control mechanism that has broken down. If an elevator button does not work, the frequency of elevators arriving at a floor, while not necessarily decreasing to zero, would nevertheless be out of the control of the operator. In other words, the correlation between the act of pressing the button and the elevator arriving at a floor would be zero. Likewise, if a water faucet breaks, the flow of water may increase drastically and be out of control. In this case, the correlation between turning the handle and the flow of water would be zero.

A zero correlation is represented by the horizontal line in the correlation plot of Figure 4.2a. Evidence that a zero correlation has been learned would be the cessation of a response. When good control (exemplified by a water faucet) breaks down, the correlation changes abruptly from a high value to zero, and organisms react appropriately. In the case of the water faucet, people would soon stop turning an ineffective faucet.

When poor control (exemplified by an elevator) breaks down, the change is less likely to have an immediate effect on behavior. When we are exposed to a positive correlation like the one in Figure 4.2b, and then switched to a zero correlation such as that of Figure 4.2a, we find it extremely difficult to realize that the correlation has changed. When the elevator button was working, even with no presses at all, there were some occasions on which the elevator stopped at that floor (when someone inside the elevator wanted to get out there). The more the button was pressed, the more times the elevator stopped at the floor. This would produce a positive correlation. The correlation shown in Figure 4.2b is a rather simplified version of such a positive correlation. When the correlation is changed to that of Figure 4.2a, when the button is out of order, it will be a long time before people stop pressing it. Very likely, people will press the button even more frequently, responding according to the old correlation which, unfortunately for them, no longer applies.

In general, the greater the change (from the old correlation function between rate of reinforcement and rate of response to the new function), the easier it is to learn; in our terms, the more likely it is to affect behavior.

Correlations versus Schedules

There are two possible areas of confusion with respect to the distinction between connections and correlations. First, correlation between responses and reinforcement must not be confused with the presentation of reinforcement on a pre-arranged schedule, such as a fixed-interval or variable-ratio schedule. Traditionally, when a schedule of reinforcement, such as those described previously, is programmed, a specific response always produces reinforcement immediately. For instance, in a fixed-ratio of ten responses, every tenth response produces reinforcement immediately and reliably. In a situation where responses are only correlated with reinforcement but not in 1:1 correspondence with reinforcement, reinforcements may come between responses or just preceding responses as well as immediately after responses.

The only relation required for a positive correlation in rate is that increased responding somehow produce increased reinforcement. While reinforcement delivered on a schedule will always determine some correlation function between responding and reinforcement, reinforcement correlated with responding does not imply that some schedule of reinforcement (as a schedule is traditionally understood) is in effect.

Correlations and Contingencies

A second area of confusion applies to the contingency tables shown in Figure 2.14. A contingency table represents a set of conditional probabilities. As long as the probabilities are 1.0 and 0, there is no difference between saying that an organism learns a set of probabilities (as in Figure 2.14a or 2.14b) and saying that an organism learns the connections shown on the left hand side of Figure 4.1.

When the conditional probabilities of the contingency table are less than unity but when reinforcement (when it comes) comes immediately after each response, the situation is like the schedules of reinforcement described above.

When the conditional probabilities of the contingency tables are less than unity *and* when reinforcement need not follow immediately upon the response, as in Figure 2.14c, the situation is like that we have been describing as based on correlations between the variables.

In general, correlation functions such as those of Figure 4.1 provide a better description of contingencies than tables such as Figure 2.14c. Conditional probabilities are usually measured in terms of relative frequencies. The correlation functions of Figure 4.1 provide a better picture of relative frequencies. However, in some experiments, conditional probabilities are deliberately set on a trial-by-trial basis. In such cases contingency tables such as that of Figure 2.14c would better represent the conditions imposed. Which of the two representations is a better picture of what is learned by the organism is an empirical question not yet fully settled.

Negative Correlations

Negative correlations between rate of responding and rate of reinforcement like that illustrated in Figure 4.2c affect behavior usually by reducing its frequency. If a rat is given food when it *doesn't* press a bar and bar-presses reduce the frequency of food, the rat will soon stop bar pressing and, in fact, avoid the vicinity of the bar, even though bar-presses were previously used to obtain food.

Studies of Correlations

In the case of a positive correlation between an act (bar pressing) and reinforcement (food), when each bar-press produces its own reinforcement, we may ask which is more important, the fact that each bar-press produces food or the fact that rapid bar pressing produces frequent reinforcement? In the simple situations of Figure 4.1, where each bar-press is specifically reinforced, it is hard to decide between 1:1 connections and correlations. It may be that *only* 1:1 connections can be learned. If so, we would have to invent connections in more complex situations, where none are provided by the environment, as in the example of the fireman stoking coal. Such invention would, in effect, be an abandonment of our strategy as behaviorists: to deal only with that which can be measured, observed, and confirmed. Fortunately, there is some evidence that correlations can be learned, in fact, that they are learned in situations in which they are not specifically arranged by an experimenter.

One experiment that tests whether correlations can be learned when they are not accompanied by direct connections between responses and their consequences is the one by Herrnstein and Hineline described previously. They found that rats would learn to press a bar when presses were not followed by any consequence other than a reduced frequency of shock. In their experiment there was no 1:1 connection between responses and shocks or even between responses and shock-free periods. Instead, when the rats pressed at a rapid rate, shocks came at a slow rate and when rats pressed at a slow rate shocks came at a rapid rate. Under these conditions rats learned to press rapidly.

Another interesting experiment in this area was done by three researchers at the University of Pennsylvania, Martin Seligman, Steven Maier, and Richard Solomon. In our example of the broken elevator button, we talked about changing from one correlation to another; before the button broke, there was a positive correlation between button pressing and elevator arrivals (Figure 4.2b). We speculated that the change from this positive correlation to zero correlation would be hard to detect. Subjects would respond according to the correlation that they had originally learned, even after that correlation was changed (that is, people would press the elevator button frequently even after it had been disconnected). Seligman, Maier, and Solomon varied a set of correlations in the opposite direction. Whereas, in the example of the elevator, the correlation between button pressing and elevator arrivals was first positive and then zero, the correlation in this experiment was first zero and then positive.

On the first day of the experiment, dogs were exposed to electric shocks programmed independently of their behavior. Nothing the dogs could do prevented the shock or enabled them to escape it (each shock lasted five seconds). Any responses the dogs made were completely uncorrelated with electric shock. On the next day, the dogs were put into a shuttle box and again shocked. This time, however, the shocks were preceded by a signal and the dogs could jump over a barrier to escape the shock (or, if they were fast enough, to avoid it). Most of the dogs in this experiment did not learn to escape. The dogs seemed to "give up" and passively "accept" the shock. Some of the dogs learned to escape after they were dragged by the experimenters across the barrier. Even then, some of them did not learn. In this respect their behavior contrasted vividly with dogs who had not been previously exposed to the inescapable shock. These dogs quickly learned to escape, and then to avoid the shock in the shuttle box. Obviously the prior exposure to inescapable shock had a strong effect on the dogs' subsequent behavior in the shuttle box. It severely retarded their learning to avoid the shocks.

Once again, it is tempting to draw analogies to human behavior. Often, when people are put in situations where they cannot avoid pain no matter what they do, and then the situation is changed so that they can avoid pain, they have a difficult time learning the proper avoidance responses. A child who is beaten regularly no matter what he does may not learn to "behave well" when conditions are changed so that beatings only follow "bad" behavior. What is it, then, about the initial conditions where responses and shocks are uncorrelated that affects behavior later when they are correlated? Seligman, Maier, and Solomon have a vivid name for the effect of the uncorrelated initial condition. They call it *learned helplessness*. The dogs learned in the initial condition that nothing they did could affect the shock. Then, when they were exposed to a situation when they could avoid shock, they had to "unlearn" the helplessness that they had previously acquired. In our terms, the dogs first learned the zero correlation between shock and responding; then, when exposed to the positive correlation they failed to react to the change in correlation. They had to "unlearn" the zero correlation.

By analogy, a zero correlation between *positive* reinforcement and behavior would also retard the acquisition of a response correlated with reward. In the human case, rewarding a child no matter what he does would be as bad as punishing a child no matter what he does because both would retard the child's acquisition of behavior that leads to reward or avoids punishment. Just as learned helplessness results from uncorrelated punishment, *learned omnipotence* could result from uncorrelated reward.

The evidence provided by the Seligman, Maier, and Solomon experiment is that correlations, even when they are zero correlations, are learned (in the sense that they have a potent effect on behavior). It would be difficult to explain this experiment in terms of connections, because the important feature of the first stage of the experiment, when shocks and responses were uncorrelated, was that there were no connections established. If there were no connections, what could have been learned? In terms of correlations, however, the experiment is easy to explain, because zero correlations exist on the same continuum as positive correlations. There is no reason why they cannot be learned just as easily as positive correlations. Then, the zero correlation, already learned, interferes with the effect of the positive correlation imposed later.

One might ask, why substitute one highly speculative notion, that organisms learn correlations, for another, that organisms learn connections. If "connections" send us off on a hunt for unobserved stimuli and reinforcers, doesn't this new "correlation" theory send us off on a hunt for unobserved correlations? The answer is, that it does, but the critical difference is not whether we must look for previously unobserved events, but *where* we must look for them. The unobserved stimuli and reinforcers postulated by connectionists have usually been postulated within the organism, where we cannot observe them, while the correlations we are speculating about must be found between the organism's responses and its environment, an area in which we are able to look.

As behaviorists, we observe the organism as it interacts with its environment. Whatever rules or laws we have uncovered are rules and laws regarding this observable interaction. It is this aspect of modern behaviorism that most distinguishes it from other approaches to psychology. When a rat presses a bar to obtain food, for instance, we focus our attention on the relation between the food and the bar-presses rather than on the relation between the food and the hopes, expectations, fears, wishes, and dreams of the rat. If the rat learns a complex series of movements, we focus on the environmental manipulations necessary for the complex series of movements to occur rather than on the way they are encoded in the rat's mind or even in its brain.

STIMULUS CONTROL

Stimulus control is another term for stimulus discrimination. If an organism comes to respond one way in the presence of a stimulus and another way in its absence, then that stimulus is said to "control" the organism's behavior much as a red light controls traffic.

Stimulus Control In Classical Conditioning

We have already discussed stimulus control (discrimination) in classical conditioning. Recall the experiment of Shenger-Krestovnikova with circles and ellipses as stimuli for dogs (Figure 2.6). The circle (CS) was followed by food powder while the ellipse was not. At first dogs salivated when circles or ellipses were presented; they later came to salivate only when circles were presented (except when the circles and ellipses were almost identical). From one point of view, the dogs learned to discriminate between the circles and ellipses. From another point of view the circles gained control of the dog's salivation.

The most common form of discrimination conditioning consists of alternating two stimuli (like the circles and ellipses), with one followed by the unconditioned stimulus and the other not followed by the unconditioned stimulus. Because this form of discrimination conditioning is so common, there are special terms for the stimuli; the stimulus followed by the unconditioned stimulus (the circle) is called the CS^+; the stimulus not followed by the unconditioned stimulus (the ellipse) is called the CS^-.

There are, however, other ways to obtain stimulus control in classical conditioning. For example, instead of circles followed by food (and ellipses followed by no food), Shenger-Krestovnikova's experiment might have had circles followed by more food and ellipses by less food. The dogs then might have come to respond during exposure to both circles and ellipses, but to respond more during circles. Alternatively, Shenger-Krestovnikova might have adjusted the amount of food proportionally to the roundness of the ellipse [In Figure 2.6, (b) would be followed by the least food, (c) by more food, (d) by still more food and (a) by the most food.] The dogs might then have come to salivate in proportion to the roundness of the stimulus. Still another alternative would have been to follow circles by food, and ellipses by electric shock to the paw. Then circles might have come to elicit salivation and ellipses, withdrawal.

Stimulus Control in Instrumental Conditioning

In instrumental conditioning the relation between behavior and reinforcement (or punishment) is very important, however, *signaling stimuli* (which are neither reinforcing nor punishing in themselves) can also play an important role. In classical conditioning the CS is correlated with reinforcement. In that sense the stimulus plays a primary role in classical conditioning. In instrumental conditioning, however, nonreinforcing stimuli play only a secondary role: They indicate changes in the correlation between behavior and reinforcement (or punishment). A good example of a stimulus serving such a secondary function in human behavior is an out-of-order sign on a Coke machine. This sign tells us about the relationship between dimes and Cokes but is not itself directly associated with either. Signs that signal a relation between responses and reinforcement are called *discriminative stimuli*.

As in classical conditioning, the most common discrimination procedures involve alternate presentation of two stimuli; in the presence of one stimulus, reinforcement is obtained; in the presence of the other, reinforcement is not obtained. As with classical conditioning, the stimuli for this special discrimination procedure also have special names. A discriminative stimulus that signals a positive correlation between responding and reinforcement is called an S^D ("ess dee"). A discriminative stimulus that signals the absence of reinforcement regardless of responding is called an S^Δ ("ess delta"). Figure 4.3 shows this common discrimination procedure with the two types of conditioning.

It is important to note, however, that alternation of stimuli signaling reinforcement and no reinforcement (as in Figure 4.3) is only one of many discrimination procedures—only one form of stimulus control. A discriminative stimulus may signal any relation between responding and reinforcement. The color of the sky in the morning, for example, gives an indication of whether a trip to the beach that afternoon will be reinforced by the opportunity to swim. But blue skies in the morning do not

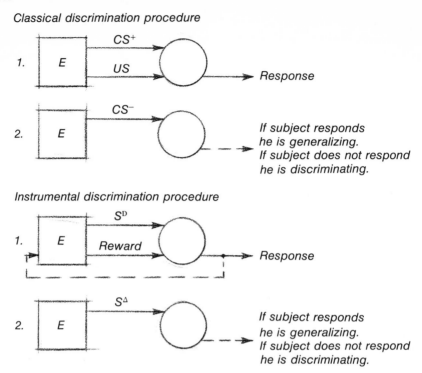

Classical discrimination procedure

Instrumental discrimination procedure

Figure 4.3 *Discrimination procedures for classical and instrumental conditioning.*

guarantee fair weather, nor do grey skies guarantee rain. Blue skies signal one relation between response and reinforcement, grey skies, another. Thus, while we may refrain from going to the beach on a grey day, such a signal is not, properly, an S^Δ because it is *possible* that our response (going to the beach) would be reinforced (nice weather at the beach) even when skies are grey in the morning.

Successive Discrimination and Simultaneous Discrimination

Within the confines of instrumental conditioning, discrimination has been studied in two ways. One way, called *successive discrimination*, is alternately presenting two different discriminative stimuli. The other way, called *simultaneous discrimination*, presents two discriminative stimuli together.

The alternating green and red of a traffic light, telling us to go (respond) in the presence of the green and stop (not respond) in the presence of the red is an example of successive discrimination. The adjacent green and red lights marking open and closed toll booths on a highway or bridge are an example of simultaneous discrimination. They tell us not whether to go or stop, but whether to go one way or another. In general, simultaneous-discrimination situations can produce finer distinctions in responses to stimuli than successive-discrimination situations. There are two reasons for this greater sensitivity of simultaneous discrimination. First of all, the stimuli themselves are easier to tell apart when presented simultaneously. It is easier, for instance, to tell a darker from a lighter shade of grey when the two greys are adjacent than when they are seen at different times. Secondly, even when the stimuli are clearly distinguishable, the properties of simultaneous procedures tend to create greater differences in performance than the properties of successive procedures. In successive discriminations, responding appropriate to one stimulus when it appears does not preclude responding appropriate to the other when it appears.

In simultaneous discriminations, on the other hand, when the organism is responding appropriately for one stimulus, it is losing time during which it might be responding appropriately for the other.

It is easy to see how simultaneous discrimination is more sensitive than successive discrimination in everyday life. At home, where dinner is put before someone, he often has the choice only of eating it or not. Observing a person's eating habits at home may tell you little about his preferences for food, since many people will eat whatever is put in front of them. In a restaurant, however, a choice is available, and eating one food often precludes eating another. Here, the same person is liable to be more "discriminating."

Connections

In classical conditioning the stimulus (the CS) is said to cause the response; in instrumental conditioning the stimulus is said to set the occasion for the response.

The CS in classical conditioning is like an airraid siren signaling an event to come and generating a direct response. The discriminative stimulus of instrumental conditioning is like the "Open" sign in a store window signaling that *if* we were to turn the knob of the door, the door would open.

This distinction rests on the distinction we previously made between elicited and emitted responses. During classical conditioning, responses are preceded by the US and are said to be elicited, or caused, by the US. After conditioning has taken place (when responses begin to occur after

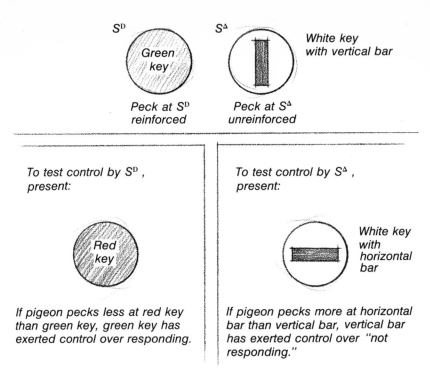

Figure 4.4 *Procedures for testing control by S^D and S^Δ.*

the CS), the responses are, by extension, said to be elicited or caused by the CS. During instrumental conditioning, on the other hand, responses are not preceded in any strict way by any stimulus. They are said to be emitted by the organism. The discriminative stimulus never invariably indicates reinforcement. It may indicate that reinforcement is available *provided* some response is made. Thus, when responding increases in frequency during the discriminative stimulus, we do not say that the stimulus elicits or causes the responses, but that the stimulus *sets the occasion* for the responses to occur.

Accordingly, when pecking of pigeons at a key is reinforced when the key is green and unreinforced when the key is dark, and the pigeon pecks more frequently at the green key, we say that the green key sets the occasion for the response as opposed to the notion that the green key *causes* the response. Similarly, when a man is paid for working on weekdays and not paid for working on weekends we say that the stimuli that tell him what day of the week it is (e.g., checking a calendar) set the occasion for his work. It would be awkward to say that checking a calendar *causes* the man to work. We also realize that these stimuli, while controlling whether the man works or not, do not exert exclusive control. It is rare to find a 1:1 correspondence of weekdays and working.

Testing for Control by S^D and S^Δ

Let us return to the procedure illustrated in the lower part of Figure 4.3. Two discriminative stimuli are alternated. One (the S^D) signals a positive correlation between responding and reinforcement. The other (the S^Δ) signals a zero correlation, with no reinforcement programmed, regardless of responding. The behavior usually observed under these conditions is straightforward: responding during the S^D, no responding during the S^Δ.

A particular instance of such a discrimination, involving a pigeon and a key, is illustrated at the top of Figure 4.4. The pigeon's pecks are reinforced when the key is green (S^D) and not reinforced when the key is white with a vertical bar (S^Δ). After alternate exposure to the two discriminative stimuli, the pigeon comes to peck at the key when it is green and not to peck at the key when it is white with a vertical bar.

What has the pigeon learned about the two discriminative stimuli? Consider these three alternatives:

a. The pigeon learns to peck when the key is green (S^D).
b. The pigeon learns not to peck when the key is white with a vertical bar (S^Δ).
c. The pigeon learns to peck when the key is green *and* not to peck when the key is white with a vertical bar.

A parallel set of questions can be raised about virtually any discrimination. A little boy may be rewarded for kissing his mother and not rewarded for kissing his father. Does he learn (1) to kiss his mother, (2) not to kiss his father, or (3) both?

Which alternative the boy learns depends on what he ordinarily does. If he ordinarily kisses nobody, he must learn to kiss his mother, and he need learn nothing specific about his father. If he ordinarily kisses everybody, he must learn not to kiss his father, but nothing specific about his mother. If he ordinarily kisses some people he must learn to kiss his mother *and* not to kiss his father.

The same sort of reasoning applies to the pigeon. If it ordinarily does not peck, it must learn to peck the green key. If it ordinarily pecks, it must learn not to peck the white key with the vertical bar. If it sometimes pecks, it must learn both.

Whether alternative (a), (b), or (c) applies in any given case depends on the organism (both its species and its previous experience), the stimuli, the reinforcement, the response, and the relation between the reinforcement and the response. The question that concerns us here is how to test the alternatives.

Alternatives (a) and (b) imply that one of the stimuli has no effect. Alternative (a) implies that the S^Δ has no effect, and alternative (b) implies that the S^D has no effect. One way to test either of these alternatives is the hypothetical experiment shown in Figure 4.5. The rationale for the tests follows a somewhat complicated argument. The stimulus that is supposed to have no effect is varied. If it is argued, as it is in alternatives (a) and (b), that one of the stimuli has no effect, then its variation also ought to have no effect.

If, on the other hand, varying either stimulus has the effect of producing variation in behavior, then alternative (c) must have been correct.

An important practical point of the tests is that the S^D and S^Δ must be capable of separate variation along different continua. In the illustration in Figure 4.5, the continuum is color for the S^D and angle of the bar for the S^Δ. Suppose otherwise, that the S^D and S^Δ varied along the same continuum—that the S^D was a simple white key, the S^Δ was a grey key (and the continuum is brightness). Then in the test phase, any new stimulus (a new shade of grey) would be a variation of both the S^D and the S^Δ. If the pigeon pecked less during the new stimulus, there would be no way of knowing whether it was because the stimulus was less like the S^D or more like the S^Δ. In the example in Figure 4.5, on the other hand, where the S^D and S^Δ are on two continua, we can be fairly certain that while the red key is not like the S^D, it is no more like the S^Δ than the green key was.

Another practical problem with the procedure in Figure 4.5, is what to do about reinforcement while the test stimuli are presented. For tests of the efficacy of S^D, for instance, the usual solution is to stop reinforcement altogether during the test and alternate the original S^D and a group of test stimuli varying along the same dimension (color, in the case of the example in Figure 4.5). This would be a simple generalization experiment where responding would be expected to fall off as the stimuli became more different from the original S^D, provided the S^D had an effect, i.e., provided either alternative (a) or (c) was true. Otherwise (if alternative

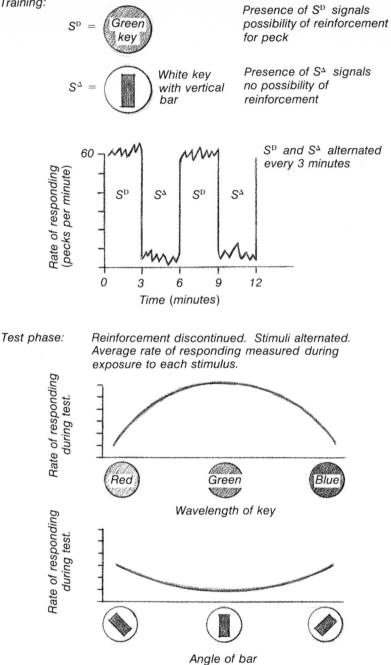

Figure 4.5 Hypothetical experiment to test discrimination.

(b) were true), responding would not drop off, but would remain at a high value as the color of the stimulus was varied.

For tests of the efficacy of S^Δ, a corresponding procedure is followed. Reinforcements are discontinued, and the original S^Δ is alternated with test stimuli varying along the same dimension (tilt of the bar across the white key in Figure 4.5). This experiment shown in Figure 4.5 (bottom curve) would test generalization of the S^Δ. Responding would be expected to increase as the stimuli became more different from the original S^Δ provided the S^Δ had an effect (provided either alternative (b) or (c) were true). Otherwise (if alternative (a) were true), responding would not increase but would remain at the same low value as the angle of the bar was changed.

While the specific hypothetical experiment of Figure 4.5 has not been performed exactly as described here, enough similar experiments have been performed for us to be certain that in the case described (pigeons pecking a key), alternative (c) is correct. Both S^D and S^Δ gradients have been found. Figure 4.5 shows a hypothetical S^D and an S^Δ test-phase gradient. Usually S^Δ gradients are somewhat shallower than S^D gradients. Some experimenters have speculated that this is because the S^D is the only stimulus signaling reinforcement, while the S^Δ shares the property of signaling nonreinforcement with the myriad other stimuli in the pigeon's environment. Since the S^D is unique and the S^Δ somewhat more general, the pigeon is likely to respond in the presence of a new stimulus as if it were another of the general, more common "S^Δ"s. In the generalization test, therefore, the particular S^Δ of training does not produce as much discrimination in responding as the S^D of training. This is another way of saying that while alternative (c) is correct, alternatives (a) and (b) are not equally incorrect. There is some truth to alternative (a) in the case of Figure 4.5.

Some psychologists interpret the test-phase gradients shown in Figure 4.5 as reflections of processes inside the organism. The S^D gradient is said to mirror an excitatory process inside the organism. The excitation is a continuous state said to underly emissions of discrete responses. The S^Δ gradient is said to mirror an inhibitory process inside the organism. The inhibition is said to underly the nonemission of the response.* It is arguable whether the concepts of excitation and inhibition are necessary to mediate between environment and behavior. As behaviorists, we would prefer to relate stimuli such as the green and white keys directly to the organism's behavior.

---

* The notion that inhibition is associated with nonreinforcement comes from Pavlov's conception of extinction as a positive inhibitory process (see Figure 2.4).

Complex Discriminations

Most experiments in the laboratory use discriminative stimuli of a simple kind—they use tones, lights, bars, and so forth. Yet, we know that humans and animals are capable of much more complex discriminations. We recognize the faces of our relatives, the handwriting of our friends, and their voices. Animals also are capable of making complex discriminations of this kind. Dogs recognize their masters' faces, and the famous RCA trademark reminds us that a dog can recognize his masters' voice as well.

As an illustration of the complex discriminations that are possible, consider the following experiment with pigeons. Thousands of photographs were taken of vehicles of various kinds. The pictures were then sorted into two groups, those that contained trucks or parts of trucks, and those that contained only cars. The pictures were shown in random order to the pigeons, but the same picture was never shown twice to the same pigeon. While the pictures were being shown, the pigeons could peck a key. Occasionally, a peck would produce some food, but most of the time pecks had no effect. The critical point of the experiment was that for some pigeons pecks were reinforced only if the picture contained a truck or part of a truck. For other pigeons, pecks were reinforced only when the picture contained cars or parts of cars. In other words, for the first group of pigeons, trucks were "S^D"s and cars were "S^Δ"s; for the other group, conditions were reversed. As far as the experimenters could tell, there was no other difference between the two groups of photographs other than the cars-versus-trucks distinction. The two groups of photographs were equally light, equally colorful, and equally complex. Yet, within a few weeks of daily exposure to the photographs, the pigeons came to peck rapidly when exposed to a picture containing a truck (if that was the S^D) or a car (if that was the S^D) and slowly or not at all when the picture contained the S^Δ vehicle. How was this discrimination made? Possibly each pigeon had its own strategy. Perhaps some counted the axles on the vehicles. Perhaps some recognized the distinctive hoods or fenders of trucks or simply discriminated the size of the vehicle. (Although this could not be a simple size discrimination, since some vehicles were close and some far away. It would have to be based on the relative size of the vehicle compared to its surroundings.) The complexity of the discrimination can be appreciated when we realize that with all our modern technology, we are now only on the threshold of our ability to build machines to make equivalent discriminations.

The important point here is that whatever the detailed strategy of the individual pigeons, there was an invariance in the molar properties of their behavior (pecking did occur in the presence of the S^D). Furthermore, whatever the strategy of the individual pigeons, their behavior is subject to manipulation in the same way by reinforcing pecks in the presence of the S^D. When differential reinforcement was discontinued, the discrimination deteriorated, and the pigeons responded equally during the two kinds of pictures. For the behaviorist, this covariance between properties of behavior (responding) and properties of the environment (cars or trucks) is the important part of the experiment. The strategy of a particular pigeon is a matter for speculation only insofar as it leads to future experiments. (For instance, if the pigeons counted axles, they would do badly in discriminating cars from two-axled trucks.) When the particular strategy hypothesized does not lead to specific behavioral consequences, the behaviorist loses interest in it.

Warning. While organisms behave with surprising uniformity under similar correlations of stimulus, response, and reinforcement, every organism comes to a conditioning situation with a host of innate and previously acquired behaviors. One of these behaviors may be contrary to the conditioning being undertaken and may require special procedures to compensate for it. (In the previous chapter we discussed a way to train cockroaches to approach light, a stimulus they usually avoid).

It is also important to realize that no stimulus is completely neutral. Stimuli will not always produce the same effects when correlated with responses and reinforcements. A vivid demonstration of this is the work of John Garcia at the State University of New York at Stony Brook. He arranged a situation in which the sickness of rats was correlated with certain lights, sounds, and tastes. The rats were later indifferent to the lights and sounds, but showed marked aversion to the tastes. Either the rats in Garcia's experiment were born with the tendency to associate whatever they had recently tasted with sickness or they had learned early in life that tastes and sickness are often correlated.

Bibliography

There is very little published specifically on connections and correlations. The previously cited theoretical accounts by Guthrie, Hull, Tolman, and Skinner, all have a point of view on the subject. Tolman was first to call himself a molar behaviorist, and *molar behaviorism* (the view that stimuli and responses need not be discrete sensory or muscular events) is probably the best way to describe the present approach. However, the most direct influence on the material in this chapter is the work of B. F. Skinner. He showed that behavior could be accounted for quantitatively without the notion of a 1:1 correspondence between stimulus and response. The present account extends his ideas to account quantitatively for behavior without a 1:1 relation between responses and reinforcement. See R. J. Herrnstein, "Method and theory in the study of avoidance" (*Psychological Review*, 76, 1969, 49–70) for a formal application of these notions to avoidance learning.

The experiment by Seligman, Maier, and Solomon is described in their paper, "Pavlovian fear conditioning and learned helplessness," in R. Church and B. Campbell (Eds.), *Aversive Conditioning and Learning* (New York: Appleton-Century-Crofts, 1969).

In the specific area of stimulus control, there are many published works. See the article by H. S. Terrace in Honig's *Operant Behavior* (cited in the bibliography at the end of Chapter 3) for a clearly written account. For descriptions of experiments on inhibition see H. M. Jenkins, "Generalization gradients and the concept of inhibition," in D. I. Mostofsky (Ed.), *Stimulus Generalization* (Stanford: Stanford University Press, 1965, pp. 55–62.) For experiments in complex discriminations in animals see "The complex discriminated operant: studies of matching-to-sample and related problems" by W. W. Cumming and R. Berryman (in the Mostofsky book). Also see R. J. Herrnstein and D. Loveland "Complex visual concept in the pigeon" (*Science*, 146, 1964, 549–551).

Chapter 5

Some New Directions

The previous chapters have briefly sketched the history and the recent progress of the science of the behavior of organisms. In this chapter we take up the question: In what directions is this emerging science moving? The following sections cover only three of the many areas in which behaviorism is being extended and applied: (1) the treatment of dysfunctional human behavior, (2) self-control, (3) the quantification of behavioral variables.

Warning. In the physical sciences, trained engineers, familiar with both the physical sciences themselves and with machines and their operation, develop practical uses for the laws that scientists discover. In behavioral sciences we are all engineers in a sense. We are, ourselves, behaving organisms and we sometimes feel a pressing need for rules that will tell us how to behave. There is thus a strong temptation to draw analogies from pigeons to people—to attempt to apply laboratory data directly to our everyday lives. However, the behavior of an organism in response to the simple contingencies of an isolated laboratory environment may be quite different from the behavior of an organism exposed to the complex contingencies of a nonlaboratory environment. We hope to eventually apply what we have learned in the laboratory to the problems of everyday life. But such application must be undertaken with the utmost care.

Perhaps the greatest danger of premature application of the findings of behavioral science to the complex world outside the laboratory is that it gives us the illusion that we are acting scientifically when, in reality, our behavior is no more effective than it would be if it were guided simply by tradition. Since we know little of the complex effects of spanking on children, it is no more scientific to tell ourselves we are spanking a child "to reduce his maladaptive behavior" than to spank him "because we are mad at him." (It is for this reason that the examples that are drawn here from everyday life should not be regarded as direct guides to action.)

DYSFUNCTIONAL BEHAVIOR

In the laboratory we are concerned with complex contingencies of reinforcement and with quantifying the variables that control behavior. We tend to take for granted the basic principles by which such control is obtained, the principles outlined in this book. At several institutions, however, researchers have been resolutely applying these principles to the treatment of dysfunctional human behavior. These applications have been successful as measured against results with more traditional methods of treating behavioral disorders.

One way to look at dysfunctional behavior is to regard it as behavior that has evolved "out of synchrony" with changes in the environment. According to this view, when the environment changes too suddenly or drastically, an organism may not be able to "keep up"—to compensate adequately, to behave so as to maximize reward under the changed contingencies.

Someone who is unhappy about his behavior may seek help from a therapist. It is up to the therapist to provide the appropriate environmental gradations that will reward the patient for approximations to the desired behavior.

Sometimes it is society, rather than the individual himself, that desires a change in his behavior. Murder is an obvious example of a dysfunctional behavior that harms human society. Then there are those individuals who cannot function in the particular society in which they live. Some cannot hold a job; some cannot interact with other people; some cannot communicate rationally; others cannot even eat or attend to their own bodily needs without constant assistance. In the United States alone, more than a quarter of a million criminals are locked up in federal and state prisons, and more than half a million mental patients are institutionalized. The basic question regarding an institutionalized person is: Do we want to use the most effective means we know to change his or her behavior for the better (that is, to bring it into conformity with the environmental contingencies)? If we refuse to try, we will continue to expose the inmate to the contingencies of reinforcement in our present institutions. This course of action often does provide a crude but effective means of modifying behavior—for the worse.

The techniques used in behavior modification are varied. At present, behavior modification outside the laboratory is more of an art than a science; each therapist evolves his own techniques for application of behavioral principles. Let us consider two examples:

(1) In a mental hospital (as in any hospital or institution where boredom is a strong factor) the attention of the staff is a potent reinforcer. Almost every mental hospital is "short staffed" and there is a tendency for staff members to pay most attention to those patients who give the most trouble. Thus, a behaviorist would contend that there is a built-in mechanism in most mental hospitals to reinforce trouble-making and disturbances of various kinds. An easy way for a patient to get personal attention under these circumstances is to refuse to eat. In fact, in many mental hospitals there is a large number of patients who must be coaxed to enter the dining room and once there, who must be fed like infants. A vicious circle develops. Patients refuse to eat, becoming the center of attention. This, in turn, reinforces their refusal to eat and gets them more attention. Clearly, positive feedback is at work in the situation.

In a report published in 1962, Teodore Ayllon and Erick Haughton, on the staff of a hospital in Saskatchewan, Canada described a technique they devised to break the vicious circle. They selected a group of thirty schizophrenic women with a history of refusal to eat. Several attendants usually took thirty minutes to get the women into the dining room. Ayllon and Haughton then changed the contingencies. The attendants were instructed to ignore the patients. A bell sounded to announce that the dining room was open. Thirty minutes later the doors of the dining room were closed and patients were no longer allowed in. Whoever did not enter within 30 minutes did not eat that meal. Although, at first, few patients entered the dining room within the allotted time, eventually almost all of them did. Then the time was decreased from 30 minutes to 20 minutes to 15 minutes and to 5 minutes. Finally, almost all of the patients entered the dining room within five minutes of the bell without the assistance of the attendants. Next, Haughton and Ayllon made entrance to the dining room contingent on a dropping a penny (which the patients received from a nurse) into a slot. Then, in order to receive the coin, each patient had to press a button simultaneously with another patient at another button. At the end of the experiment, all the patients, selected originally for their refusal to eat, were engaging in cooperative behavior in order to obtain admission to the dining hall. Here is an example of making one reinforcer (attention from staff) independent of a behavior (refusal to eat) and making another reinforcer (food) dependent on a behavior (sharing a task with another person). The first reinforcer lost its effect on the patient's behavior and the second reinforcer gained effectiveness.

(2) A second example also involves the gradual shaping of a response, this time a verbal response of a *catatonic schizophrenic* patient who had been completely mute for nineteen years prior to the incidents reported here. To say the least, the patient, referred to as S (for Subject), was withdrawn and exhibited little psychomotor activity. The case history that follows is not unique. It is from a report published in 1960 by Wayne Isaacs, James Thomas, and Israel Goldiamond of Anna State Hospital in Illinois.*

> The S was brought to a group therapy session with other chronic schizophrenics (who were verbal), but he sat in the position in which he was placed and continued the withdrawal behaviors which characterized him. He remained impassive and stared ahead even when cigarettes, which other members accepted, were offered to him and were waved before his face. At one session, when E removed cigarettes from his pocket, a package of chewing gum accidentally fell out. The S's eyes moved toward the gum and then returned to their usual position. This response was chosen by E as one with which he would start to work, using the method of successive approximation. (This method finds use where E desires to produce responses which are not present in the current repertoire of the organism and which are considerably removed from those which are available. The E then attempts to "shape" the available behaviors into the desired form, capitalizing upon both the variability and regularity of successive behaviors. The shaping process involves the reinforcement of those parts of a selected response which are successively in the desired direction and the nonreinforcement of those which are not. For example, a pigeon may be initially reinforced when it moves its head. When this movement occurs

---

* In case histories, the subject is often referred to as S, the experimenter as E.

regularly, only an upward movement may be reinforced, with downward movements not reinforced. The pigeon may now stretch its neck, with this movement reinforced. Eventually the pigeon may be trained to peck at a disc which was initially high above its head and at which it would normally never peck. In the case of the psychotic under discussion, the succession was eye movement, which brought into play occasional facial movements including those of the mouth, lip movements, vocalizations, word utterance, and finally verbal behavior.)

The S met individually with E three times a week. Group sessions also continued. The following sequence of procedures was introduced in the private sessions. Although the weeks are numbered consecutively, they did not follow at regular intervals since other duties kept E from seeing S every week.

Weeks, 1, 2. A stick of gum was held before S's face, and E waited until S's eyes moved toward it. When this response occurred, E as a consequence gave him the gum. By the end of the second week, response probability in the presence of the gum was increased to such an extent that S's eyes moved toward the gum as soon as it was held up.

Weeks 3, 4. The E now held the gum before S, waiting until he noticed movement in S's lips before giving it to him. Toward the end of the first session of the third week, a lip movement spontaneously occurred, which E promptly reinforced. By the end of this week both lip movement and eye movement occurred when the gum was held up. The E then withheld giving S the gum until S spontaneously made a vocalization, at which time E gave S the gum. By the end of this week, holding up the gum readily occasioned eye movement toward it, lip movement, and a vocalization resembling a croak.

Weeks, 5, 6. The E held up the gum, and said, "Say gum, gum," repeating these words each time S vocalized. Giving S the gum was made contingent upon vocalizations increasingly approximating gum. At the sixth session (at the end of Week 6), when E said, "Say gum, gum," S suddenly said, "Gum, please." This response was accompanied by reinstatement of other responses of this class, that is, S answered questions regarding his name and age.

Thereafter he responded to questions by E both in individual sessions and in group sessions, but answered no one else. Responses to the discriminitive stimuli of the room generalized to E on the ward; he greeted E on two occasions in the group room. He read from signs in E's office upon request by E.

Since the response now seemed to be under the strong stimulus control of E, the person, attempt was made to generalize the stimulus to other people. Accordingly, a nurse was brought into the private room; S smiled at her. After a month, he began answering her questions. Later, when he brought his coat to a volunteer worker on the ward, she interpreted the gesture as a desire to go outdoors and conducted him there. Upon informing E of the incident, she was instructed to obey S only as a consequence of explicit verbal requests by him. The S thereafter vocalized requests. These instructions have now been given to other hospital personnel, and S regularly initiates verbal requests when nonverbal requests have no reinforcing consequences. Upon being taken to the commissary, he said, "Ping pong," to the volunteer worker and played a game with her. Other patients, visitors, and members of hospital-society-at-large continue, however, to interpret non-verbal requests and to reinforce them by obeying S.

Some nonbehaviorists object to this kind of direct treament of dysfunctional behavior on the grounds that it treats "only the behavioral symptoms of the disorder" rather than "the underlying disorder," which is said to exist in "the mind" of the patient. These critics contend that as long as the basic psychological problem is not found by subtle and sophisticated techniques and revealed to the patient, elimination of one symptom will tend to be replaced by the substitution of another. In actual instances of behavioral treatment, however, dysfunctional behaviors have been eliminated, and such a hypothetical substitution of symptoms is virtually never found.*

But will a successful treatment in a mental hospital (or therapist's office), where the environment is largely under control, persist when a person returns to the normal complex environment outside of the institution? Behavioral modifications wrought in an institution could easily be extinguished in other environments. Clearly, it is important that appropriate behavior continue to be rewarded in the "outside world."

Often dysfunctional behavior seems to be subject to the effect of positive feedback. For some reason a man has a mild behavioral disturbance; his relatives and friends overreact to the mild disturbance and upset him; this increases the disturbance, which, in turn, provokes stronger reactions. A behavioral therapist's treatment of such behavior would be designed to break this pattern in a direct fashion. Relatives who have refused to have a patient home for visits because they are upset by the patient's strange appearance or behavior may change their attitude when the patient's appearance and behavior are less strange. Their changed attitude may well reinforce normal behavior outside the institution.

---

* Even if the critics were correct, and behavioral therapy treated only symptoms, surely it would be better to get rid of the symptoms and not the underlying disease than to "cure" the disease and leave all the symptoms intact. (A man would not worry about a cold without its symptoms to tell him that he has it. Similarly, he would worry a great deal if the symptoms of runny nose, headaches, sneezing and high temperature persisted even though his "basic cold" had been cured.)

SELF-CONTROL

Frequently, people want to change and better control their own behavior. Some people want to study more, some less. Some want to work harder, some to learn to relax. Some people want to be more aggressive with their employers or employees or with their relatives; some want to be less aggressive. Such behavior changes can often be brought about by behavioral techniques. The therapist rewards the patient for approaches to the desired behavior in a manner that parallels the way a pigeon is rewarded for desired approximations to a peck on a key. In a previous section we have seen that this relatively small-scale process (called *shaping*) bears certain similarities to the general process of the evolutionary development of species.

Self-control is actually a misnomer for any kind of self-induced change, for although patterns of behavior may come from within ourselves in the sense that they were acquired before birth or soon thereafter, whatever causes these patterns to appear at a given time must come from interaction with the environment at that time. Thus *self*-control really refers to certain forms of environmental control of behavior.

The kinds of behavior that come under the rubric of self-control are most easily defined by listing some examples. A person can exert self-control by biting his tongue, clapping his hand over his mouth to keep from laughing, putting a box of candy out of sight to keep from eating, or putting an alarm clock out of easy reach of his bed. All these involve overt performance of one sort of behavior in order to change the probability of later engaging in another sort. Less overt strategies of self-control may involve an overweight lady refraining from dessert or a man not taking a cocktail at a party because he is driving home later. A close look at the contingencies involved in each of these instances reveals a common feature having to do with *immediacy* versus *delay* of reinforcement and punishment.

Rational behavior might be roughly defined as that behavior producing the most reward and the least punishment. Within this definition, we all want to act rationally, but events often upset our intentions. Such upsets occur when we are offered immediate rewards of relatively low magnitude in exchange for delayed rewards of high magnitude. The reward of eating a candy now is less strong than the reward of being thin. If we were to offer the overweight lady the choice of eating the candy *next week* or being thin *next week* there is no question which she would chose. However, if we offer her the choice of eating the candy *now* or being thin next week she might find the temptation to eat the candy too strong to resist. It is relatively easy to make a decision between two rewards both far in the future. It is more difficult to make a decision when one of the rewards can occur immediately. Successful self-control seems to depend on making the easy decision early and preventing the later difficult decision from having to be made. The man who decides the night before to get up at six the next morning and puts his alarm clock across the room from his bed (forcing himself to get out of bed to turn it off) has effectively prevented himself from having to decide at six the next morning whether to accept the immediate reward of more sleep or the more distant reward of being on time for work.

There has been little laboratory research on self-control, but a recent experiment by George Ainslie at Harvard University has shown self-control of the "remote alarm clock" variety exhibited by pigeons. The pigeons in Ainslee's experiment were deprived of food until they weighed about 80 percent of what they would if they were allowed to eat freely. Then they were put into a chamber with a single key, on which they could peck, and a food hopper. The key was dark ordinarily, but every once in a while, it would be illuminated with red light for 2.5 seconds. If the pigeons pecked the key during the 2.5 seconds that the key was red, the food hopper would be available immediately for 1.5 seconds. If the pigeons refrained from pecking the key for the 2.5 seconds that the key was red, they would receive 4 seconds of access to the food without pecking for it. Now pigeons normally show strong preference for a 4-second reward over a 1.5-second reward. Yet, in this experiment all the pigeons pecked the key as soon as it turned red. The pigeons seemed to prefer a 1.5-second reward immediately to a 4-second reward that they would have to wait a short time for. In other words, they could not control their tendency to peck for an immediate reinforcement even though the long-term reinforcement for not pecking was greater. After observing this behavior Ainslie introduced a new contingency to the experiment. About eleven seconds before the key turned red, it would turn white. If the pigeons pecked the key when it was white, they would prevent the key from turning red when it ordinarily would have and they would obtain the 4-second reward at the end of the trial. In a sense, pecking the white key was like putting the alarm clock far from the bed. It insured that the larger reward would be obtained. If the pigeon did not peck the white key, the key would turn red and a peck on the red key would produce an immediate 1.5-second reward as before. Figure 5.1 diagrams the experimental procedure. A peck on the white key could not affect reward directly. It could only prevent the opportunity to make a choice later between a small immediate reward and a larger delayed reward. Ainslie's pigeons exhibited self-control. They pecked the white key about 90 percent of the time it was offered to them. Later, in a

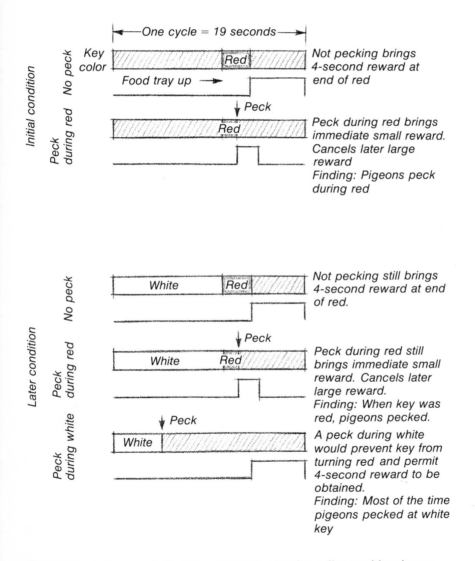

Figure 5.1 *A diagram of Ainslie's experiment, showing self-control by pigeons.*

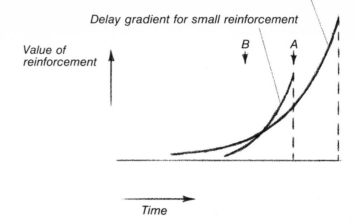

Figure 5.2 *Delay gradients. Reinforcements will be delivered at times indicated by vertical dotted lines. Prior to point of delivery, reinforcement is "discounted"—the further in the future reinforcement is to be, the less it is worth. A and B are points at which a choice must be made between the large reinforcement and the small reinforcement.*

control experiment, Ainslie allowed the key to turn red no matter what the pigeons did while the key was white. Here, the pigeons stopped pecking the white key (but continued to peck the red key).

It is possible to explain Ainslie's results in terms of *gradients* of delay of reinforcement. Figure 5.2 shows two gradients, one for the short reinforcement and one for the long reinforcement. Each gradient is highest at the point of reinforcement. The further away reinforcement is, the lower the gradient. At Point A, when the red light comes on the small reinforcement gradient is available immediately and is at its maximum. The larger reinforcement is still a few seconds away, and its gradient is low at Point A. At Point B, on the other hand, both reinforcements are far in the future, hence both are low. Because of the particular shape of the gradients, they cross so that one gradient is higher at Point A and the other is higher at Point B. The pigeons are said to chose according to whichever gradient is higher. At Point A (when the key is red) the gradient for the immediate reinforcement is higher. At Point B (when the key is white) the gradient for the delayed reinforcement is higher. The fact remains, however, that behavior at Point B, when the key is white, has no direct effect on reinforcement. Rather it affects behavior which, in turn, affects reinforcement. This is a characteristic of situations in everyday life that we would call examples of self-control.

An attempt to apply these findings in a practical setting is a device invented by Nathan H. Azrin and J. Powell. It is a cigarette box that can be locked for two hours after a cigarette is removed. When a person starts to smoke one cigarette he is most willing to postpone his next cigarette. At that point he cheerfully locks his cigarette case for two hours. Thirty minutes later, when he might ordinarily be ready for another cigarette, and, presumably, when the immediate reward of smoking outweighs the long term reward of not smoking, he is prevented from succumbing to temptation by his prior decision to lock the case. Azrin and Powell report sharp reductions in the rate of smoking of chain smokers with this device.

QUANTIFICATION OF BEHAVIORAL VARIABLES

While some applications of behavioral techniques can be made at present, true behavioral engineering awaits better quantification of behavioral variables. There is a forbidding stretch of terra incognita between the laws of conditioning and the practical manipulation of behavior. Pavlov's and Thorndike's qualitative laws say little to a mother confronted with an unruly child, a teacher struggling with a balky class, or a legislator concerned with the public good. The "controlling agency" is often without a clearly defined response to control, let alone access to potent stimuli, reinforcers or punishers. But even with the essentials for conditioning (stimuli, responses, and consequences), the quantitative ingredients for a practical course of action are still lacking. It is, for example, insufficient to assert that good driving would be encouraged by an incentive program. In order to be useful, the information must be quantitative. Will an incentive program stimulate enough good driving to justify its cost?

Where response and consequence can be measured as monetary quantities or their equivalents, classical economics has been able to deal quantitatively with behavior; the modern science of game theory is an extension of an analysis of behavior from an economist's point of view. However, the limitation of a quantification of behavior in purely economic terms is not only that it assumes men will always act rationally (to maximize money gained) but also that it focuses only on situations that permit monetary analysis. Organisms are often in situations that do not easily lend themselves to such a characterization—for example, a mother with her child. Yet in both monetary and nonmonetary situations, presumably in accordance with a single set of psychological laws, the behavior of organisms is governed by its consequences.

Laws relating the two parameters of reward and punishment to behavior can be regarded as a sort of behavioral economics. The self-control experiments of George Ainslie (described above) are a subcategory of such economic laws. Ainslie started his experiment with the idea that the relative value of two rewards seen from a distance (B in Figure 5.2) might be inverse to the relative value of the rewards seen from close-up (A in Figure 5.2). In other words, he thought that the function showing the decreasing value of the small reward as its attainment proceeded further into the future and the similar function showing the decreasing value of the large reward (economists call these *discount* functions) could cross as the functions of Figure 5.2 cross. However, Ainslie's problem in setting up his experiments was to use amounts of reinforcement and relative delays that would be most likely to demonstrate the crossing of the functions. He had to choose B so that it was near enough to the rewards so that a discernible difference between the two discount functions would remain, and far enough from the rewards so that the functions would have crossed between B and A. How could he chose the parameters of his experiment? One way would have been to simply try various parameter combinations and see which worked. However, it would have taken years to experiment with each of the combinations of amounts and delays of reinforcement possible.

Instead of guessing about parameters to use, Ainslie turned to previous quantitative results. In 1965 Frank Logan at Yale University studied rats' choices between various combinations of *delay* and *amount of reward*. He used a device similar in principle to the T-maze shown in the top part of Figure 2.25. Food was usually available in both goal boxes, but usually in different amounts, and there were different delay periods between reaching the goal box and getting the food. In a given trial, there were two alternative choices, X and Y with amounts, A_x and A_y and delays D_x and D_y. Logan tested many combinations of amount and delay one against the other; by trial and error he found the actual choices of the rats were best described by the following functions:

$$\text{Value of X} = 1 - 10^{-12A_x} - .13D_x{}^{.5}$$
$$\text{Value of Y} = 1 - 10^{-12A_y} - .13D_y{}^{.5}$$

Whichever value is bigger is the one most likely to be chosen. These equations were remarkably successful in predicting choices of 204 rats among many alternative combinations in Logan's experiment. Ainslie found that these equations also predict a shift of preference between two different amounts as they proceed further into the future. In other words, the equations predict that the functions of Figure 5.2 cross. For instance, a rat will probably prefer 1 pellet of food delayed 1 second to 3 pellets delayed 14 seconds but if we added 4 seconds to both delays a rat will probably reverse its choice and prefer 3 pellets delayed 18 seconds to 1 pellet delayed 5 seconds. Ainslie used Logan's equations (substituting time of access to food for number of pellets) to predict the points at which the pigeons' discount functions would cross. Ainslie's guesses, based on Logan's painstaking experiments, worked, in the sense that pigeons showed reversed preferences where predicted.

Another application of quantitative techniques in the area of choice was made in 1970 by Richard Herrnstein at Harvard University. Herrnstein wanted to relate the behavior of an organism in a choice situation to behavior in a single response situation (see Figure 2.25 for characteristics of the two situations). In a sense, he reasoned, all behavior is choice behavior. Figure 2.15 shows how the behavior of a single organism (in that case, a businessman) can be classified; we can think of the organism as constantly engaged in choosing between the various alternatives shown in the pie-shaped sections of the circle. The more one alternative is chosen, the longer the time the man is engaged in that activity, the bigger the section of the circle in the representation. A pigeon's pecks on a key can be represented in a similar way (as shown on the left in Figure 5.3). If we assume that each peck takes an equal amount of time, the rate of pecking is a measure of the time spent pecking; the faster the rate of pecking, the larger the section of the pie. We can therefore think of the pigeon as constantly choosing between pecking and not pecking, with choice represented by the relative sizes of the sections. However, we cannot draw an accurate pie diagram because we have no way of knowing how long a peck takes. We measure the moment that the key is depressed —but the pigeon starts to peck before our moment of measurement and continues afterward. Our measure gives us the rate of pecking, but it cannot give us the duration of each peck. We *assume* that all pecks have equal duration. Thus, if our measurements doubled we should double the size of the slice of the pie in Figure 5.3a that represents pecks. But we do not know the size of the original slice that we are to double.

Now consider two keys in the chamber. (The situation changes to that shown on the left in Figure 5.3.) With two keys we consider the pigeon to be faced with a three-way choice. The pigeon may peck on Key A or Key B, or may choose not to peck. Similarly, three keys in the chamber would mean a four-way choice: pecking on any of the three keys or not pecking.

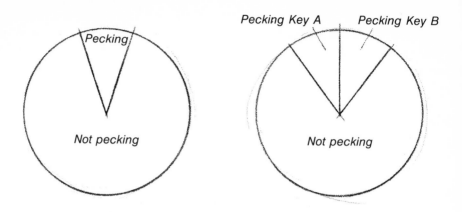

Figure 5.3 *Division of a pigeon's time into "pecking" and "not pecking" with (left) a single key and (right) with two keys.*

It is easy to measure the rate of pecking on one key and compare that rate to the rate of pecking on another key. In this comparison a remarkably simple relationship is usually found. If the pigeons are made hungry and pecks on the keys occasionally produce food, the rate of pecking on each key is a constant fraction of the rate at which food reinforcement is obtained by pecking the key. In other words, if

P_A stands for the rate of pecking Key A,
P_B stands for the rate of pecking Key B, and
R_A stands for the rate of reinforcement obtained by pecking Key A,
R_B stands for the rate of reinforcement obtained by pecking Key B,

then

$$\frac{P_A}{R_A} = \frac{P_B}{R_B} \tag{1}$$

No matter how many keys there are in the chamber, the equation above holds between any pair of the keys. Since we are assuming that each peck has the same duration (without knowing what the duration is), relative rate of pecking equals relative time spent pecking. Thus, equation (1) says that the pigeon distributes its time pecking a key in proportion to the rate at which reinforcement is produced by pecking that key. The total reinforcement may come from many small individual presentations of food or a few large food presentations. What counts is the overall rate of delivery.

Generalizing this result, we say that an organism distributes its time among several activities in proportion to the rewards to be derived from engaging in those activities. If this generalization holds, we may turn back to the case of Figure 5.3a, where the activities of the pigeon with which we were concerned were pecking a single key or not pecking that key. If we use the symbol N to represent time not pecking the key, and R_N to represent any reward involved in not pecking the key (from resting, preening, pecking the floor, and so forth), we have:

$$\frac{P_A}{R_A} = \frac{N}{R_N} \tag{2}$$

Logically, another way of saying the same thing is:

$$\frac{P_A}{P_A + N} = \frac{R_A}{R_A + R_N} \tag{3}$$

Again, as opposed to the two-key situation of Equation 1, we have no way of measuring N and R_N, but we can assume that R_N is constant for a given situation and a given pigeon, and, because $P_A + N$ exhaust whatever the organism can do with a single key, this sum equals a constant. Thus:

$$P_A = \frac{(P_A + N)R_A}{R_A + (R_N)} \tag{4}$$

where the items in brackets are constants. Equation 4 makes a prediction that can be tested. It predicts a certain relationship between the rate of an activity and the reinforcement of that activity, holding all other reinforcements constant.

Herrnstein has found that, by and large, this prediction is confirmed in experiments with animals. Figure 5.4 shows the rate at which a pigeon pecks a single available key as a function of the reinforcements delivered to that pigeon for pecking. The reinforcements were programmed on a variable-interval schedule (see Chapter 3 for a discussion of schedules). The points on the graph show the data for one particular pigeon. The solid line is Equation 4. The constant $(P_A + N)$ can be interpreted as the rate of pecking if the pigeon spent all its time pecking. The constant R_N can be interpreted as the rate of reinforcement from other sources than that specifically arranged by the experimenter.

Whether Equation 1 and Equation 4 (which is another form of Equation 1) will prove valid over the long run and whether N and R_N are meaningful in the sense that they can predict an individual's behavior in

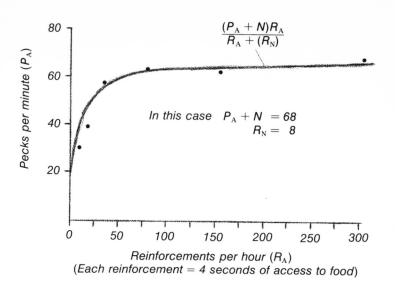

$$\frac{(P_A + N)R_A}{R_A + (R_N)}$$

In this case $P_A + N = 68$
$R_N = 8$

Pecks per minute (P_A)

Reinforcements per hour (R_A)
(Each reinforcement = 4 seconds of access to food)

Figure 5.4 *The rate of pecking of a pigeon as a function of the rate of reinforcement on a variable-interval schedule of reinforcement. The points are fitted by Equation 4. The constant ($P_A + N$) is the rate at which this pigeon would peck if it spent all its time pecking. The constant (R_N) is the equivalent rate of reinforcement for nonpecking.* [Data from A. C. Catania and G. S. Reynolds, *"A quantitative analysis of the responding maintained by interval schedules of reinforcement,"* Journal of the Experimental Analysis of Behavior, *1968,* 11, *327–383.*]

other situations are open questions and we await practical applications of this quantitative work. However, we can see from Equation 4 the direction they might take. Two ways of changing a given behavior (P_A) are by manipulating reward for that behavior (R_A) and by manipulating reward for other behavior (R_N). When faced with these alternatives in practical situations, how can we decide which to take? For instance, if a traffic engineer wants people to take an alternate route, is it better to make the first route harder to travel on or make the alternate route easier to travel on? Should a mother reduce crying in her child by reducing the reinforcement for crying (by ignoring it) or by increasing attention .to the child during periods without crying?

Equation 4 tells us the surprising fact that manipulating reward for *other* behavior will occasionally have a stronger effect on a given response than manipulating reward for that response itself. Which is more effective depends on the relative size of the two rewards in the first place. In general the change in reward that will have most effect on a response is that which involves a larger percentage change in reward. In other words, a given change in a big reward (adding $5 to $100) will have less effect than the same change made in a small reward (adding $5 to $5). Thus, a good rule to remember is to change the reward that is initially smaller in order to have the greatest effect.

Bibliography

Two books dealing directly with the application of behavioral techniques to human problems are J. Dollard and N. E. Miller, *Personality and Psychotherapy* (New York: McGraw-Hill 1950) and B. F. Skinner, *Science and Human Behavior*. New York: The Macmillan Co., 1953). Many other behaviorists have speculated about applications to human problems. A classic (but now out of date) attempt at such application is J. B. Watson's *Behaviorism*, originally published in 1924 and now available as a Phoenix paperback (Chicago: University of Chicago Press). Azrin and Powell describe their locking cigarette box in the *Journal of Applied Behavior Analysis*, 1969, 2, 39–42.

A collection of articles specifically dealing with behavior modification in clinical settings is L. Krasner and L. P. Ullman, *Research in Behavior Modification* (New York: Holt, Rinehart & Winston, 1965). Another book by these authors is *A Psychological Approach to Abnormal Behavior, I. Concepts* (New York: Prentice-Hall, 1969.) Pioneering work on clinical application of behavioral principles has been done by Joseph Wolpe. An inspiring account of successes with various techniques that he has developed can be found in a paperback by J. Wolpe and A. A. Lazarus, *Behavior Therapy Technique: A Guide to the Treatment of Neuroses* (Long Island City, New Yok: Pergamon Press, 1966).

Self-control is discussed in the above-mentioned book by Skinner (Chapter XV), and several experiments in the area have been performed by W. Mischel and reported in B. A. Maher (Ed.), *Progress in Experimental Personality Research*, Vol. 3 (New York: Academic Press, 1966). Ainslie's experiments are presently unavailable, but an interesting theoretical analysis of self-control from an economist's point of view can be found in R. H. Strotz, "Myopia and inconsistency in dynamic utility maximization" (*Review of Economic Studies*, 1956, 23, 166–180). There are several collections of studies dealing with application of behavioral work to human problems. A good one is A. W. Staats (Ed.), *Human Learning* (New York: Holt, Rinehart & Winston, 1964). In this book, an interesting experiment is reported by C. D. Ferster, J. I. Nurnberger, and E. B. Levitt on the control of eating. The Ayllon and Haughton report on "Control of the behavior of schizophrenic patients by food" appears in the *Journal of the Experimental Analysis of Behavior*, 1962, 5, 343–352.

There is no available source for the quantitative techniques discussed here. Perusal of recent issues of the *Journal of the Experimental Analysis of Behav-*

ior, Journal of Comparative and Physiological Psychology, and *Psychological Review*, is the best way to keep abreast of developments. An early attempt to quantify reinforcements in the manner discussed here was that of C. J. Warden. His "obstruction box" contained an electrified grid and he ranked various species with respect to the number of times they would cross the grid to reach a reward on the other side. His works on this subject are no longer in print.

Quantitative accounts of the interaction of reward and punishment are often subsumed under *theories of conflict*. A review of studies of conflict can be found in a paperback by A. J. Yates, *Frustration and Conflict* (New York: Wiley, 1962). Logan's experiments with rats in a straight alley may be found in F. A. Logan, *Incentive: How the Conditions of Reinforcement Affect the Performance of Rats* (New Haven: Yale University Press, 1960). Logan's studies of choice and the equations derived therefrom, which were used by Ainslie to predict crossover points in his experiment, are from F. A. Logan, "Decision-making by rats: delay versus amount of reward" (*Journal of Comparative and Physiological Psychology*, 1965, *59*, 1–12).

The equations on pages 192 and 193 are from R. H. Herrnstein, "On the law of effect" (*Journal of the Experimental Analysis of Behavior*, 1970, *13*, 243–266).

Glossary

ASSOCIATION. The connection of two or more sensations, ideas, images, or other mental phenomena. Laws of association are laws formulated to account for the establishment of such connections.

BEHAVIOR. (1) Any action of an organism. (2) The actions of an organism. (3) Actions of organisms.

BEHAVIORAL THERAPIST. A psychologist who is concerned with helping people change their behavior so as to better adapt it to their environment.

BEHAVIORISM. A branch of experimental psychology, the object of which is to discover laws describing the behavior of organisms.

BEHAVIOR RATIO. When an organism is free to make any of two or more responses in "choice" experiments, the behavior ratio is the measure of choice. It is the number of responses to one alternative divided by the total responses to all alternatives.

CHOICE. The possibility of more than one response. Essentially every situation in which behavior may vary is a choice situation. Even with one alley or one manipulandum (a lever, a disk, or the like), an organism may choose to run or not to run, to press a lever or not to press it. Choice can be measured most easily, however, when two similar alternatives are available as in a T-maze or multi-lever Skinner box. One frequently used measure of choice is the *Behavior Ratio*.

CLASSICAL CONDITIONING. As an operation, classical conditioning refers to the pairing in fixed temporal relation of (a) a neutral stimulus with (b) a stimulus correlated with a response—a reflex. (For example, a bell—a neutral stimulus—may be paired with food powder, which is originally correlated with salivation—a reflex. An organism exposed to such repeated pairings often comes to respond to the originally neutral stimulus as it did to the other stimulus. In this example, the organism would come to salivate upon presentation of the bell.)

CONDITIONED REINFORCEMENT. Another name for secondary reinforcement.

CONDITIONED RESPONSE. The response elicited by the conditioned stimulus alone (after the process of classical conditioning has taken place). In some cases this is only quantitatively different from the response originally elicited by the unconditioned stimulus (the unconditioned response). In other cases there may be qualitative differences between the conditioned and unconditioned responses.

CONDITIONED STIMULUS (CS). A stimulus that does not ordinarily elicit a certain response but that comes to elicit that response by virtue of its pairings in a classical conditioning procedure with another stimulus, an unconditioned stimulus, that does ordinarily elicit the response.

CONSCIOUSNESS. That part of one's *Mind* that one knows. A conscious mental process would be a process that one knows about, like doing mental arithmetic; an unconscious mental process would be a process about which one has no knowledge. John Stuart Mill's *Mental Chemistry*, in which sensations get combined into ideas, would be described as an unconscious mental process, since we seem to have many ideas without being aware of component sensations.

CONTINGENCY. A set of conditional probabilities relating the occurrence and nonoccurrence of events. In classical conditioning, the critical contingencies are between the conditioned and unconditioned stimuli. In instrumental conditioning the critical contingencies are between responding and reinforcement. The word "contingency" has also been used in a more general sense, as in *Contingencies of Reinforcement*, a recent book by B. F. Skinner. Here, contingency refers to the general relationships between behavior and the environment (without reference to any specific set of correlations or probabilities).

CORRELATION. In general, any relation between two variables. If the knowledge of the value of one variable helps you predict the value of the other, then the variables are correlated. In a positive correlation, increases in one variable correspond to increases in the other, as in the correlation between rising atmospheric temperature and trips to the beach. In a negative correlation, increases in one variable correspond to decreases in the other, as in the correlation between rising atmospheric temperature and skiing.

CUE. Another term for a discriminative stimulus (S^D or S^Δ).

DISCRIMINATION. Reliable differences in behavior in the presence of two or more stimuli.

DISCRIMINATIVE STIMULUS (s^D AND s^Δ). An S^D ("ess dee") is a stimulus during which there is a correlation between responding and reinforcement. An S^Δ ("ess delta") is a stimulus during which there is no correlation between responding and reinforcement. Somewhat confusingly, both S^D's and S^Δ's are called "discriminative stimuli."

DISINHIBITION. Removal of an inhibitory force, resulting in the action of the excitatory force formerly inhibited. (For instance, experimental extinction of classically conditioned salivation was thought by Pavlov to consist of the development of an inhibitory force opposing salivation. If, during extinction, a loud noise or other strong stimulus is presented, salivation suddenly increases. This is thought to be due to the disinhibitory effect of the noise.)

DUALISM. In the history of Western philosophy, the nature of man understood according to two principles—matter (the body) and spirit (the mind)—which are not derivable from each other.

ELICITED RESPONSE. When a stimulus is reliably followed by a certain response or set of responses, it is said to elicit that response or those responses. The notion of elicitation rests on an observed correlation between a stimulus and a subsequent response.

EMITTED RESPONSE. When a response is not found to be correlated with any prior stimulus it is said to be emitted. An emitted response may be brought into correlation with a subsequent stimulus by the environment, in which case the subsequent stimulus could reinforce or punish the response.

EMPIRICISM. (See *Nativism*.)

ESCAPE CONDITIONING. A form of instrumental conditioning in which responding is negatively correlated with aversive stimulation. Also called "negative reinforcement."

EVOLUTION. Gradual development. According to Darwin's theory of evolution of the structure of species, the mechanism of evolution works by survival (and reproduction) of those organisms most fitted to the environment. An analogous mechanism seems to govern functional changes of behavior in the repertoire of individual organisms. Behavior fitted to the environment is repeated while behavior not fitted to the environment is not repeated.

EXCITATION. Any increase in rate or amplitude of responding. Some psychologists refer to an "excitatory force," which is said to underlie the increases in responding actually measured.

EXPERIMENTAL PSYCHOLOGY. A branch of psychology in which behavioral observations are made in artificial and restricted environments, in which conditions can be controlled and behavior observed more easily than in natural settings.

EXTINCTION.   In classical conditioning, the removal of a correlation between the unconditioned stimulus and conditioned stimulus. In instrumental conditioning, removal of a correlation between response and reward. In most cases, this is done simply by eliminating the unconditioned stimulus or the reward. However it may also be done by continued presentations of unconditioned stimulus or reward that are not correlated with conditioned stimuli or responses.

FEEDBACK.   Any system in which a process is governed by its results. Most behavior involves feedback of some kind. (The act of picking up a pencil is governed to an extent by the position of the hand relative to the pencil. Thus the position of the hand is "fed back" by the visual system to govern further movements of the hand.)

FUNCTIONALISM.   According to the Darwinian notion of evolution, the structure of species is determined by its function. Functional (that is, useful) traits remain after dysfunctional (nonuseful) traits disappear as organisms evolve from generation to generation. The original "functional psychologists" believed that the mind evolved along with the body. Because evolution "selects according to function," the mind is best understood through its uses, or functional qualities. According to Thorndike's Law of Effect, functional behavior is strengthened and repeated while nonfunctional behavior dies out within the lifetime of a single organism. Present-day functionalists attempt to understand behavior through its function as the organism interacts with the environment.

GENERALIZATION.   In conditioning (whether classical or instrumental), an organism learns to behave in a certain way with the presentation of—or in the presence of—a certain stimulus or "stimulus situation." If this learned behavior also comes to be made in the presence of stimuli other than those used in conditioning, the organism is said to be generalizing from the training stimulus to the new stimulus. The closer the behavior in the presence of the new stimulus to the behavior in the presence of the training stimulus, the greater the generalization. The most generalization is to be found with stimuli similar to the training stimuli. Often generalization is ascribed to a failure to discriminate or pay attention to differences between stimuli.

GRADIENT.   A function that relates a measure of responding to stimuli arranged along a continuum. See also *Generalization*.

GSR (Galvanic Skin Response).   A change in resistance on the palms of the hands caused, partially, by sweating. The GSR is part of the unconditioned response to electric shock and other painful stimuli. The GSR may, by classical conditioning procedures, come to be emitted after an originally neutral stimulus, such as a bell or light. The GSR is sometimes said to reflect a "central anxiety state" of the organism.

HABIT.   Any learned behavior.

INHIBITION.   Any decrease in rate or amplitude of responding. Some psychologists refer to an "inhibitory force" which is said to underlie the decreases in responding actually measured. According to Pavlov, all decreases in responding result from an active inhibitory force opposing the force of excitation. This implies that there is a distinction between decreases in responding due to loss of excitation and decreases in responding due to the active inhibitory force.

INNATE IDEAS. "Mental contents" or "mental structures" that appear at birth or develop with maturation independently of experience.

INSTINCT. Any innate behavior or any behavior acquired by all normal members of a species through the process of maturation.

INSTRUMENTAL CONDITIONING. Instrumental conditioning involves establishment of a correlation between some aspect of behavior and reinforcement or punishment. An organism is said to have been conditioned when its behavior changes so as to obtain (or retain) the reward or avoid (or escape from) the punishment.

INTROSPECTION. A technique for observing mental events in which the mind is said to reflect on its own operations or contents.

ISOMORPHISM. Having the same form. The Gestalt psychologists believe that consciousness has the same form as its representation in the nervous system. Thus, if a figure is seen as distorted, the distortion must take place, not in consciousness, but somewhere in the nervous system.

LEARNING. Any consistent change in behavior not brought about solely by maturation.

MENTAL CHEMISTRY. John Stuart Mill's term for the association of simple sensations to form an idea. The idea's properties may differ from those of its components just as the chemical properties of a compound (e.g., water) differ from those of its components (hydrogen and oxygen). (For example, the idea of visual depth may be composed of forms, textures, and shading, yet visual depth may have conscious properties other than those of form, texture, and shading.)

MIND. The repository of consciousness, sensation, thought, feeling, and so forth. According to Descartes, man could be divided into two parts: mind and body. The mind, unlike the body, is not machinelike and does not obey physical laws—but may obey laws of its own. Originally the task of psychology was to discover mental laws by the technique of *Introspection*. More recent attempts to discover mental laws have relied on observations of behavior. Currently, two kinds of psychologists are to be found observing behavior: those interested in behavior itself and those using behavioral observations to infer mental laws.

MOLARISM. A broad classification of environment or behavior. The belief that stimuli or responses broadly classified may be lawfully described without reference to smaller units. (See also *Stimulus, Response.*)

MOLECULARISM. A narrow classification of environment or behavior. The belief that complex processes, whether mental or behavioral, may be explained in terms of small units and rules for their combination.

NATIVISM. In the mental sphere, the belief that man's most basic or important ideas come to him without experience by virture of his humanity. (Opposed to empiricism—the belief that man's most basic or important ideas come to him through experience.) In the behavioral sphere, the belief that basic behavior patterns are inborn and only modified slightly by experience or that the capacity to acquire certain behaviors is unique to certain species. (For example, while the particular language a person speaks is governed by his experience, a nativist would argue that humans are born with special mechanism that enables them to learn language and furthermore, that certain rules common to all languages are determined by the nature of this inborn mechanism. An empiricist would argue that the structure of language is determined by its function manifested only through experience.) The nativist-empiricist controversy is generally one of emphasis. There is general agreement that all behavior has innate and acquired components. The nativist stresses inborn patterns while the empiricist stresses the methods by which they may be modified.

NONSENSE SYLLABLE. A three-letter trigram (e.g., BAV, RUX, JIC, CIB) used by Ebbinghaus and others to study association. The principal advantage of nonsense syllables, according to Ebbinghaus, is that they have few previous associations; thus, any associations between them formed during an experiment can be studied independently of past experience.

OMISSION CONDITIONING. Omission is a form of instrumental conditioning in which the response is correlated with removal of a reward, otherwise continuously present.

OPERANT. All responses having a single common effect. Each instance of any response differs in some way, however small, from any other instance. Under what conditions can we say a response is repeated? One way to classify responses is by their common effect on the environment. All responses having a single common effect belong to the same operant class. For instance, all behavior that results in a bar-press could be considered a single operant. The definition of an operant is up to the observor of behavior (often the experimenter). He may base the delivery or removal of reinforcement or punishment upon the occurrence of the operant as he has defined it.

PARAMETER. A constant in an equation. A parametric experiment is one that tests a relationship with various parametric values. For instance, "days of deprivation" would affect the function relating "number of responses" in extinction to "number of prior reinforcements." An experiment that related responses in extinction to number of prior reinforcements at various deprivation levels would be a parametric experiment.

PERCEPTION. A process by which conclusions are reached as to the nature of the environment. Early mentalists believed that perceptions were sensations modified by associative experience. (For instance, when a melody is played a child and an adult might experience the same isolated sensations of individual notes but only the adult, because of his experience, will perceive the series of notes as a unit of melody.) The Gestalt psychologists, on the other hand, believed that perceptions as well as sensations could be independent of experience. (The notes of a melody might be seen as unitary by a child, not because of his experience with the notes but because the relation between the notes conformed to laws determined by the nervous system which tend to group certain of them together.)

PHENOMENOLOGY.   A type of introspection which attempts to view immediate experience as a whole, naively, without analysis. According to the Gestalt psychologists, phenomenological observation is the preferred method of collecting psychological data.

PHYSIOLOGY.   The study of the body, usually in terms of its parts (e.g., the nervous system) as opposed to study of behavior of the organism as a whole.

PSEUDOCONDITIONING.   Any conditioning obtained with a pairing that is shown to have been unnecessary for the establishment of the response is pseudo-conditioning (not genuine conditioning). The essential element in *Classical Conditioning* is the pairing or correlation between the unconditioned and conditioned stimuli. The essential element in *Instrumental Conditioning* is the pairing or correlation of response and reinforcement. If a certain response can be made to appear without that pairing, then any experiment using pairing to establish that response is suspect; the pairing may not have been necessary.

PSYCHOLOGY.   Originally a branch of philosophy devoted to the study of the mind. More recently, a science whose subject is the behavior of organisms. The observations of behavior (verbal behavior included) may or may not be used to infer mental processes.

PSYCHOPHYSICS.   The study of sensation as a function of the physical properties of stimulation.

PUNISHMENT.   A positive correlation between responding and aversive stimulation.

REFLEX.   Originally, reflex referred to stimuli and responses related by specific nervous connections within the organism. Recently the concept of reflex has been broadened to include any relationship between a stimulus and a response. The stimulus may be any event in the environment and the response may be any behavior of the organism.

REINFORCEMENT.   In *Classical Conditioning*, the presentation of the unconditioned stimulus. In *Instrumental Conditioning*, the presentation of a reward (positive reinforcement) or the removal of an aversive stimulus (negative reinforcement).

RESPONSE.   Another word for a *Behavior*. Usually a response is defined as a rather discrete form of behavior such as a knee jerk, the pressing of a bar, or the pressing of a key. However, responses can also be broadly defined, e.g., "standing on one side of a chamber," or "not pressing a key."

SECONDARY REINFORCEMENT.   A positive correlation of a response, not with reinforcement, but with a conditioned stimulus (CS) or a discriminative stimulus (S^D).

SENSATION.   The conscious correlate of simple stimulation of the sense organs. Early mentalists believed that consciousness consisted only of simple sensations combined in various ways by association.

SOUL.   The soul is said to be the spiritual and immortal part of man. Psychologists have tended to ignore the religious questions of the soul's immortality, its possible moral implications, and its role as the "essence of being." Stripped of religious implications, the concept of the soul approaches the concept of the *Mind*. The two concepts have generally been treated similarly by psychologists.

STIMULUS.   Any environmental event. Stimuli may be classified broadly (for instance, any picture of a horse) or narrowly (e.g., a tone of a particular frequency and amplitude). With respect to behavior, stimuli may be relatively neutral, having no discernable effect on the organism, or they may elicit violent behavior. Stimuli may be positively reinforcing or punishing depending on whether they increase or decrease the strength of the behavior they follow. A neutral stimulus in one situation may be non-neutral in others.

STIMULUS CONTROL.   Another word for the effects of *Discrimination* and *Generalization* in instrumental conditioning.

TEMPORAL CONTINGUITY.   Happening at the same time.

VOLUNTARY BEHAVIOR.   Behavior, the original cause of which is said to lie within the mind. Psychological theories that do not make use of mental concepts likewise ignore the concept of voluntary behavior.

Index

W9-ATM-512

.NET Framework Essentials

Other Microsoft .NET resources from O'Reilly

Related titles

Programming C#
C# in a Nutshell
Programming Visual Basic .NET
Programming ASP.NET
ASP.NET in a Nutshell
ADO.NET in a Nutshell

.NET Windows Forms in a Nutshell
Programming .NET Web Services
Mastering Visual Studio .NET
Programming .NET Components

.NET Books Resource Center

dotnet.oreilly.com is a complete catalog of O'Reilly's books on .NET and related technologies, including sample chapters and code examples.

ONDotnet.com provides independent coverage of fundamental, interoperable, and emerging Microsoft .NET programming and web services technologies.

Conferences

O'Reilly & Associates brings diverse innovators together to nurture the ideas that spark revolutionary industries. We specialize in documenting the latest tools and systems, translating the innovator's knowledge into useful skills for those in the trenches. Visit *conferences.oreilly.com* for our upcoming events.

Safari Bookshelf (*safari.oreilly.com*) is the premier online reference library for programmers and IT professionals. Conduct searches across more than 1,000 books. Subscribers can zero in on answers to time-critical questions in a matter of seconds. Read the books on your Bookshelf from cover to cover or simply flip to the page you need. Try it today with a free trial.

THIRD EDITION

.NET Framework Essentials

Thuan Thai and Hoang Q. Lam

O'REILLY®

Beijing · Cambridge · Farnham · Köln · Paris · Sebastopol · Taipei · Tokyo

.NET Framework Essentials, Third Edition
by Thuan Thai and Hoang Q. Lam

Copyright © 2003, 2002, 2001 O'Reilly & Associates, Inc. All rights reserved.
Printed in the United States of America.

Published by O'Reilly & Associates, Inc., 1005 Gravenstein Highway North, Sebastopol, CA 95472.

O'Reilly & Associates books may be purchased for educational, business, or sales promotional use. Online editions are also available for most titles (*safari.oreilly.com*). For more information, contact our corporate/institutional sales department: (800) 998-9938 or *corporate@oreilly.com*.

Editors:	John Osborn and Valerie Quercia
Production Editor:	Matt Hutchinson
Production Services:	Octal Publishing, Inc.
Cover Designer:	Ellie Volckhausen
Interior Designer:	David Futato

Printing History:

June 2001:	First Edition.
February 2002:	Second Edition.
August 2003:	Third Edition.

Nutshell Handbook, the Nutshell Handbook logo, and the O'Reilly logo are registered trademarks of O'Reilly & Associates, Inc. Microsoft, MSDN, the .NET logo, Visual Basic, Visual C++, Visual Studio, and Windows are registered trademarks of Microsoft Corporation. Many of the designations used by manufacturers and sellers to distinguish their products are claimed as trademarks. Where those designations appear in this book, and O'Reilly & Associates, Inc. was aware of a trademark claim, the designations have been printed in caps or initial caps. The association between the image of shrimp and the topic of the .NET Framework is a trademark of O'Reilly & Associates, Inc.

While every precaution has been taken in the preparation of this book, the publisher and authors assume no responsibility for errors or omissions, or for damages resulting from the use of the information contained herein.

ISBN: 0-596-00505-9

[M]

Table of Contents

Preface

A condensed introduction to the Microsoft .NET Framework, this book aims to help programmers make the transition from traditional Windows programming to the world of .NET programming. The Microsoft .NET Framework includes the Common Language Runtime (CLR) and a set of base classes that radically simplify the development of large-scale applications and services. This book examines the CLR in detail, so that you can put its new features to good use. The book also illustrates how language integration really works and guides you through component and enterprise development using the .NET Framework. In addition, it introduces you to four key .NET technologies: data (ADO.NET) and XML, web services, Web Forms (ASP.NET), and Windows Forms.

We used the latest release of Microsoft Visual Studio .NET 2003 and the .NET Framework SDK 1.1 to prepare this manuscript and to develop all the examples and figures in this book. In .NET Framework SDK 1.1, Microsoft has fixed a number of bugs, made performance and security improvements, and added a few important changes, including:

- Support for additional ADO.NET data sources (Oracle and ODBC)
- Improved support for using C++ to build .NET Windows and Web applications
- Integration of J# into VS.NET
- Inclusion of a mobile controls package for developing ASP.NET sites for small devices, such as cell phones
- Integration of mobile application development into VS.NET

Although we have done our best to ensure that the technical content of this book is up-to-date, it is possible that some items have changed slightly from the time of writing. To stay up-to-date, regularly check *http://msdn.microsoft.com/*

net, http://www.gotdotnet.com, and this book's O'Reilly page, *http://www. oreilly.com/catalog/dotnetfrmess3/*.

Audience

Although this book is for any person interested in learning about the Microsoft .NET Framework, it targets seasoned developers with experience in building Windows applications with Visual Studio 6 and the Visual Basic and Visual C++ languages. Java™ and C/C++ developers will also be well prepared for the material presented here. To gain the most from this book, you should have experience in object-oriented, component, enterprise, and web application development. COM programming experience is a plus.

About This Book

Based on a short course that Thuan has delivered to numerous companies since August 2000, this book is designed so that each chapter builds on knowledge from the previous one for those unfamiliar with each technology. To give you a heads-up, here are brief summaries for the chapters and appendixes covered in this book.

Chapter 1, *.NET Overview*, takes a brief look at Microsoft .NET and the Microsoft .NET Platform. It then describes the .NET Framework design goals and introduces you to the components of the .NET Framework.

Chapter 2, *The Common Language Runtime*, lifts the hood and peers into the CLR. This chapter surveys the rich runtime of the CLR, as well as other features.

Chapter 3, *.NET Programming*, introduces you to .NET programming. You'll examine a simple program that uses object-oriented and component-based concepts in five different languages: Managed C++, VB.NET, C#, J#, and IL. You'll also experience the benefits of language integration.

Chapter 4, *Working with .NET Components*, demonstrates the simplicity of component and enterprise development in .NET. Besides seeing the component-deployment features of the .NET Framework, you'll also find complete programs that take advantage of transaction, object pooling, role-base security, and message queuing—all in one chapter.

Chapter 5, *Data and XML*, describes the architecture of ADO.NET and its benefits. Besides being disconnected to promote scalability, the ADO.NET dataset is also tightly integrated with XML to enhance interoperability. This

chapter introduces you to the .NET data-access objects, as well as the XML namespace.

Chapter 6, *Web Services*, describes how .NET software components can be accessed through the Internet. In this chapter, we discuss the protocols that support web services, as well as how to publish and discover them. You will see how XML, used in conjunction with HTTP, breaks the proprietary nature of typical component-oriented software development and enables greater interoperability.

Chapter 7, *ASP.NET*, introduces you to ASP.NET, which now supports object-oriented and event-driven programming, as opposed to conventional ASP development. In this chapter, Web Forms and server controls take the center stage. In addition, we examine how to build custom server controls, perform data binding to various .NET controls, and survey state management features in ASP.NET.

Chapter 8, *Windows Forms*, takes conventional form-based programming a step into the future with the classes in the System.Windows.Forms namespace. Similar to Win32-based applications, Windows Forms are best used to build so-called rich or "fat" clients; however, with the new zero-effort installation procedure of .NET and the advent of web services, Windows Forms are appropriate for a host of applications.

Chapter 9, *.NET and Mobile Devices*, shows you how to build an ASP.NET application that targets smart devices and a mobile device application that is backed by SQL Server CE.

Appendix A, *.NET Languages*, contains a list of links to web sites with information regarding languages that target the CLR, including some burgeoning open-source projects.

Appendix B, *Common Acronyms*, contains a list of commonly used acronyms found in .NET literature and presentations.

Appendix C, *Common Data Types*, contains several lists of commonly used data types in .NET. This appendix also illustrates the use of several .NET collection classes.

Appendix D, *Common Utilities*, surveys the important tools that the .NET SDK provides to ease the tasks of .NET development.

Assumptions This Book Makes

This book assumes that you are a Windows or web application developer fluent in object-oriented and component-based programming. We also

assume that you have some basic knowledge of XML. While COM is not a crucial prerequisite, if you have COM programming experience, you will appreciate this book and the .NET Framework all the more.

Conventions Used in This Book

We use the following font conventions in this book.

Italic is used for:

- Pathnames, filenames, and program names
- Internet addresses, such as domain names and URLs
- New terms where they are defined

`Constant width` is used for:

- Command lines and options that should be typed verbatim
- Direct quotes and specific method names from code examples, as well as specific values for attributes and settings within code
- XML element tags

`Constant width bold` is used for:

- User input in code that should be typed verbatim
- Items in code to which we'd like to draw the reader's attention

`Constant width italic` is used for:

- Replaceable items in code, which should be replaced with the appropriate terms

In code syntax examples, we sometimes use [*value*]+ to represent one or more instances of a value and [*value*]* to mean zero or more instances of a value.

> This icon designates a tip, which contains important information about the nearby text.

> This icon designates a warning related to the nearby text.

How to Contact Us

We have tested and verified the information in this book to the best of our abilities, but you may find that features have changed (or even that we have made mistakes!). Please let us know about any errors you find, as well as your suggestions for future editions, by writing to:

O'Reilly & Associates, Inc.
1005 Gravenstein Highway North
Sebastopol, CA 95472
(800) 998-9938 (in the United States or Canada)
(707) 829-0515 (international/local)
(707) 829-0104 (FAX)

You can also send us messages electronically. To be put on the mailing list or request a catalog, send email to:

info@oreilly.com

To ask technical questions or comment on the book, send email to:

bookquestions@oreilly.com

We have a web site for the book, where we list examples, errata, and any plans for future editions. You can access this page at:

http://www.oreilly.com/catalog/dotnetfrmess3/

For more information about this book and others, see the O'Reilly web site:

http://www.oreilly.com

For more information on .NET in general, visit the O'Reilly .NET Center at *http://dotnet.oreilly.com* and the .NET DevCenter at *http://www.oreillynet.com/dotnet/*.

Acknowledgments

The folks at O'Reilly never cease to amaze us with the support that they provide. We'd like to thank O'Reilly executive editor John Osborn for extending us the contract to write this book and for his continuous support throughout the project. Thanks to O'Reilly editor Nancy Kotary for making the first and second editions of this book such a success. We'd also like to thank O'Reilly editor Valerie Quercia who did a fine job reviewing our materials and coordinating the project for this third edition.

We'd like to give many thanks to the production and design folks at O'Reilly for making this book a reality: Emma Colby, David Futato, Matt Hutchinson, Robert Romano, and Ellie Volckhausen.

We'd like to thank Brian Jepson, who has contributed significantly to this book since the beginning of the project. Brian did an unquestionably outstanding job reading, testing, and ensuring that the technical content in every chapter lined up with the latest release. He also gave us invaluable guidance and support throughout the project. We'd like to thank Matthew MacDonald for the same reason, since he's been providing invaluable feedback and recommendations in the third edition. We'd also like to thank Dennis Angeline and Brad Merrill at Microsoft for answering technical questions on the CLR and languages.

Thuan Thai

I would like to thank my parents, siblings, and Ut Nga for their constant support during this project.

Hoang Q. Lam

I would like to thank my parents and family for their support and understanding of my being missing-in-action for several months. Mom and Dad, your ongoing efforts to put your children where they are today can never be repaid.

I would like to thank my wife, Van Du, and daughter, Nina. Your smiles mean the world to me. Don't underestimate your contribution to this book.

.NET Overview

The .NET Framework is a development framework that provides a new programming interface to Windows services and APIs, and integrates a number of technologies that emerged from Microsoft during the late 1990s. Microsoft announced the .NET initiative in July 2000. In April 2003, Version 1.1 of the integral .NET Framework was released. This book describes this updated version of the .NET Framework.

The .NET platform consists of four separate product groups:

Development tools and libraries
> A set of languages, including C#, J#, and VB.NET; a set of development tools, including Visual Studio .NET; a comprehensive class library for building web services and web and Windows applications; as well as the Common Language Runtime (CLR). These components collectively form the largest part of the .NET Framework.

Web services
> An offering of commercial web services, specifically the .NET Services initiative; for a fee, developers can use these services in building applications that require them.

Specialized servers
> A set of .NET-enabled enterprise servers, including SQL Server, Exchange Server, BizTalk Server, and so on. These provide specialized functionality for relational data storage, email, and B2B commerce. Future versions of these products will increasingly support the .NET Framework.

Devices
> New .NET-enabled, non-PC devices, from cell phones to game boxes.

Behind Microsoft .NET

While the main strategy of .NET is to enable software as a service, .NET is much more than that. In addition to embracing the Web, Microsoft .NET acknowledges and responds to the following trends within the software industry:

Distributed computing
> Simplifies the development of robust client/server and multi-tier (*n*-tier) applications. Traditional distributed technologies require high vendor-affinity and are unable to interoperate with the Web. Microsoft .NET provides remoting and web services architectures that exploit open Internet standards, including the Hypertext Transfer Protocol (HTTP), Extensible Markup Language (XML), and Simple Object Access Protocol (SOAP) and WSOL.

Componentization
> Simplifies the integration of software components developed by different vendors and supports development of distributed applications. The Component Object Model (COM) has brought reality to software plug-and-play, but COM component development and deployment are too complex. Microsoft .NET provides a simpler way to build and deploy components.

Enterprise services
> Allow the development of scalable enterprise applications without writing code to manage transactions, security, or pooling. Microsoft .NET continues to support COM and component services, since these services greatly reduce the development time and effort required to build large-scale applications.

Web paradigm shifts
> Over the past decade, web application development has shifted from connectivity (TCP/IP), to presentation (HTML), to programmability (XML and SOAP). A key goal of Microsoft .NET is to enable the sharing of functionality across the Web among different platforms, devices, and programming languages.

Maturity of IT industry
> Lessons that the software industry has learned from developing large-scale enterprise and web applications. A commercial web application must support interoperability, scalability, availability, security, and manageability. Microsoft .NET facilitates all these goals.

Although these are the sources of many ideas embodied by Microsoft .NET, what's most notable about the platform is its use of open Internet standards

(HTTP, XML, and SOAP) at its core to transmit information from one machine to another across the Internet. In fact, .NET provides bidirectional mapping between XML and objects. For example, a class can be expressed as an XML Schema Definition (XSD); an object can be converted to and from an XML buffer; a method can be specified using an XML format called Web Services Description Language (WSDL); and a method call can be expressed using an XML format called SOAP.

The .NET Platform

The Microsoft .NET platform consists of five main components, as shown in Figure 1-1. At the lowest layer lies the operating system (OS), which can be one of a variety of Windows platforms, including Windows XP, Windows 2000, Windows Server 2003, Windows ME, and Windows CE. As part of the .NET strategy, Microsoft has promised to deliver more .NET device software to facilitate a new generation of smart devices.

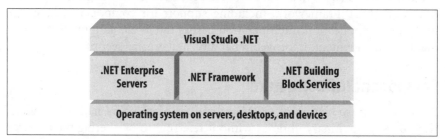

Figure 1-1. The Microsoft .NET platform

On top of the operating system is a collection of specialized server products that shortens the time required to develop large-scale business systems. These server products include Application Center, BizTalk Server, Commerce Server, Exchange Server, Host Integration Server, Internet Security and Acceleration Server, and SQL Server.

Since web services are highly reusable across the Web, Microsoft provides a number of building-block services (officially called .NET Services) that applications developers can use, for a fee. Two examples of .NET Services that Microsoft offers include .NET Passport and .NET Alerts. .NET Passport allows you to use a single username and password at all web sites that support Passport authentication. .NET Alerts allow .NET Alert providers, such as a business, to alert their consumers with important or up-to-the-minute information. Microsoft plans to add newer services, such as calendar, directory, and search services. Third-party vendors are also creating new web services of their own.

The top layer of the .NET architecture is a development tool called Visual Studio .NET (VS.NET), which makes possible the rapid development of web services and other applications. A successor to Microsoft Visual Studio 6.0, VS.NET is an Integrated Development Environment (IDE) that supports four different languages and features such as cross-language debugging and the XML Schema Editor.

And at the center of .NET is the Microsoft .NET Framework—the main focus of this book. The .NET Framework is a development and runtime infrastructure that changes the development of business applications on the Windows platform. The .NET Framework includes the CLR and a common framework of classes that can be used by all .NET languages.

.NET Framework Design Goals

The Microsoft .NET Framework embodies design goals that are both practical and ambitious. In this section, we discuss the main design goals of the Microsoft .NET Framework, including support for components, language integration, application interoperation across the Web, simplified development and deployment, improved reliability, and greater security.

Component Infrastructure

Prior to the introduction of COM technology, developers had no standard way to integrate binary libraries without referring to or altering their source code. With the advent of COM, programmers were able to integrate binary components into their applications, similar to the way we can plug-and-play hardware components into our desktop PCs. Although COM was great, the grungy details of COM gave developers and administrators many headaches.

Although COM permits you to integrate binary components developed using any language, it does require you to obey the COM identity, lifetime, and binary layout rules. You must also write the plumbing code that is required to create a COM component, such as DllGetClassObject, CoRegister-ClassObject, and others.

Realizing that these requirements result in frequent rewrites of similar code, .NET sets out to remove them. In the .NET world, all classes are ready to be reused at the binary level. You don't have to write extra plumbing code to support componentization in the .NET Framework. You simply write a .NET class, which then becomes a part of an assembly (to be discussed in Chapter 2) that inherently supports plug-and-play.

In addition to providing a framework to make development easier, .NET removes the pain of developing COM components. Specifically, .NET removes the use of the registry for component registration and eliminates the requirements for extraneous plumbing code found in all COM components, including code to support IUnknown, class factories, component lifetime, registration, dynamic binding, and others.

 "Component" is a nasty word because one person may use it to refer to an object and another may use it to refer to a compiled binary module. To be consistent, this book uses the term "COM component" (or simply "component") to refer to a binary module, such as a DLL or an EXE.

Language Integration

COM supports *language independence*, which means that you can develop a COM component in any language you want. As long as your component meets all the rules spelled out in the COM specification, it can be instantiated and used by your applications. Although this supports binary reuse, it doesn't support *language integration*. In other words, you can't reuse the code in the COM components written by someone else; you can't extend a class hosted in the COM component; you can't catch exceptions thrown by code in the COM component; and so forth.

Microsoft .NET supports not only language independence, but also language integration. This means that you can inherit from classes, catch exceptions, and take advantage of polymorphism across different languages. The .NET Framework makes this possible with a specification called the Common Type System (CTS), which all .NET components must support. For example, everything in .NET is an object of a specific class that derives from the root class called System.Object. The CTS supports the general concepts of classes, interfaces, delegates (which support callbacks), reference types, and value types. The .NET base classes provide most of the base system types, such as those that support integer, string, and file manipulation. Because every language compiler must meet a minimum set of rules stipulated by the Common Language Specification (CLS) and generate code to conform to the CTS, different .NET languages can be used in the same application. We will examine the CTS and CLS in Chapter 2.

Internet Interoperation

COM supports distributed computing through its Distributed COM (DCOM) wire protocol. A problem with DCOM is that it embeds the host TCP/IP

address inside the Network Data Representation (NDR) buffer, such that it will not work through firewalls and Network Address Translation (NAT) software. In addition, the DCOM dynamic activation, protocol negotiation, and garbage collection facilities are proprietary, complex, and expensive. The solution is an open, simple, and lightweight protocol for distributed computing. The .NET Framework uses the industry-supported SOAP protocol, which is based on the widely accepted XML standards.

Simplified Development

If you have developed software for the Windows platforms since their inception, you have seen everything from the Windows APIs to the Microsoft Foundation Classes (MFC), the Active Template Library (ATL), the system COM interfaces, and countless other environments, such as Visual Interdev, Visual Basic, JScript, and other scripting languages. Each time you set out to develop something in a different compiler, you had to learn a new API or a class library, because there is no consistency or commonality among these different libraries or interfaces.

.NET solves this problem by providing a set of framework classes that every language uses. Such a framework removes the need for learning a new API each time you switch languages.

Simplified Deployment

Imagine this scenario: your Windows application, which uses three shared Dynamic Link Libraries (DLLs), works just fine for months, but stops working one day after you've installed another software package that overwrites the first DLL, does nothing to the second DLL, and adds an additional copy of the third DLL into a different directory. If you have ever encountered such a brutal—yet entirely possible—problem, you have entered DLL Hell. And if you ask a group of seasoned developers whether they have experienced DLL Hell, they will grimace at you in disgust, not because of the question you've posed, but because they have indeed experienced the pain and suffering.

To avoid DLL Hell on Windows 2000 and subsequent Windows operating systems (at least for system DLLs), Windows 2000 stores system DLLs in a cache. If you install an application that overwrites system DLLs, Windows 2000 will overwrite the added system DLLs with the original versions from the cache.

Microsoft .NET further diminishes DLL Hell. In the .NET environment, your executable will use the shared DLL with which it was built. This is

guaranteed, because a shared DLL must be registered against something similar to the Windows 2000 cache, called the Global Assembly Cache (GAC). In addition to this requirement, a shared DLL must have a unique hash value, public key, locale, and version number. Once you've met these requirements and registered your shared DLL in the GAC, its physical file-name is no longer important. In other words, if you have two versions of a DLL that are both called *MyDll.dll*, both of them can live and execute on the same system without causing DLL Hell. This is possible because the executable that uses one of these DLLs is tightly bound to a specific version of the DLL during compilation.

In addition to eradicating DLL Hell, .NET also removes the need for component-related registry settings. A COM developer will tell you that half the challenge of learning COM is understanding the COM-specific registry entries for which the developer is responsible. Microsoft .NET stores all references and dependencies of .NET assemblies within a special section called a *manifest* (see Chapter 2). In addition, assemblies can be either private or shared. Private assemblies are found using logical paths or XML-based application configuration files, and public assemblies are registered in the GAC; in both cases, the system will find your dependencies at runtime. If they are missing, you get an exception telling you exactly what happened.

Finally, .NET brings back the concept of zero-impact installation and removal. This concept is the opposite of what you have to deal with in the world of COM. To set up a COM application, you have to register all your components after you have copied them over to your machine. If you fail to perform this step correctly, nothing will work and you'll end up pulling your hair out. Likewise, to uninstall the application, you should unregister your components (to remove the registry entries) prior to deleting your files. Again, if you fail to perform this step correctly, you will leave remnants in the registry that will be forever extant.

Unlike COM, but like DOS, to set up an application in .NET, you simply xcopy your files from one directory on a CD to another directory on your machine, and the application will run automatically.* Similarly, you can just delete the directory to uninstall the application from your machine.

Reliability

There are many programming languages and platforms in the commercial software industry, but few of them attempt to provide both a reliable language and

---

* This is true for private assemblies, but not for shared assemblies. See Chapter 4 for more details.

a robust runtime or infrastructure. The most successful language that we have seen in the commercial software industry is the Java™ language and the Java Virtual Machine™, which have brought the software-development community much satisfaction. Microsoft is positioning .NET as the next big thing.

Microsoft .NET requires type safety. Unlike C++, every class in .NET is derived from the mother of all classes, Object, which supports basic features such as returning a string representation of the object, indicating whether the object is equal to another, and so on. The CLR must recognize and verify types before they can be loaded and executed. This decreases the chances for rudimentary programming errors and prevents buffer overruns, which can be a security weakness.

Traditional programming languages don't provide a common error-handling mechanism. C++ and Java support exception handling, but many others leave you in the dust, forcing to invent your own error-handling facilities. Microsoft .NET supports exceptions in the CLR, providing a consistent error-handling mechanism. Put another way: exceptions work across all .NET-compatible languages.

When you program in C++, you must deallocate all heap-based objects that you have previously allocated. If you fail to do this, the allocated resources on your system will never be reclaimed even though they are no longer needed. And if this is a server application, it won't be robust because the accumulation of unused resources in memory will eventually bring down the system. Similar to Java, the .NET runtime tracks and garbage-collects all allocated objects that are no longer needed.

Security

When developing applications in the old days of DOS, Microsoft developers cared little about security because their applications ran on a single desktop with a single thread of execution. As soon as developers started developing client and server applications, things got a bit complicated: multiple users might then have accessed the servers, and sensitive data might be exchanged between the client and the server. The problem became even more complex in the web environment, since you could unknowingly download and execute malicious applets on your machine.

To mitigate these problems, .NET provides a number of security features. Windows NT and Windows 2000 protect resources using access-control lists and security identities, but don't provide a security infrastructure to verify access to parts of an executable's code. Unlike traditional security support in which only access to the executable is protected, .NET goes further

to protect access to specific parts of the executable code—this is known as *code access security*. For example, to take advantage of declarative security checks, you can prefix your method implementations with security attributes without having to write any code. To take advantage of imperative security checks, you write the code in your method to explicitly cause a security check. .NET provides other security features to make it harder to penetrate your applications and system.

.NET Framework

Now that you are familiar with the major goals of the .NET Framework, let's briefly examine its architecture. As you can see in Figure 1-2, the .NET Framework sits on top of the operating system, which can be a few different flavors of Windows and consists of a number of components (each of these components is discussed in greater detail starting with Chapter 4, as described in the Preface). .NET is essentially a system application that runs on Windows.

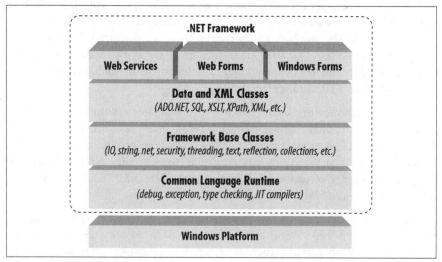

Figure 1-2. The .NET Framework

The most important component of the framework is the CLR. If you are a Java programmer, think of the CLR as the .NET equivalent of the Java Virtual Machine (JVM). If you don't know Java, think of the CLR as the heart and soul of the .NET architecture. At a high level, the CLR activates objects, performs security checks on them, lays them out in memory, executes them, and garbage-collects them.

Conceptually, the CLR and the JVM are similar in that they are both run-time infrastructures that abstract the underlying platform differences. However, while the JVM officially supports only the Java language, the CLR supports any language that can be represented in its Common Intermediate Language (CIL). The JVM executes bytecode, so it can, in principle, support many languages, too. Unlike Java's bytecode, though, CIL is never interpreted. Another conceptual difference between the two infrastructures is that Java code runs on any platform with a JVM, whereas .NET code runs only on platforms that support the CLR. In April, 2003, the International Organization for Standardization and the International Electrotechnical Committee (ISO/IEC) recognized a functional subset of the CLR, known as the Common Language Interface (CLI), as an international standard. This development, initiated by Microsoft and developed by ECMA International, a European standards organization, opens the way for third parties to implement their own versions of the CLR on other platforms, such as Linux or Mac OS X. For information on third-party and open source projects working to implement the ISO/IEC CLI and C# specifications, see Appendix A.

In Figure 1-2, the layer on top of the CLR is a set of framework base classes. This set of classes is similar to the set of classes found in STL, MFC, ATL, or Java. These classes support rudimentary input and output functionality, string manipulation, security management, network communications, thread management, text management, reflection functionality, collections functionality, as well as other functions.

On top of the framework base classes is a set of classes that extend the base classes to support data management and XML manipulation. These classes, called ADO.NET, support persistent data management—data that is stored on backend databases. Alongside the data classes, the .NET Framework supports a number of classes to let you manipulate XML data and perform XML searching and XML translations.

Classes in three different technologies (including web services, Web Forms, and Windows Forms) extend the framework base classes and the data and XML classes. Web services include a number of classes that support the development of lightweight distributed components, which work even in the face of firewalls and NAT software. These components support plug-and-play across the Internet, because web services employ standard HTTP and SOAP.

Web Forms, the key technology behind ASP.NET, include a number of classes that allow you to rapidly develop web Graphical User Interface (GUI) applications. If you're currently developing web applications with Visual Interdev, you can think of Web Forms as a facility that allows you to

develop web GUIs using the same drag-and-drop approach as if you were developing the GUIs in Visual Basic. Simply drag-and-drop controls onto your Web Form, double-click on a control, and write the code to respond to the associated event.

Windows Forms support a set of classes that allow you to develop native Windows GUI applications. You can think of these classes collectively as a much better version of the MFC in C++ because they support easier and more powerful GUI development and provide a common, consistent interface that can be used in all languages.

In the next chapter, we examine the internals of the CLR and how it supports and executes .NET components, formally called *assemblies* in .NET.

The Common Language Runtime

The most important component of the .NET Framework is the Common Language Runtime (CLR). The CLR manages and executes code written in .NET languages and is the basis of the .NET architecture, similar to the Java Virtual Machine. The CLR activates objects, performs security checks on them, lays them out in memory, executes them, and garbage-collects them.

In this chapter, we describe the CLR environment, executables (with examples in several languages), metadata, assemblies, manifests, the CTS, and the CLS.

CLR Environment

The CLR is the underlying .NET infrastructure. Its facilities cover all the goals that we spelled out in Chapter 1. Unlike software libraries such as MFC or ATL, the CLR is built from a clean slate. The CLR manages the execution of code in the .NET Framework.

 An *assembly* is the basic unit of deployment and versioning, consisting of a manifest, a set of one or more modules, and an optional set of resources.

Figure 2-1 shows the two portions of the .NET environment, with the bottom portion representing the CLR and the top portion representing the CLR executables or Portable Executable (PE) files, which are .NET assemblies or units of deployment. The CLR is the runtime engine that loads required classes, performs just-in-time compilation on needed methods, enforces security checks, and accomplishes a bunch of other runtime functionalities. The CLR executables shown in Figure 2-1 are either EXE or DLL files that consist mostly of metadata and code.

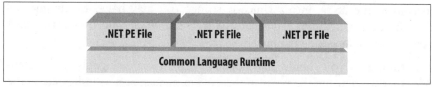

Figure 2-1. The CLR environment

CLR Executables

Microsoft .NET executables are different from typical Windows executables in that they carry not only code and data, but also metadata (see "Metadata" and "Intermediate Language (IL)" later in this chapter). In this section, we start off with the code for several .NET applications, and discuss the .NET PE format.

Hello, World: Managed C++

Let's start off by examining a simple *Hello, World* application written in Managed C++, a Microsoft .NET extension to the C++ language. Managed C++ includes a number of new CLR-specific keywords that permit C++ programs to take advantage of CLR features, including garbage collection. Here's the Managed C++ version of our program:

```
#using <mscorlib.dll>

using namespace System;

void main( )
{
   Console::WriteLine(L"C++ Hello, World!");
}
```

As you can see, this is a simple C++ program with an additional directive, #using (shown in bold). If you have worked with the Microsoft Visual C++ compiler support features for COM, you may be familiar with the #import directive. While #import reverse-engineers type information to generate wrapper classes for COM interfaces, #using makes all types accessible from the specified DLL, similar to a #include directive in C or C++. However, unlike #include, which imports C or C++ types, #using imports types for any .NET assembly, written in any .NET language.

The one and only statement within the main( ) method is self-explanatory—it means that we are invoking a static or class-level method, WriteLine( ), on the Console class. The L that prefixes the literal string tells the C++ compiler

to convert the literal into a Unicode string. You may have already guessed that the Console class is a type hosted by *mscorlib.dll*, and the WriteLine( ) method takes one string parameter.

One thing that you should also notice is that this code signals to the compiler that we're using the types in the System namespace, as indicated by the using namespace statement. This allows us to refer to Console instead of having to fully qualify this class as System::Console.

Given this simple program, compile it using the new C++ command-line compiler shipped with the .NET SDK:

```
cl hello.cpp /CLR /link /entry:main
```

The /CLR command-line option is extremely important, because it tells the C++ compiler to generate a .NET PE file instead of a normal Windows PE file.

When this statement is executed, the C++ compiler generates an executable called *hello.exe*. When you run *hello.exe*, the CLR loads, verifies, and executes it.

Hello, World: C#

Because .NET is serious about language integration, we'll illustrate this same program using C#, a language especially designed for .NET. Borrowing from Java and C++ syntax, C# is a simple and object-oriented language that Microsoft has used to write the bulk of the .NET base classes and tools. If you are a Java (or C++) programmer, you should have no problem understanding C# code. Here's *Hello, World* in C#:

```
using System;

public class MainApp
{
  public static void Main( )
  {
    Console.WriteLine("C# Hello, World!");
  }
}
```

C# is similar to Java in that it doesn't have the concept of a header file: class definitions and implementations are stored in the same *.cs* file. Another similarity to Java is that Main( ) is a public, static function of a particular class, as you can see from the code. This is different from C++, where main( ) itself is a global function.

The using keyword here functions similar to using namespace in the previous example, in that it signals to the C# compiler that we want to use types within the System namespace. Here's how to compile this C# program:

```
csc hello.cs
```

In this command, csc is the C# compiler that comes with the .NET SDK. Again, the result of executing this command is an executable called *hello.exe*, which you can execute like a normal EXE but it's managed by the CLR.

Hello, World: VB.NET

Here is the same program in Visual Basic .NET (VB.NET):

```
Imports System

Public Module MainApp
  Public Sub Main()
    Console.WriteLine ("VB Hello, World!")
  End Sub
End Module
```

If you are a VB programmer, you may be in for a surprise. The syntax of the language has changed quite a bit, but luckily these changes make the language mirror other object-oriented languages, such as C# and C++. Look carefully at this code snippet, and you will see that you can translate each line of code here into an equivalent in C#. Whereas C# uses the keywords using and class, VB.NET uses the keywords Import and Module, respectively. Here's how to compile this program:

```
vbc /t:exe /out:hello.exe hello.vb
```

Microsoft now provides a command-line compiler, *vbc*, for VB.NET. The /t option specifies the type of PE file to be created. In this case, since we have specified an EXE, *hello.exe* will be the output of this command.

Hello, World: J#

And since Microsoft has added the Visual J# compiler, which allows programmers to write Java code that targets the CLR, we'll show the same program in J# for completeness:

```
import System.*;

public class MainApp
{
  public static void main()
  {
```

```
    Console.WriteLine("J# hello world!");
  }
}
```

If you carefully compare this simple J# program with the previously shown C# program, you'll notice that the two languages are very similar. For example, the only difference (other than the obvious literal string) is that the J# version uses the import directive, instead of the using directive. Here's how to compile this program:

```
vjc hello.jsl
```

In this command, vjc is the J# compiler that comes with the .NET SDK. The result of executing this command is an executable called *hello.exe*, targeting the CLR.

 In all four versions of this *Hello, World* program, the Console class and the WriteLine( ) method have remained constant. That is, no matter which language you're using, once you know how to do something in one language, you can do it in all other languages that target the CLR. This is an extreme change from traditional Windows programming, in which if you know how to write to a file in C++, you probably won't know how to do it for VB, Java, or Cobol.

.NET Portable Executable File

A Windows executable, EXE or DLL, must conform to a file format called the *PE* file format, which is a derivative of the Common Object File Format (COFF). Both of these formats are fully specified and publicly available. The Windows OS knows how to load and execute DLLs and EXEs because it understands the format of a PE file. As a result, any compiler that wants to generate Windows executables must obey the PE/COFF specification.

A standard Windows PE file is divided into a number of sections, starting off with an MS-DOS header, followed by a PE header, followed by an optional header, and finally followed by a number of native image sections, including the .text, .data, .rdata, and .rsrc sections. These are the standard sections of a typical Windows executable, but Microsoft's C/C++ compiler allows you to add your own custom sections into the PE file using a compiler #pragma directive. For example, you can create your own data section to hold encrypted data that only you can read.

To support the CLR, Microsoft has extended the PE/COFF file format to include metadata and IL code. The CLR uses metadata to determine how to

load classes and uses the IL code to turn it into native code for execution. As shown in Figure 2-2, the extensions that Microsoft has added to the normal PE format include the CLR header and CLR data. The CLR header mainly stores relative virtual addresses (RVA) to locations that hold pertinent information to help the CLR manage program execution. The CLR data portion contains metadata and IL code, both of which determine how the program will be executed. Compilers that target the CLR must emit both the CLR header and data information into the generated PE file, otherwise the resulting PE file will not run under the CLR.

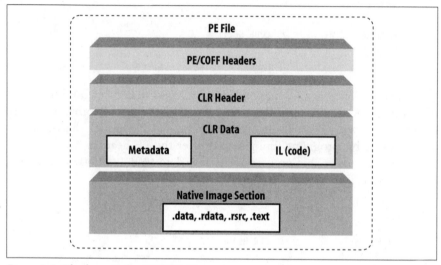

Figure 2-2. The format of a .NET PE file

If you want to prove to yourself that a .NET executable contains this information, use the *dumpbin.exe* utility, which dumps the content of a Windows executable in readable text.* For example, running the following command on the command prompt:

```
dumpbin.exe hello.exe /all
```

generates the following data (for brevity, we have shown only the main elements that we want to illustrate):

```
Microsoft (R) COFF/PE Dumper Version 7.10.2292
Copyright (C) Microsoft Corporation.  All rights reserved.
```

---

* Note that you can dump the same information, in a more readable format, using the *ildasm.exe* utility, to be discussed later in this chapter.

```
Dump of file hello.exe

PE signature found

File Type: EXECUTABLE IMAGE

FILE HEADER VALUES          /* 128-BYTE MS-DOS/COFF HEADER */
    14C machine (x86)
    ...


OPTIONAL HEADER VALUES  /* FOLLOWED BY PE AND OPTIONAL HEADERS */
        10B magic # (PE32)
        ...


SECTION HEADER #1         /* CODE SECTION */
    .text name

    ...
```

Looking at this text dump of a .NET PE file, you can see that a PE file starts off with the MS-DOS/COFF header, which all Windows programs must include. Following this header, you will find the PE header that supports Windows 32-bit programs. Immediately after the PE headers, you can find the code section for this program. The raw data (RAW DATA #1) of this section stores the CLR header, as follows:

```
RAW DATA #1
    ...


    clr Header:             /* CLR HEADER */
        48 cb
      2.00 runtime version
      207C [      214] RVA [size] of MetaData Directory
         1 flags
   6000001 entry point token
         0 [        0] RVA [size] of Resources Directory
         0 [        0] RVA [size] of StrongNameSignature Directory
         0 [        0] RVA [size] of CodeManagerTable Directory
         0 [        0] RVA [size] of VTableFixups Directory
         0 [        0] RVA [size] of ExportAddressTableJumps Directory

  Section contains the following imports:
    mscoree.dll
        ...
        0 _CorExeMain
    ...
```

As mentioned earlier, the CLR header holds a number of pertinent details required by the runtime, including:

Runtime version
    Indicates the runtime version that is required to run this program

MetaData directory
    Is important because it indicates the location of the metadata needed by the CLR at runtime

Entry point token
    Is even more important because, for a single file assembly, this is the token that signifies the entry point, such as Main( ), that the CLR executes

Below the CLR Header, note that there is an imported function called _CorExeMain, which is implemented by *mscoree.dll*, the core execution engine of the CLR.[*] At the time of this writing, Windows 98, 2000, and Me have an OS loader that knows how to load standard PE files. To prevent massive changes to these operating systems and still allow .NET applications to run on them, Microsoft has updated the OS loaders for all these platforms. The updated loaders know how to check for the CLR header, and, if this header exists, it executes _CorExeMain, thus not only jumpstarting the CLR but also surrendering to it. You can then guess that the CLR will call Main( ), since it can find the entry point token within the CLR header.[†]

Now that we've looked at the contents of the CLR header, let's examine the contents of the CLR data, including metadata and code, which are arguably the most important elements in .NET.

Metadata

Metadata is machine-readable information about a resource, or "data about data." Such information might include details on content, format, size, or other characteristics of a data source. In .NET, metadata includes type definitions, version information, external assembly references, and other standardized information.

---

[*] We invite you to run *dumpbin.exe* and view the exports of *mscoree.dll* at your convenience. You will also find _CorDllMain, _CorExeMain, _CorImageUnloading, and other interesting exports. It's interesting to note that this DLL is an in-process COM server, attesting that .NET is created using COM techniques.

[†] For brevity, we've covered only the important content of this header. If you want to learn the meanings of the rest, see this chapter's example code, which you can download from *www.oreilly.wm/catalog/dotnetfrmness3/*.

In order for two systems, components, or objects to interoperate with one another, at least one must know something about the other. In COM, this "something" is an interface specification, which is implemented by a component provider and used by its consumers. The interface specification contains method prototypes with full signatures, including the type definitions for all parameters and return types.

Only C/C++ developers were able to readily modify or use Interface Definition Language (IDL) type definitions—not so for VB or other developers, and more importantly, not for tools or middleware. So Microsoft invented something other than IDL that everyone could use, called a *type library*. In COM, type libraries allow a development environment or tool to read, reverse engineer, and create wrapper classes that are most appropriate and convenient for the target developer. Type libraries also allow runtime engines, such as the VB, COM, MTS, or COM+ runtime, to inspect types at runtime and provide the necessary plumbing or intermediary support for applications to use them. For example, type libraries support dynamic invocation and allow the COM runtime to provide universal marshaling* for cross-context invocations.

Type libraries are extremely rich in COM, but many developers criticize them for their lack of standardization. The .NET team invented a new mechanism for capturing type information. Instead of using the term "type library," we call such type information *metadata* in .NET.

Type Libraries on Steroids

Just as type libraries are C++ header files on steroids, metadata is a type library on steroids. In .NET, metadata is a common mechanism or dialect that the .NET runtime, compilers, and tools can all use. Microsoft .NET uses metadata to describe all types that are used and exposed by a particular .NET assembly. In this sense, metadata describes an assembly in detail, including descriptions of its identity (a combination of an assembly name, version, culture, and public key), the types that it references, the types that it exports, and the security requirements for execution. Much richer than a type library, metadata includes descriptions of an assembly and modules, classes, interfaces, methods, properties, fields, events, global methods, and so forth.

---

* In COM, *universal marshaling* is a common way to marshal all data types. A universal marshaler can be used to marshal all types, so you don't have to provide your own proxy or stub code.

Metadata provides enough information for any runtime, tool, or program to find out literally everything that is needed for component integration. Let's take a look at a short list of consumers that make intelligent use of metadata in .NET, just to prove that metadata is indeed like type libraries on steroids:

CLR

The CLR uses metadata for verification, security enforcement, cross-context marshaling, memory layout, and execution. The CLR relies heavily on metadata to support these runtime features, which we will cover in a moment.

Class loader

A component of the CLR, the class loader uses metadata to find and load .NET classes. This is because metadata records detailed information for a specific class and where the class is located, whether it is in the same assembly, within or outside of a specific namespace, or in a dependent assembly somewhere on the network.

Just-in-time (JIT) compilers

JIT compilers use metadata to compile IL code. IL is an intermediate representation that contributes significantly to language-integration support, but it is not VB code or bytecode, which must be interpreted. .NET JIT compiles IL into native code prior to execution, and it does this using metadata.

Tools

Tools use metadata to support integration. For example, development tools can use metadata to generate callable wrappers that allow .NET and COM components to intermingle. Tools such as debuggers, profilers, and object browsers can use metadata to provide richer development support. One example of this is the IntelliSense features that Microsoft Visual Studio .NET supports. As soon as you have typed an object and a dot, the tool displays a list of methods and properties from which you can choose. This way, you don't have to search header files or documentation to obtain the exact method or property names and calling syntax.

Like the CLR, any application, tool, or utility that can read metadata from a .NET assembly can make use of that assembly. You can use the .NET reflection classes to inspect a .NET PE file and know everything about the data types that the assembly uses and exposes. The CLR uses the same set of reflection classes to inspect and provide runtime features, including memory management, security management, type checking, debugging, remoting, and so on.

Metadata ensures language interoperability, an essential element to .NET, since all languages must use the same types in order to generate a valid .NET PE file. The .NET runtime cannot support features such as memory management, security management, memory layout, type checking, debugging, and so on without the richness of metadata. Therefore, metadata is an extremely important part of .NET—so important that we can safely say that there would be no .NET without metadata.

Examining Metadata

At this point, we introduce an important .NET tool, the IL disassembler (*ildasm.exe*), which allows you to view both the metadata and IL code within a given .NET PE file. For example, if you execute *ildasm.exe* and open the *hello.exe* .NET PE file that you built earlier in this chapter, you will see something similar to Figure 2-3.

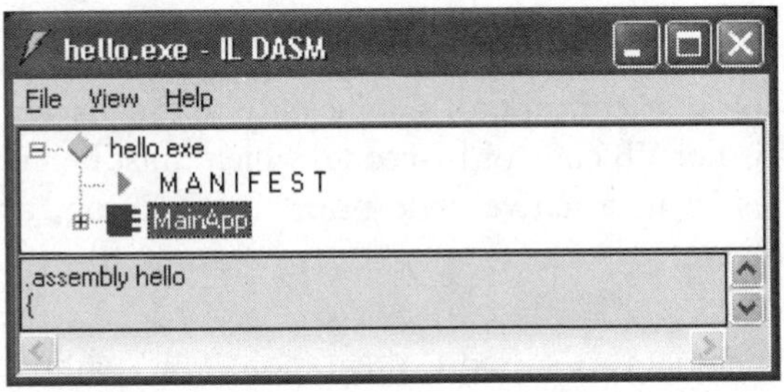

Figure 2-3. The ildasm.exe tool

The *ildasm.exe* tool displays the metadata for your .NET PE file in a tree view, so that you can easily drill down from the assembly, to the classes, to the methods, and so on. To get full details on the contents of a .NET PE file, you can press Ctrl-D to dump the contents out into a text file.* Here's an example of an *ildasm.exe* dump, showing only the contents that are relevant to the current discussion:

```
.assembly extern mscorlib
{
}
```

---

* The *ildasm.exe* tool also supports a command-line interface. You can execute *ildasm.exe* /h to view the command-line options. As a side note, if you want to view exactly which types are defined and referenced, press Ctrl-M in the *ildasm.exe* GUI, and it will show you further details.

```
.assembly hello
{
}

.module hello.exe

.class private auto ansi beforefieldinit MainApp
       extends [mscorlib]System.Object
{
  .method public hidebysig static
          void Main( ) cil managed
  {
  } // End of method MainApp::Main

  .method public hidebysig specialname rtspecialname
          instance void .ctor( ) cil managed
  {
  } // End of method MainApp::.ctor

} // End of class MainApp
```

As you can see, this dump fully describes the type information and dependencies in a .NET assembly. While the first IL instruction, .assembly extern, tells us that this PE file references (i.e., uses) an external assembly called *mscorlib*, the second IL instruction describes our assembly, the one that is called hello. We will discuss the contents of the .assembly blocks later, as these are collectively called a *manifest*. Below the manifest, you see an instruction that tells us the module name, *hello.exe*.

Next, you see a definition of a class in IL, starting with the .class IL instruction. Notice this class, MainApp, derives from System.Object, the mother of all classes in .NET. Although we didn't derive MainApp from System.Object when we wrote this class earlier in Managed C++, C#, J#, or VB.NET, the compiler automatically added this specification for us because System. Object is the implicit parent of all classes that omit the specification of a base class.

Within this class, you see two methods. While the first method, Main( ), is a static method that we wrote earlier, the second method, .ctor( ), is automatically generated. Main( ) serves as the main entry point for our application, and .ctor( ) is the constructor that allows anyone to instantiate MainApp.

As this example illustrates, given a .NET PE file, we can examine all the metadata that is embedded within a PE file. The important thing to keep in mind here is that we can do this without the need for source code or header files. If we can do this, imagine the exciting features that the CLR or a third-party tool can offer by simply making intelligent use of metadata. Of course,

everyone can now see your code, unless you use different techniques (e.g., obfuscation and encryption) to protect your property rights.

Inspecting and Emitting Metadata

To load and inspect a .NET assembly to determine what types it supports, use a special set of classes provided by the .NET Framework base class library. Unlike API functions, these classes encapsulate a number of methods to give you an easy interface for inspecting and manipulating metadata. In .NET, these classes are collectively called the *Reflection API*, which includes classes from the System.Reflection and System.Reflection.Emit namespaces. The classes in the System.Reflection namespace allow you to inspect metadata within a .NET assembly, as shown in the following example:

```
using System;
using System.IO;

using System.Reflection;

public class Meta
{
  public static int Main( )
  {
    // First, load the assembly.
    Assembly a = Assembly.LoadFrom("hello.exe");

    // Get all the modules that the assembly supports.
    Module[] m = a.GetModules( );

    // Get all the types in the first module.
    Type[] types = m[0].GetTypes( );

    // Inspect the first type.
    Type type = types[0];
    Console.WriteLine("Type [{0}] has these methods:", type.Name);

    // Inspect the methods supported by this type.
    MethodInfo[] mInfo = type.GetMethods( );
    foreach ( MethodInfo mi in mInfo )
    {
      Console.WriteLine("  {0}", mi);
    }

    return 0;
  }
}
```

Looking at this simple C# program, you'll notice that we first tell the compiler that we want to use the classes in the System.Reflection namespace because we want to inspect metadata. In Main( ), we load the assembly by a

physical name, *hello.exe*, so be sure that you have this PE file in the same directory when you run this program. Next, we ask the loaded assembly object for an array of modules that it contains. From this array of modules, we pull off the array of types supported by the module, and from this array of types, we then pull off the first type. For *hello.exe*, the first and only type happens to be MainApp. Once we have obtained this type or class, we loop through the list of its exposed methods. If you compile and execute this simple program, you see the following result:

```
Type [MainApp] has these methods:
    Int32 GetHashCode( )
    Boolean Equals(System.Object)
    System.String ToString( )
    Void Main( )
    System.Type GetType( )
```

Although we've written only the Main( ) function, our class actually supports four other methods, as is clearly illustrated by this output. There's no magic here, because MainApp inherits these method implementations from System.Object, which once again is the root of all classes in .NET.

As you can see, the System.Reflection classes allow you to inspect metadata, and they are really easy to use. If you have used type library interfaces in COM before, you know that you can do this in COM, but with much more effort. However, what you can't do with the COM type library interfaces is create a COM component at runtime—a missing feature in COM but an awesome feature in .NET. By using the System.Reflection.Emit classes, you can write a simple program to generate a .NET assembly dynamically at runtime. Given the existence of System.Reflection.Emit, anyone can write a custom .NET compiler.

Interoperability Support

Because it provides a common format for specifying types, metadata allows different components, tools, and runtimes to support interoperability. As demonstrated earlier, you can inspect the metadata of any .NET assembly. You can also ask an object at runtime for its type, methods, properties, events, and so on. Tools can do the same. The Microsoft .NET SDK ships four important tools that assist interoperability, including the .NET assembly registration utility (*RegAsm.exe*), the type library exporter (*tlbexp.exe*), the type library importer (*tlbimp.exe*), and the XML schema definition tool (*xsd.exe*).

You can use the .NET assembly registration utility to register a .NET assembly into the registry so COM clients can make use of it. The type library exporter is a tool that generates a type library file (*.tlb*) when you pass it

a .NET assembly. Once you have generated a type library from a given .NET assembly, you can import the type library into VC++ or VB and use the .NET assembly in exactly the same way as if you were using a COM component. Simply put, the type library exporter makes a .NET assembly look like a COM component. The following command-line invocation generates a type library, called *hello.tlb*:

```
tlbexp.exe hello.exe
```

Microsoft also ships a counterpart to *tlbexp.exe*, the type library importer; its job is to make a COM component appear as a .NET assembly. So if you are developing a .NET application and want to make use of an older COM component, use the type library importer to convert the type information found in the COM component into .NET equivalents. For example, you can generate a .NET PE assembly using the following command:

```
tlbimp.exe COMServer.tlb
```

Executing this command will generate a .NET assembly in the form of a DLL (e.g., *COMServer.dll*). You can reference this DLL like any other .NET assembly in your .NET code. When your .NET code executes at runtime, all invocations of the methods or properties within this DLL are directed to the original COM component.

 Be aware that the type library importer doesn't let you reimport a type library that has been previously exported by the type library exporter. In other words, if you try to use *tlbimp.exe* on *hello.tlb*, which was generated by *tlbexp.exe*, *tlbimp.exe* will barf at you.

Another impressive tool that ships with the .NET SDK is the XML schema definition tool, which allows you to convert an XML schema into a C# class, and vice versa. This XML schema:

```
<schema xmlns="http://www.w3.org/2001/XMLSchema"
 targetNamespace="urn:book:car"
 xmlns:t="urn:book:car">
  <element name="car" type="t:CCar"/>
  <complexType name="CCar">
    <all>
      <element name="vin" type="string"/>
      <element name="make" type="string"/>
      <element name="model" type="string"/>
      <element name="year" type="int"/>
    </all>
  </complexType>
</schema>
```

represents a type called CCar. To convert this XML schema into a C# class definition, execute the following:

```
xsd.exe /c car.xsd
```

The /c option tells the tool to generate a class from the given XSD file. If you execute this command, you get *car.cs* as the output that contains the C# code for this type.

The XML schema definition tool can also take a .NET assembly and generate an XSD file that contains representations for the public types within the .NET assembly. For example, if you execute the following, you get an XSD file as output:

```
xsd.exe somefile.exe
```

Before we leave this topic, we want to remind you to try out these tools for yourself, because they offer many impressive features that we won't cover in this introductory book.

Assemblies and Manifests

As we just saw, types must expose their metadata to allow tools and programs to access them and benefit from their services. Metadata for types alone is not enough. To simplify software plug-and-play and configuration or installation of the component or software, we also need metadata about the component that hosts the types. Now we'll talk about .NET assemblies (deployable units) and manifests (the metadata that describes the assemblies).

Assemblies Versus Components

During the COM era, Microsoft documentation inconsistently used the term *component* to mean a COM class or a COM module (DLLs or EXEs), forcing readers or developers to consider the context of the term each time they encountered it. In .NET, Microsoft has addressed this confusion by introducing a new concept, *assembly*, which is a software component that supports plug-and-play, much like a hardware component. Theoretically, a .NET assembly is approximately equivalent to a compiled COM module. In practice, an assembly can contain or refer to a number of types and physical files (including bitmap files, .NET PE files, and so forth) that are needed at runtime for successful execution. In addition to hosting IL code, an assembly is a basic unit of versioning, deployment, security management, side-by-side execution, sharing, and reuse, as we discuss next.

To review: an assembly is a logical DLL or EXE, and a manifest is a detailed description (metadata) of an assembly, including its version, what other assemblies it uses, and so on.

Unique Identities

Type uniqueness is important in RPC, COM, and .NET. Given the vast number of GUIDs in COM (application, library, class, and interface identifiers), development and deployment can be tedious because you must use these magic numbers in your code and elsewhere all the time. In .NET, you refer to a specific type by its readable name and its namespace. Since a readable name and its namespace are not enough to be globally unique, .NET guarantees uniqueness by using unique public/private key pairs. All assemblies that are shared (called *shared assemblies*) by multiple applications must be built with a public/private key pair. Public/private key pairs are used in public-key cryptography. Since public-key cryptography uses asymmetrical encryption, an assembly creator can sign an assembly with a private key, and anyone can verify that digital signature using the assembly creator's public key. However, because no one else will have the private key, no other individual can create a similarly signed assembly.

To sign an assembly digitally, you must use a public/private key pair to build your assembly. At build time, the compiler generates a hash of the assembly files, signs the hash with the private key, and stores the resulting digital signature in a reserved section of the PE file. The public key is also stored in the assembly.

To verify the assembly's digital signature, the CLR uses the assembly's public key to decrypt the assembly's digital signature, resulting in the original, calculated hash. In addition, the CLR uses the information in the assembly's manifest to dynamically generate a hash. This hash value is then compared with the original hash value. These values must match, or we must assume that someone has tampered with the assembly.

Now that we know how to sign and verify an assembly in .NET, let's talk about how the CLR ensures that a given application loads the trusted assembly with which it was built. When you or someone else builds an application that uses a shared assembly, the application's assembly manifest will include an 8-byte hash of the shared assembly's public key. When you run your application, the CLR dynamically derives the 8-byte hash from the shared assembly's public key and compares this value with the hash value

stored in your application's assembly manifest. If these values match, the CLR assumes that it has loaded the correct assembly for you.[*]

IL Code

An assembly contains the IL code that the CLR executes at runtime (see "Intermediate Language (IL)" later in this chapter). The IL code typically uses types defined within the same assembly, but it also may use or refer to types in other assemblies. Although nothing special is required to take advantage of the former, the assembly must define references to other assemblies to do the latter, as we will see in a moment. There is one caveat: each assembly can have at most one entry point, such as DllMain( ), WinMain( ), or Main( ). You must follow this rule because when the CLR loads an assembly, it searches for one of these entry points to start assembly execution.

Versioning

There are four types of assemblies in .NET:

Static assemblies
> These are the .NET PE files that you create at compile time. You can create static assemblies using your favorite compiler: *csc*, *cl*, *vjc*, or *vbc*.

Dynamic assemblies
> These are PE-formatted, in-memory assemblies that you dynamically create at runtime using the classes in the System.Reflection.Emit namespace.

Private assemblies
> These are static assemblies used by a specific application.

Shared assemblies
> These are static assemblies that must have a unique shared name and can be used by any application.

An application uses a private assembly by referring to the assembly using a static path or through an XML-based application configuration file. Although the CLR doesn't enforce versioning policies—checking whether the correct version is used—for private assemblies, it ensures that an application uses the

---

[*] You can use the .NET Strong (a.k.a., Shared) Name (*sn.exe*) utility to generate a new key pair for a shared assembly. Before you can share your assembly, you must register it in the Global Assembly Cache, or GAC—you can do this by using the .NET Global Assembly Cache Utility (*gacutil. exe*). The GAC is simply a directory called Assembly located under the Windows (*%windir%*) directory.

correct shared assemblies with which the application was built. Thus, an application uses a specific shared assembly by referring to the specific shared assembly, and the CLR ensures that the correct version is loaded at runtime.

In .NET, an assembly is the smallest unit to which you can associate a version number; it has the following format:

```
<major_version>.<minor_version>.<build_number>.<revision>
```

Deployment

Since a client application's assembly manifest (to be discussed shortly) contains information on external references—including the assembly name and version the application uses—you no longer have to use the registry to store activation and marshaling hints as in COM. Using the version and security information recorded in your application's manifest, the CLR will load the correct shared assembly for you. The CLR does lazy loading of external assemblies and will retrieve them on demand when you use their types. Because of this, you can create downloadable applications that are small, with many small external assemblies. When a particular external assembly is needed, the runtime downloads it automatically without involving registration or computer restarts.

Security

The concept of a user identity is common in all development and operating platforms, but the concept of a *code identity*, in which even a piece of code has an identity, is new to the commercial software industry. In .NET, an assembly itself has a code identity, which includes information such as the assembly's shared name, version number, culture, public key, and where the code came from (local, intranet, or Internet). This information is also referred to as the assembly's evidence, and it helps to identify and grant permissions to code, particularly mobile code.

To coincide with the concept of a code identity, the CLR supports the concept of *code access*. Whether code can access resources or use other code is entirely dependent on security policy, which is a set of rules that an administrator configures and the CLR enforces. The CLR inspects the assembly's evidence and uses security policy to grant the target assembly a set of permissions to be examined during its execution. The CLR checks these permissions and determines whether the assembly has access to resources or to other code. When you create an assembly, you can declaratively specify a set of permissions that the client application must have in order to use your assembly. At runtime, if the client application has code access to your

assembly, it can make calls to your assembly's objects; otherwise, a security exception will ensue. You can also imperatively demand that all code on the call stack has the appropriate permissions to access a particular resource.

Side-by-Side Execution

We have said that an assembly is a unit of versioning and deployment, and we've talked briefly about DLL Hell, something that .NET intends to minimize. The CLR allows any versions of the same, shared DLL (shared assembly) to execute at the same time, on the same system, and even in the same process. This concept is known as *side-by-side execution*. Microsoft .NET accomplishes side-by-side execution by using the versioning and deployment features that are innate to all shared assemblies. This concept allows you to install any versions of the same, shared assembly on the same machine, without versioning conflicts or DLL Hell. The only caveat is that your assemblies must be public or shared assemblies, meaning that you must register them against the GAC using a tool such as the .NET Global Assembly Cache Utility (*gacutil.exe*). Once you have registered different versions of the same shared assembly into the GAC, the human-readable name of the assembly no longer matters—what's important is the information provided by .NET's versioning and deployment features.

Recall that when you build an application that uses a particular shared assembly, the shared assembly's version information is attached to your application's manifest. In addition, an 8-byte hash of the shared assembly's public key is also attached to your application's manifest. Using these two pieces of information, the CLR can find the exact shared assembly that your application uses, and it will even verify that your 8-byte hash is indeed equivalent to that of the shared assembly. Given that the CLR can identify and load the exact assembly, the end of DLL Hell is in sight.

Sharing and Reuse

When you want to share your assembly with the rest of the world, your assembly must have a shared or strong name, and you must register it in the GAC. Likewise, if you want to use or extend a particular class that is hosted by a particular shared assembly, you don't just import that specific class, but you import the whole assembly into your application. Therefore, the whole assembly is a unit of sharing.

Assemblies turn out to be an extremely important feature in .NET because they are an essential part of the runtime. An assembly encapsulates all types that are defined within the assembly. For example, although two different

assemblies, Personal and Company, can define and expose the same type, Car, Car by itself has no meaning unless you qualify it as [Personal]Car or [Company]Car. Given this, all types are scoped to their containing assembly, and for this reason, the CLR cannot make use of a specific type unless the CLR knows the type's assembly. In fact, if you don't have an assembly manifest, which describes the assembly, the CLR will not execute your program.

Manifests: Assembly Metadata

An assembly *manifest* is metadata that describes everything about the assembly, including its identity, a list of files belonging to the assembly, references to external assemblies, exported types, exported resources, and permission requests. In short, it describes all the details that are required for component plug-and-play. Since an assembly contains all these details, there's no need for storing this type of information in the registry, as in the COM world.

In COM, when you use a particular COM class, you give the COM library a class identifier. The COM library looks up in the registry to find the COM component that exposes that class, loads the component, tells the component to give it an instance of that class, and returns a reference to this instance. In .NET, instead of looking into the registry, the CLR peers right into the assembly manifest, determines which external assembly is needed, loads the exact assembly that's required by your application, and creates an instance of the target class.

Let's examine the manifest for the *hello.exe* application that we built earlier. Recall that we used the *ildasm.exe* tool to pick up this information.

```
.assembly extern mscorlib
{
  .publickeytoken = (B7 7A 5C 56 19 34 E0 89 )
  .ver 1:0:5000:0
}

.assembly hello
{
  .hash algorithm 0x00008004
  .ver 0:0:0:0
}
.module hello.exe
// MVID: {F828835E-3705-4238-BCD7-637ACDD33B78}
```

You'll notice that this manifest starts off identifying an external or referenced assembly, with mscorlib as the assembly name, which this particular application references. The keywords .assembly extern tell the CLR that this

application doesn't implement mscorlib, but makes use of it instead. This external assembly is one that all .NET applications will use, so you will see this external assembly defined in the manifest of all assemblies. You'll notice that, inside this assembly definition, the compiler has inserted a special value called the *publickeytoken*, which is basic information about the publisher of mscorlib. The compiler generates the value for .publickeytoken by hashing the public key associated with the mscorlib assembly. Another thing to note in the mscorlib block is the version number of mscorlib.[*]

Now that we've covered the first .assembly block, let's examine the second, which describes this particular assembly. You can tell that this is a manifest block that describes our application's assembly because there's no extern keyword. The identity of this assembly is made up of a readable assembly name, hello, its version information, 0:0:0:0, and an optional culture, which is missing. Within this block, the first line indicates the hash algorithm that is used to hash selected contents of this assembly, the result of which will be encrypted using the private key. However, since we are not sharing this simple assembly, there's no encryption and there's no .publickey value.

The last thing to discuss is .module, which simply identifies the output filename of this assembly, *hello.exe*. You'll notice that a module is associated with a GUID, which means you get a different GUID each time you build the module. Given this, a rudimentary test for exact module equivalence is to compare the GUIDs of two modules.

Because this example is so simple, that's all we get for our manifest. In a more complicated assembly, you can get all this, including much more in-depth detail about the make up of your assembly.

Creating Assemblies

An assembly can be a *single-module assembly* or a *multi-module assembly*. In a single-module assembly, everything in a build is clumped into one EXE or DLL, an example of which is the *hello.exe* application that we developed earlier. This is easy to create because a compiler takes care of creating the single-module assembly for you.

If you wanted to create a multi-module assembly, one that contains many modules and resource files, you have a few choices. One option is to use the

---

[*] The fascinating details are explained in Partition II Metadata.doc and Partition III CIL.doc, which come with the .NET SDK. If you really want to understand metadata IL, read these documents.

Assembly Linker (*al.exe*) that is provided by the .NET SDK. This tool takes one or more IL or resource files and spits out a file with an assembly manifest.

Using Assemblies

To use an assembly, first import the assembly into your code, the syntax of which is dependent upon the language that you use. For example, this is how we import an assembly in C#, as we have seen previously in the chapter:

```
using System;
```

When you build your assembly, you must tell the compiler that you are referencing an external assembly. Again, how you do this is different depending on the compiler that you use. If you use the C# compiler, here's how it's done:

```
csc /r:mscorlib.dll hello.cs
```

Earlier, we showed you how to compile *hello.cs* without the /r: option, but both techniques are equivalent. The reference to *mscorlib.dll* is inherently assumed because it contains all the base framework classes.

Intermediate Language (IL)

In software engineering, the concept of *abstraction* is extremely important. We often use abstraction to hide the complexity of system or application services, providing instead a simple interface to the consumer. As long as we can keep the interface the same, we can change the hideous internals, and different consumers can use the same interface.

In language advances, scientists introduced different incarnations of language-abstraction layers, such as *p-code* and *bytecode*. Produced by the Pascal-P compiler, p-code is an intermediate language that supports procedural programming. Generated by Java compilers, bytecode is an intermediate language that supports object-oriented programming. Bytecode is a language abstraction that allows Java code to run on different operating platforms, as long as the platforms have a Java Virtual Machine (JVM) to execute bytecode.

Microsoft calls its own language-abstraction layer the Microsoft Intermediate Language (MSIL) or IL, for short. IL is an implementation of the Common Intermediate Language (CIL), a key element of the EMCA CLI specification. Similar to bytecode, IL supports all object-oriented features, including data abstraction, inheritance, polymorphism, and useful concepts such as exceptions and events. In addition to these features, IL supports other concepts, such as properties, fields, and enumeration. Any

.NET language may be converted into IL, so .NET supports multiple languages and multiple platforms, as long as the target platforms have a CLR.

Shipped with the .NET SDK, *Partition III CIL.doc* describes the important IL instructions that language compilers should use. In addition to this specification, the .NET SDK includes another important document, *Partition II Metadata.doc*. Both of these documents are intended for developers who write compilers and tools, but you should read them to further understand how IL fits into .NET. Although you can develop a valid .NET assembly using the supported IL instructions and features, you'll find IL to be very tedious because the instructions are a bit cryptic. However, should you decide to write pure IL code, you could use the IL Assembler (*ilasm.exe*) to turn your IL code into a .NET PE file.*

Enough with the theory: let's take a look at some IL. Here's an excerpt of IL code for the *hello.exe* program that we wrote earlier:†

```
.class private auto ansi beforefieldinit MainApp
  extends [mscorlib]System.Object
{
  .method public hidebysig static
          void Main( ) cil managed
  {
    .entrypoint
    .maxstack  1
    ldstr "C# hello world!"
    call void [mscorlib]System.Console::WriteLine(string)
    ret
  } // End of method MainApp::Main

  .method public hidebysig specialname rtspecialname
    instance void .ctor( ) cil managed
  {
    .maxstack  1
    ldarg.0
    call instance void [mscorlib]System.Object::.ctor( )
    ret
  } // End of method MainApp::.ctor

} // End of class MainApp
```

Ignoring the weird-looking syntactic details, you can see that IL is conceptually the same as any other object-oriented language. Clearly, there is a class

---

* You can test this utility using the IL disassembler to load a .NET PE file and dump out the IL to a text file. Once you've done this, use the IL Assembler to covert the text file into a .NET PE file.

† Don't compile this IL code: it's incomplete because we've extracted unclear details to make it easier to read. If you want to see the complete IL code, use *ildasm.exe* on *hello.exe*.

that is called MainApp that derives from System.Object. This class supports a static method called Main( ), which contains the code to dump out a text string to the console. Although we didn't write a constructor for this class, our C# compiler has added the default constructor for MainApp to support object construction.

Since a lengthy discussion of IL is beyond the scope of this book, let's just concentrate on the Main( ) method to examine its implementation briefly. First, you see the following method signature:

```
.method public hidebysig static
        void Main( ) cil managed
```

This signature declares a method that is public (meaning that it can be called by anyone) and static (meaning it's a class-level method). The name of this method is Main( ). Main( ) contains IL code that is to be managed or executed by the CLR. The hidebysig attribute says that this method hides the same methods (with the same signatures) defined earlier in the class hierarchy. This is simply the default behavior of most object-oriented languages, such as C++. Having gone over the method signature, let's talk about the method body itself:

```
{
    .entrypoint
    .maxstack 1
    ldstr "C# hello world!"
    call void [mscorlib]System.Console::WriteLine(string)
    ret
} // End of method MainApp::Main
```

This method uses two directives: .entrypoint and .maxstack. The .entrypoint directive specifies that Main( ) is the one and only entry point for this assembly. The .maxstack directive specifies the maximum stack slots needed by this method; in this case, the maximum number of stack slots required by Main( ) is one. Stack information is needed for each IL method because IL instructions are stack-based, allowing language compilers to generate IL code easily.

In addition to these directives, this method uses three IL instructions. The first IL instruction, ldstr, loads our literal string onto the stack so that the code in the same block can use it. The next IL instruction, call, invokes the WriteLine() method, which picks up the string from the stack. The call IL instruction expects the method's arguments to be on the stack, with the first argument being the first object pushed on the stack, the second argument being the second object pushed onto the stack, and so forth. In addition, when you use the call instruction to invoke a method, you must specify the

method's signature. For example, examine the method signature of
WriteLine( ):

```
void [mscorlib]System.Console::WriteLine(string)
```

and you'll see that WriteLine( ) is a static method of the Console class. The
Console class belongs to the System namespace, which happens to be a part
of the *mscorlib* assembly. The WriteLine( ) method takes a string (an alias
for System.String) and returns a void. The last thing to note in this IL snippet is that the ret IL instruction simply returns control to the caller.

 Since .NET assemblies contain IL code, your proprietary
algorithms can be seen by anyone. To protect your intellectual property, use an obfuscator, either the one that comes
with Visual Studio .NET or one that is commercially available.

The CTS and CLS

Having seen the importance of metadata and IL, let's examine the CTS and
the CLS. Both the CTS and the CLS ensure language compatibility, interoperability, and integration.

The Common Type System (CTS)

Because .NET treats all languages as equal, a class written in C# should be
equivalent to a class written in VB.NET, and an interface defined in Managed C++ should be exactly the same as one that is specified in Managed
COBOL. Languages must agree on the meanings of these concepts before
they can integrate with one another. In order to make language integration a
reality, Microsoft has specified a common type system by which every .NET
language must abide. In this section, we outline the common types that have
the same conceptual semantics in every .NET language. Microsoft .NET
supports a rich set of types, but we limit our discussion to the important
ones, including value types, reference types, classes, interfaces, and delegates.

Value types

In general, the CLR supports two different types: value types and reference
types. *Value types* represent values allocated on the stack. They cannot be
null and must always contain some data. When value types are passed into a
function, they are passed by value, meaning that a copy of the value is made
prior to function execution. This implies that the original value won't
change, no matter what happens to the copy during the function call. Since
intrinsic types are small in size and don't consume much memory, the

resource cost of making a copy is negligible and outweighs the performance drawbacks of object management and garbage collection. Value types include primitives, structures, and enumerations; examples are shown in the following C# code listing:

```
int i;                    // Primitive
struct Point { int x, y; } // Structure
enum State { Off, On }     // Enumeration
```

You can also create a value type by deriving a class from System.ValueType. One thing to note is that a value type is *sealed*, meaning that once you have derived a class from System.ValueType, no one else can derive from your class.

Reference types

If a type consumes significant memory resources, then a reference type provides more benefits over a value type. *Reference types* are so called because they contain references to heap-based objects and can be null. These types are passed by reference, meaning that when you pass such an object into a function, an address of or pointer to the object is passed—not a copy of the object, as in the case of a value type. Since you are passing a reference, the caller will see whatever the called function does to your object. The first benefit here is that a reference type can be used as an output parameter, but the second benefit is that you don't waste extra resources because a copy is not made. If your object is large (consuming lots of memory), than reference types are a better choice. In .NET, one drawback of a reference type is that it must be allocated on the managed heap, which means it requires more CPU cycles because it must be managed and garbage-collected by the CLR. In .NET, the closest concept to destruction is finalization, but unlike destructors in C++, finalization is nondeterministic. In other words, you don't know when finalization will happen because it occurs when the garbage collector executes (by default, when the system runs out of memory). Since finalization is nondeterministic, another drawback of reference types is that if reference-type objects hold on to expensive resources that will be released during finalization, system performance will degrade because the resources won't be released until these objects are garbage-collected. Reference types include classes, interfaces, arrays, and delegates, examples of which are shown in the following C# code listing:

```
class Car {}              // Class
interface ISteering {}    // Interface
int[] a = new int[5];     // Array
delegate void Process();  // Delegate
```

Classes, interfaces, and delegates will be discussed shortly.

Boxing and unboxing

Microsoft .NET supports value types for performance reasons, but everything in .NET is ultimately an object. In fact, all primitive types have corresponding classes in the .NET Framework. For example, int is, in fact, an alias of System.Int32, and System.Int32 happens to derive from System.ValueType, meaning that it is a value type. Value types are allocated on the stack by default, but they can always be converted into a heap-based, reference-type object; this is called *boxing*. The following code snippet shows that we can create a box and copy the value of i into it:

```
int i = 1;         // i - a value type
object box = i;    // box - a reference object
```

When you box a value, you get an object upon which you can invoke methods, properties, and events. For example, once you have converted the integer into an object, as shown in this code snippet, you can call methods that are defined in System.Object, including ToString( ), Equals( ), and so forth.

The reverse of boxing is of course *unboxing*, which means that you can convert a heap-based, reference-type object into its value-type equivalent, as the following shows:

```
int j = (int)box;
```

This example simply uses the cast operator to cast a heap-based object called box into a value-type integer.

Classes, properties, indexers

The CLR provides full support for object-oriented concepts (such as encapsulation, inheritance, and polymorphism) and class features (such as methods, fields, static members, visibility, accessibility, nested types, and so forth). In addition, the CLR supports new features that are nonexistent in many traditional object-oriented programming languages, including properties, indexers, and events.* Events are covered in Chapter 8. For now let's briefly talk about properties and indexers.

A property is similar to a field (a member variable), with the exception that there is a getter and a setter method, as follows:

```
using System;

public class Car
{
    private string make;
```

---

* An event is a callback that is implemented using delegates, which is covered shortly.

```
  public string Make
  {
    get { return make; }
    set { make = value; }
  }

  public static void Main( )
  {
    Car c = new Car( );
    c.Make = "Acura";  // Use setter.
    String s = c.Make; // Use getter.
    Console.WriteLine(s);
  }
}
```

Although this is probably the first time you've seen such syntax, this example is straightforward and really needs no explanation, with the exception of the keyword value. This is a special keyword that represents the one and only argument to the setter method.

Syntactically similar to a property, an indexer is analogous to operator[ ] in C++, as it allows array-like access to the contents of an object. In other words, it allows you to access an object like you're accessing an array, as shown in the following example:

```
using System;

public class Car
{
  Car( )
  {
    wheels = new string[4];
  }

  private string[] wheels;
  public string this[int index]
  {
    get { return wheels[index]; }
    set { wheels[index] = value; }
  }

  public static void Main( )
  {
    Car c = new Car( );
    c[0] = "LeftWheel";  // c[0] can be an l-value or an r-value.
    Console.WriteLine(c[0]);
  }
}
```

Unlike C++, but similar to Java, classes in .NET support only single-implementation inheritance.

Interfaces

Interfaces support exactly the same concept as a C++ abstract base class (ABC) with only pure virtual functions. An ABC is a class that declares one or more pure virtual functions and thus cannot be instantiated. If you know COM or Java, interfaces in .NET are conceptually equivalent to a COM or Java interface. You specify them, but you don't implement them. A class that derives from your interface must implement your interface. An interface may contain methods, properties, indexers, and events. In .NET, a class can derive from multiple interfaces.

Delegates

One of the most powerful features of C is its support for function pointers. Function pointers allow you to build software with hooks that can be implemented by someone else. In fact, function pointers allow many people to build expandable or customizable software. Microsoft .NET supports a type-safe version of function pointers, called *delegates*. Here's an example that may take a few minutes to sink in, but once you get it, you'll realize that it's really simple:

```
using System;
class TestDelegate
{
  // 1. Define callback prototype.
  delegate void MsgHandler(string strMsg);

  // 2. Define callback method.
  void OnMsg(string strMsg)
  {
    Console.WriteLine(strMsg);
  }

  public static void Main( )
  {
    TestDelegate t = new TestDelegate( );

    // 3. Wire up our callback method.
    MsgHandler f = new MsgHandler(t.OnMsg);

    // 4. Invoke the callback method indirectly.
    f("Hello, Delegate.");
  }
}
```

The first thing to do is to define a callback function prototype, and the important keyword here is delegate, which tells the compiler that you want an object-oriented function pointer. Under the hood, the compiler generates a nested class, MsgHandler, which derives from System.MulticastDelegate.* A multicast delegate supports many receivers. Once you've defined your prototype, you must define and implement a method with a signature that matches your prototype. Then, simply wire up the callback method by passing the function to the delegate's constructor, as shown in this code listing. Finally, invoke your callback indirectly. Having gone over delegates, you should note that delegates form the foundation of events, which are discussed in Chapter 8.

The Common Language Specification (CLS)

A goal of .NET is to support language integration in such a way that programs can be written in any language, yet can interoperate with one another, taking full advantage of inheritance, polymorphism, exceptions, and other features. However, languages are not made equal because one language may support a feature that is totally different from another language. For example, Managed C++ is case-sensitive, but VB.NET is not. In order to bring everyone to the same sheet of music, Microsoft has published the Common Language Specification (CLS). The CLS specifies a series of basic rules that are required for language integration. Since Microsoft provides the CLS that spells out the minimum requirements for being a .NET language, compiler vendors can build their compilers to the specification and provide languages that target .NET. Besides compiler writers, application developers should read the CLS and use its rules to guarantee language interoperation.

CLR Execution

Now that you understand the elements of a .NET executable, let's talk about the services that the CLR provides to support management and execution of .NET assemblies. There are many fascinating components in the CLR, but for brevity, we will limit our discussions to just the major components, as shown in Figure 2-4.

The major components of the CLR include the class loader, verifier, JIT compilers, and other execution support, such as code management, security management, garbage collection, exception management, debug management,

---

* If you want to see this, use *ildasm.exe* and view the metadata of the *delegate.exe* sample that we've provided.

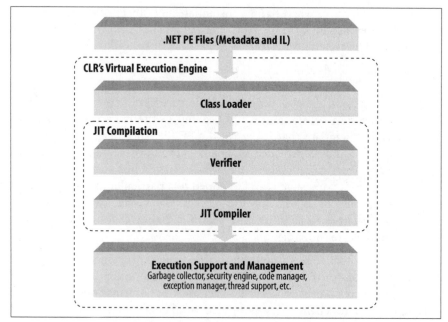

Figure 2-4. Major CLR components: the Virtual Execution System (VES)

marshaling management, thread management, and so on. As you can see from Figure 2-4, your .NET PE files lay on top of the CLR and execute within the CLR's Virtual Execution System (VES), which hosts the major components of the runtime. Your .NET PE files will have to go through the class loader, the type verifier, the JIT compilers, and other execution support components before they will execute.

Class Loader

When you run a standard Windows application, the OS loader loads it before it can execute. At the time of this writing, the default loaders in the existing Windows operating systems, such as Windows 98, Windows Me, Windows 2000, and so forth, recognize only the standard Windows PE files. As a result, Microsoft has provided an updated OS loader for each of these operating systems that support the .NET runtime. The updated OS loaders know the .NET PE file format and can handle the file appropriately.

When you run a .NET application on one of these systems that have an updated OS loader, the OS loader recognizes the .NET application and thus passes control to the CLR. The CLR then finds the entry point, which is typically Main( ), and executes it to jump-start the application. But before Main( ) can execute, the class loader must find the class that exposes Main( ) and load

the class. In addition, when Main( ) instantiates an object of a specific class, the class loader also kicks in. In short, the class loader performs its magic the first time a type is referenced.

The *class loader* loads .NET classes into memory and prepares them for execution. Before it can successfully do this, it must locate the target class. To find the target class, the class loader looks in several different places, including the application configuration file (*.config*) in the current directory, the GAC, and the metadata that is part of the PE file, specifically the manifest. The information that is provided by one or more of these items is crucial to locating the correct target class. Recall that a class can be scoped to a particular namespace, a namespace can be scoped to a particular assembly, and an assembly can be scoped to a specific version. Given this, two classes, both named Car, are treated as different types even if the version information of their assemblies are the same.

Once the class loader has found and loaded the target class, it caches the type information for the class so that it doesn't have to load the class again for the duration of this process. By caching this information, it will later determine how much memory is needed to allocate for the newly created instance of this class. Once the target class is loaded, the class loader injects a small stub, like a function prolog, into every single method of the loaded class. This stub is used for two purposes: to denote the status of JIT compilation and to transition between managed and unmanaged code. At this point, if the loaded class references other classes, the class loader will also try to load the referenced types. However, if the referenced types have already been loaded, the class loader has to do nothing. Finally, the class loader uses the appropriate metadata to initialize the static variables and instantiate an object of the loaded class for you.

Verifier

Scripting and interpreted languages are very lenient on type usages, allowing you to write code without explicit variable declarations. This flexibility can introduce code that is extremely error-prone and hard to maintain, and that is often a culprit for mysterious program crashes. Unlike scripting and interpreted languages, compiled languages require types to be explicitly defined prior to their use, permitting the compiler to ensure that types are used correctly and the code will execute peacefully at runtime.

The key here is type safety, and it is a fundamental concept for code verification in .NET. Within the VES, the verifier is the component that executes at runtime to verify that the code is type safe. Note that this type verification is done at runtime and that this is a fundamental difference between .NET and

other environments. By verifying type safety at runtime, the CLR can prevent the execution of code that is not type safe and ensure that the code is used as intended. In short, type safety means more reliability.

Let's talk about where the verifier fits within the CLR. After the class loader has loaded a class and before a piece of IL code can execute, the verifier kicks in for code that must be verified. The verifier is responsible for verifying that:

- The metadata is well formed, meaning the metadata must be valid.
- The IL code is type safe, meaning type signatures are used correctly.

Both of these criteria must be met before the code can be executed because JIT compilation will take place only when code and metadata have been successfully verified. In addition to checking for type safety, the verifier also performs rudimentary control-flow analysis of the code to ensure that the code is using types correctly. You should note that since the verifier is a part of the JIT compilers, it kicks in only when a method is being invoked, not when a class or assembly is loaded. You should also note that verification is an optional step because trusted code will never be verified but will be immediately directed to the JIT compiler for compilation.

JIT Compilers

JIT compilers play a major role in the .NET platform because all .NET PE files contain IL and metadata, not native code. The JIT compilers convert IL to native code so that it can execute on the target operating system. For each method that has been successfully verified for type safety, a JIT compiler in the CLR will compile the method and convert it into native code.

One advantage of a JIT compiler is that it can dynamically compile code that is optimized for the target machine. If you take the same .NET PE file from a one-CPU machine to a two-CPU machine, the JIT compiler on the two-CPU machine knows about the second CPU and may be able to spit out the native code that takes advantage of the second CPU. Another obvious advantage is that you can take the same .NET PE file and run it on a totally different platform, whether it be Windows, Unix, or whatever, as long as that platform has a CLR.

For optimization reasons, JIT compilation occurs only the first time a method is invoked. Recall that the class loader adds a stub to each method during class loading. At the first method invocation, the VES reads the information in this stub, which tells it that the code for the method has not been JIT-compiled. At this indication, the JIT compiler compiles the method and injects the address of the native method into this stub. During subsequent

invocations to the same method, no JIT compilation is needed because each time the VES goes to read information in the stub, it sees the address of the native method. Because the JIT compiler only performs its magic the first time a method is invoked, the methods you don't need at runtime will never be JIT-compiled.

The compiled, native code lies in memory until the process shuts down and until the garbage collector clears off all references and memory associated with the process. This means that the next time you execute the process or component, the JIT compiler will again perform its magic.

If you want to avoid the cost of JIT compilation at runtime, you can use a special tool called *ngen.exe*, which compiles your IL during installation and setup time. Using ngen, you can JIT-compile the code once and cache it on the machine so that you can avoid JIT compilation at runtime (this process is referred to as pre-JITting). In the event that the PE file has been updated, you must PreJIT the PE file again. Otherwise, the CLR can detect the update and dynamically command the appropriate JIT compiler to compile the assembly.

Execution Support and Management

By now, you should see that every component in the CLR that we've covered so far uses metadata and IL in some way to successfully carry out the services that it supports. In addition to the provided metadata and generated managed code, the JIT compiler must generate managed data that the code manager needs to locate and unwind stack frames.* The *code manager* uses managed data to control the execution of code, including performing stack walks that are required for exception handling, security checks, and garbage collection. Besides the code manager, the CLR also provides a number of important execution-support and management services. A detailed discussion of these services is beyond the scope of this book, so we will briefly enumerate a few of them here:

Garbage collection
> Unlike C++, where you must delete all heap-based objects manually, the CLR supports automatic lifetime management for all .NET objects. The garbage collector can detect when your objects are no longer being referenced and perform garbage collection to reclaim the unused memory.

---

* By the way, you can write a custom JIT compiler or a custom code manager for the CLR because the CLR supports the plug-and-play of these components.

Exception handling

Prior to .NET, there was no consistent method for error or exception handling, causing lots of pain in error handling and reporting. In .NET, the CLR supports a standard exception-handling mechanism that works across all languages, allowing every program to use a common error-handling mechanism. The CLR exception-handling mechanism is integrated with Windows Structured Exception Handling (SEH).

Security support

The CLR performs various security checks at runtime to make sure that the code is safe to execute and that the code is not breaching any security requirements. In addition to supporting code access security, the security engine also supports declarative and imperative security checks. Declarative security requires no special security code, but you have to specify the security requirements through attributes or administrative configuration. Imperative security requires that you write the code in your method to specifically cause security checks.

Debugging support

The CLR provides rich support for debugging and profiling. There is an API that compiler vendors can use to develop a debugger. This API contains support for controlling program execution, breakpoints, exceptions, control flow, and so forth. There is also an API for tools to support the profiling of running programs.

Interoperation support

The CLR supports interoperation between the managed (CLR) and unmanaged (no CLR) worlds. The *COM Interop* facility serves as a bridge between COM and the CLR, allowing a COM object to use a .NET object, and vice versa. The *Platform Invoke* (P/Invoke) facility allows you to call Windows API functions.

This is by no means an exhaustive list. The one thing that we want to reiterate is that like the class loader, verifier, JIT compiler, and just about everything else that deals with .NET, these execution-support and management facilities all use metadata, managed code, and managed data in some way to carry out their services.

Summary

As you can see from this chapter, the .NET architecture strives to support language integration and componentization in every way that makes sense. Thanks to metadata, programming becomes much easier because you no longer have to worry about the registry for component deployment and other kinks (such as CoCreateInstanceEx, CLSIDs, IIDs, IUnknown, IDL, and so

forth) in order to support componentization. Thanks to the CTS, CLS, metadata, and IL, you now have real language integration. Microsoft has shipped a CLR for several flavors of Windows, and has released their shared-source implementation of the CLR that will run on FreeBSD and will no doubt be portable to other Unix-like systems.* Non-Microsoft implementations of the CLR have also appeared, including DotGNU Portable.NET (for more information, see *http://www.southern-storm.com.au/portable_net.html*) and Mono (see *http://www.go-mono.com*). .NET is thus a multilanguage and multiplatform architecture.

---

* You can download "The Shared Source CLI 1.0 Release" from Microsoft. The CLR is submitted to ECMA as the Common Language Infrastructure (CLI).

.NET Programming

Now that you know what .NET is all about, let's talk about programming for the .NET environment. This chapter presents the common programming model that .NET provides, the core languages and features that .NET supports, and language integration—how you can take advantage of object-oriented features even across different languages that target the CLR.

Common Programming Model

Without the .NET Framework, programmers must choose from a wealth of APIs or libraries that support system services. For example, if you want to write GUI applications on Windows, you have a slew of options from which to choose, including the Win32 API, MFC, ATL, VB, and so on. Once you've chosen the library, you have to learn how to use the structures, classes, functions, interfaces, and so forth that the library provides. Unfortunately, this knowledge doesn't transfer directly into a different environment. For instance, there's a big difference between the code to manage IO in MFC and the code to manage IO in VB.

One of the goals of the .NET Framework is to bring commonality to application development by providing a framework of common classes to developers who are using compilers that generate IL. This set of classes, known as the Base Class Library (BCL), is extremely helpful: if you know how to take advantage of IO functionality in .NET using your favorite language, you can easily port that code to another language. This is possible because the namespaces, classes, methods, and so forth are equally accessible in all languages. For example, you can output a line of text to the console the same way across all .NET languages by using the WriteLine() method of the Console object, as we have seen elsewhere in this book. This consistent framework requires less development training and enables higher programmer productivity.

Since a full discussion of the entire set of classes in the .NET BCL is beyond the scope of this book (see O'Reilly's In a Nutshell .NET series), we talk about the System.Object class and present the major namespaces in the .NET Framework, opening the doors for you to step into this world.

System.Object

Every type in .NET is an object, meaning that it must derive directly or indirectly from the Object class. If you don't specify a base class when you define a class, the compiler will inject this requirement into the IL code. The Object class supports a commonality that all .NET classes inherit and, thus, automatically provide to their consumers. The Object class exposes the public methods listed in Table 3-1, which you can invoke on any given .NET object at runtime.

Table 3-1. Public methods of the Object class

Methods	Description
Equals( )	Compares two objects and determines whether they are equivalent (having the same content).
ReferenceEquals( )	Compares two object references and determines whether they are referring to the same object in memory.
GetHashCode( )	Gets the object's hash code. Hash codes are used as an added mechanism for determining object uniqueness at runtime. For instance, if you want your objects to be used as keys in a hashtable, you must override this function and provide a unique hash value for each instance of your class.
GetType( )	Obtains the object's type at runtime. Once you have obtained the object's type, you can obtain everything about that type using the Reflection API, as explained in Chapter 2.
ToString( )	Gets a string representation of the object. Often used for debugging purposes, this method spits out the fully qualified class name by default.

Examine the following program, which illustrates the use of all these methods:

```
using System;
namespace Cpm
{
  class CPModel
  {
    public static void Main( )
    {
      CPModel c = new CPModel( );

      // Test for self equivalence.
      Console.WriteLine("Equivalence:\t" +
        c.Equals(c)
      );
```

```
      // Get the hash code from this object.
      Console.WriteLine("Object hash:\t" +
        c.GetHashCode( )
      );

      // Use the type to obtain method information.
      Console.WriteLine("Object method:\t" +
        c.GetType( ).GetMethods( )[1]
      );

      // Convert the object to a string.
      Console.WriteLine("String representation:\t" +
        c.ToString( )
      );
    }
  }
}
```

If you compile and run this C# program, you get the following output:

```
Equivalence:    True
Object hash:    2
Object method:  Boolean Equals(System.Object)
Object dump:    Cpm.CPModel
```

The boldface line displays the second method of the CPModel class. If you look back at the program's code, you'll see that we use the GetType() method to get the type, and then we use the GetMethods() method to retrieve the array of methods supported by this type. From this array, we pull off the second method, which happens to be Equals( ), a method that's implemented by System.Object.

As you can see, the System.Object class provides a mechanism for runtime type identification, equivalence, and inspection for all .NET objects.

Major Namespaces

Table 3-2 is a short list of important namespaces and classes in the .NET Framework that provide support for almost any application that you will develop. These are the namespaces that you'll find yourself using again and again the more you develop .NET applications. For more information, consult MSDN Online or your SDK documentation, as a detailed discussion of these namespaces and classes is beyond the scope of this book.

Table 3-2. Important .NET namespaces and classes

Namespace	Description
System	Includes basic classes almost every program will use. Some simple classes that belong in this namespace are Object, Char, String, Array, and Exception. This namespace also includes more advanced classes such as GC and AppDomain.
System.IO	Provides a set of classes to support synchronous and asynchronous IO manipulation for data streams. Also provides classes that allow you to manipulate the file system, such as creating, managing, and deleting files and directories. Some of these classes are FileStream, MemoryStream, Path, and Directory.
System.Collections	Includes a set of classes that allow you to manage collections of objects. Some of these classes are ArrayList, DictionaryBase, Hashtable, Queue, and Stack.
System.Threading	Includes a set of classes that support multithreaded programming. Some of these classes are Thread, ThreadPool, Mutex, and AutoResetEvent.
System.Reflection	Includes a set of classes that support dynamic binding and type inspection. Some of these classes are Assembly, Module, and MethodInfo.
System.Security	Includes a set of classes and child namespaces that provide security support. The interesting child namespaces include Cryptography, Permissions, Policy, and Principal.
System.Net	Includes a set of classes and child namespaces that provide support for network programming. Some of these classes are IPAddress, Dns, and HttpWebRequest.
System.Data	Contains classes for ADO.NET. See Chapter 5.
System.Web.Services	Contains classes for XML web services. See Chapter 6.
System.Web.UI	Contains classes for ASP.NET web pages. See Chapter 7.
System.Windows.Forms	Contains classes for Windows user interface applications. See Chapter 8.

Keep in mind that if you know how to use any of the classes in these namespaces, you can write the code to take advantage of them in any language that targets the CLR, because the class and method names remain consistent across all .NET languages.

Core Features and Languages

Since one of .NET's goals is to support a common paradigm for application programming, it must specify and utilize programming concepts consistently. In this section, we will examine four core Microsoft .NET languages, including Managed C++, VB.NET, C#, and J#, and several core programming concepts that all .NET languages support, including:

Namespace
  Mitigates name collisions.

Interface
  Specifies the methods and properties that must be implemented by objects that expose the interface.

Encapsulation

> In object-oriented languages, allows a class to combine all its data and behavior.

Inheritance

> Allows a class to inherit from a parent class so that it can reuse rich functionality that the parent class has implemented, thus reducing development effort and programming errors.

Polymorphism

> Permits developers to specify or implement behaviors in a base class that can be overridden by a derived class. This is a very powerful feature because it allows developers to select the correct behavior based on the referenced runtime object.

Exception handling

> Allows us to write easier-to-understand code because it allows us to capture all errors in a common, understandable pattern—totally opposite to that of nine levels of nested conditional blocks.

Although this is not a complete list of concepts that .NET supports, it includes all the major .NET concepts that we want to cover in this section. We will show you examples of all these features in Managed C++, VB.NET, C#, and J#. These concepts are nothing new: we're merely demonstrating how they're represented in all core Microsoft .NET languages.

Before we start, you should understand first what our examples will accomplish. First, we will create a namespace, called Lang, that encapsulates an interface, ISteering. Then we will create two classes: Vehicle, which is an abstract base class that implements ISteering, and Car, which is a derivative of Vehicle. We will support an entry point that instantiates and uses Car within a try block. We will unveil other details as we work through the examples.

Managed C++ Code

Managed C++ is Microsoft's implementation of the C++ programming language with some newly added keywords and features to support .NET programming. This allows you to use C++ to develop managed objects, which are objects that run in the CLR. Using Managed C++, you can obtain the

performance* that is inherent in C++ programs, and at the same time, you can also take advantage of CLR features.†

Now let's look at an example that includes all the concepts we want to examine. As you can see in the following code listing, we start off creating a new namespace, Lang, which envelops everything except main( ). With the exception of the first line and special keywords, the code listing conforms perfectly to the C++ standard:

```
#using <mscorlib.dll>
using namespace System;

namespace Lang
{
```

Next, we specify an interface, called ISteering. If you are a C++ programmer, you will immediately notice that there are two new keywords in the following code listing, __gc and __interface. The new keyword __interface allows you to declare an interface, which is basically equivalent to an abstract base class in C++. In other words, the two method prototypes are specified, but not implemented here. The class that implements this interface provides the implementation for these methods:

```
__gc __interface ISteering
{
  void TurnLeft( );
  void TurnRight( );
};
```

If you are a COM programmer, you know that in COM you have to manage the lifetimes of your objects and components yourself. Even worse, you also have to rely on your clients to negotiate and interoperate correctly with your COM components; otherwise, extant references will never be reclaimed. Managed C++ removes this problem by adding a new keyword, __gc that tells the CLR to garbage-collect the references to your interface when they are no longer in use. Aside from these two keywords, the previous code listing requires no other explanation for programmers who have experience with C-like languages.

Now that we have an interface, let's implement it. The following code listing is a Managed C++ class (as indicated by the __gc) that implements our

---

* You can easily mix managed and unmanaged code in C++ programs. The unmanaged code will perform better. See this chapter's example code, which you can download from *http://www.oreilly.com/catalog/dotnetfrmess3/*.

† However, if you look carefully at the features and new keywords (__abstract, __box, __delegate, __gc, __nogc, __pin, etc.) that have been added to Microsoft C++, we doubt that you'll want to use Managed C++ to write new code for the CLR, especially when you have C#.

ISteering interface. One thing to notice is that this class is an abstract base class because the ApplyBrakes() method is a pure virtual function, as indicated by the =0 syntax. Vehicle doesn't provide the implementation for this method, but its derived class must supply the implementation:

```
__gc class Vehicle : public ISteering
{
  public:

  void TurnLeft()
  {
    Console::WriteLine("Vehicle turns left.");
  }

  void TurnRight()
  {
    Console::WriteLine("Vehicle turns right.");
  }

  virtual void ApplyBrakes() = 0;
};
```

Since Vehicle is an abstract base class and can't be instantiated, we need to provide a Vehicle derivative, which we will call Car. As you can see in the following listing, everything about the class is C++, with the exception of the keyword __gc. Note that the ApplyBrakes() function first dumps a text message to the console and then immediately creates and throws an exception, notifying an exception handler that there has been a brake failure.

```
__gc class Car : public Vehicle
{
  public:

  void ApplyBrakes()
  {
    Console::WriteLine("Car trying to stop.");

    throw new Exception ("Brake failure!");
  }
};

} // This brace ends the Lang namespace.
```

What is special here is that the Exception class is a part of the .NET Framework, specifically belonging to the System namespace. This is great because this class works exactly the same way in all languages and there's no longer a need to invent your own exception hierarchy.

Two important types that derive from Exception are SystemException (framework and Windows errors) and ApplicationException (your application's errors). If you create your own exception classes, they should derive from ApplicationException. .NET conventions also suggest throwing ApplicationException objects for application-specific errors.

Now that we have a concrete class, we can write the main() function to test our Car class. Notice that we have added a try block that encapsulates the bulk of our code so that we can handle any exceptions in the catch block. Looking carefully at the following code listing, you'll see that we've instantiated a new Car on the managed heap, but we've actually referred to this Car instance using a Vehicle pointer. Next, we tell the vehicle to TurnLeft()— there's no surprise here because we've implemented this method in Vehicle. However, in the following statement, we tell the Vehicle that we're applying the brakes, but ApplyBrakes() is not implemented in Vehicle. Since this is a virtual method, the correct vptr and vtbl* will be used, resulting in a call to Car::ApplyBrakes(). Of course Car::ApplyBrakes() will throw an exception, putting us into the catch block. Inside the catch block, we convert the caught exception into a string and dump it out to the console. We can do this because Exception is a class in the .NET Framework and all classes in the framework must derive from System.Object, which implements a rudimentary ToString() function to convert any object into a string:

```
void main( )
{
  try
  {
    Lang::Vehicle *pV = 0;   // Namespace qualifier
    pV = new Lang::Car( );   // pV refers to a car
    pV->TurnLeft( );         // Interface usage
    pV->ApplyBrakes( );      // Polymorphism in action
  }
  catch(Exception *pe)
  {
    Console::WriteLine(pe->ToString( ));
  }
}
```

Notice that you don't have to deallocate your objects on the managed heap when you've finished using them, because the garbage collector will do that for you in .NET.

---

* Many C++ compilers use vtbls (a vtbl is a table of function pointers) and vptrs (a vptr is a pointer to the vtbl) to support dynamic binding or polymorphism.

Although this is a simple example, we have used Managed C++ to illustrate all major object-oriented programming concepts, including namespaces, interfaces, encapsulation, inheritance, polymorphism, and exception handling. Next, we demonstrate that you can translate this code into any other .NET language because they all support these concepts. Specifically, we'll show you this same example in VB.NET, C#, J#, and IL, just to prove that these concepts can be represented the same way in all languages that targets the CLR.

VB.NET Code

Microsoft has revamped VB and added full features for object-oriented programming. The new VB language, Visual Basic .NET (or VB.NET), allows you to do all that you can do with VB, albeit much more easily. If you are a VB programmer with knowledge of other object-oriented languages, such as C++ or Smalltalk, then you will love the new syntax that comes along with VB.NET. If you are a VB programmer without knowledge of other object-oriented languages, you will be surprised by the new VB.NET syntax at first, but you will realize that the new syntax simplifies your life as a programmer.*

In addition to the VB-style Rapid Application Development (RAD) support, VB.NET is a modernized language that gives you full access to the .NET Framework. The VB.NET compiler generates metadata and IL code, making the language an equal citizen to that of C# or Managed C++. Unlike VB versions prior to VB6, there will be no interpreter in VB.NET, so there should be no violent arguments about performance drawbacks of VB versus another language.

Perhaps the most potent feature is that now you can write interfaces and classes that look very similar to those written in other .NET languages. The new syntax allows you to inherit from base classes, implement interfaces, override virtual functions, create an abstract base class, and so forth. In addition, it also supports exception handling exactly as does C# and Managed C++, making error handling much easier. Finally, VB.NET ships with a command-line compiler, *vbc.exe*, introduced in Chapter 2.

Let's see how to translate the previous Managed C++ program into VB.NET so that you can see the striking conceptual resemblance. First, we'll start by defining a namespace called Lang, shown here in bold:

```
Imports System

Namespace Lang
```

---

* To learn more about VB.NET, see O'Reilly's *VB.NET Language in a Nutshell*, Second Edition, by Steven Roman, PhD., Ron Petrusha, and Paul Lomax, or *Programming Visual Basic .NET*, Second Edition, by Jesse Liberty.

Next, we specify the ISteering interface, which is easy to do in VB.NET since the syntax is very straightforward, especially when you compare it with Managed C++. In the following code listing, you'll notice that instead of using opening and closing braces as in Managed C++, you start the interface definition by using the appropriate VB.NET keyword, Interface, and end it by prefixing the associated keyword with the word End. This is just normal VB-style syntax and shouldn't surprise any VB programmer:

```
Interface ISteering
    Sub TurnLeft( )
    Sub TurnRight( )
End Interface
```

With our interface specified, we can now implement it. Since our Vehicle class is an abstract base class, we must add the MustInherit keyword when we define it, explicitly telling the VB.NET compiler that this class cannot be instantiated. In VB.NET, the Class keyword allows you to define a class, and the Implements keyword allows you implement an interface. Another thing that you should be aware of is that ApplyBrakes( ) is not implemented in this class, and we have appropriately signaled this to the VB.NET compiler by using the MustOverride keyword:

```
MustInherit Class Vehicle
    Implements ISteering

    Public Sub TurnLeft( ) Implements ISteering.TurnLeft
        Console.WriteLine("Vehicle turns left.")
    End Sub

    Public Sub TurnRight( ) Implements ISteering.TurnRight
        Console.WriteLine("Vehicle turn right.")
    End Sub

    Public MustOverride Sub ApplyBrakes( )

End Class
```

As far as language differences go, you must explicitly describe the access (i.e., public, private, and so forth) for each method separately. This is different from C++ because all members take on the previously defined access type.

Now we are ready to translate the concrete Car class. In VB.NET, you can derive from a base class by using the Inherits keyword, as shown in the following code. Since we have said that ApplyBrakes( ) must be overridden, we provide its implementation here. Again, notice that we're throwing an exception:

```
Class Car
    Inherits Vehicle
```

```
    Public Overrides Sub ApplyBrakes()
        Console.WriteLine("Car trying to stop.")
        throw new Exception("Brake failure!")
    End Sub

End Class

End Namespace
```

Now that we have all the pieces in place, let's define a module with an entry point, Main(), that the CLR will execute. In Main(), you'll notice that we're handling exceptions exactly as we did in the Managed C++ example. You should also note that this code demonstrates the use of polymorphism because we first create a Vehicle reference that refers to a Car object at runtime. We tell the Vehicle to ApplyBrakes(), but since the Vehicle happens to be referring to a Car, the object that is stopping is the target Car object:

```
Public Module Driver

    Sub Main()

        Try

            Dim v As Lang.Vehicle  ' namespace qualifier
            v = New Lang.Car        ' v refers to a car
            v.TurnLeft()            ' interface usage
            v.ApplyBrakes()         ' polymorphism in action

        Catch e As Exception

            Console.WriteLine(e.ToString())

        End Try

    End Sub

End Module
```

This simple program demonstrates that we can take advantage of .NET object-oriented features using VB.NET. Having seen this example, you should see that VB.NET is very object oriented, with features that map directly to those of Managed C++ and other .NET languages.

C# Code

As you've just seen, VB.NET is a breeze compared to Managed C++, but VB.NET is not the only simple language in .NET—C# is also amazingly simple. Developed from the ground up, C# supports all the object-oriented features in .NET. It maps so closely to the Java and C++ languages that if

you have experience with either of these languages, you can pick up C# and be productive with it immediately.

Microsoft has developed many tools using C#; in fact, most of the components in Visual Studio .NET and the .NET class libraries were developed using C#. Microsoft is using C# extensively, and we think that C# is here to stay.*

Having said that, let's translate our previous program into C# and illustrate all the features we want to see. Again, we start by defining a namespace. As you can see, the syntax for C# maps really closely to that of Managed C++:

```
using System;

namespace Lang
{
```

Following is the IStreering interface specification in C#. Since C# was developed from scratch, we don't need to add any funny keywords like __gc and __interface, as we did in the Managed C++ version of this program:

```
interface ISteering
{
  void TurnLeft( );
  void TurnRight( );
}
```

Having defined our interface, we can now implement it in the abstract Vehicle class. Unlike Managed C++ but similar to VB.NET, C# requires that you explicitly notify the C# compiler that the Vehicle class is an abstract base class by using the abstract keyword. Since ApplyBrakes( ) is an abstract method—meaning that this class doesn't supply its implementation—you must make the class abstract, otherwise the C# compiler will barf at you. Put another way, you must explicitly signal to the C# compiler the features you want, including abstract, public, private, and so forth, each time you define a class, method, property, and so on:

```
abstract class Vehicle : ISteering
{
  public void TurnLeft( )
  {
    Console.WriteLine("Vehicle turns left.");
  }
```

---

* To learn more about C#, check out O'Reilly's *C# Essentials*, Second Edition, by Ben Albahari, Peter Drayton, and Brad Merrill; the forthcoming *C# in a Nutshell*, Second Edition, by Peter Drayton, Ben Albahari, and Ted Neward; and *Programming C#*, Third Edition, by Jesse Liberty.

```
  public void TurnRight( )
  {
    Console.WriteLine("Vehicle turn right.");
  }

  public abstract void ApplyBrakes( );
}
```

Here's our Car class that derives from Vehicle and overrides the ApplyBrakes() method declared in Vehicle. Note that we are explicitly telling the C# compiler that we are indeed overriding a method previously specified in the inheritance chain. You must add the override modifier, or ApplyBrakes() will hide the one in the parent class. Otherwise, we are also throwing the same exception as before:

```
class Car : Vehicle
{
  public override void ApplyBrakes( )
  {
    Console.WriteLine("Car trying to stop.");
    throw new Exception("Brake failure!");
  }
}

} // This brace ends the Lang namespace.
```

Finally, here's a class that encapsulates an entry point for the CLR to invoke. If you look at this code carefully, you'll see that it maps directly to the code in both Managed C++ and VB.NET:

```
class Drive
{
  public static void Main( )
  {
    try
    {
      Lang.Vehicle v = null;   // Namespace qualifier
      v = new Lang.Car( );     // v refers to a car
      v.TurnLeft( );           // Interface usage
      v.ApplyBrakes( );        // Polymorphism in action
    }
    catch(Exception e)
    {
      Console.WriteLine(e.ToString( ));
    }
  }
}
```

There are two other interesting things to note about C#. First, unlike C++ but similar to Java, C# doesn't use header files.* Second, the C# compiler generates XML documentation for you if you use XML comments in your code. To take advantage of this feature, start your XML comments with three slashes, as in the following examples:

```
/// <summary>Vehicle Class</summary>
/// <remarks>
///    This class is an abstract class that must be
///    overridden by derived classes.
/// </remarks>
abstract class Vehicle : ISteering
{
  /// <summary>Add juice to the vehicle.</summary>
  /// <param name="gallons">
  ///    Number of gallons added.
  /// </param>
  /// <return>Whether the tank is full.</return>
  public bool FillUp(int gallons)
  {
    return true;
  }
}
```

These are simple examples using the predefined tags that the C# compiler understands. You can also use your own XML tags in XML comments, as long as your resulting XML is well formed. Given that you have a source code file with XML comments, you can automatically generate an XML-formatted reference document by using the C# compiler's /doc: option, as follows:

```
csc /doc:doc.xml mylangdoc.cs
```

Although we didn't specify the types of our parameters in the XML comments shown previously, the C# compiler will detect the correct types and add the fully qualified types into the generated XML document. For example, the following generated XML listing corresponds to the XML comments for the FillUp( ) method. Notice that the C# compiler added System.Int32 into the generated XML document:

```
<member name="M:Lang.Vehicle.FillUp(System.Int32)">
  <summary>Add juice to the vehicle.</summary>
  <param name="gallons">
    Number of gallons added.
  </param>
  <return>Whether the tank is full.</return>
</member>
```

---

* If you've never used C++, a header file is optional and usually contains class and type declarations. The implementation for these classes is usually stored in source files.

Now that you have the generated XML document, you can write your own XSL document to translate the XML into any visual representation you prefer.

J# Code

Shipped with .NET Framework 1.1 (and thus with Visual Studio .NET 2003), J# is a Java language that targets the CLR. For completeness, here's the same program in J#, demonstrating that J# also supports the same object-oriented features that we've been illustrating. We simply took the preceding C# program and made a few minor changes, resulting in the J# program that we are about to examine.

Let's first look at the namespace declaration. Instead of using the keyword namespace, Java uses the keyword package, which is conceptually equivalent to the namespace concept we've been observing, since the purpose of a package is to prevent name conflicts:

```
package Lang;

import System.Console;
```

The interface specification for ISteering in J# looks exactly equivalent to the one written in C#:

```
interface ISteering
{
  void TurnLeft( );
  void TurnRight( );
}
```

For the Vehicle class, there are two changes, which are shown in bold. First, the keyword implements is used to declare that a class implements one or more interfaces. Second, since Java requires thrown exceptions to be explicitly declared within the method signature, we've added this declaration in the ApplyBrakes( ) method:

```
abstract class Vehicle implements ISteering
{
  public void TurnLeft( )
  {
    Console.WriteLine("Vehicle turns left.");
  }

  public void TurnRight( )
  {
    Console.WriteLine("Vehicle turn right.");
  }

  public abstract void ApplyBrakes( ) throws Exception;
}
```

There are also two changes for the Car class, which are shown in bold. The extends keyword is used to declare that a class derives from (or extends) another class. The declaration for ApplyBrakes( ) must match it's parents signature, so we've explicitly indicated that an exception may be thrown from this method, as shown in bold:

```
// extends - used to derive from a base class.
class Car extends Vehicle
{
  public void ApplyBrakes( ) throws Exception
  {
    Console.WriteLine("Car trying to stop.");
    throw new Exception("Brake failure!");
  }
}
```

Finally, we've made one minor change in the Drive class: we simply changed Main( ) to main( ), as required by J#:

```
class Drive
{
  public static void main( )
  {
    try
    {
      Lang.Vehicle v = null;   // Namespace qualifer
      v = new Lang.Car( );     // v refers to a car
      v.TurnLeft( );           // Interface usage
      v.ApplyBrakes( );        // Polymorphism in action
    }
    catch(Exception e)
    {
      Console.WriteLine(e.ToString( ));
    }
  }
}
```

Like C#, J# supports all the object-oriented concepts we've been studying. Also, J# and C# are syntactically very similar.

Intermediate Language (IL) Code

Since all languages compile to IL, let's examine the IL code for the program that we've been studying. As explained in Chapter 2, IL is a set of stack-based instructions that supports an exhaustive list of popular object-oriented features, including the ones that we've already examined in this chapter. It is an intermediary step, gluing .NET applications to the CLR.

Let's start by looking at the namespace declaration. Notice the `.namespace` IL declaration allows us to create our Lang namespace. Similar to C#, IL uses opening and closing braces:

```
.namespace Lang
{
```

Now for the IStreering interface. In IL, any type that is to be managed by the CLR must be declared using the `.class` IL declaration. Since the CLR must manage the references to an interface, you must use the `.class` IL declaration to specify an interface in IL, as shown in the following code listing:

```
.class interface private abstract auto ansi ISteering
{
  .method public hidebysig newslot virtual abstract
          instance void TurnLeft( ) cil managed
  {
  } // End of method ISteering::TurnLeft

  .method public hidebysig newslot virtual abstract
          instance void TurnRight( ) cil managed
  {
  } // End of method ISteering::TurnRight

} // End of class ISteering
```

In addition, you must insert two special IL attributes:

interface
>   Signals that the current type definition is an interface specification.

abstract
>   Signals that there will be no method implementations in this definition and that the implementer of this interface must provide the method implementations for all methods defined in this interface.

Other attributes shown in this definition that aren't necessarily needed to specify an interface in IL include the following:

private
>   Because we haven't provided the visibility of our interface definition in C#, the generated IL code shown here adds the private IL attribute to this interface definition. This means that this particular interface is visible only within the current assembly and no other external assembly can see it.

auto
>   Tells the CLR to perform automatic layout of this type at runtime.

ansi
>   Tells the CLR to use ANSI string buffers to marshal data across managed and unmanaged boundaries.

Now you know how to specify an interface in IL. Before we proceed further, let's briefly look at the attributes in the .method declarations—at least the attributes that we haven't examined, including:

newslot

Tells the JIT compiler to reserve a new slot in the type's vtbl, which will be used by the CLR at runtime to resolve virtual-method invocations.

instance

Tells the CLR that this method is an instance or object-level method, as opposed to a static or class-level method.

Having specified the ISteering interface in IL, let's implement it in our Vehicle class. As you can see in the following code fragment, there's no surprise. We extend the System.Object class (indicated by the extends keyword) and implement Lang.ISteering (as indicated by the implements keyword):

```
.class private abstract auto ansi beforefieldinit Vehicle
       extends [mscorlib]System.Object
       implements Lang.ISteering
{
  .method public hidebysig newslot final virtual
          instance void TurnLeft() cil managed
  {
    // IL code omitted for clarity
  } // End of method Vehicle::TurnLeft

  .method public hidebysig newslot final virtual
          instance void TurnRight() cil managed
  {
    // IL code omitted for clarity
  } // End of method Vehicle::TurnRight

  .method public hidebysig newslot virtual abstract
          instance void ApplyBrakes() cil managed
  {
  } // End of method Vehicle::ApplyBrakes

  // .ctor omitted for clarity

} // End of class Vehicle
```

Notice also that this class is an abstract class and that the ApplyBrakes() method is an abstract method, similar to what we've seen in the previous examples. Another thing to note is the final IL attribute in the .method declarations for both TurnLeft() and TurnRight(). This IL attribute specifies that these methods can no longer be overridden by subclasses of Vehicle. Having seen all these attributes, you should realize that everything in IL is explicitly declared so that all components of the CLR can take advantage of this information to manage your types at runtime.

Now let's look at the Car class that derives from the Vehicle class. You'll notice that in the ApplyBrakes() method implementation, the newobj instance IL instruction creates a new instance of the Exception class. Next, the throw IL instruction immediately raises the exception object just created:

```
.class private auto ansi beforefieldinit Car
       extends Lang.Vehicle
{
   .method public hidebysig virtual instance void
          ApplyBrakes( ) cil managed
   {
      // IL code omitted for clarity
      newobj instance void
         [mscorlib]System.Exception::.ctor(class System.String)
      throw

   } // End of method Car::ApplyBrakes

   // .ctor omitted for clarity

} // End of class Car

} // End of namespace Lang
```

Finally, let's look at our Main() function, which is part of the Drive class. We've removed most of the IL code—which you've already learned—from this function to make the following code easier to read, but we've kept the important elements that must be examined. First, the .locals directive identifies all the local variables for the Main() function. Second, you can see that IL also supports exception handling through the .try instruction. In both the .try and catch blocks, notice that there is a leave.s instruction that forces execution to jump to the IL instruction on line IL_0024, thus leaving both the .try and catch blocks:

```
.class private auto ansi beforefieldinit Drive
       extends [mscorlib]System.Object
{
   .method public hidebysig static void Main( ) cil managed
   {
      .entrypoint
      // Code size       37 (0x25)
      .maxstack  1

      .locals (class Lang.Vehicle V_0,
               class [mscorlib]System.Exception V_1)
      .try
      {
         // IL code omitted for clarity
         leave.s    IL_0024
      } // End .try
      catch [mscorlib]System.Exception
      {
```

```
        // IL code omitted for clarity
        leave.s    IL_0024
    }  // End handler
    IL_0024:  ret
 }  // End of method Drive::Main

    // .ctor omitted for clarity

 }  // End of class Drive
```

As you can see, all the major concepts that we've examined apply intrinsi-cally to IL. Since you've seen Managed C++, VB.NET, C#, J#, and IL code that support these features, we won't attempt to further convince you that all these features work in other languages that target the CLR.

Language Integration

In the previous section, we saw that you can take advantage of .NET object-oriented concepts in any .NET language. In this section, we show that you can take advantage of *language integration*—the ability to derive a class from a base that is specified in a totally different language; to catch exceptions thrown by code written in a different language; or to take advantage of poly-morphism across different languages, and so forth.

Before we discuss the examples in this section, let's first understand what we want to accomplish (see Figure 3-1). We will first use Managed C++ to develop a Vehicle class that is an abstract base class. The Vehicle class exposes three polymorphic methods, including TurnLeft(), TurnRight(), and ApplyBrakes(). We will then use VB.NET to develop a Car class that derives from Vehicle and overrides these three virtual methods. In addition, we will use C# to develop the Plane class that derives from Vehicle and overrides these three virtual methods.

In the upcoming code example, we can tell a Vehicle to TurnLeft() or TurnRight(), but what turns left or right depends on the target object, whether a Car or a Plane. Unlike the examples in the previous section, the examples here illustrate that we can inherit classes and call virtual functions from ones that are defined in another language. In addition, we will demon-strate in our test program that exception handling works across different languages.

Vehicle Class in Managed C++

Let's use Managed C++ to develop the Vehicle class, which is an abstract base class because ApplyBrakes() is a pure virtual function. Vehicle implements the

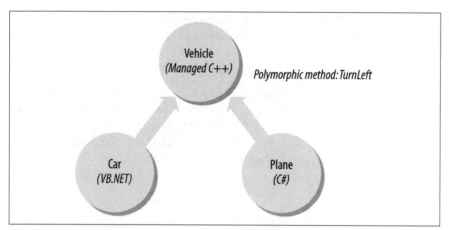

Figure 3-1. Polymorphism across languages

ISteering interface to support turning left and turning right. Since the ApplyBrakes() function is a pure virtual function, any concrete derivative of Vehicle must implement this method:

```cpp
#using <mscorlib.dll>
using namespace System;

public __gc __interface ISteering
{
  void TurnLeft();
  void TurnRight();
};

public __gc class Vehicle : public ISteering
{
  public:

    virtual void TurnLeft()
    {
      Console::WriteLine("Vehicle turns left.");
    }

    virtual void TurnRight()
    {
      Console::WriteLine("Vehicle turns right.");
    }

    virtual void ApplyBrakes() = 0;
};
```

Given this abstract base class, we can create a DLL that hosts this definition. The first command here shows how we use the Managed C++ compiler to compile (as indicated by the /c option) the *vehicle.cpp* file, which

contains the previous code. The second command shows how we use the C++ linker to create a DLL with metadata and IL code:

```
cl /CLR /c vehicle.cpp
link -dll /out:vehicle.dll vehicle.obj
```

Given just a few lines of Managed C++ code, we can build a DLL that can be used by another component. Note that there is no need to provide code for IUnknown, DllGetClassObject( ), DllCanUnloadNow( ), DllRegisterServer( ), DllUnregisterServer( ), and so forth. In the old days, you had to provide code for these functions and interfaces for legacy COM DLLs.

Car Class in VB.NET

Given this abstract Vehicle class, the Car class can derive from it and provide the implementation for the three virtual methods defined by Vehicle. In the following code, note that we've overridden and provided the implementation for TurnLeft( ), TurnRight( ), and ApplyBrakes( ). The ApplyBrakes( ) method is special in that it throws an exception, which will be caught by code written in J#, as we'll see later:

```
Imports System

Public Class Car
  Inherits Vehicle

  Overrides Public Sub TurnLeft( )
    Console.WriteLine("Car turns left.")
  End Sub

  Overrides Public Sub TurnRight( )
    Console.WriteLine("Car turns right.")
  End Sub

  Overrides Public Sub ApplyBrakes( )
    Console.WriteLine("Car trying to stop.")
    throw new Exception("Brake failure!")
  End Sub

End Class
```

With this code, we can build a DLL using the command-line VB.NET compiler, as follows:

```
vbc /r:vehicle.dll /t:library /out:car.dll car.vb
```

Since we want the VB.NET compiler to generate a DLL, we must signal this by using the /t:library option. Also, since Car derives from Vehicle, the VB.NET compiler must resolve the references to Vehicle. We can tell the VB.NET compiler the location of external references using the /r: option. It

is important to note that you don't need to have the source code for the vehicle DLL to reuse its code because all type information can be obtained from any .NET assembly. In addition, you should note that from this example, we have proven that you can derive a VB.NET class from a Managed C++ class.

Plane Class in C#

Now let's use C# to develop the Plane class, which derives from the Vehicle class written in Managed C++. Similar to the Car class, the Plane class implements the three virtual functions from the Vehicle class. Unlike the Car class, though, the ApplyBrakes() method of this class doesn't throw an exception:

```
using System;

public class Plane : Vehicle
{
  override public void TurnLeft()
  {
    Console.WriteLine("Plane turns left.");
  }

  override public void TurnRight()
  {
    Console.WriteLine("Plane turns right.");
  }

  override public void ApplyBrakes()
  {
    Console.WriteLine("Air brakes being used.");
  }
}
```

You can build a DLL from this code using the following command:

```
csc /r:vehicle.dll /t:library /out:plane.dll plane.cs
```

Notice that we have used the /r: option to tell the C# compiler that Vehicle is defined in *vehicle.dll*.

Test Driver in J#

Having developed *vehicle.dll*, *car.dll*, and *plane.dll*, we are now ready to demonstrate that polymorphism and exception handling work across different languages. Written in J#, the next code listing contains a main() method with a Vehicle reference and an exception handler.

Inside the try block, we first instantiate a Plane class and refer to this instance using the local Vehicle reference. Instead of telling the Plane to TurnLeft( ) or ApplyBrakes( ), we tell the Vehicle to do so. Similarly, we instantiate a Car and refer to this instance using the local Vehicle reference. Again, instead of telling the Car to TurnLeft( ) or ApplyBrakes( ), we tell the Vehicle to do so. In both cases, we tell the Vehicle either to TurnLeft( ) or ApplyBrakes( ), but the actual vehicle that employs TurnLeft( ) or ApplyBrakes( ) is the Plane instance in the first case and the Car instance in the second case; that's polymorphism, and it works across languages.

You should note that the second call to ApplyBrakes( ) would cause an exception because we threw an exception from Car's ApplyBrakes( ). Although Car's ApplyBrakes( ) was written using VB.NET, we could still catch the exception that it's throwing in J#, proving that exception handling works across languages:

```
class TestDrive
{
  public static void main( )
  {
    Vehicle v = null;  // Vehicle reference

    try
    {
      Plane p = new Plane( );
      v = p;
      v.TurnLeft( );
      v.ApplyBrakes( );

      Car c = new Car( );
      v = c;
      v.TurnLeft( );
      v.ApplyBrakes( );  // Exception
    }
    catch(System.Exception e)
    {
      System.Console.WriteLine(e.ToString( ));
    }

  }
}
```

If you want to test out these features, you can create an EXE using the following command:

```
vjc /r:vehicle.dll;car.dll;plane.dll /t:exe /out:drive.exe drive.jsl
```

Since we have used the Vehicle, Car, and Plane classes in this code, we must include references to *vehicle.dll*, *car.dll*, and *plane.dll*. And since we are building an EXE, we need to signal this to the J# compiler using the /t:exe

option. Once you have built this EXE and executed it, you get the following output:

```
Plane turns left.
Air brakes being used.
Car turns left.
Car trying to stop.
System.Exception: Brake failure!
   at Car.ApplyBrakes()
   at TestDrive.main()
```

As expected, the plane first turns left and then uses its air brakes. Then the car turns left, tries to stop, but can't, so it throws an exception that is caught in the main() method.

In this simple example, we have shown that you can now take advantage of inheritance, polymorphism, and exception handling across different languages that target the CLR.

Summary

We started this chapter by telling you that .NET provides a common programming model, which reduces the learning curve and increases productivity. Once you've learned how to do something using the classes in the .NET Framework, this knowledge will transfer to any .NET language. We then illustrated that we could write the same type of code, supporting major .NET features, in any given language that targets the CLR. Finally, we proved to you that .NET indeed supports language integration, which was never possible using Microsoft platforms and tools, prior to .NET.

Working with .NET Components

Having seen the language-integration examples in the previous chapter, you now know that all .NET assemblies are essentially binary components.* You can treat each .NET assembly as a component that you can plug into another component or application, without the need for source code, since all the metadata for the component is stored inside the .NET assembly. While you have to write a ton of plumbing code to build a component in COM, creating a component in .NET involves no extra work, as all .NET assemblies are components by nature.

In this chapter, we examine the more advanced topics, including component deployment, distributed components, and enterprise services, such as transaction management, object pooling, role-based security, and message queuing.

Deployment Options

For a simple program like *hello.exe* that we built in Chapter 2, deployment is easy: copy the assembly into a directory, and it's ready to run. When you want to uninstall it, remove the file from the directory. However, when you want to share components with other applications, you've got to do some work.

---

* Remember, as we explained in Chapter 1, we're using the term "component" as a binary, deployable unit, not as a COM class.

In COM, you must store activation and marshaling* information in the registry for components to interoperate; as a result, any COM developer can discuss at length the pain and suffering inherent in COM and the system registry. In .NET, the system registry is no longer necessary for component integration.

In the .NET environment, components can be *private*, meaning that they are unpublished and used by known clients, or *shared*, meaning that they are published and can be used by any clients. This section discusses several options for deploying private and shared components.

Private Components

If you have private components that are used only by specific clients, you have two deployment options. You can store the private components and the clients that use these components in the same directory, or you can store the components in a component-specific directory that the client can access. Since these clients use the exact private components that they referenced at build time, the CLR doesn't support version checking or enforce version policies on private components.

To install your applications in either of these cases, perform a simple xcopy of your application files from the source installation directory to the destination directory. When you want to remove the application, remove these directories. You don't have to write code to store information into the registry, so there's no worrying about whether you've missed inserting a registry setting for correct application execution. In addition, because nothing is stored in the registry, you don't have to worry about registry residues.

One-directory deployment

For simplicity, you can place supporting assemblies in the same directory as the client application. For example, in Chapter 3, we placed the vehicle, car, and plane assemblies in the same directory as the client application, *drive.exe*. Since both the client application and supporting assemblies are stored within the same directory, the CLR has no problem resolving this reference at runtime (i.e., find and load *plane.dll* and activate the Plane class). If you move any of the DLLs to a different directory (e.g., put *vehicle.dll* in

---

* Distributed applications require a communication layer to assemble and disassemble application data and network streams. This layer is formally known as a marshaler in Microsoft terminology. Assembling and disassembling an application-level protocol network buffer are formally known as marshaling and unmarshaling, respectively.

c:\temp), you will get an exception when you execute *drive.exe*. This is because the CLR looks for the *vehicle* assembly in the following order:

1. It looks for a file called *vehicle.dll* within the same directory as *drive.exe*.

2. Assuming that the CLR hasn't found *vehicle.dll*, it looks for *vehicle.dll* in a subdirectory with the same name as the assembly name (i.e., *vehicle*).

3. Assuming that the CLR hasn't found the vehicle assembly, it looks for a file called *vehicle.exe* in the same directory as *drive.exe*.

4. Assuming that the CLR hasn't found *vehicle.exe*, it looks for *vehicle.exe* in a subdirectory with the same name as the assembly name (i.e., *vehicle*).

5. At this point, the CLR throws and exception, indicating that it has failed to find the *vehicle* assembly.

The search for other supporting assemblies, such as *car* and *plane*, follows the same order. In steps 2 and 4, the CLR looks for the supporting assemblies in specific subdirectories. Let's investigate an example of this in the following section, which we've called multiple-directory deployment.

Multiple-directory deployment

Instead of storing all assemblies in the same directory as your client application, you can also use multiple, private subdirectories to segregate your assemblies so that they are easier to find and manage. For example, we will separate the vehicle, car, and plane assemblies into their own private directories, as shown in Figure 4-1. We will leave the *drive.exe* application in the top directory, *MultiDirectories*.

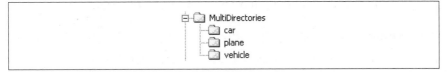

Figure 4-1. Multiple-directory tree of components

When you build the *vehicle* assembly, you don't have to do anything special, as it doesn't reference or use any third-party assemblies. However, when you build the car or plane assembly, you must refer to the correct vehicle component (i.e., the one in the *vehicle* directory). For example, to build the plane assembly successfully, you must explicitly refer to *vehicle.dll* using a specific or relative path, as shown in the following command (cd to the *plane* directory):

```
csc /r:..\vehicle\vehicle.dll /t:library /out:plane.dll plane.cs
```

You can build the car assembly the same way you build the plane assembly. To compile your client application, you must also refer to your dependencies using the correct paths (cd to the main directory, *MultiDirectories*, before you type this command all on one line):

```
vjc /r:vehicle\vehicle.dll;car\car.dll;plane\plane.dll
    /t:exe /out:drive.exe drive.jsl
```

Based on the previously discussed search algorithm, the CLR can find the supporting assemblies within the appropriate subdirectories.

Shared Components

Unlike application-private assemblies, *shared assemblies*—ones that can be used by any client application—must be published or registered in the system Global Assembly Cache (GAC). When you register your assemblies against the GAC, they act as system components, such as a system DLL that every process in the system can use. A prerequisite for GAC registration is that the component must possess originator and version information. In addition to other metadata, these two items allow multiple versions of the same component to be registered and executed on the same machine. Again, unlike COM, you don't have to store any information in the system registry for clients to use these shared assemblies.

There are three general steps to registering your shared assemblies against the GAC:

1. Use the shared named (*sn.exe*) utility to obtain a public/private key pair. This utility generates a random key pair for you and saves the key information in an output file—for example, *originator.key*.

2. Build your assembly with an assembly version number and the key information from *originator.key*.

3. Use the .NET Global Assembly Cache Utility (*gacutil.exe*) to register your assembly in the GAC. This assembly is now a shared assembly and can be used by any client.

The commands that we use in this section refer to relative paths, so if you're following along, make sure that you create the directory structure, as shown in Figure 4-2. The *vehicle, plane,* and *car* directories hold their appropriate assemblies, and the *key* directory holds the public/private key pair that we will generate in a moment. The *car-build* directory holds a car assembly with a modified build number, and the *car-revision* directory holds a car assembly with a modified revision number.

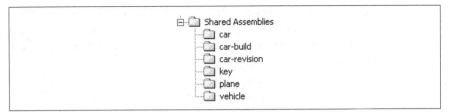

Figure 4-2. Directory structure for examples in this section

Generating a random key pair

We will perform the first step once and reuse the key pair for all shared assemblies that we build in this section. We're doing this for brevity only because you can use different key information for each assembly, or even each version, that you build. Here's how to generate a random key pair (be sure to issue this command in the *key* directory):

```
sn -k originator.key
```

The -k option generates a random key pair and saves the key information into the *originator.key* file. We will use this file as input when we build our shared assemblies. Let's now examine steps 2 and 3 of registering your shared assemblies against the GAC.

Making the vehicle component a shared assembly

In order to add version and key information into the vehicle component (developed using Managed C++), we need to make some minor modifications to *vehicle.cpp*, as follows:

```
#using<mscorlib.dll>
using namespace System;

using namespace System::Reflection;
[assembly:AssemblyVersion("1.0.0.0")];
[assembly:AssemblyKeyFile("..\\key\\originator.key")];

public _ _gc _ _interface ISteering
{
  void TurnLeft();
  void TurnRight();
};

public _ _gc class Vehicle : public ISteering
{
  public:

    virtual void TurnLeft()
    {
```

```
    Console::WriteLine("Vehicle turns left.");
  }

  virtual void TurnRight( )
  {
    Console::WriteLine("Vehicle turn right.");
  }

  virtual void ApplyBrakes( ) = 0;
};
```

The first boldface line indicates that we're using the Reflection namespace, which defines the attributes that the compiler will intercept to inject the correct information into our assembly manifest. (For a discussion of attributes, see "Attribute-Based Programming" later in this chapter.) We use the AssemblyVersion attribute to indicate the version of this assembly, and we use the AssemblyKeyFile attribute to indicate the file containing the key information that the compiler should use to derive the public-key-token value, to be revealed in a moment.

Once you've done this, you can build this assembly using the following commands, which you've seen before:

```
cl /CLR /c vehicle.cpp
link -dll /out:vehicle.dll vehicle.obj
```

After you've built the assembly, you can use the .NET GAC Utility to register this assembly into the GAC, as follows:

```
gacutil.exe /i vehicle.dll
```

Successful registration against the cache turns this component into a shared assembly. A version of this component is copied into the GAC so that even if you delete this file locally, you will still be able to run your client program.[*]

Making the car component a shared assembly

In order to add version and key information into the car component, we need to make some minor modifications to *car.vb*, as follows:

```
Imports System

Imports System.Reflection
<Assembly:AssemblyVersion("1.0.0.0")>
<assembly:AssemblyKeyFile("..\\key\\originator.key")>

Public Class Car
  Inherits Vehicle
```

---

[*] However, don't delete the file now because we need it to build the car and plane assemblies.

```
    Overrides Public Sub TurnLeft()
      Console.WriteLine("Car turns left.")
    End Sub

    Overrides Public Sub TurnRight()
      Console.WriteLine("Car turns right.")
    End Sub

    Overrides Public Sub ApplyBrakes()
      Console.WriteLine("Car trying to stop.")

      Console.WriteLine("ORIGINAL VERSION - 1.0.0.0.")

      throw new Exception("Brake failure!")
    End Sub

  End Class
```

Having done this, you can now build it with the following command:

```
vbc /r:..\vehicle\vehicle.dll /t:library /out:car.dll car.vb
```

Once you've built this component, you can register it against the GAC:

```
gacutil /i car.dll
```

At this point, you can delete *car.dll* in the local directory because it has been registered in the GAC.

Making the plane component a shared assembly

In order to add version and key information into the plane component, we need to make some minor modifications to *plane.cs*, as follows:

```
using System;

using System.Reflection;
[assembly:AssemblyVersion("1.0.0.0")]
[assembly:AssemblyKeyFile("..\\key\\originator.key")]

public class Plane : Vehicle
{
  override public void TurnLeft()
  {
    Console.WriteLine("Plane turns left.");
  }

  override public void TurnRight()
  {
    Console.WriteLine("Plane turns right.");
  }

  override public void ApplyBrakes()
  {
```

```
      Console.WriteLine("Air brakes being used.");
   }
}
```

Having done this, you can build the assembly with the following commands:

```
csc /r:..\vehicle\vehicle.dll /t:library /out:plane.dll plane.cs
gacutil /i plane.dll
```

Of course, the last line in this snippet simply registers the component into the GAC.

Viewing the GAC

Now that we've registered all our components into the GAC, let's see what the GAC looks like. Microsoft has shipped a shell extension, the Shell Cache Viewer, to make it easier for you to view the GAC. On our machines, the Shell Cache Viewer appears when we navigate to *C:\WINDOWS\Assembly*, as shown in Figure 4-3.[*]

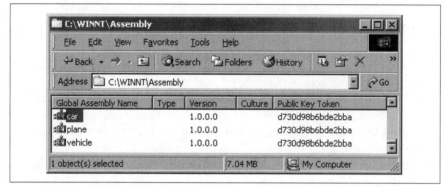

Figure 4-3. Our shared assemblies in the GAC

As you can see, the Shell Cache Viewer shows that all our components have the same version number because we used 1.0.0.0 as the version number when we built our components. Additionally, it shows that all our components have the same public-key-token value because we used the same key file, *originator.key*.

Building and testing the drive.exe

You should copy the previous *drive.jsl* source-code file into the *Shared Assemblies* directory, the root of the directory structure (shown in

---

[*] This path is entirely dependent upon the *%windir%* setting on your machine.

Figure 4-2) we are working with in this section. Having done this, you can build this component as follows (remember to type everything on one line):

```
vjc /r:vehicle\vehicle.dll;car\car.dll;plane\plane.dll
    /t:exe /out:drive.exe drive.jsl
```

Once you've done this, you can execute the *drive.exe* component, which will use the *vehicle.dll*, *car.dll*, and *plane.dll* assemblies registered in the GAC. You should see the following as part of your output:

```
ORIGINAL VERSION - 1.0.0.0.
```

To uninstall these shared components (assuming that you have administrative privileges), select the appropriate assemblies and press the Delete key (but if you do this now, you must reregister these assemblies because we'll need them in the upcoming examples). When you do this, you've taken all the residues of these components out of the GAC. All that's left is to delete any files that you've copied over from your installation diskette—typically, all you really have to do is recursively remove the application directory.

Adding new versions

Unlike private assemblies, shared assemblies can take advantage of the rich versioning policies that the CLR supports. Unlike earlier OS-level infrastructures, the CLR enforces versioning policies during the loading of all shared assemblies. By default, the CLR loads the assembly with which your application was built, but by providing an application configuration file, you can command the CLR to load the specific assembly version that your application needs. Inside an application configuration file, you can specify the rules or policies that the CLR should use when loading shared assemblies on which your application depends.

Let's make some code changes to our car component to demonstrate the default versioning support. Remember that Version 1.0.0.0 of our car component's ApplyBrakes() method throws an exception, as follows:

```
Overrides Public Sub ApplyBrakes()
   Console.WriteLine("Car trying to stop.")

   Console.WriteLine("ORIGINAL VERSION - 1.0.0.0.")

   throw new Exception("Brake failure!")
End Sub
```

Let's create a different *build* to remove this exception. To do this, make the following changes to the ApplyBrakes() method (store this source file in the *car-build* directory):

```
Overrides Public Sub ApplyBrakes()
   Console.WriteLine("Car trying to stop.")
```

```
Console.WriteLine("BUILD NUMBER change - 1.0.1.0.")

End Sub
```

In addition, you need to change the build number in your code as follows:

```
<Assembly:AssemblyVersion("1.0.1.0")>
```

Now build this component, and register it using the following commands:

```
vbc /r:..\vehicle\vehicle.dll
    /t:library /out:car.dll car.vb
gacutil /i car.dll
```

Notice that we've specified that this version is 1.0.1.0, meaning that it's compatible with Version 1.0.0.0. After registering this assembly with the GAC, execute your *drive.exe* application, and you will see the following statement as part of the output:

```
ORIGINAL VERSION - 1.0.0.0.
```

This is the default behavior—the CLR will load the version of the assembly with which your application was built. And just to prove this statement further, suppose that you provide Version 1.0.1.1 by making the following code changes (store this version in the *car-revision* directory):

```
Overrides Public Sub ApplyBrakes()
  Console.WriteLine("Car trying to stop.")

  Console.WriteLine("REVISION NUMBER change - 1.0.1.1.")

End Sub

<Assembly:AssemblyVersion("1.0.1.1")>
```

This time, instead of changing the build number, you're changing the revision number, which should still be compatible with the previous two versions. If you build this assembly, register it against the GAC and execute *drive.exe* again; you will get the following statement as part of your output:

```
ORIGINAL VERSION - 1.0.0.0.
```

Again, the CLR chooses the version with which your application was built.

As shown in Figure 4-4, you can use the Shell Cache Viewer to verify that all three versions exist on the system simultaneously. This implies that the support exists for side-by-side execution—which terminates DLL Hell in .NET.

If you want your program to use a different, compatible version of the car assembly, you have to provide an application configuration file. The name of an application configuration file is composed of the physical executable name and ".config" appended to it. For example, since our client program is named *drive.exe*, its configuration file must be named *drive.exe.config*.

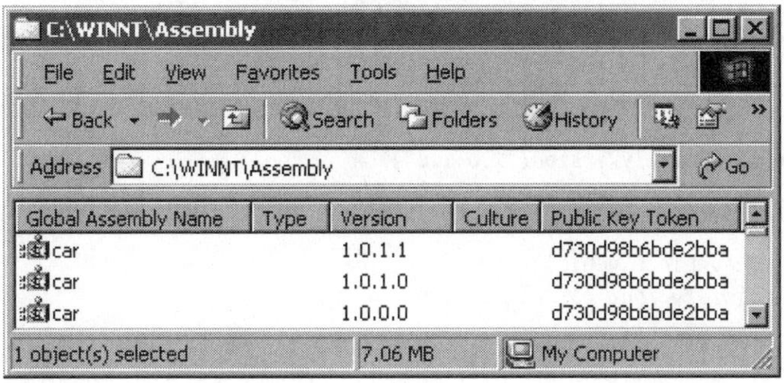

Figure 4-4. Multiple versions of the same shared assembly

Here's a *drive.exe.config* file that allows you to tell the CLR to load Version 1.0.1.0 of the car assembly for you (instead of loading the default Version, 1.0.0.0). The two boldface attributes say that although we built our client with Version 1.0.0.0 (oldVersion) of the car assembly, load 1.0.1.0 (newVersion) for us when we run *drive.exe*.

```
<?xml version ="1.0"?>
<configuration>
  <runtime>
    <assemblyBinding xmlns="urn:schemas-microsoft-com:asm.v1">
      <dependentAssembly>
        <assemblyIdentity name="car"
            publicKeyToken="D730D98B6BDE2BBA"
            culture="" />
        <bindingRedirect oldVersion="1.0.0.0"
                          newVersion="1.0.1.0" />
      </dependentAssembly>
    </assemblyBinding>
  </runtime>
</configuration>
```

In this configuration file, the name attribute of the assemblyIdentity tag indicates the shared assembly's human-readable name that is stored in the GAC. Although the name value can be anything, you must replace the publicKeyToken value appropriately in order to execute drive.exe. The publicKeyToken attribute records the public-key-token value, which is an 8-byte hash of the public key used to build this component. There are several ways to get this 8-byte hash: you can copy it from the Shell Cache Viewer, you can copy it from the IL dump of your component, or you can use the Shared Name utility to get it, as follows:

```
sn -T car.dll
```

Once you create the previously shown configuration file (stored in the same directory as the *drive.exe* executable) and execute *drive.exe*, you will see the following as part of your output:

```
BUILD NUMBER change - 1.0.1.0.
```

If you change the configuration file to newVersion=1.0.1.1 and execute *drive.exe* again, you will see the following as part of your output:

```
REVISION NUMBER change - 1.0.1.1.
```

Having gone over all these examples, you should realize that you have full control over which dependent assembly versions the CLR should load for your applications. It doesn't matter which version was built with your application: you can choose different versions at runtime merely by changing a few attributes in the application configuration file.

Distributed Components

A component technology should support distributed computing, allowing you to activate and invoke remote services, as well as services in another application domain.* Distributed COM, or DCOM, is the wire protocol that provides support for distributed computing using COM. Although DCOM is fine for distributed computing, it is inappropriate for global cyberspace because it doesn't work well in the face of firewalls and NAT software. Some other shortcomings of DCOM are expensive lifecycle management, protocol negotiation, and binary formats.

To eliminate or at least mitigate these shortcomings, .NET provides a host of different distributed support. The Remoting API in .NET allows you to use a host of channels, such as TCP and HTTP (which uses SOAP by default), for distributed computing. It even permits you to plug in your own custom channels, should you require this functionality. Best of all, since the framework is totally object-oriented, distributed computing in .NET couldn't be easier. To show you how simple it is to write a distributed application in .NET, let's look at an example using sockets, otherwise known as the *TCP channel* in .NET.

---

* Each Windows process requires its own memory address space, making it fairly expensive to run multiple Windows processes. An application domain is a lightweight or virtual process. All application domains of a given Windows process can use the same memory address space.

Distributed Hello Server

In this example, we'll write a distributed Hello application, which outputs a line of text to the console whenever a client invokes its exposed method, SayHello( ). Since we're using the TCP channel, we'll tell the compiler that we need the definitions in the System.Runtime.Remoting and System.Runtime.Remoting.Channels.Tcp namespaces.

Note that this class, CoHello, derives from MarshalByRefObject.* This is the key to distributed computing in .NET because it gives this object a distributed identity, allowing the object to be referenced across application domains, or even process and machine boundaries. A marshal-by-reference object requires a proxy to be set up on the client side and a stub to be set up on the server side, but since both of these are automatically provided by the infrastructure, you don't have to do any extra work. Your job is to derive from MarshalByRefObject to get all the support for distributed computing:

```
using System;

using System.Runtime.Remoting;
using System.Runtime.Remoting.Channels;
using System.Runtime.Remoting.Channels.Tcp;

public class CoHello : MarshalByRefObject
{
  public static void Main( )
  {
    TcpChannel channel = new TcpChannel(4000);
    ChannelServices.RegisterChannel(channel);

    RemotingConfiguration.RegisterWellKnownServiceType (
      typeof(CoHello),            // Type name
      "HelloDotNet",             // URI
      WellKnownObjectMode.Singleton // SingleCall or Singleton
    );

    System.Console.WriteLine("Hit <enter> to exit...");
    System.Console.ReadLine( );
  }

  public void SayHello( )
  {
    Console.WriteLine("Hello, Universe of .NET");
  }
}
```

---

* If you fail to do this, your object will not have a distributed identity since the default is marshal-by-value, which means that a copy of the remote object is created on the client side.

The SayHello() method is public, meaning that any external client can call this method. As you can see, this method is very simple, but the interesting thing is that a remote client application (which we'll develop shortly) can call it because the Main() function uses the TcpChannel class. Look carefully at Main(), and you'll see that it instantiates a TcpChannel, passing in a port number from which the server will listen for incoming requests.*

Once we have created a channel object, we then register the channel to the ChannelServices, which supports channel registration and object resolution. Having done this, you must then register your object with the Remoting-Configuration so that it can be activated—you do this by calling the RegisterWellKnownServiceType() method of the RemotingConfiguration class. When you call this method, you must pass in the class name, a URI, and an object-activation mode. The URI is important because it's a key element that the client application will use to refer specifically to this registered object. The object-activation mode can be either Singleton, which means that the same object will service many calls, or SingleCall, which means an object will service at most one call.

Here's how to build this distributed application:

```
csc server.cs
```

Once you've done this, you can start the server program, which will wait endlessly until you hit the Enter key. The server is now ready to service client requests.

Remote Hello Client

Now that we have a server waiting, let's develop a client to invoke the remote SayHello() method. Instead of registering an object with the remoting configuration, we need to activate a remote object. So let's jump into the code now to see how this works. As you examine the following program, note these items:

- We're using types in the System.Runtime.Remoting and System.Runtime.Remoting.Channels.Tcp namespaces, since we want to use the TCP channel.
- Our Client class doesn't need to derive from anything because it's not a server-side object that needs to have a distributed identity.
- Since we're developing a client application, we don't need to specify a client port when we instantiate the TcpChannel.

---

* Believe it or not, all you really have to do is replace TcpChannel with HttpChannel to take advantage of HTTP and SOAP as the underlying communication protocols.

Other than these items, the key thing to note is object activation, shown in the second boldface statement in the following code. To invoke remote methods, you must first activate the remote object and obtain an associated proxy on the client side. To activate the object and get a reference to the associated proxy, you call the GetObject() method of the Activator class. When you do this, you must pass along the remote class name and its fully qualified location, including the complete URI. Once you've successfully done this, you can then invoke remote methods.

```
using System;
using System.Runtime.Remoting;
using System.Runtime.Remoting.Channels;
using System.Runtime.Remoting.Channels.Tcp;

public class Client
{
  public static void Main( )
  {
    try
    {
      TcpChannel channel = new TcpChannel( );
      ChannelServices.RegisterChannel(channel);

      CoHello h = (CoHello) Activator.GetObject(
        typeof(CoHello),                      // Remote type
        "tcp://127.0.0.1:4000/HelloDotNet"   // Location
      );

      h.SayHello( );
    }
    catch(Exception e)
    {
      Console.WriteLine(e.ToString( ));
    }
  }
}
```

To build this client application, you must include references to the *server.exe* assembly:

```
csc /r:Server.exe Client.cs
```

If you're familiar with DCOM, you must be relieved to find that it's relatively simple to write distributed applications in .NET.[*]

---

[*] In fact, if you have a copy of *Learning DCOM* (O'Reilly) handy, compare these programs with their DCOM counterparts in Appendix D, and you will see what we mean.

Distributed Garbage Collector

Because the .NET distributed garbage collector is different from that of DCOM, we must briefly cover this facility. Instead of using DCOM's delta pinging, which requires few network packets when compared to normal pinging (but still too many for a distributed protocol), .NET remoting uses leases to manage object lifetimes. If you've ever renewed the lease to an IP address on your Dynamic Host Configuration Protocol (DHCP) network, you've pretty much figured out this mechanism because it's based on similar concepts.

In .NET, distributed objects give out leases instead of relying on reference counting (as in COM) for lifetime management. An application domain where the remote objects reside has a special object called the *lease manager*, which manages all the leases associated with these remote objects. When a lease expires, the lease manager contacts a sponsor, telling the sponsor that the lease has expired. A *sponsor* is simply a client that has previously registered itself with the lease manager during an activation call, indicating to the lease manager that it wants to know when a lease expires. If the lease manager can contact the sponsor, the sponsor may then renew the lease. If the sponsor refuses to renew the lease or if the lease manager can't contact the sponsor after a configurable timeout period, the lease manager will void the lease and remove the object. There are two other ways in which a lease can be renewed: implicitly, via each call to the remote object, or explicitly, by calling the Renew() method of the ILease interface.

COM+ Services in .NET

COM programming requires lots of housekeeping and infrastructure-level code to build large-scale, enterprise applications. To make it easier to develop and deploy transactional and scalable COM applications, Microsoft released Microsoft Transaction Server (MTS). MTS allows you to share resources, thereby increasing the scalability of an application. COM+ Services were the natural evolution of MTS. While MTS was just another library on top of COM, COM+ Services were subsumed into the COM library, thus combining both COM and MTS into a single runtime.

COM+ Services have been very valuable to the development shops using the COM model to build applications that take advantage of transactions, object pooling, role-based security, etc. If you develop enterprise .NET applications, the COM+ Services in .NET are a must.

In the following examples, rather than feeding you more principles, we'll show you examples for using major COM+ Services in .NET, including

examples on transactional programming, object pooling, and role-based security. But before you see these examples, let's talk about the key element—attributes—that enables the use of these services in .NET.

Attribute-Based Programming

Attributes are the key element that helps you write less code and allows an infrastructure to automatically inject the necessary code for you at runtime. If you've used IDL (Interface Definition Language) before, you have seen the in or out attributes, as in the following example:

```
HRESULT SetAge([in] short age);
HRESULT GetAge([out] short *age);
```

IDL allows you to add these attributes so that the marshaler will know how to optimize the use of the network. Here, the in attribute tells the marshaler to send the contents from the client to the server, and the out attribute tells the marshaler to send the contents from the server to the client. In the SetAge() method, passing age from the server to the client will just waste bandwidth. Similarly, there's no need to pass age from the client to the server in the GetAge() method.

Developing custom attributes

While in and out are built-in attributes the MIDL compiler supports, .NET allows you to create your own custom attributes by deriving from the System.Attribute class. Here's an example of a custom attribute:

```
using System;

public enum Skill {  Guru, Senior, Junior }
[AttributeUsage(AttributeTargets.Class      |
                AttributeTargets.Field      |
                AttributeTargets.Method     |
                AttributeTargets.Property   |
                AttributeTargets.Constructor|
                AttributeTargets.Event)]
public class AuthorAttribute : System.Attribute
{
  public AuthorAttribute(Skill s)
  {
    level = s;
  }
  public Skill level;
}
```

The AttributeUsage attribute that we've applied to our AuthorAttribute class specifies the rules for using AuthorAttribute.* Specifically, it says that AuthorAttribute can prefix or describe a class or any class member.

Using custom attributes

Given that we have this attribute, we can write a simple class to make use of it. To apply our attribute to a class or a member, we simply make use of the attribute's available constructors. In our case, we have only one and it's AuthorAttribute(), which takes an author's skill level. Although you can use AuthorAttribute() to instantiate this attribute, .NET allows you to drop the Attribute suffix for convenience, as shown in the following code listing:

```
[Author(Skill.Guru)]
public class Customer
{
    [Author(Skill.Senior)]
    public void Add(string strName)
    {
    }
    [Author(Skill.Junior)]
    public void Delete(string strName)
    {
    }
}
```

You'll notice that we've applied the Author attribute to the Customer class, telling the world that a guru wrote this class definition. This code also shows that a senior programmer wrote the Add() method and that a junior programmer wrote the Delete() method.

Inspecting attributes

You won't see the full benefits of attributes until you write a simple interceptor-like program, which looks for special attributes and provides additional services appropriate for these attributes. Real interceptors include marshaling, transaction, security, pooling, and other services in MTS and COM+.

Here's a simple interceptor-like program that uses the Reflection API to look for AuthorAttribute and provide additional services. You'll notice that we can ask a type, Customer in this case, for all of its custom attributes. In our code, we ensure that the Customer class has attributes and that the first attribute is AuthorAttribute before we output the appropriate messages to

---

* You don't have to postfix your attribute class name with the word "Attribute", but this is a standard naming convention that Microsoft uses. C# lets you name your attribute class any way you like; for example, Author is a valid class name for your attribute.

the console. In addition, we look for all members that belong to the Customer class and check whether they have custom attributes. If they do, we ensure that the first attribute is an AuthorAttribute before we output the appropriate messages to the console.

```
using System;
using System.Reflection;

public class interceptor
{
  public static void Main( )
  {
    Object[] attrs = typeof(Customer).GetCustomAttributes(false);
    if ((attrs.Length > 0) && (attrs[0] is AuthorAttribute))
    {
      Console.WriteLine("Class [{0}], written by a {1} programmer.",
          typeof(Customer).Name, ((AuthorAttribute)attrs[0]).level);
    }

    MethodInfo[] mInfo = typeof(Customer).GetMethods( );
    for ( int i=0; i < mInfo.Length; i++ )
    {
      attrs = mInfo[i].GetCustomAttributes(false);

      if ((attrs.Length > 0) && (attrs[0] is AuthorAttribute))
      {
        AuthorAttribute a = (AuthorAttribute)attrs[0];
        Console.WriteLine("Method [{0}], written by a {1} programmer.",
            mInfo[i].Name, (a.level));
        if (a.level == Skill.Junior)
        {
          Console.WriteLine("***Performing automatic " +
            "review of {0}'s code***", a.level);
        }
      }
    }
  }
}
```

It is crucial to note that when this program sees a piece of code written by a junior programmer, it automatically performs a rigorous review of the code. If you compile and run this program, it will output the following to the console:

```
Class [Customer], written by a Guru programmer.
Method [Add], written by a Senior programmer.
Method [Delete], written by a Junior programmer.
***Performing automatic review of Junior's code***
```

Although our interceptor-like program doesn't intercept any object-creation and method invocations, it does show how a real interceptor can examine attributes at runtime and provide necessary services stipulated by the

attributes. Again, the key here is the last boldface line, which represents a special service that the interceptor provides as a result of attribute inspection.

Transactions

In this section, we'll show you that it's easy to write a .NET class to take advantage of the transaction support that COM+ Services provide. All you need to supply at development time are a few attributes, and your .NET components are automatically registered against the COM+ catalog the first time they are used. Put differently, not only do you get easier programming, but you also get just-in-time and automatic registration of your COM+ application.*

To develop a .NET class that supports transactions, here's what must happen:

1. Your class must derive from the ServicedComponent class to exploit COM+ Services.

2. You must describe your class with the correct Transaction attribute, such as Transaction(TransactionOption.Required), meaning that instances of your class must run within a transaction.

Besides these two requirements, you can use the ContextUtil class (which is a part of the System.EnterpriseServices namespace) to obtain information about the COM+ object context. This class exposes the major functionality found in COM+, including methods such as SetComplete(), SetAbort(), and IsCallerInRole(), and properties such as IsInTransaction and MyTransactionVote.

In addition, while it's not necessary to specify any COM+ application installation options, you should do so because you get to specify what you want, including the name of your COM+ application, its activation setting, its versions, and so on. For example, in the following code listing, if you don't specify the ApplicationName attribute, .NET will use the module name as the COM+ application name, displayed in the Component Services Explorer (or COM+ Explorer). For example, if the name of module is *crm.dll*, the name of your COM+ application will be *crm*. Other than this attribute, we also use the ApplicationActivation attribute to specify that this component will be installed as a library application, meaning that the component will be activated in the creator's process:

---

* Automatic registration is nice during development, but don't use this feature in a production environment, because not all clients will have the administrative privilege to set up COM+ applications.

```
using System;
using System.Reflection;
using System.EnterpriseServices;

[assembly: ApplicationName(".NET Framework Essentials CRM")]
[assembly: ApplicationActivation(ActivationOption.Library)]

[assembly: AssemblyKeyFile("originator.key")]
[assembly: AssemblyVersion("1.0.0.0")]
```

The rest should look extremely familiar. In the Add() method, we simply call SetComplete() when we've successfully added the new customer into our databases. If something has gone wrong during the process, we will vote to abort this transaction by calling SetAbort().

```
[Transaction(TransactionOption.Required)]
public class Customer : ServicedComponent
{
  public void Add(string strName)
  {
    try
    {
      Console.WriteLine("New customer: {0}", strName);

      // Add the new customer into the system
      // and make appropriate updates to
      // several databases.

      ContextUtil.SetComplete();
    }
    catch(Exception e)
    {
      Console.WriteLine(e.ToString());
      ContextUtil.SetAbort();
    }
  }
}
```

Instead of calling SetComplete() and SetAbort() yourself, you can also use the AutoComplete attribute, as in the following code, which is conceptually equivalent to the previously shown Add() method:

```
[AutoComplete]
public void Add(string strName)
{
  Console.WriteLine("New customer: {0}", strName);

  // Add the new customer into the system
  // and make appropriate updates to
  // several databases.
}
```

Here's how you build this assembly:

```
csc /t:library /out:crm.dll crm.cs
```

Since this is a shared assembly, remember to register it against the GAC by using the GAC utility:

```
gacutil /i crm.dll
```

At this point, the assembly has not been registered as a COM+ application, but we don't need to register it manually. Instead, .NET automatically registers and hosts this component for us in a COM+ application the first time we use this component. So, let's write a simple client program that uses this component at this point. As you can see in the following code, we instantiate a Customer object and add a new customer:

```
using System;

public class Client
{
  public static void Main( )
  {
    try
    {
      Customer c = new Customer( );
      c.Add("John Osborn");
    }
    catch(Exception e)
    {
      Console.WriteLine(e.ToString( ));
    }
  }
}
```

We can build this program as follows:

```
csc /r:crm.dll /t:exe /out:client.exe client.cs
```

When we run this application, COM+ Services automatically create a COM+ application called .NET Framework Essentials CRM to host our *crm.dll* .NET assembly, as shown in Figure 4-5. In addition to adding our component to the created COM+ application, .NET also inspects our metadata for provided attributes and configures the associated services in the COM+ catalog.

Object Pooling

A *pool* is technical term that refers to a group of resources, such as connections, threads, and objects. Putting a few objects into a pool allows hundreds of clients to share these few objects (you can make the same assertion for threads, connections, and other objects). Pooling is, therefore, a technique

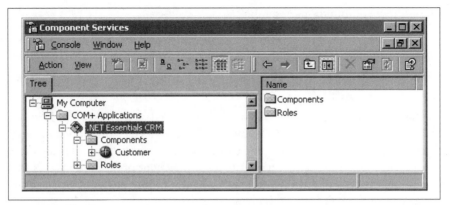

Figure 4-5. The Component Services explorer

that minimizes the use of system resources, improves performance, and helps system scalability.

Missing in MTS, *object pooling* is a nice feature in COM+ that allows you to pool objects that are expensive to create. Similar to providing support for transactions, if you want to support object pooling in a .NET class, you need to derive from ServicedComponent, override any of the Activate(), Deactivate(), and CanBePooled() methods, and specify the object-pooling requirements in an ObjectPooling attribute, as shown in the following example:*

```
using System;
using System.Reflection;
using System.EnterpriseServices;

[assembly: ApplicationName(".NET Framework Essentials CRM")]
[assembly: ApplicationActivation(ActivationOption.Library)]
[assembly: AssemblyKeyFile("originator.key")]
[assembly: AssemblyVersion("1.0.0.0")]

[Transaction(TransactionOption.Required)]
[ObjectPooling(MinPoolSize=1, MaxPoolSize=5)]
public class Customer : ServicedComponent
{
  public Customer()
  {
    Console.WriteLine("Some expensive object construction.");
  }

  [AutoComplete]
  public void Add(string strName)
  {
```

---

* Mixing transactions and object pooling should be done with care. See *COM and .NET Component Services*, by Juval Löwy (O'Reilly).

```
Console.WriteLine("Add customer: {0}", strName);
// Add the new customer into the system
// and make appropriate updates to
// several databases.
}

override protected void Activate( )
{
  Console.WriteLine("Activate");
  // Pooled object is being activated.
  // Perform the appropriate initialization.
}

override protected void Deactivate( )
{
  Console.WriteLine("Deactivate");
  // Object is about to be returned to the pool.
  // Perform the appropriate clean up.
}

override protected bool CanBePooled( )
{
  Console.WriteLine("CanBePooled");
  return true; // Return the object to the pool.
}
}
```

Take advantage of the Activate() and Deactivate() methods to perform appropriate initialization and cleanup. The CanBePooled() method lets you tell COM+ whether your object can be pooled when this method is called. You need to provide the expensive object-creation functionality in the constructor, as shown in the constructor of this class.

Given this Customer class that supports both transaction and object pooling, you can write the following client-side code to test object pooling. For brevity, we will create only two objects, but you can change this number to anything you like so that you can see the effects of object pooling. Just to ensure that you have the correct configuration, delete the current .NET Framework Essentials CRM COM+ application from the Component Services Explorer before running the following code:

```
for (int i=0; i<2; i++)
{
  Customer c = new Customer( );
  c.Add(i.ToString( ));
}
```

Running this code produces the following results:

```
Some expensive object construction.
Activate
Add customer: 0
```

```
Deactivate
CanBePooled
Activate
Add customer: 1
Deactivate
CanBePooled
```

We've created two objects, but since we've used object pooling, only one object is really needed to support our calls, and that's why you see only one output statement that says Some expensive object construction. In this case, COM+ creates only one Customer object, but activates and deactivates it twice to support our two calls. After each call, it puts the object back into the object pool. When a new call arrives, it picks the same object from the pool to service the request.

Role-Based Security

Role-based security in MTS and COM+ has drastically simplified the development and configuration of security for business applications. This is because it abstracts away the complicated details for dealing with access control lists (ACL) and security identifiers (SID). All .NET components that are hosted in a COM+ application can take advantage of role-based security. You can fully configure role-based security using the Component Services Explorer, but you can also manage role-based security in your code to provide fine-grain security support that's missing from the Component Services Explorer.

Configuring role-based security

In order to demonstrate role-based security, let's add two roles to our COM+ application, .NET Framework Essentials CRM. The first role represents Agent who can use the Customer class in every way but can't delete customers. You should create this role and add to it the local Users group, as shown in Figure 4-6. The second role represents Manager who can use the Customer class in every way, including deleting customers. Create this role and add to it the local Administrators group.

Once you create these roles, you need to enable access checks for the .NET Framework Essentials CRM COM+ application. Launch the COM+ application's Properties sheet (by selecting .NET Framework Essentials CRM and pressing Alt-Enter), and select the Security tab. Enable access checks to your COM+ application by providing the options, as shown in Figure 4-7.

Once you have enabled access checks at the application level, you need to enforce access checks at the class level, too. To do this, launch Customer's Properties sheet, and select the Security tab. Enable access checks to this .NET

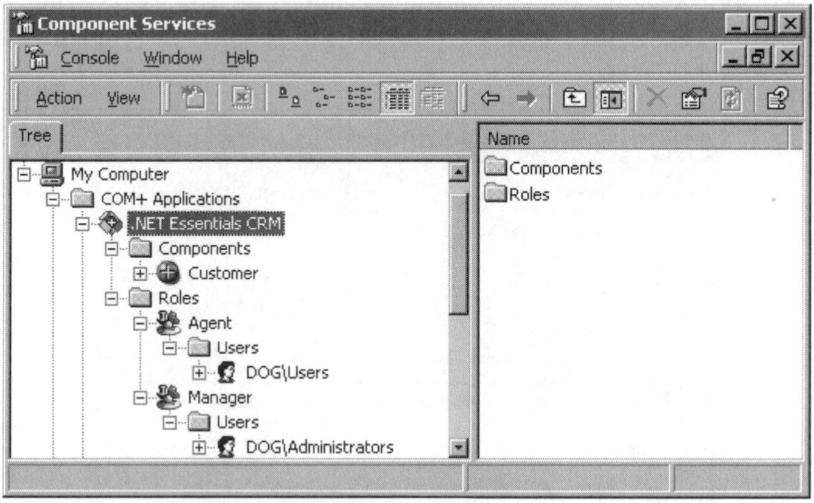

Figure 4-6. Creating roles and adding users to roles

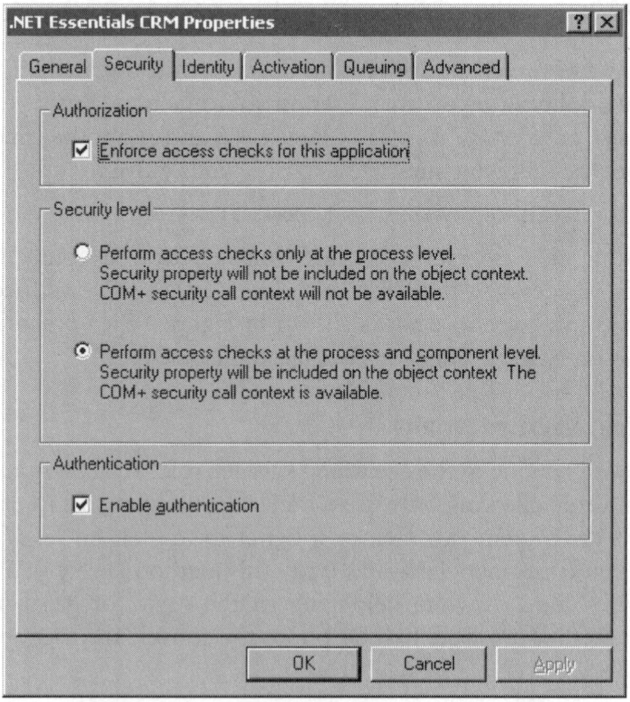

Figure 4-7. Enable authorization for this COM+ application

class by providing the options shown in Figure 4-8. Here, we're saying that no one can access the Customer class except for those that belong to the Manager or Agent role.

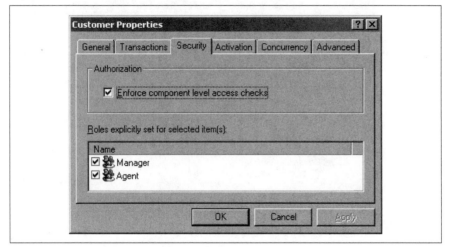

Figure 4-8. Enforce component-level access checks

Now, if you run the client application developed in the last section, everything will work because you are a user on your machine. But if you uncheck both the Manager* *and* Agent roles in Figure 4-8 and rerun the client application, you get the following message as part of your output:

```
System.UnauthorizedAccessException: Access is denied.
```

You're getting this exception because you've removed yourself from the roles that have access to the Customer class. Once you've verified this, put the configuration back to what is shown in Figure 4-8 to prepare the environment for the next test that we're about to illustrate.

Programming role-based security

We've allowed anyone in the Agent and Manager roles to access our class, but let's invent a rule allowing only users under the Manager role to delete a customer from the system (for lack of a better example). So let's add a new method to the Customer class—we'll call this method Delete( ), as shown in the following code. Anyone belonging to the Agent or Manager role can invoke this method, so we'll first output to the console the user account that

---

* Since you're a developer, you're probably an administrator on your machine, so you need to uncheck the Manager role, too, in order to see an access violation in the test that we're about to illustrate.

invokes this method. After doing this, we'll check to ensure that this user belongs to the Manager role. If so, we allow the call to go through; otherwise, we throw an exception indicating that only managers can perform a deletion. Believe it our not, this is the basic premise for programming role-based security:

```
[AutoComplete]
public void Delete(string strName)
{
  try
  {
    SecurityCallContext sec;
    sec = SecurityCallContext.CurrentCall;
    string strCaller = sec.DirectCaller.AccountName;

    Console.WriteLine("Caller: {0}", strCaller);

    bool bInRole = sec.IsCallerInRole("Manager");
    if (!bInRole)
    {
      throw new Exception ("Only managers can delete customers.");
    }

    Console.WriteLine("Delete customer: {0}", strName);
    // Delete the new customer from the system
    // and make appropriate updates to
    // several databases.
  }
  catch(Exception e)
  {
    Console.WriteLine(e.ToString( ));
  }
}
```

Here's the client code that includes a call to the Delete() method:

```
using System;

public class Client
{
  public static void Main( )
  {
    try
    {
      Customer c = new Customer( );
      c.Add("John Osborn");
      // Success depends on the role
      // under which this method
      // is invoked.
      c.Delete("Jane Smith");
    }
```

```
    catch(Exception e)
    {
      Console.WriteLine(e.ToString( ));
    }
  }
}
```

Once you've built this program, you can test it using an account that belongs to the local Users group, since we added this group to the Agent role earlier. On Windows 2000 or XP, you can use the following command to launch a command window using a specific account:

    runas /user:DEVTOUR\student cmd

Of course, you should replace DEVTOUR and student with your own machine name and user account, respectively. After running this command, you will need to type in the correct password, and a new command window will appear. Execute the client under this user account, and you'll see the following output:

```
Add customer: John Osborn
Caller: DEVTOUR\student
System.Exception: Only managers can delete customers.
    at Customer.Delete(String strName)
```

You'll notice that the Add( ) operation went through successfully, but the Delete( ) operation failed, because we executed the client application under an account that's missing from the Manager role.

To remedy this, we need to use a user account that belongs to the Manager role—any account that belongs to the Administrators group will do. So, start another command window using a command similar to the following:

    runas /user:DEVTOUR\instructor cmd

Execute the client application again, and you'll get the following output:

```
Add customer: John Osborn
Caller: DEVTOUR\instructor
Delete customer: Jane Smith
```

As you can see, since we've executed the client application using an account that belongs to the Manager role, the Delete( ) operation went through without problems.

Message Queuing

In addition to providing support for COM+ Services, .NET also supports message queuing. If you've used Microsoft Message Queuing (MSMQ) services before, you'll note that the basic programming model is the same but the classes in the System.Messaging namespace make it extremely easy to

develop message-queuing applications. The System.Messaging namespace provides support for basic functionality, such as connecting to a queue, opening a queue, sending messages to a queue, receiving messages from a queue, and peeking for messages on the queue. To demonstrate how easy it is to use the classes in System.Messaging, let's build two simple applications: one to enqueue messages onto a private queue on the local computer and another to dequeue these messages from the same queue.*

Enqueue

Here's a simple program that enqueues a Customer object onto a private queue on the local computer. Notice first that we need to include the System.Messaging namespace because it contains the classes that we want to use:

```
using System;
using System.Messaging;
```

While the following Customer structure is very simple, it can be as complex as you want because it will be serialized into an XML-formatted buffer by default before it's placed into the queue:

```
public struct Customer
{
  public string Last;
  public string First;
}
```

Our program first checks whether a private queue on the local computer exists. If this queue is missing, the program will create it. Next, we instantiate a MessageQueue class, passing in the target queue name. Once we have this MessageQueue object, we invoke its Send() method, passing in the Customer object, as shown in the following code. This will put our customer object into our private queue:

```
public class Enqueue
{
  public static void Main( )
  {
    try
    {
      string path = ".\\PRIVATE$\\NFE_queue";
      if(!MessageQueue.Exists(path))
      {
```

---

* To execute these programs, you must have MessageQueuing installed on your system. You can verify this by launching the ComputerManagement console, as shown in Figure 4-9.

```
            // Create our private queue.
            MessageQueue.Create(path);
        }

        // Initialize the queue.
        MessageQueue q = new MessageQueue(path);

        // Create our object.
        Customer c = new Customer();
        c.Last = "Osborn";
        c.First = "John";

        // Send it to the queue.
        q.Send(c);
    }
    catch(Exception e)
    {
        Console.WriteLine(e.ToString());
    }
  }
}
```

Use the following command to build this program:

```
csc /t:exe /out:enqueue.exe enqueue.cs
```

Execute this program, examine the Computer Management console, and you will see your message in the private queue called nfe_queue, as shown in Figure 4-9.

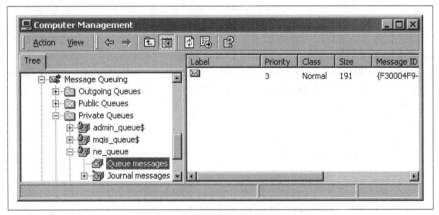

Figure 4-9. Our private queue, ne_queue, with a message

Dequeue

Now that there's a message in our private message queue, let's write a program to dequeue and examine the message. After ensuring that the private

queue we want exists, we initialize it by instantiating a MessageQueue class, passing in the path to our private queue. Next, we tell the MessageQueue object that the type of object we want to dequeue is Customer. To actually dequeue the object, we need to invoke the Receive() method, passing in a timeout in terms of a TimeSpan object, whose parameters stand for hours, minutes, and seconds, respectively. Finally, we cast the body of the received Message object into a Customer object and output its contents:

```
using System;
using System.Messaging;
using System.Runtime.Serialization;

public struct Customer
{
  public string Last;
  public string First;
}

public class Dequeue
{
  public static void Main()
  {
    try
    {
      string strQueuePath = ".\\PRIVATE$\\NFE_queue";

      // Ensure that the queue exists.
      if (!MessageQueue.Exists(strQueuePath))
      {
        throw new Exception(strQueuePath + " doesn't exist!");
      }

      // Initialize the queue.
      MessageQueue q = new MessageQueue(strQueuePath);

      // Specify the types we want to get back.
      string[] types = {"Customer, dequeue"};
      ((XmlMessageFormatter)q.Formatter).TargetTypeNames = types;

      // Receive the message (5-second timeout).
      Message m = q.Receive(new TimeSpan(0,0,5));

      // Convert the body into the type we want.
      Customer c = (Customer) m.Body;

      Console.WriteLine("Customer: {0}, {1}", c.Last, c.First);
    }
    catch(Exception e)
    {
```

```
      Console.WriteLine(e.ToString( ));
    }
  }
}
```

Compile and execute this program, look at the `Computer Management` console, press F5 to refresh the screen, and you will realize that the previous message is no longer there.

Summary

In this chapter, we've touched on many aspects of component-oriented programming, including deployment strategies, distributed computing, and enterprise services such as transaction management, object pooling, role-based security, and message queuing. We have to give due credit to Microsoft for making componentization easier in the .NET Framework. Case in point: without .NET, it would be impossible for us to show the complete code for all of these programs in a single chapter of a book.*

---

* For additional information on programming .NET component-based applications, see O'Reilly's *Programming .NET Components*, by Juval Löwy.

Data and XML

Almost everything we do in the software industry relates to data in some way. At some point, all software developers must deal with data, perhaps using a database, text file, spreadsheet, or some other method of data storage. There are many different methods and technologies for using, manipulating, and managing data, and newer methods are continually introduced to enhance existing ones. These methods range from function-based APIs to object-based frameworks and proprietary libraries.

Several years ago, it was common for a simple VB desktop application to access a private Microsoft Access database stored on the local hard disk, but this is no longer a typical scenario. Today's applications take advantage of distributed-component technologies to exploit scalability and interoperability, thus widening the reach of the application to the enterprise. Although ActiveX Data Objects (ADO) served a typical VB application well a few years ago, it fails to meet the increasing demands for better scalability, performance, and interoperability across multiple platforms that web-based applications require.

Here's where ADO.NET comes in. ADO.NET provides huge benefits that allow us to build even better enterprise applications. In this chapter, you will learn the benefits of ADO.NET, the ADO.NET architecture, the main classes in ADO.NET and how they work, and the integration of ADO.NET and XML.

ADO.NET Architecture

Microsoft ADO.NET's object model encompasses two distinct groups of classes: *content components* and *data-provider components.* The content components include the DataSet class and other supporting classes, such as DataTable, DataRow, DataColumn, and DataRelation. These classes contain the actual content of a data exchange. The data-provider components assist in data retrievals and updates. Developers can use the connection, command, and data reader objects to directly manipulate data. In more typical scenarios, developers use the DataAdapter class as the conduit to move data between the data store and the content components. The data can be actual rows from a database or any other form of data, such as an XML file or an Excel spreadsheet.

Figure 5-1 shows the high-level architecture of ADO.NET. ADO developers should have no problems understanding connection and command objects. We offer a brief overview then go into more detail in the rest of this chapter.

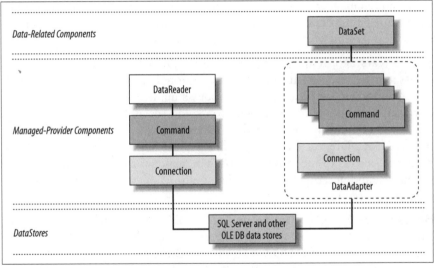

Figure 5-1. High-level architecture of ADO.NET

A data reader is a new object providing fast, forward-only, and read-only access to data. This structure is similar to an ADO Recordset, which has server-side, forward-only, and read-only cursor types.

---

* In previous releases of this book, we referred to the Data-Provider components as managed-provider components.

The DataSet class is analogous to a lightweight cache of a subset of the database from the data store for disconnected operations. It also allows reading and writing of data and schema in XML, and it is tightly integrated with XmlDataDocument, as you will see later.

The DataAdapter class serves as a higher-level abstraction of the connection and command classes. It enables you to load content from a data store into a DataSet and reconcile DataSet changes back to the data store.

ADO.NET Benefits

ADO.NET brings with it a number of benefits, which fall into the following categories:

Interoperability
> The ability to communicate across heterogeneous environments.

Scalability
> The ability to serve a growing number of clients without degrading system performance.

Productivity
> The ability to quickly develop robust data access applications using ADO.NET's rich and extensible component object model.

Performance
> An improvement over previous ADO versions due to the disconnected data model.

Interoperability

All communication involves data exchange, whether the communication between distributed components is through a request/response methodology or a message-based facility. Current distributed systems assume that the components involved in the communication are using the same protocol and data format. This assumption is too restrictive for a client base to expand across an enterprise or for multiple companies. Data-access layers should impose no such restrictions.

In current Microsoft Windows Distributed interNet Applications (DNA) Architecture, application components pass data back and forth as ADO disconnected recordsets. The data-providing components, as well as the data-consuming components, are required to use the Component Object Model (COM). The *payload*, the actual content we are passing around, is packaged in a data format called Network Data Representation (NDR). These NDR packages are streamed between components.

There are two issues with current Windows DNA systems. The first is the requirement that both ends of the communication pipe have the COM library. The second issue is that it is difficult to set up and manage these communications across firewalls. If your middle-tier components are COM/DCOM-based and you are using them within your intranet, you are in good shape. To put it another way: if all your components use Microsoft technology, you're fine. With the advent of electronic commerce (e-commerce), however, enterprise applications must interoperate with more than just Microsoft-development shops. ADO must improve for cross-platform components to seamlessly share data, breaking away from the limitations of COM/DCOM.

ADO.NET addresses the common data-exchange limitation by using XML as its payload data format. Since XML is text-based and simple to parse, it's a good choice for a common, platform-independent, and transportable data format. Furthermore, because XML is nothing more than structured text, employing XML as the data format on top of the HTTP network protocol minimizes firewall-related problems. With ADO and its XML format, the clients do not have to know COM to de-serialize the packaged data. All they need is an XML parser, which is readily available in many flavors on many different platforms. The data producers and consumers need only adhere to the XML schema to exchange data among themselves.

Scalability

In a client/server model, it is typical for a client to acquire and hold onto a connection to the server until all requests are fulfilled. While this solution works fine in small- to medium-scale applications, it is not scalable across a large enterprise. As soon as the number of clients reaches a certain threshold, the server becomes the bottleneck, as database connections eat up network and CPU resources. ADO.NET moves away from the client/server model by promoting the use of disconnected datasets. When a client requests some data, the data is retrieved, it's transferred to the client, and—as soon as possible—the connection is torn down. Since the connection between the client and the data source is short-lived, this technique allows more clients to request information from the server, thus solving the problem of limited connections.

You might think that setting up and tearing down connections is not a good idea since the cost of establishing a connection is usually high. This is a concern only in the absence of connection pooling. ADO.NET automatically keeps connections to a data source in a pool, so when an application thinks it is tearing down a connection, it's actually returning it to the resource pool.

This allows connections to be reused, avoiding the cost of reconstructing new connections from scratch.

Working with data in this disconnected fashion is not new to ADO programmers. The disconnected recordset was introduced in early versions of ADO. However, in ADO, it is up to the developer to implement this feature, whereas in ADO.NET, data is disconnected by nature.

ADO.NET has enhanced its predecessor by growing out of the client/server model and into the distributed components model. By using disconnected datasets as the paradigm for data exchange, ADO.NET is much more scalable than its predecessors.

Productivity

ADO.NET's rich data access classes allow developers to boost their productivity. Current ADO developers should have no problems getting up to speed with the object model, because ADO.NET is a natural evolution of ADO. The core functionality remains the same. We still have the connection object, representing the pipeline through which commands are executed.* With ADO.NET, the functionality is factored and distributed to each object in the model—much better than in previous versions of ADO. For example, the connection object is responsible only for connecting to and disconnecting from the data source. In ADO.NET, we can no longer execute a query directly through the connection object. Although some developers might miss this ability, it is a step in the right direction for cohesion of component development.

ADO.NET also boosts developers' productivity through extensibility. Because ADO.NET framework classes are managed code, developers can inherit and extend these classes to their custom needs. If you prefer not to do this low-level legwork, you can use the Visual Studio. NET data-design environment to generate these classes for you.

Visual Studio .NET is a great Rapid Application Development (RAD) tool for developing applications with ADO.NET. You can have the Component Designer generate ADO.NET typed DataSets. These typed DataSets are extended types, modeled for your data. You don't have to reference database fields by their names or indices but instead by their names as properties of typed objects. For example, instead of oRow(*customerName*), you can

---

* Along with the familiar connection and command objects, ADO.NET introduces a number of new objects, such as DataSet and DataAdapter. All of these objects are discussed earlier in this chapter.

use oRow.*customerName*. The generated code is much more readable, when compared to previous Microsoft code generators. In addition, these generated classes are type-safe, thus reducing the chances for errors and allowing compilers and the CLR to verify type usage.

In short, ADO.NET improves developers' productivity through its rich and extensible framework classes. These features are complemented by the rich toolsets for ADO.NET in Visual Studio .NET, which enable rapid application development.

Performance

Because ADO.NET is mainly about disconnected datasets, the system benefits from improved performance and scalability. The database server is no longer a bottleneck when the number of connection requests goes up. Data Providers in ADO.NET also enable implicit connection pooling, which reduces the time required to open a connection.

Previous marshaling of recordsets required type conversion to make sure that the data types were all COM-based. Since the disconnected dataset is in XML format, there is no need for this type conversion during transport, as opposed to dealing with data in Network Data Representation format.

With the ADO.NET architecture, the data providers can be optimized for better performance by talking directly to the database server. .NET Framework Data Provider for SQL Server is an example of this as we can see later in this chapter.

Content Components

Content components encapsulate data. In previous ADO versions, the Recordset object represented such a component. The data contained by the recordset component is in the form of a table, consisting of columns and rows. In ADO.NET, the data encapsulated by the DataSet component is in the form of a relational database, consisting of tables and relationships. This is a major improvement in data-access technology. In this section, we provide a high-level survey of the core classes that make up the content components, including DataSet, DataTable, DataColumn, DataRow, DataView, and DataRelation.[*]

---

[*] The complete list of all classes can be found in the Microsoft .NET SDK.

DataSet

If you are familiar with ADO, you know that data is typically transferred between components in *recordsets*. The recordset contains data in a tabular form. Whether the recordset includes information from one or many tables in the database, the data is still returned in the form of rows and columns as if they were from a single table. ADO.NET allows for more than just a recordset to be shared between application components. This is one of the most important features of ADO.NET: we will be transferring a DataSet instead of a recordset.

The DataSet can be viewed as an in-memory view of the database. It can contain multiple DataTable and DataRelation objects.* With previous versions of ADO, the closest you could get to this functionality was to exchange data with a chain of Recordset objects. When the client application receives this chained recordset, it can get to each of the recordsets through NextRecordset(); however, there is no way to describe the relationship between each of the recordsets in the chain. With ADO.NET, developers can navigate and manipulate the collection of tables and their relationships.

As mentioned earlier, ADO.NET involves disconnected datasets because it is geared toward a distributed architecture. Since a DataSet is disconnected, it must provide a way to track changes to itself. The DataSet object provides a number of methods so that all data manipulation done to the DataSet can be easily reconciled with the actual database (or other data source) at a later time. They include: HasChanges(), HasErrors, GetChanges(), AcceptChanges(), and RejectChanges(). You can employ these methods to check for changes that have happened to the DataSet, obtain the modifications in the form of a changed DataSet, inspect the changes for errors, and then accept or reject the changes. If you want to communicate the changes to the data store back end (which is usually the case), you would ask the DataSet for an update.

The DataSet is intended to benefit enterprise web applications, which are disconnected by nature. You don't know that the data at the back end has changed until you have updated records you were editing or performed any other tasks that required data reconciliation with the database.

As depicted in Figure 5-2, a DataSet contains two important collections. The first is the Tables (of type DataTableCollection), which holds a collection for

---

* Furthermore, the DataSet can be persisted into disconnected XML datafiles so that your application can continue to work offline. More information on this topic will be presented in later sections.

all the tables belonging to a given DataSet. The second collection contains all the relationships between the tables, and it is appropriately named the Relations (of type DataRelationCollection).

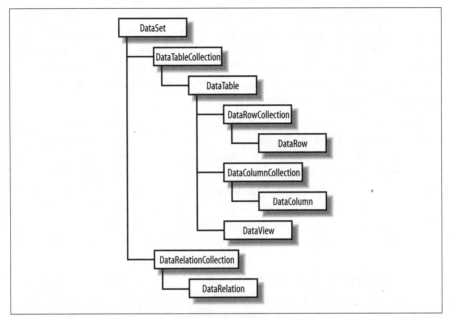

Figure 5-2. Important ADO.NET data objects, including DataSet

Creating a DataSet: An example in C#

All the tables and relations inside the DataSet are exposed through its Tables and Relations properties, respectively. Normally, you obtain tables from some data sources such as SQL Server or other databases; however, we would like to show the nuts and bolts of the DataSet here first. The following block of C# code demonstrates how to create a DataSet dynamically that consists of two tables, Orders and OrderDetails, and a relationship between the two tables:

```
using System;
using System.Data;

// Class and method declarations omitted for brevity...

// Construct the DataSet object.
DataSet m_ds = new DataSet("DynamicDS");

// Add a new table named "Order" to m_ds's collection tables.
m_ds.Tables.Add ("Order");
```

```
// Add new columns to table "Order".
m_ds.Tables["Order"].Columns.Add("OrderID",
                                Type.GetType("System.Int32"));
m_ds.Tables["Order"].Columns.Add("CustomerFirstName",
                                Type.GetType("System.String"));
m_ds.Tables["Order"].Columns.Add("CustomerLastName",
                                Type.GetType("System.String"));
m_ds.Tables["Order"].Columns.Add("Date",
                                Type.GetType("System.DateTime"));

// Register the column "OrderID" as the primary key of table "Order".
DataColumn[] keys = new DataColumn[1];
keys[0] = m_ds.Tables["Order"].Columns["OrderID"];
m_ds.Tables["Order"].PrimaryKey = keys;

// Add a new table named "OrderDetail" to m_ds's collection of tables.
m_ds.Tables.Add ("OrderDetail");

// Add new columns to table "OrderDetail".
m_ds.Tables["OrderDetail"].Columns.Add("fk_OrderID",
                                Type.GetType("System.Int32"));
m_ds.Tables["OrderDetail"].Columns.Add("ProductCode",
                                Type.GetType("System.String"));
m_ds.Tables["OrderDetail"].Columns.Add("Quantity",
                                Type.GetType("System.Int32"));
m_ds.Tables["OrderDetail"].Columns.Add("Price",
                                Type.GetType("System.Currency"));

// Get the DataColumn objects from two DataTable objects in a DataSet.
DataColumn parentCol = m_ds.Tables["Order"].Columns["OrderID"];
DataColumn childCol = m_ds.Tables["OrderDetail"].Columns["fk_OrderID"];

// Create and add the relation to the DataSet.
m_ds.Relations.Add(new DataRelation("Order_OrderDetail",
                                parentCol,
                                childCol));
m_ds.Relations["Order_OrderDetail"].Nested = true;
```

Let's highlight some important points in this block of code. After instantiating the DataSet object with the new operator, we add some tables with the Add method of the Tables object. We go through a similar process to add columns to each Table's Columns collection. Each of the added tables or columns can later be referenced by name. In order to assign the primary key for the Order table, we have to create the DataColumn array to hold one or more fields representing a key or a composite key. In this case, we have only a single key field, OrderID. We set the PrimaryKey property of the table to this array of key columns. For the relationship between the two tables, we first create the DataRelation called Order_OrderDetail with the two linking columns from the two tables, and then we add this DataRelation to the collection of relations of the DataSet. The last statement indicates that we want

to represent the relationship between the Order and OrderDetail table as a nested structure. This makes dealing with these entities easier in XML.

The following block of C# code shows how to insert data into each of the two tables:

```
DataRow newRow;
newRow = m_ds.Tables["Order"].NewRow( );
newRow["OrderID"] = 101;
newRow["CustomerFirstName"] = "John";
newRow["CustomerLastName"] = "Doe";
newRow["Date"] = new DateTime(2001, 5, 1);;
m_ds.Tables["Order"].Rows.Add(newRow);
newRow = m_ds.Tables["Order"].NewRow( );
newRow["OrderID"] = 102;
newRow["CustomerFirstName"] = "Jane";
newRow["CustomerLastName"] = "Doe";
newRow["Date"] = new DateTime(2001, 4, 29);
m_ds.Tables["Order"].Rows.Add(newRow);

newRow = m_ds.Tables["OrderDetail"].NewRow( );
newRow["fk_OrderID"] = 101;
newRow["ProductCode"] = "Item-100";
newRow["Quantity"] = 7;
newRow["Price"] = "59.95";
m_ds.Tables["OrderDetail"].Rows.Add(newRow);

newRow = m_ds.Tables["OrderDetail"].NewRow( );
newRow["fk_OrderID"] = 101;
newRow["ProductCode"] = "Item-200";
newRow["Quantity"] = 1;
newRow["Price"] = "9.25";
m_ds.Tables["OrderDetail"].Rows.Add(newRow);

newRow = m_ds.Tables["OrderDetail"].NewRow( );
newRow["fk_OrderID"] = 102;
newRow["ProductCode"] = "Item-200";
newRow["Quantity"] = 3;
newRow["Price"] = "9.25";
m_ds.Tables["OrderDetail"].Rows.Add(newRow);
```

Tables and Relations are important properties of DataSet. Not only do they describe the structure of the in-memory database, but the DataTables inside the collection also hold the content of the DataSet.

XML and tables sets

Now that you have a DataSet filled with tables and relationships, let's see how this DataSet helps in interoperability. XML is the answer. The DataSet has a number of methods that integrate DataSet tightly with XML, thus

making it universally interoperable. These methods are WriteXml(), WriteXmlSchema(), ReadXml(), and ReadXmlSchema().

WriteXmlSchema() dumps only the schema of the tables, including all tables and relationships between tables. WriteXml() can dump both the schema and table data as an XML encoded string. Both WriteXmlSchema() and WriteXml() accept a Stream, TextWriter, XmlWriter, or String representing a filename. WriteXml() accepts an XmlWriteMode as the second argument so you can optionally write the schema in addition to the data.

By default, WriteXml() writes only the data. To also write the schema, you will have to pass XmlWriteMode.WriteSchema as the second parameter to the call. You can also retrieve only the data portion of the XML by using the XmlWriteMode.IgnoreSchema property explicitly. Another mode that you can set is XmlWriteMode.DiffGram. In this DiffGram mode, the DataSet will be dumped out as both the original data and changed data. More on this topic when we get to the GetChanges() method of the DataSet.

The DataSet object also provides methods to reconstruct itself from an XML document. Use ReadXmlData() for reading XML data documents, and ReadXmlSchema() for reading XML schema documents.

The following code creates an XML document from the previously created dataset:

```
// Dump the previously shown DataSet to
// the console (and to an XML file).
m_ds.WriteXml(Console.Out, XmlWriteMode.WriteSchema);
m_ds.WriteXml("DS_Orders.xml", XmlWriteMode.WriteSchema);

// Constructing a new DataSet object
DataSet ds2 = new DataSet("RestoredDS");
ds2.ReadXml("DS_Orders.xml");
```

Let's examine the resulting XML file and its representation of the dataset:

```
<?xml version="1.0" standalone="yes"?>
<DynamicDS>
  <xs:schema id="DynamicDS"
             xmlns=""
             xmlns:xs="http://www.w3.org/2001/XMLSchema"
             xmlns:msdata="urn:schemas-microsoft-com:xml-msdata">
    <xs:element name="DynamicDS" msdata:IsDataSet="true">

      <xs:complexType>
        <xs:choice maxOccurs="unbounded">

          <xs:element name="Order">
            <xs:complexType>
              <xs:sequence>
```

```
<xs:element name="OrderID"
            type="xs:int" />
<xs:element name="CustomerFirstName"
            type="xs:string" minOccurs="0" />
<xs:element name="CustomerLastName"
            type="xs:string" minOccurs="0" />
<xs:element name="Date"
            type="xs:dateTime" minOccurs="0" />

<xs:element name="OrderDetail"
            minOccurs="0" maxOccurs="unbounded">

  <xs:complexType>
    <xs:sequence>
      <xs:element name="fk_OrderID"
                  type="xs:int" minOccurs="0" />
      <xs:element name="ProductCode"
                  type="xs:string" minOccurs="0" />
      <xs:element name="Quantity"
                  type="xs:int" minOccurs="0" />
      <xs:element name="Price"
                  msdata:DataType="System.Currency,
                  mscorlib, Version=n.n.nnnn.n,
                  Culture=neutral,
                  PublicKeyToken=nnnnnnnnnnnnnnnn"
                  type="xs:string" minOccurs="0" />
    </xs:sequence>
  </xs:complexType>

</xs:element>

      </xs:sequence>
    </xs:complexType>
  </xs:element>

</xs:choice>
</xs:complexType>

<xs:unique name="Constraint1"
        msdata:PrimaryKey="true">
  <xs:selector xpath=".//Order" />
  <xs:field xpath="OrderID" />
</xs:unique>

<xs:keyref name="Order_OrderDetail"
        refer="Constraint1"
        msdata:IsNested="true">
  <xs:selector xpath=".//OrderDetail" />
  <xs:field xpath="fk_OrderID" />
</xs:keyref>
```

```
    </xs:element>
  </xs:schema>

  <... Data Portion ...>

</DynamicDS>
```

The root element is named DynamicDS because that is the name of the dataset we created earlier. The xsd:schema tag contains all table and relationship definitions in this DynamicDS dataset. Because we've indicated that the relationship should be nested, the schema shows the xsd:element OrderDetail nested within the xsd:element Order. All columns are also represented as xsd:elements.

After the table definitions, the document holds definitions for various key types. The xsd:unique element is used with msdata:PrimaryKey for keys, as shown in the xsd:unique named Constraint1. The msdata:PrimaryKey attribute makes this a primary key, which has the added effect of enforcing uniqueness (every OrderID in the Order table must be unique).

The xsd:keyref element is used for foreign keys, as shown in the Order_OrderDetail key that refers to the Constraint1 key. This links the OrderDetail and Order tables where OrderDetail.fk_OrderID = Order.OrderID.

Let's now look at the data portion of the XML file:

```
<Order>
  <OrderID>101</OrderID>
  <CustomerFirstName>John</CustomerFirstName>
  <CustomerLastName>Doe</CustomerLastName>
  <Date>2001-05-01T00:00:00.0000000-04:00</Date>
  <OrderDetail>
    <fk_OrderID>101</fk_OrderID>
    <ProductCode>Item-100</ProductCode>
    <Quantity>7</Quantity>
    <Price>59.95</Price>
  </OrderDetail>
  <OrderDetail>
    <fk_OrderID>101</fk_OrderID>
    <ProductCode>Item-200</ProductCode>
    <Quantity>1</Quantity>
    <Price>9.25</Price>
  </OrderDetail>
</Order>
<Order>
  <OrderID>102</OrderID>
  <CustomerFirstName>Jane</CustomerFirstName>
  <CustomerLastName>Doe</CustomerLastName>
  <Date>2001-04-29T00:00:00.0000000-04:00</Date>
  <OrderDetail>
    <fk_OrderID>102</fk_OrderID>
```

```
    <ProductCode>Item-200</ProductCode>
    <Quantity>3</Quantity>
    <Price>9.25</Price>
  </OrderDetail>
</Order>
```

This part of the XML document is fairly self-explanatory. For each row of data in the Order table, we end up with one record of type Order. This is the same for the OrderDetail table. The OrderDetail that relates to a particular Order is nested inside the Order element.

Because the dataset is inherently disconnected from its source, changes to the data inside the dataset have to be tracked by the dataset itself. This is done through the following methods: HasChanges(), GetChanges(), and Merge(). The application can check the changes to the dataset and then ask the DataAdapter object to reconcile the changes with the data source through the DataAdapter Update() method.

The following block of code demonstrates how to the track and manage changes to a DataSet:

```
m_ds.AcceptChanges();
/* Make a change to the data set. */
m_ds.Tables["OrderDetail"].Rows[0]["Quantity"] = 12;

if(m_ds.HasChanges()){

    /* Get a copy of the data set containing the changes. */
    DataSet changeDS = m_ds.GetChanges();

    /* Dump the changed rows. */
    changeDS.WriteXml("ChangedDS.xml" , XmlWriteMode.DiffGram);

    /* Commit all changes. */
    m_ds.AcceptChanges();

}
```

Because we create this DataSet dynamically, we want to tell the DataSet to accept all changes made up to this point by first issuing an AcceptChange() call. Knowing that the DataSet should start tracking the changes again, we then change the quantity of one of the OrderDetail rows. Next, we ask the dataset for all the changes and dump it into a new dataset called changeDS. This dataset results in the following XML dump when using DiffGram mode. Notice that because OrderDetail is a child of Order, the change also includes the parent row:

```
<?xml version="1.0" standalone="yes"?>
<diffgr:diffgram xmlns:msdata="urn:schemas-microsoft-com:xml-msdata"
                 xmlns:diffgr="urn:schemas-microsoft-com:xml-diffgram-v1">
```

```
<DynamicDS>
  <Order diffgr:id="Order1" msdata:rowOrder="0">
    <OrderID>101</OrderID>
    <CustomerFirstName>John</CustomerFirstName>
    <CustomerLastName>Doe</CustomerLastName>
    <Date>2001-05-01T00:00:00.0000000-04:00</Date>
    <OrderDetail diffgr:id="OrderDetail1"
                 msdata:rowOrder="0" diffgr:hasChanges="modified">
      <fk_OrderID>101</fk_OrderID>
      <ProductCode>Item-100</ProductCode>
      <Quantity>12</Quantity>
      <Price>59.95</Price>
    </OrderDetail>
  </Order>
</DynamicDS>

<diffgr:before>
  <OrderDetail diffgr:id="OrderDetail1" msdata:rowOrder="0">
    <fk_OrderID>101</fk_OrderID>
    <ProductCode>Item-100</ProductCode>
    <Quantity>7</Quantity>
    <Price>59.95</Price>
  </OrderDetail>
</diffgr:before>

</diffgr:diffgram>
```

We would like to emphasize that the DataSet object is the most important construct in ADO.NET. Because DataSet does not tie to an underlying representation, such as SQL Server or Microsoft Access, it is extremely portable. Its data format is self-described in its schema, and its data is in pure XML. A DataSet is self-contained regardless of how it was created, whether by reading data from a SQL Server, from Microsoft Access, from an external XML file, or even by being dynamically generated as we have seen in an earlier example. This portable XML-based entity—without a doubt—should be the new standard for data exchange.

Enough said about DataSet. Let's drill down from DataSet to DataTable.

DataTable

DataTable represents a table of data and, thus, contains a collection of Data-Columns as a Columns property and a collection of DataRows as a Rows property. The Columns property provides the structure of the table, while the Rows property provides access to actual row data. Fields in the table are represented as DataColumn objects, and table records are represented as

DataRow objects. Here is some sample code that dumps the name of each column as a row of headers, followed by each row of data:

```
/* Walk the DataTable and display all column headers
 * along with all data rows.
 */
DataTable myTable = m_ds.Tables["OrderDetail"];

/* Display all column names. */
foreach(DataColumn c in myTable.Columns) {
  Console.Write(c.ColumnName + "\t");
}
Console.WriteLine(""); // Newline

/* Process each row. */
foreach(DataRow r in myTable.Rows) {

  /* Display each column. */
  foreach(DataColumn c in myTable.Columns) {
    Console.Write(r[c] + "\t");
  }
  Console.WriteLine(""); // Newline

}
```

Here is the output of that code:

fk_OrderID	ProductCode	Quantity	Price
101	Item-100	12	59.95
101	Item-200	1	9.25
102	Item-200	3	9.25

Typically, a DataTable has one or more fields serving as a primary key. This functionality is exposed as the PrimaryKey property. Because the primary key might contain more than one field, this property is an array of DataColumn objects. We revisit this excerpt of code here to put things in context. Note that in this example, the primary key consists of only one field; hence, the array of size one.

```
// Register the column "OrderID" as the primary key of table "Order".
DataColumn[] keys = new DataColumn[1];
keys[0] = m_ds.Tables["Order"].Columns["OrderID"];
m_ds.Tables["Order"].PrimaryKey = keys;
```

Relations and constraints

Relations define how tables in a database relate to each other. The DataSet globally stores the collection of relations between tables in the Relations property; however, each of the tables participating in the relation also has to know about the relationship. ChildRelations and ParentRelations, two properties of the DataTable object, take care of this. ChildRelations enumerates

all relations that this table participates in as a master table. ParentRelations, on the other hand, lists the relations in which this table acts as a slave table. We provide more information on the topic of relations when we explain the DataRelation object in an upcoming section of this chapter.

While we are on the topic of tables and relationships, it is important to understand how to set up constraint enforcements. There are two types of constraints that we can set up and enforce, UniqueConstraint and Foreign-KeyConstraint. UniqueConstraint enforces the uniqueness of a field value for a table. ForeignKeyConstraint enforces rules on table relationships. For ForeignKeyConstraint, we can set up UpdateRule and DeleteRule to dictate how the application should behave upon performing update or delete on a row of data in the parent table.

Table 5-1 shows the constraint settings and behavior of ForeignKeyConstraint rules.

Table 5-1. Constraint types and behaviors

Setting	Behavior
None	Nothing.
Cascade	Dependent rows (identified by foreign key) are deleted/ updated when parent row is deleted/ updated.
SetDefault	Foreign keys in dependent rows are set to the default value when parent row is deleted.
SetNull	Foreign keys in dependent rows are set to null value when parent row is deleted.

Constraints are activated only when the EnforceConstraint property of the DataSet object is set to true.

The following block of code shows how we have altered the foreign key constraint between the Order and OrderDetail tables to allow cascading deletion:

```
m_ds.Relations["Order_OrderDetail"].ChildKeyConstraint.DeleteRule =
Rule.Cascade;

m_ds.WriteXml("DS_BeforeCascadeDelete.xml");
m_ds.Tables["Order"].Rows[0].Delete( );
m_ds.WriteXml("DS_AfterCascadeDelete.xml");
```

As the result of running this code, the DataSet is left with only one order (order 102), which contains one line item.

DataView

The DataView object is similar to a *view* in conventional database programming. We can create different customized views of a DataTable, each with

different sorting and filtering criteria. Through these different views, we can traverse, search, and edit individual records. This ADO.NET concept is the closest to the old ADO recordset. In ADO.NET, DataView serves another important role—data binding to Windows Forms and Web Forms. We show the usage of DataView when we discuss data binding on Windows Forms and Web Forms in Chapters 7 and 8.

DataRelation

A DataSet object as a collection of DataTable objects alone is not useful enough. A collection of DataTable objects returned by a server component provides little improvement upon the chained recordset in previous versions of ADO. In order for your client application to make the most of the returned tables, you also need to return the relations between these Data-Tables. This is where the DataRelation object comes into play.

With DataRelation, you can define relationships between the DataTable objects. Client components can inspect an individual table or navigate the hierarchy of tables through these relationships. For example, you can find a particular row in a parent table and then traverse all dependent rows in a child table.

The DataRelation contains the parent table name, the child table name, the parent table column (primary key), and the child table column (foreign key).

Because it has multiple DataTables and DataRelations within the DataSet, ADO.NET allows for a much more flexible environment where consumers of the data can choose to use the data in whichever way they wish.

One example might be the need to display all information about a particular parent table and all of its dependent rows in a child table. You have ten rows in the parent table. Each of the rows in the parent table has ten dependent rows in the child table. Let's consider two approaches to getting this data to the data consumer. First, we will just use a join in the query string:

```
Select
    Order.CustomerFirstName, Order.CustomerLastName, Order.OrderDate,
    OrderDetail.ProductCode, OrderDetail.Quantity, OrderDetail.Price
from
    Order, OrderDetail
        where Order.OrderID = OrderDetail.fk_OrderID
```

The result set contains 100 rows, in which each group of ten rows contains duplicate information about the parent row.

A second approach is to retrieve the list of rows from the parent table first, which would be ten rows:

```
Select
    Order.OrderID,
    Order.CustomerFirstName, Order.CustomerLastName, Order.OrderDate
from
    Order
```

Then for each of the ten rows in the parent table, you would retrieve the dependent rows from the child table:

```
Select
    OrderDetail.ProductCode, OrderDetail.Quantity, OrderDetail.Price
from
    OrderDetail where fk_OrderID = thisOrderID
```

This second approach is less of a resource hog since there is no redundant data; however, you end up making 11 round-trips (one time for the parent table, and 10 times for each parent of the child table).

It's better to get the parent table, the child table, and the relation between them using one round-trip, without all the redundant data. This is one of the biggest benefits that DataSet brings. The following block of code demonstrates the power of having tables and relationships:

```
/*
 * Given an order id, display a single order.
 */
public static void DisplaySingleOrder(DataSet m_ds, int iOrderID) {

    Decimal runningTotal = 0;
    Decimal lineTotal = 0;
    Decimal dPrice = 0;
    int iQty = 0;

    DataTable oTable = m_ds.Tables["Order"];

    // Find an order from the Order table.
    DataRow oRow = oTable.Rows.Find(iOrderID);

    /* Navigate to the OrderDetail table
     * through the Order_Details relationship.
     */
    DataRow[] arrRows = oRow.GetChildRows("Order_OrderDetail");

    /* Display the order information. */
    Console.WriteLine ("Order: {0}", iOrderID);
    Console.WriteLine ("Name: {0} {1}",
                    oRow["CustomerFirstName"].ToString( ),
                    oRow["CustomerLastName"].ToString( ));
    Console.WriteLine ("Date: {0}", oRow["Date"].ToString( ));
    Console.WriteLine("--------------------------");
```

```
/*
 * Display and calculate line total for each item.
 */
for(int i = 0; i < arrRows.Length; i++)  {

  foreach(DataColumn myColumn in m_ds.Tables["OrderDetail"].Columns)
  {
    Console.Write(arrRows[i][myColumn] + " ");
  }

  iQty = System.Int32.Parse(arrRows[i]["Quantity"].ToString());
  dPrice = System.Decimal.Parse(arrRows[i]["Price"].ToString());

  lineTotal = iQty * dPrice;
  Console.WriteLine("{0}", lineTotal);

  /* Keep a running total. */
  runningTotal += lineTotal;
}

/* Display the total of the order. */
Console.WriteLine("Total: {0}", runningTotal);
}
```

DisplaySingleOrder finds a single row in the Order table with a given order ID. Once this row is found, we ask the row for an array of dependent rows from the OrderDetail table according to the Order_OrderDetail relationship. With the returned array of DataRows, we then proceed to display all fields in the row. We also calculate the lineTotal value based on the quantity ordered and the price of the item, as well as keeping a runningTotal for the whole order. The following shows the output from the DisplaySingleOrder function:

```
Order: 101
Name: John Doe
Date: 5/1/2001 12:00:00 AM
--------------------------
101 Item-100 12 59.95 719.4
101 Item-200 1 9.25 9.25
Total: 728.65
```

.NET Framework Data Providers

.NET Framework Data Provider (a.k.a. Managed Provider) is a term used for a group of .NET components that implement a fixed set of functionality put forth by the ADO.NET architecture. This enforces a common interface for accessing data. In order to build our own data provider, we must provide our own implementation of System.Data.Common.DbDataAdapter objects and implement interfaces such as IDbCommand, IDbConnection,

and IDataReader. We are not building our own data provider here;[*] however, we do dive into each of these classes and interfaces in this section.

Most of the time, developers don't have to know how to implement data providers, even though this might increase their productivity with regard to ADO. NET. Understanding how to use the stock data providers alone is sufficient to develop your enterprise application. Microsoft provides the following data providers in its current release of ADO.NET: OLE DB and SQL (Version 1 of .NET Framework) and ODBC, Oracle, SQL CE. The OLE DB data provider comes with OleDbConnection, OleDbCommand, OleDbParameter, and OleDbDataReader. The SQL Server data provider comes with a similar set of objects, whose names start with SqlClient instead of OleDb, and so on, as illustrated in Figure 5-3. The implementation of this core function set for data providers is packaged in the System.Data namespace. The assemblies are: System.Data.{Odbc, OleDb, OracleClient SqlClient, SqlServerCe}.

All of the included data providers implement a set of interfaces that access the appropriate data store. The OLE DB provider relies on OLE DB as an access layer to a broad variety of data sources, including Microsoft SQL Server. For performance reasons, the SQL data provider uses a proprietary protocol to communicate directly with SQL Server. In Version 1.1 of the .NET framework, ODBC, Oracle, and SQL CE data providers are added to provide better performance for these data store. Regardless of how the data is obtained, the resulting dataset remains the same. This clean separation of data providers and the XML-based dataset helps ADO.NET achieve portable data.

Figure 5-3 shows the base classes and the all implementations of data provider. Because all data providers, adhere to a fixed, common set of interfaces (IDbCommand, IDbConnection, IDataParameterCollection, IDataReader, and IDataAdapter), you can easily adapt your application to switch data providers as the need arises.

Connection

All Connection classes implement System.Data.IDbConnection and, thus, inherit properties such as the connection string and the state of the connection. They implement the core set of methods specified by IDbConnection, including Open and Close.

---

[*] There is a reference implementation of a .NET Framework Data Provider included in the .NET Framework documentation for any other type of data. In the near future, we are sure that the list of .NET Framework Data Providers will grow to cover even more different data sources.

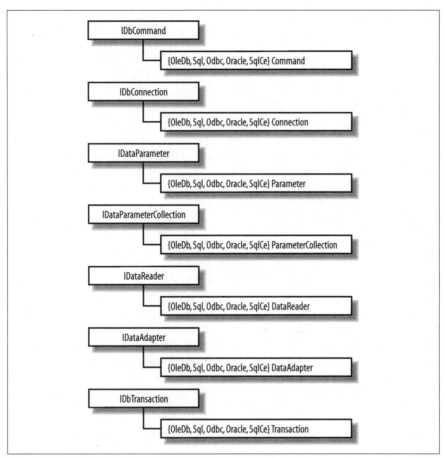

Figure 5-3. Data provider framework class hierarchy

Unlike the ADO Connection object, transaction support for the ADO.NET connection object has been moved to a Transaction object (such as OleDb-Transaction and SqlTransaction). The reason for this is that we cannot assume that all data providers implement transaction the same way, so it's better for the Connection object not to have transaction-related functionalities. To create a new transaction, execute the BeginTransaction() method of the Connection object. This returns an IDbTransaction implementation that supports transaction-oriented functionality such as Commit and Rollback. The SqlTransaction is currently the only provider that also supports saving checkpoints so that we can rollback to a specific checkpoint instead of rolling back the whole transaction. Again, if you examine the list of methods that any Connection class (such as OleDbConnection and SqlConnection) supports, you will find that the functionality is very much the same as the

old ADO Connection object's. However, none of the Connection classes allows SQL statements or provider-specific text statements to be executed directly any more. In other words, Execute( ) is no longer supported by the Connection object. This is a better way for distributing functionality between classes. All execution is done through the Command object, which is discussed in the next section along with how to initiate a connection.

The Command and Data Reader Objects

Fortunately for ADO developers, ADO.NET's Command objects behave like ADO's Command object; however, the Command objects are the only way we can make execution requests to insert, update, and delete data in ADO.NET. This makes it easier to learn the object model. Developers are not faced with as many ways of doing the same things, as in the case (with ADO) of whether to execute the query through a Connection, Command, or even a Recordset object.

Command execution

All commands are associated with a connection object through the Command's Connection property. Think of the connection object as the pipeline between the data-reading component and the database back end. In order to execute a command, the active connection has to be opened. The command object also accepts parameters to execute a stored procedure at the back end. The top left of Figure 5-5 shows the relationships between command, connection, and parameters objects.

There are two types of execution. The first type is a query command, which returns an IDataReader implementation. It is implemented by the ExecuteReader( ) method. The second type of command typically performs an update, insert, or deletion of rows in a database table. This type of execution is implemented by the ExecuteNonQuery( ) method.

One of the main differences between ADO.NET's Command objects and ADO's Command object is the return data. In ADO, the result of executing a query command is a recordset, which contains the return data in tabular form.[*] In ADO.NET, however, recordsets are no longer supported. The result of executing a query command is now a data reader object (see the following section). This data reader object can be an OleDbDataReader for OLE DB, SqlDataReader for SQL Server (as of v.1 of .NET Framework), or any class implementing the IDataReader for custom reading needs. Once

---

[*] Disconnected record set.

you've obtained a valid data reader object, you can perform a Read operation on it to get to your data.

Employing the command, connection, and data reader objects is a low-level, direct way to work with the data provider. As you will find out a little later, the data adapter encapsulates all this low-level plumbing as a more direct way to get the data from the data source to your disconnected dataset.

The data reader object

The data reader is a brand new concept to ADO developers, but it is straightforward. A data reader is similar to a stream object in object-oriented programming (OOP). If you need to access records in a forward-only, sequential order, use a data reader because it is very efficient. Since this is a server-side cursor, the connection to the server is open throughout the reading of data. Because of this continually open connection, we recommend that you exercise this option with care and not have the data reader linger around longer than it should. Otherwise, it might affect the scalability of your application.

The following code demonstrates basic use of OleDbConnection, OleDbCommand, and OleDbDataReader. Though we're using the OLE DB data provider here, the connection string is identical to the one we used earlier for ADO:*

```
using System;
using System.Data;
using System.Data.OleDb;

public class pubsdemo {

  public static void Main( ) {

    /* An OLE DB connection string. */
    String sConn =
      "provider=sqloledb;server=(local);database=pubs; Integrated
Security=SSPI";

    /* An SQL statement. */
    String sSQL = "select au_fname, au_lname, phone from authors";

    /* Create and open a new connection. */
    OleDbConnection oConn = new OleDbConnection(sConn);
    oConn.Open( );
```

---

* In addition, you can create a Command object from the current connection by using this instead:
oCmd = oConn.CreateCommand( );.

```
/* Create a new command and execute the SQL statement. */
OleDbCommand oCmd = new OleDbCommand(sSQL, oConn);
OleDbDataReader oReader = oCmd.ExecuteReader( );

/* Find the index of the columns we're interested in. */
int idxFirstName = oReader.GetOrdinal("au_fname");
int idxLastName = oReader.GetOrdinal("au_lname");
int idxPhone = oReader.GetOrdinal("phone");

/* Retrieve and display each column using their column index. */
while(oReader.Read( )) {
  Console.WriteLine("{0} {1} {2}",
                    oReader.GetValue(idxFirstName),
                    oReader.GetValue(idxLastName),
                    oReader.GetValue(idxPhone));
}

  }
}
```

The code opens a connection to the local SQL Server (using integrated security)[*] and issues a query for first name, last name, and phone number from the authors table in the pubs database.

If you don't have the pubs database installed on your system, you can load and run *instpubs.sql* in Query Analyzer (*instpubs.sql* can be found under the *MSSQL\Install* directory on your machine). For those that install the VS.NET Quickstart examples, change the server parameter of the connection string to server=(local)\\NetSDK because the Quickstart examples installation lays down the NetSDK SQL Server instance that also include the infamous Pubs database. The following example uses SqlClient to get the same information. This time, instead of obtaining the indices for the columns and getting the values based on the indices, this example indexes the column directly using the column names:

```
using System;
using System.Data;
using System.Data.SqlClient;

public class pubsdemo {

  public static void Main( ) {
```

---

[*] Please be aware that database connection pooling relies on the uniqueness of the connection strings. When using the integrated security model of SQL Server, if you make the data access code run under the security context of each of the logged-in users, database connection pooling will suffer. You must create a small set of Windows accounts to overcome this problem; we don't discuss security in great depth in this book, due to its compact size.

```
/* A SQL Server connection string. */
String sConn = "server=(local);database=pubs;Integrated Security=SSPI";

/* An SQL statement. */
String sSQL = "select au_fname, au_lname, phone from authors";

/* Create and open a new connection. */
SqlConnection oConn = new SqlConnection(sConn);
oConn.Open();

/* Create a new command and execute the SQL statement. */
SqlCommand oCmd = new SqlCommand(sSQL, oConn);
SqlDataReader oReader = oCmd.ExecuteReader();

/* Retrieve and display each column using the column names. */
while(oReader.Read()) {
  Console.WriteLine("{0} {1} {2}",
                    oReader["au_fname"],
                    oReader["au_lname"],
                    oReader["phone"]);
}

  }
}
```

We leave the example code utilizing other data providers to the readers as an exercise.

The DataAdapter Object

Along with the introduction of data reader, ADO.NET also brings the Data-Adapter object, which acts as the bridge between the data source and the disconnected DataSet. It contains a connection and a number of commands for retrieving the data from the data store into one DataTable in the DataSet and updating the data in the data store with the changes currently cached in the DataSet. Although each DataAdapter maps only one DataTable in the DataSet, you can have multiple adapters to fill the DataSet object with multiple DataTables. The class hierarchy of DataAdapter is shown in Figure 5-4. All Data Adapters are derived from DbDataAdapter, which in turn is derived from the DataAdapter abstract class. This DataAdapter abstract class implements the IDataAdapter interface, which specifies that it supports Fill and Update. IDataAdapter is specified in the System.Data namespace, as is the DataSet itself.

The data adapter can fill a DataSet with rows and update the data source when you make changes to the dataset. For example, you can use OleDb-Adapter to move data from an OLE DB provider into a DataSet using the OleDbDataAdapter.Fill() method. Then you can modify the DataSet and

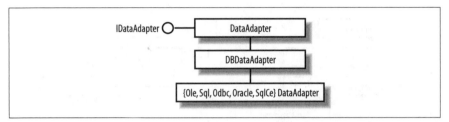

Figure 5-4. DataSetCommand class hierarchy

commit the changes you made to the underlying database using the OleDb-DataAdapter.Update() method. These adapters act as the middleman bridging the data between the database back end and the disconnected DataSet.

For data retrieval, a data adapter uses the SQL SELECT command (exposed as the SelectCommand property). This SELECT command is used in the implementation of the IDataAdapter interface's Fill method. For updating data, a data adapter uses the SQL UPDATE, INSERT, and DELETE commands (exposed as the UpdateCommand, InsertCommand, and DeleteCommand properties).

Along with the Fill and Update methods from DbDataAdapter class, All data adapters also inherit the TableMappings property, a collection of TableMapping objects that enable the mapping of actual database column names to user-friendly column names. This further isolates the DataSet from the source where the actual data comes from. Even table names and column names can be mapped to more readable names, making it easier to use the DataSet. The application developer can be more productive at what he does best, which is to implement business logic and not to decipher cryptic database column names. Figure 5-5 shows the relationship between data provider components.

Out of the four commands in the IDbDataAdapter object, only the SELECT command is required. The rest of the commands are optional since they can be generated automatically by the system. However, the auto-generation of these commands only works when certain conditions are met. For example, if your data adapter fills the data set from some database view that includes more than one table, you will have to explicitly define all four commands. Another example is when your adapter does not return key fields from the table, the system won't be able to generate the insert, update, or delete command. A typical usage of the data adapter involves the following steps:

- Create a data-adapter object.
- Set up the query string for the internal SelectCommand object.
- Set up the connection string for the SelectCommand's Connection object.

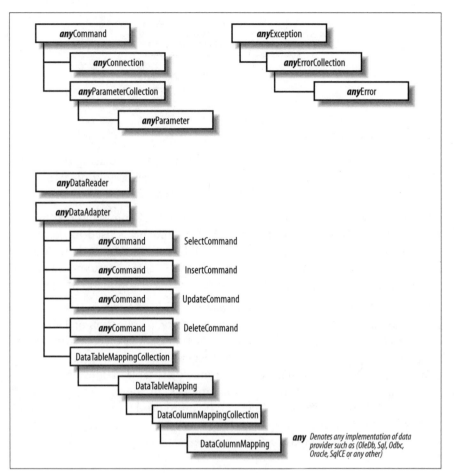

Figure 5-5. Data adapter and supporting classes

- Set up the InsertCommand, UpdateCommand, or DeleteCommand query strings and connections (Recommended).
- Call Fill( ) to fill the given dataset with the results from the query string.
- Make changes and call the adapter's Update( ) method with the changed DataSet (Optional).

The following block of code demonstrates these steps:

```
static DataSet GenerateDS( ) {

    /* Create the DataSet object. */
    DataSet ds = new DataSet("DBDataSet");
    String sConn =
        "provider=SQLOLEDB;server=(local);database=pubs; Integrated
Security=SSPI ";
```

```
/* Create the DataSet adapters. */
OleDbDataAdapter dsAdapter1 =
    new OleDbDataAdapter("select * from authors", sConn);

OleDbDataAdapter dsAdapter2 =
    new OleDbDataAdapter("select * from titles", sConn);

OleDbDataAdapter dsAdapter3 =
    new OleDbDataAdapter("select * from titleauthor", sConn);

/* Fill the data set with three tables. */
dsAdapter1.Fill(ds, "authors");
dsAdapter2.Fill(ds, "titles");
dsAdapter3.Fill(ds, "titleauthor");

// Add the two relations between the three tables. */
ds.Relations.Add("authors2titleauthor",
                ds.Tables["authors"].Columns["au_id"],
                ds.Tables["titleauthor"].Columns["au_id"]);

ds.Relations.Add("titles2titleauthor",
                ds.Tables["titles"].Columns["title_id"],
                ds.Tables["titleauthor"].Columns["title_id"]);

// Return the DataSet.
return ds;

}
```

This is a demonstration of constructing a dataset with three tables from the sample *pubs* database. The DataSet also contains two relationships that tie the three tables together. Let's take a look at the dataset in XML by trying out the next couple lines of code:

```
DataSet ds = GenerateDS();
ds.WriteXml("DBDataSet.xml", XmlWriteMode.WriteSchema);
```

The content of *DBDataSet.xml* (with some omission for brevity) is shown next:

```
<?xml version="1.0" standalone="yes"?>
<DBDataSet>
  <xsd:schema id="DBDataSet" targetNamespace="" xmlns=""
            xmlns:xsd="http://www.w3.org/2001/XMLSchema"
            xmlns:msdata="urn:schemas-microsoft-com:xml-msdata">
    <xsd:element name="DBDataSet" msdata:IsDataSet="true">
      <xsd:complexType>
        <xsd:choice maxOccurs="unbounded">

            <xsd:element name="authors">
              <xsd:complexType>
                <xsd:sequence>
                  <!-- columns simplified for brevity -->
```

```
                    <xsd:element name="au_id" type="xsd:string" />
                    <xsd:element name="au_lname" type="xsd:string" />
                    <xsd:element name="au_fname" type="xsd:string" />
                    <xsd:element name="phone" type="xsd:string" />
                    <xsd:element name="address" type="xsd:string" />
                    <xsd:element name="city" type="xsd:string" />
                    <xsd:element name="state" type="xsd:string" />
                    <xsd:element name="zip" type="xsd:string" />
                    <xsd:element name="contract" type="xsd:boolean" />
                  </xsd:sequence>
                </xsd:complexType>
              </xsd:element>

              <!-- titles and titleauthor omitted for brevity -->

            </xsd:choice>
          </xsd:complexType>

          <xsd:unique name="Constraint1">
            <xsd:selector xpath=".//authors" />
            <xsd:field xpath="au_id" />
          </xsd:unique>

          <xsd:unique name="titles_Constraint1"
                        msdata:ConstraintName="Constraint1">
            <xsd:selector xpath=".//titles" />
            <xsd:field xpath="title_id" />
          </xsd:unique>

          <xsd:keyref name="titles2titleauthor"
                        refer="titles_Constraint1">
            <xsd:selector xpath=".//titleauthor" />
            <xsd:field xpath="title_id" />
          </xsd:keyref>

          <xsd:keyref name="authors2titleauthor"
                        refer="Constraint1">
            <xsd:selector xpath=".//titleauthor" />
            <xsd:field xpath="au_id" />
          </xsd:keyref>

        </xsd:element>
      </xsd:schema>

      <!-- Most rows removed for brevity -->

      <authors>
        <au_id>899-46-2035</au_id>
        <au_lname>Ringer</au_lname>
        <au_fname>Anne</au_fname>
        <phone>801 826-0752</phone>
        <address>67 Seventh Av.</address>
        <city>Salt Lake City</city>
```

```xml
      <state>UT</state>
      <zip>84152</zip>
      <contract>true</contract>
   </authors>

   <titles>
      <title_id>PS2091</title_id>
      <title>Is Anger the Enemy?</title>
      <type>psychology  </type>
      <pub_id>0736</pub_id>
      <price>10.95</price>
      <advance>2275</advance>
      <royalty>12</royalty>
      <ytd_sales>2045</ytd_sales>
      <notes>Carefully researched study of the effects of strong
      emotions on the body. Metabolic charts included.</notes>
      <pubdate>1991-06-15T00:00:00.0000</pubdate>
   </titles>
      <title_id>MC3021</title_id>
      <title>The Gourmet Microwave</title>
      <type>mod_cook</type>
      <pub_id>0877</pub_id>
      <price>2.99</price>
      <advance>15000</advance>
      <royalty>24</royalty>
      <ytd_sales>22246</ytd_sales>
      <notes>Traditional French gourmet recipes adapted for modern
      microwave cooking.</notes>
      <pubdate>1991-06-18T00:00:00.0000</pubdate>
   </titles>

   <titleauthor>
      <au_id>899-46-2035</au_id>
      <title_id>MC3021</title_id>
      <au_ord>2</au_ord>
      <royaltyper>25</royaltyper>
   </titleauthor>
   <titleauthor>
      <au_id>899-46-2035</au_id>
      <title_id>PS2091</title_id>
      <au_ord>2</au_ord>
      <royaltyper>50</royaltyper>
   </titleauthor>

</DBDataSet>
```

The tables are represented as <xsd:element name="table name">...</xsd:element> tag pairs that contain column definitions. In addition to one xsd:element for each table, we have one xsd:unique for each key and one xsd:keyref for each relationship. The xsd:unique specifies the key of the parent table in a relationship. The tag xsd:keyref is used for child tables

in a relationship. This xsd:keyref serves as the foreign key and refers to the key in the parent table.

For brevity, we've stripped down the data portion of the XML to contain just one author, Anne Ringer, and two books she authored.

We can have many different DataAdapters populating the DataSet. Each of these DataAdapters can be going against a completely different data source or data server. In other words, you can construct a DataSet object filled with data that is distributed across multiple servers. In the previous example, we have three different DataAdapters; however, all of them are going to the same server.

XML in the .NET Framework

XML has rapidly gained popularity. Enterprise applications are using XML as the main data format for data exchanges.

ADO.NET breaks away from the COM-based recordset and employs XML as its transport data format. Because XML is platform independent, ADO.NET extends the reach to include anyone who is able to encode/decode XML. This is a big advantage over ADO because a COM-based recordset is not platform independent.

XML Parsers

Even though XML is text-based and readable by humans, you still should have some way of programmatically reading, inspecting, and changing XML. This is the job of XML parsers. There are two kinds of XML parsers: tree-based and stream-based. Depending on your needs, these two types of parsers should complement each other and serve you well.

Tree-based XML parsers read the XML file (or stream) in its entirety to construct a tree of XML nodes. Think of these XML nodes as your XML tag:

```
<car>
  <vin>VI00000383148374</vin>
  <make>Acura</make>
  <model>Integra</model>
  <year>1995</year>
</car>
```

When parsed into a tree, this information would have one root node: car; under car, there are four nodes: vin, make, model, and year. As you might have suspected, if the XML stream is very large in nature, then a tree-based XML parser might not be a good idea. The tree would be too large and consume a lot of memory.

A Stream-based XML parser reads the XML stream as it goes. SAX (Simple API for XML) is a specification for this kind of parsing. The parser raises events as it reads the data, notifying the application of the tag or text the parser just read. It does not attempt to create the complete tree of all XML nodes as does the tree-based parser. Therefore, memory consumption is minimal. This kind of XML parser is ideal for going through large XML files to look for small pieces of data. The .NET framework introduces another stream-based XML parser: the XmlReader. While SAX pushes events at the application as it reads the data, the XmlReader allows the application to pull data from the stream.

Microsoft implements both types of parsers in its XML parser. Because XML is so powerful, Microsoft, among other industry leaders, incorporates XML usage in almost all the things they do. That includes, but is not limited to, the following areas:

- XML+HTTP in SOAP
- XML+SQL in SQL2000
- XML in BizTalk
- XML+DataSet in ADO.NET
- XML in web services and Web Services Discovery (DISCO) (see Chapter 6)

In this chapter, we will discuss XML+Dataset in ADO.NET, and XML in web services will be examined in the next chapter. Because XML is used everywhere in the .NET architecture, we also provide a high-level survey of the XML classes.

XML Classes

To understand the tree-based Microsoft XML parser, which supports the Document Object Model (DOM Level 2 Core standard), there are only a handful of objects you should know:

- XmlNode and its derivatives
- XmlNodeList, as collection XmlNode
- XmlNamedNodeMap, as a collection of XmlAttribute

We will walk through a simple XML example to see how XML nodes are mapped into these objects in the XML DOM.

XmlNode and its derivatives

XmlNode is a base class that represents a single node in the XML docu-ment. In the object model, almost everything derives from XmlNode

(directly or indirectly). This includes: XmlAttribute, XmlDocument, XmlElement, and XmlText, among other XML node types.

The following XML excerpt demonstrates mapping of XML tags to the node types in the DOM tree:

```
<books>
 <book category="How To">
  <title>How to drive in DC metropolitan</title>
  <author>Jack Daniel</author>
  <price>19.95</price>
 </book>
 <book category="Fiction">
  <title>Bring down the fence</title>
  <author>Jack Smith</author>
  <price>9.95</price>
 </book>
</books>
```

After parsing this XML stream, you end up with the tree depicted in Figure 5-6. It contains one root node, which is just a derivative of XmlNode. This root node is of type XmlDocument. Under this books root node, you have two children, also derivatives of XmlNode. This time, they are of type XmlElement. Under each book element node, there are four children. The first child is category. This category node is of type XmlAttribute, a derivative of XmlNode. The next three children are of type XmlElement: title, author, and price. Each of these elements has one child of type XmlText.

As a base class, XmlNode supports a number of methods that aid in the constructing of the XML document tree. These methods include AppendChild(), PrependChild(), InsertBefore(), InsertAfter(), and Clone().

XmlNode also supports a group of properties that aid in navigation within the XML document tree. These properties include FirstChild, NextSibling, PreviousSibling, LastChild, ChildNodes, and ParentNode. You can use the ChildNodes property to navigate down from the root of the tree. For traversing backward, use the ParentNode property from any node on the tree.

XmlNodeList

Just as an XmlNode represents a single XML element, XmlNodeList represents a collection of zero or more XmlNodes. The ChildNodes property of the XmlNode is of type XmlNodeList. Looking at the root node books, we see that its ChildNodes property would be a collection of two XmlNodes. XmlNodeList supports enumeration, so we can iterate over the collection to get to each of the XmlNode objects. We can also index into the collection through a zero-based index.

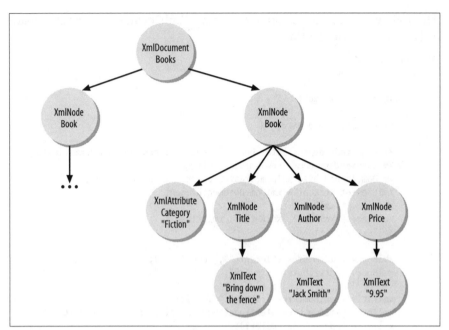

Figure 5-6. Tree representation of an XML document

Each of the book XmlElement objects would have a ChildNodes collection that iterates over `title`, `author`, and `price` XmlElements.

XmlNamedNodeMap

Similar to XmlNodeList, XmlNamedNodeMap is also a collection object. XmlNamedNodeMap is a collection of XmlAttribute objects that enable both enumeration and indexing of attributes by name. Each XmlNode has a property named Attributes. In the case of the book elements, these collections contain only one attribute, which is `category`.

XmlDocument

In addition to all methods and properties supported by XmlNode, this derivative of XmlNode adds or restricts methods and properties. Here, we inspect only XmlDocument as an example of a derivative of XmlNode.

XmlDocument extends XmlNode and adds a number of helper functions. These helper functions are used to create other types of XmlNodes, such as XmlAttribute, XmlComment, XmlElement, and XmlText. In addition to allowing for the creation of other XML node types, XmlDocument also provides the mechanism to load and save XML contents.

The following code demonstrates how an XmlDocument is programmatically generated with DOM:

```
using System;
using System.Xml;

public class XmlDemo {

  public static void Main( ) {

    // Code that demonstrates how to create XmlDocument programmatically
    XmlDocument xmlDom = new XmlDocument( );
    xmlDom.AppendChild(xmlDom.CreateElement("", "books", ""));
    XmlElement xmlRoot = xmlDom.DocumentElement;
    XmlElement xmlBook;
    XmlElement xmlTitle, xmlAuthor, xmlPrice;
    XmlText xmlText;

    xmlBook= xmlDom.CreateElement("", "book", "");
    xmlBook.SetAttribute("category", "", "How To");

    xmlTitle = xmlDom.CreateElement("", "title", "");
    xmlText = xmlDom.CreateTextNode("How to drive in DC metropolitan");
    xmlTitle.AppendChild(xmlText);
    xmlBook.AppendChild(xmlTitle);

    xmlAuthor = xmlDom.CreateElement("", "author", "");
    xmlText = xmlDom.CreateTextNode("Jack Daniel");
    xmlAuthor.AppendChild(xmlText);
    xmlBook.AppendChild(xmlAuthor);

    xmlPrice = xmlDom.CreateElement("", "price", "");
    xmlText = xmlDom.CreateTextNode("19.95");
    xmlPrice.AppendChild(xmlText);
    xmlBook.AppendChild(xmlPrice);

    xmlRoot.AppendChild(xmlBook);

    xmlBook= xmlDom.CreateElement("", "book", "");
    xmlBook.SetAttribute("category", "", "Fiction");

    xmlTitle = xmlDom.CreateElement("", "title", "");
    xmlText = xmlDom.CreateTextNode("Bring down the fence");
    xmlTitle.AppendChild(xmlText);
    xmlBook.AppendChild(xmlTitle);

    xmlAuthor = xmlDom.CreateElement("", "author", "");
    xmlText = xmlDom.CreateTextNode("Jack Smith");
    xmlAuthor.AppendChild(xmlText);
    xmlBook.AppendChild(xmlAuthor);

    xmlPrice = xmlDom.CreateElement("", "price", "");
    xmlText = xmlDom.CreateTextNode("9.95");
```

```
xmlPrice.AppendChild(xmlText);
xmlBook.AppendChild(xmlPrice);

xmlRoot.AppendChild(xmlBook);

Console.WriteLine(xmlDom.InnerXml);

    }

}
```

The XmlDocument also supports LoadXml and Load methods, which build the whole XML tree from the input parameter. LoadXml takes a string in XML format, whereas Load can take a stream, a filename or a URL, a Text-Reader, or an XmlReader. The following example continues where the previous one left off. The XML tree is saved to a file named *books.xml*. Then this file is loaded back into a different XML tree. This new tree outputs the same XML stream as the previous one:

```
...
xmlDom.Save("books.xml");
XmlDocument xmlDom2 = new XmlDocument( );
xmlDom2.Load("books.xml");
Console.WriteLine(xmlDom2.InnerXml);
```

XmlReader

The XmlReader object is a fast, noncached, forward-only way of accessing streamed XML data. There are two derivatives of XmlReader: XmlText-Reader and XmlNodeReader. Both of these readers read XML one tag at a time. The only difference between the two is the input to each reader. As the name implies, XmlTextReader reads a stream of pure XML text. XmlNode-Reader reads a stream of nodes from an XmlDocument. The stream can start at the beginning of the XML file for the whole XmlDocument or only at a specific node of the XmlDocument for partial reading.

Consider the following XML excerpt for order processing. If this file is large, it is not reasonable to load it into an XmlDocument and perform parsing on it. Instead, we should read only nodes or attributes we are interesting in and ignore the rest. We can use XmlReader derived classes to do so:

```
<Orders>
<Order id="ABC001" ...>
<Item code="101" qty="3" price="299.00" ...>17in Monitor</Item>
<Item code="102" qty="1" price="15.99" ...>Keyboard</Item>
<Item code="103" qty="2" price="395.95" ...>CPU</Item>
</Order>
<Order id="ABC002" ...>
<Item code="101b" qty="1" price="499.00" ...>21in Monitor</Item>
<Item code="102" qty="1" price="15.99" ...>Keyboard</Item>
```

```
</Order>
<...>
</Orders>
```

The following block of code traverses and processes each order from the large Orders.xml input file:

```
using System;
using System.IO;
using System.Xml;

class TestXMLReader
{

static void Main(string[] args)
{
    TestXMLReader tstObj = new TestXMLReader( );
    StreamReader myStream = new StreamReader("Orders.xml");
    XmlTextReader xmlTxtRdr = new XmlTextReader(myStream);
    while(xmlTxtRdr.Read( ))
    {
        if(xmlTxtRdr.NodeType == XmlNodeType.Element
            && xmlTxtRdr.Name == "Order")
        {
            tstObj.ProcessOrder(xmlTxtRdr);
        }
    }
}

public void ProcessOrder(XmlTextReader reader)
{
    Console.WriteLine("Start processing order: " +
                    reader.GetAttribute("id"));
    while(!(reader.NodeType == XmlNodeType.EndElement
        && reader.Name == "Order")
        && reader.Read( ))
    {
        // Process Content of Order
        if(reader.NodeType == XmlNodeType.Element
            && reader.Name == "Item")
        {
            Console.WriteLine("itemcode:" + reader.GetAttribute("code") +
                        ". Qty: " + reader.GetAttribute("qty"));
        }
    }
}

}
```

Let's take a closer look at what is going on. Once we have established the XmlTextReader object with the stream of data from the string, all we have to do is loop through and perform a Read( ) operation until there is nothing else to read. While we are reading, we start to process the order only when

we come across a node of type XmlElement and a node named Order. Inside the ProcessOrder function, we read and process all items inside an order until we encounter the end tag of Order. In this case, we return from the function and go back to looking for the next Order tag to process the next order.

XmlNodeReader is similar to XmlTextReader because they both allow processing of XML sequentially. However, XmlNodeReader reads XML nodes from a complete or fragment of an XML tree. This means XmlNodeReader is not helpful when processing large XML files.

XmlWriter

The XmlWriter object is a fast, noncached way of writing streamed XML data. It also supports namespaces. The only derivative of XmlWriter is XmlTextWriter.

XmlWriter supports namespaces by providing a number of overloaded functions that take a namespace to associate with the element. If this namespace is already defined and there is an existing prefix, XmlWriter automatically writes the element name with the defined prefix. Almost all element-writing methods are overloaded to support namespaces.

The following code shows how to use an XmlTextWriter object to write a valid XML file:

```
XmlTextWriter writer =
    new XmlTextWriter("test.xml", new System.Text.ASCIIEncoding());
writer.Formatting = Formatting.Indented;
writer.Indentation = 4;
writer.WriteStartDocument();
writer.WriteComment("Comment");
writer.WriteStartElement("ElementName", "myns");
writer.WriteStartAttribute("prefix", "attrName", "myns");
writer.WriteEndAttribute();
writer.WriteElementString("ElementName", "myns", "value");
writer.WriteEndElement();
writer.WriteEndDocument();
writer.Flush();
writer.Close();
```

This produces the following XML document in *test.xml*:

```
<?xml version="1.0" encoding="us-ascii"?>
<!--Comment-->
<ElementName prefix:attrName="" xmlns:prefix="myns" xmlns="myns">
    <prefix:ElementName>value</prefix:ElementName>
</ElementName>
```

XslTransform

XslTransform converts XML from one format to another. It is typically used in data-conversion programs or to convert XML to HTML for the purpose of presenting XML data in a browser. The following code demonstrates how such a conversion takes place:

```
using System;
using System.Xml;           // XmlTextWriter
using System.Xml.Xsl;       // XslTransform
using System.Xml.XPath;     // XPathDocument
using System.IO;            // StreamReader

public class XSLDemo {
  public static void Main( ) {
    XslTransform xslt = new XslTransform( );
    xslt.Load("XSLTemplate.xsl");
    XPathDocument xDoc = new XPathDocument("Books.xml");
    XmlTextWriter writer = new XmlTextWriter("Books.html", null);
    xslt.Transform(xDoc, null, writer, new XmlUrlResolver( ));
    writer.Close( );
    StreamReader stream = new StreamReader("Books.html");
    Console.Write(stream.ReadToEnd( ));
  }
}
```

The code basically transforms the XML in the *Books.xml* file, which we've seen earlier, into HTML to be displayed in a browser. Even though you can replace the XPathDocument with XmlDocument in the previous code, XPathDocument is the preferred class in this case because it is optimized for XSLT processing.*

Figures 5-7 and 5-8 show the source XML and the output HTML when viewed in a browser.

The template XSL file that was used to transform the XML is:

```
<xsl:stylesheet version="1.0"
  xmlns:xsl="http://www.w3.org/1999/XSL/Transform">
<xsl:template match = "/" >

<html>
<head><title>A list of books</title></head>
<style>
.hdr { background-color=#ffeedd; font-weight=bold; }
</style>
<body>
<B>List of books</B>
```

---

* XPathDocument loads data faster than XmlDocument because it does not maintain node identity and it does not perform rule checking. One catch to this advantage is that the content is read-only.

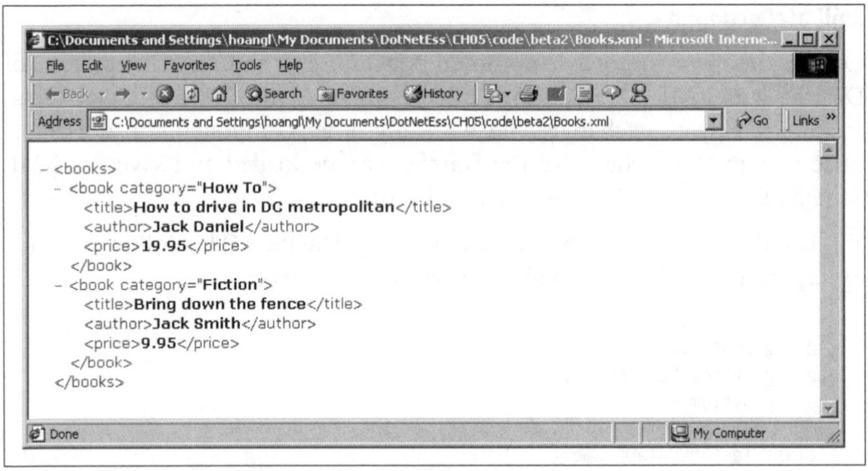

Figure 5-7. Books.xml shown in IE

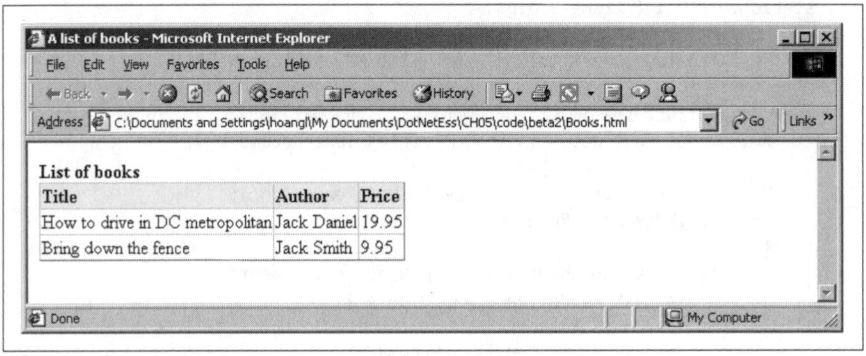

Figure 5-8. Books.html shown in IE

```
<table style="border-collapse:collapse" border="1">
<tr>
  <td class="hdr">Title</td>
  <td class="hdr">Author</td>
  <td class="hdr">Price</td>
</tr>
<xsl:for-each select="//books/book">
<tr>
  <td><xsl:value-of select="title"/></td>
  <td><xsl:value-of select="author"/></td>
  <td><xsl:value-of select="price"/></td>
</tr>
</xsl:for-each>
</table>
</body>
</html>

</xsl:template>
</xsl:stylesheet>
```

XmlDataDocument

One of the most important points in ADO.NET is the tight integration of DataSet with XML. DataSet can easily be streamed into XML and vice versa, making it easy to exchange data with any other components in the enterprise system. The schema of the DataSet can be loaded and saved as XML Schema Definition (XSD), as described earlier.

XmlDataDocument can be associated with DataSet. The following code excerpt illustrates how such an association takes place:

```
using System;
using System.Data;
using System.Data.OleDb;
using System.Xml;

class TestXMLDataDocument
{

static void Main(string[] args)
{
    TestXMLDataDocument tstObj = new TestXMLDataDocument();

    // Construct the XmlDataDocument with the DataSet.
    XmlDataDocument doc = tstObj.GenerateXmlDataDocument();

    XmlNodeReader myXMLReader = new XmlNodeReader(doc);
    while (myXMLReader.Read())
    {
        if(myXMLReader.NodeType == XmlNodeType.Element
            && myXMLReader.Name == "Orders")
        {
            tstObj.ProcessOrder(myXMLReader);
        }
    }
}

public void ProcessOrder(XmlNodeReader reader)
{
    Console.Write("Start processing order: ");
    while(!(reader.NodeType == XmlNodeType.EndElement
        && reader.Name == "Orders")
        && reader.Read())
    {
        if(reader.NodeType == XmlNodeType.Element
            && reader.Name == "OrderID")
        {
            reader.Read();
            Console.WriteLine(reader.Value);
        }
```

```
            if(reader.NodeType == XmlNodeType.Element
                && reader.Name == "OrderDetails")
            {
                ProcessLine(reader);
            }
        }
}

public void ProcessLine(XmlNodeReader reader)
{
    while(!(reader.NodeType == XmlNodeType.EndElement
        && reader.Name == "OrderDetails")
        && reader.Read())
    {
        if(reader.NodeType == XmlNodeType.Element && reader.Name ==
"ProductID")
        {
            reader.Read();
            Console.Write(".  ItemCode: " + reader.Value);
        }
        if(reader.NodeType == XmlNodeType.Element && reader.Name ==
"Quantity")
        {
            reader.Read();
            Console.WriteLine(".  Quantity: " + reader.Value);
        }
    }
}
public XmlDataDocument GenerateXmlDataDocument()
{
    /* Create the DataSet object. */
    DataSet ds = new DataSet("DBDataSet");
    String sConn =
        "provider=SQLOLEDB;server=(local);database=NorthWind;Integrated
Security=SSPI";

    /* Create the DataSet adapters. */
    OleDbDataAdapter dsAdapter1 =
        new OleDbDataAdapter("select * from Orders", sConn);

    OleDbDataAdapter dsAdapter2 =
        new OleDbDataAdapter("select * from [Order Details]", sConn);

    /* Fill the data set with three tables. */
    dsAdapter1.Fill(ds, "Orders");
    dsAdapter2.Fill(ds, "OrderDetails");

    DataColumn[] keys = new DataColumn[1];
    keys[0] = ds.Tables["Orders"].Columns["OrderID"];
    ds.Tables["Orders"].PrimaryKey = keys;
```

```
    // Add the two relations between the three tables. */
    ds.Relations.Add("Orders_OrderDetails",
        ds.Tables["Orders"].Columns["OrderID"],
        ds.Tables["OrderDetails"].Columns["OrderID"]);

    ds.Relations["Orders_OrderDetails"].Nested = true;
    //ds.WriteXml("NorthWindOrders.xml");

    return new XmlDataDocument(ds);

    }

}
```

The previous section describing DataSet has already shown you that once we have a DataSet, we can persist the data inside the DataSet into an XML string or file. This time, we demonstrated how to convert the DataSet into an XmlDataDocument that we can manipulate in memory.

Summary

This chapter describes the core of ADO.NET. Having focused on the disconnected dataset, ADO.NET enables us not only to build high-performance, scalable solutions for e-commerce, but also allows the applications to reach other platforms through the use of XML. This chapter serves as a high-level survey into the classes that make up ADO.NET and serves to familiarize you with the System.Xml library.* In the next chapter, we delve into building software as services. We will make use of ADO.NET as the data-access and exchange mechanism in our software services.

---

* For additional information on ADO.NET, see O'Reilly's *ADO.NET in a Nutshell*, by Bill Hamilton and Matthew MacDonald, and *ADO.NET Cookbook*, by Bill Hamilton.

Web Services

Web services allow access to software components through standard web protocols such as HTTP and SMTP. Using the Internet and XML, we can now create software components that communicate with others, regardless of language, platform, or culture. Until now, software developers have progressed toward this goal by adopting proprietary componentized software methodologies, such as DCOM; however, because each vendor provides its own interface protocol, integration of different vendors' components is a nightmare. By substituting the Internet for proprietary transport formats and adopting standard protocols such as SOAP, web services help software developers create building blocks of software, which can be reused and integrated regardless of their location.

In this chapter, we describe the .NET web services architecture and provide examples of a web service provider and several web service consumers.

Web Services in Practice

You may have heard the phrase "software as a service" and wondered about its meaning. The term *service*, in day-to-day usage, refers to what you get from a service provider. For example, you bring your dirty clothing to a cleaner to use its cleaning *service*. Software, on the other hand, is commonly thought of as an application, either an off-the-shelf product, or a custom application developed by a software firm. You typically buy the software (or in our case, build the software). It usually resides on some sort of media such as floppy diskette or CD and is sold in a shrink-wrapped package through retail outlets, or, in the case of a web application, the software application is not distributed, but is accessed through a browser.

How can software be viewed as a service? The example we are about to describe might seem far-fetched; however, it is possible with current tech-

nology. Imagine the following. As you grow more comfortable with the Internet, you might choose to replace your computer at home with something like an Internet Device, a large-screen PDA designed for use with the Internet. Let's call the device an iDev. Let's suppose that with this device, you can be on the Internet immediately through your cell phone, WiFi, or some other means. When you want to do word processing, your iDev is configured to print to a Microsoft Word service somewhere in Redmond, so you can type away without the need to install word-processing software. When you are done, the document can be saved at an iStore server where you can later retrieve it. Notice that for you to do this, the iStore server must host a software service that allows you to store documents. Microsoft might charge you a service fee based on the amount of time your word processor is running and the features you use (such as the grammar and spell checkers). The iStore service charges might vary based on the size of your document and how long it is stored. Of course, none of these charges would come in the mail, but rather through an escrow service where the money would be withdrawn from your bank account or credit card.

As long as your document is in a standard format, such as XML, you're free to switch word processors at any time. Of course, the document that you store at the iStore server is already in a standard data format. Since iStore utilizes the iMaxSecure software service from a company called iNNSA (Internet Not National Security Agency), the security of your files is assured. And because you use the document storage service at iStore, you also benefit from having your document authenticated and decrypted upon viewing, as well as encrypted at storing time.

While this particular vision of software as a service has yet to be realized, a variety of for-fee and free services have begun to appear. In early 2001, Microsoft announced plans for an integrated collection of consumer-oriented services (known first by their codename, "Hailstorm," and later as ".NET My Services") but was forced to abandon the initiative for a variety of reasons, some technical and others legal, political, or market-related. Today, Microsoft offers a variety of user-centric services for identification and authentication, email, instant messaging, automated alerts, calendar, address book, and personal information storage. These are available through its MSN online services, and through Passport (*http://www.passport.net*), Alerts (*http://alerts.microsoft.com*), MSN Wallet (*http://wallet.msn.com*), and Hotmail.

Of greater interest to developers, however, is the availability of these services for use as building blocks in third-party web applications. Hosted by Microsoft and known as Microsoft .NET Services, Passport, Alerts, and MSN Wallet can each be licensed and incorporated into any application that

adheres to XML web services standards, regardless of platform. A more recently announced web service is Microsoft MapPoint .NET, which is a set of services that allows you to incorporate maps, driving directions, distance calculations, proximity searches, and other location intelligence into your applications.

In addition to Microsoft, other companies are beginning to offer information and functionality as services over the Web. A recent poster child is Saleforce.com, which offers customer relations management (CRM) software over the Web, either as a standalone product or as a set of services that can be incorporated into third-party applications. The Liberty Alliance is at work defining an authentication service that can be offered as an alternative to Microsoft Passport. And both Google and Amazon now make portions of their business information available through public web service interfaces.

The potential for consumer-oriented and business-to-business web services like Microsoft .NET Services is great, although there are serious and well-founded concerns about security and privacy. In the mean time, web services can be great in interoperability areas where there are needs to expose legacy functionalities or to enable interaction between multiple heterogeneous systems. In one form or another, though, web services are here to stay, so let's dive in and see what's underneath.

Web Services Framework

Web services combine the best of both distributed componentization and the World Wide Web, extending distributed computing to broader ranges of client applications. The best thing is that this is done by seamlessly marrying and enhancing existing technologies.

Web Services Architecture

Web services are distributed software components accessible through standard web protocols. The first part of the definition is similar to that for COM/DCOM components. However, it is the second part that distinguishes web services from the crowd. Web services enable software to interoperate with a much broader range of clients. While COM-aware clients can understand only COM components, web services can be consumed by any application that understands how to parse an XML-formatted stream transmitted through HTTP channels. XML is the key technology used in

web services and is used in the following areas of the Microsoft .NET web services framework:

Web service wire formats
> The technology enabling universal understanding of how to perform data exchanges between the service provider and consumer; the format of data for the request and response.

Web service description in Web Services Description Language (WSDL)
> The language describing how the service can be used. Think of this as the instructions on the washing machine at the laundromat telling you where to put quarters, what buttons to push, etc.

Web service discovery
> The process of advertising or publishing a piece of software as a service and allowing for the discovery of this service.

Figure 6-1 depicts the architecture of web applications using Windows DNA, while Figure 6-2 shows .NET-enabled web applications architecture. As you can see, communication between components of a web application does not have to be within an intranet. Furthermore, intercomponent communication can also use HTTP/XML.

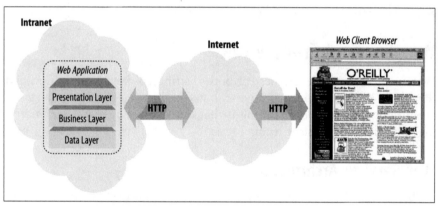

Figure 6-1. Windows Distributed interNet Architecture (DNA)

Web Services Wire Formats

You may have heard the phrase "DCOM is COM over the wire." Web services are similar to DCOM except that the wire is no longer a proprietary communication protocol. With web services, the wire formats rely on more open Internet protocols such as HTTP or SMTP.

A web service is more or less a stateless component running on the web server, exposed to the world through standard Internet protocols. Microsoft

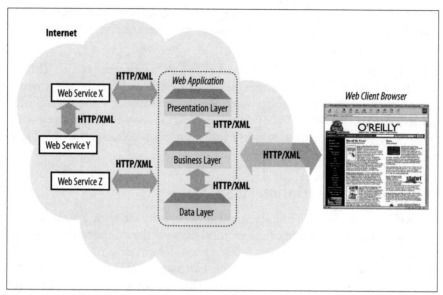

Figure 6-2. .NET-enabled web application framework

.NET web services currently supports three protocols: HTTP GET, HTTP POST, and SOAP over HTTP (Simple Object Access Protocol), explained in the next sections. Because these protocols are standard protocols for the Web, it is very easy for the client applications to use the services provided by the server.

HTTP GET and HTTP POST

As their names imply, both HTTP GET and HTTP POST use HTTP as their underlying protocol. The GET and POST methods of the HTTP protocol have been widely used in ASP (Active Server Pages), CGI, and other server-side architectures for many years now. Both of these methods encode request parameters as name/value pairs in the HTTP request. The GET method creates a query string and appends it to the script's URL on the server that handles the request. For the POST method, the name/value pairs are passed in the body of the HTTP request message.

SOAP

Similar to HTTP GET and HTTP POST, SOAP serves as a mechanism for passing messages between the clients and servers. In this context, the clients are web services consumers, and the servers are the web services. The clients simply send an XML-formatted request message to the server to get the service over an HTTP channel. The server responds by sending back yet

another XML-formatted message. The SOAP specification describes the format of these XML requests and responses. It is simple, yet it is extensible, because it is based on XML.

SOAP is different than HTTP GET and HTTP POST because it uses XML to format its payload. The messages being sent back and forth have a better structure and can convey more complex information compared to simple name/value pairs in HTTP GET/POST protocols. Another difference is that SOAP can be used on top of other transport protocols, such as SMTP in addition to HTTP.*

Web Services Description (WSDL)

For web service clients to understand how to interact with a web service, there must be a description of the method calls, or the interface that the web service supports. This web service description document is found in an XML schema called *Web Services Description Language (WSDL)*. Remember that type libraries and IDL scripts are used to describe a COM component. Both IDL and WSDL files describe an interface's method calls and the list of in and out parameters for the particular call. The only major difference between the two description languages is that all descriptions in the WSDL file are done in XML.

In theory, any WSDL-capable SOAP client can use the WSDL file to get a description of your web service. It can then use the information contained in that file to understand the interface and invoke your web service's methods.

WSDL structure

The root of any web service description file is the <definitions> element. Within this element, the following elements provide both the abstract and concrete description of the service:

Types
    A container for data type definitions.

Message
    An abstract, typed definition of the data being exchanged between the web service providers and consumers. Each web method has two messages: input and output. The input describes the parameters for the web method; the output describes the return data from the web method.

---

* SOAP is recognized as the cross-platform standard protocol to use for web services both inside and outside the Microsoft circle.

Each message contains zero or more <part> parameters. Each parameter associates with a concrete type defined in the <types> container element.

Port type

An abstract set of operations supported by one or more endpoints.

Operation

An abstract description of an action supported by the service. Each operation specifies the input and output messages defined as <message> elements.

Binding

A concrete protocol and data-format specification for a particular port type. Similar to port type, the binding contains operations, as well as the input and output for each operation. The main difference is that with binding, we are now talking about actual transport type and how the input and output are formatted.

Service

A collection of network endpoints—ports. Each of the web service wire formats defined earlier constitutes a port of the service (HTTP GET, HTTP POST, and SOAP ports).

Port

A single endpoint defined by associating a binding and a network address. In other words, it describes the protocol and data-format specification to be used as well as the network address of where the web service clients can bind to for the service.

The following shows a typical WSDL file structure:

```
<definitions name="" targetNamespace="" xmlns:...>

  <types>...</types>

  <message name="">...</message>
  ...

  <portType name="">
    <operation name="">
      <input message="" />
      <output message="" />
    </operation>
    ...
  </portType>
  ...

  <binding name="">
    <protocol:binding ...>
    <operation name="">
      <protocol:operation ...>
```

```
      <input>...</input>
      <output>...</output>
    </operation>
    ...
  </binding>
  ...

  <service name="">
    <port name="" binding="">
      <protocol:address location="" />
    </port>
    ...
  </service>
</definitions>
```

The <types> element contains physical type descriptions defined in XML Schema (XSD). These types are being referred to from the <message> elements.

For each of the web methods in the web service, there are two messages defined for a particular port: input and output. This means if a web service supports all three protocols: SOAP, HTTP GET, and HTTP POST, there will be six <message> elements defined, one pair for each port. The naming convention used by the Microsoft .NET autogenerated WSDL is:

```
MethodName + Protocol + {In, Out}
```

For example, a web method called GetBooks( ) has the following messages:

```
<message name="GetBooksSoapIn">...</message>
<message name="GetBooksSoapOut">...</message>
<message name="GetBooksHttpGetIn">...</message>
<message name="GetBooksHttpGetOut">...</message>
<message name="GetBooksHttpPostIn">...</message>
<message name="GetBooksHttpPostOut">...</message>
```

For each protocol that the web service supports, there is one <portType> element defined. Within each <portType> element, all operations are specified as <operation> elements. The naming convention for the port type is:

```
WebServiceName + Protocol
```

To continue our example, here are the port types associated with the web service that we build later in this chapter, PubsWS:

```
<portType name="PubsWSSoap">
  <operation name="GetBooks">
    <input message="GetBooksSoapIn" />
    <output message="GetBooksSoapOut" />
  </operation>
</portType>

<portType name="PubsWSHttpGet">
  <operation name="GetBooks">
    <input message="GetBooksHttpGetIn" />
```

```
      <output message="GetBooksHttpGetOut" />
    </operation>
  </portType>

  <portType name="PubsWSHttpPost">
    <operation name="GetBooks">
      <input message="GetBooksHttpPostIn" />
      <output message="GetBooksHttpPostOut" />
    </operation>
  </portType>
```

We have removed namespaces from the example to make it easier to read.

While the port types are abstract operations for each port, the bindings provide concrete information on what protocol is being used, how the data is being transported, and where the service is located. Again, there is a <binding> element for each protocol supported by the web service:

```
<binding name="PubsWSSoap" type="s0:PubsWSSoap">
  <soap:binding transport="http://schemas.xmlsoap.org/soap/http"
                style="document" />
  <operation name="GetBooks">
    <soap:operation soapAction="http://tempuri.org/GetBooks"
                    style="document" />
    <input>
      <soap:body use="literal" />
    </input>
    <output>
      <soap:body use="literal" />
    </output>
  </operation>
</binding>

<binding name="PubsWSHttpGet" type="s0:PubsWSHttpGet">
  <http:binding verb="GET" />
  <operation name="GetBooks">
    <http:operation location="/GetBooks" />
    <input>
      <http:urlEncoded />
    </input>
    <output>
      <mime:mimeXml part="Body" />
    </output>
  </operation>
</binding>

<binding name="PubsWSHttpPost" type="s0:PubsWSHttpPost">
  <http:binding verb="POST" />
  <operation name="GetBooks">
    <http:operation location="/GetBooks" />
    <input>
      <mime:content type="application/x-www-form-urlencoded" />
    </input>
```

```
    <output>
      <mime:mimeXml part="Body" />
    </output>
  </operation>
</binding>
```

For SOAP protocol, the binding is <soap:binding>, and the transport is SOAP messages on top of HTTP protocol. The <soap:operation> element defines the HTTP header soapAction, which points to the web method. Both input and output of the SOAP call are SOAP messages.

For the HTTP GET and HTTP POST protocols, the binding is <http:binding> with the verb being GET and POST, respectively. Because the GET and POST verbs are part of the HTTP protocol, there is no need for the extended HTTP header (like soapAction for SOAP protocol). The only thing we need is the URL that points to the web method; in this case, the <soap:operation> element contains the attribute location, which is set to /GetBooks.

The only real difference between the HTTP GET and POST protocols is the way the parameters are passed to the web server. HTTP GET sends the parameters in the query string, while HTTP POST sends the parameters in the form data. This difference is reflected in the <input> elements of the operation GetBooks for the two HTTP protocols. For the HTTP GET protocol, the input is specified as <http:urlEncoded />, whereas for the HTTP POST protocol, the input is <mime:content type="application/x-www-form-urlencoded" />.

Looking back at the template of the WSDL document, we see that the only thing left to discuss is the <service> element, which defines the ports supported by this web service. For each of the supported protocol, there is one <port> element:

```
<service name="PubsWS">

  <port name="PubsWSSoap" binding=s0:PubsWSSoap">
    <soap:address
      location="http://.../PubsWs.asmx" />
  </port>

  <port name="PubsWSHttpGet" binding="s0:PubsWSHttpGet">
    <http:address
      location="http://.../PubsWs.asmx" />
  </port>

  <port name="PubsWSHttpPost" binding="s0:PubsWSHttpPost">
    <http:address
      location="http://.../PubsWs.asmx" />
  </port>

</service>
```

Even though the three different ports look similar, their binding attributes associate the address of the service with a binding element defined earlier. Web service clients now have enough information on where to access the service, through which port to access the web service method, and how the communication messages are defined.

Although it is possible to read the WSDL and manually construct the HTTP* conversation with the server to get to a particular web service, there are tools that autogenerate client-side proxy source code to do the same thing. We show such a tool in "web services Consumers" later in this chapter.

Web Services Discovery

Even though advertising of a web service is important, it is optional. Web services can be private as well as public. Depending on the business model, some business-to-business (B2B) services would not normally be advertised publicly. Instead, the web service owners would provide specific instructions on accessing and using their service only to the business partner.

To advertise web services publicly, authors post discovery files on the Internet. Potential web services clients can browse to these files for information about how to use the web services—the WSDL. Think of it as the yellow pages for the web service. All it does is point you to where the actual web services reside and to the description of those web services.

The process of looking up a service and checking out the service description is called *web service discovery*. Currently in .NET, there are two ways of advertising the service: static and dynamic. In both of these, XML conveys the locations of web services.

Static discovery

Static discovery is easier to understand because it is explicit in nature. If you want to advertise your web service, you must explicitly create the .disco discovery file and point it to the WSDL.†

All *.disco* files contain a root element discovery, as shown in the following code sample. Note that discovery is in the namespace http://schemas.xmlsoap.org/disco/, which is referred to as disco in this sample.

```
<?xml version="1.0" ?>
<disco:discovery xmlns:disco="http://schemas.xmlsoap.org/disco/">
</disco:discovery>
```

---

* Current Microsoft .NET SOAP implementation runs on top of HTTP.

† If you use Visual Studio .NET to create your web service, the discovery file is created automatically.

Inside the discovery element, there can be one or more of contractRef or discoveryRef elements. Both of these elements are described in the namespace http://schemas.xmlsoap.org/disco/scl/. The contractRef tag is used to reference an actual web service URL that would return the WSDL or the description of the actual web service contract. The discoveryRef tag, on the other hand, references another discovery document.

This XML document contains a link to one web service and a link to another discovery document:

```
<?xml version="1.0" ?>
<disco:discovery
        xmlns:disco="http://schemas.xmlsoap.org/disco/"

    xmlns:scl="http://schemas.xmlsoap.org/disco/scl/">

    <scl:contractRef ref="http://yourWebServer/yourWebService.asmx?WSDL"/>

    <scl:discoveryRef ref="http://yourBrotherSite/hisWebServiceDirectory.disco"/>

</disco:discovery>
```

This sample *disco* file specifies two different namespaces: disco, which is a nickname for the namespace http://schemas.xmlsoap.org/disco/; and scl, short for http://schemas.xmlsoap.org/disco/scl/. The contractRef element specifies the URL where *yourWebService* WSDL can be obtained. Right below that is the discoveryRef element, which links to the discovery file on *yourBrotherSite* web site. This linkage allows for structuring networks of related discovery documents.

Dynamic discovery

As opposed to explicitly specifying the URL for all web services your site supports, you can enable *dynamic discovery*, which enables all web services underneath a specific URL on your web site to be listed automatically. For your web site, you might want to group related web services under many different directories and then provide a single dynamic discovery file in each of the directories. The root tag of the dynamic discovery file is *dynamicDiscovery* instead of *discovery*:

```
<?xml version="1.0" encoding="utf-8"?>
<dynamicDiscovery xmlns="urn://schemas-dynamic:disco.2000-03-17" />
```

You can optionally specify exclude paths so that the dynamic mechanism does not have to look for web services in all subdirectories underneath the

location of the dynamic discovery file. Exclude paths are in the following form:

```
<exclude path="pathname" />
```

If you run IIS as your web server, you'd probably have something like the following for a dynamic discovery file:[*]

```
<?xml version="1.0" encoding="utf-8"?>
<dynamicDiscovery xmlns="urn://schemas-dynamic:disco.2000-03-17">
    <exclude path="_vti_cnf" />
    <exclude path="_vti_pvt" />
    <exclude path="_vti_log" />
    <exclude path="_vti_script" />
    <exclude path="_vti_txt" />
    <exclude path="Web References" />
</dynamicDiscovery>
```

Discovery setting in practice

A combination of dynamic and static discovery makes a very flexible configuration. For example, you can provide static discovery documents at each of the directories that contain web services. At the root of the web server, provide a dynamic discovery document with links to all static discovery documents in all subdirectories. To exclude web services from public viewing, provide the exclude argument to XML nodes to exclude their directories from the dynamic discovery document.

UDDI

Universal Description, Discovery, and Integration (UDDI) Business Registry is like a yellow pages of web services. It allows businesses to publish their services and locate web services published by partner organizations so that they can conduct transactions quickly, easily, and dynamically with their trading partner.

Through UDDI APIs, businesses can find services over the web that match their criteria (e.g., cheapest fare), that offer the service they request (e.g., delivery on Sunday), and so on. Currently backed by software giants such as Microsoft, IBM, and Ariba, UDDI is important to web services because it enables access to businesses from a single place.[†]

---

[*] VS.NET uses vsdisco as the extension for its dynamic discovery files.

[†] UDDI SDK can be downloaded from Microsoft as a .NET assembly.

The System.Web.Services Namespace

Now that we have run through the basic framework of Microsoft .NET web services, let us take a look inside what the .NET SDK provides us in the System.Web.Services namespace.

There are only a handful of classes in the System.Web.Services namespace and the most important ones for general use are:

WebService
   The base class for all web services.

WebServiceAttribute
   An attribute that can be associated with a web service–derived class.

WebMethodAttribute
   An attribute that can be associated with public methods within a web service–derived class.

The two essential classes for creating web services are the WebService base class and WebMethodAttribute. We make use of these classes in the next section, where we implement a web service provider and several web service consumers. WebService is the base class from which all web services inherit. It provides properties inherent to legacy ASP programming such as Application, Server, Session, and a new property, Context, which now includes Request and Response.

The WebMethodAttribute class allows you to apply attributes to each public method of your web service. Using this class, you can assign specific values to the following attributes: description, session state enabling flag, message name, transaction mode, and caching. See the following section for an example of attribute setting in C# and VB.

The WebServiceAttribute class is used to provide more attributes about the web service itself. You can display a description of the web service, as well as the namespace to which this web service belongs.

Web Services Provider

In this section, we describe how to develop a web service, first from the point of view of service providers and then of the consumers. Web services providers implement web services and advertise them so that the clients can discover and make use of the services. Because web services run on top of HTTP, there must be a web server application of some sort on the machine that hosts the web services. This web server application can be Microsoft Internet Information Services (IIS), Apache, or any other program that can

understand and process the HTTP protocol. In our examples, we use Microsoft IIS, since that is the only web server currently supported by .NET.

Web Service Provider Example

We will be building a web service called *PubsWS* to let consumers get information from the sample *Pubs* database. All data access will be done through ADO.NET, so read Chapter 5 before attempting the examples.

Creating a web service is a three-step process:

1. Create a new *asmx* file for the web service. This must contain the <% webservice ... %> directive, as well as the class that provides the web service implementation. To the web service clients, this *asmx* file is the entry point to your web service. You need to put this in a virtual directory that has the executescripts permission turned on.

2. Inherit from the WebService class of the System.Web.Services namespace. This allows the derived class to access all the normal ASP.NET objects exposed in the WebService base class such as Application, Session, Server, Request, and Response.* It is highly recommended that you specify a namespace for your web service before publishing it publicly because the default namespace, *http://tempuri.org/*, will not uniquely identify your web service from other web services. To do this, tag the WebService class with the Namespace attribute, specifying your own namespace.

3. Tag the public methods with WebMethod attributes to make *web methods*—public methods of a distributed component that are accessible via the Web. You don't have to tag a method as WebMethod unless you want that method to be published as a web method.

The following C# code demonstrates a simple web service† that exposes four methods to Internet clients.

---

* Access to the Request and Response objects *can* be done through the Context property of the WebService class.

† For security reasons, the current release of ASP.NET runs as the account ASPNET. If you are using integrated security to access database resources, you must grant database access to the ASP-NET account. You can also enable impersonation in the *web.config* or *machine.config* file:

```
<system.web>
 <identity impersonate="true" userName="." password=""/>
</system.web>
```

If you set impersonate to true but leave UserName and password blank, the application will run as *MachineName\IUSR_MachineName*, so make sure to grant this user (or whatever userName you specify) database access.

We emphasize "Internet" because anyone that can access this *asmx* file on the web server can access these methods, as opposed to your COM component, which can be accessed only by COM clients:

```
<%@ WebService Language="C#" Class="PubsWS.PubsWS" %>


namespace PubsWS
{
  using System;
  using System.Data;
  using System.Data.OleDb;
  using System.Web;
  using System.Web.Services;

  [WebService(Namespace="http://Oreilly/DotNetEssentials/")]
  public class PubsWS : WebService
  {
    private static string m_sConnStr =
"provider=sqloledb;server=(local);database=pubs; Integrated Security=SSPI";


    [WebMethod(Description="Returns a DataSet containing all authors.")]

    public DataSet GetAuthors()
    {
      OleDbDataAdapter oDBAdapter;
      DataSet oDS;

      oDBAdapter = new OleDbDataAdapter("select * from authors",
                                        m_sConnStr);
      oDS = new DataSet();
      oDBAdapter.Fill(oDS, "Authors");
      return oDS;
    }


    [WebMethod]

    public DataSet GetAuthor(string sSSN)
    {
      OleDbDataAdapter oDBAdapter;
      DataSet oDS;

      oDBAdapter = new OleDbDataAdapter(
                "select * from authors where au_id ='"
                + sSSN + "'", m_sConnStr);
      oDS = new DataSet();
      oDBAdapter.Fill(oDS, "SelectedAuthor");
      return oDS;
    }
```

```csharp
[WebMethod(MessageName="GetBooksByAuthor",

          Description="Find books by author's SSN.")]

public DataSet GetBooks(string sAuthorSSN)
{
  OleDbDataAdapter oDBAdapter;
  DataSet oDS;

  oDBAdapter = new OleDbDataAdapter(
              "select * from titles inner join titleauthor on " +
              "titles.title_id=titleauthor.title_id " +
              "where au_id='" + sAuthorSSN + "'", m_sConnStr);
  oDS = new DataSet();
  oDBAdapter.Fill(oDS, "Books");
  oDBAdapter = new OleDbDataAdapter("select * from authors " +
              "where au_id='" + sAuthorSSN + "'", m_sConnStr);
  oDBAdapter.Fill(oDS, "Author");

  return oDS;
}


[WebMethod]

public DataSet GetBooks()
{
  OleDbDataAdapter oDBAdapter;
  DataSet oDS;

  oDBAdapter = new OleDbDataAdapter("select * from titles" ,
                                    m_sConnStr);
  oDS = new DataSet();
  oDBAdapter.Fill(oDS, "Books");
  return oDS;
}

} // End PubsWS
}
```

If you are familiar with ASP, you may recognize the usage of the @ symbol in front of keyword WebService. This WebService directive specifies the language of the web service so that ASP.NET can compile the web service with the correct compiler. This directive also specifies the class that implements the web service so it can load the correct class and employ reflection to generate the WSDL for the web service.

Because *PubsWS* also uses ADO.NET's OLE DB provider for its data-access needs, we have to add a reference to System.Data and System.Data.OleDb, in addition to the System, System.Web, and System.Web.Services namespaces.

Class PubsWS inherits from WebService with the colon syntax that should be familiar to C++ or C# developers:

```
public class PubsWS : WebService
```

The four methods that are tagged with WebMethod attributes are GetAuthors(), GetAuthor(), GetBooks(*string*), and GetBooks(). In C#, you can tag public methods with a WebMethod attribute using the [] syntax. In VB, you must use <>. For example, in VB, the second method would be declared as:

```
<WebMethod()> Public Function GetAuthor(sSSN As String) As DataSet
```

By adding [WebMethod] in front of your public method, you make the public method callable from any Internet client. What goes on behind the scenes is that your public method is associated with an *attribute*, which is implemented as a WebMethodAttribute class. WebMethodAttribute has six properties:

BufferResponse (boolean)
Controls whether or not to buffer the method's response.

CacheDuration
Specifies the length of time in seconds to keep the method response in cache; the default is not to hold the method response in cache (0 seconds). A cache hit is when an identical call with identical parameters is requested. The cached response is used to avoid re-processing.

Description
Provides additional information about a particular web method.

EnableSession (boolean)
Enables or disables session state. If you don't want to use session state for the web method, you should make sure that this flag is disabled so the web server doesn't have to generate and manage session IDs for each user accessing the method.

MessageName
Distinguishes web methods with the same names. For example, if you have two different methods called GetBooks (one method retrieves all books while the other method retrieves only books written by a certain author) and you want to publish both of these methods as web methods, the system will have a problem trying to distinguish the two methods since their names are duplicated. You have to use the MessageName property to make sure all service signatures within the WSDL are unique. If the protocol is SOAP, MessageName is mapped to the SOAPAction request header and nested within the soap:Body element. For HTTP GET and HTTP POST, it is the PathInfo portion of the URI (as in *http:// localhost//PubsWS/PubsWS.asmx/GetBooksByAuthor*).

TransactionOption

Can be one of five modes: Disabled, NotSupported, Supported, Required, and RequiresNew. Even though there are five modes, web methods can only participate as the root object in a transaction. This means both Required and RequiresNew result in a new transaction being created for the web method. The Disabled, NotSupported, and Supported settings result in no transaction being used for the web method. The TransactionOption property of a web method is set to Disabled by default.

To set up these properties, pass the property name and its value as a *name = value* pair:

```
[WebMethod(Description="Returns a DataSet containing all authors.")]
public DataSet GetAuthors( )
```

You can separate multiple properties with a comma:

```
[WebMethod(MessageName="GetBooksByAuthor",
           Description="Find books by author's SSN.")]
public DataSet GetBooks(string sAuthorSSN)
```

Web.Config

If you set up your web services from scratch, you should also need to provide the configuration file (web.config) in the same directory as your asmx file. This configuration file allows you to control various application settings about the virtual directory. Here, we set the authentication mode to None to make our web services development and testing a little easier. When you release your web services to the public, you should change this setting to Windows, Forms, or Passport instead of None:

```
<configuration>
  <system.web>
    <authentication mode="None" />
  </system.web>
</configuration>
```

The following list shows the different modes of authentication:

Forms

Basic Forms authentication is where unauthenticated requests are redirected to a login form.

Windows

Authentication is performed by IIS in one of three ways: basic, digest, or Integrated Windows Authentication.

Passport

Unauthenticated requests to the resource are redirected to Microsoft's centralized authentication service. When authenticated, a token is passed back and used by subsequent requests.

In v1.1 of .NET Framework, for security reasons, HttpGet and HttpPost protocol are disabled by default. To override the default and enable or disable any particular protocols, the web.config can be modified as the following:

```
<configuration>
...
  <webServices>
    <protocols>
      <add name="HttpGet" />
      <add name="HttpPost" />
    </protocols>
  </webServices>
...
</configuration>
```

Discover files

After creating the web service, you can provide the supporting files to help in the discovery of the service. The static discovery disco file is:[*]

```
<?xml version="1.0" ?>
<disco:discovery xmlns:disco="http://schemas.xmlsoap.org/disco/"
                 xmlns:scl="http://schemas.xmlsoap.org/disco/scl/">
<scl:contractRef ref="http://localhost/PubsWS/PubsWS.asmx?WSDL"/>
</disco:discovery>
```

Web Services Consumers

Now that you have successfully created a web service, let's take a look at how this web service is used by web clients. Web services clients communicate with web services through standard web protocols. They send and receive XML-encoded messages to and from the web services. This means any application on any platform can access the web services as long as it uses standard web protocols and understands the XML-encoded messages. As mentioned earlier, there are three protocols that the web clients can employ to communicate with the servers (web services): HTTP GET, HTTP POST, and SOAP. We demonstrate next how to build client applications that utilize each of these protocols. These web services–client applications

---

[*] This code snippet assumes the virtual directory you set up is /PubsWS on your local web server.

are done in legacy languages such as VB6 and Perl,[*] and .NET languages, such as C# and VB.NET, to demonstrate the cross-language/cross-platform benefits of web services.

HTTP GET Consumer

Let's look at how it is done using HTTP GET first, since it is the simplest. In the examples that follow, we use *localhost* as the name of the web server running the service and *PubsWS* as the virtual directory. If you have deployed the sample web service on a remote server, you'll need to substitute the name of the server and virtual directory as appropriate.

If you point your web browser at the web service URL (*http://localhost/PubsWS/PubsWS.asmx*), it will give you a list of supported methods. To find out more about these methods, click one of them. This brings up a default web service consumer. This consumer, autogenerated through the use of reflection, is great for testing your web services' methods.[†] It uses the HTTP GET protocol to communicate with the web service. This consumer features a form that lets you test the method (see Figure 6-3), as well as descriptions of how to access the method via SOAP, HTTP GET, or HTTP POST.

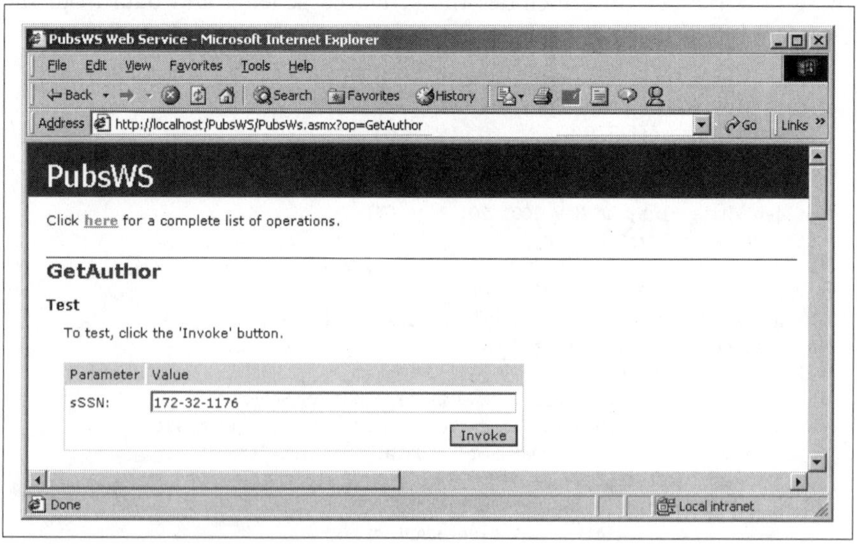

Figure 6-3. An autogenerated web services consumer

---

[*] We use SOAP::Lite PERL modules. See *http://www.soaplite.com/*.

[†] A simple reflection example can be found in Section 4.3.1 in Chapter 4.

Here is the description of the GET request and response supplied by the default consumer:

The following is a sample HTTP GET request and response. The
placeholders shown need to be replaced with actual values.

```
GET /PubsWS/PubsWS.asmx/GetAuthor?sSSN=string HTTP/1.1
Host: localhost

HTTP/1.1 200 OK
Content-Type: text/xml; charset=utf-8
Content-Length: length


<?xml version="1.0" encoding="utf-8"?>
<DataSet xmlns="http://Oreilly/DotNetEssentials/">
  <schema xmlns="http://www.w3.org/2001/XMLSchema">schema</schema>xml
</DataSet>
```

Using HTTP GET protocol, the complete URL to invoke the web method, along with parameters, can be the following:

```
http://localhost/PubsWS/PubsWS.asmx/GetAuthor?sSSN=172-32-1176
```

Here is the response; including HTTP response headers and the raw XML (note how the response includes the serialized schema and data from the DataSet object):

```
Cache-Control: private, max-age=0
Date: Tue, 08 May 2001 20:53:16 GMT
Server: Microsoft-IIS/5.0
Content-Length: 2450
Content-Type: text/xml; charset=utf-8
Client-Date: Tue, 08 May 2001 20:53:16 GMT
Client-Peer: 127.0.0.1:80

<?xml version="1.0" encoding="utf-8"?>
<DataSet xmlns="http://Oreilly/DotNetEssentials/">
  <xs:schema id="NewDataSet"
             xmlns=""
             xmlns:xs="http://www.w3.org/2001/XMLSchema"
             xmlns:msdata="urn:schemas-microsoft-com:xml-msdata">
    <xs:element name="NewDataSet" msdata:IsDataSet="true">
      <xs:complexType>
        <xs:choice maxOccurs="unbounded">
          <xs:element name="SelectedAuthor">
            <xs:complexType>
              <xs:sequence>
                <xs:element name="au_id" type="xs:string"
                            minOccurs="0" />
                <xs:element name="au_lname" type="xs:string"
                            minOccurs="0" />
```

```xml
            <xs:element name="au_fname" type="xs:string"
                        minOccurs="0" />
            <xs:element name="phone" type="xs:string"
                        minOccurs="0" />
            <xs:element name="address" type="xs:string"
                        minOccurs="0" />
            <xs:element name="city" type="xs:string"
                        minOccurs="0" />
            <xs:element name="state" type="xs:string"
                        minOccurs="0" />
            <xs:element name="zip" type="xs:string"
                        minOccurs="0" />
            <xs:element name="contract" type="xs:boolean"
                        minOccurs="0" />
          </xs:sequence>
        </xs:complexType>
      </xs:element>
    </xs:choice>
  </xs:complexType>
</xs:element>
</xs:schema>
<diffgr:diffgram
        xmlns:msdata="urn:schemas-microsoft-com:xml-msdata"
        xmlns:diffgr="urn:schemas-microsoft-com:xml-diffgram-v1">
  <NewDataSet xmlns="">
    <SelectedAuthor diffgr:id="SelectedAuthor1" msdata:rowOrder="0">
      <au_id>172-32-1176</au_id>
      <au_lname>White</au_lname>
      <au_fname>Johnson</au_fname>
      <phone>408 496-7223</phone>
      <address>10932 Bigge Rd.</address>
      <city>Menlo Park</city>
      <state>CA</state>
      <zip>94025</zip>
      <contract>true</contract>
    </SelectedAuthor>
  </NewDataSet>
</diffgr:diffgram>
</DataSet>
```

HTTP POST Consumer

In the section "HTTP GET Consumer," we saw the automatic creation of a web services consumer by merely hitting the URL of the web services, *http://localhost/PubsWS/PubsWS.asmx*. It is now time for us to see how a web client can use HTTP POST and SOAP to access a web service. This time around, we are going write a C# web service consumer.

The Microsoft .NET SDK has a rich set of tools to simplify the process of creating or consuming web services. We are going to use one of these tools, wsdl, to generate source code for the proxies to the actual web services:*

```
wsdl /l:CS /protocol:HttpPost http://localhost/PubsWS/PubsWS.asmx?WSDL
```

This command line creates a proxy for the PubsWS web service from the WSDL document from the URL *http://localhost/PubsWS/PubsWS.asmx?WSDL*. The proxy uses HTTP POST as its protocol to talk to the web service; it is generated as a C# source file. The wsdl tool can also take a WSDL file as its input instead of a URL pointing to the location where the WSDL can be obtained.

This C# proxy source file represents the proxy class for the PubsWS web service that the clients can compile against. This generated C# file contains a proxy class PubsWS that derives from HttpPostClientProtocol class. If you use the /protocol:HttpGet or /protocol:SOAP2† parameters, the PubsWS derives from either the HttpGetClientProtocol or SoapHttpClientProtocol class.

After generating the C# source file *PubsWS.cs*, we have two choices for how this proxy can be used. One way is to include this source file in the client application project using Visual Studio .NET. The project has to be a C# project if you choose this route.‡ To make use of the proxy, you also have to add to your project any references that the proxy depends on. In this example, the necessary references for the proxy file are System.Web.Services, System.Web.Services.Protocols, System.Xml.Serialization, and System.Data.

The other way to use the proxy is more flexible. You can compile the C# source file into a dynamic link library (DLL) and then add a reference to this DLL to any project you want to create. This way you can even have a VB project use the DLL.

Below is the command line used to compile the C# proxy source into a DLL. Notice that the three references are linked to *PubsWS.cs* so that the resulting *PubsWS.DLL* is self-contained (type the entire command on one line):

```
csc /t:library
    /r:system.web.services.dll
```

---

* *wsdl.exe* generates the proxy source code similar to the way IDL compilers generate source files for DCOM proxies. The only difference is that WSDL is the language that describes the interface of the software component, which is XML-based.

† In .NET Framework 1.1, SOAP 1.2 is also supported via /protocol:SOAP12. All this does is generate the SOAP derived proxy for SOAP Version 1.2.

‡ For other languages, use wsdl with the /l option to specify the language. See Appendix D for more details.

```
/r:system.xml.dll
/r:system.data.dll
PubsWS.cs
```

Regardless of how you choose to use the proxy, the client application code will still look the same. Consider the next two code examples containing C# and VB code. For both languages, the first lines create an instance of the proxy to the web service, PubsWS. The second lines invoke the GetAuthors web method to get a DataSet as the result. The remaining lines bind the default view of the table Authors to the data grid, add the data grid to a form, and display the form. Note that these examples use the Windows Forms API, which we'll discuss in Chapter 8. Here is the C# web service client, *TestProxy.cs*:

```
using System;
using System.Drawing;
using System.Windows.Forms;
using System.Data;

public class TestProxy
{

  public static void Main( )
  {

    /* Create a proxy. */
    PubsWS oProxy = new PubsWS( );

    /* Invoke GetAuthors( ) over HTTPPOST and get the data set. */
    DataSet oDS = oProxy.GetAuthors( );

    /* Create a data grid and connect it to the data set. */
    DataGrid dg = new DataGrid( );
    dg.Size = new Size(490, 270);
    dg.DataSource = oDS.Tables["Authors"].DefaultView;

    /* Set the properties of the form and add the data grid. */
    Form myForm = new Form( );
    myForm.Text = "DataGrid Sample";
    myForm.Size = new Size(500, 300);
    myForm.Controls.Add(dg);

    /* Display the form. */
    System.Windows.Forms.Application.Run(myForm);

  }

}
```

If you created the DLL as previously directed, you can compile this with the following command:

```
csc TestProxy.cs /r:PubsWS.dll
```

This creates the executable *TestProxy.exe*, which gets a DataSet using a HTTP POST call, and displays a data grid containing that dataset. Figure 6-4 shows the output of the C# client after obtaining the data from the PubsWS web service via HTTP POST protocol.

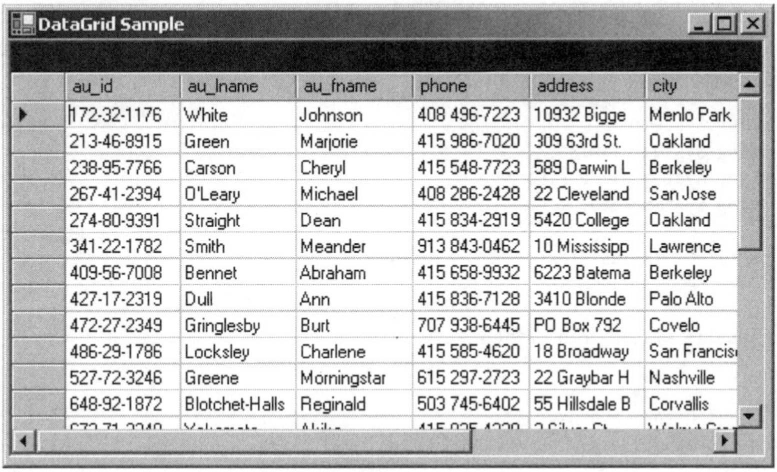

Figure 6-4. C# web service client after calling GetAuthors()

Here is the VB web service client, *TestProxyVB.vb*:

```
imports System
imports System.Drawing
imports System.Windows.Forms
imports System.Data

Module TestProxyVB
  Sub Main()
    ' Create a proxy.
    dim oProxy as PubsWS = new PubsWS()

    ' Invoice GetAuthors() over SOAP and get the data set.
    dim oDS as DataSet = oProxy.GetAuthors()

    ' Create a data grid and connect it to the data set.
    dim dg as DataGrid = new DataGrid()
```

```
      dg.Size = new Size(490, 270)
      dg.DataSource = oDS.Tables("Authors").DefaultView

      ' Set the properties of the form and add the data grid.
      dim myForm as Form = new Form( )
      myForm.Text = "DataGrid Sample"
      myForm.Size = new Size(500, 300)
      myForm.Controls.Add(dg)

      ' Display the form.
      System.Windows.Forms.Application.Run(myForm)
   End Sub
End Module
```

You can compile the VB web service client with this command (type the entire command on one line):

```
vbc TestProxyVB.vb
    /r:System.Drawing.dll
    /r:System.Windows.Forms.dll
    /r:System.Data.dll
    /r:PubsWS.dll
    /r:System.Web.Services.dll
    /r:System.dll
    /r:System.xml.dll
```

Instead of using wsdl to generate and include the proxy in your application, you can also rely on VS.NET to automate the whole process. In VS.NET, you can just add a Web Reference to your application. The process of adding a Web Reference to an application involves the discovery of the web service, obtaining the WSDL, generating the proxy, and including the proxy into the application.[*]

Non-.NET Consumers

This section shows how to develop non-.NET web service consumers using HTTP GET, HTTP POST, and SOAP protocols. Because we cannot just create the proxy class from the WSDL and compile it with the client code directly, we must look at the WSDL file to understand how to construct and interpret messages between the web service and the clients. We trimmed down the WSDL file for our PubsWS web service to show only types, messages, ports, operations, and bindings that we actually use in the next several

---

[*] You can find the proxy source file under Web References\ReferenceName as *reference.cs* (if you're working with C#). If you have not renamed the reference name, it is *localhost* by default. (You might have to select the option to "show all files" in VS.NET Solution Explorer.)

web service-client examples. In particular, we will have our VB6 client access the following:

Web method	Protocol
GetBooks( )	HTTP GET protocol
GetAuthor(ssn)	HTTP POST protocol
GetBooksByAuthor(ssn)	SOAP protocol

As a reference, here is the simplified version of the WSDL file while you experiment with the VB6 client application:

```
<?xml version="1.0" encoding="utf-8"?>
<definitions xmlns:...
    xmlns:s0="http://Oreilly/DotNetEssentials/"
    targetNamespace="http://Oreilly/DotNetEssentials/" >

 <types>
    <!-- This data type is used by the HTTP POST call -->
    <s:element name="GetAuthor">
      <s:complexType>
        <s:sequence>
          <s:element minOccurs="1" maxOccurs="1"
                     name="sSSN" type="s:string" />
        </s:sequence>
      </s:complexType>
    </s:element>
    <!-- This data type is used by the HTTP POST call -->
    <s:element name="GetAuthorResponse">
      <s:complexType>
        <s:sequence>
          <s:element minOccurs="1" maxOccurs="1"
                     name="GetAuthorResult"">
            <s:complexType>
              <s:sequence>
                <s:element ref="s:schema" />
                <s:any />
              </s:sequence>
            </s:complexType>
          </s:element>
        </s:sequence>
      </s:complexType>
    </s:element>

    <!-- This data type is used by the SOAP call -->
    <s:element name="GetBooksByAuthor">
      <s:complexType>
        <s:sequence>
          <s:element minOccurs="1" maxOccurs="1"
            name="sAuthorSSN" type="s:string" />
        </s:sequence>
```

```
          </s:complexType>
        </s:element>
        <!-- This data type is used by the SOAP call -->
        <s:element name="GetBooksByAuthorResponse">
          <s:complexType>
            <s:sequence>
              <s:element minOccurs="1" maxOccurs="1"
                         name="GetBooksByAuthorResult"">
                <s:complexType>
                  <s:sequence>
                    <s:element ref="s:schema" />
                    <s:any />
                  </s:sequence>
                </s:complexType>
              </s:element>
            </s:sequence>
          </s:complexType>
        </s:element>

        <!-- This data type is used by the HTTP GET call -->
        <s:element name="GetBooks">
          <s:complexType />
        </s:element>
        <!-- This data type is used by the HTTP GET call -->
        <s:element name="GetBooksResponse">
          <s:complexType>
            <s:sequence>
              <s:element minOccurs="1" maxOccurs="1"
                         name="GetBooksResult">
                <s:complexType>
                  <s:sequence>
                    <s:element ref="s:schema" />
                    <s:any />
                  </s:sequence>
                </s:complexType>
              </s:element>
            </s:sequence>
          </s:complexType>
        </s:element>

        <!-- This data type is used by the HTTP GET/POST responses -->
        <s:element name="DataSet"
          <s:complexType>
            <s:sequence>
              <s:element ref="s:schema" />
              <s:any />
            </s:sequence>
          </s:complexType>
        </s:element>

    </types>
```

```
<!-- These messages are used by the SOAP call -->
<message name="GetBooksByAuthorSoapIn">
  <part name="parameters" element="s0:GetBooksByAuthor" />
</message>
<message name="GetBooksByAuthorSoapOut">
  <part name="parameters" element="s0:GetBooksByAuthorResponse" />
</message>

<!-- These messages are used by the HTTP GET call -->
<message name="GetBooksHttpGetIn" />
<message name="GetBooksHttpGetOut">
  <part name="Body" element="s0:DataSet" />
</message>

<!-- These messages are used by the HTTP POST call -->
<message name="GetAuthorHttpPostIn">
  <part name="sSSN" type="s:string" />
</message>
<message name="GetAuthorHttpPostOut">
  <part name="Body" element="s0:DataSet" />
</message>

<!-- SOAP port -->
<portType name="PubsWSSoap">
  <operation name="GetBooks">
    <documentation>Find books by author's SSN.</documentation>
    <input name="GetBooksByAuthor"
           message="s0:GetBooksByAuthorSoapIn" />
    <output name="GetBooksByAuthor"
            message="s0:GetBooksByAuthorSoapOut" />
  </operation>
</portType>

<!-- HTTP GET port -->
<portType name="PubsWSHttpGet">
  <operation name="GetBooks">
    <input message="s0:GetBooksHttpGetIn" />
    <output message="s0:GetBooksHttpGetOut" />
  </operation>
</portType>

<!-- HTTP POST port -->
<portType name="PubsWSHttpPost">
  <operation name="GetAuthor">
    <input message="s0:GetAuthorHttpPostIn" />
    <output message="s0:GetAuthorHttpPostOut" />
  </operation>
</portType>

<!-- SOAP binding -->
<binding name="PubsWSSoap" type="s0:PubsWSSoap">
  <soap:binding
        transport="http://schemas.xmlsoap.org/soap/http"
```

```
          style="document" />
  <operation name="GetBooks">
    <soap:operation
        soapAction="http://Oreilly/DotNetEssentials/GetBooksByAuthor"
        style="document" />
    <input name="GetBooksByAuthor">
      <soap:body use="literal" />
    </input>
    <output name="GetBooksByAuthor">
      <soap:body use="literal" />
    </output>
  </operation>
</binding>

<!-- HTTP GET binding -->
<binding name="PubsWSHttpGet" type="s0:PubsWSHttpGet">
  <http:binding verb="GET" />
  <operation name="GetBooks">
    <http:operation location="/GetBooks" />
    <input>
      <http:urlEncoded />
    </input>
    <output>
      <mime:mimeXml part="Body" />
    </output>
  </operation>
</binding>

<!-- HTTP POST binding -->
<binding name="PubsWSHttpPost" type="s0:PubsWSHttpPost">
  <http:binding verb="POST" />
  <operation name="GetAuthor">
    <http:operation location="/GetAuthor" />
    <input>
      <mime:content type="application/x-www-form-urlencoded" />
    </input>
    <output>
      <mime:mimeXml part="Body" />
    </output>
  </operation>
</binding>

<!-- The whole web service and address bindings -->
<service name="PubsWS">

  <port name="PubsWSSoap" binding="s0:PubsWSSoap">
    <soap:address location="http://localhost/PubsWS/PubsWS.asmx" />
  </port>

  <port name="PubsWSHttpGet" binding="s0:PubsWSHttpGet">
    <http:address location="http://localhost/PubsWS/PubsWS.asmx" />
  </port>
```

```
      <port name="PubsWSHttpPost" binding="s0:PubsWSHttpPost">
        <http:address location="http://localhost/PubsWS/PubsWS.asmx" />
      </port>

    </service>

  </definitions>
```

In both the HTTP GET and HTTP POST protocols, you pass parameters to the web services as name/value pairs. With the HTTP GET protocol, you must pass parameters in the query string, whereas the HTTP POST protocol packs the parameters in the body of the request package. To demonstrate this point, we will construct a simple VB client using both HTTP GET and HTTP POST protocols to communicate with the PubsWS web service.

Let's first create a VB6 standard application. We need to add a reference to Microsoft XML, v3.0 (*msxml3.dll*), because we'll use the XMLHTTP object to help us communicate with the web services. For demonstrative purposes, we will also use the Microsoft Internet Controls component (*shdocvw.dll*) to display XML and HTML content.

First, add two buttons on the default form, form1, and give them the captions GET and POST, as well as the names cmdGet and cmdPost, respectively. After that, drag the WebBrowser object from the toolbar onto the form, and name the control myWebBrowser. If you make the WebBrowser navigate to about:blank initially, you will end up with something like Figure 6-5.

Figure 6-5. VB client form to test web services

Now all we need is some code similar to the following to handle the two buttons' click events:

```
Private Sub cmdGet_Click()
  Dim oXMLHTTP As XMLHTTP
  Dim oDOM As DOMDocument
  Dim oXSL As DOMDocument

  ' Call the web service to get an XML document
  Set oXMLHTTP = New XMLHTTP
```

```
oXMLHTTP.open "GET",_
                "http://localhost/PubsWS/PubsWS.asmx/GetBooks", _
                False
oXMLHTTP.send
Set oDOM = oXMLHTTP.responseXML

' Create the XSL document to be used for transformation
Set oXSL = New DOMDocument
oXSL.Load App.Path & "\templateTitle.xsl"

' Transform the XML document into an HTML document and display
myWebBrowser.Document.Write CStr(oDOM.transformNode(oXSL))
myWebBrowser.Document.Close

Set oXSL = Nothing
Set oDOM = Nothing
Set oXMLHTTP = Nothing
End Sub

Private Sub cmdPost_Click( )
    Dim oXMLHTTP As XMLHTTP
    Dim oDOM As DOMDocument
    Dim oXSL As DOMDocument

    ' Call the web service to get an XML document
    Set oXMLHTTP = New XMLHTTP
    oXMLHTTP.open "POST", _
                    "http://localhost/PubsWS/PubsWS.asmx/GetAuthor", _
                    False
    oXMLHTTP.setRequestHeader "Content-Type", _
                              "application/x-www-form-urlencoded"
    oXMLHTTP.send "sSSN=172-32-1176"
    Set oDOM = oXMLHTTP.responseXML

    ' Create the XSL document to be used for transformation
    Set oXSL = New DOMDocument
    oXSL.Load App.Path & "\templateAuthor.xsl"

    ' Transform the XML document into an HTML document and display
    myWebBrowser.Document.Write oDOM.transformNode(oXSL)
    myWebBrowser.Document.Close

    Set oXSL = Nothing
    Set oDOM = Nothing
    Set oXMLHTTP = Nothing
End Sub
```

The two subroutines are similar in structure, except that the first one uses
the HTTP GET protocol and the second one uses the HTTP POST protocol
to get to the PubsWS web service. Let's take a closer look at what the two
subroutines do.

For the HTTP GET protocol, we use the XMLHTTP object to point to the URL for the web method, as specified in the WSDL. Since the GetBooks web method does not require any parameters, the query string in this case is empty. The method is invoked synchronously because the async parameter to XMLHTTP's open method is set to `false`. After the method invocation is done, we transform the XML result using *templateTitle.xsl* and display the HTML on the `myWebBrowser` instance on the form. Figure 6-6 displays the screen of our web services testing application after invoking the GetBooks web method at URL *http://localhost/PubsWS/ PubsWS.asmx/* through HTTP GET protocol.

List of books

Title	Type	Price	Notes
The Busy Executive's Database Guide	business	19.99	An overview of available database systems with emphasis on common business applications. Illustrated.
Cooking with Computers: Surreptitious Balance Sheets	business	11.95	Helpful hints on how to use your electronic resources to the best advantage.
You Can Combat Computer Stress!	business	2.99	The latest medical and psychological techniques for living with the electronic office. Easy-to-understand explanations.
Straight Talk About Computers	business	19.99	Annotated analysis of what computers can do for you: a no-hype guide for the critical user.
Silicon Valley Gastronomic Treats	mod_cook	19.99	Favorite recipes for quick, easy, and elegant meals.
The Gourmet Microwave	mod_cook	2.99	Traditional French gourmet recipes adapted for modern microwave cooking.
The Psychology of Computer Cooking	UNDECIDED		
But Is It User Friendly?	popular_comp	22.95	A survey of software for the naive user, focusing on the

Figure 6-6. VB client form after calling GetBooks

For the HTTP POST protocol, we also point the XMLHTTP object to the URL for the web method—in this case, method GetAuthor. Because this is a POST request, we have to specify in the HTTP header that the request is coming over as a form by setting the `Content-Type` header variable to `application/x-www-form-urlencoded`. If this variable is not set, XMLHTTP by default passes the data to the server in XML format.

Another difference worth noticing is that the GetAuthor method requires a single parameter, which is the SSN of the author as a string. Since this is a post request, we are going to send the name/value pair directly to the server in the body of the message. Because the `Content-Type` header has been set to `application/x-www-form-urlencoded`, the server will know how to get to the parameters and perform the work requested. This time, we

use *templateAuthor.xsl* to transform the XML result to HTML and display it. Figure 6-7 shows our application after invoking the GetAuthor web method of PubsWS web service through HTTP POST protocol.

Figure 6-7. VB client form after calling GetAuthor

The following code is the XSL used to transform the XML result from the GetBooks web method call to HTML to be displayed on the web browser instance on the VB form:

```
<html version="1.0" xmlns:xsl="http://www.w3.org/TR/WD-xsl">
<head><title>A list of books</title></head>
<style>
.hdr { background-color=#ffeedd; font-weight=bold; }
</style>
<body>
<B>List of books</B>
<table style="border-collapse:collapse" border="1">
<tr>
  <td class="hdr">Title</td>
  <td class="hdr">Type</td>
  <td class="hdr">Price</td>
  <td class="hdr">Notes</td>
</tr>
<xsl:for-each select="//Books">
<tr>
  <td><xsl:value-of select="title"/></td>
  <td><xsl:value-of select="type"/></td>
  <td><xsl:value-of select="price"/></td>
  <td><xsl:value-of select="notes"/></td>
</tr>
</xsl:for-each>
</table>
</body>
</html>
```

Here is the XSL used to transform the XML result from the GetAuthor web method call to HTML to be displayed on the web browser instance on the VB form:

```
<html version="1.0" xmlns:xsl="http://www.w3.org/TR/WD-xsl">
<head><title>Selected author</title></head>
<STYLE>
.hdr { background-color:'#ffeedd';
       text-align:'right'; vertical-align:'top';
       font-weight=bold; }
</STYLE>
<body>
<B>Selected author</B>
<xsl:for-each select="//SelectedAuthor">
<table style="border-collapse:'collapse'" border="1">
<tr><td class="hdr">ID</td>
    <td><xsl:value-of select="au_id"/></td></tr>
<tr><td class="hdr">Name</td>
    <td><xsl:value-of select="au_fname"/>
        <xsl:value-of select="au_lname"/></td></tr>
<tr><td class="hdr">Address</td>
    <td><xsl:value-of select="address"/><br>
        <xsl:value-of select="city"/>,
        <xsl:value-of select="state"/>
        <xsl:value-of select="zip"/></br></td></tr>
<tr><td class="hdr">Phone</td>
    <td><xsl:value-of select="phone"/></td></tr>
</table>
</xsl:for-each>
</body>
</html>
```

We can also use SOAP protocol to access the web service. Because the web service is exposed through HTTP and XML, any clients on any platform can access the service as long as they conform to the specification of the service. Again, this specification is the WSDL file. By inspecting the WSDL file—specifically, the SOAP section—we can use XMLHTTP again to communicate in SOAP dialog. Let's see how this can be done.

Let's go back to the example of consumer web services using VB6 and XMLHTTP. Add another button on the form, and call it cmdSOAP with caption SOAP. This time, we will ask the web service to return all books written by a particular author:

```
Private Sub cmdSOAP_Click()
  Dim oXMLHTTP As XMLHTTP
  Dim oDOM As DOMDocument
  Dim oXSL As DOMDocument
```

```
' Call the web service to get an XML document
Set oXMLHTTP = New XMLHTTP
oXMLHTTP.open "POST", "http://localhost/PubsWS/PubsWS.asmx", False

Dim sBody As String

sBody = "" & _
"<soap:Envelope" & _
" xmlns:xsi=""http://www.w3.org/2001/XMLSchema-instance""" & _
" xmlns:xsd=""http://www.w3.org/2001/XMLSchema""" & _
" xmlns:soap=""http://schemas.xmlsoap.org/soap/envelope/"">" & _
"<soap:Body>" & _
"<GetBooksByAuthor xmlns=""http://Oreilly/DotNetEssentials/"">" & _
"<sAuthorSSN>213-46-8915</sAuthorSSN>" & _
"</GetBooksByAuthor>" & _
"</soap:Body>" & _
"</soap:Envelope>"

oXMLHTTP.setRequestHeader "Content-Type", "text/xml"
oXMLHTTP.setRequestHeader "SOAPAction",
                    "http://Oreilly/DotNetEssentials/GetBooksByAuthor"

oXMLHTTP.send sBody

Set oDOM = oXMLHTTP.responseXML

' Create the XSL document to be used for transformation
Set oXSL = New DOMDocument
oXSL.Load App.Path & "\templateAuthorTitle.xsl"

' Transform the XML document into an HTML document
myWebBrowser.Document.Write oDOM.transformNode(oXSL)
myWebBrowser.Document.Close

Set oXSL = Nothing
Set oDOM = Nothing
Set oXMLHTTP = Nothing
End Sub
```

This method is structurally similar to the ones used for HTTP GET and
HTTP POST; however, it has some very important differences. In SOAP,
you have to set the Content-Type to text/xml instead of application/x-www-
form-urlencoded as for the HTTP POST. By this time, it should be clear to
you that only HTTP POST and SOAP care about the Content-Type because
they send the data in the body of the HTTP request. The HTTP GET protocol does not really care about the Content-Type because all of the parameters are packaged into the query string. In addition to the difference in
format of the data content, you also have to refer to the WSDL to set the
SOAPAction header variable to the call you want. Looking back at the SOAP
section of the WSDL, if you want to call the GetBooks(sAuthorSSN) method

of the web service, you will set the SOAPAction header variable to http://
Oreilly/DotNetEssentials/GetBooksByAuthor. On the other hand, if you
want to call the GetBooks() method instead, the SOAPAction variable has to
be set to http://Oreilly/DotNetEssentials/GetBooks. The reason the
namespace is http://Oreilly/DotNetEssentials/ is because we set it up as
the attribute of the PubsWS web service class.

After setting up the header variables, pass the parameters to the server in the
body of the message. While HTTP POST passes the parameters in name/
value pairs, SOAP passes the parameters in a well-defined XML structure:

```
<soap:Envelope ...namespace omitted... >
  <soap:Body>
    <GetBooksByAuthor xmlns="http://Oreilly/DotNetEssentials/">
      <sAuthorSSN>213-46-8915</sAuthorSSN>
    </GetBooksByAuthor>
  </soap:Body>
</soap:Envelope>
```

Both the SOAP request and response messages are packaged within a Body
inside an Envelope. With the previously specified request, the response
SOAP message looks like this:

```
<?xml version="1.0"?>
<soap:Envelope ...namespace omitted...>
  <soap:Body>
    <GetBooksByAuthorResult xmlns="http://Oreilly/DotNetEssentials/">
      <result>
        <xsd:schema id="NewDataSet" ...>

        <... content omitted ...>

      </xsd:schema>
      <NewDataSet xmlns="">
        <Books>
          <title_id>BU1032</title_id>
          <title>The Busy Executive's Database Guide</title>
        <... more ...>
        </Books>
        <Books>
          <title_id>BU2075</title_id>
          <title>You Can Combat Computer Stress!</title>
          <... more ...>
        </Books>
        <Author>
          <au_id>213-46-8915</au_id>
          <au_lname>Green</au_lname>
          <au_fname>Marjorie</au_fname>
          <phone>415 986-7020</phone>
          <address>309 63rd St. #411</address>
          <city>Oakland</city>
          <state>CA</state>
```

```
            <zip>94618</zip>
            <contract>True</contract>
          </Author>
        </NewDataSet>
      </result>
    </GetBooksByAuthorResult>
  </soap:Body>
</soap:Envelope>
```

Figure 6-8 shows the result of the test form after invoking the GetBooksBy-Author web method using the SOAP protocol.

Figure 6-8. VB client form after calling GetBooksByAuthor

The XSL stylesheet used for transformation of the resulting XML to HTML is included here for your reference. Notice that since GetBooksByAuthor returns two tables in the dataset, author and books, we can display both the author information and the books that this author wrote:

```
<html version="1.0" xmlns:xsl="http://www.w3.org/TR/WD-xsl">
<head><title>A list of books</title></head>
<style>
.hdr { background-color=#ffeedd; font-weight=bold; }
</style>
<body>
<B>List of books written by
  <I><xsl:value-of select="//Author/au_fname"/>
     <xsl:value-of select="//Author/au_lname"/>
     (<xsl:value-of select="//Author/city"/>,
     <xsl:value-of select="//Author/state"/>)
  </I>
</B>
<table style="border-collapse:collapse" border="1">
<tr>
  <td class="hdr">Title</td>
  <td class="hdr">Type</td>
  <td class="hdr">Price</td>
  <td class="hdr">Notes</td>
```

```
</tr>
<xsl:for-each select="//Books">
<tr>
  <td><xsl:value-of select="title"/></td>
  <td><xsl:value-of select="type"/></td>
  <td><xsl:value-of select="price"/></td>
  <td><xsl:value-of select="notes"/></td>
</tr>
</xsl:for-each>
</table>
</body>
</html>
```

It's ok to go through the previous exercise to understand how to write a VB application as a front-end client for web services. However, for your real-life applications, you should use a SOAP toolkit (such as the Microsoft SOAP toolkit) to make things easier.

The next couple of examples take a step further. This time, we will use Perl to access our sample web service PubWS with the help of ActiveState Perl and SOAP::Lite Perl Library (author: Paul Kulchenko).[*]

With SOAP::Lite Perl Library, all you have to do is to create a SOAP::Lite object (similar to the proxy object in the C# example) and setup its uri and proxy properties. Once this is done, you can ask the proxy object to run the remote web methods. The uri property maps to the first part of the soapAction and the web method name maps to the second part. The proxy property maps to the physical location of the web service itself.

In our first Perl example, we want to call the GetAuthors web method. This method does not take any parameter and returns a DataSet object. The SOAP portion of the WSDL states that the soapAction for this method is *http://Oreilly/DotNetEssentials/GetAuthors*. By default, SOAP::Lite library constructs the soapAction as *<uri string>* + *"#"* + *<web method name>*. This does not agree with web services written on the .NET Framework, where the soapAction is *uri_string* + *"/"* + *web method name*. Fortunately, the SOAP::Lite library provides a callback-like kind of feature so that we can plug in a sub-routine to override the default construction of the soapAction string. The highlighted line of PERL script below basically just concatenates the uri string and the web method name. For simplicity, we rely on the fact

---

[*] *http://www.ActiveState.com/* and *http://www.soaplite.com/*, respectively.

that the uri string already has the trailing slash.* To run the program, just type *perl <program name>*:

```
use SOAP::Lite
  on_action => sub {sprintf '%s%s', @_};

my $proxy = SOAP::Lite
  -> uri('http://Oreilly/DotNetEssentials/')
  -> proxy('http://localhost/PubsWS/PubsWS.asmx');

my $method = SOAP::Data->name('GetAuthors')
    ->attr({xmlns => 'http://Oreilly/DotNetEssentials/'});
my $xmlDataSet = $proxy->call($method);
# my $xmlDataSet = $proxy->GetAuthors( ); # You can also do this
my @authorsNodes = $xmlDataSet->valueof('//Authors');
foreach $author (@authorsNodes) {
  print $author->{'au_lname'}, ", ", $author->{'au_fname'}, "\n";
  print "\t", $author->{'address'}, "\n";
  print "\t", $author->{'city'}, ", ",
              $author->{'state'}, " ", $author->{'zip'}, "\n";
  print "\t", $author->{'phone'}, "\n";
}
```

The output of this program is the following:

```
White, Johnson
        10932 Bigge Rd.
        Menlo Park, CA 94025
        408 496-7223
Green, Marjorie
        309 63rd St. #411
        Oakland, CA 94618
        415 986-7020
  . . .
```

Once the $proxy object is created, we call the GetAuthors web method knowing that the generated soapAction will be '*http://Oreilly/DotNetEssentials/*' + 'GetAuthors' and the location of the web service where SOAP::Lite library will try to contact is *http://localhost/PubsWS/PubsWS.asmx*. Because this web method returns a DataSet, which translates to an XML document, we can parse it with XPATH-like syntax to obtain the list of authors and traverse the list to display the information for each author.

Now we want to call the GetBooksByAuthor web method as the second Perl program. This method takes one string parameter, the SSN for the author, and returns a DataSet object containing the author's name and all books he

---

* The trace for the SOAP::Lite library turns out to be extremely useful because it shows the SOAP request and response as well as other vital information. Insert trace => all at the end of the first line of the example.

has published. The SOAP portion of the WSDL document states that the soapAction for this method is named *http://Oreilly/DotNetEssentials/GetBooksByAuthor*, and the parameter is named sAuthorSSN:

```perl
use SOAP::Lite
  on_action => sub { sprintf '%s%s', @_ };

my $proxy = SOAP::Lite
  -> uri('http://Oreilly/DotNetEssentials/')
  -> proxy('http://localhost/PubsWS/PubsWS.asmx');

my $method = SOAP::Data->name('GetBooksByAuthor')
  ->attr({xmlns => 'http://Oreilly/DotNetEssentials/'});

my @params = (SOAP::Data->name(sAuthorSSN => '998-72-3567'));

my $xmlDataSet = $proxy->call($method => @params);

my $author = $xmlDataSet->valueof('//Author');
print "Books by author:\n";
print $author->{'au_lname'}, ", ", $author->{'au_fname'}, "\n";
print $author->{'address'}, "\n";
print $author->{'city'}, ", ",
      $author->{'state'}, " ", $author->{'zip'}, "\n";
print $author->{'phone'}, "\n\n";

my @books = $xmlDataSet->valueof('//Books');
foreach $book (@books) {
  print "Type  : ", $book->{'type'}, "\n";
  print "Title : ", $book->{'title'}, "\n";
  print "Price : \$", $book->{'price'}, "\n";
  print "Notes : ", $book->{'notes'}, "\n";
  print "\n";
}
```

Type `perl yourPerlFile.pl` to run the program. The output is:

```
Books by author:
Ringer, Albert
67 Seventh Av.
Salt Lake City, UT 84152
801 826-0752

Type  : psychology
Title : Is Anger the Enemy?
Price : $10.95
Notes : Carefully researched study of the effects of strong emotions on the
body. Metabolic charts included.

Type  : psychology
Title : Life Without Fear
Price : $7
```

Notes : New exercise, meditation, and nutritional techniques that can reduce
the shock of daily interactions. Popular audience. Sample menus included,
exercise video available separately.

As you can see, you can easily use any type of web service client to access a
.NET web service. Clients of web services need to know how to communicate in HTTP and understand the WSDL. By the same token, you can
develop a web service in any language and on any platform as long as it
adheres to its WSDL specification.

Now that you have seen how simple it is to create and consume web services, we should let you in on a small but important point—that XML web
services is not the solution for everything. As responsible developers, we
have to evaluate the requirements as well as the applicability of certain technology before applying it. On one hand, it's great to use web services as a
way to expose legacy functionalities, or to enable integration of disparate
systems on different locations, different platforms, or different companies.
But there is no real reason to make a web service out of something that can
be implemented as a simple component, or through .NET Remoting, which
is discussed in Chapter 4. The decision is up to you. Again, the technology is
just a tool; how you use it is another story.

Async Web Services

All of the web service client examples we've used so far make a call to the
web service and wait for data before continuing work. While this approach
might be appropriate for small, quick calls, such synchronous calls might
yield an unacceptable response time. The web service has to perform a time-
consuming task. Asynchronous web service calls are the answer in this case.
This section explores how the .NET Framework web services enable clients
to call web methods asynchronously, yielding a better overall response time
for an application.

If you look back at the generated source for the web service proxy in the previous section, you will find that for every web method there are three separate proxy methods generated. The following shows the three proxy
methods: GetAuthors( ), BeginGetAuthors( ), and EndGetAuthors( ):

```
public System.Data.DataSet GetAuthors() {
 object[] results = this.Invoke("GetAuthors", new object[0]);
 return ((System.Data.DataSet)(results[0]));
}

public System.IAsyncResult BeginGetAuthors(System.AsyncCallback callback,
        object asyncState) {
 return this.BeginInvoke("GetAuthors",new object[0],callback,asyncState);
}
```

```
public System.Data.DataSet EndGetAuthors(System.IAsyncResult asyncResult) {
  object[] results = this.EndInvoke(asyncResult);
  return ((System.Data.DataSet)(results[0]));
}
```

In the earlier web service consumer example, we've used the proxy method GetAuthors( ) to call the web method on the other side of the HTTP channel. The following example shows how the other two methods can be used to perform an asynchronous web method call.

As it turns out, there are a couple of different ways to use the Begin*MethodName*( ) and End*MethodName*( ) to call the web method asynchronously. We will show you each one and describe how they are different from one another.

The first way will be calling Begin*MethodName*( ) passing in null for both the callback and the asyncState objects. We will poll on the IAsyncResult object until it is completed while simulating other works. When the call is done, we call End*MethodName*( ) to complete the web method call and obtain the DataSet result:*

```
WSPubsWS.PubsWS oProxy = new WSPubsWS.PubsWS( );
IAsyncResult result;
// Async call polling (cannot run this in debugger)
Console.Write("Async Polling");
result = oProxy.BeginGetAuthors(null, null);
while(!result.IsCompleted) {
  Console.Write("..."); Thread.Sleep(5);
}
DataSet oDSAsync = oProxy.EndGetAuthors(result);
oDSAsync.WriteXml("outputpolling.xml");
Console.WriteLine("done");
```

Although this might not be the best way, it demonstrates one way of performing an asynchronous call to a web method.

The second way still does not use the callback mechanism. Be patient. Again, we use the IAsyncResult object to perform a block waiting on the remote call. Block waiting put the current thread to sleep, giving up the CPU to other processes or threads until the wait handle is signaled. Depending on your application, this might be how you would want to do it:

```
// Async call with waithandle
Console.WriteLine("Async, processing then wait for handle");
result = oProxy.BeginGetAuthors(null, null);
Console.WriteLine("...Processing some more...");
result.AsyncWaitHandle.WaitOne( );// block on handle
```

---

* The proxy in this example was generated with a namespace "WSPubsWS" instead of the default global namespace.

BUSINESS REPLY MAIL

FIRST CLASS MAIL   PERMIT NO. 80   SEBASTOPOL, CA

Postage will be paid by addressee

O'Reilly & Associates, Inc.
Book Registration
1005 Gravenstein Highway North
Sebastopol, CA 95472-9910

NO POSTAGE
NECESSARY IF
MAILED IN THE
UNITED STATES

Register Your O'Reilly Book

Register your book with O'Reilly and receive a FREE copy of our latest catalog, email notification of new editions of this book, information about new titles, and special offers available only to registered O'Reilly customers.

Register online at register.oreilly.com or complete and return this postage paid card.

Which book(s) are you registering? Please include title and ISBN # (above bar code on back cover)

Title _____ ISBN # _____

Title _____ ISBN # _____

Title _____ ISBN # _____

Name _____

Company/Organization _____ Job Title _____

Address _____

City _____ State _____ Zip/Postal Code _____ Country _____

Telephone _____ Email address _____

register.oreilly.com

```
DataSet oDSAsyncWait = oProxy.EndGetAuthors(result);
oDSAsyncWait.WriteXml("outputWaiting.xml");
Console.WriteLine("done");
```

The third and fourth ways use the callback mechanism so we will know exactly when to complete the web method call with the End*MethodName*( ). We make the call to the Begin*MethodName*( ) passing in the callback delegate. When the web method call completes, we will get called back. Since this example is done as a console application, a little more setting up is required; otherwise, the application might exit before the callback occurs. This is done through the AutoResetEvent object (a synchronization primitive similar to a mutex). Basically, we want to set up a wait object, call the async web method, and wait for the signal from the callback before continuing with the application:

```
// Async call with callback 1
AutoResetEvent oWait = new AutoResetEvent(false);
Console.WriteLine("Async, processing then wait for callback");
CallBack cb = new CallBack(oProxy, oWait);
Result =oProxy.BeginGetAuthors(new AsyncCallback(cb.CallBackMethod), null);
Console.WriteLine("...Processing some more...");
Console.WriteLine("Application waits for callback rendezvous");
oWait.WaitOne( );
Console.WriteLine("done");
```

The CallBack class needs to have the proxy to complete the web method call. It also needs the AutoResetEvent to signal the main application flow to continue. The following is the definition of the CallBack class at this moment:

```
public class CallBack {
  public CallBack(WSPubsWS.PubsWS oProxy, AutoResetEvent oWait) {
    m_oProxy = oProxy;
    m_oWait = oWait;
  }
  public void CallBackMethod(IAsyncResult result) {
    DataSet oDSAsyncCB;
    oDSAsyncCB = m_oProxy.EndGetAuthors(result);
    oDSAsyncCB.WriteXml("outputCallback.xml");
    m_oWait.Set( );
  }
  private WSPubsWS.PubsWS m_oProxy;
  private AutoResetEvent m_oWait;
}
```

In the next example, we pass both the callback and the asyncState object to the Begin*MethodName*( ) method. We already know all about the callback object. What about this asyncState thing? It actually can be *anything* you want to pass to the callback object. We will pass the proxy object itself via this asyncState object so we will know how to complete the web method call

when the callback is invoked. The following code segment shows how this is done:

```
// async call with callback 2
oWait.Reset();
Console.WriteLine("Async, processing then wait for callback also");
CallBack cbWithData = new CallBack(oWait);
result=oProxy.BeginGetAuthors(new AsyncCallback(cbWithData.CallBackMethod),
oProxy);
Console.WriteLine("Processing some more data");
Console.WriteLine("Application waits for callback rendezvous");
oWait.WaitOne();
Console.WriteLine("done");
```

This time, the CallBack object is instantiated with only one parameter. Changes to the CallBack class are highlighted in the following code block. When the callback method is invoked, you can cast the IAsyncResult object's AsyncState back to whatever type you passed into the second parameter of the Begin*MethodName*( ) method. In this case, we cast the Async-State object back to the proxy in order to complete the web method call with End*MethodName*( ) to obtain the resulting DataSet:

```
public class CallBack {
   public CallBack(WSPubsWS.PubsWS oProxy, AutoResetEvent oWait) {
     m_oProxy = oProxy;
     m_oWait = oWait;
   }
   public CallBack(AutoResetEvent oWait) {
     m_oWait = oWait;
   }
   public void CallBackMethod(IAsyncResult result) {
     DataSet oDSAsyncCB;
     if(m_oProxy == null) {
       WSPubsWS.PubsWS oTmp = (WSPubsWS.PubsWS)result.AsyncState;
       oDSAsyncCB = oTmp.EndGetAuthors(result);
       oDSAsyncCB.WriteXml("outputCallbackWithData.xml");
     } else {
       oDSAsyncCB = m_oProxy.EndGetAuthors(result);
       oDSAsyncCB.WriteXml("outputCallback.xml");
     }
     m_oWait.Set();
   }
   private WSPubsWS.PubsWS m_oProxy;
   private AutoResetEvent m_oWait;
}
```

In a Windows Form application, you can start the web service call via a button clicked or a menu clicked and still can have other parts of the application be responsive to the user. We will leave that example to you as an exercise.

SOAP Header in Web Services

As you have seen from the web service consumer using SOAP, the data being passed back and forth as is structured XML inside the body of the HTTP package. In particular it has the following format:

```
<Envelope>
  <Header>
    <...>
  </Header>
  <Body>
    <...>
  </Body>
</Envelope>
```

We have seen how to pass data from the client to the web service through the Body of the Envelope. In this section, we show how to use the Header of the Envelope.

Through this optional header node, the developers can pass information that does not relate to any particular web method or information that is common to all web methods. Of course, you can pass information that does not related to any particular web method in a method call itself, such as InitiateService(param) enforcing a usage rule that this method has to be called first. This is not an elegant solution. Just add the param of the InitiateService to the header. On the other hand, if all web methods of your service require a common parameter, wouldn't it be nice if you could just set up the header and didn't have to worry about this parameter for each of the web methods. Examples of header information are a security token, a payment token, priority, and so on; there is no reason to pass these pieces of common information via every web method.

Once you construct your web service to use a SOAP header, the WSDL will instruct the client that a header node is in place so that a web service client knows how to set up the header information before making a call to the web service methods. The following example should provide some clarification:

```csharp
<%@ WebService Language="C#" Class="TestHeader.PayWS" %>

namespace TestHeader {
  using System;
  using System.Web;
  using System.Web.Services;
  using System.Web.Services.Protocols;

  public class Payment : SoapHeader {
    public string CreditCardNumber;
  }
```

```
[WebService(Namespace="http://Oreilly/DotNetEssentials/")]
public class PayWS : WebService {

public Payment clientPayment;

[WebMethod, SoapHeader("clientPayment")]
public string Task1( ) {
  return string.Format("Task1 performed.   " +
    "Charging $25,000.00 on credit card: {0}",
    clientPayment.CreditCardNumber);
  }

[WebMethod, SoapHeader("clientPayment")]
public string Task2( ) {
  return string.Format("Task2 performed.   " +
    "Charging $4,500.00 on credit card: {0}",
    clientPayment.CreditCardNumber);
  }
 }
}
```

In this example, we create a web service with two methods, Task1 and Task2. Both of these methods use the Payment object in the soap header.

The SOAP request and response format for Task1 follows:

```
POST /SOAPHeader/PayWS.asmx HTTP/1.1
Host: localhost
Content-Type: text/xml; charset=utf-8
Content-Length: length
SOAPAction: "http://Oreilly/DotNetEssentials/Task1"

<?xml version="1.0" encoding="utf-8"?>
<soap:Envelope
    xmlns:xsi="http://www.w3.org/2001/XMLSchema-instance"
    xmlns:xsd="http://www.w3.org/2001/XMLSchema"
    xmlns:soap="http://schemas.xmlsoap.org/soap/envelope/">
  <soap:Header>
    <Payment xmlns="http://Oreilly/DotNetEssentials/">
      <CreditCardNumber>string</CreditCardNumber>
    </Payment>
  </soap:Header>
  <soap:Body>
    <Task1 xmlns="http://Oreilly/DotNetEssentials/" />
  </soap:Body>
</soap:Envelope>

HTTP/1.1 200 OK
Content-Type: text/xml; charset=utf-8
Content-Length: length

<?xml version="1.0" encoding="utf-8"?>
<soap:Envelope
```

```
    xmlns:xsi="http://www.w3.org/2001/XMLSchema-instance"
    xmlns:xsd="http://www.w3.org/2001/XMLSchema"
    xmlns:soap="http://schemas.xmlsoap.org/soap/envelope/">
  <soap:Body>
    <Task1Response xmlns="http://Oreilly/DotNetEssentials/">
      <Task1Result>string</Task1Result>
    </Task1Response>
  </soap:Body>
</soap:Envelope>
```

This is different than the soap envelope we've seen for PubsWS where there was no SOAP header. In this case, the header is an object of type Payment and this Payment class has a string property called CreditCardNumber.

Our example expects the clients to this web service to pass in the Payment object. The following is the client code. Of course, you will have to generate the proxy class for the PayWS web service using *wsdl.exe* and compile this proxy along with the client code:

```
public class ClientWS {
  public static void Main( ) {
    // Create a proxy
    PayWS oProxy = new PayWS( );

    // Create the payment header.
    Payment pmt = new Payment( );
    pmt.CreditCardNumber = "1234567890123456";

    // Attach the payment header to the proxy.
    oProxy.PaymentValue = pmt;

    // Call Task1.
    System.Console.WriteLine(oProxy.Task1( ));

    // Call Task2.
    System.Console.WriteLine(oProxy.Task2( ));
  }
}
```

The output of the client:

```
Task1 performed.  Charging $25,000.00 on credit card: 1234567890123456
Task2 performed.  Charging $4,500.00 on credit card: 1234567890123456
```

The above is a trivial usage of SOAP header. In reality, the SOAP headers are probably not as simple as our Payment class.

Microsoft, IBM, and a number of other companies have been working on the Global XML web services Architecture (GXA) that defines a framework on how to build standardized web services incorporating security, reliability, referral, routing, transaction, and so on. A number of GXA specifications use SOAP Header as the means for this infrastructure.

Web Services and Security

This section demonstrates how to incorporate security into your web service. We will do so in two ways: system security and application security. System-level security allows for restricting access to the web services from unauthorized clients. It is done in a declarative fashion, whereas application-level security is more flexible. With system-level security, you will most likely have the list of authorized clients' IP addresses that you will let access your web service through the use of some configuration-management tools. With application-level security, you will incorporate the authentication into your web service, thus providing a more flexible configuration.*

System Security

Because web services communication is done through HTTP, you can apply system-level security on web services just as you do for other web pages or resources on your web site.

There are a number of different ways you can secure your web services. For a business-to-business (B2B) solution, you can use the IIS Administration Tool to restrict or grant permission to a set of IP addresses, using the Internet Protocol Security (IPSec) to make sure that the IP address in the TCP/IP header is authenticated. When you rely only on the client to provide the IP in the TCP/IP header, hackers can still impersonate other host IPs when accessing your web services. IPSec authenticates the host addresses using the Kerberos authentication protocol. You can also use a firewall to restrict access to your web services for your partner companies. For a business-to-consumer (B2C) scenario, you can take advantage of the authentication features of the HTTP protocol.

To show you how to use the authentication feature of the HTTP protocol to secure your web services, let's revisit the example web service we have in this chapter, PubsWS. All we have to do to secure PubsWS web service is go to the IIS Admin Tool and choose to edit the File Security properties for the *PubsWS.asmx*. Instead of keeping the default setting, which leaves this file accessible to all anonymous users, we change this setting to "Basic Authentication" only, which means unchecking "Anonymous Access" and checking only "Basic Authentication" in the Authenticated Access frame. After this change, only users that pass the authentication can make use of the web service.

---

* As always, consult your security expert on this decision.

For real-life situations, of course, we are not going to use just the Basic Authentication method, because it sends the username and password in clear text through the HTTP channel. We would choose other methods, such as Secure Sockets Layer (SSL) underneath Basic Authentication, so that the data passed back and forth is secure. Available methods include:

Basic Authentication
Sends the username and password to the Web Server in clear text. IIS authenticates the login against the database of users for the domain.

Basic over SSL Authentication
Similar to Basic Authentication, except that the username and password are sent with SSL encryption.

Digest Authentication
Uses a hashing technique, as opposed to SSL encryption, to send client credentials securely to the server.

Integrated Windows Authentication
Good for intranet scenarios only. Uses the login information of the client for authentication.

Client Certificates Authentication
Requires each of the clients to obtain a certificate that is mapped to a user account. The use of client-side digital certificates is not widespread at this time.

Application Security

A less systematic way of securing your web services involves taking security into your own hands. You can program your web services so that all of their methods require an access token, which can be obtained from the web service after sending in the client's username and password. The client credentials can be sent to the server through SSL, which eliminates the risk of sending clear-text passwords across the wire. Through this SSL channel, the server returns an access token to the caller, who can use it to invoke all other web service methods. Of course, all of the other web methods that you publish must have one parameter as the token. A simple pseudocode example of a bank account web service can be the following:

```
web service Bank Account
  Web Methods:
    Login(user id, password) returns access token or nothing
    Deposit(access token, account number, amount, balance) returns boolean
    Withdraw(access token, account number, amount, balance) returns boolean
```

The only method that should be on SSL is the Login method. Once the token is obtained, it can be used for other web methods. Of course, you should be able to make sure that subsequent calls using this token are coming from the same IP as the Login( ) call. You can also incorporate an expiration timestamp on this access token to ensure that the token only exists in a certain time frame until a renewal of the access token is needed.

You can also use public/private keys (asymmetric) encryption for better key-management. The following scenario might suit your needs.

The client gets the server's public key and uses it to encrypt the requesting data (possibly including the client's private symmetric encryption key) before calling the web service. This ensures that the requesting data is encrypted and only the server can decrypt it. The server decrypts the data using the private key, figures out what the request is and uses the client's private key to encrypt the response before sending it back to the client. This time, the response data is encrypted. The client then decrypts the response package with its private symmetric key to view clear data. Since asymmetric cryptography operations are always much slower than symmetric, it's probably best if you only use asymmetric cryptography for key distribution. Once the key is communicated, you can use the symmetric operation for better performance. Rolling your own security is always harder than using a standard security solution. There are numerous areas you will have to manage yourself such as identity authentication, message authentication, and so on. Be forewarned if you choose this route.

The Microsoft .NET Cryptographic Services can be very useful if you choose to apply application security for your web services. DES, RC2, RC4, Triple-DES, and RSA cryptography algorithms are supported along with hashing methods such as SHA and MD5. These implementations in the .NET library enable developers to avoid low-level grunt work and focus on the application logic.

Summary

In this chapter, we've introduced you to the new paradigm of applications—the enterprise application. You are no longer restricted to homogeneous platforms for implementing your solutions. With Microsoft web services, your solutions can span many different platforms because the communication between web services is done through standard Internet protocols such as HTTP and XML. The distributed components in Windows DNA with which you may be familiar are now replaced by web services. Using web services as

components in a distributed environment allows for a heterogeneous system. The web services in your system can not only be implemented in different languages, but can even be on different platforms. Because of this greater interoperability, web services are eminently suitable for B2B integration.

CHAPTER 7

ASP.NET

This chapter introduces the next technology for providing dynamic and interactive web pages. ASP.NET takes Active Server Pages (ASP) a step further to simplify the development process of web pages and enhance scalability of web applications. First, we review the conventional way of developing web applications using ASP to uncover some of the pitfalls that ASP.NET overcomes. We then discuss the benefits of ASP.NET and provide a high-level survey of the classes in the ASP.NET, such as control and page, as well as the complete syntax of ASP.NET Web Forms. To wrap up the chapter, we discuss the many aspects of ASP.NET development: how ASP.NET supports web services development, how to use custom server controls, and how session management has been improved to provide more scalable web solutions. This overview chapter is designed to provide experienced developers with a solid introduction to ASP.NET and Web Forms; for additional in-depth information, see *Programming ASP.NET* by Liberty and Hurwitz (O'Reilly) and *ASP.NET in a Nutshell* by Duthie and MacDonald (O'Reilly).

ASP

Microsoft ASP is a server-side scripting technology enabling dynamic web pages. An ASP page contains HTML markup and server-side scripts that generate HTML content dynamically. The server-side scripts run when a request for the ASP page arrives at the web server. Inputs to the ASP page come from the client browsers through HTTP POST and GET methods. ASP provides an object model to simplify developers' tasks. Besides objects from the ASP object model like Application, Server, Request, Response, and Session, developers can use any COM components on the server.

If you've already been developing web applications using ASP, you probably agree that it is very easy to end up with intertwined, possibly conflicting

HTML markups and server-side scripts. The poor encapsulation model of ASP pages makes them difficult to manage and reuse. Attempts have been made to improve upon this model, including server-side include files and parameterized functions in scripts; however, these attempts come with trade-offs such as time, the management of a network of include files, the performance impact of having nested includes, as well as object ID and variable-scope management.

Developers that deal with cross-browser web applications also run into problems generating HTML according the client's browser capability. Most of the time, we end up generating only the simplest HTML tags and client-side scripts, which can be understood by many browsers, and foregoing the features of the more advanced browsers. The resulting web application can be only as good as the worst browser it supports. Sometimes, we also attempt to generate different HTML markups for different browsers to take advantage of browser-specific features, resulting in a much better client-side experience; however, this involves much more development time and effort.

Since scripting in ASP is available only to late-bound languages such as VBScript and JavaScript, type-safety is not an option. In addition, server-side scripts in ASP pages get reinterpreted each time the page is accessed, which is not ideal for performance.

Form-state maintenance in an ASP-based application is also labor-intensive—developers must do everything manually, including reposting data, using hidden fields, and session variables. At times, web applications are configured to run in web farm environments where there is more than one web server available to the client. Maintaining session states becomes much harder in these scenarios because it is not guaranteed that the client would return to the same server for the next request. Basically, the developers have to save states manually to SQL Server or other external storage.

Although ASP is a great technology to build dynamic web pages, it has room for improvement. ASP.NET evolved from ASP and overcomes most, if not all, of its shortfalls.

ASP.NET

Visual Basic developers have long enjoyed the ease of programming with forms and controls. Writing a VB form-based application is as simple as dragging some controls onto a form and writing some event-handling functions. This is one of the reasons VB has attracted lots of programmers interested in speed of development. Microsoft wisely built this feature into ASP.NET.

ASP.NET simplifies web page development with form-based programming. In ASP.NET, these forms are called *Web Forms* and are analogous to VB forms, replacing ASP pages. Similar to VB, Web Forms programming is also event based. We don't have to write in-line ASP scripts and rely on the top-down parsing interpretation as in ASP programming. To match the rich set of ActiveX controls that VB programmers love in their toolset, ASP.NET equips ASP programmers with *server controls*. To further enhance the productivity of developers, ASP.NET's Web Forms also allow for the separation of the application logic and the presentation layer.

ASP.NET evolves from the ASP programming model with the following additional benefits:

- Clean separation between the application logic (server-side code) and the presentation layer (HTML markup)—no more spaghetti code
- A rich set of server controls that automatically render HTML suitable for any clients and that additionally manage their states
- Enhanced session-state management
- An event-based programming model on the server side, which is simpler and more intuitive than an older script-based model like ASP
- Application logic that can be written in any Microsoft .NET language (VB, C#, Managed C++, etc.); application server-side code is compiled for better performance
- Visual Studio .NET as a RAD tool, which simplifies the development process of Web Forms

The System.Web.UI Namespace

Before getting into developing your favorite *Hello, World!* application in ASP.NET, it's important that you become familiar with the underlying structure of ASP.NET. This section describes some of the most important classes packaged in the System.Web.UI namespace in the ASP.NET framework.

The System.Web.UI namespace defines classes and interfaces used in constructing and rendering elements on a Web Form. The most important class in the System.Web.UI is the Control class, which defines properties, methods, and events that are common in all server controls in the Web Forms framework. Another important class in this namespace is Page, which is a derivative of the Control class. All ASP.NET web pages are instances of derivatives of the Page class. To have an extensible framework, the System. Web.UI namespace also includes the UserControl class, which is similar to

the Page class except that it is used as the base class for user controls. We will make use of the UserControl and Page classes in "ASP.NET Application Development" and "Custom Server Controls" sections later in this chapter.

Control Class

The Control class is the root of all controls. For example, a text box is a control; a button or a combo box is also a control. The Control class basically encapsulates common functionalities and properties of all user-interface widgets. As you get deeper into ASP.NET development, everything you see is a Control derivative of some sort.

Control's properties

The Control class has the following important properties: Controls, ID, ClientID, Parent, EnableViewState, Visible, Context, and ViewState. We will go over each of these properties briefly to show you what the Control class is made up of and how deriving from Control class would create a model that is consistent and easy to work with.

The Controls property represents the children of the control instance; the Parent property defines the parent of the control. These properties enable a hierarchy of controls on a web page. The ID property allows the control to be accessed programmatically by just using the ID and the dot notation to get to the object's properties and methods (i.e., MyObjectId.property-name). While the ID property allows us to program the control on the server side, ClientID allows us to setup client-side script to access the control on the client side. More information on using ClientID will be shown later in this chapter.

The EnableViewState flag indicates whether the control will maintain its view state, as well as all view states of its child controls. If this flag is set to true, the control will remember its previous view state when the page posts back to itself.* For example, if EnableViewState is set to true, the user's previous selection or form-field data are preserved automatically when the user performs some operation that requires a postback. When the page is sent back to the browser, the user can just continue filling in the form as if he never left it. This is how all derivatives of the Control class maintain their

---

* Postback is the condition when an ASP page posts the data back to itself for processing. In conventional ASP programming, the states of the fields in the form have to be managed manually. In ASP.NET, we can have these field states managed automatically with a simple EnableViewState flag.

states between requests and free ASP developers from having to simulate view-state behavior with hidden form fields.

The Context property enables us to get to information about the current HTTP request, such as the Application, Server, Session, Request, and Response objects. ASP developers should be familiar with these intrinsic objects. You will likely use the Context property when you are processing the web page's Load event to get to application- or session-level variables and request parameters to set up your page. Through the Context property, you can also get other information, such as cached resources, including database connection for performance improvement; the trace property for debugging purposes; and the user property for security validation.

The ViewState property is an instance of the StateBag class, which is used to store name/value pairs of information that can be made accessible across multiple requests for the same web page. These name/value pairs are instances of the StateItem class. ViewState allows ASP.NET controls to maintain their own state across multiple client roundtrips; it is implemented as a hidden form field on the page. If you've attempted to maintain state for your form in ASP development, you will appreciate this because it is now automatically done for you.

Control class methods

The list of methods for the Control class is much longer than what we've covered in this section; however, this short list is probably all you need to know to get started with the Control class:

DataBind method
> Binds the control to a data source. This method is used in conjunction with the data-binding expression syntax on the Web Form. When this method is called, all data-binding tags, <%# %>, are re-evaluated so that the new data is bound to the appropriate tag location. Also, any controls that have their DataSource property set, retrieve the data from the DataSource and fill themselves.

CreateChildControls method
> Called before any compositional custom control is rendered. A compositional custom control is similar to a user control. Both of them are composed of other controls to create more complex controls. You would not employ this method simply to use the control. When developing custom controls, this method can be overridden so that custom control developers can create and layout child controls prior to rendering the controls, whether for the first time or for postbacks.

Render method

Similar to the CreateChildControls, primarily used to develop custom controls. Control developers override this method to render the control content through the provided HtmlTextWriter parameter.

We will revisit the Render and CreateChildControls methods when we show you how to create custom controls in "Customer Server Controls" later in this chapter.

SaveViewState and LoadViewState methods

Save and reload the state for the control. Server controls maintain their state between requests via these methods.

Page Class

As mentioned earlier, the Page class is actually a derivative* of the Control class. This means it inherits all properties, methods, and events exposed by the Control class. In addition to the inherited things, the Page class defines more specific properties, methods, and events for a web page in the ASP.NET framework.

If you've done ASP development, you already know that Application, Request, Response, Server, and Session are intrinsic objects that you can access while scripting your ASP page. With ASP.NET, these objects are actually properties of the Page class. In addition to these familiar objects, the Page class also exposes other properties such as Cache, ErrorPage, IsPostBack, IsValid, Trace, and Validators.

Page class properties and methods

This list is not complete; however, it includes some of the more important features that we want to introduce:

Cache property

Points to a Cache object of the Context for the current page. Here, resources such as DataSet with information retrieved from a database are stored for reuse while the cache item is not yet expired.

ErrorPage property

Specifies the page to display when an error occurs. You can also specify the error page by using the @Page directive, as shown in the section "Web Form Syntax."

---

* The Page class derives from TemplateControl, which derives from the Control class.

IsPostBack property

Indicates whether the page request is an original request or a postback, since the interaction between the user and the server controls requires a postback to the current page. If IsPostBack is true, you should not redo all your page initialization to improve performance.

Validators property

Groups together server controls that can validate themselves inside the Validators property of the Page. (In ASP.NET, a web page usually consists of a number of server controls.) This is so that when the Page needs to validate itself, it can delegate the validation to all of these controls and then set the IsValid property to the appropriate value.

Trace property

References a TraceContext object, through which you can issue warning or error messages. Tracing can be switched on or off at any time from the web.config setting. web.config is an XML-based text file that stores the runtime configuration for an ASP.NET application. Changes to this file take effect immediately. The main configuration file is at the root of your web application; however, you can have a configuration file for each subdirectory in your web application. The closest configuration file overrides the settings of distant configuration files. Being able to switch off tracing in a configuration file like this is much better than doing so manually in ASP development, where you must go through all ASP files to remove all instances of Response.Write debugging messages when you are ready to deploy your application.

LoadControl method

Loads server controls from a file into the page programmatically. This is especially for user controls in ascx files. For ordinary server controls, they can be instantiated directly and added to the page's Controls collection. You can also have static server control declared on the page using the server-side object syntax as described in "Web Form Syntax" later in this chapter.

MapPath method

Maps a virtual path to a physical path for file I/O. This should be familiar to ASP developers.

Validate method

Works with the Server Validation Controls on the page to validate data on the page. If any of the server controls fail to validate, this method returns false, and the failed server-validation control renders the error message to the user.

CreateHtmlTextWriter method

Produces an HtmlTextWriter object to write HTML to the response stream. This is similar to ASP's Response.Write method; however, the HtmlTextWriter object is much smarter than the raw Write method. It helps you write well-formed HTML.

LoadPageStateFromPersistenceMedium, SavePageStateToPersistenceMedium methods

By default, save and load view state for all controls as hidden fields on the page. If you don't want this setting, you can override the SavePage-StateFromPersistenceMedium method to save the view state anywhere other than hidden fields. You will also have to override the LoadPage-StateFromPersistenceMedium method to have the saved view states loaded back onto the page prior to rendering.

UserControl Class

The UserControl class is similar to the Page class (see the previous section) with the omission of page-specific properties or methods such as ErrorPage, IsValid, User, Validators, MapPath, Validate, and CreateHtmlTextWriter.

The UserControl class is typically used as the base class for custom controls. We can also build custom controls by inheriting directly from the Control class; however, it's better to start from UserControl because it is not as raw as the Control class. If you find that UserControl supports a number of properties and methods that you don't really want in your custom control, you might choose to inherit the raw Control class instead. We show you how to create custom controls in the "Custom Server Controls" section later in this chapter.

System.Web.UI.HtmlControls Namespace

If you've done any client-side DHTML scripting, you know how all HTML tags are mapped to scriptable objects. ASP.NET brings this mapping to the server side. Before the web page is rendered and sent back the client, you can access and manipulate each of the objects on the page.

ASP.NET maps HTML tags with objects in the hierarchy of server-side classes defined in the System.Web.UI.HtmlControls namespace. These server objects are called *HtmlControls* because they closely map to standard HTML elements.

For example, here is a simple HTML page that relies on client-side scripting to change the output page dynamically. (This page won't run on browsers

that do not support VBScript client-side scripting or browsers that have client-side scripting turned off.)

```
<html>
<head>
  <script language=vbscript>
  sub cmd1_onclick( )
    txtMessage.InnerHtml = _
        "(Client-side) Your name is: " & frm1.txtName.value
  end sub
  </script>
</head>
<body>
  <form id=frm1>
    Enter Name: <input id="txtName" type="text" size="40">
    <input type=button id="cmd1" value="Click Me">
    <span id="txtMessage"></span>
  </form>
</body>
</html>
```

We will convert this page so that it relies on server control instead of the IE Document Object Model. Since the output of the page is controlled from the server side, the page works regardless of what kind of browser you are using. One drawback to this is that all interaction with the page requires a postback to the server.

To take advantage of server controls mapping, all you have to do is to add the id and runat attributes, and your server-side script will be able to access and manipulate the server controls:

```
<html>
<head>
  <script id="scr1" language="c#" runat="server">
    void svr_cmd1_onclick(Object o, EventArgs e)
    {
      txtMessage.InnerHtml =
          "(Server-side) Your name is: " + txtName.Value;
    }
  </script>
</head>
<body>
  <form id="frm1" runat="server">
    Enter Name: <input id="txtName" type="text" size="40" runat="server">
    <input type="button" id="cmd1" value="Click Me"
        onserverclick="svr_cmd1_onclick" runat="server">
    <span id="txtMessage" runat="server"></span>
  </form>
</body>
</html>
```

By adding the runat="server" attribute to the HTML form and its controls, you have exposed an HtmlForm object, an HtmlInputText object, an Html-InputButton object, and an HtmlGenericControl object (the span) to your server-side script, as depicted in Figure 7-1. As you can see in the previous script, you can manipulate the HtmlGenericControl object's txtMessage to set its InnerHtml property.

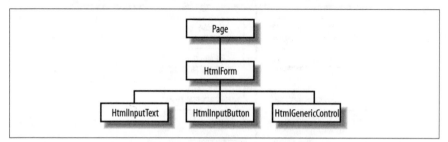

Figure 7-1. Server-side scriptable objects for the code example

Even though the results of the two simple examples appear to be the same, they are drastically different from the technical point of view. Client-side scripting, as the name implies, runs in the client browser process. On the other hand, when we have controls tagged to run on the server, we can have accesses to other server resources.

Most classes in the System.Web.UI.HtmlControls namespace are derivatives of the HtmlControl class, which in turn derives from the Control class of the System.Web.UI namespace. See Figure 7-2 for a graphical presentation of the hierarchy. The HtmlControl class serves as the base class for these HtmlControls because most HTML elements share common characteristics that are defined in this HtmlControl base class. They share properties such as ID, Disabled, Value, Style, and TagName. Because these HtmlControls ultimately are derivatives of the Control class, they also have methods and events that the Control class exposes.

Table 7-1 maps the HtmlControls to standard HTML tags. This means when you have an HTML tag that is flagged to run on the server side with runat="server", ASP.NET creates an appropriate HtmlControl that you can program against.

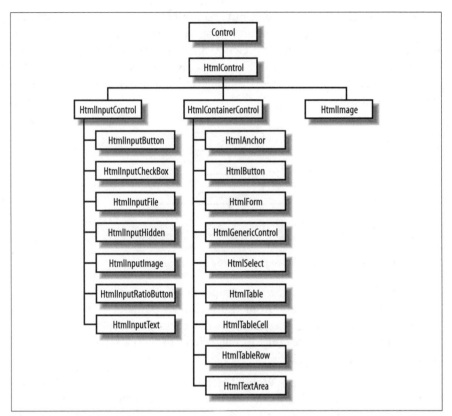

Figure 7-2. HtmlControls object hierarchy

Table 7-1. HtmlControls mapping to HTML tags

HTMLControl	Description	HTML tag
HtmlImage	Image tag	`<img>`
HtmlInputFile	File selector	`<input type="file">`
HtmlInputHidden	Used for hidden form fields	`<input type="hidden">`
HtmlInputImage	Image input	`<input type="image">`
HtmlInputRadioButton	Radio button	`<input type="radio">`
HtmlInputText	Standard text input	`<input type="text">`
HtmlInputButton	Standard HTML button	`<input type="button">`
HtmlInputCheckBox	Standard HTML checkbox	`<input type="checkbox">`
HtmlForm	Form tag	`<form>`
HtmlGenericControl	Miscellaneous generic HTML tags	`<span, div, etc.>`
HtmlSelect	Standard HTML drop-down control	`<select>`
HtmlTable	Standard HTML table	`<table>`

Table 7-1. HtmlControls mapping to HTML tags (continued)

HTMLControl	Description	HTML tag
HtmlTableCell	A cell in a table row	`<td>`
HtmlTableRow	A row in a table	`<tr>`
HtmlTextArea	Multiline text area	`<textarea rows=n cols=n>`
HtmlAnchor	Standard HTML hyperlink control	`<a href=...>` or `<a name=...>`
HtmlButton	HTML button	`<button>`

System.Web.UI.WebControls Namespace

While providing HtmlControls, which map to standard HTML elements, ASP.NET also provides another group of UI controls, the WebControl class (see Figure 7-3). In addition to providing all traditional controls similar to HtmlControls, WebControls also provide much richer controls such as calendars, grids, and validators.

WebControls are richer, more powerful, and more flexible than HtmlControls. It seems that it is the natural choice for new ASP.NET applications; however, HtmlControls are better if you are migrating ASP applications. Another thing that might make you consider using HtmlControls is that with it, your client-side scripts can still access and manipulate the objects.

Most classes in this namespace are based on WebControl, which is again a derivative of the Control class. The WebControl class provides the common properties and methods inherited by all of its descendants, including access key, tab index, tool tip, color, font, and border setting.

Web Form Syntax

Similar to Active Server Pages, Web Forms are text files consisting of HTML tags and other controlling tags such as directives and script blocks. The default extension for web forms is *aspx;* however, you can use the IIS administration tool to map other file extensions explicitly with *aspnet_isapi.dll* to have them parsed and compiled when accessed, as if they were ASP.NET resources.

There are 10 different syntax elements in ASP.NET; because most of them are carried over from ASP, we list here the familiar ones and discuss only those that are important in ASP.NET:

Directives
Code declaration blocks
Code-rendering blocks

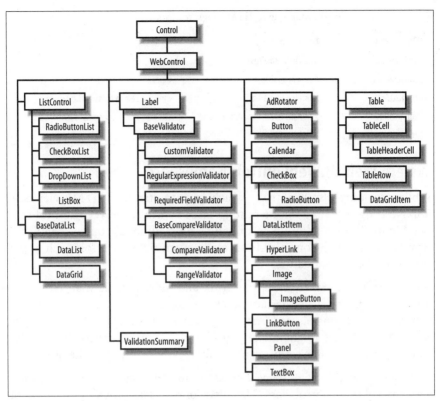

Figure 7-3. WebControls object hierarchy

> HTML control syntax
> Custom control syntax
> Data-binding expressions
> Server-side object tags
> Server-side include directives
> Server-side comments
> Literal text

Directives

Previously, all ASP directives were formatted as `<%@ [attribute=value]+ %>` because there was only one type of directive.*

---

* As noted in the Preface, the plus sign indicates one or more instances of the preceding term in brackets.

ASP.NET adds a number of directives to ASP.NET files. With the new list of directives—Page, Control, Import, Implements, Register, Assembly, OutputCache, and Reference—the syntax for directive is now `<%@ directive [attribute=value]+ %>`. All of the old ASP directives are attributes under the Page directive. If you use the old syntax by omitting the directive name, the attribute/value pairs will be applied to the default directive, which is Page.

@ Page

In addition to containing all previous ASP directives (CodePage, EnableSessionState, Language, LCID, and Transaction), the ASP.NET Page directive also supports the important attributes ErrorPage, Inherits, Src, and EnableViewState, which we will make use of in this chapter. The complete list of all attributes for the Page directive can be found in the *.NET Framework Developers' Guide*:

```
<@ Page Language="VB" ErrorPage="URL" EnableViewState="true">
```

@ Control

Similar to the way the Page directive is used for an ASP.NET page (an *.aspx* file), the Control directive is used for an ASP.NET control (an *.ascx* file). (We get into developing ASP.NET controls in the "Custom Server Controls" section later in this chapter.)

@ Import

We can use the Import directive to add namespace references to the current page. Your code can access all classes and interfaces of imported namespaces. For example, if you want to use ADO.NET, you would include the following code:

```
<%@ Import Namespace="System.Data" %>
<%@ Import Namespace="System.Data.OleDb" %>
```

A number of namespaces are automatically imported into all ASP.NET pages to simplify the developers' task:

System
System.Collections
System.Collections.Specialized
System.Configuration
System.IO
System.Text
System.Text.RegularExpressions
System.Web
System.Web.Caching

System.Web.Security
System.Web.SessionState
System.Web.UI
System.Web.UI.HtmlControls
System.Web.UI.WebControls

@ Implements

Because an *aspx* file is basically a Page class derivative, it too can also implement an interface. The @ Implements directive is used to declare that the *aspx* implements the specified interface. For example, the following line declares that the page implements the IPostBackEventHandler interface:

```
<%@ Implements Interface="System.Web.UI.IPostBackEventHandler" %>
```

@ Register

This directive registers custom server controls for use in the current page by specifying the aliases to be used as prefixes for class names. It is used in conjunction with the custom server-control elements to provide a concise way of specifying server-control names. The following line of code registers a custom control to be used in this page:

```
<%@ Register Tagprefix="Ch07"
             TagName="MyCustomControl"
             Src="MyCustomControl.ascx" %>
```

The name of the control is MyCustomControl; the prefix used when declaring the control is Ch07; the source for the control is in MyCustomControl.ascx. (We demonstrate this when we develop our ASP.NET controls later in this chapter.)

If the server custom control was not done through *.ascx* but instead, through inheriting UserControl, the syntax for the Register directive is the following:

```
<%@ Register Tagprefix="MyCustomCtrl"
             Namespace="MyNamespace"
             Assembly="MyDll.dll" %>
```

@ Assembly

The Assembly directive specifies the assembly to which the current page belongs. This effectively makes all the classes and interfaces belonging to the assembly accessible to the current page. For example, the following line of code specifies that the current page belong to the Ch07 assembly:

```
<%@ Assembly Name="Ch07" %>
```

This means that code in this page can access anything in the Ch07 assembly as long as the Ch07 assembly is compiled and placed in the *bin* subdirectory of this web application.

@ OutputCache

You can use the OutputCache directive to control the output-caching duration for the current page. This is similar to setting up the expiration for the response object in ASP programming. The Duration attribute of the OutputCache directive defines the time in seconds until the page expires.

@ Reference

The @ Reference directive is used to add a reference to a page or a control to this *aspx* page.

Code Declaration Blocks

As in ASP, *code declaration blocks* define the code to be parsed and run for the page. In these blocks, the runat attribute specifies whether the code block is client-side or server-side code. For server-side programming, set this attribute to server. If you ignore the runat attribute, IIS will interpret the code block as client-side code, which is used for Dynamic HTML (DHTML).

```
<script runat="server" [language="codelanguage"]>
  Code
</script>
```

For both client- and server-side code declaration blocks, you can also use the src attribute to point to an external source file containing the code. This helps separate the code from the HTML content of the page. The value for src can be a relative path or a URL to a source file. The URL can be on the same or a different web server:

```
<script runat="server"
  [language="codelanguage"]
  [src="externalfilename"] />
```

Code-Rendering Blocks

There are no changes to this syntax versus that in ASP. Inline code or inline expressions specified in these code-rendering blocks are executed when the page is rendered. All these blocks are enclosed between the tags <% and %>. The language used in these tags is specified in the language attribute of the Page directive.

HTML-Control Syntax

HTML controls are very similar to standard HTML elements, with the exception of the id and the runat attributes. If you've developed web applications with DHTML, you should be familiar with the id attribute of an HTML element and how to programmatically reference the client-side control representing the HTML element. The difference in this case is that the control is not on the client side but on the server side. For example, the following code represents an HTML server button control:

```
<input id="cmd1" runat="server"
    type="button" value="Click Me" />
```

All HTML server controls must be inside a <form runat="server"> control because Web Forms use the POST method to maintain the controls' states.

When encountering an HTML element tagged with id and the runat attribute set to server, ASP.NET creates the appropriate scriptable server HtmlControl object. For example, the previous HTML snippet generates a server HtmlControl of type HtmlInputButton that has an id of cmd1.

You can bind an event handler to this control's event to handle notification from this control, such as the onclick event. There are two ways to bind an event handler to a control's event, the declarative way and the programmatic way. The declarative is done inside the HTML element tag as an attribute/value pair. The attribute is the name of the event, and the value is the name of the event-handling function. For example, to handle the onclick event, add this to the previous HTML tag:

```
onserverclick="handleServerClick"
```

The programmatic way to bind an event to the handler involves a line of code that assigns a delegate to the event property of the control. In C#, the code to bind the ServerClick event of the button to the event handler handleServerClick is:

```
cmd1.ServerClick += new System.EventHandler(handleServerClick);
```

If you've used client-side DHTML in your web applications, event binding should be nothing new to you, except for some subtle differences. The first difference is obvious: the event handler runs on the server before the page is sent back to the browser, instead of running on the client side. The other difference is that all event-handler functions for server-side must have two parameters: Sender and Event. The Sender parameter is of type object, indicating the source element that caused the event to happen; the Event parameter is of type EventArgs, which is the actual event fired. In DHTML scripting, we would inspect the window.event object to find out which element was the source of the event and other event information.

Custom-Control Syntax

Similar to HTML Server Controls, *custom controls* also have id and runat attributes; however, custom controls are not standard HTML elements. To insert a custom control into a page, use the following syntax:

```
<tagprefix:tagname id="controlID" runat="server" eventname=
  "eventHandler" />
```

Notice that all custom controls' tags have a tag prefix, which is an alias to the namespace in which the control is defined. See the Register directive earlier in this chapter for information on registering namespaces' aliases. Binding events to their handlers for custom controls is the same as for HTML controls. Even though we show the two ways of binding events, it is preferable to bind events using the second method because it cleanly separates the HTML tags from the code behind the screen.

All web controls mentioned in the WebControls namespace can be inserted in the same manner (these controls have the prefix asp). For example, you can have the following tags in your *aspx* page:

```
<asp:TextBox id=txt1 runat=server></asp:TextBox>
<asp:Button id=cmd1 runat=server Text="Web Button"></asp:Button>
<asp:Label id=label1 runat=server></asp:Label>
```

These tags result in three objects generated from the three classes: TextBox, Button, and Label, from the System.Web.UI.WebControls namespace. In your server script, you can access and manipulate these objects to render your page appropriately.

Data-Binding Expressions

Data-binding expressions bind the server controls with some data sources. The syntax to bind data is:

```
<%# data-binding-expression %>
```

Examine the following block of code to see the simplest data binding:

```
<asp:Label text='<%# TestData %>' runat=server/>
```

The data-binding expression here indicates that the label's text content is bound to a publicly defined property, TestData, of the Web Form. This means that when data binding occurs for the form, <%# TestData %> will be replaced by the content of the TestData property. Let's define this property for the Web Form:

```
public string TestData = "Hello World";
```

The Web Forms page framework does not perform data binding automatically. The developers must explicitly call the DataBind() method to activate

the evaluation of the data-binding expression and perform the substitution. We can call the page's DataBind method upon the page-load event or whenever we change the TestData property and want it reflected on the page. This example calls DataBind() upon page load to bind the Label's text to the TestData variable:

```html
<html>
  <head><title>Data Binding Sample</title></head>
  <body>

    <script language="C#" runat=server>
      /* Declare the variable we want to bind to. */
      public string TestData;
      void Page_Load(Object oSender, EventArgs oEvent) {
        TestData = "Hello World!\n";
        Page.DataBind();
      }
    </script>

    <asp:Label text='<%# TestData %>' runat=server/>

  </body>
</html>
```

Let's try something a little more complicated. In the next block of tags, we have three labels bound to three different properties of an object called currStudent:

```
Name: <asp:Label text='<%# currStudent.FirstName %>' runat=server/>
<asp:Label text='<%# currStudent.LastName %>' runat=server/> <br/>
SSN: <asp:Label text='<%# currStudent.SSN %>' runat=server/>
```

The currStudent object is a publicly accessible property of the current page:

```
<script language="C#" runat=server>
  public class CStudent {
    /* Declare the variable we want to bind to. */
    public string FirstName;
    public string LastName;
    public string SSN;
  }
  public CStudent currStudent;

  void Page_Load(Object oSender, EventArgs oEvent) {
    currStudent = new CStudent();
    currStudent.FirstName = "Jack";
    currStudent.LastName = "Daniel";
    currStudent.SSN = "123-45-6789";
    Page.DataBind();
  }

</script>
```

You can have this currStudent object filled with data coming from any source then perform a DataBind call to update the page with the current student's information. The assumption here, of course, is that the Student class provides the previously mentioned properties.

Server-Side Object Tags

Server-side object tags statically declare and instantiate COM and .NET objects. The syntax to declare server-side objects in *global.asax* is:

```
<object id="id" runat="server" scope="scope" class=".NET class name">
<object id="id" runat="server" scope="scope" progid="COM ProgID">
<object id="id" runat="server" scope="scope" classid="COM classID">
```

Scope can be pipeline, application, or session, which means the object is available on the page, as an application variable, or as a session variable, respectively. To dynamically add a server-side object to the page, you would use the Page.LoadControl( ) method or just instantiate the control directly.

Other Elements

Server-side includes server-side comments and literal text which are exactly the same as in ASP. Therefore, we will not go over them here.

ASP.NET Application Development

In conventional ASP programming, developers typically access the Request object to get the parameters needed to render the page and render the content of the page through either the Response object or code-rendering blocks. We also use other ASP objects such as the Application, Session, and Server objects to manage application variables, session variables, server settings, and so on.

As mentioned earlier, ASP.NET is intended to change all this spaghetti madness by introducing a much cleaner approach to server-side scripting framework: Web Forms, or programmable pages, and server controls.

In the following sections, we cover the components of a Web Form, its life cycles, the server controls that the Web Form contains, event-handling for these server controls, as well as how to create your own server controls.

Web Form Components

Similar to VB Forms, a Web Form consists of two components: the form with its controls, and the code behind it that handles events associated with

the form's controls. A Web Form has the file extension *.aspx* and contains HTML elements, as well as server controls. The code behind the form is usually located in a separate class file. Note that while it is possible to have both the form and the code in one file, it is better to have separate files. This separation of user interface and application code helps improve the spaghetti-code symptom that most ASP-based applications are plagued with.

ASP.NET provides the Page class in the System.Web.UI namespace. This class encapsulates all common properties and methods associated with web pages. The code behind the class derives from this Page class to provide extensions specific to the page we're implementing. The *aspx* file provides the form layout and control declarations. Figure 7-4 illustrates the relationship between the Page base class, the Web Form code behind the class, and the Web Form user interface (UI).

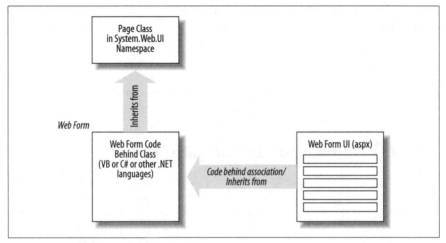

Figure 7-4. Web Form components

As a Web Form developer, you will have to provide the latter two. The Web Form UI is where you declare server controls with appropriate IDs. The code behind the class is where you programmatically access server controls declared in the Web Form UI, as well as handle events from these controls. The following simple example shows the *aspx* page, the code behind source file, and how they work together. The *aspx* file (*TestEvent.aspx*) contains only HTML tags and a directive that links to the code behind:

```
<%@ Page language="c#" codebehind="TestEvents.cs" inherits="CTestEvents"%>
<html>
  <head><title>Testing Page Events with codebehind</title></head>
  <body>
    <form runat=server>
      Init Time: <asp:Label id=labelInit runat=server/><br/>
```

```
      Load Time: <asp:Label id=labelLoad runat=server/><br/>
      <input type=submit />
   </form>
  </body>
</html>
```

The code-behind, *TestEvents.cs*, contains the class CTestEvents to which the *aspx* page is referring:

```
using System;

public class CTestEvents : System.Web.UI.Page {
  protected System.Web.UI.WebControls.Label labelInit;
  protected System.Web.UI.WebControls.Label labelLoad;

  public CTestEvents() {
    labelInit = new System.Web.UI.WebControls.Label();
    labelLoad = new System.Web.UI.WebControls.Label();
  }

  public void Page_Init(Object oSender, EventArgs oEvent) {
    labelInit.Text = DateTime.Now.ToString();
  }

  public void Page_Load(Object oSender, EventArgs oEvent) {
    labelLoad.Text = DateTime.Now.ToString();
    if(IsPostBack) {
      labelLoad.Text += "(PostBack)";
    }
  }
}
```

You must compile *TestEvents.cs* and place the DLL in the */bin* directory under your web application's virtual directory before trying to access the *aspx* page.[*]

The command to compile this C# file is:

```
csc /t:library TestEvents.cs
```

ASP.NET parses the Web Form files to generate a tree of programmable objects, where the root is the Page-derived object representing the current Web Form. This is similar to how the IE browser parses the HTML file and generates a tree of scriptable objects to be used in DHTML; however, the tree of objects for the Web Form files resides on the server side.

As you are already aware from our survey of the System.Web.UI namespace, the Page class actually derives from the Control class. In a sense, a Web

---

[*] The Web Application directory is the root virtual directory where your web application resides. To set up the virtual directory, use the IIS Administration Tool.

Form is a hierarchy of Control-derived objects. These objects establish the parent-child relationship through the Parent and Controls properties.

Besides the Controls and Parent properties, the Page class also provides other useful properties, which are familiar to ASP developers—such as the Request, Response, Application, Session, and Server properties.

Because the Web Form is nothing but a programmable page object, using this object-oriented model is much more intuitive and cleaner than the conventional ASP development. As opposed to the linear execution of server-side scripts on an ASP page, ASP.NET enables an event-based object-oriented programming model.

Let's take an example of a web page that contains a form with numerous fields. One or more of these fields display list information from a database. Naturally, we have code in the ASP page to populate these fields so that when a user requests this ASP page, the generated page would have the content ready. As soon as the last line of data is written to the browser, the ASP page is done. This means that if there were errors when the user submits the form, we will have to repopulate all the database-driven form fields, as well as programmatically reselect values that the user chose prior to submitting the form. In ASP.NET, we don't have to repopulate the database-driven fields if we know that the page has already been populated. Furthermore, selected values stay selected with no manual handling. The next couple of sections describe the concept in more detail.

Web Form events

The Page class exposes events such as Init, Load, PreRender, and Unload. Your job as a developer is to handle these events and perform the appropriate task for each of these stages. This is much better than the linear execution model in ASP programming because you don't have to worry about the location of your initialization scripts.

The first event that happens in the life of a Web Form is the Init event. This is raised so that we can have initialization code for the page. Please note that because the controls on the page are not yet created at this point, this initialization should only contain code that does not rely on any controls. This event is raised once for each user of the page.

Most developers are more familiar with the Load event that follows the Init event. Subsequently, it is raised each time the page is requested. When this event is raised, all child controls of the Web Form are loaded and accessible. You should be able to retrieve data and populate the controls so that they can render themselves on the page when sent back to the client.

The following example shows the how the Init and Load events can be handled in ASP.NET. In this example, we show both the HTML and its code together in one file to make it simpler:

```html
<html>
  <head><title>Testing Page Events</title></head>
  <body>

    <script language="C#" runat="server">
      void Page_Init(Object oSender, EventArgs oEvent) {
        labelInit.Text = DateTime.Now.ToString();
      }

      void Page_Load(Object oSender, EventArgs oEvent) {
        labelLoad.Text = DateTime.Now.ToString();
        if(IsPostBack) {
          labelLoad.Text += "(PostBack)";
        }
      }
    </script>

    <form runat="server">
      Init Time: <asp:Label id="labelInit" runat="server"/><br />
      Load Time: <asp:Label id="labelLoad" runat="server"/><br />
      <input type="submit" />
    </form>
  </body>
</html>
```

The first time you access this page, the Init event happens, followed by the Load event. Because these events happen quickly, both the Init Time and Load Time will probably show the same time. When you click on the submit button to cause the page to reload, you can see that the Init Time stays what it was, but the Load Time changes each time the page is reloaded.

The PreRender event happens just before the page is rendered and sent back to the client. We don't often handle this event; however, it depends on the situation. You might want to alter the state of some of the "server-side" objects before rendering the page content.

The last event in the life of a Web Form is the Unload event. This happens when the page is unloaded from memory. Final cleanup should be done here. For example, while unloading you should free the unmanaged resources that you've allocated at the Init event.

Beside these page-level events, controls on the page can raise events such as ServerClick and ServerChange for HtmlControls, as well as Click, Command, CheckedChanged, SelectedIndexChanged, and TextChanged events for WebControls. It is the handling of these events that makes ASP.NET truly dynamic and interactive.

The Life Cycle of a Web Form

In ASP, the web page starts its life when a client requests a particular page. IIS parses and runs the scripts on the ASP page to render HTML content. As soon as the page rendering is complete, the page's life ceases. If you have forms that pass data back to the ASP page to be processed, the ASP page runs as a new request, not knowing anything about its previous states. Passing data back to the original page for processing is also referred to as postback.

In ASP.NET, things are a little different. The page still starts at the client's request; however, it appears to stay around for as long as the client is still interacting with the page. For simplicity's sake, we say that the page stays around, but in fact, only the view states of the page persist between requests to the page. These view states allow the controls on the server to appear as if they are still present to handle server events. We can detect this postback state of the page via the IsPostBack property of the Page object and forego certain costly reinitialization. The handling of events during these postbacks is what makes ASP.NET so much different than conventional ASP development.

In the following example, we extend the previous example to handle the postback. When the Load event is handled for the first time, we populate the drop-down list box with data. Subsequently, we indicate only the time the event is raised without reloading the data. This example also demonstrates the server event handler handleButtonClick that was bound to the ServerClick event of the button:

```
<html>
  <head><title>Testing Page Events</title></head>
  <body>

    <script language="C#" runat="server">
      void Page_Init(Object oSender, EventArgs oEvent) {
        labelInit.Text = DateTime.Now.ToString();
      }

      void Page_Load(Object oSender, EventArgs oEvent) {
        labelLoad.Text = DateTime.Now.ToString();
        if(!IsPostBack) {
          selectCtrl.Items.Add("Acura");
          selectCtrl.Items.Add("BMW");
          selectCtrl.Items.Add("Cadillac");
          selectCtrl.Items.Add("Mercedes");
          selectCtrl.Items.Add("Porche");
        } else {
```

```
        labelLoad.Text += " (Postback)";
      }
    }

    void handleButtonClick(Object oSender, EventArgs oEvent) {
      labelOutput.Text = "You've selected: " + selectCtrl.Value;
      labelEvent.Text = DateTime.Now.ToString( );
    }
  </script>

  <form runat="server">
    Init Time: <asp:Label id="labelInit" runat="server"/><br/>
    Load Time: <asp:Label id="labelLoad" runat="server"/><br/>
    Event Time: <asp:Label id="labelEvent" runat="server"/><br/>
    Choice: <select id="selectCtrl" runat="server"></select><br/>
    <asp:Label id="labelOutput" runat="server"/><br/>
    <input type=button value="update"
           OnServerClick="handleButtonClick" runat="server" />
  </form>

 </body>
</html>
```

The life cycle of a Web Form consists of three main stages: Configuration, Event Handling, and Termination. As mentioned earlier, these stages span across many requests to the same page, as opposed to the serving-one-page-at-a-time policy found in ASP.

Init and Load events map to the configuration stage (i.e., when the page is first requested and each time the page is reloaded via postbacks). Events such as Button.Click and ListControl.SelectedIndexChanged map to the Event Handling stage, where user interactions with the page are handled via postbacks. The Termination stage involves the Dispose method and the Unload event. The postbacks allow the ASP.NET web page to appear like a continuous thread of execution while spanning multiple, full round-trips. In the old ASP world, each round-trip is a brand new request to the page unless the developer has built in a custom and elaborated framework similar to that of ASP.NET.

Configuration

In the Configuration stage, the page's Load event is raised. It is your job to handle this event to set up your page. Because the Load event is raised when all the controls are already up and ready, your job is now to read and update control properties as part of setting up the page. In the previous code example, we handled the Load event to populate the drop-down list with some

data. We also updated the labelLoad control's Text to display the time the Load event happens. In your application, you will probably load the data from a database and initialize form fields with default values.

The page's IsPostBack property indicates whether this is the first time the page is loaded or if it is a postback. For example, if you have a control that contains a list of information, you will only want to load this control the first time the page is loaded by checking the IsPostBack property of the page. When IsPostBack is true, you know that the list control object is already loaded with information. There is no need to repopulate the list. In the previous code example, we skipped over the population of the drop-down and just displayed a string "(Postback)".

You might need to perform data binding and re-evaluate data-binding expressions on the first and subsequent round trips to this page.

Event handling

In this middle stage, the page's server event-handling functions are being called as the result of some events being triggered from the client side. These events are from the controls you've placed on the Web Form. Figure 7-5 depicts the life cycle of an event.

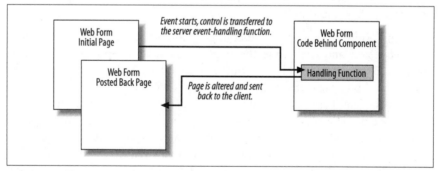

Figure 7-5. The Web Form event life cycle

Termination

At this stage, the page has finished rendering and is ready to be discarded. You are responsible for cleaning up file handles, releasing database connections, and freeing objects. Although you can rely on the CLR to perform garbage collection of managed resources for you, we strongly advise you to clean up after yourself because garbage collection only happens periodically.

On heavily loaded systems, if the garbage-collection cycle is not optimal, the unfreed resources can still exhaust memory and bring your system to a halt.*

We can perform the cleanup for the previous example with the Unload event handler shown as follows. Because there is nothing to clean up in this simple example, we just show you the function as a template:

```
void Page_Unload(Object oSender, EventArgs oEvent) {
  // Cleaning up code here
}
```

Server Controls

As we saw from the System.Web.UI.HtmlControls and System.Web.UI. WebControls namespaces, server controls are programmable controls that run on the server before the page is rendered by ASP.NET. They manage their own states between requests to the same page on the server by inserting a hidden field that stores the view state of the form. This eliminates the need to repopulate the value of form fields with the posted value before sending the page back the client.

Server controls are also browser-independent. Because they are run on the server side, they can rely on the Request.Browser property to get the client's capability and render appropriate HTML.

Since the server controls are just instantiations of .NET classes, programming the server controls yields easy-to-maintain code. Especially when you have custom server controls that encapsulate other controls, web application programming becomes nothing more than gluing these blocks together.

All HTML controls and web controls mentioned in System.Web.UI.Html-Controls and System.Web.UI.WebControls are server controls shipped with ASP.NET.

---

* These so-called logical memory leaks equate to areas where large blocks of memory (managed or unmanaged) were allocated and used for a brief amount of time but won't be free automatically until it is out of scope. Because in ASP.NET the scope from the configuration phase to the termination phase is rather small, this problem does not appear to be that bad. For Windows Form applications or Windows Services, this problem, if undetected, could be catastrophic. The way to expedite the deallocation of objects is to set long-lived objects to null (or nothing in VB). If the object implements the IDisposable interface, call its Dispose method as soon as you can. The garbage collector won't pick up this kind of unintentional memory usage if you have references to objects that are unused, yet remain in scope throughout the life of the application.

Custom Server Controls

As you become more familiar with the ASP.NET framework and the use of server controls on your Web Form, you will eventually need to know how to develop these server controls yourself. In ASP.NET, there are two ways of creating custom server controls: the *pagelet* approach, which is easy to do but rather limited in functionality, and the Control base class (or UserControl) *derivative* approach, which is more complicated but also more powerful and flexible.

Pagelets

Until recently, code reuse in ASP development has been in the form of server-side includes. If you have common UI blocks or scripts, you can factor them into an include file. Use the syntax `<!-- #include file="url" -->` to include the common file into the main page to return to the browser. This approach is fine, but it has serious limitations. The main thing is to make sure the HTML tag IDs and script variable names are unique. This is because IIS does nothing more than merge the include file when it parses server-side includes. The include file ends up being in the same scope with the container file. You cannot include the same file twice because there will be tag ID and script conflicts.

With ASP.NET, you can factor out common HTML and scripts into what is currently called a pagelet and reuse it without worrying about the ID conflicts. A pagelet is a Web Form without a body or a form tag, accompanied by scripts. The HTML portion of the pagelet is responsible for the layout and the user interface, while the scripts provide the pagelet with programmability by exposing properties and methods. Because the pagelet is considered a user control, it provides an independent scope. You can insert more than one instance of the user control without any problem.

The container Web Form must register the pagelet as a user control with the @Register directive and include it on the page with the `<prefix:tagname>` syntax. If more than one copy of the pagelet is used in a container page, each of them should be given different IDs for the container page's script to work correctly. The script on the container Web Form can access and manipulate the pagelet the same way it does any other server controls. The next example shows how an address form is reused as a pagelet. You might display this address form to allow the web user to register with your application or to display the shipping and billing addresses when the web user checks out:

```
<table>
  <tr>
    <td><asp:Label id="labelName" runat="server">Name</asp:Label></td>
```

```
      <td><asp:TextBox id="txtUserName" runat="server"
          Width="332" Height="24"></asp:TextBox></td>
    </tr>
  <tr>
    <td><asp:Label id="labelAddr1" runat="server">Address</asp:Label></td>
    <td><asp:TextBox id="txtAddr1" runat="server"
        Width="332" Height="24"></asp:TextBox></td>
    </tr>
  <tr>
    <td><asp:Label id="labelAddr2" runat="server"></asp:Label></td>
    <td><asp:TextBox id="txtAddr2" runat="server"
        Width="332" Height="24"></asp:TextBox></td>
    </tr>
  <tr>
    <td><asp:Label id="labelCity" runat="server">City</asp:Label></td>
    <td>
    <asp:TextBox id="txtCity" runat="server"></asp:TextBox>
    <asp:Label id="labelState" runat="server">State</asp:Label>
    <asp:TextBox id="txtState" runat="server" Width="34" Height="24">
      </asp:TextBox>
    <asp:Label id="labelZIP" runat="server">ZIP</asp:Label>
    <asp:TextBox id="txtZIP" runat="server" Width="60" Height="24">
      </asp:TextBox>
    </td>
    </tr>
  <tr>
    <td><asp:Label id="labelEmail" runat="server">Email</asp:Label></td>
    <td><asp:TextBox id="txtEmail" runat="server"
        Width="332" Height="24"></asp:TextBox></td>
    </tr>
</table>

<script language="C#" runat="server" ID="Script1">
  public String UserName {
    get { return txtUserName.Text; }
    set { txtUserName.Text = value; }
  }
  public String Address1 {
    get { return txtAddr1.Text; }
    set { txtAddr1.Text = value; }
  }
  public String Address2 {
    get { return txtAddr2.Text; }
    set { txtAddr2.Text = value; }
  }
  public String City {
    get { return txtCity.Text; }
    set { txtCity.Text = value; }
  }
  public String State {
    get { return txtState.Text; }
    set { txtState.Text = value; }
  }
```

```
public String ZIP {
  get { return txtZIP.Text; }
  set { txtZIP.Text = value; }
}
</script>
```

To use your pagelet, register it as a server control via the @Register directive, as shown in the next block of code. After registering, include the tag for the pagelet as if it was a normal server control. Specify the prefix, the tag name, the server control's ID, and set the runat property to server:

```
<%@ Register TagPrefix="Acme" TagName="Address" Src="Address.ascx" %>
<%@ Page language="c#"%>
<html>
<head>
  <script language="C#" runat="server">
    void Page_Load(Object oSender, EventArgs evt) {
      addr.UserName = "Jack Daniel";
    }
  </script>
</head>
<body>
    Welcome to the E-Shop.
    Registering with E-Shop will allow for monthly updates of bargains...
  <form method="post" runat="server">
    <p><Acme:Address id="addr" runat="server"></Acme:Address></p>
    <p><asp:Button id="cmdClear" runat="server" Text="Clear"></asp:Button>
      <asp:Button id="cmdSubmit" runat="server" Text="Submit">
      </asp:Button></p>
  </form>
</body>
</html>
```

You should be able to programmatically access the properties of the pagelet through the server control's ID (addr in this case). In the previous example, we accessed the UserName property of the Address pagelet via its ID:

```
addr.UserName = "Jack Daniel";
```

For an e-commerce checkout page, you could have two instances of <Acme: Address> on the same page: one for the billing and the other for the shipping address. Your script should access these instances of the pagelet via the ID you assign to each address control.

You can also programmatically instantiate instances of the pagelet through the use of the Page's LoadControl method. The first thing is to declare a variable of type Control in your script to host your pagelet. This is because the Control is the root of all objects, including your pagelet. Then instantiate the variable with a call to the LoadControl, passing in the filename of the control page. To make the control visible on the page, add the control to the Page's collection of controls. Because you currently have an instance of the Control

object, you won't be able to call the pagelet's properties and methods until you *cast* the variable from Control type to your pagelet type. This is similar to having an Object variable in Visual Basic to hold a COM component. To access the COM-component methods and properties, you would cast the Object variable to the component type. Pagelets when loaded are automatically typed as pagename_extension. For example, if your pagelet were named *myControl.ascx*, the type generated for it would be myControl_ascx. The bold-face line in the following example shows you how to cast addr1 from Control to type Address_ascx in order to access the UserName property of the pagelet:

```
<%@ Register TagPrefix="Acme" TagName="Address" Src="Address.ascx" %>
<%@ Page language="C#" %>
<html>
<head>
  <script language="C#" runat="server">
    void Page_Load(Object oSender, EventArgs evt) {
      addr.UserName = "Jack Daniel";
      Control addr1;
      addr1 = LoadControl("Address.ascx");
      ((Address_ascx)addr1).UserName = addr.UserName;
      this.frm.Controls.AddAt(3, addr1);
    }
  </script>
</head>
<body>
  <form id="frm" method="post" runat="server">
    Billing Address:<br/>
    <Acme:Address id="addr" runat="server"></Acme:Address>
    Shipping Address:<br/>
    <p><asp:Button id="cmdClear" runat="server" Text="Clear">
      </asp:Button>
      <asp:Button id="cmdSubmit" runat="server" Text="Submit">
      </asp:Button>
    </p>
  </form>
</body>
</html>
```

This example, the checkout page, shows you how to declare a pagelet statically in your page with the <Acme:Address> tag, as well as how to dynamically create an instance of the custom control Address with the Page's LoadControl() method. Once you've created the control dynamically, you must cast the object to the control type before manipulating it.

The AddAt() method is used to insert the Address pagelet at a particular location in the checkout page. Instead of declaring the dynamic pagelet as a Control, you can also declare it as its type, which is Address_ascx. This way, you have to cast it only once when loading the dynamic control:

```
Address_ascx addr2 = (Address_ascx)LoadControl("Address.ascx");
addr2.UserName = "ABC";
```

Control derivatives

Although it is easy to create custom controls using the pagelet approach, this technique is not flexible enough to create more powerful custom controls, such as ones that expose events or hierarchy of controls. With ASP. NET, you can also create custom controls by inheriting from the Control base class and overriding a couple of methods.

The following example shows you how to create the simplest custom control as a Control derivative:

```
namespace MyWebControls
{
  using System;
  using System.Web.UI;
  using System.Web.UI.WebControls;
  using System.ComponentModel;

  public class MyWebControl : System.Web.UI.WebControls.WebControl
  {
    //protected override void Render(HtmlTextWriter output)
    //{
    //    output.Write("custom control testing via Render()");
    //}

    protected override void CreateChildControls()
    {
      Table tbl = new Table();
      TableRow row = new TableRow();
      TableCell cell = new TableCell();
      HyperLink a = new HyperLink();
      a.NavigateUrl = "http://msdn.microsoft.com";
      a.ImageUrl = "image url";
      cell.Controls.Add (a);
      row.Cells.Add(cell);
      tbl.Rows.Add(row);

      row = new TableRow();
      cell = new TableCell();
      cell.Controls.Add (new LiteralControl("custom control testing"));
      row.Cells.Add(cell);
      tbl.Rows.Add(row);

      tbl.BorderWidth = 1;
      tbl.BorderStyle = BorderStyle.Ridge;

      Controls.Add(tbl);
    }
  }
}
```

As you can see, the MyWebControl object derives from the WebControl class. We have seen that WebControl ultimately derives from the base Control class. All we really do here is override either the Render or the CreateChildControls methods to construct the custom web control. If you choose to override the Render method, you will have to generate the HTML for your custom control through the HtmlTextWriter object, output. You can use methods such as Write, WriteBeginTag, WriteAttribute, and WriteEndTag.

In our example, we override the CreateChildControls method. Instead of worrying about the actual HTML tag and attribute names, we then create ASP.NET objects directly by their class names, such as Table, TableRow, TableCell, HyperLink, and LiteralControl, to construct a hierarchy of objects under a *table*. We can also manipulate attributes for the objects via their properties. At the end of the method, we add the *table* to the custom control's collection of controls.

You will have to compile the previous control code to generate a DLL assembly (i.e., csc /t:library MyWebControls.cs). To use the control, deploy the assembly by copying it to the */bin* directory of your web application. Then you should be able to register the control with the @Register directive and use it as if it was a server control provided by ASP.NET. If you are using Visual Studio .NET, you can add a reference to the control assembly file or the control project for the test web project that uses the control.

Your custom-control test page should now look like the following:

```
<%@ Page language="c#"%>
<%@ Register TagPrefix="WC" Namespace="MyWebControls"
            Assembly="MyWebControls"%>
<html>
<head>
  <script language="C#" runat=server>
    void Page_Load(object sender, EventArgs e) {
      MyWebControls.MyWebControl myCtrl;
      myCtrl = new MyWebControls.MyWebControl();
      this.Controls.Add(myCtrl);
    }
  </script>
</head>
<body>
  <form method="post" runat="server">
    This is the main page
    <WC:MyWebControl id="myControl1" runat="server" />
  </form>
</body>
</html>
```

As you can see, we register the custom control with the @Register directive and alias the namespace MyWebControls with the WC prefix. In the body of the Web Form, we can add the custom-control tag as <WC:MyWebControl>.

In addition to inserting the custom control onto the page declaratively, as shown earlier, we can also programmatically create the custom control at runtime. The Page_Load code demonstrates this point:

```
MyWebControls.MyWebControl myCtrl;
myCtrl = new MyWebControls.MyWebControl();
this.Controls.Add(myCtrl);
```

The output page is shown in Figure 7-6.

Figure 7-6. Custom control test output, statically and dynamically

Event-Driven Programming

There are two ways to associate event handlers—functions that handle the event—to the UI controls.

Refer to the section earlier in this chapter on "Web Form Syntax," particularly where we describe the syntax for server controls. All we do to bind an event from a control to an event handler is use the *eventname=eventhandlername* attribute/value pair for the control. For example, if we want to handle the onclick event for the HTML control input, all we do is the following. Note that for the HTML controls, the server-side click event is named onserverclick, as opposed to the client-side click event, onclick, which can still be used in DHTML scripting:

```
<input id="cmd1" runat="server"
  onserverclick="OnClickHandler"
  type="button" value="click me">
```

For an ASP.NET web control, the syntax is the same:

```
<asp:Button id="cmd2" runat="server"
  onclick="OnclickHandler2"
  Text="click me too"></asp:Button>
```

After binding the event to the event-handling function name, we have to provide the actual event handler:

```
void OnClickHandler(object sender, EventArgs e)
{
  // Code to retrieve and process the posted data
}
```

The second way of binding events is delegation. You don't have to have any notion of code in the *aspx* file, not even the event-handling function name. All you have to do is register the event handler with the control's event-handler property. For web controls, the event-handler property for button click is Click. For HTML controls, it's ServerClick:

```
ControlID.Click += new System.EventHandler (this.EventHandlerName);

ControlID.ServerClick += new System.EventHandler (this.EventHandlerName);
```

Custom Server Controls and Client Script

Although ASP allows for the generating of dynamic pages from the server, the HTML generated usually needs the help of client-side scripting to provide a richer user experience. Again, in ASP.NET, the Server Controls are not meant to just generate static HTML. Client-side scripts can still be incorporated to further enhance the user interaction. There are two general way of doing this. The first is to include the client-side scripts within the body of the ASPX page, or somewhere the custom control can get to. The second way is to make the custom control emit its related client-side script while rendering. Either way, the client-side events will need to be tied to the script either through declarative means (i.e., *attributeEvent=eventHandler*) or programmatically through adding attributes to the rendering control dynamically. This is also where we can use the ClientId property of the Control object to allow client-side script to refer to the control on the client side.

We show two examples in this section to describe how you can do both. The pros and cons for each of these should be weighed technically as by other factors, such as time and usage of the control. For example, if you write the custom control for internal use in your company and the time-to-market is extremely short, you might opt to just include the client-side script manually because it might be easier to debug and change client or server-side code

independently. On the other hand, if the custom control you are writing will be distributed widely, you might want to package it so that the control users do not have to worry about having to set up any external scripts. Enough said, let's see some examples. In this first example, we change the simple custom control shown earlier to include some invocation of client-side script and add the client script to the test page that uses the control:

```
namespace MyWebControls
{
    ...

    public class MyWebControlWithClientScriptV1 :
    System.Web.UI.WebControls.WebControl
    {
        protected override void CreateChildControls( )
        {
            ...
            cell.Controls.Add (new LiteralControl("custom control testing"));
            cell.Attributes.Add("onmouseover", "MouseOverHandler(this);");
            cell.Attributes.Add("onmouseout", "MouseOutHandler(this);");
            row.Cells.Add(cell);
            ...
        }
    }
}
```

The changes from the custom control are highlighted. Basically, we just add two attributes "onmouseover" and "onmouseout" to the cell that contains the text "custom control testing" to call two client-side functions: MouseOverHandler and MouseOutHandler, respectively. What we need to do now is add these two client-side script functions to the custom control test page:

```
<%@ Page language="c#" Trace="true"%>
<%@ Register TagPrefix="WC" Namespace="MyWebControls"
             Assembly="MyWebControlWithClientScriptV1"%>
<html>
<head>
  <script language="javascript">
    function MouseOverHandler(ctl) {
      ctl.style.color="red";
    }
    function MouseOutHandler(ctl) {
      ctl.style.color="black";
    }
  </script>
</head>
<body>
  <form id="myForm1" method="post" runat="server">
    <WC:MyWebControlWithClientScriptV1 id="myControl1" runat="server" />
```

```
        </form>
      </body>
    </html>
```

The two client-side script functions change the color of the text within the custom control when the mouse moves over and out of it.

As you can see, in order to use this version of the custom control, you have to know to include the client-side script functions to avoid errors. This is not ideal if you are writing custom control for a living. We move on to the second example where you don't have to do anything special to use the custom control.

Let's start with the test ASPX page:

```
<%@ Page language="c#" Trace="true"%>
<%@ Register TagPrefix="WC" Namespace="MyWebControls"
             Assembly="MyWebControlWithClientScriptV2"%>
<html>
<head>
</head>
<body>
  <form id="myForm1" method="post" runat="server">
    <WC:MyWebControlWithClientScriptV2 id="myControl1" runat="server" />
  </form>
</body>
</html>
```

Notice that there is no client-side script block and the class name for the control is V2.

Now on the control side, we add the following block of code in the overridden CreateChildControls method:

```
        if(!Page.IsClientScriptBlockRegistered("myScript")) {
            string sScript =
@"
<!-- ctrl generated -->
<script language=""javascript"">
    function MouseOverHandler(ctl) {
      ctl.style.color=""red"";
    }
    function MouseOutHandler(ctl) {
      ctl.style.color=""black"";
    }
</script>
<!-- ctrl generated -->
";
        Page.RegisterClientScriptBlock("myScript", sScript);
```

Here, we basically ask the Page (that hosts the control) to see if "myScript" has been registered. If not, we register the included script with the name

"myScript". When the control is rendered to the browser, the script will be rendered only once for this version of the control.

This example is just to demonstrate how client-side scripts can be inserted into the stream rendering to the browser. In practice, you might only render the script header block that points to an external script file that you've installed on a specific location on the web server. This improves performance in the long run by having the client-side script file cached by the browser. In case you really don't want anybody to change the client-side script that you have installed on the web server, you can include the client-side script file in your assembly as a resource. You can then load and register the script block from the DLL file.

ASP.NET and Caching

When talking about caching in ASP.NET, there are two kind of caching you should know. "Output caching" involves caching the generated HTML for part or the whole ASPX page so that it can be resent to the client without regenerating the cache content. The second type of caching in ASP.NET is application specific "Application data caching". Here you write code to cache data generated via expensive operations so that you don't have to regenerate the data for every request. Output caching is done through a declarative mean and it's automatic while Application data caching is programmable and flexible but not automatic.

Let's look at the following simple ASPX file:

```
<%@ Page language="c#" %>
<html>
<body>
  <form id="frm1" runat="server">
    Page generated: <% DateTime t = DateTime.Now; Response.Write(t); %><br/>
  </form>
</body>
</html>
```

If you browse to this ASPX file, you will see the time the page was generated on the server. Every time you refresh your browser, the page is regenerated.

You can cache the content of this page by just adding the output cache directive:

```
<%@ OutputCache duration="30" varybyparam="none" %>
```

With this change, every time you refresh the browser within 30 seconds from the first request, the page does not get regenerated.

There are attributes associating with the OutputCache directive dealing with:

Duration
How long the item stays in the cache (in seconds).

Location
Where the cache is stored (for an ASPX file).

Shared
Whether the cached item can be shared with multiple pages (for an ASCX file).

The rest of the attributes specify how to uniquely cache the item based on differences by control IDs, by HTTP header variables, by QueryString variables or Form variables, and by custom management (VaryByControl, VaryByCustom, VaryByHeader, VaryByParam).

The example shows that we cache the page with no distinction on param. Of course, you can set it up so that the system will cache multiple versions of the page based on params.

Now that we know how to cache pages or controls on a page, let's take a look at how application content caching has changed from ASP. In ASP, developers have used Application variables or even Session variables as the cache mechanism. This works fine, but there are a number of considerations the developers have to worry about around issues such as memory resource and freshness of data. ASP.NET introduces the Cache object that is associated with each instance of ASP.NET application. You can add items into this Cache collection with priority, duration (absolute duration or relative to latest access), file or key dependencies (so that when the file, directory, or dependent cache item changes, the cache item is cleared. In addition, you can also have call-back function so you will know when the cache item is removed from the cache.

```
<%@ Page language="c#" %>
<script runat="server" language="c#">
  void Page_Load( ) {
    if(Cache["myItem"] == null) {
      Cache.Insert("myItem", // Cache name
              DateTime.Now, // Cache data
              null, // Cache dependency
              DateTime.Now.AddSeconds(30), // Absolute
              TimeSpan.Zero // Relative
                  );
    }
    myLabel.Text = Cache["myItem"].ToString( );
  }
</script>
<html>
```

```
<body>
  <form id="frm1" runat="server">
    <asp:Label id="myLabel" runat="server"></asp:Label>
  </form>
</body>
</html>
```

The above code behaves similar to the output cache example we had earlier. The cache item, which is the current date time value is stored for 30 seconds. In the real world, you would probably cache something that would cost a little more than DateTime.Now, such as a DataSet that contains a number of rows or tables from a database.

For the second example, let's see how we can cause the cache to refresh the data using the dependency. We continue with the previous example and add the following code to Page_Load to load *myDoc.xml* into the cache and display this *xml* content in myLabel2. The cache dependency specifies that when *myDoc.xml* is changed, this cache item should be invalidated:

```
if(Cache["myItem2"] == null) {
    System.Xml.XmlDocument oDoc = new System.Xml.XmlDocument( );
    oDoc.Load(Server.MapPath("myDoc.xml"));
    Cache.Insert("myItem2",
            oDoc,
            new CacheDependency(Server.MapPath("myDoc.xml")));
    myLabel2.Text = "<br/>Refresh time: " + DateTime.Now.ToString( );
}
myLabel2.Text += "<xmp>"
            + ((System.Xml.XmlDocument)Cache["myItem2"]).InnerXml
            + "</xmp>";
```

We also have to add another label object inside the form tag:

```
<br/>
<asp:Label id="myLabel2" runat="server"></asp:Label>
```

Now if you navigate to this test page for the first time, the first label will be the date time on the server and the second label will contain "Refresh time" and the xml in *myDoc.xml*. Refreshing the page won't reload the xml file until this file is modified.*

ASP.NET and Web Services

The ASP.NET framework simplifies development of web services.† All the low-level work, such as packaging and unpackaging data in XML format

---

* This is merely an example to demonstrate the CacheDependency. Reading a file in a web application is dangerous, especially when there is no error handling code.

and utilizing HTTP protocol to transport the web messages between distributed components, are done by the framework. This allows the developers to focus on the application logic.

The .NET Framework uses *asmx* as the default file extension for web services, as opposed to *aspx* for Web Forms and *ascx* for web controls.

The WebService Directive

All *asmx* files start with the @WebService directive that instructs ASP.NET on how to compile the code, as well as the main class name. The WebService directive has the following attributes:

Language
Specifies the language in which the code was written. This instructs the ASP.NET framework to use the appropriate compiler to build your web service. Use VB for Visual Basic, C# for C#, and JS for JScript .NET. As other languages emerge, obviously you can specify other languages.

Class
Specifies the main class, which exposes web methods. The ASP.NET framework instantiates this class in order to serve the web methods to the clients.

Codebehind
Specifies the source file for your code, which allows for complete code/ASP separation.

You can easily create a simple Web Service similar to the following *asmx* file:

```
<%@ WebService Language="VB" class="MathClass" %>
imports System.Web.Services
Public Class MathClass
  <WebMethod> _
  public function Add(a as integer, b as integer) as integer
    return(a + b)
  end function
end class
```

Note the line continuation symbol right after <WebMethod>. If you prefer to separate your code completely from any ASP.NET elements, you could have the code for your Web Service saved in a separate file and specify the Codebehind attribute of the @WebService directive to point to the code file:

† We've seen web services in detail in Chapter 6. This section reviews web services briefly to remind you that the underlying support for web services is ASP.NET.

```
<%@ WebService Language="VB" Codebehind="MathClass.vb" Class="MathClass" %>
```

The source for *MathClass.vb* looks exactly like the *asmx* shown earlier minus the first line. You can use the following command line to compile *MathClass.dll*:

```
vbc /t:library /r:System.Web.Services.dll MathClass.vb
```

As with all code-behind, the binary has to be deployed in the */bin* directory under the application.

The WebMethod Attribute

Public methods of any classes can be tagged with the WebMethod attribute to be made accessible from the Web. The syntax for tagging attributes to methods is different for each .NET language. For example, in C# the tag takes the following form:

```
[WebMethod(attribute="value" attribute="value" ...)]
    public returnType FunctionName(paramsList)
```

In VB, angle brackets are used instead of square brackets and the assignment symbol is ":=" instead of just "=". Also note that the whole web method declaration is on a single line. If you want to separate them for readability, use the line continuation symbol "_":

```
<WebMethod(attribute:="value" attribute="value" ...)> Public Function
    FunctionName(paramsList) as returnType
```

```
<WebMethod(attribute:="value" attribute="value" ...)> Public Sub
    SubName(paramsList)
```

Using Web Services

If you are using Visual Studio .NET, you can choose Project/Add Web Reference and then type in the URL where the Web Service resides.* For our purpose, we'll point to the Web Service we created in the last chapter, PubsWS. The URL to this Web Service on our server is *http://localhost/PubsWS/ PubsWS.asmx*. The default web reference name is the server name where the Web Service was found. After adding the web reference, you can access the proxy object to the Web Service you are calling via the type servername. proxyObjectName. For your case, it is localhost.PubsWS.†

---

* In VS.NET 1.1, you can also browse the web services on your local machine in addition to browsing web services on UDDI servers.

† You can rename the web reference when adding it to your project. This way the Web Service will be <*yourwebservicename*>.*proxyObjectName* instead of *servername*.*proxyObjectName*.

The following code excerpt demonstrates how to use the Web Service through the proxy. We create an instance of the proxy object and then ask it to relay the message to the real Web Service to get the list of authors. The result will be streamed back in XML format, which is reconstructed into a DataSet object. We then bind DataGrid1, which is just a DataGrid object that we have on the Web Form, to the default view of the first table of the DataSet. Finally, we ask for the actual binding to take place. The resulting page is the grid populated with rows from the Authors table of the Pubs sample database:

```csharp
localhost.PubsWS ws = new localhost.PubsWS( );
DataSet ds = ws.GetAuthors( );
DataGrid1.DataSource = ds.Tables[0].DefaultView;
DataGrid1.DataBind( );
```

Instead of using Visual Studio .NET to locate and automatically generate the proxy class, you can also use the information from the previous chapter to generate the source for the proxy class yourself. You can then include or compile the source into a DLL and add the DLL to the project as a reference. In any case, the end result is the same. Here is an example that links against the proxy we created in the previous chapter and fills a grid with data:

```
<%@ Page Language="C#" %>
<%@ Import Namespace="System.Data" %>

<!-- Link to the proxy generated by wsdl.exe -->
<%@ Assembly Src="PubsWS.cs" %>

<html>
  <head>
    <title>SOAP Client</title>
  </head>
  <body>

  <!-- Make the SOAP call and fill the data grid. -->
  <%
    PubsWS ws = new PubsWS( );
    DataSet ds = ws.GetAuthors( );
    dg.DataSource = ds.Tables[0].DefaultView;
    dg.DataBind( );
  %>

  <!-- Create a data grid. -->
  <asp:DataGrid id="dg" runat="server"/>

  </body>
</html>
```

Data Binding and the Use of Templates

Although all web controls can be data bound, only DataGrid, DataList, and Repeater use a template to control the display of data items. In this section, we show you how to perform simple data binding with some common web controls and how to use an HTML template to provide fully customized data-bound controls.

In ASP.NET, data binding between a control and its data source simply means that the data is copied from the source and placed onto the control upon the call to the DataBind() method. This is different than data binding in Windows Forms, where a link is maintained between the control and the data source. We cover Windows Forms and data binding in the next chapter.

In its simplest form, data binding is the act of binding a control to a data source. Previously, data binding required that an ADO recordset be a data source, which is not too flexible. There was no way to bind, for example, an array or a collection of objects to a control. With ASP.NET, the whole data-binding business is revamped. The only requirement to make your data source bindable to web controls is that your data source implements the System.Collections.ICollection interface. In other words, a bindable data source is a collection of homogeneous objects that the web controls can obtain data items from.

Although it is possible to write your own data classes that implement the ICollection interface and bind them to web controls, numerous classes exist that do this for you, such as Array, ArrayList, DataView, HashTable, Queue, SortedList, and Stack. All you have to do is put your data in these forms, and you can bind your data to web controls.

Here is the simplest form of data binding. In the form file, all we have are two list boxes with ids list0 and list1:

```
<asp:listbox id="list0" runat="server"></asp:listbox>
<asp:listbox id="list1" runat="server"></asp:listbox>
```

In the Page_Load event handler in the code-behind source file, we construct the data sources of type Array, which implement the ICollection interface we mentioned earlier, and then bind the list controls with the data sources:

```
int[] myArray0 = new int[7] { 1, 2, 3, 5, 7, 11, 13 };
string[] myArray1 = new string[7] {
                        "Monday",
                        "Tuesday",
                        "Wednesday",
                        "Thursday",
                        "Friday",
                        "Saturday",
```

```
                    "Sunday"
                    };
list0.DataSource = myArray0;
list0.DataBind( );
list1.DataSource = myArray1;
list1.DataBind( );
```

Figure 7-7 shows the output of this page.

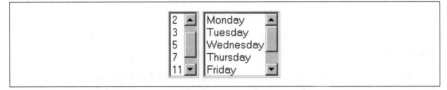

Figure 7-7. Data binding with data from arrays

Most of the time, we tend to bind data from data sources that come from a database. The next example pulls data from the Categories table of the familiar NorthWind database. We can still use the asp:listbox control, but this time, we specify the item's property we want for the text, as well as the value property of the list box. We did not have to do this for the previous example because the items that the list box binds to are of simple types (int and string). If we were to have an array of objects, we would have to specify the property we want to bind to datavaluefield and datatextfield the way we do in the following example:

```
<asp:listbox id=ListBox1 runat="server"
    datavaluefield="CategoryID"
    datatextfield="CategoryName">
</asp:listbox>
```

Again, in the code-behind source file, we have the code to construct the data source and to bind the data source to the list control. Note that because we are using ADO.NET to get the data from the database, we must have references to System.Data and System.Data.OleDb namespaces. The Default-View property of class Table is of type DataView, which implements the ICollection interface:

```
System.Data.DataSet m_ds = new System.Data.DataSet( );
String sConn =
    "provider=SQLOLEDB;server=(local);database=NorthWind;Integrated
Security=SSPI";
String sSQL =
    "select * from Categories";

System.Data.OleDb.OleDbDataAdapter da =
    new System.Data.OleDb.OleDbDataAdapter(sSQL, sConn);
da.Fill(m_ds, "Categories");

ListBox1.DataSource = m_ds.Tables["Categories"].DefaultView;
ListBox1.DataBind( );
```

Figure 7-8 shows the output for this example.

Figure 7-8. Data binding with data from a database

DataGrid

The DataGrid control takes data binding a step further by allowing more than one property of the bound item to be displayed. This section's example shows you how to control the binding of data columns to the grid, as well as how to customize the look and feel of the DataGrid using style.

By default, the DataGrid automatically binds all columns of the data source in the order that they come from the database. Sometimes this is not the behavior you would want. To fully control what columns bind and in which order you want the binding to happen, switch off the autogeneratecolumns attribute of the DataGrid, and provide the columns property, as shown in the following sample:

```
<asp:DataGrid id=DataGrid1 runat="server"
    ForeColor="Black"
    autogeneratecolumns=false>

<columns>
  <asp:boundcolumn datafield=CategoryID
                   headertext="ID" readonly=True/>
  <asp:boundcolumn datafield=CategoryName
                   headertext="Category" />
  <asp:boundcolumn datafield=Description
                   headertext="Description" />
</columns>

<SelectedItemStyle backcolor="#ffcc99" font-bold=True/>

<AlternatingItemStyle BackColor="Gainsboro"/>

<FooterStyle BackColor="Silver" ForeColor="White"/>

<ItemStyle BackColor="White"/>

<HeaderStyle BackColor="Navy" Font-Bold="True" ForeColor="White"/>

</asp:DataGrid>
```

Figure 7-9 shows the result of this example.

ID	Category	Description
1	Beverages	Soft drinks, coffees, teas, beers, and ales
2	Condiments	Sweet and savory sauces, relishes, spreads, and seasonings
3	Confections	Desserts, candies, and sweet breads
4	Dairy Products	Cheeses
5	Grains/Cereals	Breads, crackers, pasta, and cereal
6	Meat/Poultry	Prepared meats
7	Produce	Dried fruit and bean curd
8	Seafood	Seaweed and fish

Figure 7-9. DataGrid data binding

In addition to using `asp:boundcolumn` to bind a column of the DataGrid to a column of the data source, you can also use `asp:buttoncolumn` to insert a column with buttons that generate notifications. You can handle these notifications to perform predefined tasks such as selecting the item, removing it, and adding it to the shopping basket. You can also have `asp:hyperlinkcolumn` insert links to other pages in a column, `asp:editcommandcolumn` control editing of the selected row of data, or `asp:templatecolumn` customize the display of your column of data.

There are a number of styles that you use to control the visual formatting of your DataGrid control. The HeaderStyle and FooterStyle, as the names imply, control the style for the header and the footer of the DataGrid. The ItemStyle, AlternatingItemStyle, SelectedItemStyle, and EditItemStyle are used for each type of items in the list. The PagerStyle controls the visual appearance and layout of the paging interface.

The code-behind source file for binding data to the DataGrid is similar to that of the previous example. Basically, we bind the set of the DataSource property of the DataGrid to the DefaultView of the Categories table and perform the binding with the DataBind method:

```
DataGrid1.DataSource = m_ds.Tables["Categories"].DefaultView;
DataGrid1.DataBind();
```

DataList

Unlike the DataGrid control, where the data binding is still in a tabular form, the DataList control allows to you lay out the list in any way* through the use of HTML templates.

Within a DataList tag, you can customize a number of templates. The templates that can be customized include:

    AlternatingItemTemplate
    EditItemTemplate
    FooterTemplate
    HeaderTemplate
    ItemTemplate
    SelectedItemTemplate
    SeparatorTemplate

Specific tags are used to set up the style for each type of items you want to display. Similar to the previous list, you also have ItemStyle, SelectedItemStyle, and so on.

In the following example, we only show you one template, the ItemTemplate, which is applied to all items in the list. In this template, we use Web Form data-binding syntax to bind two properties of the data item, the CategoryID and CategoryName fields. In this simple template, the CategoryID will always be shown with Verdana font in size 10.

You can also control the flow of the DataList by setting attributes such as `repeatcolumns`, `repeatdirection` (vertical, horizontal), or `repeatlayout` (flow, table):

```
<asp:DataList id=DataList1 runat="server"
    repeatcolumns=3
    repeatdirection=Horizontal>

<AlternatingItemStyle BackColor="Gainsboro"/>
<ItemTemplate>
  <font face=Verdana size=10>
    <%# DataBinder.Eval(Container.DataItem, "CategoryID") %>
  </font>
  <%# DataBinder.Eval(Container.DataItem, "CategoryName") %>
</ItemTemplate>

</asp:DataList>
```

---

* For both the DataList and DataGrid controls, the table HTML tag is used to lay out the output. The difference is that the DataGrid actually uses the table to display tabular data while the DataList uses the table for the lay out only and flows the data into the rows in the table.

The code behind the data binding is shown here:

```
DataList1.DataSource = m_ds.Tables["Categories"].DefaultView;
DataList1.DataBind();
```

Figure 7-10 shows the output of this DataList data-binding example.

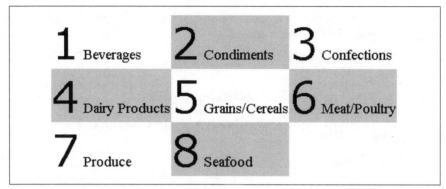

Figure 7-10. DataList data binding with template

Repeater

The ASP.NET Repeater control is completely driven by an HTML template to repeatedly display each of the data items bound to it. When the page renders, the Repeater control loops through all the records in the data source and generates HTML to display the record according to the HTML template. This is as free-form as you can get for data binding. You can have templates to generate bulleted lists, numbered lists, comma-separated lists, and tabs. Unlike the DataGrid or DataList that use an HTML table to control the layout of the data, the Repeater control does not add any HTML of its own. You can specify the layout however you want using the templates described below.

There are only five templates in the Repeater control:

> AlternatingItemTemplate
> FooterTemplate
> HeaderTemplate
> ItemTemplate
> SeparatorTemplate

We will use two of these templates to control the display of the item and its separator.

Again, we bind two fields of each item to the template. The end result is a comma-separated list of URLs that link another Web Form to display more

detailed information about the clicked category. As you can see, we also use Web Form data-binding tags, <%# and %>, to perform the binding. The CategoryID fills the cat parameter of the query string to the fictitious *Display-Category.aspx* Web Form, and the CategoryName is the display text for the anchor tag.

You could also replace the anchor tag and comma with graphical images to make your page more visually appealing:

```
<asp:Repeater id=Repeater1 runat="server">

  <ItemTemplate>
    <A HREF="http://YourURL/DisplayCategory.aspx?cat=
    <%# DataBinder.Eval(Container.DataItem, "CategoryID") %>"
    ><%# DataBinder.Eval(Container.DataItem, "CategoryName") %>
    </A>
  </ItemTemplate>
  <SeparatorTemplate>, </SeparatorTemplate>

</asp:Repeater>
```

Figure 7-11 shows the result of using the data repeater to bind data.

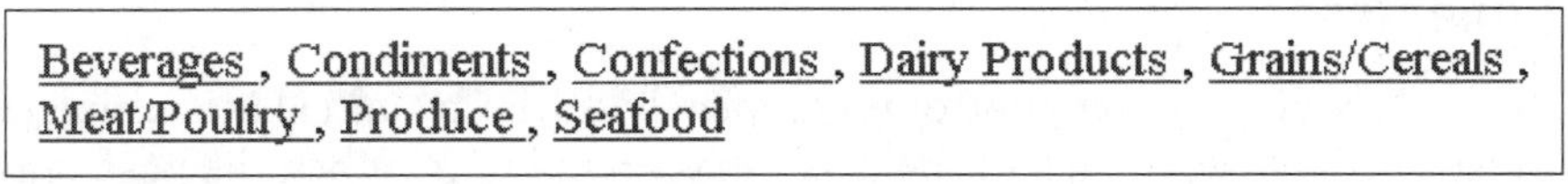

Beverages , Condiments , Confections , Dairy Products , Grains/Cereals , Meat/Poultry , Produce , Seafood

Figure 7-11. Data binding using repeater and template

As with the other controls, the Repeater needs to be bound to a data source:

```
Repeater1.DataSource = m_ds.Tables["Categories"].DefaultView;
Repeater1.DataBind( );
```

As you can see, using a template to bind data to these list-bound controls can be very simple, yet powerful. However, you should be aware of how the generated HTML will look. You should not have complicated, bloated templates that will result in unappealing, large files. In web application development, the page size is directly proportional to the response time the customer experiences.

State Management and Scalability

ASP.NET overcomes all major limitations of ASP when it comes to managing session states. As you are aware from ASP development, a session state is nothing but a named variable that is cached at the server for the duration of the web user's session. As the user navigates through the web application, the session state retains its value as long as the session is not expired.

ASP session-state management can be summarized as follows:

- The session starts, and the web application assigns a unique key to the user.
- This key is stored in an HTTP cookie. Along each subsequent request, the client browser sends the unique key back to the server.
- The server looks up the states stored for this particular key and processes the request accordingly.

Although this has worked fine for all these years, we've found out that there were a number of limitations to live with or work around. The biggest limitation is that the session state is process-dependent, which is impossible to implement in a web farm environment without custom session management.

ASP.NET Session-State Management

ASP.NET improves on ASP session-state management by giving you the option to move to an out-of-process model. By having all web servers in the farm pointing to a common server that hosts the out-of-process state manager, the web client can be redirected around the farm without losing the session states.

By using an out-of-process model, we no longer have the problem of losing session states when the IIS process is cycled. This means that if the web server application crashed for whatever reason and restarted within the session timeout duration, the web clients could still have all their session states intact. Of course, if the out-of-process state manager crashed, that is a whole different issue. This leads to the next improvement of ASP.NET—the ability to persist session state to a database.

The idea of persisting session state to a database is not new. Many of us have implemented this as the workaround for dealing with web farm configuration. However, ASP.NET makes it easier.

Similar to all other configurations in ASP.NET, session management is done through the use of the *web.config* files. There are two levels of configuration: machine and application. Machine-level configuration associates with the *machine.config* file stored in *WinNT\Microsoft.NET\ Framework\<version>\CONFIG\machine.config*, while the application-level configuration uses the *web.config* file in the application root directory. The application-level configuration overrides the machine-level configuration.

The following code is a portion of the *web.config* file dealing with session-state management:*

```
<configuration>
  <system.web>
    <sessionState
      mode="InProc"
      cookieless="false"
      timeout="20" />
  </system.web>
</configuration>
```

Table 7-2 lists the properties of the SessionState class.

Table 7-2. Properties of the SessionState class

Property	Description
mode	Off indicates that session state is disabled; InProc stores session data locally; StateServer stores session state on a remote server; and SQLServer stores it on a SQL Server.
Cookieless	Specifies whether to rely on the client acceptance of cookie. If this property is set to true, ASP.NET inserts the unique key to the URL for navigation between pages within the application instead of setting it in the client's cookie.
Timeout	Specifies session timeout in minutes. This is a sliding window of time: it starts counting down for each request. The default is 20 minutes.
stateConnectionString	Specifies the server and port of the remote session-state server (not a SQL Server). The format is tcpip=HOST:PORT, as in tcpip=192.168.254.1:42424. Use this only when mode=StateServer.
sqlConnectionString	Represents a SQL Server connection string, such as user id=sa;password=;database=ASPState;server=(local). This is required when mode=SQLServer.

Out-of-process session-state management

When you set the session-state mode to run on a remote server (mode=StateServer), you must prepare the remote server to run the state management service automatically.

ASP.NET SDK includes an NT service call *ASP.NET State Service* to be used for out-of-process session-state management. Before setting your *web.config* files to use the out-of-process mode, you will have to start the ASP State service by going to the NT Services Management Console and start the service. You might want to change the *startup type* to automatic so that this service will start automatically at subsequent reboots.

---

* The content of this file is case-sensitive.

SQL Server session-state management

To use this mode, the SQL Server machine has to be prepared. ASP.NET SDK includes a SQL script to create the ASP State database, which is where all session states are stored. Find this SQL script (*InstallSqlState.sql*) at *%SystemRoot%\Microsoft.NET\Framework\BUILDNUMBER*. To apply the script to your SQL Server, use the SQL Server command-line tool *osql.exe* or SQL Query Analyzer. We use the latter because it allows us to inspect the script to get a better understanding of how this mode of session management is implemented. You will have to stop and restart SQL Server because the script alters the master to run the ASPState_Startup helper procedure at SQL startup time.

Cookieless session-state management

In ASP development, it is a usual practice to impose the requirement that the clients' web browsers be set up to accept cookies so that we can use session state the way it is meant to be used. However, when this requirement is not in place, especially for business-to-consumer (B2C) kinds of applications, the developers have to package the session ID along with the URL as a variable in the query string or as a form field and manage the session states manually.

With ASP.NET, as you can see from the sessionstate section of the configuration file, all you do is flip the setting of cookieless to true, and everything is automatically done for you. Session state can be used as if nothing has changed.

To setup and experiment with these session-state configuration, we've created two fictitious *asp.net* pages: login.aspx and main.aspx. The main page redirects the user to the login page if the user has not logged in. The login page redirects the user to the main page when the user is authenticated. When the user logs in, session variable UserName will be populated.

The following is the source for the simplified login page:

```
<HTML>

<script language="VB" runat="server">
Sub cmdLogin_Click(ByVal sender As System.Object, _
                   ByVal e As System.EventArgs)
   ' more processing here
   Session("UserName") = txtUID.Text
   Response.Redirect("Main.aspx")
End Sub
</script>
```

```
<body>
<form id="Form1" method="post" runat="server">
<table>
  <tr>
    <td>User ID</td>
    <td><asp:TextBox id="txtUID"
                     runat="server"></asp:TextBox></td>
  </tr>
  <tr>
    <td>Password</td>
    <td><asp:TextBox id="txtPWD"
                     textmode="password"
                     runat="server">
                     </asp:TextBox></td>
  </tr>
  <tr>
    <td></td>
    <td><asp:Button id="cmdLogin"
                    runat="server"
                    Text="Login"
                    onclick="cmdLogin_Click">
                    </asp:Button></td>
  </tr>
</table>
</form>
</body>
</HTML>
```

The skeleton for the main page is as follows:

```
<HTML>

<script language="VB" runat="server">
Sub Page_Load(ByVal sender As System.Object, ByVal e As System.EventArgs)
  If (Session("UserName") <> "") Then
    labelData.Text = "Welcome back, " + Session("UserName")
  Else
    Response.Redirect("Login.aspx")
  End If
End Sub
</script>

<body>
<form id="Form1" method="post" runat="server">
  <asp:Label id="labelData" runat="server"></asp:Label>
</form>
</body>
</HTML>
```

In the first scenario, we will use session-state mode InProc. Because the IIS process handles the session state, if we simulate a web server restart by issuing the command iisreset and trying to refresh the main page, it will redirect us to the login page.

In the second scenario, we change the session-state mode to StateServer and start the ASP.NET Session State Service (i.e., the command line net start aspnet_state). Note that here we are running the Session State Service on the same machine as the web server even though we can have this service running on a separate server for more reliability. This time around, the session state persists through the resetting of the web server. Of course, if we restart the ASP.NET Session State Service itself, the main page will still redirect us to the login page.

Now that we've seen in-process and out-of-process session-state management, the last scenario we try will be to have session state persisted to a database. This is as simple as setting the mode and the sqlConnectionString attributes of the sessionState node in the web.config file. Of course, we ran InstallSqlState.sql on the SQL server to generate theschema and supporting stored procedures needed by ASP.NET to persist state into the database. The result is similar to the previous trials, however. Because the session data are stored in tempdb, they are cleared when the SQL server is restarted. As a side note, remember to have SQL Server Agent start automatically so that the cleanup session-state job can be run correctly.

Performance Versus Scalability and Reliability

As we've said, ASP.NET introduces an out-of-process model of session-state management, which enables more scalable solutions, but not without a cost. Out-of-process communication performs much worse than in-process communication, not to mention persisting the session states to a database. You should weigh the benefits of each of the different modes of state managements to find the one that is most suitable for your application. Table 7-3 summarizes the different modes and their trade-offs.

Table 7-3. Session-state management communication modes

Mode	Description
In-process	This mode gives you the best performance. It is not reliable, because it is memory-based. It is not scalable, because it is process-based. If you are setting up a web farm, you will have to make sure that subsequent requests are going to the same server.
Out-of-process	The reliability factor is still in question because this mode is still memory based. However, because a separate process manages the session state, it is more reliable than the in-process mode. Because of the out-of-process communication overhead, it is much slower than in-process mode. It is scalable for use in web farms.
SQL Server	This mode gives you the highest level of reliability at the cost of performance. It is scalable for use in web farms.

Forms Authentication in ASP.NET

The previous example in the session management section only demonstrates how session state can be managed in ASP.NET. If you want to expand the example to handle your application authentication, every single *aspx* file in addition to *main.aspx* should check for the session variable "UserName" and redirect to the *Login.aspx* file if this session variable is not found. This is too much work, at least in the .NET world. We take this opportunity to show you how to do forms authentication in ASP.NET. By definition, forms authentication is basically a setup where unauthenticated requests are automatically redirected to a designated login form. Once the user provides the login information and the login form processes it successfully, the user is then redirected back to the original page along with an "authenticated cookie." Subsequent requests do not get redirected to the login form until the cookie expires.

The first thing you will have to do is edit the web.config file to set the authentication mode to "Forms" and setup the URL for the login page and the name of the authentication cookie:

```
<configuration>
  <system.web>
    <authentication mode="Forms">
      <forms loginUrl="login.aspx" name=".authToken"/>
    </authentication>
    <authorization>
      <deny users="?" />
    </authorization>
  </system.web>
</configuration>
```

In this web.config file, we've specified that the authentication mode is "Forms" for form-based authentication. Other settings are "Windows," "Passport," and "None" (case-sensitive), which we will not cover in this book because of its size. The loginUrl is where the system should redirect the request if the user is not yet authenticated and the name attribute is the name of the cookie to store the authentication info. We also have to set up the authorization so that this web application will deny all unauthenticated users.

Since we specify that the login URL is *login.aspx*, let's see the content of this file:

```
<HTML>
<script language="VB" runat="server">
Sub cmdLogin_Click(ByVal sender As System.Object, _
                ByVal e As System.EventArgs)
  ' more processing here
```

```
        FormsAuthentication.RedirectFromLoginPage(txtUID.Text, false)
End Sub
</script>
<body>
...
</body>
</HTML>
```

Once we have authenticated the credentials, we call a helper method of FormsAuthentication object to redirect to whatever page the client was from. The first parameter is the user name and the second Boolean variable tells the function not to persist the cookie across browser sessions. Note the difference between this and the home-grown authentication via the session example we had earlier. Here, we don't have to remember what URL to return to.

The *main.aspx* page now looks like this:

```
<HTML>
<body>
<script language="VB" runat="server">
Sub Page_Load(ByVal sender As System.Object, ByVal e As System.EventArgs)
    labelData.Text = "Welcome back, " + Context.User.Identity.Name
End Sub
Sub Logout(ByVal sender As System.Object, ByVal e As System.EventArgs)
    FormsAuthentication.Signout()
    Response.Redirect("Login.aspx")
End Sub
</script>
<form id="Form1" method="post" runat="server">
  <asp:Label id="labelData" runat="server">Label</asp:Label>
  <asp:Button id="cmdLogout" runat="server" onclick="Logout" Text="Logout">
</asp:Button>
</form>
</body>
</HTML>
```

Summary

Throughout this chapter, we've introduced you to ASP.NET and the benefits that it brings to web application development. These benefits include a new and extended web page life cycle that involves events driven from the client browsers, server controls that manage their own states, the separation of user interface and the code behind, the replacement of late-bound scripting languages with strong-typed compiled languages, and the new and improved session-state management that improves scalability.

If you are trying to embrace the web paradigm by using ASP.NET for your web application, along with web services for integration between sites, you

are right on target. However, not all applications are suitable for the Web. There is a huge market of standard applications where the development is done in traditional VB, C, C++, Java, and so on, and there is no need for it to be web-based. In the next chapter, we cover Windows Forms, which map to traditional Windows applications.

CHAPTER 8

Windows Forms

If the goal of Microsoft .NET is to embrace the Web, what will happen to conventional Windows applications? It turns out the .NET Framework not only benefits the development of web applications, but improves the way standard Windows applications are built. In this chapter, we provide you with an understanding of what Windows Forms are, how to use Windows Forms .NET classes to create Windows Forms-based applications, and how you can still "embrace the Web" while creating Windows applications.*

Introducing Windows Forms

If you have developed Windows applications since the early 1990s, chances are you have used raw Windows APIs such as RegisterClass, CreateWindow, ShowWindow, GetMessage, TranslateMessage, and DispatchMessage. You certainly had a WinMain entry point in your application. Inside this function, you registered your application with Windows, created and showed the window, and handled messages from the system. Every Windows application has to have a message loop that collects Windows messages and dispatches them to the message-handler function that you've registered through RegisterClass function. As a developer, much of your job is handling Windows messages, such as WM_CREATE, WM_SIZE, or WM_CLOSE, that you create and pump into the system with PostMessage or SendMessage.

Classic Windows development is tedious and error-prone. The result is that application frameworks were built as an abstraction on top of all these Windows APIs. Frameworks such as the Microsoft Foundation Class Library

---

* For further information, see O'Reilly's *.NET Windows Forms in a Nutshell*, by Ian Griffiths and Matthew Adams, and *Programming .NET Windows Applications*, by Jesse Liberty.

(MFC) and Active Template Library (ATL) were created to help Windows application developers focus more on the task of solving business problems than on how to handle certain Windows messages. These frameworks provide the plumbing, or the template, of a Windows application. The developer's responsibility is to deal with business logic.

Although it is much easier to develop Windows applications using these frameworks, it is again sometimes necessary to go down to the Windows API level when the Framework does not give you the controls you need. This situation causes inconsistency in the code. Moreover, there exist numerous frameworks similar to MFC and ATL, such as the Object Windows Library (OWL) from Borland, zApp from Rogue Wave, Windows add-on scripts for Python such as the Win32 Extensions or PythonWin GUI Extensions, Visual Basic, and other homegrown frameworks, causing developers much grief when switching from one to another.

Windows Forms provides a unified programming model for standard Windows application development. It is similar to the native Windows API with regard to level of abstraction; however, it is much richer and more powerful. Instead of depending on functions such as the native Windows API, Windows Forms provides a hierarchy of classes. Instead of calling CreateWindow for any type of user-interface widgets, you create the particular type of user-interface control using the appropriate class. You might think that MFC and other frameworks already provide hierarchy of classes. What other benefits can Windows Forms bring that make it stand out from the crowd? The answer is the language-independent aspect of this new framework. Any .NET language can use this collection of classes that make up the Windows Forms object model.

If you've developed Windows applications in C++ and Visual Basic, you might think that it would be nice to have the power of C++ to work in an integrated development environment like that of VB. It is now possible with Visual Studio .NET and Windows Forms. Windows Forms brings a VB-like integrated development environment to C#, Managed C++, and other languages.

In current Windows application development, if you use COM, DCOM, or ActiveX components, deployment of your application requires extensive configuration. You would probably at least use the *regsvr32* utility to register and unregister components from the Windows Registry on the client machine. All these setup-related deployment tasks are eliminated by Microsoft .NET—by Windows Forms in particular. Now, all you have to do to install an application is copy the executable onto the client machine.

Because Windows Forms is part of the Microsoft .NET grand scheme, it fully supports and integrates with web services, ADO.NET, and the .NET classes. You can have Windows Forms as the frontend to your web application by using .NET classes such as HttpWebRequest and HttpWebResponse. These classes allow your Windows Forms application to communicate with web servers. You can make also use web services from your Windows Forms application. Remember that Windows Forms applications are no longer just stand-alone applications.

The System.Windows.Forms Namespace

In this section, we describe the architecture of Windows Forms and introduce the classes that make up the Windows Forms namespace.

Windows Forms architecture is rather simple. It takes the form of *controls* and *containers*. This is similar to Java JFC model, where container types of classes are Panel, Window, JComponent, and so on, and control types of classes are Button, Checkbox, Label, and so on. Most user-interface classes in the Windows.Forms namespace derive from the Control class. In a sense, everything that you see in a Windows Forms application is a control. If a control can contain other controls, it is a container. The application user interface consists of a form object acting as the main container, as well as the controls and other containers that reside on the form.

Similar to the native Windows API common functions, the System.Windows.Forms namespace provides a common set of classes you can use and derive from to build Windows Forms applications. The classes and interfaces in this namespace allow you to construct and render the user-interface elements on a Windows Form.

As we have seen from the last chapter, the System.Web.UI namespace provides the classes for building web applications. Similarly, the System.Windows.Forms namespace provides the classes for building standard applications. The System.Windows.Forms namespace is analogous to the System.Web.UI namespace, as described in the previous chapter.

Similar to the Control and Page classes in the System.Web.UI namespace, Control and Form are the two most important classes in the System.Windows.Forms namespace.

Control Class

Control is the base class of all UI controls in Windows Forms applications. It provides common properties for all controls, as well as common user-interface control behaviors, such as accepting user input through the keyboard or mouse and raising appropriate events.

Table 8-1 is a list of some representative properties, methods, and events that you will most likely encounter. For the complete list, check out the Microsoft .NET SDK.

Table 8-1. Common Control properties, methods, and events

Properties	Description
Controls, Parent	These properties allow for constructing hierarchy of controls. The Controls property lists all child controls, while the Parent property points to the parent of the current control.
Enabled, Focused, Visible	These properties control the visual states of the control.
Left, Right, Top, Bottom, Width, Height, Size, Location	These properties control the location and size of the control.
Methods	**Description**
Show, Hide, Focus, Select	These methods manipulate the control's visual state.
Refresh, Invalidate, Update	These methods control when and what portion of the screen needs redrawing. The Refresh method immediately forces the control to redraw itself and all of its children. The Invalidate and Update methods selectively control the portion of the screen that needs to be redrawn.
ProcessCmdKey, WndProc	If you develop your own controls, override these methods to intercept the Windows messages. This is similar to how Windows developers handled Windows messages when they developed Win32 applications using the native Win32 API.
Events	**Description**
Click, MouseDown, MouseUp, MouseMove, MouseWheel	You have to write event handlers to handle these events for your applications.
KeyDown, KeyUp, KeyPress	Similar to the mouse events, these keyboard-events can be handled via custom event handlers.

The Control class also provides behaviors, such as data binding, context menu, drag and drop, anchoring and docking; and properties, such as font, color, background, cursor, and so on.

Form Class

A *form* in Windows Forms is similar in concept to a *page* in Web Forms. It is a container type of control that hosts other UI controls. You manipulate the properties of the Form object to control the appearance, size, and color

of the displayed form. A Windows Form is basically a representation of any window displayed in your application.

A standard form contains a titlebar, which contains an icon, title text, and control box for the Minimize, Maximize, and Close buttons (see Figure 8-1). Most of the time, a form also contains a menu right under the titlebar. The working area of the form is where child controls are rendered. A border around the whole form shows you the boundary of the form and allows for resizing of the form. Sometimes, the form also contains scrollbars so that it can display more controls or larger controls than the size of the working area of the form.

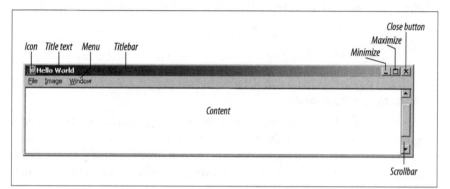

Figure 8-1. An empty application

You can manipulate the form's standard visual elements with properties such as Icon, Text, ControlBox, MinimizeBox, MaximizeBox, and FormBorderStyle. For example, if you want the title text of the form to read Hello World, you include the assignment formName.Text = "Hello World";. To have a form without the control box in the top right corner, set the ControlBox property to false. If you want to selectively hide the Maximize or the Minimize button in the control box, set the MaximizeBox or MinimizeBox property to false.

You can assign a menu to your form by setting the Menu property of the form with an instance of the MainMenu class. We will show you how to do this in the "Windows Forms Development" section later in this chapter.

Similar to Submit and Reset buttons in a web page's form, a form will frequently include OK and Cancel buttons to submit or to reset the form. In Windows Forms, you can assign any button to the AcceptButton property of the form to make it the default button when the user hits the Enter key. Similarly, you can set up the CancelButton property to handle the Escape key.

The Form class supports a number of methods itself, along with the methods it inherits from the base class. Activate, Show, Hide, ShowDialog, and Close are a few of the imperative methods used in any form to control the window-management functionality of a form. As we get into "Windows Forms Development" later in this chapter, you will see these methods in action.

Extending existing controls

Because Windows Forms API is object oriented, extending controls is as easy as deriving from the control you want to extend and adding methods, properties, and events, or overriding the default behavior of the control:

```
class MyCustomTextBox : TextBox
{
  // Customization goes here.
}
```

Creating composite controls

Composite controls are controls that contain other controls. By definition, it ought to be derived from the ContainerControl class; however, the Windows Forms object model provides the UserControl class, which is a better starting point for your custom composite controls (UserControl actually derives from ContainerControl):

```
class MyCustomComposite : UserControl
{
  // Composite controls go here.
}
```

While deriving from UserControl class to create your custom composite controls is not a hard task, Microsoft Visual Studio .NET is an excellent tool for making this task even easier. It truly is an effort to raise the bar on RAD tools. Developers' productivity benefits greatly from support tools like these.

Application Class

The Application class provides static methods to start, stop, or filter Windows messages in an application. All Windows Forms applications contain a reference to this Application class. More specifically, all Windows Forms applications start with something like the following:

```
System.Windows.Forms.Application.Run(new MyForm( ));
```

While this class provides other methods and properties beside the Run method, this method is really the only essential one. The rest of the methods (listed in the rest of this section) are low-level and not frequently used.

The Run method starts the application thread's message loop. This method has two signatures. The first signature involves no parameters, which are normally used for non-GUI applications:

```
System.Windows.Forms.Application.Run( );
```

The second signature takes a form as a parameter, as you can see from the first example. The form MyForm is the entry point to a GUI Windows Forms application.

Table 8-2 summarizes the Application class.

Table 8-2. Common Application properties and methods

Properties	Description
CommonAppDataRegistry	This is the common application registry key under which common data is stored and shared among all users. It is application specific. If a path does not exist, one is created in the following format: *Base Path\CompanyName\ ProductName\ ProductVersion.*
StartupPath	This property is the path in which the executable started.
UserAppDataRegistry	This is the registry key where roaming user's data are kept.
Methods	**Description**
Run	This method starts the application whether it is GUI-based or not.
Exit	This method stops the application by sending the stop message to all message loops in all threads in the application.
ExitThread	Similarly, this method stops the current message loop in the current thread.
AddMessageFilter	You can also add a message filter to the application to intercept and filter Windows messages.[a]
RemoveMessageFilter	You can also remove the message filter.
DoEvents	This method processes all Windows messages currently in the message queue.

[a] The only parameter you need to provide to this method is an object that implements the IMessageFilter interface. Currently, the only method in this interface is PreFilterMessage, which you have to override to intercept and filter any message. If your PreFilterMessage method returns `true`, the Windows message is consumed and not dispatched to its destination. You can let the message pass through by returning `false` in this method.

Figure 8-2 illustrates the hierarchy of Windows Controls in the System.Windows.Forms namespace. These controls are placed on the form to create Windows Forms applications and on a UserControl container to create UI Controls (similar to current ActiveX controls). This figure does not include the Application class.

Windows Forms Development

The Form class in the System.Windows.Forms namespace represents a standard window that contains Windows controls. In this section, we walk you

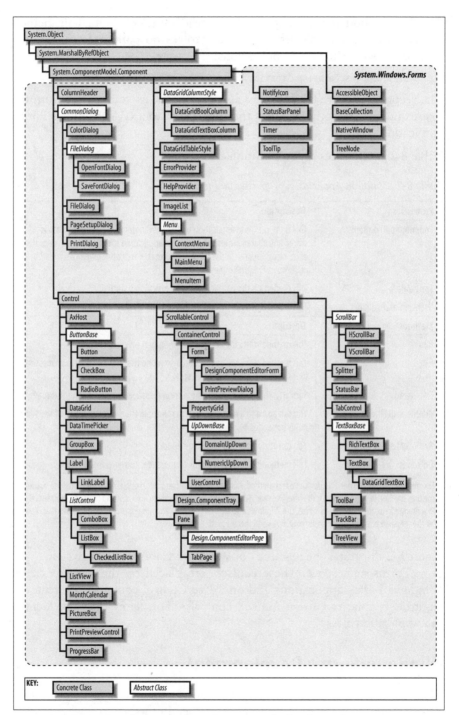

Figure 8-2. System.Windows.Forms Windows Controls class hierarchy

through the development of a Windows Forms application and introduce you to the rich set of Windows controls that can be used on a Windows Form.

Windows Forms Application

All Windows Forms applications start out with a derived class from the System.Windows.Forms.Form class. A simple Windows Forms application looks like the following:

```
public class MyForm : System.Windows.Forms.Form
{
  public MyForm( )
  {
    Text = "Hello World";
  }
  public static void Main( )
  {
    System.Windows.Forms.Application.Run(new MyForm( ));
  }
}
```

Basically, you define a class MyForm, which derives from the System.Windows.Forms.Form class. In the constructor of MyForm class, you set the Text property of the Form to Hello World. That's all there is to it. The static Main function is the entry point to all applications. In the entry-point function, you call the static method Application.Run, which starts the message loop for the application. Because you also pass a form-derived object MyForm to the Run method, what we have is a Windows Forms application.

You can also include references to the namespaces to avoid typing the fully qualified name of classes such as System.Windows.Forms.Form or System.Windows.Forms.Application. To do this, include the following line at the beginning of the source file and omit the System.Windows.Forms prefix to your class names:

```
using System.Windows.Forms;
```

To build the previously listed application, we use the command-line C# compiler. Notice that the target type is an executable, not a DLL, as when we compiled our web service PubsWS (type this command all on one line):*

```
csc /t:winexe
    /r:system.dll
    /r:System.Windows.Forms.dll
    MyForm.cs
```

---

* You can also compile the simple file with csc MyForm.cs but it's better to know how to specify the target type and the references that your source relies on.

The standard Form object that is shown on the screen doesn't do much; however, it demonstrates the simplicity of creating a Windows Forms application. You can exit the application by clicking on the Close button of the Control Box on the titlebar of the form. When you do this, a quit message is injected into the message loop, and, by default, it is processed and the Application instance will stop.

Windows Controls

Windows Forms applications can be much more involved than the application shown earlier; however, the underlying concepts are the same. In this section, we introduce you to the rich set of Windows controls that you can use on your form, as well as data binding to some of these controls. We also show how event handling works in Windows Forms applications.

Adding controls onto the form

First of all, we create and add the control to the Controls collection of the form:

```
Button btn1 = new Button( );
btn1.Text = "Click Me";
this.Controls.Add(btn1);
```

Adding other types of controls follows the same convention. There are three basic steps:

1. Create the control.
2. Set up the control's properties.
3. Add the control to the Controls collection of the Form object.

Binding the event handler

This is swell, but what does the application do when you click on the button? Nothing. We have not yet bound the event handler to the button's event. To do that, we first have to create the event handler. An event handler is nothing more than a normal function, but it always has two parameters: object and EventArgs. The object parameter is filled with event originator. For example, if you clicked on a button on a form, causing the Click event to fire, the object parameter to the event handler will point to the button object that you actually clicked on. The EventArgs object represents the event itself. Using the same example, the EventArgs parameter will be the Click event with event arguments, such as the coordinates of the

mouse, which button got clicked and so on. The following code excerpt shows the event handler for the Click event on a button:

```
void btn1_onclick(Object sender, EventArgs e)
{
    Text = "Sender: " + sender.ToString() + " - Event: " + e.ToString();
}
```

That event handler changes the title of the form each time the button is clicked. Now that we have created the event handler, we assign it to the event Click of the button:

```
btn1.Click += new EventHandler(btn1_onclick);
```

That line of code constructs an EventHandler object from the method we passed in and passes the newly created object to the Click event of the button. We basically register a callback function when Click happens. (You may want to review Chapter 2 where we discuss delegates.) Here is the complete example:

```
using System;
using System.Windows.Forms;

public class MyForm : Form
{

    void btn1_onclick(object sender, EventArgs e)
    {
        Text = "Sender: " + sender.ToString() +
               " - Event: " + e.ToString();
    }

    public MyForm()
    {
        Text = "Hello World";

        Button btn1 = new Button();
        btn1.Text = "Click Me";
        this.Controls.Add(btn1);

        btn1.Click += new EventHandler(btn1_onclick);
    }

    public static void Main()
    {
        Application.Run(new MyForm());
    }

}
```

When the user clicks on the button, our event handler is called because we've already registered for the click event. It is possible to add more than

one event handler to a single event by repeating the assignment line for other event handlers. All handlers that are registered to handle the event are executed in the order in which they're registered. For example, we add the following function to the code:

```
void btn1_onclick2(object sender, EventArgs e)
{
    MessageBox.Show(String.Format("Sender: {0} - Event: {1}",
                    sender.ToString(), e.ToString( )));
}
```

and one more line to associate this function as an event handler in the case button btn1 is clicked:

```
btn1.Click += new EventHandler(btn1_onclick);
btn1.Click += new EventHandler(btn1_onclick2);
```

The result is as expected. Both event handlers get called.

You can also easily remove the event handler. Replace += with -=:

```
btn1.Click -= new EventHandler(btn1_onclick);
```

Binding event handlers to events at runtime provides the developer with unlimited flexibility. You can programmatically bind different event handlers to a control based on the state of the application. For example, a button click can be bound to the *update function* when the data row exists or to the *insert function* when it's a new row.

As you can see, the process of binding event handlers to events is the same in Windows Forms as in Web Forms. This consistency of programming model is possibly due their shared substrate, the CLR in both environments.

Data binding

There are two kinds of data binding in Windows Forms. The first involves simple Windows controls such as Label, TextBox, and Button. These simple controls can be bound to a single value only. The second involves Windows controls that can manage lists of data such as ListBox, ComboBox, and DataGrid. These list controls are bound to lists of values.

Let's look at the first type of data binding. In the following example, we bind text boxes to fields in a table from the Pubs database. We extend the simple *Hello, World* Windows Form application to include data access and data binding.

The first thing is to obtain the data from the database. (It's a good time to review ADO.NET in Chapter 5 if you did not read the book in the order presented.) Let's take a look at the following example of a C# file:

```
using System;
using System.Windows.Forms;
```

```csharp
using System.Data;
using System.Data.OleDb;

public class MyForm : Form
{
  public static void Main( )
  {
    Application.Run(new MyForm( ));
  }

  private TextBox m_txtFirstName, m_txtLastName, m_txtPhone;
  private Button m_btnPrev, m_btnNext;
  private CurrencyManager m_lm;
  private DataSet m_ds;

  public MyForm( )
  {
    Text = "Simple Controls Data Binding";

    // Create the first name text box.
    m_txtFirstName = new TextBox( );
    m_txtFirstName.Dock = DockStyle.Top;

    // Create the last name text box.
    m_txtLastName = new TextBox( );
    m_txtLastName.Dock = DockStyle.Top;

    // Create the phone text box.
    m_txtPhone = new TextBox( );
    m_txtPhone.Dock = DockStyle.Top;

    // Add both first name and last name to the panel1.
    Panel panel1 = new Panel( );
    panel1.Dock = DockStyle.Left;
    panel1.Controls.Add(m_txtFirstName);
    panel1.Controls.Add(m_txtLastName);
    panel1.Controls.Add(m_txtPhone);
    // Add panel1 to the left of the form.
    this.Controls.Add(panel1);

    // Create the up button and bind click to event handler.
    m_btnPrev = new Button( );
    m_btnPrev.Text = "Up";
    m_btnPrev.Dock = DockStyle.Top;
    m_btnPrev.Click += new EventHandler(btnPrev_onclick);

    // Create the down button and bind click to event handler.
    m_btnNext = new Button( );
    m_btnNext.Text = "Down";
    m_btnNext.Dock = DockStyle.Top;
    m_btnNext.Click += new EventHandler(btnNext_onclick);
```

```
      // Add both the up and down buttons to panel2.
      Panel panel2 = new Panel();
      panel2.Dock = DockStyle.Right;
      panel2.Width = 50;
      panel2.Controls.Add(m_btnNext);
      panel2.Controls.Add(m_btnPrev);
      // Add panel2 to the right of the form.
      this.Controls.Add(panel2);

      // Fill the dataset with the authors table from Pubs database.
      m_ds = new DataSet();
      string oSQL = "select au_fname, au_lname, phone from authors";
      string oConnStr =
        "provider=sqloledb;server=(local);database=pubs;Integrated Security=SSPI";
      OleDbDataAdapter oDA = new OleDbDataAdapter(oSQL, oConnStr);
      oDA.Fill(m_ds, "tbl");

      // Bind the Text property of last name text box to field au_lname.
      m_txtLastName.DataBindings.Add("Text",
                                     m_ds.Tables["tbl"],
                                     "au_lname");

      // Bind the Text property of first name text box to field au_fname.
      m_txtFirstName.DataBindings.Add("Text",
                                      m_ds.Tables["tbl"],
                                      "au_fname");

      // Bind the Text property of phone text box to field phone.
      m_txtPhone.DataBindings.Add("Text",
                                  m_ds.Tables["tbl"],
                                  "phone");

      // Obtain the list manager from the binding context.

      m_lm = (CurrencyManager)this.BindingContext[m_ds.Tables["tbl"]];

    }

    protected void btnNext_onclick(object sender, EventArgs e)
    {
      // Move the position of the list manager.
      m_lm.Position += 1;
    }
    protected void btnPrev_onclick(object sender, EventArgs e)
    {
      // Move the position of the list manager.
      m_lm.Position -= 1;
    }
}
```

UI controls derive from the Control class, and inherit the DataBindings property (which is of type ControlsBindingCollection). This DataBindings

property contains a collection of Binding objects that is used to bind any property of the control to a field in the list data source.

To bind a simple control to a record in the data source, we can add a Binding object to the DataBindings collection for the control using the following syntax:

```
controlName.DataBindings.Add("Property", datasource, "columnname");
```

where `controlName` is name of the simple control that you want to perform the data binding. The `Property` item specifies the property of the simple control you want to be bound to the data in column `columnname`.

The C# source file shows how to bind the Text property of the TextBox control `m_txtLastName` to the `au_lname` column of Authors table of the DataSet `m_ds`, as well as `m_txtFirstName` and `m_txtPhone` to columns `au_fname` and `phone`.

To traverse the list in the data source, we will use the BindingManagerBase object. The following excerpt of code shows you how to get to the binding manager for the data source bound to the controls on the form. In this case, because the data is of list type, the binding manager returned from the BindingContext is a CurrencyManager:*

```
// Obtain the list manager from the binding context.
m_lm = (CurrencyManager)this.BindingContext[m_ds.Tables["tbl"]];
```

To demonstrate the use of BindingManagerBase to traverse the data source, we add two buttons onto the form, btnNext and btnPrev. We then bind the two buttons' click events to btnNext_onclick and btnPrev_onclick, respectively:

```
protected void btnNext_onclick(object sender, EventArgs e)
{
  m_lm.Position += 1;
}

protected void btnPrev_onclick(object sender, EventArgs e)
{
  m_lm.Position -= 1;
}
```

As you use BindingManagerBase to manage the position of the list—in this case, the current record in the Authors table—the TextBox controls will be updated with new values. Figure 8-3 illustrates the user interface for the simple controls data-binding example.

---

* If the data source returns only one data value, the BindingManagerBase actually points to an object of type PropertyManager. When the data source returns a list of data value, the type is CurrencyManager.

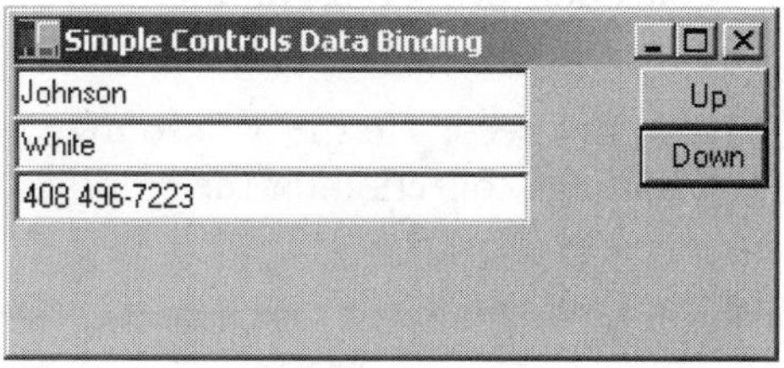

Figure 8-3. Simple controls data binding

Now let's take a look at the other type of data binding. In this example, we will bind the whole authors table to a DataGrid:

```csharp
using System;
using System.Windows.Forms;
using System.Data;
using System.Data.OleDb;

public class MyForm : Form
{
  public static void Main( )
  {
    Application.Run(new MyForm( ));
  }

  private Button m_btn1;
  private TextBox m_txt1;
  private DataGrid m_dataGrid1;

  public MyForm( )
  {
    Text = "Hello World";

    m_txt1 = new TextBox( );
    m_txt1.Text = "select * from authors";
    m_txt1.Dock = DockStyle.Top;
    this.Controls.Add(m_txt1);

    m_btn1 = new Button( );
    m_btn1.Text = "Retrieve Data";
    m_btn1.Dock = DockStyle.Top;
    m_btn1.Click += new EventHandler(btn1_onclick);
    this.Controls.Add(m_btn1);

    m_dataGrid1 = new DataGrid( );
    m_dataGrid1.Dock = DockStyle.Fill;
    this.Controls.Add(m_dataGrid1);

    this.AcceptButton = m_btn1;
  }
```

```
protected void btn1_onclick(object sender, EventArgs e)
{
  try {
    DataSet ds = new DataSet( );
    string oConnStr =
      "provider=sqloledb;server=(local);database=pubs;Integrated
Security=SSPI";
    OleDbDataAdapter oDA =
      new OleDbDataAdapter(m_txt1.Text, oConnStr);
    oDA.Fill(ds, "tbl");

    /* You can specify the table directly like this
     *
     *    m_dataGrid1.DataSource = ds.Tables["tbl"];
     *
     * or specify the datasource and the table separately
     * like this:
     */
    m_dataGrid1.DataSource = ds;
    m_dataGrid1.DataMember = "tbl";

  } catch(Exception ex) {
    MessageBox.Show("An error has occured. " + ex.ToString( ));
  }
 }
}
```

Data binding for controls of type List in Windows Forms is similar to that of Web Forms. However, you don't have to call the DataBind method of the control. All you have to do is set the DataSource property of the UI control to the data source. The data source then has to implement the IEnumerable or IListSource (or IList, which implements IEnumerable) interfaces. As it turns out, there are hundreds of classes that can be used as data source, including DataTable, DataView, DataSet, and all array or collection type of classes.

The process for DataGrid data binding is also simple: just set the Data-Source property of the DataGrid object to the data source, and you're all set. We name the table tbl when we add it to DataSet with the data adapter's Fill() method; therefore, the following line of code just indexes into the collection of tables in the DataSet using the table name:

```
m_dataGrid1.DataSource = ds.Tables["tbl"];
```

If the data source contains more than one table, you will also have to set the DataMember property of the DataGrid to the name of the table you want the control to bind to:

```
m_dataGrid1.DataSource = ds;
m_dataGrid1.DataMember = "tbl";
```

The results of binding the two tables to the DataGrid are shown in Figures 8-4 and 8-5.

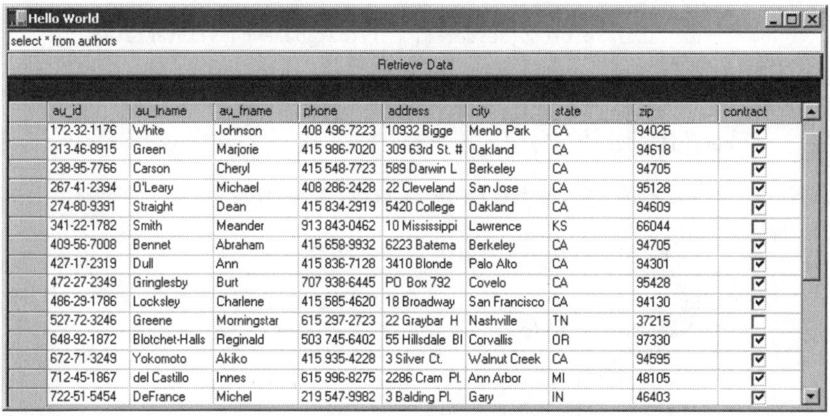

au_id	au_lname	au_fname	phone	address	city	state	zip	contract
172-32-1176	White	Johnson	408 496-7223	10932 Bigge	Menlo Park	CA	94025	☑
213-46-8915	Green	Marjorie	415 986-7020	309 63rd St. #	Oakland	CA	94618	☑
238-95-7766	Carson	Cheryl	415 548-7723	589 Darwin L	Berkeley	CA	94705	☑
267-41-2394	O'Leary	Michael	408 286-2428	22 Cleveland	San Jose	CA	95128	☑
274-80-9391	Straight	Dean	415 834-2919	5420 College	Oakland	CA	94609	☑
341-22-1782	Smith	Meander	913 843-0462	10 Mississippi	Lawrence	KS	66044	☐
409-56-7008	Bennet	Abraham	415 658-9932	6223 Batema	Berkeley	CA	94705	☑
427-17-2319	Dull	Ann	415 836-7128	3410 Blonde	Palo Alto	CA	94301	☑
472-27-2349	Gringlesby	Burt	707 938-6445	PO Box 792	Covelo	CA	95428	☑
486-29-1786	Locksley	Charlene	415 585-4620	18 Broadway	San Francisco	CA	94130	☑
527-72-3246	Greene	Morningstar	615 297-2723	22 Graybar H	Nashville	TN	37215	☐
648-92-1872	Blotchet-Halls	Reginald	503 745-6402	55 Hillsdale Bl	Corvallis	OR	97330	☑
672-71-3249	Yokomoto	Akiko	415 935-4228	3 Silver Ct.	Walnut Creek	CA	94595	☑
712-45-1867	del Castillo	Innes	615 996-8275	2286 Cram Pl.	Ann Arbor	MI	48105	☑
722-51-5454	DeFrance	Michel	219 547-9982	3 Balding Pl.	Gary	IN	46403	☑

Figure 8-4. Binding the authors table to the DataGrid

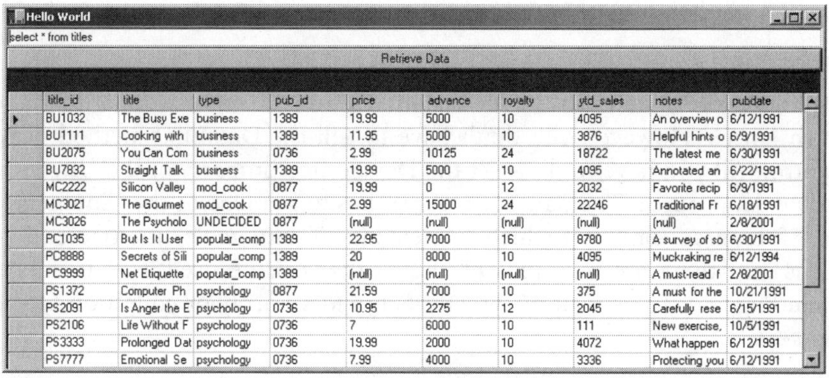

title_id	title	type	pub_id	price	advance	royalty	ytd_sales	notes	pubdate
BU1032	The Busy Exe	business	1389	19.99	5000	10	4095	An overview o	6/12/1991
BU1111	Cooking with	business	1389	11.95	5000	10	3876	Helpful hints o	6/9/1991
BU2075	You Can Com	business	0736	2.99	10125	24	18722	The latest me	6/30/1991
BU7832	Straight Talk	business	1389	19.99	5000	10	4095	Annotated an	6/22/1991
MC2222	Silicon Valley	mod_cook	0877	19.99	0	12	2032	Favorite recip	6/9/1991
MC3021	The Gourmet	mod_cook	0877	2.99	15000	24	22246	Traditional Fr	6/18/1991
MC3026	The Psycholo	UNDECIDED	0877	(null)	(null)	(null)	(null)	(null)	2/8/2001
PC1035	But Is It User	popular_comp	1389	22.95	7000	16	8780	A survey of so	6/30/1991
PC8888	Secrets of Sili	popular_comp	1389	20	8000	10	4095	Muckraking re	6/12/1994
PC9999	Net Etiquette	popular_comp	1389	(null)	(null)	(null)	(null)	A must-read f	2/8/2001
PS1372	Computer Ph	psychology	0877	21.59	7000	10	375	A must for the	10/21/1991
PS2091	Is Anger the E	psychology	0736	10.95	2275	12	2045	Carefully rese	6/15/1991
PS2106	Life Without F	psychology	0736	7	6000	10	111	New exercise,	10/5/1991
PS3333	Prolonged Dat	psychology	0736	19.99	2000	10	4072	What happen	6/12/1991
PS7777	Emotional Se	psychology	0736	7.99	4000	10	3336	Protecting you	6/12/1991

Figure 8-5. Binding the titles table to the DataGrid

Arranging controls

After adding controls onto the form and setting the event handlings and data bindings, you are fully functional. However, for the visual aspect of your application, you might want to change the layout of the controls on the form. You can do this by setting up physical locations of controls with respect to the container to which the controls belong,* or you can dock or anchor the controls inside the container.

* This is similar to VB programming. Controls initially have absolute positions on the form, but they can be programmatically moved and resized while the application is running.

Docking of a control is very simple. You can dock your control to the top, left, right, or bottom of the container. If you dock your control to the top or the bottom, the width of your control will span the whole container. On the same token, if you dock the control to the left or the right, its height will span the height of the container. You can also set the Dock property to DockStyle.Fill, which will adjust the control to fill the container.

The anchoring concept is a bit different. You can anchor your control inside your container by tying it to one or more sides of the container. The distance between the container and the control remains constant at the anchoring side.

You can also use a combination of these techniques by grouping controls into multiple panels and then organizing these panels on the form. With docking and anchoring, there is no need to programmatically calculate and reposition or resize controls on the form.

If you've ever done Java Swing development, you might notice that the current Microsoft .NET Windows Forms framework is similar to JFC with respect to laying out controls; however, it is missing the Layout Manager classes such as GridLayout and FlowLayout to help lay out controls in the containers. We hope that in future releases of the .NET SDK, some sort of layout manager will be included.* Currently, if you are writing your Windows Forms application using Visual Studio .NET, you will have more than enough control over the layout of controls on your form.

Visual Inheritance

Visual inheritance was never before possible on the Windows platform using Microsoft technologies. Prior to the release of Microsoft .NET (and we are only talking about VB development here), developers used VB templates to reuse a form. This is basically a fancy name for copy-and-paste programming. Each copy of a VB template can be modified to fit the current use. When the template itself is modified, copies or derivatives of the template are not updated. You either have to redo each one using copy-and-paste or just leave them alone.

With the advent of Microsoft .NET, where everything is now object-oriented, you can create derived classes by inheriting any base class. Since a form in Windows Forms application is nothing more than a derived class of

---

* Microsoft provides some interesting examples of how you can develop layout managers. The URL is *http://msdn.microsoft.com/library/en-us/dndotnet/html/custlaywinforms.asp.*

the base Form class, you can actually derive from your Form class to create other Form classes.

This is extremely good for something like a wizard-based application, where each of the forms looks similar to the others. You can create the common look-and-feel form as your base class and then create each of the wizard forms by deriving from this base class.

MDI Applications

There are two main styles of user interfaces for Windows-based applications: Single Document Interface (SDI) and Multiple Document Interface (MDI).* For SDI applications, each instance of the application can have only one document. If you would like more than one open document, you must have multiple instances of the application running. MDI, on the other hand, allows multiple documents to be open at one time in one instance of the application. Another good thing about MDI application is that, depending of the type of document currently open, the main menu for the application changes to reflect the operations that you can perform on the document.

While it is easy to implement both SDI and MDI applications using the Windows Forms architecture, we only show an example of MDI in this section.

MDI application architecture borrows the same pattern of Windows Forms architecture. Basically, you have one form acting as the container form and other forms acting as child forms.

The Form class provides a number of properties and methods to help in the development of MDI applications, including IsMdiContainer, IsMdiChild, MdiParent, MdiChildren, ActiveMdiChild, and LayoutMdi().

The first thing we want to show you is the bare minimum main form for our MDI application:

```
using System;
using System.Windows.Forms;

public class MdiMainForm : Form
{
  public MdiMainForm( )
  {
    this.Text = "MDI App for Text and Images";
    // This is the MDI container.
    this.IsMdiContainer = true;
  }
```

---

* Other styles are Explorer, Wizard, etc., but we are not going discuss all of them in this book.

```
public static void Main(string[] args)
{
  Application.Run(new MdiMainForm( ));
}
}
```

Believe it or not, this is basically all you have to do for the main form of the MDI application! For each of the child forms that we will be spawning from this main form, we will set its MdiParent property to point to this main form.

In the following code excerpt, we load a child form of the main form:

```
...
Form a = new Form( );
a.MdiParent = this;
a.Show( );

Form b = new Form( );
b.MdiParent = this;
b.Show( );
...
```

Again, all it takes to spawn a child form of the MDI application is a single property, MdiParent. In your application, you will replace the type for forms a and b with your own form classes. (As shown later in this chapter, we have ImageForm and TextForm.)

One other point that makes MDI applications interesting is the fact that there is one set of main menus and it is possible for child forms to merge their menus with the MDI frame. We also show you how to incorporate menus into our main MDI form, and later in this section, how the child form's menus are merged to this main menu.

The whole menu architecture in Windows Forms application revolves around two classes:* MainMenu and MenuItem. MainMenu represents the complete menu for the whole form. A MenuItem represents one menu item; however, each menu item contains child menu items in the MenuItems property. Again, you start to see the pattern of controls and containers here, too, although the menu classes are not controls.† For example, if we are to have two top-level menus (e.g., File and Window), then basically, we have to set up the MainMenu object so that it contains two menu items in its MenuItems property. We can do so using the Add method of the Menu-Items property to insert menu items dynamically into the collection. If we

---

* The third class is ContextMenu, but we won't discuss it in the scope of this book.

† MainMenu, MenuItem and ContextMenu derive from Menu.

know ahead of time the number of menu items, we can declaratively assign an array of menu items to this property. Recursively, we can have the File or the Window menu items contain a number of sub-menu items in their MenuItems property the same way we set up the main menu.

Let's take a look at the source code:

```
using System;
using System.Windows.Forms;

public class MdiMainForm : Form
{
  // Menu Items under File Menu
  private MenuItem mnuOpen, mnuClose, mnuExit;

  // Menu Items under the Window Menu
  private MenuItem mnuCascade, mnuTileHorz, mnuTileVert,
                   mnuSeparator, mnuCloseAll, mnuListMDI;

  // The File and Window Menus
  private MenuItem mnuFile, mnuWindow;

  // The Main Menu
  private MainMenu mnuMain;

  public MdiMainForm( )
  {
    this.Text = "MDI App for Text and Images";

    // File Menu Item
    mnuFile = new MenuItem( );
    mnuFile.Text = "&File";
    mnuFile.MergeOrder = 0;

    // Window Menu Item
    mnuWindow = new MenuItem( );
    mnuWindow.MergeOrder = 2;
    mnuWindow.Text = "&Window";

    // Main Menu contains File and Window
    mnuMain = new MainMenu( );
    mnuMain.MenuItems.AddRange(
        new MenuItem[2] {mnuFile, mnuWindow});

    // Assign the main menu of the form.
    this.Menu = mnuMain;

    // Menu Items under File menu
    mnuOpen = new MenuItem( );
    mnuOpen.Text = "Open";
    mnuOpen.Click += new EventHandler(this.OpenHandler);
    mnuClose = new MenuItem( );
```

```
    mnuClose.Text = "Close";
    mnuClose.Click += new EventHandler(this.CloseHandler);
    mnuExit = new MenuItem();
    mnuExit.Text = "Exit";
    mnuExit.Click += new EventHandler(this.ExitHandler);
    mnuFile.MenuItems.AddRange(
        new MenuItem[3] {mnuOpen, mnuClose, mnuExit});

    // Menu Items under Window menu
    mnuCascade = new MenuItem();
    mnuCascade.Text = "Cascade";
    mnuCascade.Click += new EventHandler(this.CascadeHandler);
    mnuTileHorz = new MenuItem();
    mnuTileHorz.Text = "Tile Horizontal";
    mnuTileHorz.Click += new EventHandler(this.TileHorzHandler);
    mnuTileVert = new MenuItem();
    mnuTileVert.Text = "Tile Vertical";
    mnuTileVert.Click += new EventHandler(this.TileVertHandler);
    mnuSeparator = new MenuItem();
    mnuSeparator.Text = "-";
    mnuCloseAll = new MenuItem();
    mnuCloseAll.Text = "Close All";
    mnuCloseAll.Click += new EventHandler(this.CloseAllHandler);
    mnuListMDI = new MenuItem();
    mnuListMDI.Text = "Windows...";
    mnuListMDI.MdiList = true;

    mnuWindow.MenuItems.AddRange(
        new MenuItem[6] {mnuCascade, mnuTileHorz, mnuTileVert,
                         mnuSeparator, mnuCloseAll, mnuListMDI});

    // This is the MDI container.
    this.IsMdiContainer = true;
    }
    public static void Main(string[] args)
    {
        Application.Run(new MdiMainForm());
    }
    ...
}
```

(Note that this source-code listing is completed in the event handlers listing that follows.)

We first declare all the menu items that we would like to have, along with one MainMenu instance in the class scope. In the main-application constructor, we then instantiate the menu items and set their Text properties. For the two top-level menu items, we also set the MergeOrder property so that we can control where the child forms will merge their menu to the main form menu. In this case, we've set up the File menu to be of order 0 and the Window menu to be of order 2. As you will see later, we will have the child

menu's MergeOrder set to 1 so that it is between the File and Window menus.

We then add both the File and the Window menus to the main menu's MenuItems collection by using the AddRange() method:

```
mnuMain.MenuItems.AddRange(
        new MenuItem[2] {mnuFile, mnuWindow});
```

Note that at this time, the File and Window menus are still empty. We then assign mnuMain to the MainMenu property of the Form object. At this point, we should be able to see the File and Window menus on the main form; however, there is no drop-down yet.

Similar to how we create menu items and add them to the main menu's MenuItems collection, we add menu items into both the File and Window menu. However, one thing is different. We also bind event handlers to the Click events of the menu items. Let's take one example, the Open menu item:

```
mnuOpen = new MenuItem( );
mnuOpen.Text = "Open";
mnuOpen.Click += new EventHandler(this.OpenHandler);
```

Note that the syntax for binding the event handler OpenHandler to the event Click of the MenuItem class is similar to any other event binding that we've seen so far. Of course, we will have to provide the function body in the MDI main class.

While we are talking about menus, another interesting piece of information is the mnuListMDI MenuItem at the end of the Window menu. We set the MdiList property of this MenuItem to true, as shown in the following code fragment, so that it will automatically show all the opened documents inside the MDI application.

```
mnuListMDI.Text = "Windows...";
mnuListMDI.MdiList = true;
```

See Figure 8-6 for an example of how this feature shows up at runtime.

The following code is for the event handlers that we've set up for various menu items in this main form (this completes the MdiMainForm class listing):

```
protected void OpenHandler(object sender, EventArgs e)
{
  //MessageBox.Show("Open clicked");
  OpenFileDialog openFileDlg = new OpenFileDialog( );
  if(openFileDlg.ShowDialog( ) == DialogResult.OK)
  {
    try
    {
      String sFN = openFileDlg.FileName;
```

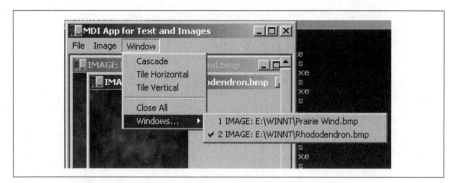

Figure 8-6. MdiList autogenerated menu entries

```
String sExt = sFN.Substring(sFN.LastIndexOf("."));
sExt = sExt.ToUpper();
//MessageBox.Show(sFN + " " + sExt);
if(sExt == ".BMP" || sExt == ".JPG" || sExt == ".GIF")
{
    ImageForm imgForm = new ImageForm();
    imgForm.SetFileName(sFN);
    imgForm.MdiParent = this;
    imgForm.Show();
}
else if(sExt == ".TXT" || sExt == ".VB" || sExt == ".CS")
{
    TextForm txtForm = new TextForm();
    txtForm.SetFileName(sFN);
    txtForm.MdiParent = this;
    txtForm.Show();
}
else
{
    MessageBox.Show("File not supported.");
}
}
catch(Exception ex)
{
    MessageBox.Show ("Error: " + ex.ToString());
}
}
}

protected void CloseHandler(object sender, EventArgs e)
{
    if(this.ActiveMdiChild != null)
    {
        this.ActiveMdiChild.Close();
    }
}
```

```
protected void ExitHandler(object sender, EventArgs e)
{
  this.Close();
}

protected void CascadeHandler(object sender, EventArgs e)
{
  this.LayoutMdi(MdiLayout.Cascade);
}

protected void TileHorzHandler(object sender, EventArgs e)
{
  this.LayoutMdi(MdiLayout.TileHorizontal);
}

protected void TileVertHandler(object sender, EventArgs e)
{
  this.LayoutMdi(MdiLayout.TileVertical);
}

protected void CloseAllHandler(object sender, EventArgs e)
{
  int iLength = MdiChildren.Length;
  for(int i=0; i<iLength; i++)
  {
    MdiChildren[0].Dispose();
  }
}
```

The functionality of the OpenHandler event handler is simple. We basically open a common file dialog box to allow the user to pick a file to open. For simplicity's sake, we will support three image formats (BMP, GIF, and JPG) and three text file extensions (TXT, CS, and VB). If the user picks the image-file format, we open the ImageForm as the child form of the MDI application. If a text-file format is selected instead, we use the TextForm class. We will show you the source for both the ImageForm and TextForm shortly.

To arrange the children forms, we use the LayoutMdi method of the Form class. This method accepts an enumeration of type MdiLayout. Possible values are Cascade, ArrangeIcons, TileHorizontal, and TileVertical.

The form also supports the ActiveMdiChild property to indicate the current active MDI child form. We use this piece of information to handle the File Close menu item to close the currently selected MDI child form.

To handle the CloseAll menu click event, we loop through the collection of all MDI child forms and dispose them all.

The following is the source for ImageForm class:

```
using System;
using System.Drawing;
using System.Windows.Forms;
```

```csharp
public class ImageForm : System.Windows.Forms.Form
{
  private MenuItem mnuImageItem;
  private MenuItem mnuImage;
  private MainMenu mnuMain;
  private Bitmap m_bmp;

  public ImageForm( )
  {

    mnuImageItem = new MenuItem( );
    mnuImageItem.Text = "Image Manipulation";
    mnuImageItem.Click += new EventHandler(this.HandleImageItem);

    mnuImage = new MenuItem( );
    mnuImage.Text = "&Image";
    mnuImage.MergeOrder = 1;    // Merge after File but before Window.
    mnuImage.MenuItems.AddRange(new MenuItem[1] {mnuImageItem});

    mnuMain = new MainMenu( );
    mnuMain.MenuItems.AddRange( new MenuItem[1] {mnuImage});
    this.Menu = mnuMain;
  }

  public void SetFileName(String sImageName)
  {
    try
    {
      m_bmp = new Bitmap(sImageName);
      Invalidate( );
      this.Text = "IMAGE: " + sImageName;
    }
    catch(Exception ex)
    {
      MessageBox.Show ("Error: " + ex.ToString( ));
    }
  }

  protected override void OnPaint(PaintEventArgs e)
  {
    if(m_bmp != null)
    {
      Graphics g = e.Graphics;
      g.DrawImage(m_bmp, 0, 0, m_bmp.Width, m_bmp.Height);
    }
  }

  protected void HandleImageItem(object sender, EventArgs e)
  {
    MessageBox.Show("Handling the image.");
  }
}
```

Because this ImageForm class needs to draw the image file on the form, we include a reference to the System.Drawing namespace. To render the image file onto the form, we rely on the Bitmap and Graphics classes. First of all, we get the input filename and construct the Bitmap object with the content of the input file. Next, we invalidate the screen so that it will be redrawn. In the overriden OnPaint method, we obtained a pointer to the Graphics object and asked it to draw the Bitmap object on the screen.

One other point that we want to show you is the fact that the Image menu item has its MergeOrder property set to 1. We did this to demonstrate the menu-merging functionality of MDI applications. When this form is displayed, the main menu of the MDI application changes to File, Image, and Window.

To complete the example, following is the source to the TextForm class:

```
using System;
using System.Windows.Forms;
using System.IO;

public class TextForm : Form
{
  private MenuItem mnuTextItem;
  private MenuItem mnuText;
  private MainMenu mnuMain;
  private TextBox textBox1;

  public TextForm( )
  {
    mnuTextItem = new MenuItem( );
    mnuTextItem.Text = "Text Manipulation";
    mnuTextItem.Click += new EventHandler(this.HandleTextItem);

    mnuText = new MenuItem( );
    mnuText.Text = "&Text";
    mnuText.MergeOrder = 1;     // Merge after File but before Window.
    mnuText.MenuItems.AddRange(new MenuItem[1] {mnuTextItem});

    mnuMain = new MainMenu( );
    mnuMain.MenuItems.AddRange(new MenuItem[1] {mnuText});
    this.Menu = mnuMain;

    textBox1 = new TextBox( );
    textBox1.Multiline = true;
    textBox1.Dock = System.Windows.Forms.DockStyle.Fill;
    this.Controls.Add (this.textBox1);
  }

  public void SetFileName(String sFileName)
  {
    StreamReader reader = File.OpenText(sFileName);
```

```
    textBox1.Text = reader.ReadToEnd( );
    reader.Close( );
    textBox1.SelectionLength = 0;
    this.Text = "TEXT: " + sFileName;
}

protected void HandleTextItem(object sender, EventArgs e)
{
    MessageBox.Show("Handling the text file.");
}

}
```

Similar to the ImageForm class, the TextForm class also has its menu inserted in the middle of File and Window. When a TextForm becomes the active MDI child form, the menu of the MDI application becomes File, Text, and Window. This menu-merging is done automatically. All we have to do is set up the MergeOrder properties of the menu items.

For the functionality of the TextForm, we have a simple TextBox object. We set its Multiline property to true to simulate a simple text editor and have its docking property set to fill the whole form. When the main form passes the text filename to this form, we read the input file and put the content into the text box.

Figure 8-7 illustrates the screen shot for this MDI application at runtime. In this instance, we have three TextForms and three ImageForms open concurrently.

The following script is used to build this MDI application. As you can see, the target parameter is set to winexe to indicate that the result of the compilation will be an executable instead of library, which would result in a DLL. Because we make use of the graphics package for our image rendering, we also have to add the reference to the System.drawing.dll assembly. We have three forms in this application: the main form, which is named MDIApp, and the two MDI child forms, ImageForm and TextForm (make sure you type these commands all on one line).[*]

```
csc /t:winexe
    /r:System.Windows.Forms.dll
    /r:system.drawing.dll
    MDIApp.cs
    ImageForm.cs
    TextForm.cs
```

---

[*] Again, you can compile the executable without specifying the target type or the references.

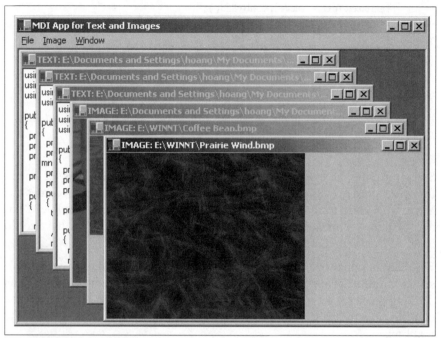

Figure 8-7. The MDI application

Stage Deployment

Imagine the MDI application from the previous example with hundreds of different types of files supported. For each of the file types, we'd probably have a class similar to the ImageForm and TextForm classes. Instead of compiling and linking all of these classes into your application, wouldn't it be nice if we could download and install a class on the fly when we use the appropriate file type? In this section, we show how you can convert the previous MDI application to allow just that.

Conceptually, we will have the main executable act as a controller. It will be the first assembly downloaded onto the client machine. Once the user chooses to open a particular file type, this controller determines which supporting DLLs should be downloaded to handle the file type, downloads and installs the DLL, and then asks the class in the downloaded assembly to display the selected file.

In order for the controller to communicate with all supporting classes, we abstract the commonality out of ImageForm and TextForm to create the abstract class BaseForm:*

```
using System;
using System.Windows.Forms;
using System.Security;
[assembly:AllowPartiallyTrustedCallers]
namespace BaseForm
{
 abstract public class BaseForm : Form
 {
  abstract public void SetFileName(String sFileName);
 }
}
```

We will rewrite both ImageForm and TextForm to make them inherit from BaseForm. Any other form that you will need to write for other file types will have to also inherit from BaseForm. This way, all the controller module has to do is to know how to talk to BaseForm and everything should be fine.

The followings are the changes to *ImageForm.cs* source file. All we did was to wrap the class inside a namespace call ImageForm, make ImageForm class inherit from BaseForm, and providing the implementation for the abstract method SetFileName(). The rest of the code is the same with the original *ImageForm.cs*.

```
// ...

namespace ImageForm
{
  public class ImageForm : BaseForm.BaseForm
  {

    // ...

    override public void SetFileName(String sImageName)
    {
      // ...
    }

    // ...

  }
}
```

---

* Because we will demonstrate running MDIApp.exe from a browser later, *BaseForm.dll* has to be explicitly flagged to grant *MDIApp.exe* usage via the AllowPartiallyTrustedCallers attribute. This is to accommodate the Version 1.1 security changes for Microsoft .NET Framework from RCs.

We apply the same thing to *TextForm.cs* as we do for *ImageForm.cs*. The following summarizes the changes:

```
// ...

namespace TextForm
{
  public class TextForm : BaseForm.BaseForm
  {

   // ...

  override public void SetFileName(String sFileName)
    {
      // ...
    }

    // ...

  }
}
```

Now, instead of having the MDIApp compiled and linked with *ImageForm.cs* and *TextForm.cs* and directly using ImageForm and TextForm class in OpenHandler() function, we utilize the reflection namespace to load each assembly from a predetermined URL on the fly. Replace the old code for handling images in OpenHandler():

```
ImageForm imgForm = new ImageForm( );
imgForm.SetFileName(sFN);
```

with:

```
Assembly ass = Assembly.LoadFrom("http://localhost/MDIDLLS/ImageForm.dll");
BaseForm.BaseForm imgForm =
          (BaseForm.BaseForm) ass.CreateInstance("ImageForm.ImageForm");
imgForm.SetFileName(sFN);
```

The three lines of code essentially do the following:

1. Download the assembly from the specified URL if the client does not already have the latest version of the assembly.

2. Create an instance of ImageForm class in ImageForm namespace and cast it to BaseForm.

3. Instruct the BaseForm derived class to deal with the image file.

For the TextForm, replace the following old code for handling text files in OpenHandler():

```
TextForm txtForm = new TextForm( );
txtForm.SetFileFile(sFN);
```

with:

```
Assembly ass = Assembly.LoadFrom("http://localhost/MDIDLLS/TextForm.dll");
BaseForm.BaseForm txtForm =
        (BaseForm.BaseForm) ass.CreateInstance("TextForm.TextForm");
txtForm.SetFileName(sFN);
```

The last thing to do is to make MDIApp use the Reflection namespace by inserting the following line of code:

```
using System.Reflection;
```

You will have to compile *BaseForm.cs*, *ImageForm.cs*, and *TextForm.cs* into *BaseForm.dll*, *ImageForm.dll*, and *TextForm.dll* in that order because Image-Form and TextForm derive from BaseForm.

The following command lines will do the job:

```
csc /t:library /r:System.Windows.Forms.dll baseform.cs
csc /t:library /r:System.Windows.Forms.dll;baseform.dll imageform.cs
csc /t:library /r:System.Windows.Forms.dll;baseform.dll textform.cs
```

You will also have to compile the main module *MDIApp.cs*. Notice that the only thing the *MDIApp.cs* needs to know is BaseForm:

```
csc /t:winexe
    /r:System.Windows.Forms.dll;system.drawing.dll;baseform.dll MDIApp.cs
```

Once you have all the components compiled, copy them all into a virtual directory call MDIDLLs because this is the predefined location where these components are to be downloaded.*

One last step you will have to do is to use the .NET Framework Configuration tool to give file I/O permission to "adjust zone security" and give Local Intranet full trust level. The tool can be found at Administrative Tools/ Microsoft .NET Framework Configuration. Choose to Configure Code Access Security and then Adjust Zone Security. Give Local Intranet full trust level for the duration of this experiment. It is not recommended that you use this setting without knowing all consequences; however, this is the simplest thing to do to quickly demonstrate the experiment. For your enterprise application, consult the .NET security documentation for further recommendations.

And now everything is set up. All you have to do is to point your browser to *http://localhost/MDIDLLs/MDIApp.exe* and see how the components are automatically downloaded and run.

Another utility you might want to use to inspect the global assembly cache (where the downloaded components reside) is gacutil. Use gacutil /ldl to

---

* Make sure this virtual directory execute permission does not have executable enabled. In other words, just create the virtual directory with the default settings.

list all downloaded assemblies and `gacutil /cdl` to clear the downloaded assemblies. When you first see the MDIApp main form, the only assembly downloaded is MDIApp. But as soon as you try to open an image file or a text file, ImageForm or TextForm along with BaseForm will be downloaded.

As you can see, with this setup, you won't need to have hundreds of DLLs when you only use a couple of file types. Another cool thing is that when the DLLs on the server are updated, you will automatically have the latest components.

Of course, you can make this MDIApp more production-like by having the main module accessing a Web Service that lists the *file types* this application supports and the *class names* as well as the *assembly filenames* needed to be downloaded. Once this is setup, you can have conditioning code based on the file type; you can pass the *assembly filename URL* to Assembly. LoadFrom() method; you can use the class name to create the class instance; all of these make the main module more generic. Suppose the Web Service that lists the supporting file types for this MDIApp reads information from a database or an XML file. When you need to introduce new file type and supporting assembly to deal with the new file type, all you have to do is add an entry to your database or your XML file and add the assembly file into the virtual directory. We think this is an exercise you should definitely try.

Windows Forms and Web Services

Previously, Windows DNA tended not to use fat clients, rich Windows applications on PCs, because of the need for an intrusive installation program. With .NET "copy" deployment, there is no such problem. Now fat Windows clients can interface easily with business logic in the middle tier through XML/HTTP. The rich client application will, in fact, perform better than a web-based front end. However, everything depends on the requirements of the application.

You can still add web references to web services that auto-generate proxy classes for use in your Windows Forms applications just as for Web Forms applications. This is further evidence that .NET as a whole is intended to embrace the Web. In Windows Forms, data binding is automatic once you've set the control's DataSource to the appropriate data source, as seen in the next block of code. Note that there is no explicit call to the DataBind method as in Web Forms data binding:

```
localhost.PubsWS ws = new localhost.PubsWS( );
DataSet ds = ws.GetAuthors( );
DataGrid1.DataSource = ds.tables[0].DefaultView;
```

Again, you can also generate the source for the proxy class yourself using the *wsdl.exe* tool, along with the WSDL obtained from the web service. You can then include this source to your Windows Forms project or compile the source into a DLL and add the DLL to the project as a reference.

Summary

Windows Forms provides a unified programming model for standard Windows application development. It does not matter what language you are using—you can always be productive because the common substrate has been developed to benefit all.

Windows Forms brings a true object-oriented programming model to Windows GUI development, allowing for an extensible framework that is much cleaner and easier to use compared to previous attempts.

In this chapter, we've shown you the architecture of the Windows Forms application. The Controls and Containers architecture, while very simple, is powerful and flexible for developing Windows-based applications. We have also shown you how to build a Windows Forms application, starting with a simple do-nothing application, then data binding, a multiple-document interface application, a self-downloading client application, and finally a Windows Forms application that pulls data from a web service.

CHAPTER 9
.NET and Mobile Devices

The increased use by employees of devices other than traditional PCs and laptops, such as personal digital assistants (PDAs) and web-enabled phones, has increased pressure on corporate IT departments to open corporate databases and intranets to a range of non-standard devices. The explosion in use of these devices, and the proliferation of embedded systems and specialized network protocols, has made it important for developers to design their applications in ways that keep it independent of the clients that will access it.

.NET embraces mobile device users and offers developers tools to meet their needs in two ways:

ASP.NET Mobile Controls
> Mobile Controls are web server controls that dynamically generate code that renders web content appropriately on devices such as web-enabled phones and PDAs as well as traditional web browsers.

.NET Compact Framework
> The .NET Compact Framework is a version of the .NET Platform that runs on Windows CE or Pocket PC mobile devices and can be used to develop clients and applications that run on the devices themselves.

Both ASP.NET Mobile Controls and the .NET Compact Framework are supported by Visual Studio .NET 2003.*

ASP.NET Mobile Controls

ASP.NET Mobile Controls are special Web Controls that run on the web server and render the appropriate web content targeting a wide array of

---

* In Version 1.0 of the .NET Framework, you have to download separate packages to write ASP.NET mobile applications or applications for smart devices.

mobile devices such as mobile phones using Wireless Markup Language (WML) via Wireless Application Protocol (WAP) to PDAs such as Pocket PC, Palm Pilot, and so on. The web server receives requests from the web browsers on the mobile devices just the same as it would receive requests from a full-fledged browser; however, the Mobile Controls on these specialized web pages know how to render the content based on the capability of the requesting web browsers. For example, if the request came from a WML-capable mobile phone, the Mobile Controls would render WML. If the request came from a Pocket PC web browser, the Mobile Controls would render HTML.

System.Web.UI.MobileControls namespace

In the same way that the System.Web.UI.WebControls namespace provides classes for building web pages that can be rendered by traditional web browsers, the MobileControls namespace include classes that for constructing web pages that will be rendered by mobile devices. Instead of the Page class discussed in Chapter 7, for example, the MobileControls namespace provides a MobilePage class. MobilePage is the base class to all mobile device Web Forms and derives class from the ASP.NET Page class. All ASP.NET Mobile Controls derive from the MobileControl base class, which derives from the corresponding ASP.NET Control class.

Here, you also have the choice to use the stock controls provided to you similar to ASP.NET Web Controls and Html Controls. You can also customize controls by deriving and extending stock controls, creating user control or composite server controls or even create your own Mobile Control from deriving directly from MobileControl class. Notice that the programming paradigm is still very similar to how you would do it in the normal ASP.NET world.*

ASP.NET Web Server Controls Versus Mobile Controls

Table 9-1 shows the mobile controls and their counterparts in ASP.NET where the mapping is one-to-one.

---

* The programming paradigm for creating user controls or composite server controls is similar to that of ASP.NET. However, if you are to create device-specific custom controls, you will have to be familiar with writing device-specific control adapters to render the control. ASP.NET mobile architecture depends on a device adapter model so that the controls are device-independent. In order for a control to support different devices, a set of adapters are created to adapt the control to the device specific capabilities. We do not cover how to create device-specific custom mobile controls in this book.

Table 9-1. ASP.NET to mobile controls'

Web Server control	Mobile control
AdRotator	AdRotator
Calendar	Calendar
CompareValidator	CompareValidator
CustomValidator	CustomValidator
DataGrid	ObjectList
Image	Image
HyperLink	Link
Panel	Panel
RangeValidator	RangeValidator
RegularExpressionValidator	RegularExpressionValidator
RequiredFieldValidator	RequiredFieldValidator
TextBox	TextBox
ValidationSummary	ValidationSummary

Although most of Web Server controls map one-to-one to a mobile control, others are mapped down to a simpler control that serves the same purpose. Table 9-2 shows such mappings.

Table 9-2. ASP.NET Web Server controls without one-to-one mappings to Mobile controls

For these ASP.NET controls	Use this Mobile control
Button, ImageButton, LinkButton	Command
DataList, Repeater	List
CheckBox, CheckBoxList, DropDown, DropDownList, ListBox, RadioButton, RadioButtonLists	SelectionList

Other controls, such as PhoneCall, DeviceSpecific, Form, StyleSheet, TextView, are controls that are specific to the mobile environment and do not exist in the standard ASP.NET.

ASP.NET Mobile Web Application

In this section, you will learn how ASP.NET Mobile Controls can be used to create a mobile web application that utilizes the PubsWS Web Service developed in Chapter 6. This application queries and displays the list of books found in the Pubs database. Using the application, mobile device users can view general information about a book and either buy a hard copy of the title or download it to a mobile device.

Let's start by opening a new ASP.NET Mobile Web Application in Visual Studio .NET. To open a Mobile Web application, simply select Mobile Web application in the New Project window.

To view information in the Pubs database, you will use an `ObjectList` control. To add the control to your form, you add the following tags in HTML view:

```
<mobile:ObjectList id="bookList" runat="server"
   AutoGenerateFields="False">
   <Field DataField="title"></Field>
   <Field DataField="type" DataFormatString="Type: {0}"></Field>
   <Field DataField="price" DataFormatString="Price: ${0}"></Field>
   <Field DataField="title_id" DataFormatString="RefID: {0}"></Field>
   <Field DataField="notes"></Field>
   <Command Name="buy" Text="Buy"></Command>
   <Command Name="dnload" Text="Download"></Command>
</mobile:ObjectList>
```

The previous code snippet is similar to how you would have a DataGrid on an ASP.NET page. In this case the ObjectList control is used instead. Similar to the Column tags of the DataGrid control, the Field tags are data bound fields that also provide some formatting. The two Command tags represent the two operation that the user will be able to perform on a data item. In this example, the user can buy or download the book.

If you prefer using the VS.NET visual environment, you can drag an ObjectList onto the form directly from the Mobile Web Forms menu of the VS.NET Toolbox and then set its properties using the Property window. The preceding code creates an ObjectList control, binds it to specific fields of the Pubs database, and provides for two commands—Buy and Download—that that the user can issue on any item selected from the list.

Next, you need to add a web reference to the PubsWS Web Service and name it PubsWSProxy (see Chapter 6 to review how this is done). Finally, you can switch to the code behind page of your application and write a page load handler that uses the PubsWS proxy to load the Pubs data into a DataSet that the ObjectList can bind to, as shown in the following code fragment:

```
If Not IsPostBack Then
   Dim oProxy As PubsWSProxy.PubsWS = New PubsWSProxy.PubsWS
   oProxy.Credentials = New Net.NetworkCredential("uid", "pwd", "domain")
   Dim oDS As DataSet = oProxy.GetBooks()
   bookList.DataSource = oDS.Tables(0).DefaultView
   bookList.DataBind()
End If
```

There is no need to set up the Credentials for the proxy object if your Web Service allows anonymous access.

Now if you run the application, the page shown in Figure 9-1 will display in your browser.

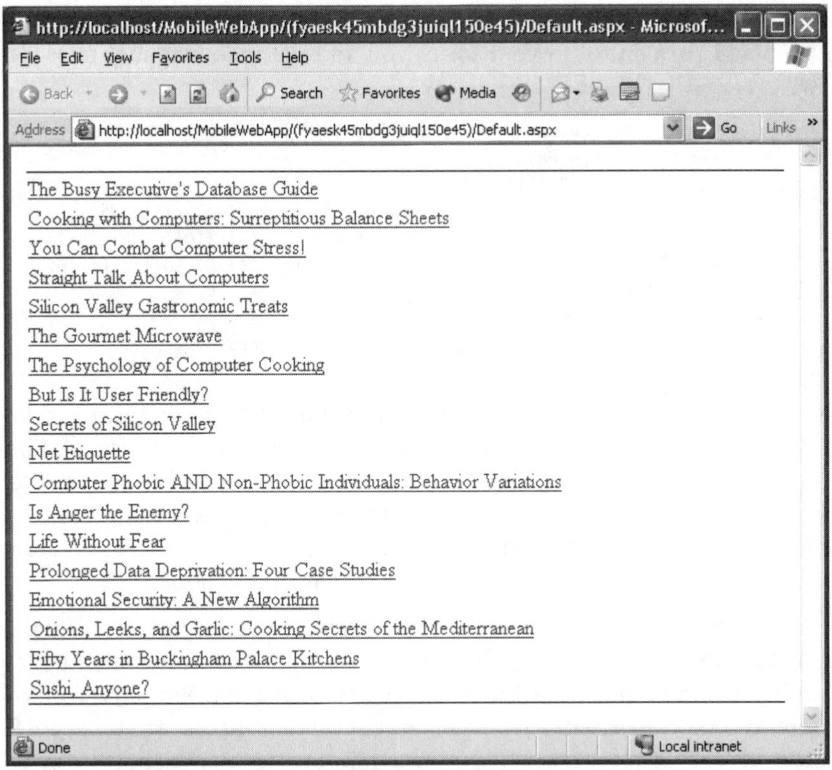

Figure 9-1. Book listing in Microsoft Internet Explorer (IE)

We are viewing this application using a desktop Internet Explorer to test it out. Notice that in Figure 9-1 the ObjectList control does not show the bound data as a grid,* but instead as a list of hyper links to the first fields of each record.† Clicking on any book in the list will cause all fields of the selected item to be displayed, as shown in Figure 9-2. Note that the commands that apply to the selected item are also shown on the form.

---

* If you want to display an actual table of data on that tiny screen, you will have to set the TableFields property of the ObjectList. This property takes a set of field names, separated by semicolons. Because the screens of the mobile devices are normally small, by default the ObjectList shows the data as a list instead of a table. One other thing to note is that when the page is rendered to WML browsers, the table cannot be displayed, and the ObjectList falls back to the list approach.

† Depending on the device, this list can be a list of commands instead of hyperlinks.

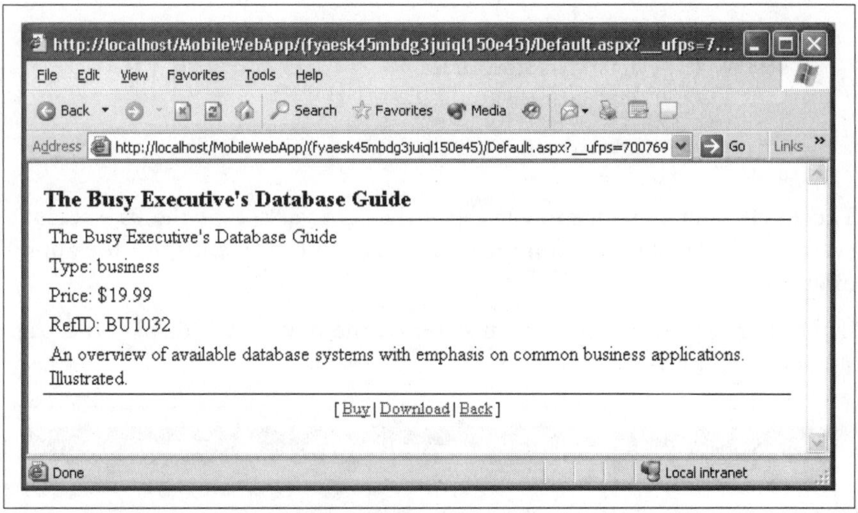

Figure 9-2. Book detail screen in IE

Now let's add another form to the mobile web application to handle the buying and downloading of the book:

```
<mobile:Form id=FormPurchase runat="server">
  <mobile:TextView id=txtPurchaseInfo runat="server"></mobile:TextView>
  <mobile:Label id=labelCC runat="server">Credit Card #</mobile:Label>
  <mobile:TextBox id=txtCC runat="server"></mobile:TextBox>
  <mobile:Command id=cmdSubmit runat="server">Submit</mobile:Command>
</mobile:Form>
```

The purchase form uses a TextView control that displays some simple formatted text and a TextBox control to collect a credit card number. The form also makes use of a submit button to post the form data back to the server for processing.

To complete this part of the application, you must write an event handler for the ItemCommand event of the ObjectList that is triggered when the user chooses to buy or download the book:

```
Private Sub bookList_ItemCommand _
    ( _
    ByVal sender As Object, _
    ByVal e As System.Web.UI.MobileControls.ObjectListCommandEventArgs _
    ) Handles bookList.ItemCommand
  Dim sTmp As String
  Dim oListItem As MobileControls.ObjectListItem = _
                CType(e.CommandArgument, MobileControls.ObjectListItem)
  If e.CommandName = "buy" Then
    sTmp = "<b>Buying</b> "
  ElseIf e.CommandName = "dnload" Then
    sTmp = "<b>Downloading</b> "
```

```
      End If
      sTmp += "book " + oListItem.Item("title_id")
      sTmp += " " + oListItem.Item("price")
      CType(FormPurchase.FindControl("txtPurchaseInfo"), _
            MobileControls.TextView).Text = sTmp
   ActiveForm = FormPurchase
End Sub
```

The ItemCommand function inspects the CommandName of the ObjectList's event to decide which button the user clicked in order to display the appropriate form.

If the user chooses to buy the first book, the device will display the page shown in Figure 9-3.

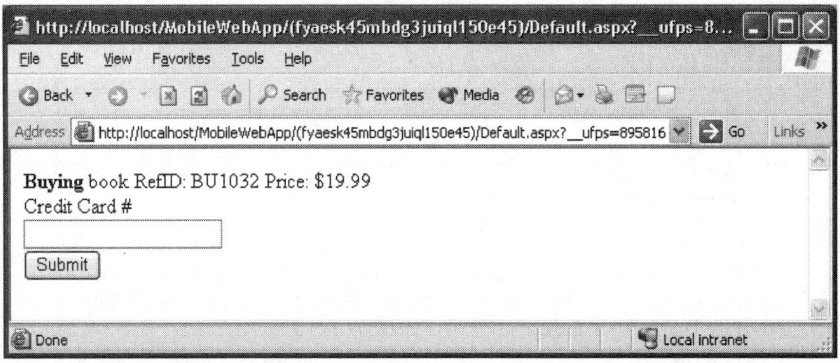

Figure 9-3. Purchase form in IE

For the submit click, we don't really process any ordering but just navigate the user back to the default page:

```
Private Sub cmdSubmit_Click _
          ( _
          ByVal sender As Object, ByVal e As System.EventArgs _
          ) Handles cmdSubmit.Click
   'More Processing Code Here
   RedirectToMobilePage("default.aspx")
End Sub
```

A primary motivation for using mobile controls in this sample application is to make it accessible to browsers other than IE. We can use the actual device to test the application or to use the emulator that comes with .NET Framework SDK (see the sidebar "Working with Microsoft Emulators"). Figure 9-4 shows how the book list page is rendered by the Pocket PC's Internet Explorer.

This display is very similar the output from IE that we've have seen earlier because Pocket PC Internet Browser is capable of displaying HTML.

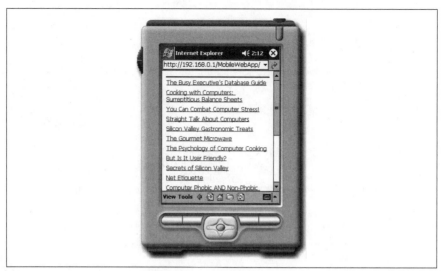

Figure 9-4. Book listing on Pocket PC

Figure 9-5 shows the page that is displayed when the user selects the first book in the list.

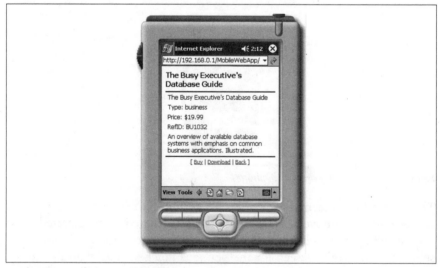

Figure 9-5. Book detail screen on Pocket PC

Finally, Figure 9-6 shows the purchase form displayed when a mobile device user chooses to download the book.

From an emulated web phone (or any WML viewer), however, the screens are drastically different. The reason is that the mobile controls sense the

Figure 9-6. Purchase form on Pocket PC

capability of the phone browser and only render WML instead of full blown HTML. Figure 9-7 shows the same application from a phone emulator.

Figure 9-7. Book listing on mobile phone

This is the first screen showing the list of books. You can use the center rocker button to move up and down the list. The currently selected book will be highlighted. When you decided on a book, press the center button to select it. Because the screen for the phone is much smaller than the Pocket PC, the WML translation of the page content decided to show the three choices that you can pick for the selected book (View the details, buy, or download the book), as shown in Figure 9-8.

Let's press the center button one more time to see the book detail screen. Again, this screen is scrollable via the center rocker button. Figures 9-9 and 9-10 show the progression through the data.

Figure 9-8. Intermediate form for commands

Figure 9-9. Book detail screen on mobile phone

Figure 9-10. Book detail screen on mobile phone, part 2

Now that we've seen the detail for this book and it's quite interesting, we press the right button (underneath the word "Back") to go back a screen and press the down button to highlight "Buy," as in Figure 9-11.

When the user chooses to buy the book, the purchase form appears. Again, the user will have to use the up/down button to scroll down to select the text box to enter the credit card number, as in Figures 9-12 and 9-13.

Figure 9-11. Choosing Buy option on mobile phone

Figure 9-12. Purchase form on mobile phone

Figure 9-13. Purchase form on mobile phone, part 2

Once the credit card text box is selected, an input box type of screen shows up to collect the credit card number, as in Figures 9-14 and 9-15.

Figure 9-14. Credit card field input on mobile phone

Figure 9-15. Purchase form with credit card info to be submitted on mobile phone

.NET Compact Framework

Instead of accessing a web application from a browser, the .NET Compact Framework allows you to write rich clients and stand-alone applications that actually run on the mobile devices themselves. These applications allow the device users to be productive without being connected to the network.

Unless you like to deal with the complexity of writing code directly to the device's operating system API, .NET Compact Framework is the answer to writing mobile device applications. Being the subset of the .NET Framework, the Compact Framework provides the same common language runtime and managed code execution. Architecturally, the .NET Compact Framework acts as the abstraction layer on top of the device-specific API so that the mobile applications written on the .NET Framework can be device independent. Figure 9-16 shows the .NET Compact Framework in relation to the mobile application and the device API.

In addition to being abstracted from the native operating system services, these mobile applications also inherit other advantages such as fault isolation,

Working with Microsoft Emulators

Microsoft provides an emulator program that comes with VS.NET to allow developers to emulate Pocket PC 2002 and Windows CE WebPad. The command line to start up the Pocket PC emulator outside of VS.NET is:

```
In directory
C:\Program Files\Microsoft Visual Studio .NET 2003\
CompactFrameworkSDK\ConnectionManager\Bin>
Execute
emulator /CEImage Images\Pocket PC\2002\1033\pPC2002.bin
/ethernet true
/skin Images\Pocket PC\2002\1033\PPC2002.xml
```

In order to communicate with the emulated Pocket PC when you are off-line:

- Install the Microsoft Loopback Adapter in your network setting.
- Configure the IP for this adapter to 192.168.0.1.
- Set the subnet mask to 255.255.255.0.

Now you should be able to create share on your desktop/laptop and access it from the Pocket PC emulator.

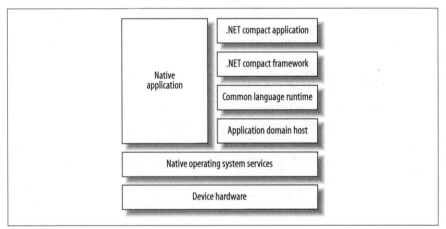

Figure 9-16. NET Compact Framework application architecture

security, and better resource management, because they run within separate application domain hosts.

Currently, the .NET Compact Framework supports Pocket PC and Windows CE .NET-based platforms.

The .NET Framework Versus the .NET Compact Framework

Having a much smaller footprint than the .NET Framework, the .NET Compact Framework provides only the core functionality for writing applications for mobile devices. The following list summarizes the main differences between the two frameworks.

ASP.NET

ASP.NET is not supported by the .NET Compact Framework for the obvious reason that currently, the reason for running web servers on these mobile device are not compelling enough.* This has nothing to do with ASP.NET application running on the servers serving ASP.NET pages to the mobile devices as we've shown you earlier in this chapter.

Data access

Only SQL Server CE .NET data provider is provided. OleDB or Oracle providers are not provided.

Classes

Being less than one tenth of the size of the full .NET Framework, the number of classes would obviously be smaller. We've already previously mentioned that the .NET Compact Framework only provides an essential subset of the full framework for the mobile environment.

Visual Studio .NET 2003 fully support the development and deployment of .NET applications on mobile devices.

To show how easy it is to write a mobile device application with the Compact Framework, let's write and demonstrate (using an emulator) a simple Hello World program that displays the words "Hello World" in a Windows message box on a Pocket PC.

The first thing you do is to create a New Project in Visual Studio .NET 2003. Choose the language of your choice and pick the Smart Device Application template in the New Project window. Click OK. The Smart Device Application Wizard window shown in Figure 9-17 will be displayed.

The two platforms currently supported are Pocket PC and Windows CE. For each of these platforms, there are a number of project templates you can choose from: Windows Application, Class Library, Non-graphical Application, or Empty Project.

---

* This does not mean that it's impossible. Maybe these devices can soon publish their services to a community of services the way JINI works. Maybe we can write a scaled-down web server that is able to serve ASP.NET applications, yet small enough to not hog all the resources of the device.

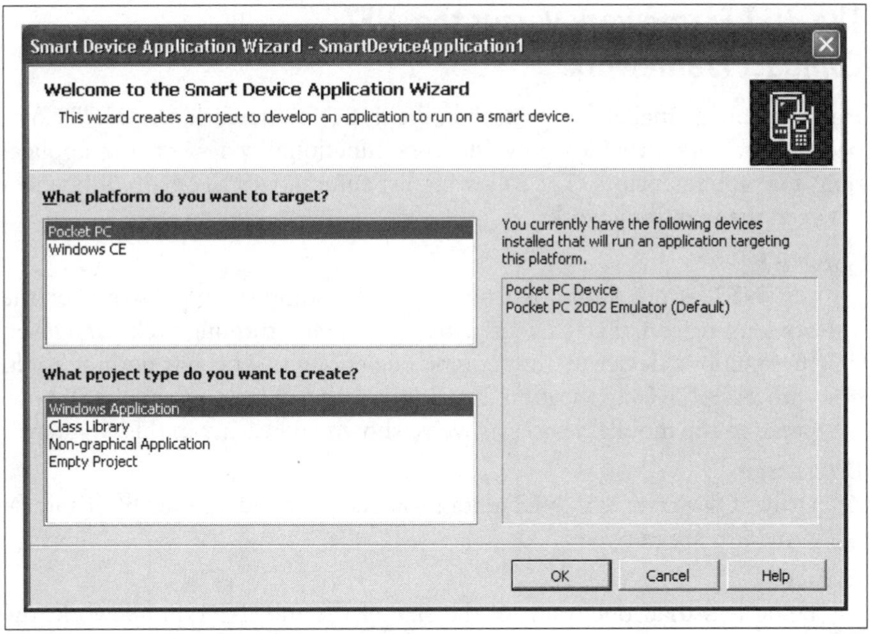

Figure 9-17. Smart device wizard

Because you want to write a standard Windows style application that targets a Pocket PC, you will accept the Wizard's default settings by clicking OK.

VS.NET uses the Smart Device Application Template to generate all the files necessary for your application and presents you a blank form with a default menu attached to it. In this first example, you will not want to do anything with this default menu. You can also start to drag and drop controls from the toolbox onto the form and write code that associates with events for these controls the way you've always done it in previous VB environments. Again, in this example, we will not add any controls to the form but only write code to handle the Load event of the form and display a message box that says "Hello World!" To do this, just double click on the form itself. VS.NET creates the default handler for the load event and moves you to the code view where you can type the following VB.NET statement:

```
Messagebox.Show("Hello World!")
```

That's all to it. Now you start the debugging process by pressing the F5 key. The message shown in Figure 9-18 will appear to ask you to name the type of device to which you wish to deploy the program. We have defaulted our

setting to the emulator so all we have to do at this point is click the Deploy button. VS.NET starts the emulator and deploys the application.[*]

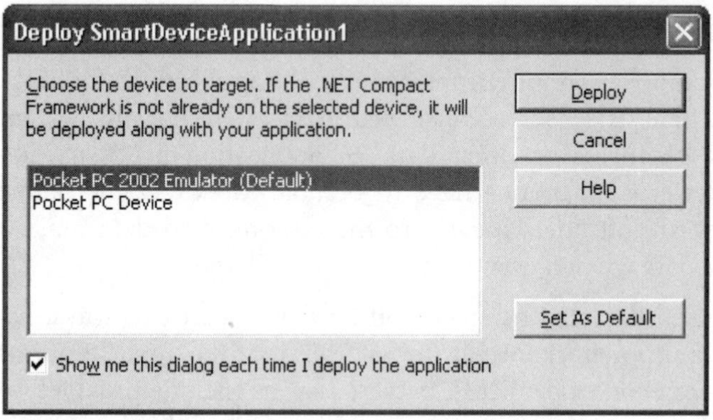

Figure 9-18. Smart Device Application Deployment

Figure 9-19 shows the output of our first Compact Framework–enabled mobile device application.

Figure 9-19. Hello World application running on Pocket PC

---

[*] The first time the emulator starts up, the .NET Compact Framework is installed. The .NET Compact Framework is less than 2MB in size.

Now that you know the process, you're ready for something a little more involved.

Mobile Devices and SQL Server 2000 CE

A primary motivation for writing stand-alone applications for mobile devices (or any offline device) is because such devices are not always connected to enterprise resources or other data an application needs to do its work. Mobile device applications have to be able to extract the data they need when they are off line. Updates to the disconnected data must be merged enterprise data when it comes time for reconciliation.

Disconnected data can be stored off-line in at least two ways. Data can be stored in a proprietary format file as XML that the application manipulates using custom code or an XML parser, such as the one provided with .NET. With SQL Server 2000 CE, the off-line data can also be stored in a relational database format and manipulated via traditional database management tools.

The following two samples show a movie listing application where you can pick a movie and see where it's shown and the show times or you can pick a nearby theater and see the movies that the selected theater shows (also with show times).

The first sample shows how this is done with just XML. The XML file represents the off-line data store that is downloaded into the mobile device periodically. For simplicity, we do not show how this file is generated (let's assume that there is a Web Service out there somewhere that we can ask for local theater and showing information). The example does not have any update to the data, hence, there is no data reconciliation needed.

The second sample shows how the application can be implemented with SQL Server for CE. Here the .sdf file replaces the XML file, but the part of generating the .sdf file is conveniently omitted in order to simplify the presentation.

SQL Server CE provides three methods for synchronization of data between the device and the enterprise data source: Pull, Push, and SubmitSQL. The Pull and Push methods allow your mobile device application to pull tables from and push tables to the enterprise database. Once the tables are on the mobile device, you don't need to have network connectivity in order for your application to work until you are ready to sync back to the enterprise database. The SubmitSQL method allows the mobile device application to send SQL directly to the enterprise database. This is obviously to keep the database state as synced as possible but it requires constant network connectivity.

You can also setup SQL Server replication so that the application on the mobile device can subscribe and replicate part or the whole database. The replication is similar to how the standard SQL Server Replication works except that your node is on a mobile device and the connectivity between the mobile node and the publisher is through HTTP. As intended, our examples do not cover how to set up your development environment to enable Remote Data Access or SQL Server CE Replication.

Storing off-line data as XML

In this example, we omit how the enterprise data (in this case, movie listing for a selected group of local theaters) XML is generated, and synced to the device. We start out with the assumption that the mobile device application will have the xml to consume. This application basically just parses the xml data and provides a GUI where the user queries movies or theaters information.

The XML for the movie listing is in the following format:

```
<?xml version="1.0" encoding="utf-8" ?>
<root>
  <theaters>
    <theater id="1" name="Centreville Multiplex" ... />
    <theater id="2" name="Lee Highway Multiplex" ... />
    <...>
  </theaters>
  <movies>
    <movie mid="1" name="Narc (R)" summary="..." />
    <movie mid="2" name="25th Hour (R)" summary="..." />
    <...>
  </movies>
  <xrefs>
    <xref theaterid="1">
      <movietime refmid="5"
      time="0:5 Fri - Feb 07: 8:00 12:30 | Sat - Feb 08: 12:30 | ... " />
      <movietime refmid="2"
      time="0:4 Fri - Feb 07: 7:00 10:30 | Sat - Feb 08: 8:00 11:30 ..." />
      <...>
    </xref>
    <xref theaterid="2">
      <movietime refmid="5" time="..." />
      <movietime refmid="4" time="..." />
      <...>
    </xref>
    <...>
  </xrefs>
</root>
```

There are basically three collections of data: theaters, movies, and xrefs. As the names imply, the theaters and movies collections hold basic information for the

theater and movie entities. The xrefs collection serves as the cross-reference between the theaters and the movies to hold the movie show times.

The application starts with the loading of the offline content into the menus and building appropriate data structures to store the theaters, movies, and references between them:

```
XmlDocument doc = new XmlDocument( );
doc.Load("\\Program Files\\XMLMovieListing\\listing.xml");
XmlNodeReader oReader = new XmlNodeReader(doc.DocumentElement);

oReader.Read( );
while(oReader.Read( )) {
  if(oReader.Name == "theaters" && oReader.IsStartElement( )) {
    ProcessTheaters(oReader);
  } else if(oReader.Name == "movies" && oReader.IsStartElement( )) {
    ProcessMovies(oReader);
  } else if(oReader.Name == "xrefs" && oReader.IsStartElement( )) {
    ProcessCrossRef(oReader);
  }
}
```

For example, the ProcessTheaters creates the menu with theaters as items, associates the menu click with mnuTheater_Click event handler. This function also creates two hashtables: one to store general theater information keying on the theater ID and the other is a hashtable that points to another hashtable that stores movie show times based on movie ID for the current theater. Because this application is just an example and the list of local theaters and movies are small, it is ok to store the information in memory. Remember, when you are developing for these mobile devices, memory resource can be scarce and some alternative design should be considered:

```
private void ProcessTheaters(XmlNodeReader oReader) {
  bool bDone = false;
  string sTheaterKey = "";
  while(!bDone && oReader.Read( )) {
    if(oReader.Name == "theater" && oReader.IsStartElement( )) {
      MenuItem mnuItem = new MenuItem( );
      string sText = oReader["id"] + " " + oReader["name"];
      mnuItem.Text = sText;
      mnuItem.Click += new EventHandler(this.mnuTheater_Click);
      this.mnuTheater.MenuItems.Add(mnuItem);
      sTheaterKey = oReader["id"];
      THEATERS_TIME.Add(sTheaterKey, new Hashtable( ));
      THEATERS.Add(sTheaterKey,
          new Theater(oReader["name"], oReader["addr1"],
                      oReader["addr2"], oReader["phone"]));
    }
```

```
      if(oReader.Name == "theaters" && oReader.IsStartElement( ) == false) {
        bDone = true;
      }
    }
  }
}
```

At this point, you probably wonder if you can just rely on the XPath query to find movie/theater associations. As it turns out, because you are using the "compact" framework, some of the functionality that you might be familiar with in the desktop/web world might not be implemented here. In this case, XPath is not implemented so you won't be able to do SelectNodes to simplify your life.

Similar to the ProcessTheaters function, the ProcessMovies creates the menu with movies as items, associates the menu click with mnuMovie_Click event handler. This function also creates two hashtables: one to store general movie information keying on the movie ID and the other is a hashtable that points to another hashtable that stores movie times based on theater ID for the current movie:

```
private void ProcessMovies(XmlNodeReader oReader) {
  bool bDone = false;
  while(!bDone && oReader.Read( )) {
    if(oReader.Name == "movie" && oReader.IsStartElement( )) {
      MenuItem mnuItem = new MenuItem( );
      string sText = oReader["mid"] + " " + oReader["name"];
      mnuItem.Text = sText;
      mnuItem.Click += new EventHandler(this.mnuMovie_Click);
      this.mnuMovie.MenuItems.Add(mnuItem);
      string sMovieKey = oReader["mid"];
      MOVIES_TIME.Add(sMovieKey, new Hashtable( ));
      MOVIES.Add(sMovieKey,
                 new Movie(oReader["name"], oReader["summary"]));
    }
    if(oReader.Name == "movies" && oReader.IsStartElement( ) == false) {
      bDone = true;
    }
  }
}
```

The ProcessCrossRef function fills in the two cross-ref structure so that we can list showing times for a particular movie across all theater or showing times for all movies at a particular theater:

```
private void ProcessCrossRef(XmlNodeReader oReader) {
  bool bDone = false;
  string sTheaterKey = "";
  while(!bDone && oReader.Read( )) {
    if(oReader.Name == "xref" && oReader.IsStartElement( )) {
      sTheaterKey = oReader["theaterid"];
    }
```

```
if(oReader.Name == "movietime" && oReader.IsStartElement( )) {
  Hashtable o = (Hashtable)THEATERS_TIME[sTheaterKey];
  o.Add(oReader["refmid"], oReader["time"]);
  Hashtable o1 = (Hashtable)MOVIES_TIME[oReader["refmid"]];
  o1.Add(sTheaterKey, oReader["time"]);
}
if(oReader.Name == "xrefs" && oReader.IsStartElement( ) == false) {
  bDone = true;
}
      }
    }
  }
```

The menu click handler: mnuTheater_Click and mnuMovie_Click perform similar tasks, which basically setup the current mode of selection (by theater or by movie), the current theater or movie based on the mode, the list of movie and show times if the mode is by theater, or the list of theater and show times if the mode is by movie. Other supporting functions help in navigating to show movies and show times by theater or theater and show times by movie.*

Figures 9-20 and 9-21 show the application running on a Pocket PC while having the Movies and Theaters menu expanded.

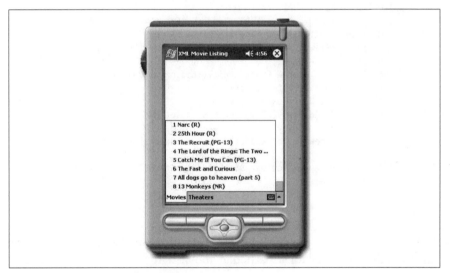

Figure 9-20. XML movie listing by movie

When you select a movie, the application traverses all theaters that show the selected movie and display the show times (see Figures 9-22 and 9-23).

---

* Download the complete code online at *http://www.oreilly.com/catalog/dotnetfrmess3/*.

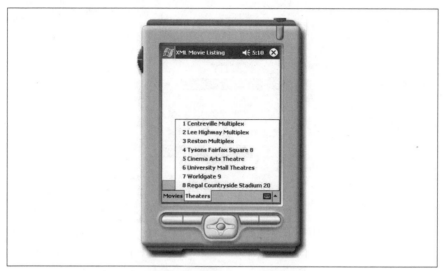

Figure 9-21. XML movie listing by theater

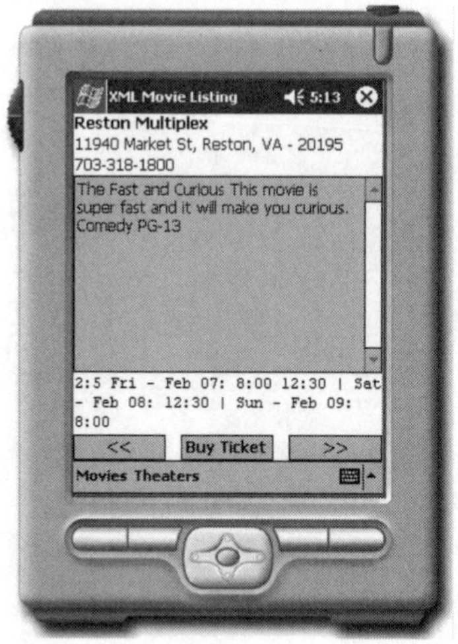

Figure 9-22. By movie

When you pick a theater instead of a movie, the application starts to traverse all movies showing at the selected theater (see Figures 9-24 and 9-25).

Storing off-line data in SQL Server for Windows CE

In the next example, you will rely on SQL Server CE for the data instead of an XML file. This change simplifies the code you write but requires the

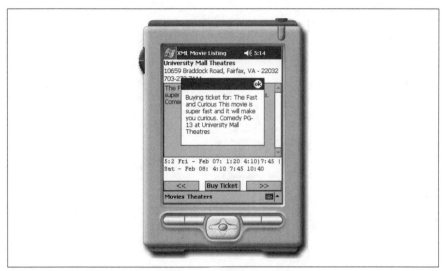

Figure 9-23. Same movie, other theater, also buying ticket

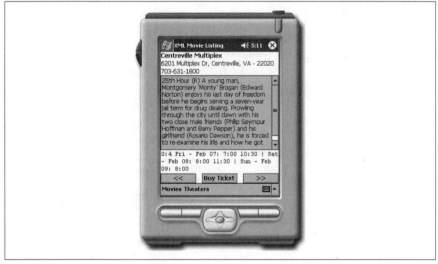

Figure 9-24. By theater

installation of SQL Server CE on the mobile device, thus the total amount of memory used might be higher than the xml version of the application. We can ignore the resource problem and exchange it with the simplification of the code and, fortunately, VS.NET automatically deploys SQL Server CE on the device the same way it does the .NET Compact Framework.

This version of the application starts by opening a database connection and generating the Theater and Movie menus. Unlike the previous version, you

Figure 9-25. Same theater, another movie, also buying ticket

don't have to build your own data structure to hold the data and cross references. The tables and their references are managed by the database in this example:

```
m_oConn = new SqlCeConnection(
            "Data Source=\\Program Files\\SQLCEMovieListing\\moviedb.sdf"
            );
m_oConn.Open();
GenerateMenus("select theaterid, name from theater",
            new EventHandler(this.mnuTheater_Click),
            this.mnuTheater);
GenerateMenus("select movieid, name from movie",
            new EventHandler(this.mnuMovie_Click),
            this.mnuMovie);
```

The GenerateMenus function just creates the menu items and associates the event handler to each item:

```
private void GenerateMenus(string sCommand,
                            EventHandler handler,
                            MenuItem mnuBranch) {
  SqlCeCommand oCmd = new SqlCeCommand();
  SqlCeDataReader oReader = null;
  oCmd.Connection = m_oConn;
  oCmd.CommandText = sCommand;
  oReader = oCmd.ExecuteReader();
  while(oReader.Read()) {
    MenuItem mnuItem = new MenuItem();
    mnuItem.Text = oReader["name"].ToString();
    mnuItem.Click += handler;
```

```
      mnuBranch.MenuItems.Add(mnuItem);
   }
   oReader.Close( );
}
```

Here are the handlers for Theater and Movie:

```
private void mnuMovie_Click(object o, System.EventArgs e) {
   // Get information from the menu item.
   string sName = ProcessMenuClick((MenuItem)o);
   // Obtain the current movie information.
   SqlCeCommand oCmd = new SqlCeCommand(
       "select summary from movie where name = '" + sName + "'"
                                    );
   oCmd.Connection = m_oConn;
   SqlCeDataReader oReader = oCmd.ExecuteReader( );
   oReader.Read( );
   m_oCurrentMovie = new Movie(sName, oReader["summary"].ToString( ));
   // Obtaining all theaters and their show times for this movie
   SqlCeDataAdapter oAdapter = new SqlCeDataAdapter
     (
@"
select t.name, t.addr1, t.addr2, t.phone, st.showtime
from theater t inner join showtime st on t.theaterid = st.theaterid
inner join movie m on m.movieid = st.movieid
where m.name = '" + sName + "'",
     m_oConn
     );
   m_oDS.Clear( );
   oAdapter.Fill(m_oDS);
   // Start in-memory cursor.
   m_iMode = 0;
   m_iCurrentIndex = 0;
   displayCurrent( );
}

private void mnuTheater_Click(object o, System.EventArgs e) {
   // Get information from the menu item.
   string sName = ProcessMenuClick((MenuItem)o);
   // Obtain the current theater information.
   SqlCeCommand oCmd = new SqlCeCommand(
       "select addr1, addr2, phone from theater where name = '" + sName + "'"
                                    );
   oCmd.Connection = m_oConn;
   SqlCeDataReader oReader = oCmd.ExecuteReader( );
   oReader.Read( );
   m_oCurrentTheater = new Theater(sName,
                                oReader["addr1"].ToString( ),
                                oReader["addr2"].ToString( ),
                                oReader["phone"].ToString( ));
   // Obtain all movie and show times at this theater.
   SqlCeDataAdapter oAdapter = new SqlCeDataAdapter
     (
```

```
@"
select m.name, m.summary, st.showtime
from movie m inner join showtime st on m.movieid = st.movieid
inner join theater t on t.theaterid = st.theaterid
where t.name = '" + sName + "'",
    m_oConn
    );
  m_oDS.Clear( );
  oAdapter.Fill(m_oDS);
  // Start in-memory cursor.
  m_iMode = 1;
  m_iCurrentIndex = 0;
  displayCurrent( );
}
```

The rest of the code can be found at *www.oreilly.com/catalog/dotnetfrmess3/*.

Summary

As you can see, writing applications for mobile devices can now be fun and productive. Whether you are going to write Web Application targeting mobile devices or applications that actually run on these devices, .NET would have you well covered. The Mobile Controls as well as the Compact Framework are now part of the standard .NET 1.1 to ensure that all aspects of the enterprise are taken care of. Thanks to great tools such as VS.NET, application developers no longer worry about the tedious legwork of setting up the environment, debugging tools, the SDK, emulators, and so on, and devote all their time to developing the business logic for the mobile application.

.NET Languages

This appendix contains two lists of languages (Microsoft-supported and third party) with compilers that generate IL to target the CLR.

Microsoft-Supported Languages for .NET

Table A-1 lists commercial languages that Microsoft supports. You can find more information about each of these languages by browsing the provided URLs.

Table A-1. Microsoft-supported languages for .NET

Language	Link
Visual C# .NET	*http://msdn.microsoft.com/vcsharp/*
Visual J# .NET (Java)	*http://msdn.microsoft.com/vjsharp/*
Visual C++ .NET (Managed C++)	*http://msdn.microsoft.com/visualc/*
Visual Basic .NET	*http://msdn.microsoft.com/vbasic/*
JScript for the CLR	*http://msdn.microsoft.com/workshop/languages/clinic/ scripting07142000.asp*

Third-Party Languages for .NET

Table A-2 shows a list of third-party languages with compilers that target the CLR. Some of these are research languages, while others are commercial languages that target .NET. Browse the provided web sites to read more about the languages that interest you. As noted earlier, this list of languages could grow by the time this book hits the market, so be sure to check the following site for the most up-to-date listings: *http://www.gotdotnet.com.*

Table A-2. Third-party languages

Language	Link
APL	http://www.dyadic.com
COBOL	http://www.adtools.com/info/whitepaper/net.html
Component Pascal	http://www.citi.qut.edu.au/research/plas/projects/component_pascal.jsp
Delta Forth	http://www.dataman.ro/dforth/
Eiffel#	http://www.eiffel.com/doc/manuals/technology/dotnet/eiffelsharp/white_paper.html
Fortran	http://www.lahey.com/dotnet.htm, http://www.salfordsoftware.co.uk/compilers/ftn95/dotnet.shtml
Haskell	http://haskell.cs.yale.edu/ghc
Mercury	http://www.cs.mu.oz.au/research/mercury/dotnet.html
Mondrian	http://www.mondrian-script.org
Oberon	http://www.oberon.ethz.ch/lightning
Perl	http://www.activestate.com/ASPN/NET
Python	http://www.activestate.com/ASPN/NET
RPG	http://www.asna.com/pr2%5F20%5F01.asp
Scheme	http://rover.cs.nwu.edu/~scheme
Smalltalk	http://www.lesser-software.com/en/content/products/lswvst/LSWVSt.htm
S#	http://www.smallscript.net
Standard ML	http://www.research.microsoft.com/Projects/SML.NET
TMT Pascal	http://www.tmt.com/net.htm

For more information, visit the O'Reilly .NET Center at *http://dotnet.oreilly.com* and the .NET DevCenter at *http://www.oreillynet.com/dotnet.*

Common Acronyms

Table B-1 provides a listing of common acronyms or terms that you will come across in .NET-related reading materials and conversations. Some of these acronyms or terms have little relevance to .NET, but appear occasionally in this book, so we've provided them in this table for your convenience.

Table B-1. List of common acronyms

Acronym	Description
.ASMX	File extension for web services source-code files.
.ASPX	File extension for ASP.NET source-code files.
.config	File extension of .NET application configuration files.
ADO	ActiveX Data Objects.
ADO.NET	With goals similar to ADO, ADO.NET is the way to access data sources in .NET.
API	Application Programming Interface.
AppDomain	Short term to mean an application domain.
ASP	Active Server Pages.
ASP.NET	With goals similar to ASP, ASP.NET is the technology that supports the rapid development of Web Forms.
ATL	Active Template Library.
BLOB	Binary Large Object.
CAB Files	Cabinet files.
CCW	COM Callable Wrapper.
CLI	Common Language Infrastructure. This is the specification of the infrastructure and base-class libraries that Microsoft has submitted to ECMA so that a third-party vendor can build a .NET runtime on another platform. The CLR is Microsoft's implementation of the CLI.
CLR	Common Language Runtime.
CLS	Common Language Specification.

Acronym	Description
CLSID	Class identifier used in COM.
COFF	Common Object File Format.
COM	Component Object Model.
COM Interop	Short for COM interoperation.
COM+ 2.0	This term is no longer used as of Beta 1 of the .NET SDK. The new, accepted term is .NET Framework.
COM+ Runtime	This term is no longer used as of Beta 1 of the .NET SDK. The new, accepted term is Common Language Runtime.
CTS	Common Type System.
DB	Database.
DCOM	Distributed Component Object Model.
DHTML	Dynamic HyperText Markup Language.
DISCO	Discovery of web services. A Web Service has one or more .DISCO files that contain information on how to access its WSDL.
DISPID	Dispatch identifier. Used in COM to identify a method or a property for dynamic invocation.
DLL	Dynamically Linked Library.
DNA	Distributed interNet Applications Architecture.
DOM	Document Object Model.
DTD	Data Type Document. This has been superceded by XSD.
EXE	Executable.
GC	Garbage Collector.
GDI	Graphical Device Interface.
GDI+	A .NET library that supports advanced graphics management.
Global.asax	The global configuration file for an ASP.NET application.
GUID	Globally Unique Identifier.
HTML	HyperText Markup Language.
HTTP	HyperText Transfer Protocol.
IDE	Integrated Development Environment.
IDL	Interface Definition Language.
IE	Internet Explorer.
IID	Interface Identifier.
IIS	Internet Information Server.
IJW	It Just Works.
IL	Intermediate Language.
ILDASM	Intermediate Language Disassembler.

Table B-1. List of common acronyms (continued)

Acronym	Description
Inproc	In-Process.
ISAPI	Information Server Application Programming Interface.
Machine.config	Configuration file for administrative policy for an entire machine.
MBR	Marshal-By-Reference.
MBV	Marshal-By-Value.
MFC	Microsoft Foundation Classes.
MSI	Microsoft Windows Installer Package.
MSIL	Microsoft Intermediate Language.
MSVCRT	Microsoft Visual C++ Runtime.
MSXML	Microsoft eXtensible Markup Language.
MTS	Microsoft Transaction Server.
NGWS	Stands for Next Generation Windows Services, the original name for .NET before it was previewed at PDC 2000 in Orlando, Florida. This term is no longer used.
NTFS	NT File System.
N-Tier	Multi-tier.
NTLM	NT Lan Manager.
OBJREF	Object Reference.
Out of proc	Out-of-process.
P/Invoke	Platform Invoke.
PE	Portable Executable.
perm	Permissions.
RAD	Rapid Application Development.
RCW	Runtime Callable Wrapper.
REGASM	Register Assembly tool.
RPC	Remote Procedure Call.
SCL	SOAP Contract Language.
SDK	Software Development Kit.
SEH	Structured Exception Handling.
SMTP	Simple Mail Transfer Protocol.
SOAP	Simple Object Access Protocol.
SQL	Structured Query Language.
STL	Standard Template Library.
TCP	Transport Control Protocol.
TLB	Type Library.
TLBEXP	Type Library Exporter Tool.

Table B-1. List of common acronyms (continued)

Acronym	Description
TLBIMP	Type Library Importer Tool.
UDDI	Universal Description, Discovery, and Integration Service. UDDI is a platform-independent framework for describing and discovering web services.
UDF	Uniform Data Format.
UI	User Interface.
URI	Uniform Resource Identifier.
URL	Uniform Resource Locator.
URT	Universal Runtime. This term is no longer used as of Beta 1 of the .NET SDK. The new, accepted term is the .NET Framework.
VB	Visual Basic.
VBRUN	Visual Basic Runtime.
VES	Virtual Execution System. The VES is a subset of the CLR. The VES doesn't include features such as debugging, profile, and COM interoperation.
VOS	Virtual Object System. This is now called the CTS.
VS.NET	Visual Studio .NET.
WAP	Wireless Application Protocol.
web.config	Configuration file for ASP.NET. You define HTTP modules, handlers, session state management, and other ASP.NET configurable parameters in this file.
WebForms	This term is no longer used as of Beta 1 of the .NET SDK. The new and accepted term is Web Forms (with a space).
WebServices	This term is no longer used as of Beta 1 of the .NET SDK. The new, accepted term is web services (with a space).
Win32	Windows 32-bit.
WinForms	This term is no longer used as of Beta 1 of the .NET SDK.
WML	Wireless Markup Language.
WSDL	Web Service Description Language. Think of this as IDL for web services. Unlike IDL, WSDL is expressed using only XML schemas. SDL is used in Beta1 of the .NET SDK, but WSDL replaced SDL in Beta 2 and later installments.
XML	Extensible Markup Language.
XPath	XML Path.
XSD	XML Schema Definition.
XSL	Extensible Stylesheet Language.
XSLT	Extensible Stylesheet Language Transformations.

Common Data Types

Each of the .NET languages can provide its own keywords for the types it supports. For example, a keyword for an integer in VB is Integer, whereas in C# or C++ it is int; a boolean is Boolean in VB, but bool in C# or C++. In any case, the integer is mapped to the class Int32, and the boolean is mapped to the class Boolean in the System namespace. Table C-1 lists all simple data types common to the .NET Framework. Non-CLS-compliant types are not guaranteed to interoperate with all CLS-compliant languages.

Table C-1. Common data types

Type	Description
Boolean	True or false.
Byte	8-bit unsigned integer: 0 to 255.
Char	Character. Unicode 16-bit character.
DateTime	Represents a date and time value.
Decimal	Can represent positive and negative values with 28 significant digits: −79,228,162,514,264,337,593,543,950,335 to 79,228,162,514,264,337,593,543,950,335.
Double	Stores 64-bit floating-point values: −1.79769313486231570e308 to 1.79769313486231570e308.
Guid	Represents a globally unique identifier (GUID); this is stored internally as a 128-bit integer. Commonly represented as a series of lowercase hexadecimal digits in groups of 8, 4, 4, 4, and 12 digits and separated by hyphens (e.g., 382c74c3-721d-4f34-80e5-57657b6cbc27).
Int16	Stores 16-bit signed integers: −32,768 to 32,767.
Int32	Stores 32-bit signed integers: −2,147,483,648 to 2,147,483,647.
Int64	Stores 64-bit signed integers: −9,223,372,036,854,775,808 to 9,223,372,036,854,775,807.
SByte	Represents an 8-bit signed integer. The SByte type is not CLS-compliant. −128 to 127.
Single	Represents an IEEE 754f, single precision, 32-bit value: −3.40282346638528859e38 to 3.40282346638528859e38.
String	Represents a string of Unicode characters.

Table C-1. Common data types (continued)

Type	Description
UInt16	Represents a 16-bit unsigned integer. The UInt16 type is not CLS- compliant. 0 to 65,535.
UInt32	Represents a 32-bit unsigned integer. The UInt32 type is not CLS- compliant. 0 to 4,294,967,295
UInt64	Represents a 64-bit unsigned integer. The UInt64 type is not CLS- compliant. The UInt64 data type can represent positive integers with 18 significant digits: 0 to 184,467,440,737,095,551,615.
Void	Void.

Table C-2 shows a number of useful container types that the .NET Framework provides.

Table C-2. Container types

Type	Description
Array	General array construct.
ArrayList	This class implements the IList interface. The array can grow or shrink dynamically in size.
BitArray	This class represents a compact array of bit values. Each element represents a Boolean value (true/false).
HashTable	This class represents a collection of associated keys and values that are organized based on the hash code of the key.
Queue	This class represents a first-in, first-out collection construct.
SortedList	This class is similar to HashTable except that all elements are sorted by their actual keys (not hashed) and elements are accessible through either key or index.
Stack	This class represents a first-in, last-out stack construct.

Usage

This section demonstrates how you can take advantage of container types. We don't illustrate all methods and properties, but we show the important characteristics of these types. All examples in this chapter are in C#; however, you can use these CLS types from any other CLS-compliant languages.

Array

Array, by definition, stores homogeneous information in a structure that allows for indexing, enumerating, and so on. It is very important in the daily programmer's life. In the following code listing, we demonstrate some of the syntax for using Array. In C#:

```
using System;
public class TestArray {
```

```csharp
    public static void Main( )  {

        string[] strArray = new string[7] { "Monday", "Tuesday", "Wednesday",
"Thursday", "Friday", "Saturday", "Sunday" };
        for(int i=0; i<strArray.Length; i++) {
            Console.WriteLine(String.Format("item at {0} is {1}",
                                            i, strArray[i]));
        }

        int[] iArray;
        iArray = new int[7];

        for(int i=0; i<iArray.Length; i++) {
            iArray[i] = i;
        }
        for(int i=0; i<iArray.Length; i++) {
            Console.WriteLine(iArray[i]);
        }

    }
}
```

and in VB:

```vb
Imports System
Public Class TestArray

    Public Shared Sub Main( )

        Dim i as Integer
        Dim strArray( ) as String = { "Monday", "Tuesday", "Wednesday",
"Thursday", "Friday", "Saturday", "Sunday" }

        For i = 0 To strArray.Length - 1
            Console.WriteLine(String.Format("item at {0} is {1}", _
                                            i, strArray(i)))
        Next

        Dim iArray(6) as Integer

        For i = 0 To iArray.Length - 1
            iArray(i) = i
        Next
        For i = 0 to iArray.Length - 1
            Console.WriteLine(iArray(i))
        Next

    End Sub
End Class
```

Notice the differences in the declaration of the array for the highlighted code. In VB, the number represents the upper bound of the array, not the size.

ArrayList

In the following code listing, we demonstrate some of the critical usages of the ArrayList class, such as adding data to the end of the list, inserting data anywhere in the list, iterating through the list, and sorting the list:

```
using System;
using System.Collections;
public class TestArrayList {

    public static void Main()  {

        ArrayList arrList = new ArrayList();
        arrList.Add("Monday");
        arrList.Add("Tuesday");
        arrList.Add("Wednesday");
        arrList.Add("Thursday");

        // We'll try to insert Friday afterward.
        // arrList.Add("Friday");

        arrList.Add("Saturday");
        arrList.Add("Sunday");

        int i = 0;
        IEnumerator arrIterator = arrList.GetEnumerator();
        Console.WriteLine("There are: {0} days in a week.", arrList.Count);
        while(arrIterator.MoveNext()) {
            Console.WriteLine("[{0}] {1}", i++, arrIterator.Current);
        }

        Console.WriteLine("Insert Friday");
        arrList.Insert(4, "Friday");

        i = 0;
        arrIterator = arrList.GetEnumerator();
        Console.WriteLine("There are: {0} days in a week.", arrList.Count);
        while(arrIterator.MoveNext()) {
            Console.WriteLine("[{0}] {1}", i++, arrIterator.Current);
        }

        arrList.Sort();

        i = 0;
        arrIterator = arrList.GetEnumerator();
        Console.WriteLine("Sorted as text");
        while(arrIterator.MoveNext()) {
            Console.WriteLine("[{0}] {1}", i++, arrIterator.Current);
        }

        Object oDay = "Friday";
        Console.WriteLine("Index for Friday using BinarySearch: {0}",
                            arrList.BinarySearch(oDay));
```

```
        Console.WriteLine("Index for Sunday using BinarySearch: {0}",
                    arrList.BinarySearch("Sunday"));
    }
}
```

BitArray

The sample code for BitArray is self-explanatory, as shown in the following code listing. We use the bit array to store and retrieve access rights in the following example. You can use the Set and Get methods as well as the [] operator:

```
using System;
using System.Collections;
public class TestBitArray  {

    enum Permissions {canRead, canWrite, canCreate, canDestroy};

    public static void Main( )  {

        BitArray bitArr = new BitArray(4);
        bitArr.Set((int)Permissions.canRead, true);
        bitArr[(int)Permissions.canWrite] = false;
        bitArr[(int)Permissions.canCreate] = true;
        bitArr[(int)Permissions.canDestroy] = false;

        Console.WriteLine("bitArr count: {0}\tlength: {1}",
                        bitArr.Count,
                        bitArr.Length);

        Console.WriteLine("Permissions:");
        Console.WriteLine("Read: {0}",
                        bitArr[(int)Permissions.canRead]);
        Console.WriteLine("Write: {0}",
                        bitArr[(int)Permissions.canWrite]);
        Console.WriteLine("Create: {0}",
                        bitArr[(int)Permissions.canCreate]);
        Console.WriteLine("Destroy: {0}",
                        bitArr[(int)Permissions.canDestroy]);
    }
}
```

HashTable

The HashTable data type is similar to the dictionary object, which is basically an associated array. Each element stored in the table is associated with a key. Because HashTable implements the IDictionaryEnumerator, we can obtain the enumerator to help us iterate through the data collection. As you

can see from the sample code, we can also loop through the data using the keys or values collection:

```csharp
using System;
using System.Collections;
public class TestHashtable  {

    public static void Main()  {

        Hashtable hashTbl = new Hashtable();
        hashTbl.Add("Param1", "UserName");
        hashTbl.Add("Param2", "Password");

        IDictionaryEnumerator hashEnumerator = hashTbl.GetEnumerator();
        Console.WriteLine();
        Console.WriteLine("Loop through with enumerator:");
        while (hashEnumerator.MoveNext()) {
            Console.WriteLine("Key: {0}\tValue: {1}",
                            hashEnumerator.Key,
                            hashEnumerator.Value);
        }

        Console.WriteLine();
        Console.WriteLine("Loop through Keys:");
        foreach(string key in hashTbl.Keys) {
            Console.WriteLine(key);
        }

        Console.WriteLine();
        Console.WriteLine("Loop through Values:");
        foreach(string val in hashTbl.Values) {
            Console.WriteLine(val);
        }

        Console.WriteLine();
        Console.WriteLine("Loop through Keys:");
        foreach(string key in hashTbl.Keys) {
            Console.WriteLine("Key: {0}\tValue: {1}", key, hashTbl[key]);
        }
    }
}
```

Queue

To demonstrate the use of a queue Abstract Data Type (ADT), we created a fictitious order-processing code listing. Each enqueued item represents a line item in a typical order. We will then dequeue each line item and perform the total calculation:

```csharp
using System;
using System.Collections;
```

```
public class TestQueue  {

    public static void Main( )  {
        string sLineItem1, sLineItem2;
        Queue myQueue = new Queue( );

        sLineItem1 = "123\tItem 123\t4\t3.39";
        sLineItem2 = "ABC\tItem ABC\t1\t9.49";
        myQueue.Enqueue(sLineItem1);
        myQueue.Enqueue(sLineItem2);

        Console.WriteLine("\nProcessing Order:\n");
        String sLineItem = "";
        String [] lineItemArr;
        Decimal total = 0;
        while(myQueue.Count > 0) {
            sLineItem = (String)myQueue.Dequeue( );
            Console.WriteLine( "\t{0}", sLineItem);
            lineItemArr = sLineItem.Split(new Char[] {'\t'});
            total += Convert.ToInt16(lineItemArr[2]) *
                    Convert.ToDecimal(lineItemArr[3]);
        }
        Console.WriteLine("\nOrder Total: {0}\n", total);
    }
}
```

SortedList

The following code demonstrates the sorted list ADT. A sorted list is similar
to a hash table or a dictionary type. Each item of data is associated with the
key with which the list is sorted. Notice that the strings are added to the list
in no particular order. However, when we iterate through the list, all strings
are sorted by their associated keys:

```
using System;
using System.Collections;
public class TestSortedList  {

    public static void Main( )  {

        SortedList mySortedList = new SortedList( );
        mySortedList.Add("AA", "Hello");
        mySortedList.Add("AC", "!");
        mySortedList.Add("AB", "World");

        Console.WriteLine("\nLoop through manually:\n");
        for(int i=0; i< mySortedList.Count; i++) {
            Console.WriteLine("Key: {0}\tValue: {1}",
                            mySortedList.GetKey(i),
                            mySortedList.GetByIndex(i));
        }
```

```
IDictionaryEnumerator myIterator = mySortedList.GetEnumerator( );
Console.WriteLine("\nLoop through with enumerator:\n");
while (myIterator.MoveNext( )) {
   Console.WriteLine("Key: {0}\tValue: {1}",
                        myIterator.Key,
                        myIterator.Value);
   }
 }
}
```

Stack

The following code demonstrates the first-in, last-out characteristics of the stack abstract data type. The output from the pop operation initially shows the fourth item, the third item, and so on:

```
using System;
using System.Collections;
public class TestStack{

   public static void Main( )  {

      Stack myStack = new Stack( );
      myStack.Push("Item 1");
      myStack.Push("Item 2");
      myStack.Push("Item 3");
      myStack.Push("Item 4");

      while(myStack.Count > 0) {
         Console.WriteLine(myStack.Pop( ));
      }
   }
}
```

Common Utilities

Microsoft .NET Framework provides many tools to help developers make the best use of the Framework. In the following sections, we document the commonly used subset of .NET tools that we've used throughout this book:

- Assembly Generation Utility (*al.exe*)
- Assembly Registration Utility (*gacutil.exe*)
- MSIL Assembler (*ilasm.exe*)
- MSIL Disassembler (*ildasm.exe*)
- C++ Compiler (*cl.exe*)
- C# Compiler (*csc.exe*)
- VB Compiler (*vbc.exe*)
- PE File viewer (*dumpbin.exe*)
- Type Library Exporter (*tlbexp.exe*)
- Type Library Importer (*tlbimp.exe*)
- XML Schema Definition Tool (*xsd.exe*)
- Shared Name Utility (*sn.exe*)
- Web Service Utility (*wsdl.exe*)

Assembly Generation Utility (al.exe)

al.exe is generally used to generate assemblies with manifests. Table D-1 shows some of the common uses of the Assembly Generation Utility.

Table D-1. Assembly Generation Utility common uses

Option	Description
/flags:*flags*	Specifies a value for the Flags field in the assembly.
	0x0000: side-by-side compatible
	0x0010: cannot execute with other versions in the same application domain.
	0x0020: cannot execute with other versions in the same process
	0x0030: cannot execute with other versions on the same computer
/help or /?	Use to get help for this command.
/keyfile:*keyfilename* or /keyf:*keyfilename*	Use to create shared components. *keyfilename* contains a key pair generated with the Shared Name Utility (*sn.exe*). The compiler inserts the public key into the assembly manifest and then signs the assembly with the private key.
/keyname:*keycontainer* or /keyn:*keycontainer*	Use to create shared components. *keycontainer* contains a key pair generated and installed into a key container with the Shared Name Utility (*sn. exe*). The compiler inserts the public key into the assembly manifest and then signs the assembly with the private key.
/main:*entrymethod*	Specifies the entry-point method name when converting a module to an executable.
/out:*filename*	Specifies the output filename.
/target:lib|exe|win or /t:lib|exe|win	Specifies the file format of the output file (lib for library, exe for console executable, and win for win32 executable). The default setting is lib.
/version:*major.minor. revision.build*	Specifies version information for the assembly. The default value is 0.

Assembly Registration Utility (gacutil.exe)

You can use *gacutil.exe* to install and uninstall an assembly, as well as to list the content of the GAC. Table D-2 shows some of the common uses of the Assembly Registration Utility.

Table D-2. Assembly Registration Utility common uses

Option	Description
/l	To list the content of the GAC.
/ldl	To list the content of the downloaded files cache.
/cdl	To clear the content of the downloaded file cache.
/i *filename*	To install an assembly with file named *filename* into the GAC.
/u *assemblyname*	To uninstall an assembly from the GAC by specifying the assembly name. If multiple versions of the same assembly exist, all of them will be removed unless a version is specified with the *assemblyname* (i.e., gac -u myAssembly, ver=1.0.0.1).
/h or /help or /?	To display command syntax and options.

MSIL Assembler (ilasm.exe)

This tool takes MSIL as input and generates a portable executable (PE) file containing the MSIL and the metadata required to run on the .NET Framework. This is most useful to vendors who would like to create MSIL-compliant compilers. All they have to do is write the compiler to translate the source language to MSIL. *Ilsam.exe* will take the second step to put the MSIL content into the PE format where it can be executed on the .NET Framework. The general syntax for MSIL assembler is:

```
ilasm [options] MSILfilename
```

Table D-3 shows some of the common uses of the assemblers.

Table D-3. Assemblers common uses

Option	Description
/debug	This option ensures that the output PE contains debugging information such as local variables, argument names, and line numbers. This is useful for debug build.
/dll	This option produces a .dll output.
/exe	This option produces an .exe output.
/listing	This option produces a listing of the output on STDOUT.
/output=*filename*	*filename* is the output filename.
/?	This option is used to obtain command-line help.

MSIL Disassembler (ildasm.exe)

This tool extracts the MSIL code from a PE file targeted for .NET Framework. The general syntax for this tool is:

```
Ildasm [options] PEFilename
```

Table D-4 shows some of the common uses of the disassembler.

Table D-4. Disassembler common uses

Option	Description
/linenum	This includes references to original source lines.
/output=*filename*	The output goes to a file instead of in a GUI dialog box.
/source	This shows original source lines as comments.
/text	The output goes in a console window.
/tokens	This shows metadata tokens of classes and members.

C++ Compiler (cl.exe)

Table D-5 shows some of the common uses of the C++ compiler.

Table D-5. C++ compiler common uses

Option	Description
/CLR	This option flags the compiler to compile .NET-runtime managed code.
/entry:*methodname*	For C++ managed code, this link setting should point to the main entry-point function.
/link	This option combines the compile and link steps.
/subsystem:|windows|windowsce|console|	This link option specifies the type of output.
/out:*filename*	This option allows for the output filename.

C# Compiler (csc.exe)

Table D-6 shows some of the common uses of the C# compiler.

Table D-6. C# compiler common uses

Option	Description
/debug	With this option, the compiler will emit debugging information in the output file.
/define:*symbol* or /d:*symbol*	This option is similar to C++. Use this option to define preprocessor symbols.
/doc:*docname*	*docname* is the XML output file for the autogenerated XML comment embedded in C# code.
/help	This option shows the command-line help for the C# compiler.
/main:*classname*	If there is more than one Main entry in different classes, you will have to specify the Main entry in which class you want the entry point of the application.
/out:*filename*	This option represents the output filename.
/reference:*libname* or /r: *libname*	This option allows single or multiple libraries be included with this compilation. For multiple libraries to be included, use a semicolon as the delimiter.
/target: exe|library|winexe|module or /t: exe|library|winexe|module	This option allows you to specify the type of the output: exe for console executables, library for DLLs, and winexe for Windows Form applications. When you set the target to module, the compiler outputs binary for the module but not a .NET assembly. Modules can be added to a .NET assembly later.
/unsafe	If you use unsafe keywords in your C# code, you will have to use this option when compiling your source.

Visual Basic Compiler (vbc.exe)

Table D-7 shows some of the common uses of the Visual Basic compiler.

Table D-7. Visual Basic compiler common uses

Option	Description
/debug	With this option, the compiler will emit debugging information in the output file.
/define:*symbol* or / d:*symbol*	Use this option to define preprocessor symbols.
/help or /?	This option shows the command-line help for the Visual Basic compiler.
/keycontainer:*keycontainer*	*keycontainer* specifies the key container that contains the key pair for signing the assembly. See *sn.exe* for information on generating the key container.
/keyfile:*keyfile*	*keyfile* specifies the key file that contains the key pair for signing the assembly. See *sn.exe* for information on generating the key file.
/main:*classname*	If there is more than one Main entry in different classes, you will have to specify the Main entry in which class you want the entry point of the application.
/out:*filename*	This option represents the output filename.
optionexplicit[+/-]	Turn on or off optionexplicit to enforce explicit or implicit declaration of variables. The default setting is on.
optionstrict[+/-]	Turn on or off optionstrict to disallow or allow casting with truncation. The default setting is on.
/reference:*libname* or /r: *libname*	This option allows single or multiple libraries be included with this compilation. For multiple libraries to be included, use a semicolon as the delimiter.
/target: exe|library|winexe|module or /t: exe|library|winexe|module	This option allows you to specify the type of the output: exe for console executables, library for DLLs, and winexe for Windows Form applications. When you set the target to module, the compiler outputs binary for the module but not a .NET assembly. Modules can be added to a .NET assembly later.

PE File Format Viewer (dumpbin.exe)

dumpbin is not a new utility. However, since .NET Framework stores the IL inside the extended PE format, this old utility is still very useful for examining the structure of executable or DLLs, as well as listing import and export entries of the binaries. The general syntax for this utility is:

```
Dumpbin [options] PEFilename
```

Table D-8 shows some of the common *dumpbin* uses.

Table D-8. Dumpbin common uses

Option	Description
/all	Displays all information from the PE file.
/exports	Displays all exports from the PE file.
/header	Displays the header information from the PE file.
/clrheader	Display the .NET Framework header information for an image built with /clr (see CL.exe).
/imports	Displays all imports for the PE file.

Type Library Exporter (tlbexp.exe)

Type library exporter and importer are the two tools necessary for COM interop. The exporter generates a type library for a .NET Framework assembly so that other COM components can interop with .NET components. The general syntax for *tlbexp.exe* is:

```
tlbexp AssemblyName [options]
```

Table D-9 shows some of the common uses of *tlbexp.exe*.

Table D-9. Type Library Exporter common uses

Option	Description
/nologo	This option suppresses the logo of the tlbexp executable.
/out:*filename*	*filename* is the name of the type library file.
/silent	This option suppresses all messages from the tlbexp executable.
/verbose	This option displays extra information while converting the component.
/? or /help	This option displays the help information for the tool.

Type Library Importer (tlbimp.exe)

Because it is the reverse tool of the type library exporter, the importer generates a .NET proxy component for a COM component so that .NET components can use legacy COM components. The general syntax for *tlbimp.exe* is:

```
tlbimp PEFile [options]
```

Table D-10 shows some of the common uses of *tlbimp.exe*.

Table D-10. Type Library Importer common uses

Option	Description
/keycontainer: keycontainer	This option signs the resulting assembly with the private key in the keycontainer. The public key in the keyfile will be used in the assembly manifest. See sn.exe for the keycontainer generation.
/keyfile: keyfile	This options signs the resulting assembly with the private key in the keyfile. The public key in the keyfile will be used in the assembly manifest. See sn.exe for keyfile generation.
/nologo	This option suppresses the logo of the tlbimp executable.
/out:filename	filename is the name of the type library file.
/silent	This option suppresses all messages from the tlbimp executable.
/unsafe	This option produces interfaces without .NET Framework security checks.
/verbose	This option displays extra information while converting the component.
/? or /help	This option displays the help information for the tool.

XML Schema Definition Tool (xsd.exe)

XML Schema Definition (XSD) is useful when working with XML schemas that follow the XSD language. With XSD, you can perform the following transformations:

- XDR to XSD
- XML to XSD
- Classes to XSD
- XSD to Classes
- XSD to DataSet

XDR to XSD

To convert an XDR-formatted file to XSD, use the following syntax:

```
xsd [options] file.xdr
```

Note that the file extension *.xdr* dictates the conversion from XDR to XSD.

XML to XSD

To convert an XML-formatted file to XSD, use the following syntax:

```
xsd [options] file.xml
```

Note that the file extension *.xml* dictates the conversion from XML to XSD.

Classes to XSD

You can convert classes to XSD by specifying the runtime assembly file (*.exe* or *.dll* extension) as the filename to the utility. You can also specify a particular type within the assembly you want to convert to XSD using the /type flag. The typename can be a wildcard match. If you omit the /type flag, all types in the assembly will be converted. The syntax follows:

```
Xsd [/TYPE:typename] assemblyFile
```

or:

```
Xsd [/T:typename] assemblyFile
```

XSD to Classes

To convert XSD back to classes, use the /classes or /c flag. You can specify a particular element in the XSD schema to be converted to a class. You can also specify the language for the class source file. The general syntax follows:

```
xsd /CLASSES
    /ELEMENT:element
    /NAMESPACE:namespace
    /LANGUAGE:language /URI:uri file.xsd
```

or:

```
xsd /C E:element /N:namespace /L:language /U:uri file.xsd
```

Note that namespace, language, and uri can be specified only once.

XSD to DataSet

To convert XSD to dataset, use the /dataset or /d flag. Again, you can narrow down to a particular element in the XSD schema to be converted. The general syntax follows:

```
xsd /D [/DATASET] file.xsd
```

Strong Name Utility (sn.exe)

The Strong Name Utility (*sn.exe*) guarantees unique names for shared components because these components will end up in the GAC. Each shared component is signed with a private key and published with the public key. Table D-11 shows some common uses of *sn.exe*.

Table D-11. Strong Name Utility common uses

Option	Description
/?	This option displays more command-line help.
-d *keycontainer*	This option is used to remove the *keycontainer* from the CSP.
-i *keyfile keycontainer*	This option reads the key pair in *keyfile* and installs it in the key container *keycontainer* in the Cryptographic Service Provider (CSP).
-k *keyfile*	This option generates a new key pair and writes it to *keyfile*.
-v *assembly*	This option is used to verify the shared name in an *assembly*.

Web Service Utility (wsdl.exe)

wsdl.exe helps create ASP.NET web services and proxies for their clients. The most common usage of *wsdl.exe* is to generate proxy classes for Web services:

```
wsdl
    /language:language
    /namespace:namespace
    /out:output
    /protocol:protocol
    path
```

The *path* parameter is a local path to a service-description file or URI where the SDL file can be retrieved. The *language* parameter specifies the language for the output-proxy source file. It can be C#, VB, JS or VJS. The generated class will be in the specified namespace. The output source file is controlled by the *output* option. The *protocol* controls which protocol the proxy will use to communicate with the Web Service. The choices of protocols provided by the .NET Framework are SOAP, SOAP12, HttpGet, and HttpPost. You can also have your own protocol here if you've extended the WebClientProtocol or HttpWebClientProtocol class.

For short names options, use the following:

```
wsdl
    /l:language
    /n:namespace
    /o:output
    /protocol:protocol
    path
```

The rest of the syntax can be obtained with wsdl /?.

Index

We'd like to hear your suggestions for improving our indexes. Send email to *index@oreilly.com*.

extends keyword in C#, 66
Extensible Markup Language (see XML)
Extensible Stylesheet Language
        Transformation (XSLT), 330
Extensible Stylesheet Language
        (XSL), 330

F

file selectors (HTML), 214
FileStream class, 52
Fill( ) method, 134, 279
firewalls, using DCOM with, 85
FooterStyle, controlling visual
        formatting of DataGrid
        control, 251
FooterTemplate, 252
ForeignKeyConstraint rules, 123
Form class, 266, 282
    LayoutMdi( ) method, using, 288
    Windows Forms development, 269
forms
    authentication, 169
    class, 282
    controls, adding, 272
    HTML, 214
    Web/Windows, 10
Framework (.NET), 9
    design goals of, 4

G

GAC (Global Assembly Cache), 7, 31
    shared components and, 77
    viewing, 81
gac.exe (Assembly Registration
        Utility), 339, 340
garbage collecting, 46
    allocated objects, 8
    distributed, 89
    terminating web forms, 230
GC class, 52
_ _gc keywords in C++, 54
GDI (Graphical Device Interface), 328
GET methods of HTTP protocol, 155
GetChanges( ) method, 113, 120
GetHashCode( ) method, 50
GetMessage Windows API, 263
GetMethods( ) method, 51
GetObject( ) method, 88
GetType( ) method, 50

Global Assembly Cache (see GAC)
globally unique identifier (GUID), 328
Graphical Device Interface (GDI), 328
Graphical User Interfaces (GUIs), 10
Guid datatype, 331
GUID (globally unique identifier), 328
GUIs (Graphical User Interfaces), 10

H

handleButtonClick event handler, 228
HasChanges( ) method, 113, 120
HasErrors method, 113
HashTable class, 52, 248, 332, 335
Haskell language, 326
HeaderStyle, controlling visual
        formatting of DataGrid
        control, 251
HeaderTemplate, 252
hidebysig attribute, 36
Host Integration Server 2000, 3
HTML (Hypertext Markup
        Language), 328
    ASP pages and, 204
    components, 224
    control syntax, 215
    DataList control, laying out lists
        through the use of, 252
    HtmlControls mapping to tags, 213
    lifecycle of, 228
    Repeater control and, 253
    System.Web.UI.HtmlControls
        namespace and, 211
HtmlAnchor HTML Control, 215
HtmlButton HTML Control, 215
HtmlControls class, 211, 227
HtmlForm HTML Control, 214
HtmlGenericControl HTML
        Control, 214
HtmlGenericControl object, 213
HtmlImage HTML Control, 214
HtmlInputButton HTML Control, 214
HtmlInputCheckBox HTML
        Control, 214
HtmlInputFile HTML Control, 214
HtmlInputHidden HTML Control, 214
HtmlInputImage HTML Control, 214
HtmlInputRadioButton HTML
        Control, 214
HtmlInputText HTML Control, 214

About the Authors

Thuan Thai is also the author of *Learning DCOM*, published by O'Reilly & Associates. He has been giving technical presentations on the .NET platform to clients since the announcement of the initiative in July 2000.

Hoang Q. Lam is an independent software consultant in the D.C. Metropolitan area. He specializes in .NET and other Microsoft technologies.

Colophon

Our look is the result of reader comments, our own experimentation, and feedback from distribution channels. Distinctive covers complement our distinctive approach to technical topics, breathing personality and life into potentially dry subjects.

The animals on the cover of *.NET Framework Essentials*, Third Edition, are shrimp. Different species of shrimp are found in marine and fresh water—shallow and deep—all over the world. Swimming backward by rapidly flexing its abdomen and tail, and with the assistance of specialized legs for swimming, the shrimp feeds on smaller plants and animals, as well as carrion. In fact, several species engage in symbiotic (mutually beneficial or dependent) relationships with other organisms. The coral shrimp (*Stenopus hispidus*) cleans the scales of the coral fish, while the fish in turn swims backward through the shrimp's pincers (presumably to clean them).

Matt Hutchinson was the production editor for *.NET Framework Essentials*, Third Edition. Octal Publishing, Inc. provided production services. Jane Ellin, Phil Dangler, and Claire Cloutier provided quality control.

Ellie Volckhausen designed the cover of this book, based on a series design by Edie Freedman. The cover image is a 19th-century engraving from the Dover Pictorial Archive. Emma Colby produced the cover layout with QuarkXPress 4.1 using Adobe's ITC Garamond font.

David Futato designed the interior layout. This book was converted to FrameMaker 5.5.6 by Andrew Savikas. The text font is Linotype Birka; the heading font is Adobe Myriad Condensed; and the code font is LucasFont's TheSans Mono Condensed. The illustrations that appear in the book were produced by Robert Romano and Jessamyn Read using Macromedia Free-Hand 9 and Adobe Photoshop 6. The tip and warning icons were drawn by Christopher Bing. This colophon was written by Jeff Holcomb.

Other Titles Available from O'Reilly

Microsoft .NET Programming

Mastering Visual Studio .NET

*By Ian Griffiths, Jon Flanders
& Chris Sells*
1st Edition March 2003
352 pages, ISBN 0-596-00360-9

Mastering Visual Studio .NET
provides you, as an experienced
programmer, with all the infor-
mation needed to get the most out of the latest and
greatest development tool from Microsoft. Written
by experienced developers and trainers John Flanders,
Ian Griffiths, and Chris Sells, this book not only covers
the fundamentals, but also shows how to customize
and extend the toolkit to your specific needs.

Programming C#, 2nd Edition

By Jesse Liberty
2nd Edition February 2002
650 pages, ISBN 0-596-00309-9

The first part of *Programming
C#*, 2nd Edition introduces C#
fundamentals, then goes on to
explain the development of desk-
top and Internet applications, including Windows
Forms, ADO.NET, ASP.NET (including Web
Forms), and Web Services. Next, this book gets to
the heart of the .NET Framework, focusing on
attributes and reflection, remoting, threads and
synchronization, streams, and finally, it illustrates
how to interoperate with COM objects.

Learning Visual Basic .NET

By Jesse Liberty
1st edition October 2002
320 pages, ISBN 0-596-00386-2

*Learning Visual Basic .NET is a
complete introduction to
VB.NET and object-oriented programming. By using hundreds of
examples, this book demonstrates how to develop
various kinds of applications—including those that
work with databases—and web services. *Learning
Visual Basic .NET* will help you build a solid foundation in .NET.

Programming ASP.NET

By Jesse Liberty & Dan Hurwitz
1st Edition February 2002
960 pages, ISBN 0-596-00171-1

The ASP.NET technologies are so
complete and flexible; your main
difficulty may lie simply in weav-
ing the pieces together for maxi-
mum efficiency. *Programming ASP.NET* shows you
how to do just that. Jesse Liberty and Dan Hurwitz
teach everything you need to know to write web
applications and web services using both C# and
Visual Basic .NET.

C# in a Nutshell

*By Peter Drayton & Ben
Albarhari*
1st Edition March 2002
856 pages, ISBN 0-596-00181-9

C# is likely to become one of the
most widely used languages for
building .NET applications. *C#
in a Nutshell* contains a concise
introduction to the language and its syntax, plus
brief tutorials used to accomplish common programming tasks. It also includes O'Reilly's classic-
style, quick-reference material for all the types and
members in core .NET namespaces, including System, System.Text, System.IO, and System.Collec-
tions.

ASP.NET in a Nutshell

*By G. Andrew Duthie &
Matthew MacDonald*
1st Edition June 2002
816 pages, ISBN 0-596-00116-9

As a quick reference and tutorial
in one, *ASP.NET in a Nutshell*
goes beyond the published documentation to highlight little-
known details, stress practical uses for particular
features, and provide real-world examples that
show how features can be used in a working application. This book covers application and web service development, custom controls, data access,
security, deployment, and error handling. There is
also an overview of web-related class libraries.

O'REILLY®

To order: 800-998-9938 • *order@oreilly.com* • *www.oreilly.com*
Online editions of most O'Reilly titles are available by subscription at *safari.oreilly.com*
Also available at most retail and online bookstores.

Microsoft .NET Programming

Learning C#

By Jesse Liberty
1st Edition September 2002
368 pages, ISBN 0-596-00376-5

With *Learning C#*, best-selling author Jesse Liberty will help you build a solid foundation in .NET and show how to apply your skills by using dozens of tested examples. You will learn how to develop various kinds of applications—including those that work with databases—and web services. Whether you have a little object-oriented programming experience or you are new to programming altogether, *Learning C#* will set you firmly on your way.

.NET Windows Forms in a Nutshell

By Ian Griffiths & Matthew Adams
1st Edition March 2003
896 pages, ISBN 0-596-00338-2

.NET Windows Forms in a Nutshell offers an accelerated introduction to this next-generation of rich user inter- face development. The book provides an all-inclusive guide for experienced programmers along with a compact but remarkably complete reference to the .NET Framework Class Library (FCL) Windows Forms namespaces and types. Included on CD is an add-in that will integrate the book's reference directly in to the help files of Visual Studio .NET.

ADO.NET in a Nutshell

By Bill Hamilton
& Matthew MacDonald
1st Edition April 2003
640 pages, ISBN 0-596-00361-7

ADO.NET in a Nutshell is the most complete and concise source of ADO.NET information available. Besides being a valuable reference, this book covers a variety of issues that programmers face when developing web applications or web services that rely on database access. Most examples use Microsoft's C# language. The book's CD includes an add-in to integrate the reference with Visual Studio .NET help files.

Programming .NET Web Services

By Alex Ferrara & Matthew MacDonald
1st Edition October 2002
414 pages, ISBN 0-596-00250-5

This comprehensive tutorial teaches programmers the skills they need to develop XML web services hosted on the Microsoft .NET platform. *Programming .NET Web Services* also shows you how to consume these services on both Microsoft and non-Windows clients, and how to weave them into well-designed and scalable applications. For those interested in building industrial-strength web services, this book is full of practical information and good old-fashioned advice.

Object-Oriented Programming with Visual Basic .NET

By J.P. Hamilton
1st Edition September 2002
308 pages, ISBN 0-596-00146-0

Visual Basic .NET is a language that facilitates object-oriented programming, but does not guarantee good code. That's where *Object-Oriented Programming with Visual Basic .NET* comes in. It will show you how to think about similarities in your application logic and how to design and create objects that maximize the benefit and power of .NET. Packed with examples that will guide you through every step, *Object-Oriented Programming with Visual Basic .NET* is for those with some programming experience.

O'REILLY®

To order: *800-998-9938* • *order@oreilly.com* • *www.oreilly.com*
Online editions of most O'Reilly titles are available by subscription at *safari.oreilly.com*
Also available at most retail and online bookstores.

O'REILLY NETWORK

Safari® Bookshelf™

Search Over 1,000 Books and Find Answers Fast

The Safari Bookshelf is a powerful online reference tool, a must have when you need to pinpoint exact answers in an instant. With access to over 1000 of the top technical reference books by leading publishers including O'Reilly, Addison-Wesley, and the Microsoft Press, Safari Bookshelf provides developers with the technical reference and code samples needed to develop quality, timely code.

Try it today with a FREE TRIAL
Visit www.oreilly.com/safari/free

How to stay in touch with O'Reilly

1. Visit our award-winning web site

http://www.oreilly.com/

★ "Top 100 Sites on the Web"—PC Magazine
★ CIO Magazine's Web Business 50 Awards

Our web site contains a library of comprehensive product information (including book excerpts and tables of contents), downloadable software, background articles, interviews with technology leaders, links to relevant sites, book cover art, and more. File us in your bookmarks or favorites!

2. Join our email mailing lists

Sign up to get email announcements of new books and conferences, special offers, and O'Reilly Network technology newsletters at:

http://elists.oreilly.com

It's easy to customize your free elists subscription so you'll get exactly the O'Reilly news you want.

3. Get examples from our books

To find example files for a book, go to:

http://www.oreilly.com/catalog

select the book, and follow the "Examples" link.

4. Work with us

Check out our web site for current employment opportunites:

http://jobs.oreilly.com/

5. Register your book

Register your book at:

http://register.oreilly.com

6. Contact us

O'Reilly & Associates, Inc.
1005 Gravenstein Hwy North
Sebastopol, CA 95472 USA
TEL: 707-827-7000 or 800-998-9938
(6am to 5pm PST)
FAX: 707-829-0104

order@oreilly.com
For answers to problems regarding your order or our products. To place a book order online visit:

http://www.oreilly.com/order_new/

catalog@oreilly.com
To request a copy of our latest catalog.

booktech@oreilly.com
For book content technical questions or corrections.

corporate@oreilly.com
For educational, library, government, and corporate sales.

proposals@oreilly.com
To submit new book proposals to our editors and product managers.

international@oreilly.com
For information about our international distributors or translation queries. For a list of our distributors outside of North America check out:

http://international.oreilly.com/distributors.html

adoption@oreilly.com
For information about academic use of O'Reilly books, visit:

http://academic.oreilly.com

O'REILLY®

To order: *800-998-9938* • *order@oreilly.com* • *www.oreilly.com*
Online editions of most O'Reilly titles are available by subscription at *safari.oreilly.com*
Also available at most retail and online bookstores.